CliffsNotes®

Praxis® Mathematics: Content Knowledge (5161)

CliffsNotes®

Praxis® Mathematics: Content Knowledge (5161)

3RD EDITION

by

Sandra Luna McCune, Ph.D.

Houghton Mifflin Harcourt

Boston • New York

About the Author

Sandra Luna McCune, Ph.D., is professor emeritus and a former Regents professor in the Department of Elementary Education at Stephen F. Austin State University, where she received the Distinguished Professor Award. She now is a full-time author and consultant and resides near Austin, Texas.

Author Acknowledgments

Sandra Luna McCune wishes to thank her late husband Donice for his brilliant understanding of mathematics that made this book possible.

Dedication

With much love, this book is dedicated to my grandchildren: Richard, Rose, Jude, Sophia, Josephine, and Myla.

Editorial

Executive Editor: Greg Tubach

Senior Editor: Christina Stambaugh

Production Editor: Erika West

Copy Editor: Donna Wright

Technical Editors: Mary Jane Sterling and Tom Page

Proofreader: Lynn Northrup

CliffsNotes® Praxis® Mathematics: Content Knowledge (5161), 3rd Edition

Library of Congress Control Number: 2016930859
ISBN: 978-0-544-62826-7 (pbk)

Printed in the United States of America
DOO 10 9 8 7 6 5 4 3 2 4500637964

For information about permission to reproduce selections from this book, write to trade.permissions@hmhco.com or to Permissions, Houghton Mifflin Harcourt Publishing Company, 3 Park Avenue, 19th Floor, New York, New York 10016.

www.hmhco.com

Table of Contents

Introduction

General Description

The Praxis Mathematics: Content Knowledge test (test code 5161, Praxis Math CK test) is designed to assess the mathematical knowledge and skills that an entry-level teacher of secondary school mathematics needs to possess. According to the *Praxis Study Companion* (http://www.ets.org/s/praxis/pdf/5161.pdf), the Praxis Math CK test addresses two broad content categories:

I. Number and Quantity, Algebra, Functions, and Calculus
II. Geometry, Probability and Statistics, and Discrete Mathematics

The computer-delivered test consists of 60 questions. Of the 60 questions, 10 are pretest items and do not count toward your score. No penalty is imposed for wrong answers (you merely score a 0 for that test question). You are given 2½ hours to complete the test.

The test provides an on-screen mathematics reference sheet containing information organized under three labels: NOTATIONS, DEFINITIONS, and FORMULAS (see "Notations, Definitions, and Formulas" in Chapter 1 to review this reference information).

Tip: To get up-to-date information about the Praxis Math CK test, go to http://www.ets.org/praxis/prepare/materials/5161 on the ETS website. If new information about the test becomes available, it will be posted on this site.

Allocation of the Test Content

According to the *Praxis Study Companion* (see "General Description," above for the Internet address), the approximate number of questions and percentage of the test for each content category are as follows:

Allocation of the Test Content

Content Category	Approximate Number of Questions	Approximate Percent of Test
Number and Quantity, Algebra, Functions, and Calculus	41	68%
Geometry, Probability and Statistics, and Discrete Mathematics	19	32%

Question Types

There are a variety of question types on the Praxis Math CK test. You may be asked to choose one correct answer choice from among four options, select all correct answer choices from a list of options presented, select a response from a drop-down menu, drag and drop an answer choice to an on-screen area where it belongs, or fill in a numeric response in an answer box. There is no set number for each question type nor do the question types appear in a specific order.

This section presents examples of the three main question types you can expect to see on the Praxis Math CK test: multiple-choice (select one answer), multiple-choice (select one or more answers), and numeric entry (fill in a numeric response in an answer box).

Read the directions carefully before you answer each question. If a question has answer choices with **ovals**, then you must select a single answer choice. If a question has answer choices with **square boxes**, then you must select one or more answer choices. If a question presents no answer choices, you are provided with a **blank rectangular box** (or two stacked boxes for answers with fractions) and you must manually enter your answer.

Ovals	⬭	Multiple-choice question (select one answer choice)
Square Boxes	☐	Multiple-choice question (select one or more answer choices)
Rectangular Box	▭	Numeric-entry question (fill in your answer)
Two Stacked Boxes	▭ ▭	Numeric-entry question (fill in your fraction answer)

Note: The example questions and practice tests in this book label each multiple-choice answer choice with a letter for clarity. These letters do not appear on the computer screen when you take the actual test. Instead, you will click on the oval or square(s) next to the answer you choose.

Multiple-Choice (Select One Answer Choice) Questions

The multiple-choice (select one answer choice) questions require you to choose one correct answer choice from among four options.

Praxis Mathematics: Content Knowledge (5161)

Answer the question by selecting the correct response.

In the *xy* plane, what is the center of the circle that has equation $x^2 + 6x + y^2 - 8y = 24$?

⬭ (–3, 4)

⬭ (3, –4)

⬭ (–6, 8)

⬭ (3, –4)

← Previous | Question 9 of 60 | Next →

Multiple-Choice (Select One or More Answer Choices) Questions

The multiple-choice (select one or more answer choices) questions require you to choose ALL of the correct answer choices and *no others* from among a list of options presented. The correct answer might be just one of the answer choices or it could be as many as all of the answer choices. The question is scored as incorrect unless you select all of the correct choices and no others. There is no partial credit.

Praxis Mathematics: Content Knowledge (5161)

Answer the question by selecting all that apply.

The number 200 lies between $\frac{1}{4}x$ and $\frac{1}{3}x$. Which of the following numbers could be values of x?

- ☐ 550
- ☐ 650
- ☐ 750
- ☐ 850

Previous | Question 56 of 60 | Next

Numeric-Entry (Fill in a Numeric Answer) Questions

Numeric-entry (fill in a numeric answer) questions do not present answer choices. Instead, you are required to fill in a numeric answer to the question. Here are guidelines.

- If you are answering a question that shows a single rectangular box for the answer, click on the box and use the keyboard to type in your answer.
- If a question asks specifically for the answer as a fraction, there will be two boxes—a numerator box and a denominator box. Click on the upper box and use the keyboard to type in the numerator of your answer. Then click on the lower box to type in the denominator of your answer. Do NOT use decimals in fractions.
- Type in the exact answer unless the question requires you to round the answer.
- For a decimal point, type a period.
- For a negative sign, type a hyphen.
- Use the backspace key to erase.
- Equivalent forms of an answer in decimal notation are all correct. For example, if the answer is 45, then answers such as 45, 45., or 45.0 are all correct. If the answer is 3.7, then answers such as 3.7, 3.70, or 03.7 are all correct.
- Fractions do not have to be reduced to lowest terms (although you might have to reduce a fraction so that it fits in the answer boxes). For example, if the answer is $\frac{2}{5}$, then fractions that are equivalent to $\frac{2}{5}$, such as $\frac{4}{10}$ and $\frac{20}{50}$, are also correct.

Praxis Mathematics: Content Knowledge (5161)

Answer the question by entering the correct response in the box below the question.

What is the least integer k such that $\frac{1}{4^k} < 0.001$?

Previous | Question 54 of 60 | Next

Praxis Mathematics: Content Knowledge (5161)

Answer the question by entering a correct number in each box below the question.

The enrollment at a small community college for the fall semester is 10% higher than the enrollment in the fall semester a year ago. The number of female students increased by 5%, and the number of male students increased by 20%. Female students make up what portion of the current enrollment at the community college?

Give your answer as a fraction.

Previous | Question 48 of 60 | Next

ETS On-Screen Graphing Calculator

While you are taking the Praxis Math CK test, an on-screen graphing calculator will be available to you. Practice using the ETS on-screen graphing calculator while working through this CliffsNotes book. You can download a 90-day free trial version at http://www.infinitysw.com/ets. Online tutorials are available on the website, and the downloadable calculator manual is available at http://infinitysw.s3.amazonaws.com/ets/ets_calculator_manual.pdf. *Note:* Hereafter in this book, the ETS on-screen graphing calculator that you will be allowed to access when you are taking the Praxis Math CK test is referred to simply as "the ETS graphing calculator."

Scoring of the Test

Educational Testing Service (ETS) does not release the exact details of the way the Mathematics CK test is scored. For each question you answer correctly you get 1 raw point, and your total raw score is the number of questions you answer correctly out of the 50 questions on the test that count.

Your raw point score is converted to a scaled score that adjusts for the difficulty level of the particular edition of the test that you took. Your score report for the test will show a scaled score ranging from 100 to 200. You can find additional information about the scoring of the test in *Understanding Your Praxis Scores* (available at http://www.ets.org/s/praxis/pdf/uyps_1415.pdf).

The recommended passing score is 32 out of a possible 50 raw-score points. The scaled score corresponding to a raw score of 32 (64% correct) is 160 on a 100–200 scale.

Note: For the practice tests in this study guide, you are provided a guideline for converting your raw score to a percent-correct score. A percent-correct score of 64% (about 38 correct out of 60 questions) or higher should roughly equate to a passing scaled score.

The Role of the Praxis Math CK Test in Teacher Certification

The Praxis Math CK test is one of the Praxis Subject Assessment tests designed by Educational Testing Service (ETS). The Praxis Subject Assessment tests are part of a national teacher assessment program and are used as part of the certification or licensing requirements in states across the U.S. This means you should be able to transfer your score on the Praxis Math CK test from state to state for those states that use the Praxis Subject Assessment tests.

If your state has selected the Praxis Math CK test to assess secondary teacher candidates' mathematical knowledge and skills, you will find this CliffsNotes book a useful resource to help you achieve the passing score for your state. Test scores needed to obtain certification vary from state to state because each state sets its own passing score. ETS maintains a list of passing scores by state at http://www.ets.org/s/praxis/pdf/passing_scores.pdf. Here is a current listing of state passing scores (as of November 2015):

Alabama—145
Alaska—160
Arkansas—160
Colorado—160
Connecticut—160
Delaware—160
District of Columbia—160
Hawaii—160
Idaho—160
Iowa—132
Kansas—152
Kentucky—160
Louisiana—160
Maine—160
Maryland—160
Mississippi—160
Montana—160
Nebraska—146
Nevada—160
New Hampshire—160
New Jersey—160
North Carolina—160
North Dakota—160
Pennsylvania—160
Rhode Island—160
South Carolina—160
South Dakota—160
Tennessee—160
Utah—160
Vermont—160
Virginia—160
West Virginia—160
Wisconsin—160
Wyoming—160

State testing requirements are subject to change. For the most up-to-date score requirements, visit your state department of education or your state page on the Praxis website, at http://www.ets.org/praxis/states.

Studying for the Praxis Math CK Test

When you read through the descriptions of the Praxis Math CK test content category topics, you may feel overwhelmed by the task of preparing for the test. Here are some suggestions for developing an effective study program using this book.

1. Set up a regular schedule of study sessions. Try to set aside approximately 2 hours for each session. If you complete one session per day (including weekends), it should take you about 4 to 6 weeks to work your way through the review and practice material in this book. Of course, if your test date is coming up soon, you might need to lengthen your study time per day.
2. Reserve a place for studying where you will have few distractions, so you can concentrate. Make sure you have adequate lighting and a room temperature that is comfortable—not too warm or too cold. Be sure you have an ample supply of water to keep your brain hydrated, and you might also want to have some light snacks available. To improve mental alertness, choose snacks that are high in protein and low in carbohydrates. Gather all the necessary study aids (paper, pencils, note cards, and so on) beforehand. Let your voicemail answer your phone during your study time.
3. Take Practice Test 1 (Chapter 12) before you begin reading the review material to help you discover your strengths and weaknesses. Read the answer explanations for all the questions, not just the ones you missed, because you might have gotten some of your correct answers by guessing. Make a list of the content category topics with which you had the most difficulty. Plan your study program so you can spend more time on topics that your Practice Test 1 results indicate are weak areas for you. For example, if you did very well on algebra and geometry, but poorly in calculus, you should plan to spend more time studying the review material for calculus.
4. Carefully study the review material in Chapters 2–11 of this book to refresh your memory about the key ideas for each of the content category topics, being sure to concentrate as you go through the material. Work through the examples and make sure you understand them thoroughly.

5. Make flashcards to aid you in memorizing key definitions and formulas and keep them with you at all times. When you have a few spare minutes, take out the flashcards and go over the information you've recorded on them.
6. Take several 2- to 3-minute breaks during your study sessions to give your mind time to absorb the review material you just read. According to brain research, you remember the first part and last part of something you've read more easily than you remember the middle part. Taking several breaks will allow you to create more beginnings and endings to maximize the amount of material you remember. It's best not to leave your study area during a break. Try stretching or simply closing your eyes for a few minutes.
7. Periodically review material you have already studied to reinforce what you have learned and to help you identify topics you might need to revisit.
8. When you complete your first review, take Practice Test 2 (Chapter 13). Use a timer and take the test under the same conditions you expect for the actual test, being sure to adhere to the $2\frac{1}{2}$-hour time limit for the test. When you finish taking the test, as you did for Practice Test 1, carefully study the answer explanations for *all* the questions. Then, go back and review again any topics in which you performed unsatisfactorily.
9. When you complete your second review, take Practice Test 3 (Chapter 14) under the same conditions you expect for the actual test, adhering to the $2\frac{1}{2}$-hour time limit, again by using a timer. When you finish taking the test, carefully study the answer explanations for *all* the questions and do additional study, if needed.
10. Organize a study group, if possible. A good way to learn and reinforce the material is to discuss it with others. If feasible, set up a regular time to study with one or more classmates or friends. Take turns explaining to each other how to work problems. This strategy will help you not only to clarify your own understanding of the underlying mathematics, but also to discover new insights into how to approach various problems.

After completing your study program, you should find yourself prepared and confident to achieve a passing score on the Praxis Math CK test.

How to Prepare for the Day of the Test

There are several things you can do to prepare yourself for the day of the test.

1. Know how to get to the test center and how to get into the room where you will be testing.
2. Make sure you have dependable transportation to get to the test center and know where you should park (if you plan to go by car).
3. Keep all the materials you will need to bring to the test center—especially your admission ticket and identification—in a secure place so you easily can find them on the day of the test.
4. The night before the test, try to get a good night's rest. Avoid taking nonprescription drugs or consuming alcohol, as the use of these products might impair your mental faculties on test day.
5. On the day of the test, get to the test center early—at least 30 minutes before your test is scheduled to begin.
6. Dress in comfortable clothing and wear comfortable shoes. Even if it is warm outside, wear layers of clothing that can be removed or put on, depending on the temperature in the test center.
7. Eat a light meal. Select foods that give you the most energy and stamina.
8. Drink plenty of water to make sure your brain remains hydrated for optimal thinking during the test.
9. Make a copy of this list and post it in a strategic location. Check it before you leave for the test center.

Tip: Go to http://www.ets.org/s/praxis/flash/prometric/18204_praxis-prometric-video.html for a video tutorial of what to expect at the test center on test day.

Test-Taking Strategies for the Praxis Math CK Test

Here are some general test-taking strategies to help maximize your score on the test:

1. When you receive the test, take several deep, slow breaths before you begin, exhaling slowly while mentally visualizing yourself performing successfully on the test.
2. During the test, follow all the directions, including the test center administrator's (TCA) oral directions and the written directions on the computer screen. If you do not understand something in the directions, raise your hand and ask the TCA for clarification.
3. Move through the test at a steady pace. The test consists of 60 questions. When you get to question 30, check the on-screen timer to see how much time has passed. If more than 1 hour and 15 minutes has gone by, you will need to pick up the pace. Otherwise, continue to work as rapidly as you can without being careless, but do not rush.
4. Try to answer the questions in order. However, if a question is taking too much time, use the Mark button to mark the question to review later, and move on.
5. Read each question entirely. Skimming to save time can cause you to misread a question or miss important information.
6. For multiple-choice (select one answer choice) questions, read all the answer choices before you select an answer. You might find an answer that immediately strikes you as correct, but this determination might have occurred because you jumped to a false conclusion or made an incorrect assumption. Also, eliminate as many wrong choices as you can. When applicable, estimate the answer to help you decide which choices are unreasonable.
7. For multiple-choice (select one or more answer choices) questions, systematically assess each answer choice one by one and either select it or eliminate it.
8. For numeric-entry questions, enter the exact answer unless the question tells you to round your answer. If you must round your answer, do not round until you have completed all your calculations. For answers that must be given as fractions, save time by not reducing to lowest terms.
9. Don't read too much into a question. For example, don't presume a geometric figure is drawn accurately or to scale.
10. With application problems, always double-check to be sure you are answering the question asked.
11. Refer to the notations, definitions, and formulas provided as an on-screen mathematics reference sheet under the Help button as often as needed.
12. Use the on-screen calculator, but use it wisely. Keep in mind that graphing calculators are powerful tools, but they can make errors. See the discussion about graphing calculators that follows this section.
13. Change an answer only if you have a good reason to do so.
14. If you are trying to recall information during the test, close your eyes and try to visualize yourself in your study place. This may trigger your memory.
15. Before ending your test, be sure you have answered every test question. You are not penalized for a question you answer incorrectly (you merely score a 0 for that test question), so even if you have no clue about the correct response, make a guess.
16. Remain calm during the test. If you find yourself getting anxious, stop and take several deep, slow breaths and exhale slowly, while mentally visualizing yourself in a peaceful place, to help you relax. Keep your mind focused on the task at hand—completing your test. Trust yourself. You should not expect to know the correct response to every question on the test. Think only of doing your personal best.
17. As you work through the practice tests provided in this book, consciously use the strategies suggested in this section as preparation for the actual Praxis Math CK test. Try to reach a point where the strategies are automatic for you.

Tip: Go to https://www.ets.org/s/praxis/flash/cbt/praxis_cdt_demo_web1.html for an interactive Praxis computer-delivered testing demonstration. The demonstration explains main features that are common to all Praxis computer-delivered tests, including how to log in and how to navigate through a test.

Graphing Calculators and the Praxis Math CK Test

Graphing calculators are very powerful tools, but you should be aware that they can make errors!

One situation in which errors might occur is when the calculator is finding the roots or zeros of a high-degree polynomial (for example, a polynomial of degree 8). The algorithm that the calculator uses to find the roots of the polynomial forces the calculator to round numbers to a certain number of decimal places before the final result is obtained, thus yielding inaccurate answers.

Errors can also occur when the calculator is drawing the graph of a function. Your choice of viewing window dimensions can give results that are visually very misleading. For example, you can be led to believe that a function has only two zeros when, in fact, it has three zeros. Changing the dimensions for the viewing window can clear up the problem in most cases; however, not every time. Most notably, for some graphing calculators, the graph of $y = \sin\left(\frac{1}{x}\right)$ at values near $x = 0$ will never be correct no matter what window dimensions you select.

The point of this discussion is to make you aware that such mistakes can happen. Therefore, you should use your mathematical expertise to evaluate *all* calculator results for reliability and accuracy.

You will benefit greatly from this CliffsNotes book. By using the recommendations in this chapter as you complete your study program, you should be prepared to walk into the testing room with confidence. Good luck on the test and in your future career as a mathematics teacher!

Chapter 1

Review for the Praxis Mathematics: Content Knowledge (5161) Test

The review of the Praxis Mathematics: Content Knowledge (5161) test (Praxis Math CK test) in this CliffsNotes book is designed around the two broad content categories assessed on the test:

I. Number and Quantity, Algebra, Functions, and Calculus
II. Geometry, Probability and Statistics, and Discrete Mathematics

Each content category topic (for example, Number and Quantity) is defined by a list of specific knowledge and skills (see the *Mathematics: Content Knowledge (5161) Study Companion* at https://www.ets.org/s/praxis/pdf/5161.pdf for detailed descriptions of each content category topic). The review presents key ideas and formulas that are important for you to know for the Praxis Math CK test.

Mathematical notations, definitions, and formulas similar to those that will be provided for you under the Help button when you take the official test are included on the following three pages.

Notations, Definitions, and Formulas

Notations

(a, b)	$\{x: a < x < b\}$
$[a, b)$	$\{x: a \le x < b\}$
$(a, b]$	$\{x: a < x \le b\}$
$[a, b]$	$\{x: a \le x \le b\}$
$\text{gcf}(m, n)$	greatest common factor of two integers m and n
$\text{lcm}(m, n)$	least common multiple of two integers m and n
$[x]$	greatest integer n such that $n \le x$
$m \equiv n \pmod{k}$	m and n are congruent modulo k (m and n have the same remainder when divided by k, or equivalently, $m - n$ is a multiple of k)
f^{-1}	inverse of a one-to-one function f; (*not* equal to $\frac{1}{f}$)
$\lim\limits_{x \to a^+} f(x)$	right-hand limit of $f(x)$; limit of $f(x)$ as x approaches a from the right (if it exists)
$\lim\limits_{x \to a^-} f(x)$	left-hand limit of $f(x)$; limit of $f(x)$ as x approaches a from the left (if it exists)
$\varnothing$ or $\{\ \}$	the empty set
$x \in A$	x is an element of set A
$A \subset B$	set A is a proper subset of set B
$A \subseteq B$	either set A is a proper subset of set B or $A = B$
$A \cup B$	union of sets A and B
$A \cap B$	intersection of sets A and B

Definitions

Discrete Mathematics

A relation $\Re$ on a set A is

reflexive if $x \Re x$ for all $x \in A$
symmetric if $x \Re y \Rightarrow y \Re x$ for all $x, y \in A$
transitive if $(x \Re y$ and $y \Re z) \Rightarrow x \Re z$ for all $x, y, z \in A$
antisymmetric if $(x \Re y$ and $y \Re x) \Rightarrow x = y$ for all $x, y \in A$

An *equivalence* relation is a reflexive, symmetric, and transitive relation.

Formulas

Angle Sum and Difference Identities	$\sin(x \pm y) = \sin x \cos y \pm \cos x \sin y$ $\cos(x \pm y) = \cos x \cos y \mp \sin x \sin y$ $\tan(x \pm y) = \dfrac{\tan x \pm \tan y}{1 \mp \tan x \tan y}$	
Half-Angle Identities (sign depends on the quadrant of $\frac{\theta}{2}$)	$\sin\frac{\theta}{2} = \pm\sqrt{\frac{1-\cos\theta}{2}}$; $\cos\frac{\theta}{2} = \pm\sqrt{\frac{1+\cos\theta}{2}}$	
Range of Inverse Trigonometric Functions	$\sin^{-1} x: \left[-\frac{\pi}{2}, \frac{\pi}{2}\right]$; $\cos^{-1} x: [0, \pi]$; $\tan^{-1} x: \left(-\frac{\pi}{2}, \frac{\pi}{2}\right)$	
Law of Sines	$\frac{\sin A}{a} = \frac{\sin B}{b} = \frac{\sin C}{c}$	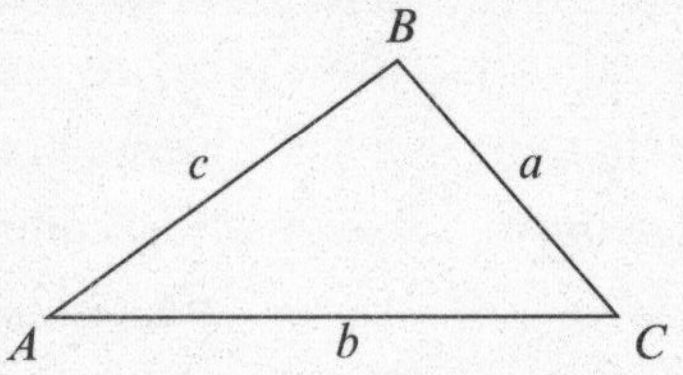
Law of Cosines	$c^2 = a^2 + b^2 - 2ab(\cos C)$	
De Moivre's Theorem	$(\cos\theta + i\sin\theta)^k = \cos(k\theta) + i\sin(k\theta)$	
Coordinate Transformation		
Rectangular (x, y) to polar (r, θ): **Polar (r, θ) to rectangular (x, y):**	$r^2 = x^2 + y^2$; $\tan\theta = \frac{y}{x}$, provided $x \neq 0$ $x = r\cos\theta$; $y = r\sin\theta$	
Distance from point (x_1, y_1) to line $Ax + By + C = 0$	$d = \dfrac{\lvert Ax_1 + By_1 + C\rvert}{\sqrt{A^2 + B^2}}$	

Volume	
Sphere: radius r	$V = \frac{4}{3}\pi r^3$
Right circular cone: height h, base of radius r	$V = \frac{1}{3}\pi r^2 h$
Right circular cylinder: height h, base of radius r	$V = \pi r^2 h$
Pyramid: height h, base of area B	$V = \frac{1}{3}Bh$
Right prism: height h, base of area B	$V = Bh$
Surface Area	
Sphere: radius r Right circular cone: radius r, slant height s	$A = 4\pi r^2$ $A = \pi rs + \pi r^2$
Differentiation	
$\left(f(x)g(x)\right)' = f(x)g'(x) + g(x)f'(x)$; $\left(\frac{f(x)}{g(x)}\right)' = \frac{g(x)f'(x) - f(x)g'(x)}{\left(g(x)\right)^2}$ provided $g(x) \neq 0$; $\left(f(g(x))\right)' = f'(g(x))g'(x)$	
Integration by Parts	$\int u\,dv = uv - \int v\,du$

While you are practicing for the Praxis Math CK test, make sure you become very familiar with the information given to you on the Notations, Definitions, and Formulas pages included in this chapter and at the beginning of the practice tests. In addition, you will need to know other familiar formulas relevant to the content categories, such as the formulas for the area and perimeter of common geometric shapes. The most important formulas for you to know are given in the review chapters. You also may find it helpful to know other common mathematical formulas, such as those provided in Appendix A.

Chapter 2

Number and Quantity

The Real and Complex Number Systems

For this topic, you must understand the structure of the natural, integer, rational, real, and complex number systems and perform basic operations on numbers in these systems.

Sets of Numbers

Important sets of numbers for you to know are the following:

natural numbers (or **counting numbers**) = {1, 2, 3, ...}

whole numbers = {0, 1, 2, 3, ...}

integers = {..., −3, −2, −1, 0, 1, 2, 3, ...}

rational numbers = $\left\{\frac{p}{q}\right.$, where p and q are integers with $\left.q \neq 0\right\}$

irrational numbers = {nonterminating, nonrepeating decimals} = {numbers that *cannot* be written as $\frac{p}{q}$, where p, q are integers with $q \neq 0$}

real numbers = rational numbers ∪ irrational numbers. The natural numbers, whole numbers, integers, rational numbers, and irrational numbers are subsets of the real numbers. The real numbers can be represented on a number line. Every real number corresponds to a point on the number line, and every point on the number line corresponds to a real number. Here are examples.

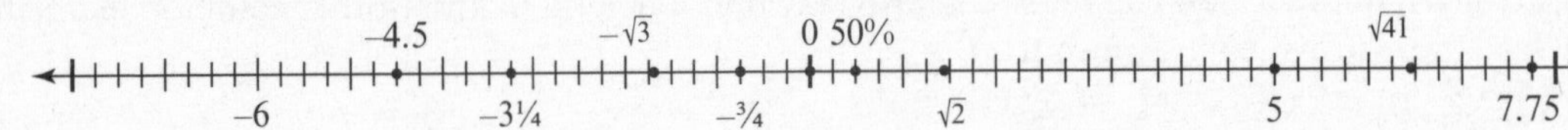

complex numbers = $\{x + yi$, where x and y are real numbers and $i^2 = -1\}$. For the complex number $z = x + yi$, the coefficients x and y are the real part and imaginary part, respectively, of z. When x is 0, the resulting set of numbers consists of pure imaginary numbers. When y is 0, the resulting set of numbers consists of the real numbers. Thus, the real numbers are a subset of the complex numbers. The complex numbers can be represented on the complex plane, where the horizontal axis is the **real axis** and the vertical axis is the **imaginary axis**. The complex numbers $z_1 = 2 + i$, $z_2 = 3 - 2i$, $z_3 = -3 + 2i$, and $z_4 = -2 - 4i$ are shown in the complex plane in the following figure.

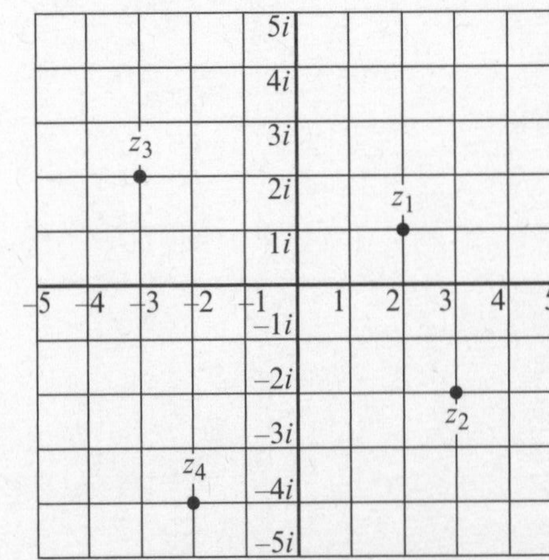

Intervals and Interval Notation

Intervals show sets of numbers on the real number line. **Open intervals** do not include the endpoints. **Closed intervals** include both endpoints. **Half-open** (or **half-closed**) intervals include only one endpoint. **Finite intervals** are bounded intervals. Intervals that extend indefinitely to the right or left or both are **unbounded intervals.**

To graph an interval on the number line, shade the number line to show the numbers included in the interval. Use a solid circle to indicate an endpoint is included and an open circle to indicate an endpoint is not included. The following table summarizes intervals and interval notation.

Interval	Notation and Type	Graph
$x < b$	$(-\infty, b)$, unbounded, open	b
$x > a$	(a, ∞), unbounded, open	a
$x \leq b$	$(-\infty, b]$, unbounded, half-open	b
$x \geq a$	$[a, \infty)$, unbounded, half-open	a
$a < x < b$	(a, b), bounded, open	a b
$a \leq x < b$	$[a, b)$, bounded, half-open	a b
$a < x \leq b$	$(a, b]$, bounded, half-open	a b
$a \leq x \leq b$	$[a, b]$, bounded, closed	a b

Computing with Real Numbers

Computations using real numbers are performed using the absolute values of the numbers. The **absolute value** of a real number is its distance from 0 on the real number line. The absolute value is always positive or 0. Therefore, the absolute value of a real number x is either x or $-x$, whichever of these is nonnegative.

For sums and differences of real numbers, use the following rules.

Rule	Examples
Rule 1. The sum of 0 and any number is the number.	$2.5 + 0 = 2.5$; $-8 + 0 = -8$
Rule 2. The sum of a number and its negative is 0. ***Tip:*** The negative of a number is also called its "opposite."	$\frac{1}{2}+\left(-\frac{1}{2}\right)=0$; $-100+100=0$
Rule 3. To add two numbers that have the same sign: Add their absolute values and give the sum their common sign.	$-\frac{1}{7}+\left(-\frac{3}{7}\right)=-\frac{4}{7}$; $4.95+3.68=8.63$
Rule 4. To add two numbers that have opposite signs: Subtract the lesser absolute value from the greater absolute value and give the sum the sign of the number with the greater absolute value.	$-150+100=-50$; $\frac{5}{9}+\left(-\frac{3}{9}\right)=\frac{2}{9}$
Rule 5. To subtract one number from another: Add the opposite of the second number to the first. (That is, "subtracting a number" and "adding the opposite of the number" give the same answer.)	$-150-200=-350$; $4.5-(-2.7)=7.2$

For products and quotients of real numbers, use the following rules.

Rule	Examples
Rule 1. Zero times any number is zero.	$\frac{3}{4}\cdot 0 = 0$; $(0)(923.99) = 0$
Rule 2. To multiply two *nonzero* real numbers that have the same sign: Multiply their absolute values and keep the product positive (no sign is necessary).	$(-30)(-6) = 180$; $(8.96)(100) = 896$
Rule 3. To multiply two *nonzero* real numbers that have opposite signs: Multiply their absolute values and make the product negative.	$\left(-\frac{1}{3}\right)(15) = -5$; $(5.2)(-8.4) = -43.68$
Rule 4. When 0 is one of the factors, the product is *always* 0; otherwise, products involving an *even* number of negative factors are positive, whereas those with an *odd* number of negative factors are negative.	$(2)(0)(-1.1)\left(\frac{3}{2}\right) = 0$; $(-1)(3)(2)(-5) = 30$; $(-2)(-5.4)\left(-\frac{3}{2}\right)(4) = -64.8$
Rule 5. To divide one *nonzero* real number by another: Multiply the first number by the reciprocal of the second number using the same rules for the signs as for multiplication. ***Tip:*** In practice, you might find it convenient to divide the absolute value of the first number by the absolute value of the second number, and then determine the sign of the result by using the rules for multiplication of real numbers.	$-\frac{2}{5}\div\left(\frac{1}{5}\right) = -\frac{2}{5}\times\left(\frac{5}{1}\right) = -2$; $\frac{-36}{-4} = 9$
Rule 6. The quotient is 0 when the dividend is 0 and the divisor is a nonzero number.	$\frac{0}{10} = 0$; $\frac{0}{-8} = 0$
Rule 7. The quotient is *undefined* when the divisor is 0.	$\frac{35}{0} =$ undefined; $\frac{0}{0} =$ undefined

Tip: To avoid sign errors when you are performing computations with real numbers, change instances of – – to + and change instances of – + or + – to –. Thereafter, keep a – sign with the number that follows it.

Sums, Differences, and Products of Even and Odd Numbers

An **even number** is an integer that can be written as $2n$, where n is an integer. An **odd number** is an integer that can be written as $2m + 1$, where m is an integer. ***Tip:*** Zero is an even number.

Here is helpful information to know about sums, differences, and products of even and odd numbers.

The sum or difference of two even numbers is even. Examples: $24 + 8 = 32$; $(-30) + (-4) = -34$; $100 - 56 = 44$

The product of two even numbers is even. Examples: $(4)(-28) = -112$; $(18)(12) = 216$

The sum or difference of an even number and an odd number is odd. Examples: $24 + 7 = 31$; $(-15) + (-4) = -19$; $101 - 70 = 31$

The product of an even number and an odd number is even. Examples: $(4)(-25) = -100$; $(18)(3) = 54$

The product of two odd numbers is odd. Examples: $(3)(-25) = -75$; $(19)(3) = 57$

If n is an integer, and n^2 is even, then n is even. Examples: If $n^2 = 36$, then $n = 6$ or -6; If $n^2 = 256$, then $n = 16$ or -16.

If n is an integer, and n^2 is odd, then n is odd. Examples: If $n^2 = 81$, then $n = 9$ or -9; If $n^2 = 625$, then $n = 25$ or -25.

Sums, Differences, and Products of Rational and Irrational Numbers

Here is helpful information to know about sums, differences, and products of rational and irrational numbers.

The sum or difference of two rational numbers is rational. Examples: $1.75 + \frac{3}{2} = 3.25$; $-\frac{1}{3} - \left(-\frac{5}{6}\right) = \frac{1}{2}$

The product of two rational numbers is rational. Examples: $(2.5)(-1.1) = -2.75$; $\left(\frac{3}{4}\right)(90.8) = 68.1$

The sum or difference of a rational number and an irrational number is irrational. Examples: $\sqrt{2} + 9$; $1\frac{3}{4} - \sqrt{41}$

The product of a nonzero rational number and an irrational number is irrational. Examples: $(0.5)\left(\sqrt{2}\right) = 0.5\sqrt{2}$; $(-1)\left(-\sqrt{23}\right) = \sqrt{23}$

The sum or difference of two irrational numbers can be rational or irrational. Examples: $4\sqrt{5} - 4\sqrt{5} = 0$; $4\sqrt{5} + 2\sqrt{5} = 6\sqrt{5}$

The product of two irrational numbers can be rational or irrational. Examples: $\left(4\sqrt{3}\right)\left(-5\sqrt{3}\right) = -60$; $\left(7\sqrt{2}\right)\left(3\sqrt{8}\right) = 84$; $\left(5\sqrt{2}\right)\left(\sqrt{3}\right) = 5\sqrt{6}$

Computing with Complex Numbers

The rules for performing operations with complex numbers follow. Keep in mind that because the coefficients x and y in a complex number $x + yi$ are *real* numbers, the computations involving these real number coefficients must adhere to the rules given previously in the section "Computing with Real Numbers."

For sums and differences of complex numbers, use the following rules.

Rule	Example
Rule 1. Addition of two complex numbers: $(x + yi) + (u + vi) = (x + u) + (y + v)i$ ***Tip:*** Add the real parts. Add the imaginary parts.	$(8 + 3i) + (-5 + 7i) = (8 - 5) + (3 + 7)i = 3 + 10i$
Rule 2. Subtraction of two complex numbers: $(x + yi) - (u + vi) = (x - u) + (y - v)i$ ***Tip:*** Subtract the real parts. Subtract the imaginary parts.	$(-5 + 9i) - (2 + 11i) = (-5 - 2) \div (9 - 11)i = -7 - 2i$

When multiplying complex numbers, it is important to remember that $i^2 = -1$.

For products of complex numbers, use the following rule.

Rule	Example
Rule 3. Multiplication of two complex numbers: $(x + yi)(u + vi) = (xu - yv) + (xv + yu)i$ ***Tip:*** In practice, to avoid errors, use F.O.I.L. (First terms, Outer terms, Inner terms, and Last terms) to perform the multiplication.	$(2 + 3i)(-4 + 5i) = -8 + 10i - 12i + 15i^2 =$ $-8 + 10i - 12i - 15 = -23 - 2i$

The complex numbers $x + yi$ and $x - yi$ are **complex conjugates** of each other. The product of a complex number and its conjugate is a real number. Specifically, $(x + yi)(x - yi) = x^2 - xyi + xyi - y^2i^2 = x^2 - y^2(-1) = x^2 + y^2$.

This concept is used in the division of complex numbers.

For quotients of complex numbers, use the following rule using the complex conjugate.

Rule	Example
Rule 4. Division of two complex numbers: $\frac{x+yi}{u+vi} = \frac{(x+yi)}{(u+vi)} \cdot \frac{(u-vi)}{(u-vi)} = \frac{xu+yv}{u^2+v^2} + \frac{yu-xv}{u^2+v^2}i$ ***Tip:*** Multiply the numerator and denominator by the conjugate of the denominator.	$\frac{6+5i}{3+4i} = \frac{(6+5i)}{(3+4i)} \cdot \frac{(3-4i)}{(3-4i)} = \frac{18-24i+15i-20i^2}{9-16i^2}$ $= \frac{18-24i+15i+20}{9+16}$ $= \frac{38-9i}{25} = \frac{38}{25} - \frac{9}{25}i$

Use the definition of multiplication and the fact that $i^2 = -1$ to compute whole number powers of the imaginary unit i. For example, $i^1 = i$; $i^2 = -1$; $i^3 = i \cdot i^2 = i \cdot -1 = -i$; $i^4 = i^2 \cdot i^2 = -1 \cdot -1 = 1$; $i^5 = i \cdot i^4 = i \cdot 1 = i$; $i^6 = i^2 \cdot i^4 = -1 \cdot 1 = -1$; $i^7 = i^3 \cdot i^4 = -i \cdot 1 = -i$; $i^8 = i^4 \cdot i^4 = 1 \cdot 1 = 1$. As you look at this list, you see a pattern of $i, -1, -i, 1, i, -1, -i, 1, \ldots$. This pattern will continue through higher powers of i. In general, $(i^4)^n = 1$ for any integer. Thus, for example: $i^{103} = \left(i^4\right)^{25} i^3 = (1)(-i) = -i$.

Field Properties of the Real and Complex Numbers

The set of real numbers has the following **field properties** under the binary operations of addition and multiplication for all real numbers a, b, and c:

Field Properties of the Real Numbers

Field Property	Explanation
Closure Property	$a + b$ and ab are real numbers. The sum or product of any two real numbers is a real number.
Commutative Property	$a + b = b + a$ and $ab = ba$. Switching the order of any two addends or any two factors does not affect the final sum or product.
Associative Property	$(a + b) + c = a + (b + c)$ and $(ab)c = a(bc)$. The way the addends or factors are grouped does not affect the final sum or product.
Additive Identity Property	There exists a real number, denoted 0, such that $a + 0 = a$ and $0 + a = a$. This property ensures that 0 is a real number and that its sum with any real number is the number.
Multiplicative Identity Property	There exists a real number, denoted 1, such that $a \cdot 1 = a$ and $1 \cdot a = a$. This property ensures that one is a real number and that its product with any real number is the number.
Additive Inverse Property	For every real number a, there exists a real number, denoted $-a$, such that $a + (-a) = 0$ and $(-a) + a = 0$. This property ensures that for every real number, there is another real number, opposite to it in sign, which, when added to the number, gives 0.
Multiplicative Inverse Property	For every nonzero real number a, there exists a real number, denoted a^{-1}, such that $a(a^{-1}) = 1$ and $(a^{-1})a = 1$. This property ensures that for every real number, except 0, there is another real number, which, when multiplied by the number, gives 1.
Distributive Property	$a(b + c) = ab + ac$ and $(b + c)a = ba + ca$. When you have a factor times a sum, you can either add first and then multiply, or multiply first and then add. Either way, the answer works out to be the same.

Note: A **binary operation** is an operation that is performed on two numbers to obtain another number.

Similarly, for all complex numbers $x + yi$, $u + vi$, $a + bi$, and $c + di$, you have the following:

Field Properties of the Complex Numbers

Field Property	Explanation
Closure Property of Addition	$(x + yi) + (u + vi) = (x + u) + (y + v)i$ is a complex number.
Closure Property of Multiplication	$(x + yi)(u + vi) = (xu - yv) + (xv + yu)i$ is a complex number.
Commutative Property of Addition	$(x + yi) + (u + vi) = (u + vi) + (x + yi)$
Commutative Property of Multiplication	$(x + yi)(u + vi) = (u + vi)(x + yi)$
Associative Property of Addition	$[(x + yi) + (u + vi)] + (a + bi) = (x + yi) + [(u + vi) + (a + bi)]$
Associative Property of Multiplication	$[(x + yi)(u + vi)](a + bi) = (x + yi)[(u + vi)(a + bi)]$
Additive Identity Property	There exists a complex number, 0, such that $(x + yi) + (0) = x + yi$ and $(0) + (x + yi) = x + yi$.
Multiplicative Identity Property	There exists a complex number, 1, such that $(x + yi)(1) = x + yi$ and $(1)(x + yi) = x + yi$.
Additive Inverse Property	For every complex number $x + yi$, there exists a complex number, $(-x) + (-y)i$, such that $(x + yi) + ((-x) + (-y)i) = 0$ and $((-x) + (-y)i) + (x + yi) = 0$.
Multiplicative Inverse Property	For every nonzero complex number $x + yi$, there exists a complex number, $\left(\frac{x}{x^2 + y^2}\right) + \left(\frac{-y}{x^2 + y^2}\right)i$, such that $(x + yi)\left(\left(\frac{x}{x^2 + y^2}\right) + \left(\frac{-y}{x^2 + y^2}\right)i\right) = 1$ and $\left(\left(\frac{x}{x^2 + y^2}\right) + \left(\frac{-y}{x^2 + y^2}\right)i\right)(x + yi) = 1$.
Distributive Property	$(x + yi)[(a + bi) + (c + di)] = (x + yi)(a + bi) + (x + yi)(c + di)$ and $[(a + bi) + (c + di)](x + yi) = (a + bi)(x + yi) + (c + di)(x + yi)$

Note: Proof of each of these properties relies on the corresponding field property for the real numbers.

In general, a system consisting of a set S and two binary operations defined on S is a **field** if the field properties are satisfied for S under the two operations.

Properties of the Integers

For this topic, you must understand the structure of the integers and their properties.

Subsets of the Integers

The **positive integers** are the integers that are greater than zero. The **negative integers** are the integers that are less than zero. The integer 0 is neither positive nor negative.

Integers that are greater than 1 are either prime or composite. A **prime number** is an integer greater than 1 that has exactly two distinct positive factors: itself and 1. The first ten prime numbers are 2, 3, 5, 7, 11, 13, 17, 19, 23, and 29. ***Tip:*** The integer 2 is the only even prime number.

The integers greater than 1 that are *not* prime are the **composite numbers.** The first ten composite numbers are 4, 6, 8, 9, 10, 12, 14, 15, 16, and 18.

The integer 1 is neither prime nor composite.

Integers that are multiples of 2 are even. The **even integers** are {… –6, –4, –2, 0, 2, 4, 6, …}. ***Tip:*** Note that 0 is an even integer.

Integers that are *not* multiples of 2 are odd. The **odd integers** are {–5, –3, –1, 1, 3, 5, …}.

See "Sums, Differences, and Products of Even and Odd Numbers" earlier in this chapter for an additional discussion of even and odd integers.

Divisibility Rules and Factoring

An integer is **divisible** by another integer if, after dividing by that number, the remainder is 0. You write $a|b$ to mean a divides b evenly or, equivalently, b "is divisible by" a (for example: 3|36, which means 36 is divisible by 3—therefore, 3 is a **factor** of 36). The following table shows some common divisibility rules that are useful to know.

Common Divisibility Rules

Divisibility by	Rule	Example
2	A number is divisible by 2 if and only if the last digit of the number is even.	2|2,347,854 because 4 (the last digit) is even.
3	A number is divisible by 3 if and only if the sum of its digits is divisible by 3.	3|151,515 because 3 divides (1 + 5 + 1 + 5 + 1 + 5) = 18 (the sum of the digits).
4	A number is divisible by 4 if and only if the last two digits form a number that is divisible by 4.	4|47,816 because 4 divides 16 (the number formed by the last two digits).
5	A number is divisible by 5 if and only if the last digit of the number is 0 or 5.	5|42,115 because the last digit is 5.
6	A number is divisible by 6 if and only if it is divisible by both 2 and 3.	6|18,122,124 because 2|18,122,124 (the last digit is even) and 3|18,122,124 (21, the sum of the digits, is divisible by 3).
7	To test for divisibility by 7, double the last digit and subtract the product from the number formed by the remaining digits. If the result is a number divisible by 7, the original number is also divisible by 7.	7|875 because 7 divides (87 – 10) = 77 (87 minus 2 times 5).
8	A number is divisible by 8 if and only if the last three digits form a number that is divisible by 8.	8|55,864 because 8 divides 864 (the number formed by the last three digits).
9	A number is divisible by 9 if and only if the sum of its digits is divisible by 9.	9|151,515 because 9 divides (1 + 5 + 1 + 5 + 1 + 5) = 18 (the sum of the digits).
10	A number is divisible by 10 if and only if the last digit of the number is 0.	10|66660 because the last digit is 0.
11	To test for divisibility by 11, alternately add and subtract the digits. If the result is a number divisible by 11, the original number is also divisible by 11.	11|2574 because 11 divides (2 – 5 + 7 – 4) = 0 (the sum of the digits with alternate signs).

Here is helpful information to know about divisibility and factors.

If an integer divides evenly into an integer n, then it divides evenly into any multiple of n. For example, $3|36$, so $3|13(36) = 3|468$.

If an integer divides evenly into both of the integers m and n, then it divides evenly into $am + bn$, for any integers a and b. For example, $9|36$ and $9|81$, so $9|(2 \cdot 36 + 5 \cdot 81)$; that is, $9|477$.

If the prime factorization of a positive integer z is $p_1^{k_1} p_2^{k_2} \cdots p_n^{k_n}$, where the ps are distinct prime numbers and the ks are their corresponding exponents, then the number of positive factors (or divisors) of z is the product $(k_1 + 1)(k_2 + 1) \ldots (k_n + 1)$. Here are examples.

The number of positive factors (or divisors) of $z = a^3bc^2d^5$, where a, b, c, and d are prime numbers, is $(3 + 1)(1 + 1)(2 + 1)(5 + 1) = (4)(2)(3)(6) = 144$.

Tip: Recall that if no exponent is written on a variable or number, the exponent is understood to be 1 (for example, $b = b^1$).

The number of factors (positive and negative) of 18 is 12. The number of positive factors of 18, which equals $(2)(3^2)$, is $(1 + 1)(2 + 1) = (2)(3) = 6$. Because integers can have negative factors as well, the total number of factors of 18 is $2(6) = 12$.

Division Algorithm: If an integer m is divided by a positive integer d, the result is a quotient q with remainder r, where $0 \le r < d$, and $m = dq + r$. In addition, $r = 0$ if and only if m is a multiple of d. ***Tip:*** The remainder r equals $m - dq$ and is always greater than or equal to zero and less than d. Here are examples.

When 21 is divided by 5, the quotient is 4 and the remainder is 1; and $21 = (5)(4) + 1$.

When 30 is divided by 5, the quotient is 6 and the remainder is 0; and $30 = (5)(6)$.

Tip: The division algorithm applies if d is negative as well, in which case $m = dq + r$, with $0 \le r < |d|$.

If $ab = n$, where a, b, and n are integers, then a and b are **factors,** or **divisors,** of n; and n is a **multiple** of a (and of b) and is **divisible** by a (and by b).

Tip: The terms *factor, divisor,* and *divisible* apply only to integers. However, the term *multiple* can be used with any number x as in nx, provided n is an integer.

Greatest Common Factor and Least Common Multiple

The **greatest common factor** (or gcf) of two or more nonzero integers is the greatest positive integer that will divide evenly into each of the numbers. You can obtain it by writing the prime factorization of each number and building a product consisting of each factor the *highest* number of times it appears as a *common* factor of integers in the set. The greatest common factor of two nonzero integers m and n is denoted gcf (m, n). For example, gcf $(72, 48)$ = gcf $(2^3 \cdot 3^2, 2^4 \cdot 3) = 2^3 \cdot 3 = 24$. This is true because the positive factors of 72 are 1, 2, 3, 4, 6, 8, 9, 12, 18, 24, 36, and 72, and the positive factors of 48 are 1, 2, 3, 4, 6, 8, 12, 16, 24, and 48. Thus, the common positive factors of 72 and 48 are 1, 2, 3, 4, 6, 8, 12, and 24, and 24 is the greatest of these.

Note: The **greatest common divisor** of two nonzero integers m and n, denoted gcd (m, n), is the greatest common factor of m and n.

You use the gcf for word problems in which you must find the greatest common number, the greatest common measure, the greatest common size, and so forth that could be used to divide or distribute objects or things evenly from unequal-size sets so that none are left over. Here is an example.

> A high school club has 18 boys and 12 girls as members. For an activity, the club's faculty sponsor wants to evenly divide the boys and girls into groups, so that each group has the same number of boys and the same number of girls as the other groups, and no one is left out. What is the greatest number of groups the sponsor can make?

The greatest number of groups is the gcf $(18, 12) = 6$. Each of the 6 groups will have 5 students in it: 3 boys and 2 girls. ***Tip:*** Notice that $5 \times 6 = 30$, which is the total number of student members $(18 + 12 = 30)$.

The **least common multiple** (or lcm) of two or more nonzero integers is the least positive integer that is a multiple of each of the numbers. That is, it is the minimum number that all of the numbers evenly divide into. You can obtain it by factoring each number and building a product consisting of each factor the *most* number of times it appears as a factor in any *one* of the numbers. The least common multiple of nonzero integers m and n is denoted lcm (m, n). For example, lcm $(36, 48) =$ lcm $(2^2 \cdot 3^2, 2^4 \cdot 3) = 2^4 \cdot 3^2 = 144$. This is true because the positive multiples of 36 are 36, 72, 108, 144, 180, 216, and so on, and the positive multiples of 48 are 48, 96, 144, 192, 240, 288, and so on. Thus, the least common positive multiple of 36 and 48 is 144.

You use the lcm for word problems in which you must find the minimum common number, the minimum common measure, the minimum common time, and so forth between multiple events or items. Here is an example.

> At the entrance to a concert, every 75th person gets a coupon for a free music download and every 100th person gets a coupon for an autographed picture of the performer. What is the minimum number of people who must enter for a person to receive both coupons?

The minimum number of people is the lcm $(75, 100) = 300$. The 300th person will be the first person to receive both coupons.

The product of two positive integers m and n equals their greatest common factor times their least common multiple; that is, $mn = \text{gcf}\,(m, n) \cdot \text{lcm}\,(m, n)$. For example, $24 \cdot 36 = 864$, which equals gcf $(24, 36) \cdot$ lcm $(24, 36) = 12 \cdot 72 = 864$.

Thus, a quick way to compute the lcm of two numbers is to divide their product by their gcf. For example,

$$\text{lcm}\,(75, 100) = \frac{(75)(100)}{\text{gcf}\,(75, 100)} = \frac{(75)(100)}{25} = \frac{\left({}^{3}\cancel{75}\right)(100)}{{}_{1}\cancel{25}} = 300$$

Mathematical Induction and the Fundamental Theorem of Arithmetic

Principle of Mathematical Induction: Any set of positive integers that contains the numbers 1 and $(k + 1)$, whenever it contains the positive integer k, contains all the positive integers.

Fundamental Theorem of Arithmetic: Every integer greater than or equal to 2 is either a prime number or can be factored into a product of prime numbers in one and only one way, except for the order in which the factors appear.

Roots and Radicals

You **square** a number by multiplying the number by itself. The reverse of squaring is finding the **square root.** Every positive number has two square roots that are equal in absolute value, but opposite in sign. For example, $(5)^2 = 25$ and $(-5)^2 = 25$ implies 5 and –5 are square roots of 25. The positive square root is the **principal square root** of the number. The **square root radical** $\left(\sqrt{\ }\right)$ denotes the principal square root. Thus, $\sqrt{(5)(5)} = \sqrt{25} = 5$ and $\sqrt{(-5)(-5)} = \sqrt{25} = 5$. In general, $\sqrt{x^2} = |x|$. Zero has only one square root, namely 0. The principal square root of 0 is 0.

Tip: The $\sqrt{\ }$ symbol always gives one number as the answer and that number is nonnegative: positive or 0. For example, $\sqrt{25} = 5$, not ±5. Also, $\sqrt{(-5)^2} = |-5| = 5$, not –5.

A number that is an exact square of another number is a perfect square. For example, the integers 4, 9, 16, and 25 are perfect squares.

Tip: On the ETS graphing calculator, you can use the $\boxed{\sqrt{x}}$ key under the math menu to find square roots.

You **cube** a number by using it as a factor three times. The inverse of cubing a number is finding the **cube root.** Every real number has exactly *one* real cube root, called its **principal cube root.** The **cube root radical** $\left(\sqrt[3]{\ }\right)$ denotes the principal cube root. The principal cube root of a negative number is negative, and the principal cube root of a positive number is positive. For example, $\sqrt[3]{8} = 2$ and $\sqrt[3]{-8} = -2$.

A number that is an exact cube of another number is a **perfect cube.** Here is a list of principal cube roots of some positive perfect cubes.

$$\sqrt[3]{0} = 0 \quad \sqrt[3]{1} = 1 \quad \sqrt[3]{8} = 2 \quad \sqrt[3]{27} = 3 \quad \sqrt[3]{64} = 4 \quad \sqrt[3]{125} = 5 \quad \sqrt[3]{1{,}000} = 10$$

In general, if $\underbrace{a \cdot a \cdot a \cdot \cdots \cdot a}_{n \text{ factors of } a} = x$ where n is a positive integer, a is an ***n*th root** of x. The **principal *n*th root** of x is denoted $\sqrt[n]{x}$. The expression $\sqrt[n]{x}$ is a **radical.** The number x is the **radicand.** The number n is the **index** and indicates which root is desired. If no index is written, it is understood to be 2 and the radical expression indicates the principal square root of the radicand. A *positive* real number has exactly *one* real positive nth root whether n is even or odd; and *every* real number has exactly one real nth root when n is odd. Negative numbers do not have real nth roots when n is even. Finally, the nth root of 0 is 0, whether n is even or odd: $\sqrt[n]{0} = 0$ (always).

Tip: On the ETS graphing calculator, you can use the $\boxed{\sqrt[x]{y}}$ key under the math menu to find cube roots or other roots. See the calculator manual available at http://infinitysw.s3.amazonaws.com/ets/ets_calculator_manual.pdf for instructions.

The following rules are for radicals when x and y are real numbers, m and n are positive integers, and the radical expression denotes a real number.

Rules for Radicals

$\sqrt[n]{x^n} = x$ if n is odd $\sqrt[n]{x^n} = |x|$ if n is even $\sqrt[n]{x^m} = \left(\sqrt[n]{x}\right)^m$ $\left(\sqrt[n]{x}\right)\left(\sqrt[n]{y}\right) = \sqrt[n]{xy}$

$\frac{\sqrt[n]{x}}{\sqrt[n]{y}} = \sqrt[n]{\frac{x}{y}}, (y \neq 0)$ $\sqrt[m]{\sqrt[n]{x}} = \sqrt[mn]{x}$ $\sqrt[pn]{x^{pm}} = \sqrt[n]{x^m}$ $a\left(\sqrt[n]{x}\right) + b\left(\sqrt[n]{x}\right) = (a+b)\left(\sqrt[n]{x}\right)$

These rules form the basis for simplifying radical expressions. (See Appendix B for a discussion on simplifying radicals.)

Exponents and Logarithms

For this topic, you will demonstrate your understanding of exponents and logarithms and their interrelationship.

Exponents

In mathematical expressions, **exponentiation** is indicated by a small raised number, called the **exponent,** written to the upper right of a quantity, which is the **base** for the exponential expression. Common types of exponents are summarized in the following table.

Common Types of Exponents

Type of Exponent	Definition	Examples
Positive Integer	If x is any real number and n is a positive integer, then $x^n = \underbrace{x \cdot x \cdot x \cdot \cdots \cdot x}_{n \text{ factors of } x}$, where x^n is read "x to the nth power" or as "x to the n."	$6^2 = 6 \cdot 6 = 36$; $2^5 = 2 \cdot 2 \cdot 2 \cdot 2 \cdot 2 = 32$
Zero	For any real number x (except 0), $x^0 = 1$.	$(-12.78)^0 = 1$; $(8^{100})^0 = 1$
Positive Rational Number	If x is any real number and m and n are positive integers, then $x^{\frac{1}{n}} = \sqrt[n]{x}$; and $x^{\frac{m}{n}} = \left(\sqrt[n]{x}\right)^m$ or $\sqrt[n]{x^m}$; provided, in all cases, over the real numbers, that $x \geq 0$ when n is even.	$16^{\frac{1}{2}} = \sqrt{16} = 4$; $(-64)^{\frac{4}{3}} = \left(\sqrt[3]{-64}\right)^4 = (-4)^4 = 256$
Negative Rational Number	If x is any real number (except 0) and m and n are positive integers so that $-n$ and $-\frac{m}{n}$ are negative numbers, then $x^{-n} = \frac{1}{x^n}$; $\frac{1}{x^{-n}} = x^n$; $x^{-\frac{m}{n}} = \frac{1}{x^{\frac{m}{n}}} = \frac{1}{\left(\sqrt[n]{x}\right)^m}$; and $\frac{1}{x^{-\frac{m}{n}}} = x^{\frac{m}{n}} = \left(\sqrt[n]{x}\right)^m$; provided, in all cases, over the real numbers, $x > 0$ when n is even.	$5^{-3} = \frac{1}{5^3} = \frac{1}{125}$; $\frac{1}{5^{-3}} = 5^3 = 125$

Tip: The exponent 2 on a number is usually read "squared" rather than "to the second power." Likewise, the exponent 3 is usually read "cubed" rather than "to the third power."

The rules for exponents are in the following table.

Rules for Exponents

Rule	Examples
$b^m b^n = b^{m+n}$ (product rule)	$(2^3)(2^4) = 2^{3+4} = 2^7$; $(4^{-3})(4^5) = 4^{-3+5} = 4^2$
$\frac{b^m}{b^n} = b^{m-n} = \frac{1}{b^{n-m}}$, $b \neq 0$ (quotient rule)	$\frac{3^6}{3^2} = 3^{6-2} = 3^4$; $\frac{5^4}{5^7} = 5^{4-7} = \frac{1}{5^{7-4}} = \frac{1}{5^3}$
$\left(b^m\right)^p = b^{mp}$ (power of a power)	$\left(5^3\right)^2 = 5^{3 \cdot 2} = 5^6$
$(ab)^p = a^p b^p$ (power of a product)	$(5 \cdot 2)^3 = 5^3 2^3$
$\left(\frac{a}{b}\right)^p = \frac{a^p}{b^p}$, $b \neq 0$ (power of a quotient)	$\left(\frac{10}{2}\right)^3 = \frac{10^3}{2^3}$ and $\frac{10^3}{2^3} = \left(\frac{10}{2}\right)^3$
$\left(\frac{a}{b}\right)^{-p} = \left(\frac{b}{a}\right)^p$, $a \neq 0$, $b \neq 0$	$\left(\frac{3}{4}\right)^{-2} = \left(\frac{4}{3}\right)^2$
$(a+b)^n = \underbrace{(a+b)(a+b)\cdots(a+b)}_{n \text{ times}}$, for n a positive integer	$(a+b)^2 = (a+b)(a+b) = a^2 + 2ab + b^2$ ***Tip:*** Expand the product using rules for multiplying binomials.
If $a^m = a^n$, then $m = n$, provided $a \neq 1$, (one-to-one property)	$2^x = 2^9$ implies $x = 9$

Here are some things to remember about exponents.

The product and quotient rules for exponential expressions can be used only when the exponential expressions have exactly the same base:

$$x^2x^3 = x^{2+3} = x^5 \text{ and } \frac{x^5}{x^3} = x^{5-3} = x^2\text{; but } x^2y^3 \text{ and } \frac{x^5}{y^3} \text{ cannot be simplified further.}$$

Exponentiation is *not* "commutative": $2^5 \neq 5^2$; $2^5 = 32$, but $5^2 = 25$.

Exponentiation does not distribute over addition (or subtraction): $(3+2)^3 \neq 3^3 + 2^3$; $(3+2)^3 = 5^3 = 125$, but $3^3 + 2^3 = 27 + 8 = 35$.

Exponentiation takes precedence over negation: $-5^2 \neq (-5)^2$; $-5^2 = -(5 \cdot 5) = -25$, but $(-5)^2 = -5 \cdot -5 = 25$.

An exponent applies only to the base to which it is attached: $3 \cdot 5^2 \neq 3^2 \cdot 5^2$; $3 \cdot 5^2 = 3 \cdot 25 = 75$, but $3^2 \cdot 5^2 = 9 \cdot 25 = 225$; $-3^2 \neq (-3)^2$; $-3^2 = -(3 \cdot 3) = -9$, but $(-3)^2 = -3 \cdot -3 = 9$.

Use parentheses around the factors for which the exponent applies: $(3 \cdot 5)^2 = 3^2 \cdot 5^2 = 9 \cdot 25 = 225$.

A negative number raised to an even power yields a positive product: $(-2)^4 = -2 \cdot -2 \cdot -2 \cdot -2 = 16$.

A negative number raised to an odd power yields a negative product: $(-2)^5 = -2 \cdot -2 \cdot -2 \cdot -2 \cdot -2 = -32$.

A negative exponent means to write a reciprocal; not to make your answer negative: $2^{-6} = \frac{1}{2^6} = \frac{1}{64}$, not $-\frac{1}{64}$.

A nonzero number or mathematical expression raised to the 0 power is 1:

$$(\text{nonzero number or mathematical expression})^0 = 1 \text{ ALWAYS!}$$

Logarithms

Logarithms are exponents. If $c = \log_b(a)$, then c is the exponent you use on b to get a; that is, $b^c = a$. The number b is the **base** for the logarithm. It must be a positive number and not equal to 1.

Here are examples.

$\log_2(16) = 4$ because 4 is the exponent you use on 2 to get 16; that is, $2^4 = 16$.

$\log_2\left(\frac{1}{8}\right) = -3$ because -3 is the exponent you use on 2 to get $\frac{1}{8}$; that is, $2^{-3} = \frac{1}{8}$.

The **common logarithm** has base 10. Here are examples.

$\log_{10}(100) = 2$ because 2 is the exponent you use on 10 to get 100; that is, $10^2 = 100$.

$\log_{10}(0.001) = -3$ because -3 is the exponent you use on 10 to get 0.001; that is, $10^{-3} = \frac{1}{10^3} = \frac{1}{1{,}000} = 0.001$.

Tip: Generally, if no base is shown on a log, it is assumed to be base 10, the common logarithm.

The **natural logarithm** has the base e, where e is the irrational number whose rational decimal approximation is 2.718281828 (to nine digits). The natural logarithm of a number x is usually written $\ln x$. Here are examples.

$\ln(e^5) = 5$ because 5 is the exponent you use on e to get e^5; that is, $(e)^5 = e^5$.

$\ln\left(\frac{1}{e}\right) = -1$ because -1 is the exponent you use on e to get $\frac{1}{e}$; that is, $e^{-1} = \frac{1}{e}$.

The following rules for logarithms are based on the rules for exponents.

Rules for Logarithms

Rule	Example
$\log_b 1 = 0$	$\log_2(1) = 0$
$\log_b b = 1$	$\log_5(5) = 1$
$\log_b b^x = x$	$\log_2 2^5 = 5$
$\log_b\left(\frac{1}{x}\right) = -\log_b x$ (reciprocal rule)	$\log_2\left(\frac{1}{8}\right) = -\log_2(8) = -3$
$\log_b(uv) = \log_b u + \log_b v$ (product rule)	$\log_2(8 \cdot 16) = \log_2(8) + \log_2(16) = 3 + 4 = 7$
$\log_b\left(\frac{u}{v}\right) = \log_b u - \log_b v$ (quotient rule)	$\log_3\left(\frac{243}{27}\right) = \log_3(243) - \log_3(27) = 5 - 3 = 2$
$\log_b(x^p) = p\log_b x$ (power rule)	$\log_2(8^{12}) = 12\log_2(8) = 12 \cdot 3 = 36$
Change-of-base formula: $\log_b x = \frac{\log_a x}{\log_a b} = \frac{\ln x}{\ln b} = \frac{\log_{10} x}{\log_{10} b}$ $(a > 0, a \neq 1)$	$\log_5 600 = \frac{\ln 600}{\ln 5} \approx 3.97$; $\log_2 100 = \frac{\log_{10} 100}{\log_{10} 2} \approx 6.64$
If $\log_b x = \log_b k$, then $x = k$ (one-to-one property)	$\ln x = \ln 7$ implies $x = 7$.

Note: See "Features of Common Functions" in Chapter 4 for a discussion of the exponential and logarithmic functions.

Order of Operations

When more than one operation is involved in a numerical expression, you must follow the **order of operations** to evaluate the expression. A commonly used mnemonic is "Please Excuse My Dear Aunt Sally"—abbreviated as **PEMDAS.** The first letters of the words remind you of the following:

> First, operations enclosed in Parentheses (or other grouping symbols, if present)
> Next, Exponentiation
> Then, Multiplication and Division in the order in which they occur from left to right
> Last, Addition and Subtraction in the order in which they occur from left to right

Tip: Note that multiplication does not have to be done before division, or addition before subtraction. You multiply and divide in the order they occur in the problem. Similarly, you add and subtract in the order they occur in the problem.

Grouping symbols such as parentheses ( ), brackets [ ], and braces { } are used to keep things together that belong together. Parentheses are used also to indicate multiplication as in (–2)(–5) or for clarity as in –(–15). Fraction bars, absolute value bars | |, and square root (or higher-order roots) symbols $\sqrt{\ }$ are grouping symbols, too.

When you are performing computations, perform operations in grouping symbols first. It is *very important* to do this when addition or subtraction is inside the grouping symbol. For example: $(1 + 1)^3 = 2^3$, $|3 - 10| = |-7| = 7$, and $\sqrt{16+9} = \sqrt{25} = 5$. The exception is when the exponent on a grouping symbol is zero. If you are certain that the sum or difference inside the grouping symbol is nonzero, you can evaluate the expression to be 1 without performing the operations inside the grouping symbol first.

If there is more than one operation inside a grouping symbol, follow the order of operations to do the computations inside the grouping symbol. If there are grouping symbols within grouping symbols, start with the innermost grouping symbol.

Here is an example.

$$100-5\cdot 3^2+\frac{(40+2)}{\sqrt{100-64}}=100-5\cdot 3^2+\frac{42}{\sqrt{36}}$$ First, compute inside grouping symbols.

$$=100-5\cdot 9+\frac{42}{6}$$ Next, evaluate exponents and roots.

$$=100-45+7$$ Then, multiply and divide from left to right.

$$=62$$ Finally, add and subtract from left to right.

Sometimes, you might find it convenient to transform exponential expressions by applying the rules of exponents *before* proceeding through the order of operations.

Here is an example.

> Evaluate $(3\cdot 10)^2-\frac{5^7}{5^4}$.

Transforming exponential expressions *first* simplifies the calculations in this problem.

$(3\cdot 10)^2-\dfrac{5^7}{5^4}=3^2\cdot 10^2-\dfrac{5^7}{5^4}$ Transform $(3\cdot 10)^2$ instead of multiplying inside the parentheses first.

$=3^2\cdot 10^2-5^3$ Transform $\dfrac{5^7}{5^4}$ instead of doing the exponentiation first.

$=9\cdot 100-125$

$=900-125$

$=775$

Scientific Notation

Scientific notation is a way to write very large or very small numbers in a shortened form. Scientific notation helps keep track of the decimal places and makes performing computations with these numbers easier.

A number written in scientific notation is written as a product of two factors. The first factor is a number that is greater than or equal to 1, but less than 10. The second factor is a power of 10. The idea is to make a product that will equal the given number. Any decimal number can be written in scientific notation. Here are examples of numbers written in scientific notation.

Written in scientific notation, 34,000 is $3.4\cdot 10^4$.
Written in scientific notation, 6.5 is $6.5\cdot 10^0$.
Written in scientific notation, 0.00047 is $4.7\cdot 10^{-4}$.

Dimensional Analysis

On the Praxis Math CK test, you will have to demonstrate your knowledge of measurement using the U.S. customary system and the metric system. See Appendix C for a list of common measurement units and conversions.

Convert from one measurement unit to another by using an appropriate "conversion fraction." You make conversion fractions by using a conversion fact, such as 1 gallon = 4 quarts. For each conversion fact, you can write *two* conversion fractions. For example, for the conversion fact given, you have $\dfrac{1\text{ gal}}{4\text{ qt}}$ and $\dfrac{4\text{ qt}}{1\text{ gal}}$ as your two conversion fractions.

Every conversion fraction is equivalent to the number 1 because the numerator and denominator are different names for measures of the same quantity. Therefore, multiplying a quantity by a conversion fraction does not change the value of the quantity.

To change one measurement unit to another unit, multiply by the conversion fraction whose *denominator is the same as the units of the quantity to be converted.* This strategy falls under **dimensional analysis,** a powerful tool used by scientists (including mathematicians) and engineers to analyze units and to guide or check equations and calculations. When you do the multiplication, the units you started out with will "cancel" (divide) out, and you will be left with the desired new units. If this doesn't happen, you used the wrong conversion fraction. Do it over again with the correct conversion fraction.

Additionally, for some conversions you might need to make a "chain" of conversion fractions to obtain the desired units. Here is an example.

> Convert 3 gallons to cups.

Start with your quantity to be converted and keep multiplying by conversion fractions until you obtain the desired units.

$$\frac{3\text{ gal}}{1}\cdot\frac{4\text{ qt}}{1\text{ gal}}\cdot\frac{2\text{ pt}}{1\text{ qt}}\cdot\frac{2\text{ c}}{1\text{ pt}}=\frac{3\cancel{\text{gal}}}{1}\cdot\frac{4\cancel{\text{qt}}}{1\cancel{\text{gal}}}\cdot\frac{2\cancel{\text{qt}}}{1\cancel{\text{qt}}}\cdot\frac{2\text{ c}}{1\cancel{\text{pt}}}=48\text{ cups}$$

Thus, 3 gallons equals 48 cups.

It is a good idea to assess your final answer to see if it makes sense. When you are converting from a larger unit to a smaller unit, you should expect that it will take more of the smaller units to equal the same amount. When you are converting from a smaller unit to a larger unit, you should expect that it will take fewer of the larger units to equal the same amount.

Here is an example of converting from a larger unit to a smaller unit.

$$5\text{ yards}=\frac{5\text{ yd}}{1}\times\frac{3\text{ ft}}{1\text{ yd}}=\frac{5\cancel{\text{yd}}}{1}\times\frac{3\text{ ft}}{1\cancel{\text{yd}}}=15\text{ feet}$$

Feet are smaller than yards, so it should take more of them to equal the same length as 5 yards.

Here is an example of converting from a smaller unit to a larger unit.

$$250\text{ centimeters}=\frac{250\text{ cm}}{1}\times\frac{1\text{ m}}{100\text{ cm}}=\frac{250\cancel{\text{cm}}}{1}\times\frac{1\text{ m}}{100\cancel{\text{cm}}}=\frac{250\text{ m}}{100}=2.5\text{ meters}$$

Meters are larger than centimeters, so it should take fewer of them to equal the same length as 250 centimeters.

Precision, Accuracy, and Approximate Error

In the physical world, measurement of continuous quantities is always approximate. The precision and accuracy of the measurement relate to the worthiness of the approximation.

Precision refers to the degree to which a measurement is repeatable and reliable; that is, consistently getting the same data each time the measurement is taken. The precision of a measurement depends on the magnitude of the smallest measuring unit used to obtain the measurement (for example, to the nearest meter, to the nearest centimeter, to the nearest millimeter, and so on). In theory, the smaller the measurement unit used, the more precise the measurement.

Accuracy refers to the degree to which a measurement is true or correct. A measurement can be precise without being accurate. This can occur, for example, when a measuring instrument needs adjustment, so that the measurements obtained, no matter how precisely measured, are inaccurate.

The amount of error involved in a physical measurement is the **approximate error** of the measurement. The **maximum possible error** of a measurement is half the magnitude of the smallest measurement unit used to obtain the measurement. For example, if the smallest measurement unit is 1 inch, the maximum possible error is 0.5 inch. The most accurate way of expressing a measurement is as a **tolerance interval.** For example, a measurement of 10 inches, to the nearest inch, should be reported as 10 inches ± 0.5 inches. In other words, the true measurement lies between 9.5 inches and 10.5 inches. Closer approximations can be obtained by refining the measurement to a higher degree of precision (for example, by measuring to the nearest half-inch).

When you do calculations with measurements that are reported as tolerance intervals, you need to consider the amount of error that will ensue. The results of such calculations should be reported as tolerance intervals that indicate the potential minimum and maximum error.

Here is an example.

> The length of a rectangular field is 100 ft ± 1 ft, and the width is 50 ft ± 1 ft. Determine a tolerance interval for the area of the field.

Since the area of the field equals length times width, the tolerance interval for the area is (100 ft ± 1 ft)(50 ft ± 1 ft), which implies that (99 ft)(49 ft) ≤ area ≤ (101 ft)(51 ft), or 4,851 ft^2 ≤ area ≤ 5,151 ft^2.

Two ways of conveying the magnitude of error in a measurement are absolute error and relative error (which can be expressed as a decimal or a percent). The **absolute error** of the measurement is the amount of physical error in the measurement, and the **relative error** of the measurement is the ratio of the absolute error to the correct value, or, if the correct value is unknown, to the measurement taken. The formula for relative error is $\frac{\text{absolute error}}{\text{correct value}}$ or $\frac{\text{absolute error}}{\text{measured value}}$ (if the correct value is unknown). When relative error is expressed as a percent, it is called **percent error.**

Here are examples.

> If a protractor is used to measure the sum of the measures of the interior angles of a triangle yielding a measurement of 178.2°, what is the absolute error, relative error, and percent error of the measurement?

The absolute error is the difference between the correct value 180° and the measured value 178.2°. That is, the absolute error = 180° – 178.2° = 1.8°. The relative error is $\frac{1.8°}{180°} = 0.01$, and the percent error is 1%.

> Find the percent error of the measurement 25 ft ± 0.5 ft.

Since the correct value is unknown, the absolute error is 0.5 ft, and the percent error is $\frac{0.5\ \cancel{ft}}{25\ \cancel{ft}} = 0.02 = 2\%$.

Tip: Notice that the absolute error has the same units as the units of the measurement, while the relative error and percent error have no units.

Results of calculations with approximate measurements should not be reported with a degree of precision that would be misleading; that is, suggesting a degree of accuracy greater than the actual accuracy that could be obtained using the approximate measurements. Generally, such calculations should be rounded, *after* all calculations have been made, to have the same precision as the measurement with least precision in the calculation. ***Caution:*** Rounding before final calculations can compound errors.

Chapter 3

Algebra

Algebraic Expressions

For this topic, you work with algebraic expressions; add, subtract, multiply, and divide polynomials; and add, subtract, multiply, and divide algebraic fractions.

Basic Concepts About Algebraic Expressions

A **variable** is a placeholder for a number (or numbers, in some cases) whose value may vary. Symbols (often upper or lowercase letters such as x, y, z, A, B, or C) represent variables. The symbol that represents a variable is the variable's name.

A **constant** is a numerical quantity whose value does not change. For example, all the real and complex numbers are constants. Each has a fixed, definite value. Thus, when a letter is used to name a constant, the letter has one fixed value. For example, the Greek letter π stands for the number that equals the ratio of the circumference of a circle to its diameter, which is approximately 3.14159.

A **numerical expression** is any constant or combination of two or more constants joined by explicit or implied operational symbols.

An **algebraic expression** is a symbol or combination of symbols that represents a number. Algebraic expressions consist of one or more variables joined by one or more operations with or without constants (explicitly) included. Juxtaposition is commonly used to indicate multiplication. That is, when constants and variables or two or more variables (with or without constants) are written side-by-side, they are products. For example, the quantity $2x$ is the result of multiplying 2 and x. Thus, $2 \cdot x = x \cdot 2 = (2)(x) = (2)x = x(2) = 2x$. Similarly, axy means a times x times y.

In an algebraic expression, **terms** are the parts of the expression that are connected to the other parts by plus or minus symbols. If the algebraic expression has no plus or minus symbols, then the algebraic expression itself is a term. For example, $2x$ is a term. Quantities enclosed within grouping symbols are considered single terms, even though they may contain + or – symbols. Thus, the algebraic expression $10(x + 5) - 8$ has two terms.

In a term consisting of a constant times a variable, the constant is the variable's **numerical coefficient.** Thus, in the term $2x$, 2 is the numerical coefficient of x. In a term that is a product of two or more factors, the **coefficient** of a factor is the product of the other factors in that term. For example, in the term $5y(x + 2)$, $5y$ is the coefficient of $(x + 2)$, and $5(x + 2)$ is the coefficient of y. The product of the numerical factors of a term is the numerical coefficient of the term. If no numerical coefficient is explicitly written, the numerical coefficient is understood to be 1.

A **monomial** is a term that when simplified is a constant or a product of one or more variables raised to nonnegative integer powers, with or without an explicit coefficient. The **degree of a monomial** is the sum of the exponents of its variables. For example, the degree of the monomial $8x^4y$ is 5. The degree of a nonzero constant c is 0 because $c = cx^0$ for any constant c. The degree of the monomial 0 is undefined.

Like terms are monomial terms that differ only in their numerical coefficients. For example, $8x^4y$ and $-6x^4y$ are like terms; however, $8x^4y$ and $8xy^4$ are unlike terms. All constants are like terms.

A **polynomial** is an algebraic expression composed of one or more monomials. Thus, a **monomial** is a polynomial that has exactly one term, such as $8x^4y$. A **binomial** is a polynomial of exactly two terms, such as $8x^4y + 5$. A **trinomial** is a polynomial of three terms, such as $16x^2 + 8x + 1$.

Performing Operations with Polynomials

The following table summarizes rules for addition and subtraction of polynomials.

Addition and Subtraction of Polynomials

Operation	Rule	Example
Addition	Combine like monomial terms by adding their numerical coefficients, use the result as the coefficient of the common variable factor or factors, and simply indicate the sum of unlike terms.	$(5x^2 + 10x - 6) + (3x^2 - 2x + 4) = 5x^2 + 10x - 6 + 3x^2 - 2x + 4 = 8x^2 + 8x - 2$
Subtraction	Keep the first polynomial, change the sign of every term in the second polynomial, and proceed as in addition.	$(5x^2 + 10x - 6) - (3x^2 - 2x + 4) = 5x^2 + 10x - 6 - 3x^2 + 2x - 4 = 2x^2 + 12x - 10$

Tip: When simple parentheses (or brackets or braces) are immediately preceded by a + symbol, they can be removed without changing the signs of the terms within, but if the parentheses are immediately preceded by a – symbol, the sign of every term within the grouping must be changed when the parentheses are removed.

To multiply polynomials, multiply each term in the first polynomial by each term in the second polynomial. The following table summarizes rules for multiplication of polynomials.

Multiplication of Polynomials

Operation	Rule	Example
Multiplication: Monomial by Monomial	Multiply both the numerical coefficients and the variable factors.	$(-5x^2y)(10xy) = -50x^3y^2$
Multiplication: Polynomial by Monomial	Use the distributive property to multiply each term of the polynomial by the monomial.	$2x^2(3x^2 - 5x + 1) = 6x^4 - 10x^3 + 2x^2$
Multiplication: Polynomial by Polynomial	Use the distributive property to multiply each term in the second polynomial by each term of the first polynomial, and then combine like terms.	$(x + 2)(x^2 - 2x + 4) = x^3 - 2x^2 + 4x + 2x^2 - 4x + 8 = x^3 + 8$
Multiplication: Binomial by Binomial	Use the distributive property to multiply each term in the second binomial by each term of the first binomial, and then combine like terms. (See "F.O.I.L." below for an efficient way to multiply two binomials.)	$(2x - 3)(x + 4) = 2x^2 + 8x - 3x - 12 = 2x^2 + 5x - 12$

F.O.I.L.

Use F.O.I.L. (First terms, Outer terms, Inner terms, and Last terms) to obtain the product of two binomials. Here is an example.

Last
First
$$(2x - 3)(x + 4) = 2x^2 + 8x - 3x - 12 = 2x^2 + 5x - 12$$
Inner
Outer

Tip: When multiplying polynomials, if possible, arrange the terms of the polynomials in descending or ascending powers of a common variable.

Special Products

Some special products are the following:

$(x+y)^2 = (x+y)(x+y) = x^2 + 2xy + y^2$	Perfect Trinomial Square
$(x-y)^2 = (x-y)(x-y) = x^2 - 2xy + y^2$	Perfect Trinomial Square
$(x+y)(x-y) = x^2 - y^2$	Difference of Two Squares
$(x+y)(x^2 - xy + y^2) = x^3 + y^3$	Sum of Two Cubes
$(x-y)(x^2 + xy + y^2) = x^3 - y^3$	Difference of Two Cubes
$(x+y)^3 = x^3 + 3x^2y + 3xy^2 + y^3$	Perfect Cube
$(x-y)^3 = x^3 - 3x^2y + 3xy^2 - y^3$	Perfect Cube

Division of Polynomials

Division of polynomials is analogous to division of real numbers. Because division by 0 is undefined, you must exclude values for the variable or variables that would make the divisor 0. For convenience, you can assume such values are excluded as you review the rules in this section.

The following table summarizes rules for division of polynomials by monomials.

Division by a Monomial

Operation	Rule	Example
Division: Monomial by Monomial	Divide the numerical coefficients. Divide the variable factors that have a common base. Leave other variable factors alone. Use the quotient of the numerical coefficients as the coefficient for the answer.	$\frac{-50x^3y^2z}{-5x^2y} = 10xyz$
Division: Polynomial by Monomial	Divide each term of the polynomial by the monomial.	$\frac{25x^5y^3 + 35x^3y^2 - 10x^2y}{-5x^2y} = -5x^3y^2 - 7xy + 2$

Tip: To avoid sign errors when you are doing division of polynomials, keep a – symbol with the number that follows it.

Long division of polynomials is performed like long division in arithmetic. The result is usually written as a mixed expression: quotient + $\frac{\text{remainder}}{\text{divisor}}$. Synthetic division is a shortcut method commonly used to divide a polynomial by a binomial of the form $x - r$. See Appendix D for examples of long division and a discussion of synthetic division.

Simplifying Polynomials

A polynomial is **simplified** when all indicated operations have been performed and it contains no uncombined like terms. The **degree of a polynomial** is the same as the greatest of the degrees of its monomial terms after the polynomial has been simplified.

To simplify a polynomial expression, follow these steps:

1. Perform all operations within grouping symbols, starting with the innermost grouping symbol and working outward.
2. Perform all indicated multiplication, starting with exponentiation, being sure to enclose the product in parentheses if it is to be multiplied by an additional factor.
3. Remove all remaining parentheses and combine like terms.

Tip: Simplifying polynomials follows PEMDAS, which makes sense since the variables in the polynomials represent numbers.

Here is an example.

$$\begin{aligned}2+4(x+3y-10)+2(x+3)(x-3)-(x+3)^2 &= 2+4x+12y-40+2\left(x^2-9\right)-\left(x^2+6x+9\right)\\ &= 2+4x+12y-40+2x^2-18-x^2-6x-9\\ &= x^2-2x+12y-65\end{aligned}$$

Tip: Don't make the mistake of writing $2 + 4(x + 3y - 10)$ as $6(x + 3y - 10)$. Remember PEMDAS—multiplication takes precedence over addition (or subtraction) unless grouping symbols indicate otherwise.

Factoring Polynomials Completely

Factoring a polynomial completely means to factor the polynomial as a product of prime polynomial factors, if possible. A **prime polynomial** is one whose only factors are itself and 1. Before you can say a polynomial is a prime factor, you must specify the set of numbers that are available as coefficients when you are factoring. For example, over the integers, the polynomial $x^2 - 3$ is prime; but over the real numbers, $x^2 - 3$ is $\left(x+\sqrt{3}\right)\left(x-\sqrt{3}\right)$. Similarly, over the real numbers, $x^2 + 4$ is prime; but over the complex numbers, $x^2 + 4$ is $(x + 2i)(x - 2i)$. As a general rule, you can safely limit the coefficients of variable terms in polynomials to real numbers. However, when you have polynomial equations, the roots of the equations can be real or complex numbers. When you factor polynomials, proceed systematically as follows.

1. Check for a greatest common monomial factor.
2. If a factor is a binomial, check for

   difference of two squares: $x^2-y^2=(x+y)(x-y)$

   sum of two cubes: $x^3+y^3=(x+y)\left(x^2-xy+y^2\right)$

   difference of two cubes: $x^3-y^3=(x-y)\left(x^2+xy+y^2\right)$

3. If a factor is a trinomial, check for

   perfect trinomial square: $x^2+2xy+y^2=(x+y)^2$

   $x^2-2xy+y^2=(x-y)^2$

   general factorable quadratic: $x^2+(a+b)x+ab=(x+a)(x+b)$

   $acx^2+(ad+bc)x+bd=(ax+b)(cx+d)$

4. If a factor has four terms, first try grouping some of the terms together and factoring the groups separately, and then factoring the entire expression.
5. Write the original polynomial as the product of all the factors obtained. Check to make sure that all polynomial factors except monomial factors are prime.

Tip: After making sure all factors are prime polynomials, check by multiplying the factors to obtain the original polynomial.

Here are examples.

$x^2 - 3x - 4 = (x - 4)(x + 1)$

$64a^2b^4 - 4a^2 = 4a^2(16b^4 - 1) = 4a^2(4b^2 + 1)(4b^2 - 1) = 4a^2(4b^2 + 1)(2b + 1)(2b - 1)$

$80x^3y - 270y^4 = 10y(8x^3 - 27y^3) = 10y(2x - 3y)(4x^2 + 6xy + 9y^2)$

$3x^4y + 3x^3y - 27x^2y - 27xy = 3xy(x^3 + x^2 - 9x - 9) = 3xy[(x^3 + x^2) - (9x + 9)] = 3xy[x^2(x + 1) - 9(x + 1)]$
$= 3xy[(x + 1)(x^2 - 9)] = 3xy[(x + 1)(x + 3)(x - 3)] = 3xy(x + 1)(x + 3)(x - 3)$

Rational Expressions

A rational expression is an algebraic fraction in which both the numerator and denominator are polynomials.

Values for which the denominator evaluates to 0 are excluded. For example, $\frac{2x}{5}$ (no excluded value); $\frac{5}{2x}$, $(x \neq 0)$; $\frac{10x}{x-1}$, $(x \neq 1)$; $\frac{x^2-4}{x^2-3x-4} = \frac{(x+2)(x-2)}{(x-4)(x+1)}$, $(x \neq 4,\ x \neq -1)$; and all polynomials (no excluded values) are rational expressions. Hereafter, whenever a rational expression is written, it will be understood that any values for which the expression is undefined are excluded.

To perform computations with algebraic fractions, often you will need to factor the polynomials used in the algebraic fractions. For example, factoring is frequently necessary when reducing algebraic fractions to lowest terms and when finding a common denominator for algebraic fractions. The following table summarizes the process.

Reducing Algebraic Fractions to Lowest Terms

Type of Algebraic Fraction	Rule	Example
$\frac{\text{monomial}}{\text{monomial}}$	Divide numerator and denominator by the greatest common factor of the two monomials.	$\frac{9x^5y^2z}{12x^2y^3} = \frac{3x^2y^2 \cdot 3x^3z}{3x^2y^2 \cdot 4y} = \frac{\cancel{3x^2y^2} \cdot 3x^3z}{\cancel{3x^2y^2} \cdot 4y} = \frac{3x^3z}{4y}$
$\frac{\text{monomial}}{\text{polynomial}}$ or $\frac{\text{polynomial}}{\text{mononomial}}$	Factor out the greatest monomial factor, if any, from the polynomial, and then divide numerator and denominator by the greatest common factor. Then simplify the polynomial, if possible.	$\frac{-9x^2y}{12x^3y - 36x^2y - 48xy} = \frac{-9x^2y}{12xy(x^2-3x-4)} = \frac{3xy(-3x)}{3xy(4)(x^2-3x-4)}$ $= \frac{\cancel{3xy}(-3x)}{\cancel{3xy}(4)(x^2-3x-4)} = \frac{-3x}{4(x^2-3x-4)}$ $= -\frac{3x}{4(x-4)(x+1)}$ $\frac{12x^3y - 36x^2y - 48xy}{9x^2y} = \frac{12xy(x^2-3x-4)}{3xy(3x)} = \frac{4(x^2-3x-4)}{3x} = \frac{4(x-4)(x+1)}{3x}$
$\frac{\text{polynomial}}{\text{polynomial}}$	Factor the polynomials completely, and then divide numerator and denominator by the greatest common factor.	$\frac{9x^2y - 9y}{12x^3y - 36x^2y - 48xy} = \frac{9y(x^2-1)}{12xy(x^2-3x-4)} = \frac{3y(3)(x+1)(x-1)}{3y(4x)(x+1)(x-4)}$ $= \frac{\cancel{3y}(3)\cancel{(x+1)}(x-1)}{\cancel{3y}(4x)\cancel{(x+1)}(x-4)} = \frac{3(x-1)}{4x(x-4)}$

Tip: When reducing algebraic fractions, make sure you divide by factors only. For example, $\frac{x+2}{4}$ cannot be reduced further. Even though 2 is a factor of the denominator, it is not a factor of the numerator—it is a term of the numerator. Remember, divide the numerator and denominator by common factors, not terms.

The following table summarizes computations with algebraic fractions.

Computations with Algebraic Fractions

Operation	Rule	Example
Addition/ Subtraction: Like Denominators	Add/subtract the numerators to find the numerator of the answer, which is placed over the common denominator. Simplify and reduce to lowest terms, if needed.	$\frac{x+2}{x-3}+\frac{2x-11}{x-3}=\frac{3x-9}{x-3}=\frac{3(x-3)}{x-3}=\frac{3}{1}=3$
	When subtracting, you must change the sign of every term of the numerator of the second fraction.	$\frac{5x^2}{3(x+1)}-\frac{4x^2+1}{3(x+1)}=\frac{5x^2-4x^2-1}{3(x+1)}=\frac{x^2-1}{3(x+1)}=\frac{\cancel{(x+1)}(x-1)}{3\cancel{(x+1)}}=\frac{x-1}{3}$
Addition/ Subtraction:Unlike Denominators	Factor each denominator completely. Find the common denominator, which is the product of each prime factor the highest number of times it is a factor in any one denominator. Write each algebraic fraction as an equivalent fraction having the common denominator as a denominator. Add/subtract the numerators to find the numerator of the answer, which is placed over the common denominator. Simplify and reduce to lowest terms, if needed.	$\frac{1}{x^2-3x-4}+\frac{2}{x^2-1}=\frac{1}{(x+1)(x-4)}+\frac{2}{(x+1)(x-1)}$ $=\frac{1(x-1)}{(x+1)(x-4)(x-1)}+\frac{2(x-4)}{(x+1)(x-1)(x-4)}$ $=\frac{x-1}{(x+1)(x-4)(x-1)}+\frac{2x-8}{(x+1)(x-1)(x-4)}$ $\frac{3x-9}{(x+1)(x-1)(x-4)}=\frac{3(x-3)}{(x+1)(x-1)(x-4)}$

continued

Operation	Rule	Example
Multiplication	Factor all numerators and denominators completely and then divide numerators and denominators by their common factors (as in reducing). The product of the remaining numerator factors is the numerator of the answer, and the product of the remaining denominator factors is the denominator of the answer.	$\frac{a^2+4a+4}{a^2+a-2}\cdot\frac{a^2-2a+1}{a^2-4}=\frac{(a+2)(a+2)}{(a+2)(a-1)}\cdot\frac{(a-1)(a-1)}{(a+2)(a-2)}$ $=\frac{\cancel{(a+2)}\cancel{(a+2)}}{\cancel{(a+2)}\cancel{(a-1)}}\cdot\frac{\cancel{(a-1)}(a-1)}{\cancel{(a+2)}(a-2)}$ $=\frac{a-1}{a-2}$
Division	Multiply the first algebraic fraction by the reciprocal of the second algebraic fraction.	$\frac{a^2+4a+4}{a^2+a-2}\div\frac{a^2-4}{a^2-2a+1}=\frac{a^2+4a+4}{a^2+a-2}\cdot\frac{a^2-2a+1}{a^2-4}$ $=\frac{(a+2)(a+2)}{(a+2)(a-1)}\cdot\frac{(a-1)(a-1)}{(a+2)(a-2)}$ $=\frac{\cancel{(a+2)}\cancel{(a+2)}}{\cancel{(a+2)}\cancel{(a-1)}}\cdot\frac{\cancel{(a-1)}(a-1)}{\cancel{(a+2)}(a-2)}$ $=\frac{a-1}{a-2}$

Complex Fractions

A **complex fraction** is a fraction that has fractions in its numerator, denominator, or both. One way to simplify a complex fraction is to interpret the fraction bar of the complex fraction as meaning division. For example,

$$\frac{\frac{1}{x}+\frac{1}{y}}{\frac{1}{x}-\frac{1}{y}}=\frac{\frac{y}{xy}+\frac{x}{xy}}{\frac{y}{xy}-\frac{x}{xy}}=\frac{\frac{y+x}{xy}}{\frac{y-x}{xy}}=\frac{y+x}{xy}\div\frac{y-x}{xy}=\frac{y+x}{xy}\cdot\frac{xy}{y-x}=\frac{y+x}{y-x}$$

Another way to simplify a complex fraction is to multiply its numerator and denominator by the least common denominator of all the fractions used in its numerator and denominator. For example,

$$\frac{\frac{1}{x}+\frac{1}{y}}{\frac{1}{x}-\frac{1}{y}}=\frac{xy\left(\frac{1}{x}+\frac{1}{y}\right)}{xy\left(\frac{1}{x}-\frac{1}{y}\right)}=\frac{xy\cdot\frac{1}{x}+xy\cdot\frac{1}{y}}{xy\cdot\frac{1}{x}-xy\cdot\frac{1}{y}}=\frac{y+x}{y-x}$$

One-Variable Linear Equations and Inequalities

For this topic, you must solve one-variable linear equations and inequalities.

Solving One-Variable Linear Equations

An **equation** is a statement that two mathematical expressions are equal. An equation has two sides. Whatever is on the left side of the equal sign is the left side (LS) of the equation, and whatever is on the right side of the equal sign is the right side (RS) of the equation. Equations containing only numerical expressions are either true or false. For example, $1 + 2 = 3$ is true, but $1 + 2 = 5$ is false. An equation containing one or more variables is an **open sentence**. For example, $x + 2 = 3$ and $x + 2y = 8$ are open sentences. Generally, you can determine whether an open sentence is true or false only after numerical quantities are substituted for the variables in the sentence.

A **one-variable linear equation** has only one variable. The variable has an exponent of 1 (commonly not written, but understood), and no products of variables or variable divisors occur in the equation. A **solution** (or **root**) of a one-variable equation is a number that when substituted for the variable makes the equation true. An equation is true when the LS has the same value as the RS. To determine whether a number is a solution of a one-variable equation, replace the variable with the number and perform all operations indicated on each side of the equation. If the resulting statement is true, the number is a solution of the equation. This process is called **checking a solution**.

The **solution set** of an equation is the set consisting of all the solutions of the equation. **Equivalent equations** are equations that have the same solution set. If the solution set is the set of all possible values of the variable, the equation is an **identity**. For example, $x + 7 = x + 5 + 2$ is an identity because any number substituted for x will make the equation true. Thus, an identity has an infinite number of solutions. If the solution set is empty, the equation has no solution. For example, $x + 7 = x + 5$ has no solution because there is no number that will make the equation true. To **solve an equation** means to find its solution set.

A one-variable linear equation can be written in the form $ax + b = 0$, where $a \neq 0$ and b is a constant in the discussion. For example, $2x + 6 = 0$, $12x + 1 = 5(x - 4)$, and $\frac{2y}{3} - 45 = y$ are one-variable linear equations. Unless the equation is an identity or has no solution, the solution set of a one-variable linear equation consists of one number.

The strategy in solving a one-variable linear equation is to proceed through a series of steps until you produce an equivalent equation that has the form variable = solution (or solution = variable). The equal sign in an equation is like a balance point. To keep the equation in balance, what you do to one side of the equation you must do to its other side. You decide what to do by inspecting what has been done to the variable. You undo what's been done until the variable is by itself on one side of the equation only, the variable's coefficient is understood to be 1, and the other side of the equation is a single number all by itself.

When you are solving an equation, the two main actions that will result in equivalent equations are the following:

1. Addition or subtraction of the same quantity on both sides of the equation.
2. Multiplication or division by the same *nonzero* quantity on both sides of the equation.

Tip: It is important to remember that when you are solving an equation, you must never multiply or divide both sides by 0.

To solve a one-variable linear equation, use the following steps.

1. Remove grouping symbols, if any, by applying the distributive property and then simplify.
2. If the variable appears on both sides of the equation, eliminate the variable from one side of the equation. Undo indicated addition or subtraction to get all terms containing the variable on one side and all other terms on the other side. Then simplify.

3. If a number is added to the variable term, subtract that number from both sides of the equation. If a number is subtracted from the variable term, add that number to both sides of the equation. Then simplify.
4. If necessary, factor the side containing the variable so that one of the factors is the variable.
5. Divide both sides of the equation by the coefficient of the variable. If the coefficient is a fraction, divide by multiplying both sides of the equation by the fraction's reciprocal.

Tip: You should always check the solution of a linear equation in the original equation.

Here is an example.

Solve $\frac{2}{3}x - 45 = -\frac{1}{2}(x + 48)$.

$$\begin{aligned}
\frac{2}{3}x - 45 &= -\frac{1}{2}(x + 48) \\
\frac{2}{3}x - 45 &= -\frac{1}{2}x - 24 \\
\frac{2}{3}x - 45 + \frac{1}{2}x &= -\frac{1}{2}x - 24 + \frac{1}{2}x \\
\frac{7}{6}x - 45 &= -24 \\
\frac{7}{6}x - 45 + 45 &= -24 + 45 \\
\frac{7}{6}x &= 21 \\
\frac{\cancel{6}}{\cancel{7}} \cdot \frac{\cancel{7}}{\cancel{6}}x &= \frac{6}{\cancel{7}} \cdot \cancel{21}^{3} \\
x &= 18
\end{aligned}$$

Tip: Of course, as long as you keep the equation in balance, you can modify the equation-solving process based on the particular equation you are trying to solve. For example, if an equation contains fractions, you first might multiply both sides of the equation by the lcm of all the denominators to eliminate fractions from both sides of the equation. You also might do some of the steps mentally to save time.

Transforming Formulas and Two-Variable Equations

An equation that expresses the relationship between two or more variables is a **formula**. The procedure for solving one-variable linear equations can be used to solve a formula for a specific variable when the value(s) of the other variable(s) are known. The procedure also can be used to solve a formula or **literal equation** (an equation with no numbers, only letters) for a specific variable in terms of the other variable(s). In general, isolate the specific variable and treat all other variable(s) as constants. This is called changing the subject of the formula or literal equation. Here is an example.

Solve $C = \frac{5}{9}(F - 32)$ for F.

$$\begin{aligned} C &= \frac{5}{9}(F-32) \\ C &= \frac{5}{9}F - \frac{5}{9}\cdot 32 \\ C &= \frac{5}{9}F - \frac{160}{9} \\ C + \frac{160}{9} &= \frac{5}{9}F \\ \frac{9}{5}\left(C + \frac{160}{9}\right) &= \frac{\cancel{9}}{\cancel{5}}\cdot\frac{\cancel{5}}{\cancel{9}}F \\ \frac{9}{5}C + 32 &= F \\ F &= \frac{9}{5}C + 32 \end{aligned}$$

The procedure for solving one-variable linear equations can be used to solve a two-variable equation for one variable in terms of the other variable. Another common use for the procedure for solving one-variable linear equations is to transform equations of lines into the form $y = mx + b$, where m and b are constants. Here is an example.

> Write $-2x + 3y = 1$ in the form $y = mx + b$.

$$\begin{aligned} -2x + 3y &= 1 \\ -2x + 3y + 2x &= 1 + 2x \\ 3y &= 2x + 1 \\ y &= \frac{2}{3}x + \frac{1}{3} \end{aligned}$$

Solving One-Variable Linear Inequalities

If you replace the equal sign in a one-variable linear equation with either < (less than), > (greater than), ≤ (less than or equal), or ≥ (greater than or equal), the result is a **one-variable linear inequality**. The graph of the solution set of the inequality can be illustrated on a number line. When you solve one-variable linear inequalities, treat them just like one-variable linear equations *except* for one important difference: If you multiply or divide both sides of the inequality by a negative number, *reverse* the direction of the inequality. Here is an example.

> Solve $-3x + 5 > 29 + x$.

$$\begin{aligned} -3x + 5 &> 29 + x \\ -3x + 5 - x &> 29 + x - x \\ -4x + 5 &> 29 \\ -4x + 5 - 5 &> 29 - 5 \\ -4x &> 24 \\ \frac{\cancel{-4}x}{\cancel{-4}} &< \frac{\cancel{24}^{-6}}{\cancel{-4}} \\ x &< -6 \end{aligned}$$

Reverse the direction of the inequality because you divided by a negative number.

Sometimes two statements of inequality apply to a variable expression simultaneously and, thus, can be combined into a **double inequality**. For example, $5x + 3 > -7$ and $5x + 3 < 13$ can be written as $-7 < 5x + 3 < 13$. To solve a double inequality, undo what has been done to the variable expression. Apply the undoing operations to all three parts of the double inequality.

Here is an example.

Solve $-7 < 5x + 3 < 13$.

$$-7 < 5x + 3 < 13$$
$$-7 - 3 < 5x + 3 - 3 < 13 - 3$$
$$-10 < 5x < 10$$
$$\frac{\cancel{-10}^{-2}}{\cancel{5}} < \frac{\cancel{5}x}{\cancel{5}} < \frac{\cancel{10}^{2}}{\cancel{5}}$$
$$-2 < x < 2$$

One-Variable Absolute Value Equations and Inequalities

For this topic, you must solve one-variable absolute value equations and inequalities.

Solving One-Variable Absolute Value Equations

Solve one-variable absolute value equations using the procedure for solving one-variable linear equations. Here are some useful facts about absolute value equations:

$|ax + b| = 0$ if and only if $ax + b = 0$.

If $c > 0$, $|ax + b| = c$ if and only if either $ax + b = -c$ or $ax + b = c$.

Here is an example.

Solve $|x + 3| = 5$.

$$|x + 3| = 5 \text{ implies}$$
$$x + 3 = -5 \quad \text{or} \quad x + 3 = 5$$
$$x = -8 \quad \text{or} \quad x = 2$$

Tip: Notice that for equations like $|ax + b| = c$, you must solve two linear equations. Don't forget the second equation!

One-variable absolute value inequalities can be solved using the procedure for solving one-variable linear inequalities. Here are some useful facts about absolute value inequalities:

If $c > 0$, $|ax + b| < c$ if and only if $-c < ax + b < c$; and

$|ax + b| > c$ if and only if either $ax + b < -c$ or $ax + b > c$.

Here are examples.

Solve $|x + 3| < 5$.

$$\begin{aligned} |x+3| &< 5 \text{ implies} \\ -5 &< x+3 < 5 \\ -5-3 &< x+3-3 < 5-3 \\ -8 &< x < 2 \end{aligned}$$

> Solve $|x + 3| > 5$.

$$|x+3| > 5 \text{ implies}$$

$$\begin{aligned} x+3 &< -5 && \text{or} && x+3 > 5 \\ x+3-3 &< -5-3 && \text{or} && x+3 > 5-3 \\ x &< -8 && \text{or} && x > 2 \end{aligned}$$

Tip: Notice that for absolute value inequalities you must solve two linear inequalities.

Note: In the above discussion, you can replace < and > with ≤ and ≥, respectively, without loss of generality.

One-Variable Quadratic Equations and Inequalities

A **one-variable quadratic equation** is an equation that can be written in the standard form $ax^2 + bx + c = 0$, where $a \neq 0$ and a, b, and c are real-valued constants in the discussion. Specifically, a is the numerical coefficient of x^2, b is the numerical coefficient of x, and c is the constant coefficient, or simply the constant term. The solutions of a quadratic equation are its **roots**. A quadratic equation may have exactly *one* real root, exactly *two* real unequal roots, or *no* real roots.

Solving Quadratic Equations of the Form $x^2 = C$

Quadratic equations that can be written in the form $x^2 = C$ have the solution $x = \pm\sqrt{C}$. If the quantity C is 0, there is *one* real root that has the value 0; if *positive*, there are *two* unequal real roots; and if *negative*, there are *no* real roots.

Here is an example.

> Solve $3x^2 = 48$.

$$\begin{aligned} 3x^2 &= 48 \\ x^2 &= 16 \\ x &= \pm\sqrt{16} \\ x &= \pm 4 \end{aligned}$$

Solving Quadratic Equations by Factoring

The procedure for solving quadratic equations by factoring is based on the **property of zero products for numbers:** If the product of two quantities is zero, at least one of the quantities is zero.

To solve a quadratic equation by factoring, use the following procedure:

1. Express the equation in standard form: $ax^2 + bx + c = 0$.
2. Factor the LS of the equation.

3. Set each factor containing the variable equal to 0.
4. Solve each of the resulting linear equations.

Tip: You should always check each root of a quadratic equation by substituting it into the original equation.

Here is an example.

Solve $x(x + 8) = 20$ by factoring.

$$\begin{aligned} x(x+8)&=20 \\ x^2+8x-20&=0 \\ (x+10)(x-2)&=0 \\ x+10=0 \quad &\text{or} \quad x-2=0 \\ x=-10 \quad &\text{or} \quad x=2 \end{aligned}$$

Solving Quadratic Equations by Completing the Square

To solve a quadratic equation by completing the square, use the following procedure:

1. Get all terms containing the variable on the equation's LS, and all other terms on the RS.
2. If the coefficient of the squared term is not 1, divide each term by it.
3. Add the square of half the coefficient of x (the first-degree term) to both sides of the equation.
4. Factor the perfect trinomial square on the equation's LS as the square of a binomial.
5. Take the square root of both sides.
6. Solve each of the resulting linear equations.

Here is an example.

Solve $x(x + 8) = 20$ by completing the square.

$$\begin{aligned} x(x+8)&=20 \\ x^2+8x&=20 \\ x^2+8x+4^2&=20+4^2 \\ x^2+8x+16&=36 \\ (x+4)^2&=36 \\ (x+4)&=\pm\sqrt{36} \\ x+4&=\pm 6 \\ x+4=-6 \quad &\text{or} \quad x+4=6 \\ x=-10 \quad &\text{or} \quad x=2 \end{aligned}$$

Note: In most instances, solving a quadratic equation by completing the square is not an efficient way to solve a quadratic equation on the Praxis Math CK test. Use the quadratic formula instead. The method is shown here because completing the square is the method commonly used to derive the quadratic formula.

Solving Quadratic Equations by Using the Quadratic Formula

To solve a quadratic equation by using the quadratic formula, use the following procedure:

1. Express the equation in standard form: $ax^2 + bx + c = 0$.
2. Determine the values of the coefficients a, b, and c.
3. Substitute into the quadratic formula: $x = \dfrac{-b \pm \sqrt{b^2 - 4ac}}{2a}$.
4. Evaluate and simplify.

Tip: When determining the values of coefficients for the quadratic formula, keep a – symbol with the number that follows it.

Here is an example.

Solve $x(x + 8) = 20$ by using the quadratic formula.

$$x(x+8) = 20$$
$$x^2 + 8x - 20 = 0$$

$a = 1$, $b = 8$, $c = -20$ (include the – sign).

$$x = \frac{-8 \pm \sqrt{8^2 - 4(1)(-20)}}{2(1)}$$
$$x = \frac{-8 \pm \sqrt{64 + 80}}{2}$$
$$x = \frac{-8 \pm \sqrt{144}}{2}$$
$$x = \frac{-8 \pm 12}{2}$$
$$x = \frac{-8 - 12}{2} \quad \text{or} \quad x = \frac{-8 + 12}{2}$$
$$x = -10 \quad \text{or} \quad x = 2$$

Note: This method is an efficient way to solve a quadratic equation on the Praxis Math CK test.

The quantity $b^2 - 4ac$ is the **discriminant** of the quadratic equation. The quadratic equation $ax^2 + bx + c = 0$ has exactly *one* real root if $b^2 - 4ac = 0$, *two* real unequal roots if $b^2 - 4ac > 0$, and *no* real roots if $b^2 - 4ac < 0$.

Tip: When solving quadratic equations, never divide both sides of the equation by the variable or by an expression containing the variable because you run the risk of unknowingly dividing by 0.

Solving Equations That Have the Form of a Quadratic Equation

Equations that are not quadratic equations but that can be written in the form of a quadratic equation can be solved using the methods for solving quadratic equations. It naturally follows that equations that can be written so one side is a factorable higher degree polynomial and the other side contains only 0 can be solved by factoring completely, setting each factor equal to 0, and then solving the resulting equations. Here is an example.

Solve $x^4 - 13x^2 + 36 = 0$.

$$x^4 - 13x^2 + 36 = 0$$
$$\left(x^2 - 9\right)\left(x^2 - 4\right) = 0$$
$$(x+3)(x-3)(x+2)(x-2) = 0$$
$$x = -3,\ 3,\ -2, \text{ or } 2$$

Solving One-Variable Quadratic Inequalities

Quadratic inequalities have the standard forms $ax^2 + bx + c < 0$, $ax^2 + bx + c > 0$, $ax^2 + bx + c \le 0$, and $ax^2 + bx + c \ge 0$. The solution sets for quadratic inequalities in standard form are based on the rules for multiplying signed numbers: If two factors have the same sign, their product is positive; if they have opposite signs, their product is negative. To solve a quadratic inequality, put it in standard form with $a > 0$ and apply the following.

If $ax^2 + bx + c = 0$ has no real roots, $ax^2 + bx + c$ is always positive (and $-ax^2 - bx - c$ is always negative).

If $ax^2 + bx + c = 0$ has exactly one real root, $ax^2 + bx + c$ is 0 at that root.

If $ax^2 + bx + c = 0$ has two real roots, $ax^2 + bx + c$ is negative between them, positive to the left of the leftmost root, positive to the right of the rightmost root, and 0 only at its roots.

For example, $x^2 + 2x - 24 = (x + 6)(x - 4) = 0$ has two real roots, –6 and 4. So $x^2 + 2x - 24$ is negative in the interval $(-6, 4)$ and positive in the intervals $(-\infty, -6)$ and $(4, \infty)$.

Note: If you have a quadratic inequality in which $a < 0$, to put the inequality in standard form with $a > 0$, multiply both sides of the inequality by -1 and reverse the direction of the inequality.

Other Common One-Variable Equations

In this section, you will solve fractional equations, radical equations, exponential equations, and logarithmic equations.

Solving Fractional Equations

A **fractional equation** is one in which a variable appears in the denominator of one or more terms. For example, $\frac{1}{2} + \frac{1}{x} = \frac{5}{6}$ and $\frac{x-2}{x} = \frac{4}{x(x-2)}$ are fractional equations. (***Note:*** Linear equations that have fractional coefficients, such as $\frac{1}{2}x - 6 = 4$, are not fractional equations.) Many fractional equations can be transformed into linear or quadratic equations by multiplying both sides of the equation by the lcm of the equation's fractions. However, this action does not necessarily result in an equivalent equation. Check your result against the excluded values for the equation's variable. A result that is an excluded value is called an **extraneous root**. It cannot be in the solution set.

Here are examples.

Solve $\frac{1}{2} + \frac{1}{x} = \frac{5}{6}$.

$$\frac{1}{2} + \frac{1}{x} = \frac{5}{6}$$
$$6x\left(\frac{1}{2} + \frac{1}{x}\right) = 6x\left(\frac{5}{6}\right)$$
$$3x + 6 = 5x$$
$$6 = 2x$$
$$3 = x$$

Check: The equation $\frac{1}{2}+\frac{1}{x}=\frac{5}{6}$ has one excluded value; x cannot be 0. Thus, $\frac{1}{2}+\frac{1}{x}=\frac{5}{6}$ has solution $x=3$.

Solve $\frac{x-2}{x}=\frac{4}{x(x-2)}$.

$$\frac{x-2}{x}=\frac{4}{x(x-2)}$$

$$\cancel{x}(x-2)\left(\frac{x-2}{\cancel{x}}\right)=\cancel{x}\cancel{(x-2)}\left(\frac{4}{\cancel{x}\cancel{(x-2)}}\right)$$

$$(x-2)(x-2)=4$$

$$x^2-4x+4=4$$

$$x^2-4x=0$$

$$x(x-4)=0$$

$$x=0 \text{ or } x=4$$

Check: The equation $\frac{x-2}{x}=\frac{4}{x(x-2)}$ has two excluded values; x cannot be 0 or 2. Thus, 0 is an extraneous root, meaning $x=4$ is the only solution of $\frac{x-2}{x}=\frac{4}{x(x-2)}$.

Solving Radical Equations

A **radical equation** is one in which the variable appears in a radical. For example, $\sqrt{2x-4}+1=7$ and $x+3=\sqrt{x+5}+4$ are radical equations. To solve a radical equation that contains only one radical, use the following procedure:

1. Get the radical on one side of the equation and all other terms on the other side.
2. Eliminate the radical by raising both sides of the equation to an appropriate power. For square root radicals, square both sides. For cube root radicals, cube both sides; and so forth.
3. Solve the resulting equation.
4. Check for extraneous roots by substituting your obtained value(s) in the original radical equation.

Here are examples.

Solve $\sqrt{2x-4}+1=7$.

$$\sqrt{2x-4}+1=7$$

$$\sqrt{2x-4}=6$$

$$\left(\sqrt{2x-4}\right)^2=6^2$$

$$2x-4=36$$

$$2x=40$$

$$x=20$$

Check:

$$\sqrt{2x-4}+1=7$$

$$\sqrt{2\cdot 20-4}+1\stackrel{?}{=}7$$

$$\sqrt{40-4}+1\stackrel{?}{=}7$$

$$\sqrt{36}+1\stackrel{?}{=}7$$

$$6+1\stackrel{?}{=}7$$

$$7\stackrel{\checkmark}{=}7$$

The solution of $\sqrt{2x-4}+1=7$ is $x=20$.

Solve $x+3=\sqrt{x+5}+4$.

$$\begin{aligned} x+3&=\sqrt{x+5}+4 \\ x-1&=\sqrt{x+5} \\ (x-1)^2&=\left(\sqrt{x+5}\right)^2 \\ x^2-2x+1&=x+5 \\ x^2-3x-4&=0 \\ (x+1)(x-4)&=0 \\ x=-1 &\text{ or } x=4 \end{aligned}$$

Check $x=-1$:

$$\begin{aligned} x+3&=\sqrt{x+5}+4 \\ (-1)+3&\overset{?}{=}\sqrt{(-1)+5}+4 \\ 2&\overset{?}{=}\sqrt{4}+4 \\ 2&\overset{?}{=}2+4 \\ 2&\neq 6 \text{ (Reject } x=-1) \end{aligned}$$

Check $x=4$:

$$\begin{aligned} x+3&=\sqrt{x+5}+4 \\ (4)+3&\overset{?}{=}\sqrt{(4)+5}+4 \\ 7&\overset{?}{=}\sqrt{9}+4 \\ 7&\overset{?}{=}3+4 \\ 7&\overset{\checkmark}{=}7 \end{aligned}$$

The solution of $x+3=\sqrt{x+5}+4$ is $x=4$.

Solving Exponential Equations

An **exponential equation** is one in which the variable appears in an exponent. For example, $5^{2x-1}=125$ and $2^x=20$ are exponential equations. In some cases, you can solve exponential equations by equating exponents of like bases. Here is an example.

Solve $5^{2x-1}=125$.

$$\begin{aligned} 5^{2x-1}&=125 \\ 5^{2x-1}&=5^3, \text{ which implies} \\ 2x-1&=3 \\ 2x&=4 \\ x&=2 \end{aligned}$$

However, solving $2^x=20$ requires the use of logarithms because 2 and 20 are not integral powers of the same base.

In general, to solve an exponential equation, use the following procedure:

1. Isolate the exponential term.
2. Take the natural log (or the common log) of both sides of the equation.
3. Use $\ln b^x = x\ln b$ (or $\log b^x = x\log b$) to simplify the logarithmic term.
4. Solve the resulting equation for the variable, using the ln key (or the log key) on the ETS graphing calculator to approximate the solution.

Tip: The solution is the same whether you use the natural log or the common log to transform the equation to logarithmic form.

Here is an example.

Solve $2^x=20$ (round to the nearest tenth).

$$\begin{aligned} 2^x &= 20 \\ \ln\left(2^x\right) &= \ln(20) \\ x\ln 2 &= \ln 20 \\ x &= \frac{\ln 20}{\ln 2} \\ x &\approx 4.3 \end{aligned}$$

Note: See "Exponents and Logarithms" in Chapter 2 for a review of these concepts.

Solving Logarithmic Equations

A **logarithmic equation** is one in which the variable appears in the argument of a logarithm. For example, $\log_5(x) + \log_5(10) = 4$ is a logarithmic equation.

In general, to solve a logarithmic equation, use the following procedure:

1. If needed, use the properties of logarithms to create one logarithmic term.
2. Isolate the logarithmic term.
3. Write the logarithmic equation in exponential form.
4. Solve the resulting equation for the variable.

Here is an example.

> Solve $\log_5(x) + \log_5(10) = 4$.

$$\begin{aligned} \log_5(x) + \log_5(10) &= 4 \\ \log_5(10x) &= 4, \text{ which implies} \\ 10x &= 5^4 \\ 10x &= 625 \\ x &= 62.5 \end{aligned}$$

Note: See "Exponents and Logarithms" in Chapter 2 for a review of these concepts.

Systems of Equations and Inequalities

For this topic, you solve and graph systems of equations and inequalities.

Basic Concepts About Systems of Equations

A set of equations, each with the same set of variables, is called a **system** when all the equations in the set are considered simultaneously. The system possesses a solution when the equations in the system are all satisfied by at least one set of values of the variables. A system that has a solution is **consistent**. A system that has no solution is **inconsistent**.

The standard form of a two-variable linear equation is $Ax + By = C$, where A, B, and C are constants and A and B are not both zero. A **system of two linear equations in two variables** consists of a pair of linear equations in the same two variables. The system has the form $\begin{aligned} A_1x + B_1y &= C_1 \\ A_2x + B_2y &= C_2 \end{aligned}$.

To solve a system of two linear equations in two variables means to find all pairs of values for the two variables that make *both* equations true simultaneously. A pair of values—for example, an x-value paired with a corresponding y-value—is called an **ordered pair** and is written as (x, y). An ordered pair that makes an equation true is said to satisfy the equation. When an ordered pair makes both equations in a system true, the ordered pair satisfies the system. The solution set is the collection of all solutions. There are three possibilities: The system has exactly *one solution, no solution,* or *infinitely many solutions.*

Geometrically, the two equations of a system of linear equations in two variables can be represented as lines in the coordinate plane. For the two lines, there are three possibilities that can occur, corresponding to the three possibilities for the solution set. If the system is consistent and has *exactly one solution,* then the two lines intersect in a unique point in the plane. The ordered pair that corresponds to the point of intersection is the solution to the system. If the system is consistent and has *infinitely many solutions,* then the two lines are **coincident** (that is, have all points in common). If the system is inconsistent and has *no solution,* then the two lines are parallel in the plane. Here are illustrations.

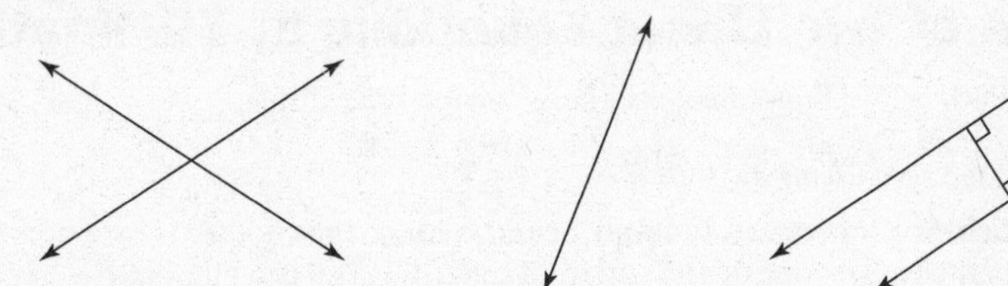

Exactly One Solution   Infinitely Many Solutions   No Solution

Note: See "Basic Function Concepts" in Chapter 4 for a discussion of the coordinate plane.

A quick way to decide whether a system of two linear equations has exactly one solution, infinitely many solutions, or no solution is to look at ratios of the coefficients of the two equations. If $\frac{A_1}{A_2} \neq \frac{B_1}{B_2}$, the system has exactly one solution; if $\frac{A_1}{A_2} = \frac{B_1}{B_2} = \frac{C_1}{C_2}$, the system has infinitely many solutions; and if $\frac{A_1}{A_2} = \frac{B_1}{B_2} \neq \frac{C_1}{C_2}$, the system has no solution.

Three algebraic methods commonly used to solve a system of linear equations are substitution, elimination, and transformation of the augmented matrix (see Chapter 10, "Matrices," for this latter method).

Solving a System of Two Linear Equations by Substitution

To solve a system of two linear equations by **substitution,** use the following procedure:

1. Select the simpler equation and solve for one of the variables in terms of the other. Use your judgment to decide which variable to solve first.
2. Substitute the result from Step 1 into the other equation, simplify, and solve, if possible.
3. Substitute the result from Step 2 into one of the original equations and solve for the other variable.

Tip: You should always check the solution to a system of linear equations in the original equations.

Here is an example (for convenience, the equations are numbered).

> Solve the system: (1) $x + y = 1,950$ by the method of substitution.
>
> (2) $9x + 6y = 13,950$

The system has exactly one solution because $\frac{1}{9} \neq \frac{1}{6}$.

Solve equation (1) for x to obtain $x = 1,950 - y$. Substitute this result into equation (2) and solve for y.

$$\begin{aligned} 9x + 6y &= 13,950 \\ 9(1,950 - y) + 6y &= 13,950 \\ 17,550 - 9y + 6y &= 13,950 \\ 17,550 - 3y &= 13,950 \\ -3y &= -3,600 \\ y &= 1,200 \end{aligned}$$

Using equation (1), $x = 1,950 - y = 1,950 - 1,200 = 750$.

The solution is $x = 750$, $y = 1,200$.

Solving a System of Two Linear Equations by Elimination

To solve a system of linear equations by **elimination,** use the following procedure:

1. Write both equations in standard form: $Ax + By = C$.
2. Eliminate one of the variables. If necessary, multiply one or both of the equations by a nonzero constant or constants to make the coefficients of one of the variables sum to 0. You can eliminate either variable. Use your judgment to decide.
3. Add the transformed equations and solve for the variable that was not eliminated.
4. Substitute the result in Step 3 into one of the original equations and solve for the other variable.

Here is an example (for convenience, the equations are numbered).

> Solve the system: (1) $3y = 2x + 1$ by the method of elimination.
> (2) $3x - 7y = 6$

Write both equations in standard form: (1) $-2x + 3y = 1$
(2) $3x - 7y = 6$

The system has exactly one solution because $\frac{-2}{3} \neq \frac{3}{-7}$.

To eliminate x, multiply equation (1) by 3 and equation (2) by 2.

$$\begin{matrix} -2x + 3y = 1 \\ 3x - 7y = 6 \end{matrix} \quad \text{implies} \quad \begin{matrix} 3(-2x + 3y) = 3(1) \\ 2(3x - 7y) = 2(6) \end{matrix} \quad \text{implies} \quad \begin{matrix} -6x + 9y = 3 \\ 6x - 14y = 12 \end{matrix}$$

Add the transformed equations and solve for y.

$$\begin{aligned} -6x + 9y &= 3 \\ \underline{6x - 14y} &= \underline{12} \\ 0 - 5y &= 15 \\ y &= -3 \end{aligned}$$

Substitute $y = -3$ into equation (1) and solve for x.

$$\begin{aligned} -2x + 3y &= 1 \\ -2x + 3(-3) &= 1 \\ -2x - 9 &= 1 \\ -2x &= 10 \\ x &= -5 \end{aligned}$$

The solution is $x = -5$, $y = -3$.

Note: Another way to solve a system of two linear equations in two variables is to use the Intersection feature under the Analysis menu of the ETS graphing calculator. See the tutorial at http://www.infinitysw.com/exams/tutorials for a demonstration of this feature.

The solution to a system of three equations with three or more variables can be solved using substitution, elimination, or transformation of the augmented matrix. In general, it is most efficient to solve such systems by using the augmented matrix. This method will be discussed in Chapter 10, "Matrices."

Formulas Used in a Two-Dimensional Coordinate Plane

To find the **slope** m of the line that connects the points (x_1, y_1) and (x_2, y_2) in a coordinate plane, use the formula

$$\text{Slope of line} = m = \frac{y_2 - y_1}{x_2 - x_1},\ (x_1 \neq x_2)$$

When a line slopes *upward* to the right, its slope is *positive;* when a line slopes *downward* to the right, its slope is *negative*. All horizontal lines have slope 0. Vertical lines have no slope. If two lines are parallel, their slopes are equal. If two lines are perpendicular, their slopes are negative reciprocals of each other.

Note: See "Features of Common Functions" in Chapter 4 for an additional discussion of slope.

To find the distance d between two points (x_1, y_1) and (x_2, y_2) in a coordinate plane, use the formula

$$\text{Distance between two points} = d = \sqrt{(x_2 - x_1)^2 + (y_2 - y_1)^2}$$

The distance d between two points (x_1, y_1) and (x_2, y_2) in a coordinate plane can be interpreted geometrically as the hypotenuse of a right triangle having legs of length $x_2 - x_1$ and $y_2 - y_1$ as illustrated below.

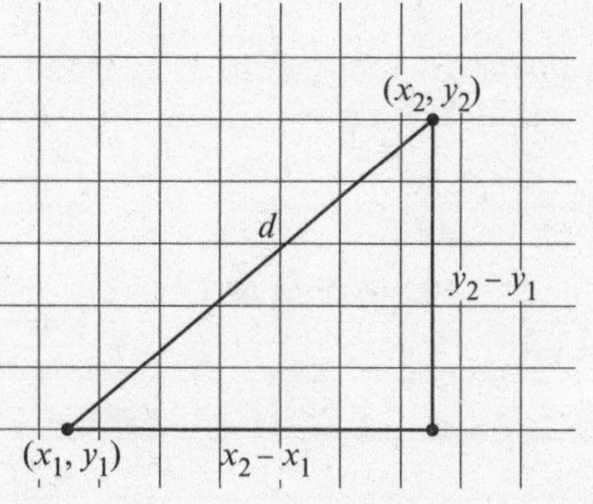

To find the midpoint between two points (x_1, y_1) and (x_2, y_2) in a coordinate plane, use the formula

$$\text{Midpoint between two points} = \left(\frac{x_1 + x_2}{2}, \frac{y_1 + y_2}{2}\right)$$

Tip: Notice that you add, not subtract, the coordinates in the numerator.

To find the distance d from point (x_1, y_1) to line $Ax + By + C = 0$, use the formula

$$d = \frac{|Ax_1 + By_1 + C|}{\sqrt{A^2 + B^2}}$$

Note: The formula to find the distance from a point to a line is given on the Notations, Definitions, and Formulas reference sheet that is available under the Help button when you are taking the Praxis Math CK test.

Tip: When substituting values into formulas, enclose any negative substituted value in parentheses to avoid making a sign error.

The Equation of a Line

The equation of a nonvertical line can be determined using one of the following:

- The **slope-intercept form:** $y = mx + b$, where the line determined by the equation has slope = m and y-intercept = b
- The **standard form:** $Ax + By = C$, where the line determined by the equation has slope $= -\frac{A}{B}$ and y-intercept $= \frac{C}{B}$, $(B \neq 0)$
- The **point-slope form:** $y - y_1 = m(x - x_1)$, where m is the slope of the line and (x_1, y_1) is a point on the line

Here is an example.

> Find the slope-intercept form of the equation of the line that passes through the points (–3, 4) and (–5, 2).

The slope of the line is $m = \frac{y_2 - y_1}{x_2 - x_1} = \frac{2-4}{(-5)-(-3)} = \frac{2-4}{-5+3} = \frac{-2}{-2} = 1$. Selecting (–3, 4) from the two points and substituting into $y - y_1 = m(x - x_1)$ gives $(y - 4) = 1(x - (-3))$ or, equivalently, $y - 4 = x + 3$, which yields the equation $y = x + 7$.

Note: See the previous section "Formulas Used in a Two-Dimensional Coordinate Plane" for the formula for finding the slope of a line given two points on the line.

Two special cases of linear equations are the equations for horizontal and vertical lines. Horizontal lines have equations of the form $y = k$ $(m = 0)$. Vertical lines have equations of the form $x = h$ (undefined slope).

Here is a summary of equations of lines.

Equations of Lines

Slope-intercept form (functional form)	$y = mx + b$
Point-slope form	$y - y_1 = m(x - x_1)$
Standard form	$Ax + By = C$ (A and B not both zero)
Horizontal line	$y = k$ for any constant k
Vertical line (not a function)	$x = h$ for any constant h

Tip: Not all authorities agree on the standard form. Some write the standard form as $Ax + By + C = 0$; others designate $y = mx + b$ as the standard form. We do not anticipate that your correct responses on the Praxis Math CK test will be jeopardized by this inconsistency.

Systems of Two-Variable Linear Inequalities

For this topic, you will graph two-variable linear inequalities and find the maximum (or minimum) value of an equation that is subject to inequality constraints.

Graphing Two-Variable Linear Inequalities

The graph of a two-variable linear inequality, such as $3x + y \le 5$, $3x - y \ge 1$, and $x - y < 0$, is a half-plane.

To graph a two-variable inequality, follow these steps:

1. Rewrite the inequality in an equivalent form with only y on the LS of the inequality symbol.
2. Graph the linear equation that results when the inequality symbol is replaced with an equal sign. Use a dashed line for $<$ or $>$ inequalities and a solid line for $\le$ or $\ge$ inequalities. This is the boundary line.
3. If the inequality contains $<$ or $\le$, shade the portion of the plane beneath the line. If the inequality contains $>$ or $\ge$, shade the portion of the plane above the line.

Here is an example.

Graph the inequality $3x + y \le 5$.

Rewrite the inequality as $y \le -3x + 5$. Graph $y = -3x + 5$. Make the line a solid line and shade the portion of the plane beneath the line as shown here.

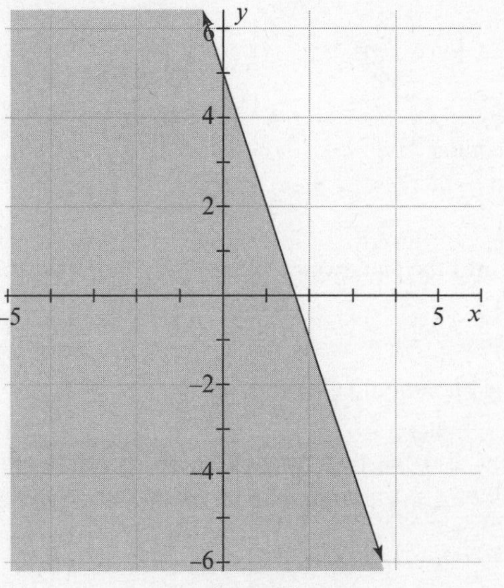

Graph of $y \le -3x + 5$

Find the Maximum Value of an Equation Subject to Inequality Constraints

Suppose you want to find the maximum value of the equation $z = 2x + 5y$ subject to the following constraints:

$$\begin{aligned} 3x + y &\le 5 \\ 3x - y &\ge 1 \\ x - y &\le 0 \end{aligned}$$

The general process to find the maximum value of the given equation (called the **"optimization"** equation) is to graph the set of constraint inequalities to produce a region in the plane that represents their intersections. The maximum value of the equation will occur at one of the corners of the region. To algebraically determine the corner points, find the points of intersection of the boundary lines of the region. In other words, systematically pair the constraint equations and solve for the intersection of each pair. Here are the constraint equations (for convenience, the equations are numbered and written in the form $y = mx + b$):

(1) $3x + y = 5$ or, equivalently, $y = -3x + 5$

(2) $3x - y = 1$ or, equivalently, $y = 3x - 1$

(3) $x - y = 0$ or, equivalently, $y = x$

Solve equations (1) and (2) to obtain the corner point (1, 2). Solve equations (1) and (3) to obtain the corner point (1.25, 1.25). Solve equations (2) and (3) to obtain the corner point (0.5, 0.5). Here is the graph.

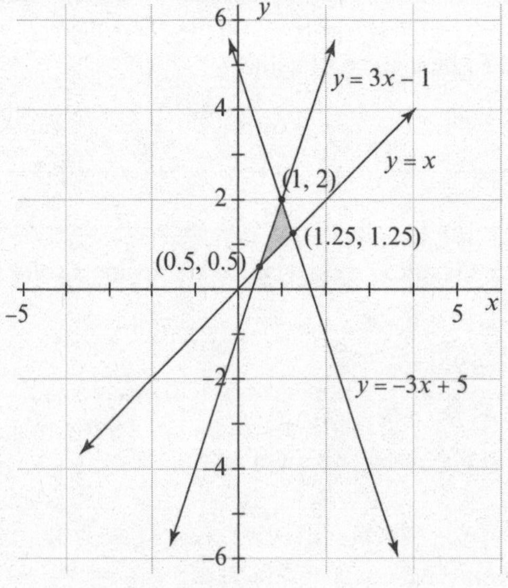

Substitute the corner point values into the equation, $z = 2x + 5y$, to find the maximum.

At (1, 2), $z = 2(1) + 5(2) = 12$; at (1.25, 1.25), $z = 2(1.25) + 5(1.25) = 8.75$; and at (0.5, 0.5), $z = 2(0.5) + 5(0.5) = 3.5$.

Subject to the given constraints, the maximum value for $z = 2x + 5y$ is 12.

Tip: As this problem demonstrates, you can find the maximum (or minimum) of an equation that is subject to inequality constraints by determining the corner points of the intersection region of the set of constraint inequalities.

Ratios, Proportions, and Percents

In this section, you will work with ratios, proportions, and percents.

Ratios

A **ratio** is the result of a multiplicative comparison of two quantities or measures. You can express the ratio "three to four" in three different forms. You can write the ratio as 3 to 4, 3:4, or $\frac{3}{4}$. The numbers 3 and 4 are the terms of the ratio. On the Praxis Math CK test, if two quantities are in the ratio a to b and you are given their sum is c, solve $ax + bx = c$ for x, then compute ax or bx—whichever one is needed. Here is an example.

> The ratio of boys to girls in a group of 35 students is 3 to 4. How many girls are in the group?

Solve $3x + 4x = 35$.

$$\begin{aligned} 3x + 4x &= 35 \\ 7x &= 35 \\ x &= 5 \\ 4x &= 20 \end{aligned}$$

There are 20 girls in the group.

Tip: You can extend this strategy to three or more quantities.

Proportions

A **proportion** is a mathematical statement that the values of two ratios are equal. The **terms** of the proportion are the four numbers that make up the two ratios. For example, the proportion $\frac{a}{b} = \frac{c}{d}$ has terms *a*, *b*, *c*, and *d*. The **fundamental property of proportions** is the following: $\frac{a}{b} = \frac{c}{d}$ if and only if $ad = bc$. In other words, **cross products,** *ad* and *bc*, of a proportion are equal. To solve for a missing term of a proportion, find a cross product that results in a numerical value, and then divide by the numerical term you didn't use. For example, in the proportion, $\frac{5}{x} = \frac{2}{13}$, $x = \frac{(5)(13)}{2} = 32.5$.

To solve an application problem that calls for a proportion, find a sentence or phrase that provides information for the left ratio of the proportion. Then find another sentence or phrase that provides information for the right ratio. Next, write and solve the proportion. Here is an example.

> On a map, the distance between two cities is 15.5 inches. The scale on the map shows that 0.5 inch represents 20 miles. What is the distance, in miles, between the two cities?

Let d = the distance, in miles, between the two cities.

Write a proportion that represents the facts given. The first sentence provides information for the left ratio of the proportion (15.5 inches represents *d* miles on the map). The second sentence provides information for the right ratio (0.5 inch represents 20 miles on the map).

Write the proportion.

$$\frac{d}{15.5 \text{ in}} = \frac{20 \text{ miles}}{0.5 \text{ in}}$$

Check to make sure that the units in the left ratio match up with the units in the right ratio. On the left, you have miles in the numerator and inches in the denominator, and on the right, you have miles in the numerator and inches in the denominator as well. If the units in the left and right ratios don't match up, the proportion is incorrect.

Solve the proportion, omitting the units for convenience.

$$d = \frac{(15.5)(20)}{0.5} = 620$$

The distance between the two cities is 620 miles.

Percents

Percent means "per hundred." The percent sign is a short way of writing $\frac{1}{100}$ or 0.01. When you see a percent sign, you can substitute multiplying by $\frac{1}{100}$ or 0.01 for the percent sign.

Basic Percentage Problems

In basic percentage problems, use the formula $P = RB$, where P is the percentage (the "part of the whole"), R is the rate (the quantity with a % sign or the word *percent* attached), and B is the base (the "whole amount").

Tip: For convenience, when P is unknown, write the formula as $P = RB$, but when B or R is unknown, write the formula as $RB = P$.

Here are examples.

> Lonnie works at a computer store that pays a commission rate of 3% to employees for all sales. Last week, Lonnie's sales totaled $4,500. What is Lonnie's commission for last week?

Tip: In application problems, a percent without a base is usually meaningless. Be sure to identify the base associated with each percent mentioned in a problem.

In this problem, Lonnie's commission is P, which is unknown, R is 3%, and B is $4,500. Write and solve an equation that represents the facts, omitting the units for convenience.

$$\begin{aligned} P &= RB \\ P &= 3\%(4,500) \\ P &= 0.03(4,500) \\ P &= 135 \end{aligned}$$

Lonnie's commission for last week is $135.

Tip: Change percents to equivalent decimals or fractions to perform calculations. Or, if you prefer, use the x% key on the ETS graphing calculator. See the calculator manual available at http://infinitysw.s3.amazonaws.com/ets/ets_calculator_manual.pdf for instructions.

> A department store offers a 25% discount on all clothing items during a two-day sale. Karlie got $74.25 off the price of a jacket she purchased during the sale. What was the jacket's original price?

In this problem, the original price of the jacket is B, which is unknown, R is 25%, and P is $74.25. Write an equation that represents the facts given.

$$\begin{aligned} RB &= P \\ 25\%B &= \$74.25 \end{aligned}$$

Solve the equation, omitting the units for convenience.

$$\begin{aligned} 25\%B &= 74.25 \\ 0.25B &= 74.25 \\ B &= 297 \end{aligned}$$

The jacket's original price was \$297.

> A customer pays a sales tax of \$7.60 at a restaurant on a meal that costs \$95.00. What is the sales tax rate for the purchase?

In this problem, the sales tax rate is R, which is unknown, P is \$7.60, and B is \$95.00. Write and solve an equation that represents the facts, omitting the units for convenience.

$$\begin{aligned} RB &= P \\ R(95.00) &= 7.60 \\ 95R &= 7.60 \\ R &= 0.08 \\ R &= 8\% \end{aligned}$$

The sales tax rate is 8%.

Percent Change

To compute percent change (increase or decrease) in the value of an item, use the following formula:

$$\text{Percent Change} = \frac{|\text{New Value} - \text{Old Value}|}{\text{Old Value}} \times 100\%$$

Tip: Always divide by the value that occurred first in time.

Here are examples.

> A collectible toy increased in value from \$345 to \$414. What is the percent increase in the value of the toy?

Omitting the units, the percent increase is

$$\frac{|\text{New Value} - \text{Old Value}|}{\text{Old Value}} \times 100\% = \frac{|414 - 345|}{345} \times 100\% = \frac{|69|}{345} \times 100\% = \frac{69}{345} \times 100\% = 0.2 \times 100\% = 20\% \text{ increase}$$

> A necklace decreased in value from \$250.00 to \$212.50. What is the percent decrease in the value of the necklace?

Omitting the units, the percent decrease is

$$\frac{|\text{New Value} - \text{Old Value}|}{\text{Old Value}} \times 100\% = \frac{|212.50 - 250.00|}{250.00} \times 100\% = \frac{|-37.50|}{250.00} \times 100\% = \frac{37.50}{250.00} \times 100\% = 0.15 \times 100\% = 15\% \text{ decrease}$$

Tip: Percent change, whether it is an increase or a decrease, is *always* positive.

Algebraic Representations of Conic Sections and Spheres

This section presents algebraic representations of geometric figures.

Algebraic Representations of Conic Sections

The four basic kinds of conics are the circle, parabola, ellipse, and hyperbola. Geometrically, these conic sections are two-dimensional figures realized as the result of cutting a double-napped right-circular cone with a plane. They are formed by altering the angle of the cutting plane as shown here.

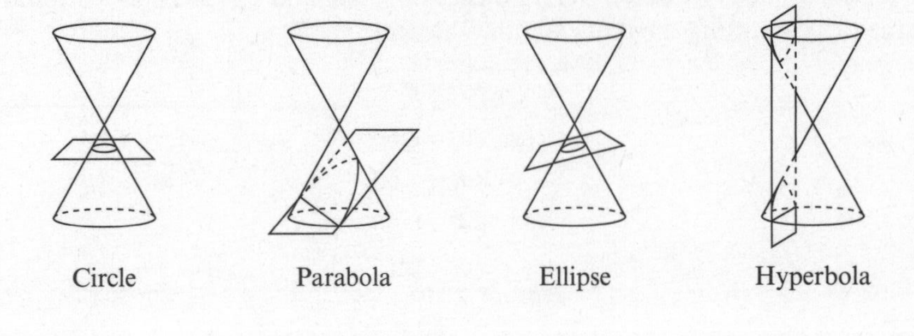

The **equation of a conic** with axis (or axes) on or parallel to a coordinate axis (or axes) can be written as $Ax^2 + By^2 + Cx + Dy + E = 0$, where A, B, C, D, and E are constants and A and B are not both 0.

This equation defines a relation that has different graphs depending on the values of the coefficients A and B according to the following:

- If $A = B$, the equation is a circle. A **circle** is a set of points in the plane such that each point is equidistant from a fixed point in the circle's center. It has standard form: $(x-h)^2 + (y-k)^2 = r^2$, where (h, k) is the circle's **center** and the **radius** is $|r|$ units. Here is the graph of the circle, $x^2 + y^2 = 25$, with center at (0, 0) and radius 5.

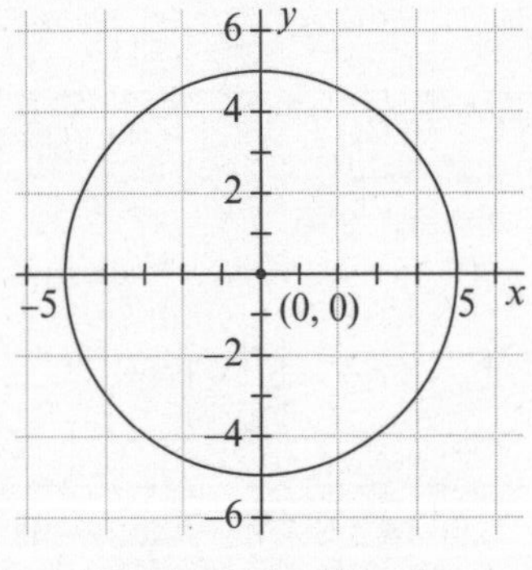

Graph of $x^2 + y^2 = 25$

- If either A or B is 0, the equation is a parabola. A **parabola** is a set of points in the plane such that each point is equidistant from a line, called the **directrix,** and a fixed point, called the **focus**. It has the following standard forms, where p (> 0) is the distance from the vertex of the parabola to the focus or directrix:
  - $(x-h)^2 = 4p(y-k)$. This parabola opens upward with vertex (h, k), focus $(h, k+p)$, and directrix $y = k - p$. It is symmetric about a vertical line through its vertex at $x = h$.
  - $(x-h)^2 = -4p(y-k)$. This parabola opens downward with vertex (h, k), focus $(h, k-p)$, and directrix $y = k + p$. It is symmetric about a vertical line through its vertex at $x = h$.
  - $(y-k)^2 = 4p(x-h)$, with vertex (h, k). This parabola opens right with vertex (h, k), focus $(h+p, k)$, and directrix $x = h - p$. The parabola is symmetric about a horizontal line through its vertex at $y = k$.
  - $(y-k)^2 = -4p(x-h)$, with vertex (h, k). This parabola opens left with vertex (h, k), focus $(h-p, k)$, and directrix $x = h + p$. The parabola is symmetric about a horizontal line through its vertex at $y = k$.

Here is the graph of the parabola, $x^2 = 8y$, with vertex at (0, 0), focus (0, 2), and directrix $y = -2$.

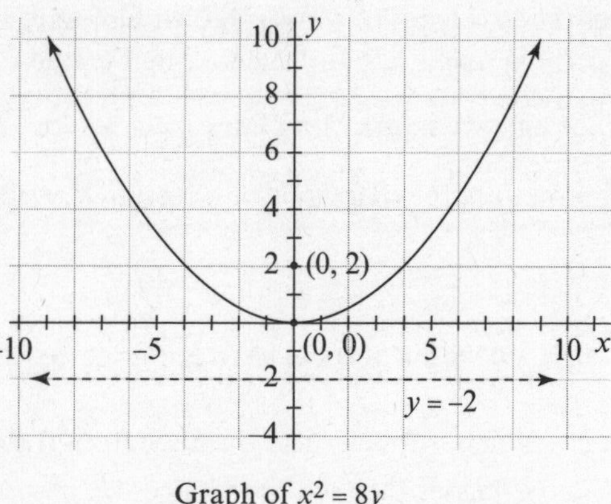

Graph of $x^2 = 8y$

- If $AB > 0$, the equation is an ellipse. An **ellipse** is a set of points, the sum of whose distances from two fixed points, called the **foci,** is a constant. It has the following standard forms:
  - $\frac{(x-h)^2}{a^2} + \frac{(y-k)^2}{b^2} = 1$, $a > b > 0$ with a horizontal axis, center at (h, k), vertices at $(h \pm a, k)$, co-vertices at $(h, k \pm b)$, and foci at $(h \pm c, k)$, where $c = \sqrt{a^2 - b^2}$, which is the horizontal distance from the center to each foci. The line segment joining the vertices $(h - a, k)$ and $(h + a, k)$ is the major axis, is a horizontal axis of symmetry, and has length $2a$. The line segment joining the co-vertices $(h, k - b)$ and $(h, k + b)$ is the minor axis, is a vertical axis of symmetry, and has length $2b$.
  - $\frac{(x-h)^2}{b^2} + \frac{(y-k)^2}{a^2} = 1$, $a > b > 0$ with a vertical axis, center at (h, k), vertices at $(h, k \pm a)$, co-vertices at $(h \pm b, k)$, and foci at $(h, k \pm c)$, where $c = \sqrt{a^2 - b^2}$, which is the vertical distance from the center to each foci. The line segment joining the vertices $(h, k - a)$ and $(h, k + a)$ is the major axis, is a vertical axis of symmetry, and has length $2a$. The line segment joining the co-vertices $(h - b, k)$ and $(h + b, k)$ is the minor axis, is a horizontal axis of symmetry, and has length $2b$.

Here is the graph of the ellipse, $\frac{x^2}{25} + \frac{y^2}{9} = 1$, with a horizontal axis, center at (0, 0), vertices at (± 5, 0), co-vertices at (0, ± 3), and foci at (± 4, 0).

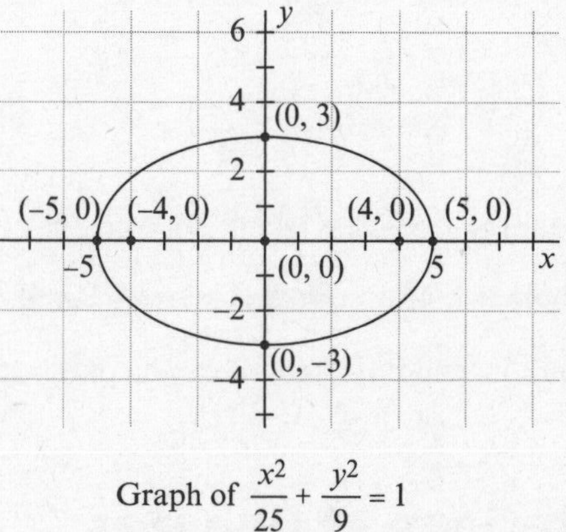

Graph of $\frac{x^2}{25} + \frac{y^2}{9} = 1$

- If $AB < 0$, the equation is a hyperbola. A **hyperbola** is a set of points, the difference of whose distances from two fixed points, called the **foci,** is a constant. It has the following standard forms:
  - $\frac{(x-h)^2}{a^2} - \frac{(y-k)^2}{b^2} = 1$, $a > 0$, $b > 0$ with a horizontal axis, center at (h, k), vertices at $(h \pm a, k)$, and foci at $(h \pm c, k)$, where $c = \sqrt{a^2 + b^2}$, which is the horizontal distance from the center to each foci. The line

segment joining the vertices $(h - a, k)$ and $(h + a, k)$ is the major axis, is a horizontal axis of symmetry, and has length $2a$. The hyperbola opens left and right along the line $y = k$, and it passes through the vertices $(h - a, k)$ and $(h + a, k)$. It has two intersecting lines $y = k + \frac{b}{a}(x - h)$ and $y = k - \frac{b}{a}(x - h)$ as (slanting) asymptotes. The asymptotes are the diagonals of a rectangle with dimensions $2a$ by $2b$ centered at (h, k).

- $\frac{(y-k)^2}{a^2} - \frac{(x-h)^2}{b^2} = 1$, $a > 0$, $b > 0$ with a vertical axis, center at (h, k), vertices at $(h, k \pm a)$, and foci at $(h, k \pm c)$, where $c = \sqrt{a^2 + b^2}$, which is the vertical distance from the center to each foci. It opens up and down along the line $x = h$, and it passes through the vertices $(h, k - a)$ and $(h, k + a)$. It has two intersecting lines $y = k + \frac{a}{b}(x - h)$ and $y = k - \frac{a}{b}(x - h)$ as (slanting) asymptotes. The asymptotes are the diagonals of a rectangle with dimensions $2a$ by $2b$ centered at (h, k).

Here is the graph of the hyperbola, $\frac{x^2}{16} - \frac{y^2}{9} = 1$, with a horizontal axis, center at (0, 0), vertices at (± 4, 0), foci at (± 5, 0), and asymptotes $y = \pm\frac{3}{4}x$.

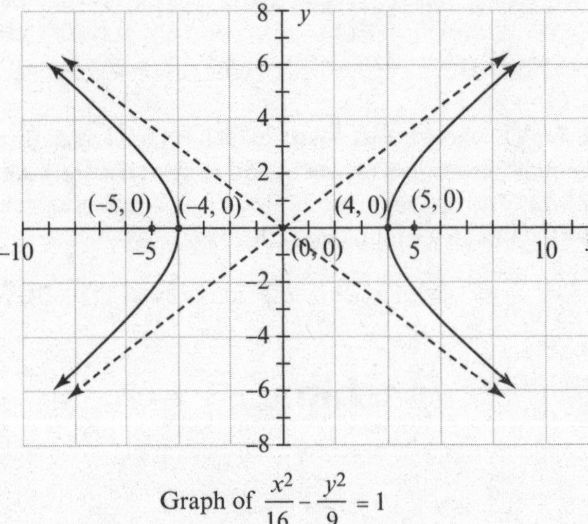

Graph of $\frac{x^2}{16} - \frac{y^2}{9} = 1$

The **eccentricity,** $e = \frac{c}{a}$, of a conic section is a measure of the degree to which the shape varies from circular. The eccentricity of a circle is 0, of a parabola is 1, of an ellipse is between 0 and 1, and of a hyperbola is greater than 1.

If the equation of a conic section is not in standard form, it can be put in standard form by completing the squares on the x and y terms.

Algebraic Representations of Spheres

A **sphere** is a three-dimensional figure, all of whose points are equidistant from a fixed point within the sphere called its center. The general equation for a sphere in a three-dimensional coordinate system is $(x - x_0)^2 + (y - y_0)^2 + (z - z_0)^2 = r^2$, with **center** (x_0, y_0, z_0) and **radius** $|r|$.

Algebraic Problem Solving

You can expect to encounter application problems on the Praxis Math CK test. This section presents some helpful ideas for algebraically dealing with application problems.

General Problem-Solving Guidelines

Here are some general problem-solving guidelines for solving application problems using algebraic techniques.

1. **Analyze the problem**. Ask yourself: What is the question's primary focus? Is the problem a familiar type (for example, an age problem)? Determine what you need to find. Look for words like *find, determine, what is, how many, how far, how much, what time,* and the like.

   Decide how many unknowns are in the problem. If there is one unknown, let the variable represent this unknown quantity. (***Tip:*** Be precise in specifying a variable. State its units, if any.) Sometimes you will have two or more unknowns in a problem. In this case, you can assign the unknowns different variable names. As another option, you might assign a variable name to one unknown and express the other unknowns in terms of that variable. For example, if a first unknown is described in terms of a second unknown, assign the variable name to the *second* unknown. No matter whether you use one variable or two or more variables, the process will culminate in a one-variable linear equation (or its equivalent).
2. **Write one or more equations that represent the facts in the problem**. Identify the information in the problem. Is there a formula that you should know? If measurement units are given, determine what units the answer should have. Decide whether making a table or sketching a diagram would be helpful. Try to relate the current problem to problems you have worked in the past. Keep in mind that you will need as many equations as you have variables in order to solve for the variables. Make sure your solution answers the question.
3. **Solve the equation(s)**. Carefully work out your solution. Make sure you copy all information accurately. Write neatly so that you can check over your work. If the answer should have units, check whether your calculations will result in the proper units for the answer. ***Tip:*** When solving an equation, you might find it convenient to omit the units, given that you have already checked that the answer will have the proper units.
4. **Check back**. Did you answer the question that was asked? Mentally check your solution in the context of the problem. Does it make sense? Is it reasonable? Are the units correct?

Translating Verbal Relationships

The following table summarizes commonly used algebraic symbolism for verbal relationships. The letter x is used in the table to represent an unknown number.

Signal Words or Phrases	Example	Algebraic Symbolism
add, plus, sum of, increased by, added to, more than, exceeds	a number that exceeds x by 10	$x + 10$
minus, subtracted from, difference between, less than, decreased by, reduced by, diminished by	10 less than x	$x - 10$
times, multiplied by, product of, twice, double, triple, quadruple, fraction of, percent of	twice x	$2x$, $2 \cdot x$, $2(x)$, $(2)(x)$, or $(2)x$
divided by, quotient of, ratio of, for each, x for every, per	ratio of x and 5	$\frac{x}{5}$
equals, is, was, are, were, will be, gives, yields, results in	50% of x is 20 more than the quotient of x and 4.	$50\%x = \frac{x}{4} + 20$

Geometry Problems

> The length of a rectangular garden is 3 meters more than its width. The garden's perimeter is 54 meters. Find the garden's area.

The garden is rectangular. Its perimeter is 54 meters. The formula for the perimeter of a rectangle is $P = 2l + 2w = 2(l + w)$; and the formula for the area of a rectangle is $A = lw$, where l is the rectangle's length and w is its width. (See "Perimeter, Area, and Volume" in Chapter 7 for common geometric formulas.) You do not know the length or the width of the garden. You will need both to find the garden's area, so this problem has two unknowns.

Make a sketch.

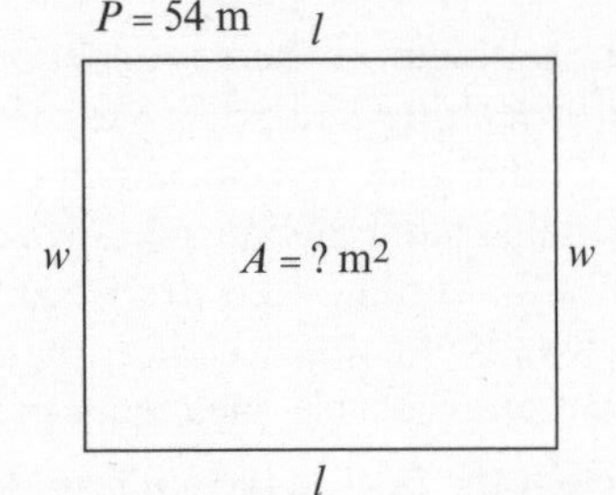

Tip: For geometry problems, making a sketch helps you visualize the problem.

Method 1. Use one variable.

The garden's length is described in terms of its width. Let w = the garden's width, in meters. Then $w + 3$ meters = the garden's length, in meters. Write an equation that represents the facts given in the question.

$$2[(w + 3 \text{ meters}) + w] = 54 \text{ meters}$$

Solve the equation, omitting the units for convenience.

$$\begin{aligned} 2[(w+3) \ + w] &= 54 \\ 2[w+3 \ + w] &= 54 \\ 2[2w+3] &= 54 \\ 4w+6 &= 54 \\ 4w &= 48 \\ w &= 12 \\ w+3 &= 15 \end{aligned}$$

The area of the garden is (12 m)(15 m) = 180 m^2.

Method 2. Use two variables.

Let w = the garden's width, in meters, and l = the garden's length, in meters. Write two equations that represent the facts given in the question. For convenience, number the equations.

(1) $l = w + 3$ meters
(2) $2(l + w) = 54$ meters

Simultaneously solve the two equations, omitting the units for convenience.

(1) $l = w + 3$
(2) $2(l + w) = 54$

Using the substitution method, substitute $l = w + 3$ from equation (1) into equation (2) to obtain

$$2[(w+3)+w]=54$$

Complete the solution as shown in Method 1.

Make sure you answer the question that was asked. In this question, after you obtain the length and width of the answer, you must calculate the garden's area to answer the question.

Note: Hereafter, only one solution method will be shown.

Age Problems

> Josie is twice as old as Daroi. In 5 years, Josie's age will be 55 years minus Daroi's age. What is Josie's age now?

You don't know Josie's age or Daroi's age now. Josie's age now is described as "twice as old as Daroi," so designate the variable as Daroi's age now.

Let d = Daroi's age in years now, and $2d$ = Josie's age in years now.

Make a table to organize the information in the question.

When?	Daroi's Age	Josie's Age
Now	d	$2d$
5 years from now	$d + 5$ years	$2d + 5$ years

From the question, you know that Josie's age 5 years from now is 55 years minus Daroi's age 5 years from now. Use the information in the table to set up an equation to match the facts in the question.

$$2d + 5 \text{ years} = 55 \text{ years} - (d + 5 \text{ years})$$

Solve the equation, omitting the units for convenience.

$$\begin{aligned} 2d+5&=55-(d+5) \\ 2d+5&=55-d-5 \\ 2d+5&=50-d \\ 3d+5&=50 \\ 3d&=45 \\ d&=15 \\ 2d&=30 \end{aligned}$$

Josie's age now is 30 years.

Make sure you answer the question asked. In this question, after you obtain Daroi's age now, calculate Josie's age now.

Coin Problems

> A collection of 250 U.S. quarters and dimes has a total value of $40.00. How many quarters are in the collection?

Note: In coin problems, assume there are no rare coins in a collection.

You don't know the number of quarters or the number of dimes, so use two variables. Let q = the number of quarters and d = the number of dimes. Make a table to organize the information given.

Denomination	Quarters	Dimes	Total
Face Value per Coin	\$0.25	\$0.10	N/A
Number of Coins	q	d	250
Value of Coins	\$0.25q	\$0.10d	\$40.00

Use the table to write two equations to represent the facts given. ***Remember:*** You need two equations when you have two variables.

$$q + d = 250$$
$$\$0.25q + \$0.10d = \$40.00$$

Solve the system, omitting the units for convenience.

$$(1)\ \ q + d = 250$$
$$(2)\ \ 0.25q + 0.10d = 40.00$$

Solve equation (1) for d, and substitute the result into equation (2). Then solve for q.

$$(1)\ d = 250 - q$$
$$(2)\ 0.25q + 0.10(250 - q) = 40.00$$

$$\begin{aligned} 0.25q + 0.10(250 - q) &= 40 \\ 0.25q + 25 - 0.10q &= 40 \\ 0.15q + 25 &= 40 \\ 0.15q &= 15 \\ q &= 100 \end{aligned}$$

There are 100 quarters in the collection.

Mixture Problems

A chemist has a 36% alcohol and a 90% alcohol solution. How many milliliters of each should be used to make 1,200 milliliters of a 72% alcohol solution?

You have two unknowns. Let x = the number of milliliters of the 36% alcohol solution to be used, and let y = the number of milliliters of the 90% alcohol solution to be used.

Make a table to organize the mixture information.

When?	Percent Alcohol Strength	Number of Milliliters	Amount of Alcohol
Before mixing	36%	x	36%x
	90%	y	90%y
After mixing	72%	1,200	72%(1,200)

Use the table to write two equations to represent the facts given.

$$x + y = 1{,}200$$
$$36\%x + 90\%y = 72\%(1{,}200)$$

The amount of alcohol before mixing equals the amount of alcohol after mixing.

Solve the system, changing percents to decimals before proceeding.

$$(1)\ x + y = 1,200$$
$$(2)\ 0.36x + 0.90y = 0.72(1,200)$$

Solve equation (1) for y, and substitute the result into equation (2). Then solve for x.

$$(1)\ y = 1,200 - x$$
$$(2)\ 0.36x + 0.90(1,200 - x) = 0.72(1,200)$$

$$\begin{aligned} 0.36x + 0.90(1,200 - x) &= 0.72(1,200) \\ 0.36x + 1,080 - 0.90x &= 864 \\ -0.54x + 1,080 &= 864 \\ -0.54x &= -216 \\ x &= 400 \\ y &= 1,200 - x = 1,200 - 400 = 800 \end{aligned}$$

400 milliliters of the 36% alcohol solution and 800 milliliters of the 90% alcohol solution should be used to make 1,200 milliliters of a 72% alcohol solution.

Tip: In mixture problems, the "before mixing" amount (or value) of a substance equals the "after mixing" amount (or value) of that substance.

Distance-Rate-Time Problems

> A car and a truck leave the same location at the same time. The car travels due east at 70 miles per hour. The truck travels due west at 65 miles per hour. If the two vehicles continue to travel at their respective rates, in how many hours will the two vehicles be 405 miles apart?

The distance, d, a vehicle travels at a uniform rate of speed, r, for a given length of time, t, is $d = rt$.

There is one unknown. Let t = the time in hours the two vehicles will be 405 miles apart. Make a table to organize the vehicle information. You might find a rough sketch helpful as well.

Vehicle	Rate (in mph)	Time (in hours)	Distance (in miles)
Car	70 mph	t	$70t$
Truck	65 mph	t	$65t$
Total	N/A	N/A	405 miles

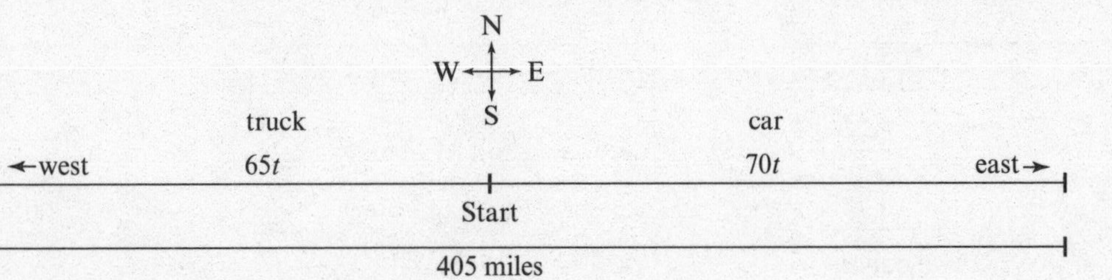

Write an equation that represents the facts given.

$$70t + 65t = 405 \text{ miles}$$

Solve the equation, omitting the units for convenience.

$$70t + 65t = 405$$
$$135t = 405$$
$$t = 3$$

In 3 hours, the two vehicles will be 405 miles apart.

Work Problems (Quick Solution Method)

> Working alone, machine A can make 500 units of a product in 4 hours. Working alone, machine B can make 500 units of the product in 3 hours. How long will it take both machines, working together, to make 500 units of the product?

In this problem, you have two machines that will work together to produce 500 units of a product. When you have two "workers" (in this case, the two machines) that can do the same job, a quick way to determine the time t it will take them to do it together is to *multiply* their individual times, then divide this product by the *sum* of their individual times. ***Tip:*** Think, "product over sum."

In the problem given, machine A's time working alone is 4 hours, and machine B's time working alone is 3 hours. Omitting units, their time working together is $t = \frac{(3)(4)}{3+4} = \frac{12}{7} = 1\frac{5}{7}$.

Working together, it will take the two machines $1\frac{5}{7}$ hours (or about 1 hour and 43 minutes) to make 500 units of the product.

Tip: Their time working together will be less than either of their times working alone.

Consecutive Integer Problems

> The greatest of four consecutive integers is $-\frac{1}{3}$ times the sum of the other three integers. What is the value of the greatest integer?

Tip: For consecutive integer problems, let n = the least integer, $n + 1$ = the next integer, and so on.

Let n = the first integer (the least one), $n + 1$ = the second integer, $n + 2$ = the third integer, and $n + 3$ = the fourth integer (the greatest one).

Write and solve an equation that represents the facts given.

$$-\frac{1}{3}[(n)+(n+1)+(n+2)] = (n+3)$$
$$-\frac{1}{3}[n+n+1+n+2] = n+3$$
$$-\frac{1}{3}[3n+3] = n+3$$
$$-n-1 = n+3$$
$$-2n = 4$$
$$n = -2$$
$$n+3 = 1$$

The greatest of the four integers is 1.

For consecutive even or odd integers, let n = the first integer, $n + 2$ = the second integer, $n + 4$ = the third integer, and so on.

Tip: If you know the sum of three consecutive integers, the middle integer is the sum divided by 3. For example, if the sum of three consecutive even integers is 102, the middle integer is $\frac{102}{3} = 34$, and the other two even integers are 32 and 36.

A Note About Using the ETS Graphing Calculator to Solve Equations

This chapter presented algebraic methods for solving equations. You can solve equations that have real zeros by using the Solver feature of the ETS graphing calculator. View a tutorial on using the Solver at http://www.infinitysw.com/exams/tutorials. The calculator's manual (available at http://infinitysw.s3.amazonaws.com/ets/ets_calculator_manual.pdf) has detailed instructions for using the Solver. The manual explains that the Solver uses an iterative method that could take a significant amount of time to complete and might return inexact results. If an equation has multiple solutions (for example, a quadratic equation can have two solutions), the Solver will return only one of the solutions at a time. It gives the solution that is closest to your guess and within the limits that you set. You also, instead, could use the Solve command that lets you input a variable equation that you want to solve. Like Solver, the Solve command returns only one solution at a time, regardless of the number of solutions in the solution set. You should spend time practicing with Solver and the Solve command so that you can determine all solutions for equations you want to solve.

Another way to use the ETS graphing calculator to solve a one-variable equation is to put the equation in the form y = expression and graph it. Then use modes from the Analysis menu (such as Trace/Evaluate, Zero, and Table) to determine x values that correspond to y values of zero. You can view a tutorial on analyzing a graph at http://www.infinitysw.com/exams/tutorials. Also, see the calculator manual for detailed instructions.

Tip: The ETS graphing calculator is a useful tool, but you need to make sure you can use its features correctly when you take the Praxis Math CK test. You should practice using them while you are working through this book.

Chapter 4

Functions

Basic Function Concepts

For this topic, you must demonstrate an ability to identify, define, and evaluate functions.

Relations

An **ordered pair** of numbers, denoted (x, y), is a pair of numbers expressed in a specific order so that one number is written first in the ordered pair, and the other number is written second. In the ordered pair (x, y), x is the first component, or ***x*-coordinate,** and y is the second component, or ***y*-coordinate.** Two ordered pairs are equal if and only if they have *exactly* the same coordinates in the same order; that is, $(a, b) = (c, d)$ if and only if $a = c$ and $b = d$. The set consisting of all possible ordered pairs of real numbers is denoted $R \times R$, or simply R^2. A **relation** $\mathfrak{R}$ in R^2 is any subset of R^2. The set consisting of all the first components in the ordered pairs contained in $\mathfrak{R}$ is the domain of $\mathfrak{R}$, and the set of all second components is the range of $\mathfrak{R}$.

Graphically, R^2 is represented by the **Cartesian coordinate plane.** Two intersecting real number lines form the axes of the Cartesian coordinate plane. The horizontal axis with positive direction to the right is commonly designated the ***x*-axis,** and the vertical axis with positive direction upward is commonly designated the ***y*-axis.** Their point of intersection is the **origin.** The axes divide the coordinate plane into four **quadrants.** The Roman numerals I, II, III, and IV name the quadrants. The numbering process starts in the upper right quadrant and proceeds counterclockwise. Here is an illustration.

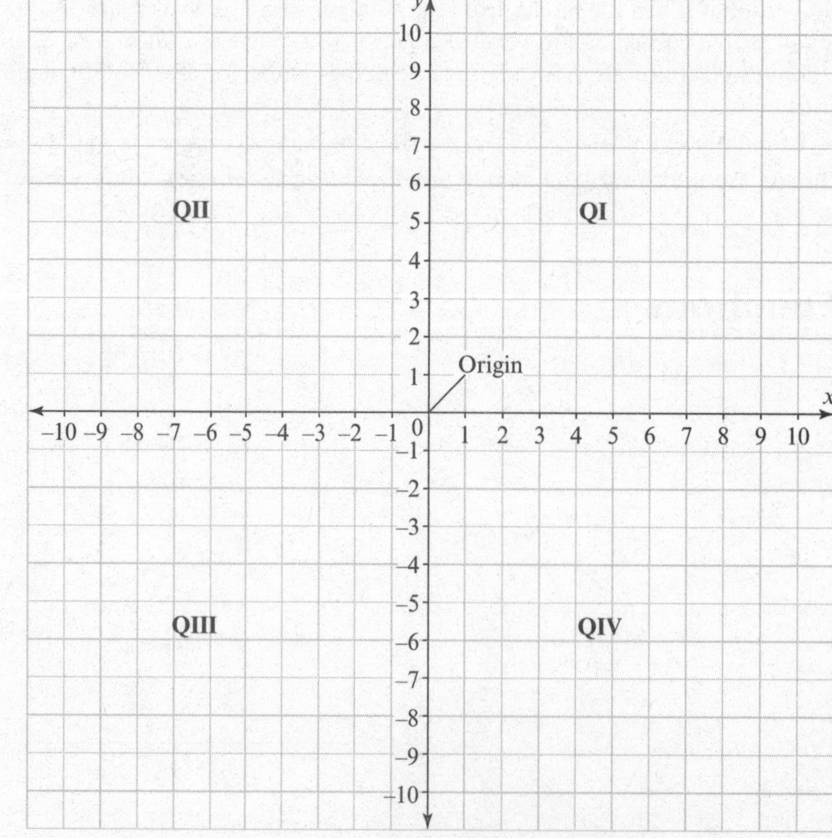

Every ordered pair, (x, y), of real numbers defines a point in the coordinate plane, and every point in the coordinate plane has a location defined by an ordered pair, (x, y), of real numbers. The numbers x and y are the coordinates of the point.

Definition and Representations of a Function

A **function** is a set of ordered pairs for which each first component is paired with *one and only one* second component. In other words, a function is a relation in which no two ordered pairs have the same first component but different second components; that is, if (a, b) and (a, d) are ordered pairs in the function, then $b = d$. Thus, the ordered pairs (1, 2) and (2, 3) can be elements of a function, but the ordered pairs (1, 2) and (1, 3) cannot.

Single letters, such as f and g, are commonly used as names for functions. For the function f, the ordered pairs are written $(x, f(x))$ or (x, y), where $y = f(x)$. You read the function notation $f(x)$ as "f of x."

Functions are represented in various ways. If a function consists of a *finite* number of ordered pairs, you can define the function by listing or showing its ordered pairs in a set, in a table, as an arrow diagram, or as a graph in a coordinate plane. You also might define the function by giving a rule or an equation. When the number of ordered pairs is *infinite,* more often than not the function is defined by either an equation or a graph. ***Note:*** In this book, equations that define functions will use only real numbers as coefficients or constants.

In the function defined by $y = f(x)$, x is the **independent variable** and y is the **dependent variable.** The variable y is "dependent" on x in the sense that you substitute a value of x, called an **argument** of f, into $y = f(x)$ to find y, the value of f at x (also called the **image** of x under f).

The set of possible x values for f is the **domain** of f, denoted D_f, and the set of possible y values is the **range** of f, denoted R_f (see "Determining Domain and Range" on the next page for further discussion of the domain and range of functions). In a **real-valued function,** the range consists of real numbers.

Note: The functions on the Praxis Math CK test are real-valued functions. Hereafter in this book, all functions are real-valued functions.

Two functions f and g are equal, written $f = g$, if and only if their domains are equal and they contain exactly the same set of ordered pairs; that is, $D_f = D_g$ and $f(x) = g(x)$ for all x in their common domain.

Evaluating Functions

Think of a function as a process f that takes an **input** number $x \in D_f$ and produces from it the **output** number $f(x) \in R_f$. Here are examples.

> For every input, x, the function $y = 2x + 1$ produces exactly one output, y. When $x = -5$, $y = 2(-5) + 1 = -10 + 1 = -9$; when $x = 3$, $y = 2(3) + 1 = 6 + 1 = 7$; and so forth.
>
> For every input, x, the function $y = x^2$ produces exactly one output, y. When $x = -2$, $y = (-2)^2 = 4$; when $x = 2$, $y = (2)^2 = 4$; and so forth.

Tip: Notice in the second example that the output for the input -2 is the same as the output for the input 2. This situation is permissible in a function. It's okay that the outputs of distinct ordered pairs are the same, as long as their inputs are different.

Evaluating a function means finding the corresponding output for a given input. Here are examples.

When $f(x) = 8x - 13$, $f\left(\frac{3}{4}\right) = 8\left(\frac{3}{4}\right) - 13 = 6 - 13 = -7$.

When $g(x)=\frac{2x+3}{x-1}$, $x\neq 1$, $g(5a+1)=\frac{2(5a+1)+3}{(5a+1)-1}=\frac{10a+2+3}{5a+1-1}=\frac{10a+5}{5a}=\frac{2a+1}{a}$, $a\neq 0$.

When $h(x)=x^2+x+1$, $h\left(-\frac{1}{2}+\frac{\sqrt{3}}{2}i\right)=\left(-\frac{1}{2}+\frac{\sqrt{3}}{2}i\right)^2+\left(-\frac{1}{2}+\frac{\sqrt{3}}{2}i\right)+1$

$$=\frac{1}{4}+2\left(-\frac{1}{2}\right)\left(\frac{\sqrt{3}}{2}i\right)-\frac{3}{4}+\left(-\frac{1}{2}+\frac{\sqrt{3}}{2}i\right)+1=\frac{1}{4}+\left(-\frac{\sqrt{3}}{2}i\right)-\frac{3}{4}-\frac{1}{2}+\frac{\sqrt{3}}{2}i+1=0.$$

Properties of Functions

This section presents properties of a function (such as domain and range).

Determining Domain and Range

The **domain,** D_f, of a real-valued function $f=\{(x,y)|\,y=f(x)\}$, where no domain is specified, is the largest possible subset of the real numbers for which each x value gives a corresponding y value that is a *real* number.

To determine the domain of a real-valued function f, start with the set of real numbers and exclude all values for x, if any, that would make the equation undefined over the real numbers. If $y=f(x)$ contains a rational expression, to avoid division by 0, exclude values for x, if any, which would make a denominator 0. If $y=f(x)$ contains a radical with an *even* index, to avoid even roots of negative numbers, exclude all values for x, if any, that would cause the expression under the radical to be negative.

Tip: Division by 0 and even roots of negative numbers are the two types of domain problems you are most likely to encounter on the Praxis Math CK test; however, you should be aware that other problems can arise. For example, the domain of the logarithm function, which will be discussed later in this chapter, cannot include 0 or negative values for *x*.

The **range,** denoted R_f, of a function f defined by $y=f(x)$ is the set of all real numbers y for which y is the image of at least one x value in the domain. When you can solve the equation $y=f(x)$ explicitly for x, you can determine the range of f in a manner similar to that used to find the domain of f. Otherwise, you can examine $y=f(x)$ for insight into the possible values for y.

Here are examples of finding the domain and range of a function.

Determine the domain, D_f, and the range, R_f, of the function f defined by $y=\frac{1}{x-3}$.

When $x=3$, the rational expression $\frac{1}{x-3}$ is $\frac{1}{0}$, which is undefined. Therefore, the number 3 is excluded from D_f.

For every real number x, except 3, the quantity $\frac{1}{x-3}$ is a real number. Thus, the domain of f consists of all real numbers except 3, written $D_f=\{x|\,x\neq 3\}$. To determine the range of f, solve $y=\frac{1}{x-3}$ explicitly for x to obtain $x=\frac{1+3y}{y}$. For every real number y, except 0, the quantity $\frac{1+3y}{y}$ is a real number. So, the range of f consists of all real numbers except 0, written $R_f=\{y|\,y\neq 0\}$.

Tip: The ETS graphing calculator can be helpful if you need to determine a function's domain and/or range while taking the Praxis Math CK test. You can find a tutorial for graphing functions using the on-screen graphing calculator at http://www.infinitysw.com/exams/tutorials. When using the graphing calculator to explore a function, use trial and error and the Zoom feature to find a good viewing window of its graph; otherwise, you might be misled by the graph displayed.

Here is the graph of $y = \frac{1}{x-3}$. For your reference, a dashed vertical line has been constructed at $x = 3$. Observe that the graph is composed of a portion to the left of $x = 3$ and a portion to the right of $x = 3$. The graph never crosses the dashed vertical line at $x = 3$, meaning that 3 is excluded from D_f. Also, the graph never crosses the x-axis, meaning that y is never zero. These observations affirm that $D_f = \{x \mid x \neq 3\}$ and $R_f = \{y \mid y \neq 0\}$.

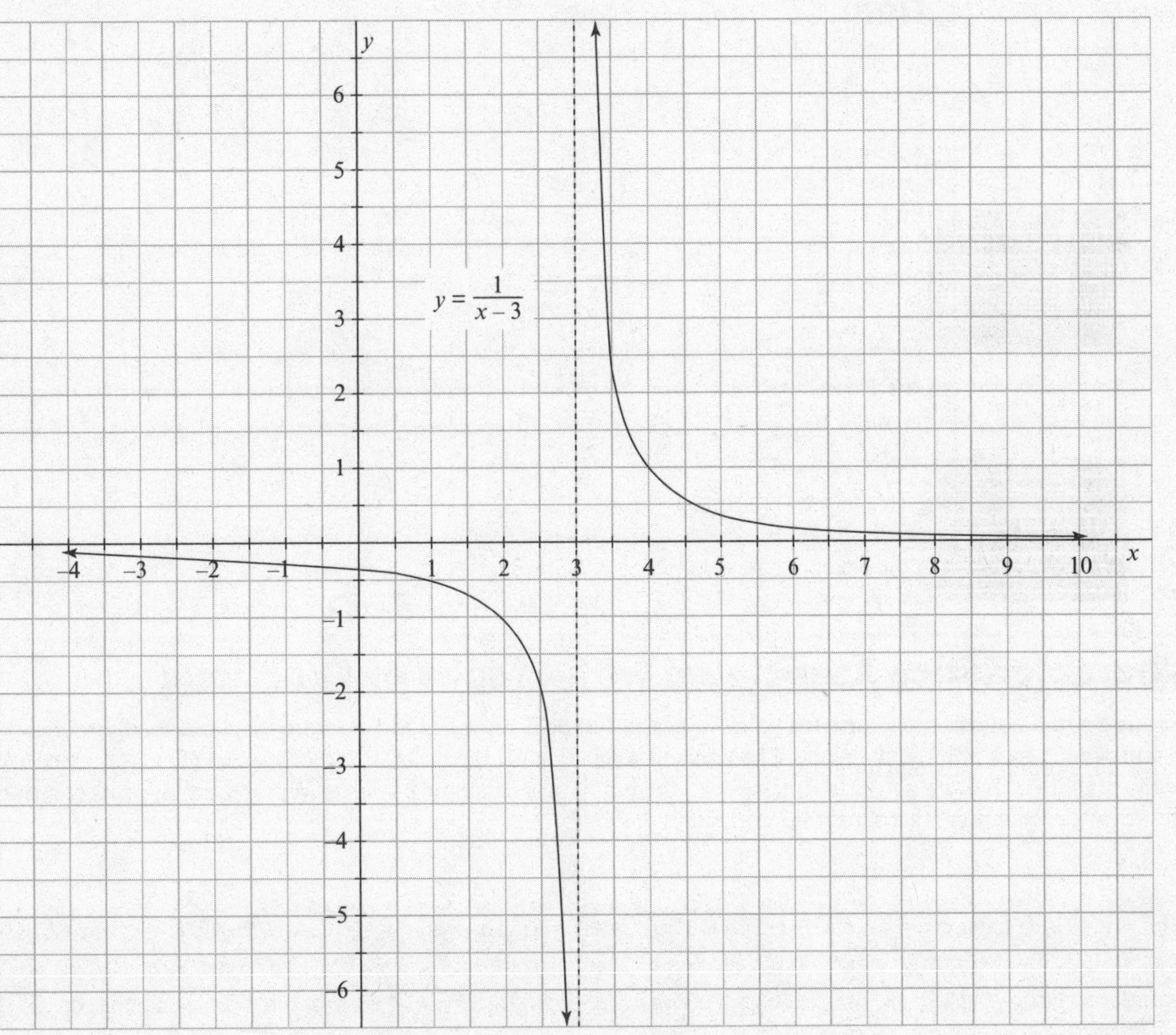

Determine the domain and range of the function g defined by $g(x) = \sqrt{x-5} + 2$.

When $x - 5 < 0$, the expression $\sqrt{x-5}$ is the square root of a negative number, so it is not defined over the real numbers. However, for every real number x for which $x - 5 \geq 0$, the quantity $\sqrt{x-5}$ is a real number. Therefore, the domain of g is all real numbers such that $x - 5 \geq 0$; therefore, $D_g = \{x| x \geq 5\}$. For all real numbers x, the quantity $\sqrt{x-5}$ is nonnegative. So, $y = g(x) = \sqrt{x-5} + 2 \geq 2$. Therefore, $R_g = \{y| y \geq 2\}$.

Here is the graph of $g(x) = \sqrt{x-5} + 2$. For your reference, a dashed horizontal line has been constructed at $y = 2$. Observe that the graph starts at $x = 5$, meaning that x is always greater than or equal to 5, and that it remains at or above the horizontal line $y = 2$, meaning that y is always greater than or equal to 2. These observations affirm that $D_g = \{x| x \geq 5\}$ and $R_g = \{y| y \geq 2\}$.

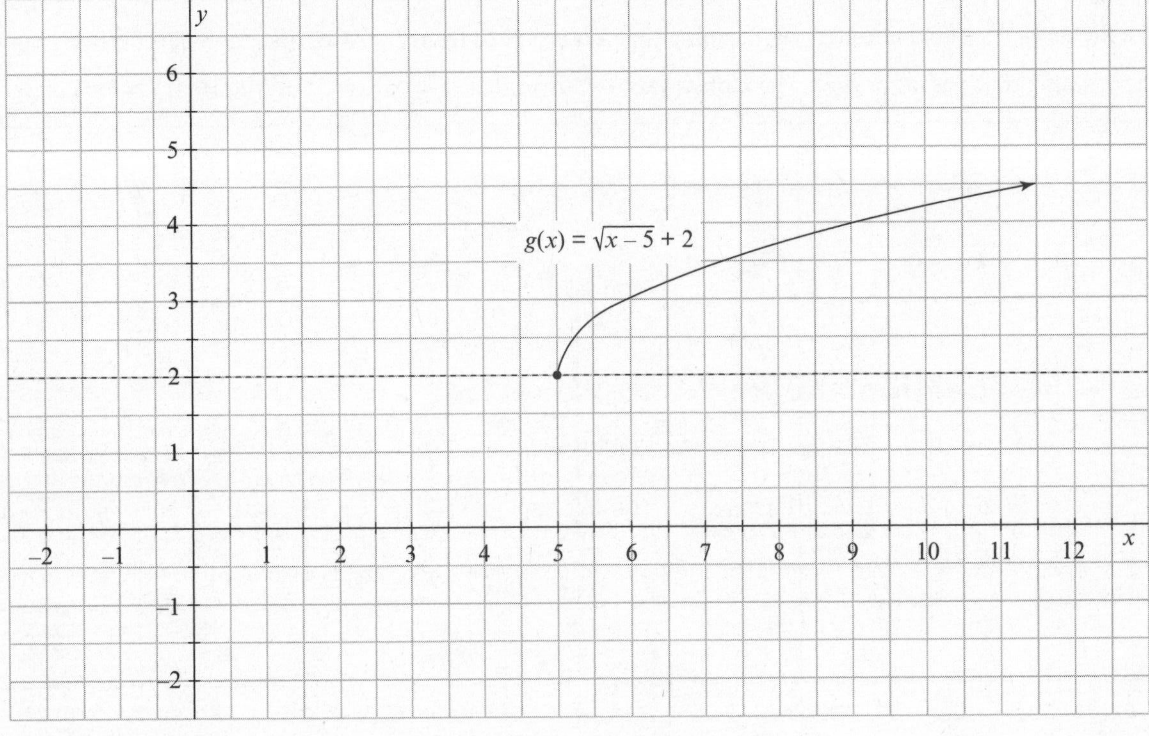

Characteristics Associated with Graphs of Functions

Because a function is a set of ordered pairs, its graph can be determined in a coordinate plane. Each ordered pair is represented by a point in the plane. The **graph of a function** f is the set of all ordered pairs (x, y) for which x is in the domain of f and $y = f(x)$. In other words, the graph of a function is a visual representation of its solutions, the set of ordered pairs that satisfy the equation $y = f(x)$.

Tip: A graphing calculator is an indispensable tool when you are exploring graphs of functions. Most graphing calculators require that you enter the equation of the graph in the form y = f(x). This form excludes graphs of relations that are not functions (such as graphs of circles, ellipses, and so on). For such relations, break the equation into two parts, so that each part defines a function, and then graph the two parts on the same coordinate grid.

Vertical Line Test

By definition, each element in the domain of a function is paired with exactly one element in the range. Thus, if a vertical line can be drawn so it cuts the graph of a relation in more than one point, the relation is *not* a function. This fact is known as the **vertical line test:** A relation is a function if any vertical line in the plane intersects the graph of the relation in no more than one point. Here is an example of a relation that does *not* pass the vertical line test, so it is *not* a function. There are two points on the graph that correspond to $x = 2$, namely (2, 1.7) and (2, −1.7).

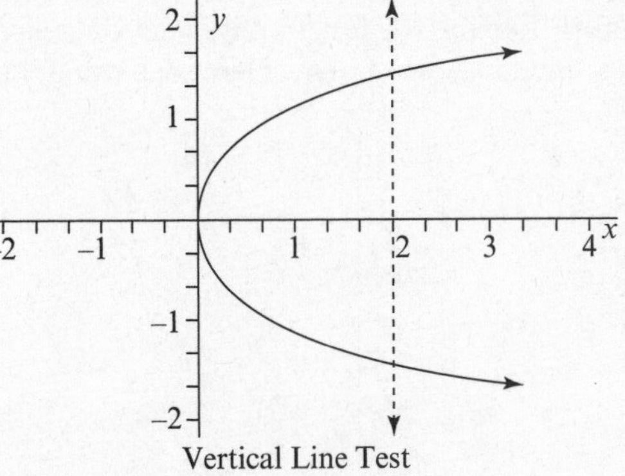

Vertical Line Test

One-to-One Function and Horizontal Line Test

A function f is **one-to-one** if and only if $f(a) = f(b)$ implies that $a = b$; that is, if (a, c) and (b, c) are elements of f, then $a = b$. In a one-to-one function, each first component is paired with *exactly one* second component *and* each second component is paired with *exactly one* first component. Therefore, you have the **horizontal line test:** A function is one-to-one if any horizontal line in the plane intersects the graph of the function in no more than one point. Here is an example of a function that does *not* pass the horizontal line test, so it is *not* a one-to-one function.

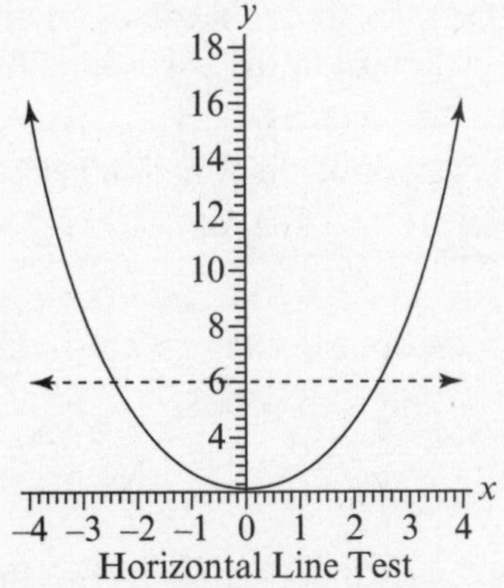

Horizontal Line Test

Increasing-Decreasing-Constant Behavior

Suppose a function f is defined over an interval. Then the following are true:

- f is **increasing** on the interval if, for every pair of numbers x_1 and x_2 in the interval, $f(x_1) < f(x_2)$ whenever $x_1 < x_2$.
- f is **decreasing** on the interval if, for every pair of numbers x_1 and x_2 in the interval, $f(x_1) > f(x_2)$ whenever $x_1 < x_2$.
- f is **constant** on the interval if $f(x_1) = f(x_2)$ for every pair of numbers x_1 and x_2 in the interval.

Thus, a function is increasing on an interval if its graph moves upward from left to right as the independent variable assumes values from left to right in the interval. A function is decreasing on an interval if its graph moves downward from left to right as the independent variable assumes values from left to right in the interval. A function is constant on an interval if the function value stays the same as the independent variable assumes values from left to right in the interval.

Monotonic Function

A function is **monotonic** if, on its entire domain, the function is either only increasing or only decreasing. A monotonic increasing or decreasing function is **one-to-one.** Here is an example.

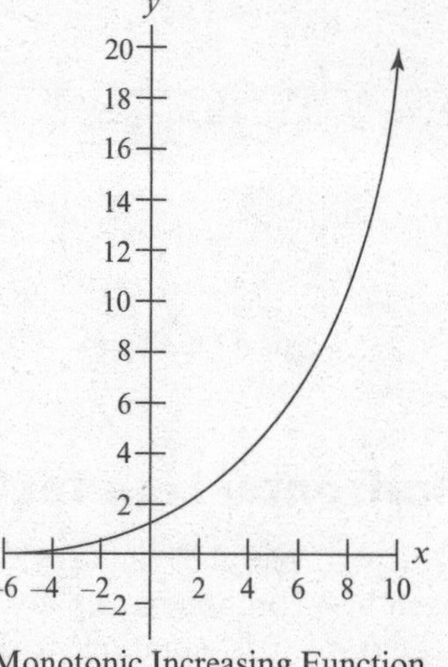

Monotonic Increasing Function

Positive and Negative Behavior

A function *f* is **positive** on an interval if its graph lies above the *x*-axis for all *x* values in the interval; similarly, a function *f* is **negative** on an interval if its graph lies below the *x*-axis for all *x* values in the interval. Here is an example.

> Describe the positive and negative behavior of the function *f* shown that crosses the *x*-axis at (−1, 0), (0, 0), (2, 0), and (3, 0).

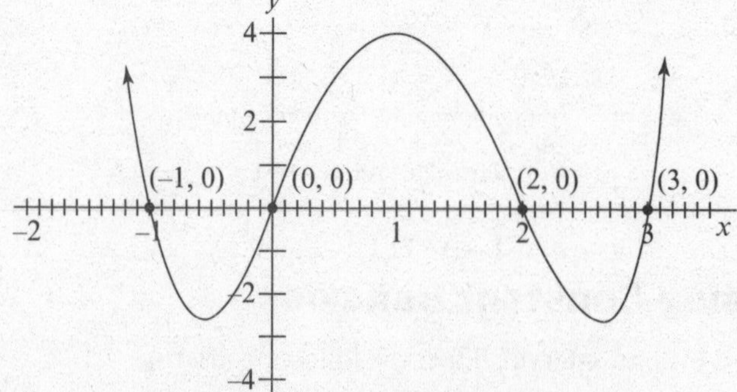

Positive and Negative Behavior of the Function *f*

The function *f* is positive in the intervals (−∞, −1), (0, 2), and (3, ∞), and negative in the intervals (−1, 0) and (2, 3).

Even and Odd Functions

A function is **even** if for every x in D_f, $-x$ is in D_f and $f(-x) = f(x)$. A function is **odd** if for every x in D_f, $-x$ is in D_f and $f(-x) = -f(x)$. The graphs of even functions are symmetric about the y-axis. The graphs of odd functions are symmetric about the origin. Here are examples.

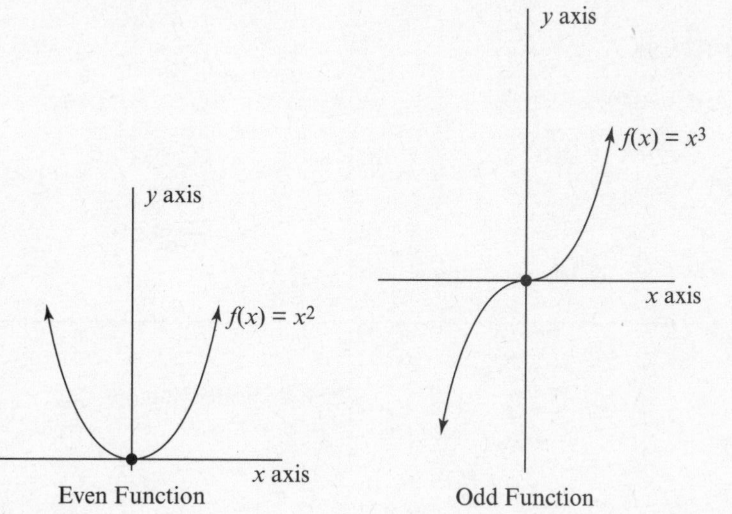

Even Function Odd Function

Note: Many functions are neither even nor odd. Their graphs show no symmetry with respect to either the y-axis or the origin.

Asymptotes

An **asymptote** of the graph of a function f is a line to which the graph gets closer and closer in at least one direction along the line. The vertical line $x = a$ is a **vertical asymptote** of the graph of a function f if as x draws close to a from the left or right, the graph goes toward either $-\infty$ or ∞. A horizontal line $y = b$ is a **horizontal asymptote** of the graph of f if $f(x)$ approaches b as x approaches either $-\infty$ or ∞. See the following figure.

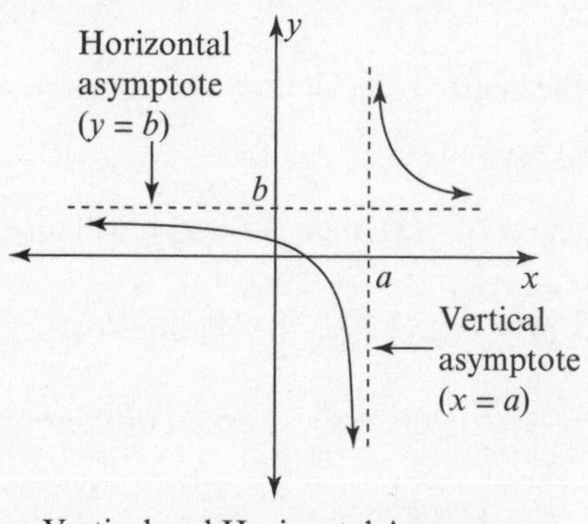

Vertical and Horizontal Asymptotes

Commonly, asymptotes are associated with rational functions (see "Rational Functions" later in this chapter for a more detailed discussion of rational functions). For a rational function f, defined by $f(x) = \frac{p(x)}{q(x)}$, you find vertical asymptotes by setting the denominator $q(x)$ equal to 0 and solving for x (provided the rational function is in simplified form and the degree of $q(x)$ is at least 1). A line $y = g(x)$ is an **oblique asymptote** (or slant asymptote) of a function f if the graph of the function approaches $y = g(x)$ as x approaches either ∞ or $-\infty$. See the following figure that shows an oblique asymptote (along with a vertical asymptote).

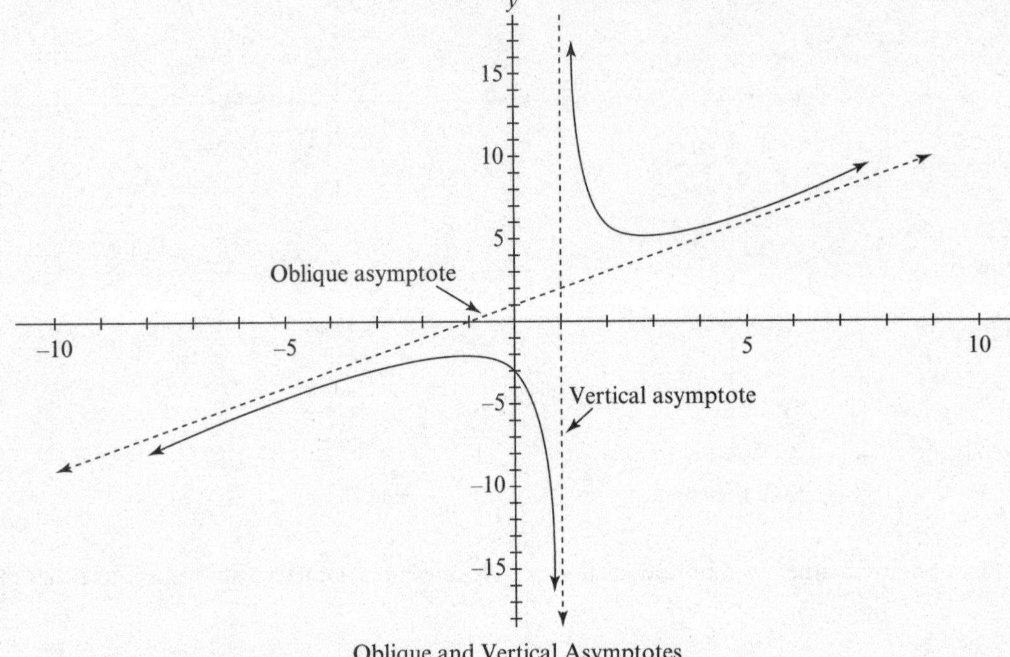

Oblique and Vertical Asymptotes

You find horizontal asymptotes by determining the value that $y = f(x)$ approaches as x approaches either ∞ or $-\infty$ (again, provided the rational function is in simplified form and the degree of $q(x)$ is at least 1).

A rational function will have at most one horizontal asymptote. The following guidelines will help you identify a horizontal asymptote of a rational function defined by $f(x) = \frac{p(x)}{q(x)}$, where $f(x)$ is in simplified form and the degree of $q(x)$ is at least 1:

- If the degree of $p(x)$ is less than the degree of $q(x)$, then the x-axis ($y = 0$) is a horizontal asymptote. For example, the x-axis is a horizontal asymptote of $f(x) = \frac{1}{x-3}$.
- If the degree of $p(x)$ equals the degree of $q(x)$, then the graph will have a horizontal asymptote at $y = \frac{a_n}{b_m}$, where a_n is the leading coefficient of $p(x)$ and b_m is the leading coefficient of $q(x)$. For example, $y = \frac{3}{4}$ is a horizontal asymptote of $g(x) = \frac{3x^2 - 4}{4x^2 + 1}$. Here is the graph. For your reference a dashed horizontal line has been constructed at $y = \frac{3}{4}$.

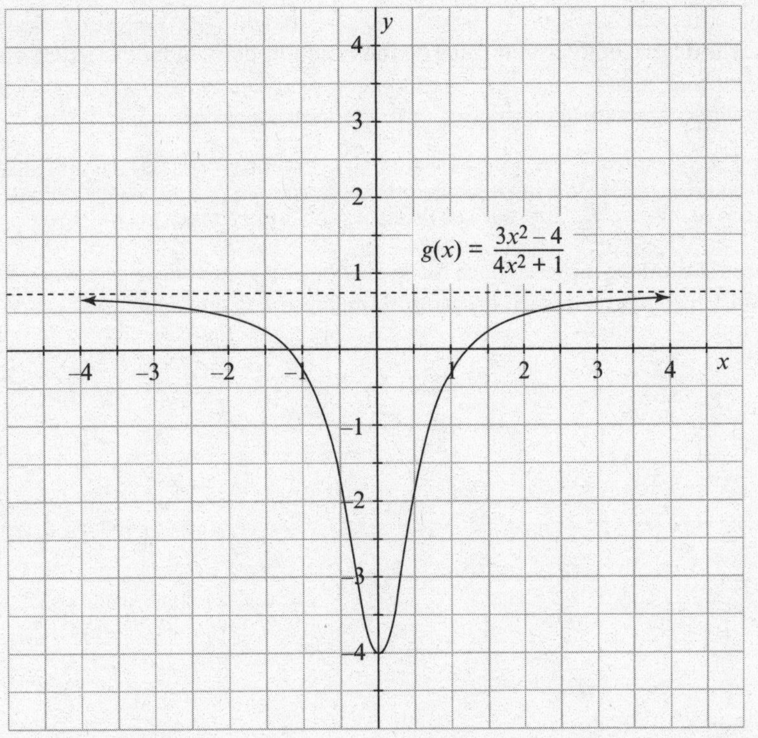

- If the degree of $p(x)$ exceeds the degree of $q(x)$ by more than 1, the graph will *not* have a horizontal asymptote. For example, $g(x) = \frac{x^6 - 1}{x^2 + 2}$ has no horizontal asymptote. Here is the graph.

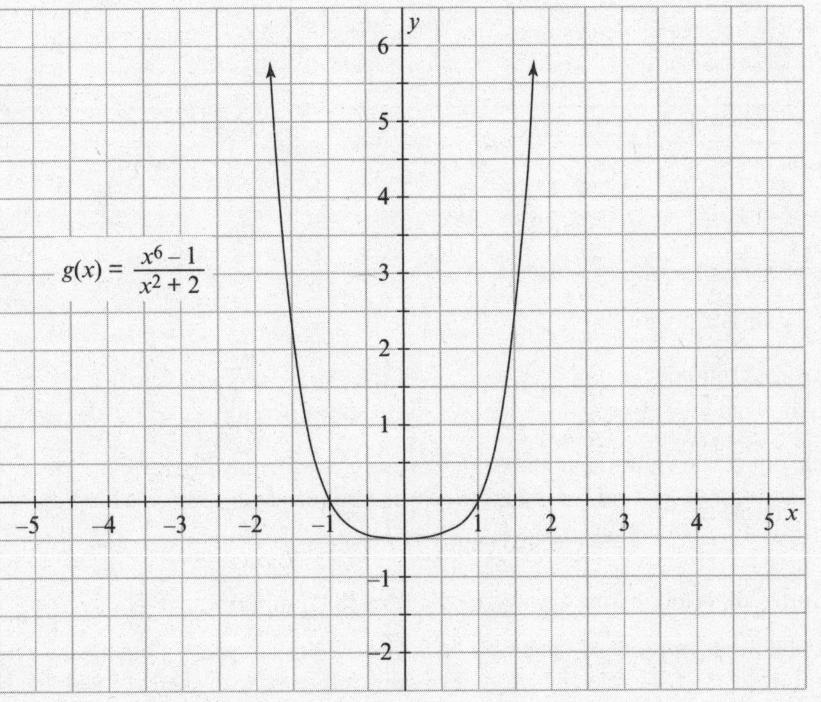

Here is an example of finding vertical and horizontal asymptotes.

Find the vertical and horizontal asymptotes of the function defined by the equation $y = \frac{1}{x^2 - 9} + 5$.

The denominator $x^2 - 9$ equals 0 when $x = 3$ or -3. Thus, the graph has vertical asymptotes at $x = 3$ and $x = -3$. As x approaches either ∞ or $-\infty$, $\frac{1}{x^2 - 9}$ approaches 0. Thus, as x approaches ∞ or $-\infty$, $\frac{1}{x^2 - 9} + 5$ approaches $0 + 5 = 5$, so $y = 5$ is a horizontal asymptote. Here is the graph. For your reference dashed vertical lines have been constructed at $x = 3$ and $x = -3$ and a dashed horizontal line has been constructed at $y = 5$.

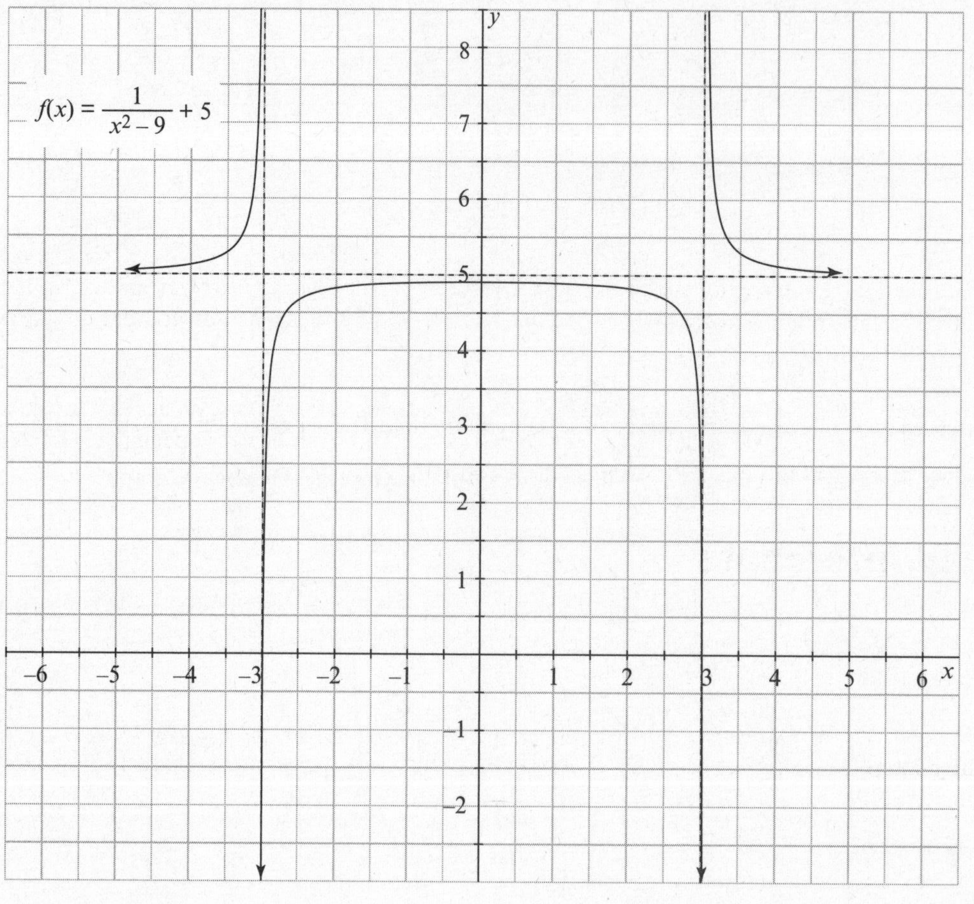

A rational function, defined by $f(x) = \frac{p(x)}{q(x)}$, where $f(x)$ is in simplified form and the degree of $q(x)$ is at least 1, will have at most one oblique asymptote. If the degree of $p(x)$ exceeds the degree of $q(x)$ by *exactly* 1, the graph will have an oblique asymptote. To find the equation of the oblique asymptote, use long division to rewrite $f(x) = \frac{p(x)}{q(x)}$ as quotient plus $\frac{\text{remainder}}{q(x)}$ (see Appendix D for a review of long division of polynomials). The line with equation, $y =$ quotient, is an oblique asymptote. For example, suppose that $f(x) = \frac{x^2 + 3}{x - 1} = (x + 1) + \frac{4}{x - 1}$, then $y = x + 1$ is an oblique asymptote of the graph of f. The denominator $x - 1$ equals 0 when $x = 1$, so the graph has a vertical asymptote at $x = 1$. Here is the graph. For your reference, a dashed vertical line has been constructed at $x = 1$ and a dashed oblique line has been constructed representing $y = x + 1$.

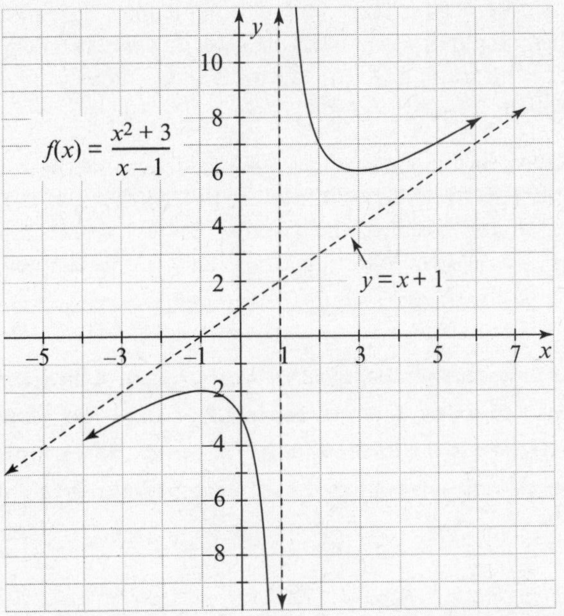

The graph of a function can *never* intersect a vertical asymptote of the function. However, the graph of a function may cross a line that is a horizontal or oblique asymptote as long as the graph eventually draws asymptotically close to the line.

In an informal sense, a function has **discontinuities** if the graph of the function has vertical asymptotes, holes, or jumps that make it impossible to sketch the graph of the function without lifting the pencil. See Chapter 6, "Calculus," for a mathematically rigorous discussion of continuity and discontinuity.

Zeros and Intercepts

A **zero** of a function f is a solution to the equation $f(x) = 0$. It is an input value that produces a zero output value. For example, −2 is a zero of the function f defined by $f(x) = x^2 - 4$ because $f(-2) = (-2)^2 - 4 = 4 - 4 = 0$. The zeros are determined by finding all x values for which $f(x) = 0$.

An ***x*-intercept** of the graph of a function is the x-coordinate of a point at which the graph intersects the x-axis, and the ***y*-intercept** is the y-coordinate of the point at which the graph intersects the y-axis. See the following figure.

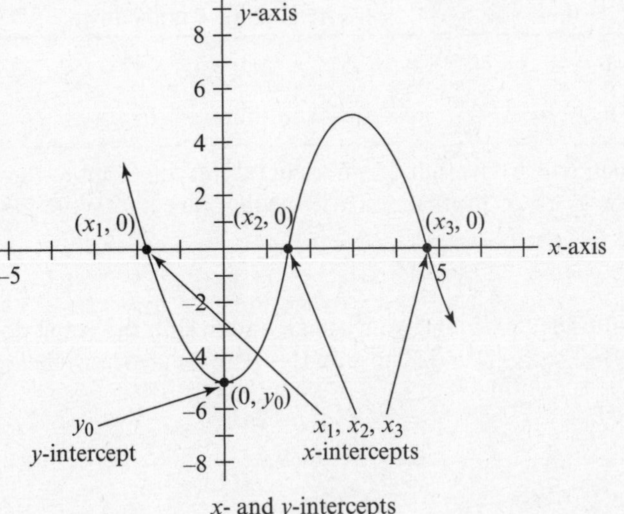

x- and y-intercepts

The graph of a function has at most *one* y-intercept. A function f cannot have more than one y-intercept because, by definition, each x value in the domain of f is paired with *exactly one* y value in the range. If 0 is in the domain of f, then $f(0)$ is the y-intercept of the graph of f. To determine the y-intercept of a function f, let $x = 0$, provided that 0 is in the domain of f, and then solve $f(0) = y$ for y.

A graph can have many x-intercepts, or it might not have any. To determine the x-intercept(s), if any, of a function f, set $f(x) = 0$ and then solve for x. The x-intercepts, if any, are the real zeros of f. You can describe a real zero of a function as one of the following: an x-intercept of the graph of $y = f(x)$, a real number x for which $f(x) = 0$, or a real root of the equation $f(x) = 0$. See "Polynomial Functions" later in this chapter for an illustration of the zeros of a function.

Tip: It is important that you understand the distinction between *x*-intercepts and zeros. To clarify the relationship in general: For any function *f*, *x*-intercepts (if any) of the graph of *f* are *always* zeros of *f*; however, only *real* zeros (if any) of *f* are *x*-intercepts of its graph. Some functions have zeros that are not real numbers, so these zeros do not correspond to *x*-intercepts because these values do not lie on the *x*-axis.

Horizontal and Vertical Translations

A **translation,** or shift, is a geometric transformation of the graph of a function f that results in a new graph congruent to the graph of f, but for which every point P **(preimage)** on the graph of f is "moved" the same distance and in the same direction along a straight line to a new point P' **(image).** Informally, a translation is a slide of the graph of a function in a horizontal or vertical direction.

You perform a horizontal shift by adding or subtracting a positive constant h to or from the independent variable x. You perform a vertical shift by adding or subtracting a positive constant k to or from $f(x)$. The following table contains a summary of vertical and horizontal shifts. ***Note:*** The numbers h and k in the table are both positive.

Horizontal and Vertical Shifts

Type of Translation	Effect on Graph of f
$y = f(x + h)$	horizontal shift: h units to left
$y = f(x - h)$	horizontal shift: h units to right
$y = f(x) + k$	vertical shift: k units up
$y = f(x) - k$	vertical shift: k units down

Here is an example.

> The graph of the function g is the result of a horizontal shift of 1 unit to the right and a vertical shift of 2 units down of the graph of the function f defined by $f(x) = x^2$. Write the equation for the graph of the function g.

To shift the graph of f 1 unit to the right, subtract 1 from x and to shift the graph down 2 units, subtract 2 from $f(x)$ to obtain $g(x) = f(x - 1) - 2 = (x - 1)^2 - 2$. The graphs of f and g are shown below.

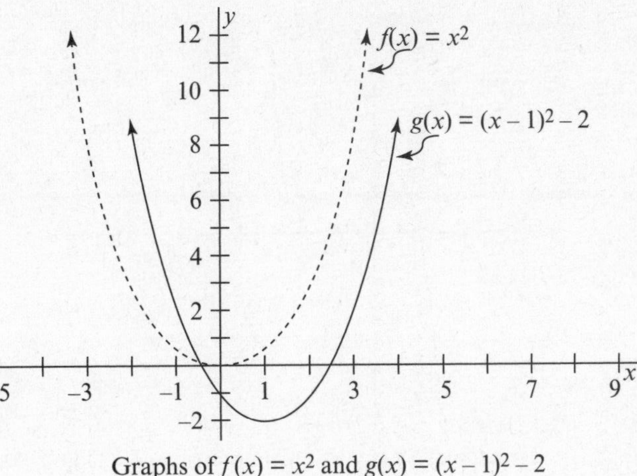

Graphs of $f(x) = x^2$ and $g(x) = (x - 1)^2 - 2$

Dilations

A **dilation** is a geometric transformation of the graph of a function f that results in a new graph that is geometrically similar in shape to the graph of f, but for which the graph of f has undergone a vertical stretch or compression or a horizontal stretch or compression.

When $a > 1$, the graph defined by $g(x) = af(x)$ is a **vertical stretch** *away* from the horizontal axis of the graph defined by $y = f(x)$; and when $0 < a < 1$, the graph defined by $g(x) = af(x)$ is a **vertical compression** *toward* the horizontal axis of the graph defined by $y = f(x)$. In either case, if (x, y) is on the graph defined by $y = f(x)$, then (x, ay) is on the graph defined by $g(x) = af(x)$. See the following figure.

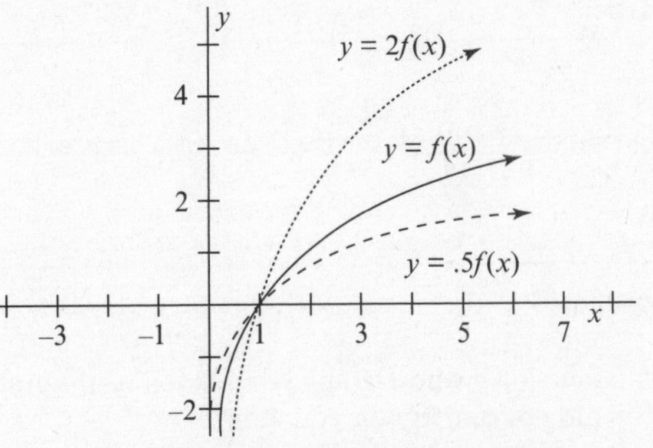

Vertical Stretch and Compression of $f(x)$

When $b > 1$, the graph defined by $g(x) = f(bx)$ is a **horizontal compression** *toward* the vertical axis of the graph defined by $y = f(x)$; and when $0 < b < 1$, the graph defined by $g(x) = f(bx)$ is a **horizontal stretch** *away* from the vertical axis of the graph defined by $y = f(x)$. In either case, if (x, y) is on the graph defined by $y = f(x)$, then $\left(\frac{x}{b}, y\right)$ is on the graph defined by $g(x) = f(bx)$. See the following figure.

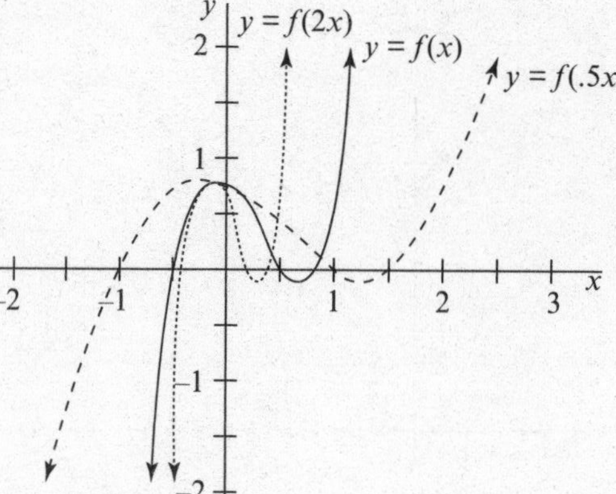

Horizontal Stretch and Compression of $f(x)$

Here are examples.

Given that the graph of the function g defined by $g(x)=\frac{3}{4}x^3$ is a dilation of the graph of the function f defined by $f(x) = x^3$, describe the dilation as one of the following:

(a) a vertical stretch

(b) a vertical compression

(c) a horizontal stretch

(d) a horizontal compression

Given that $g(x)=\frac{3}{4}x^3=\frac{3}{4}f(x)$ and that $0<\frac{3}{4}<1$, the function g is a vertical compression of the function f, choice (b).

For the function f, defined by $f(x) = x^3$,

(a) write an equation for a function g whose graph is a dilation of the graph of f satisfying the condition that $g(x) = f(3x)$ (do not simplify the equation).

(b) for the point $(-5, -125)$ on the graph defined by $f(x) = x^3$, give the coordinates of the corresponding point on the graph defined by $g(x) = f(3x)$.

(a) $g(x) = f(3x) = (3x)^3$

(b) Given $(-5, -125)$ is on the graph defined by $f(x) = x^3$, then $\left(-\frac{5}{3}, -125\right)$ is its corresponding point on the graph defined by $g(x) = (3x)^3$.

Reflections

A **reflection** is a mirror image of a function. The function $-f(x)$ reflects $f(x)$ over the x-axis and $f(-x)$ reflects $f(x)$ over the y-axis. See the following figures.

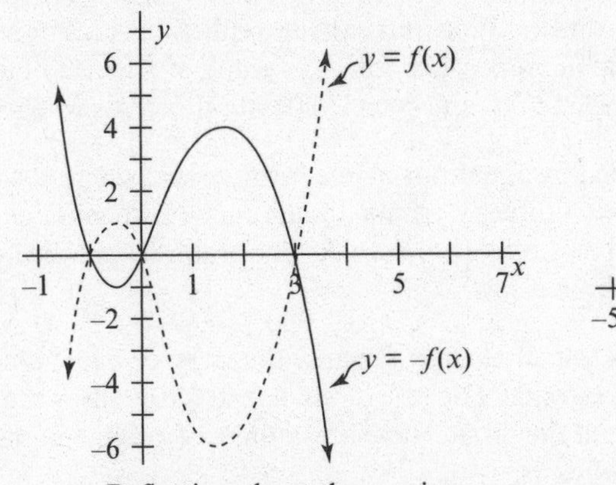

Reflection about the x-axis

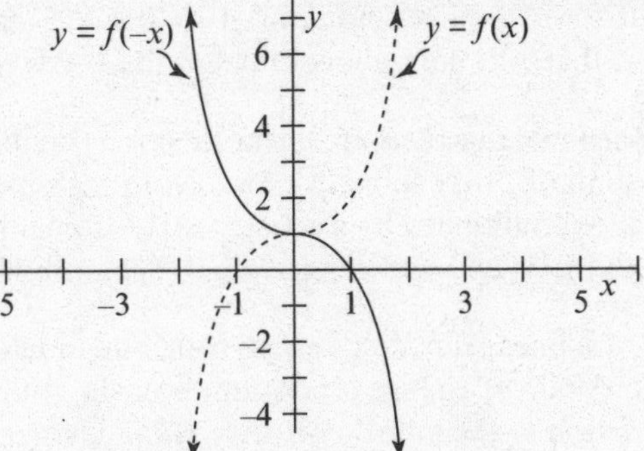

Reflection about the y-axis

Note: For a general discussion of geometric transformations, see "Geometric Transformations" in Chapter 7.

Features of Common Functions

This section presents features of common functions including their defining equations, domains and ranges, zeros, and intercepts.

Linear Functions

Linear functions are defined by equations of the form $f(x) = mx + b$. The domain for all linear functions is R, the set of real numbers. When $m \neq 0$, the range is R. When $m = 0$, the range is the set $\{b\}$, containing the single value b. The equation $y = mx + b$ is the **slope-intercept form** of the equation of a line.

The graph of a linear function f defined by $f(x) = mx + b$ is always a nonvertical line with slope m and y-intercept b. When $m \neq 0$, the graph has exactly one y-intercept b and exactly one x-intercept $-\frac{b}{m}$. Thus, the points $(0, b)$ and $\left(-\frac{b}{m}, 0\right)$ are contained in the graph. The only zero is the real number $-\frac{b}{m}$; thus, the graph crosses the x-axis at the point $\left(-\frac{b}{m}, 0\right)$. If $m > 0$, f is increasing; if $m < 0$, f is decreasing. The following figure shows the graph of the linear function $y = -\frac{1}{2}x + 6$ that has slope of $-\frac{1}{2}$, y-intercept of 6, and x-intercept of 12.

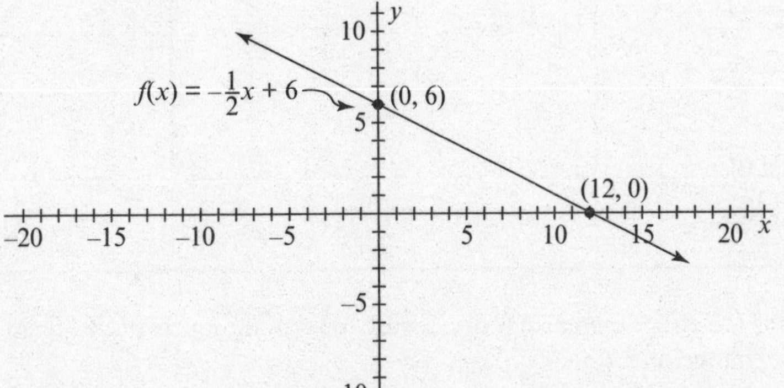

The **identity function** is the linear function defined by the equation $f(x) = x$. This function maps each x value to an identical y value. The domain and range are both R. The graph has slope of 1. The graph passes through the origin, so both the x- and y-intercepts are 0. The only zero is $x = 0$.

Constant functions are linear functions defined by equations of the form $f(x) = b$, where $b \in R$. The domain is R, and the range is the set $\{b\}$, containing the single element b. Constant functions can have either no zeros or infinitely many zeros: If $b \neq 0$, they have no zeros; if $b = 0$, every real number x is a zero. The graph of a constant function is a horizontal line that is $|b|$ units above or below the x-axis when $b \neq 0$ and coincident with the x axis when $b = 0$.

Directly proportional functions are linear functions defined by equations of the form $y = kx$, where $k \in R$ is the nonzero constant of proportionality. Simply, a function is a directly proportional function when the output is equal to the input multiplied by a constant. The domain and range are both R. The graph passes through the origin, so both the x- and y-intercepts are 0. The only zero is $x = 0$.

The slope m of a linear function's graph is the function's **rate of change.** Because the slope of a line is constant, a linear function's rate of change is constant over the entire graph. The rate of change describes how the output changes in relation to the input. For every 1-unit change in the input, there are m units of change in the output. If the input changes by k units, the output changes by km units.

For example, for the function $y = 3x + 5$, for every 1-unit change in x, there is a 3-unit change in y.

In general, if (x_1, y_1) and (x_2, y_2) are any two distinct ordered pairs in a linear function's graph, the function's rate of change is $m = \dfrac{\text{change in } y}{\text{change in } x} = \dfrac{y_2 - y_1}{x_2 - x_1}$.

Rates of change can be positive, negative, or zero. A **positive rate of change** corresponds to an increase in the output when the input increases. When you trace the input, x, as it increases from left to right, you will observe that the output, y, increases from lower to higher values. The result is that the graph slants upward from left to right.

A **negative rate of change** corresponds to a decrease in the output when the input increases. When you trace the input, x, as it increases from left to right, you will observe that the output, y, decreases from higher to lower values. The result is that the graph slants downward from left to right.

A **zero rate of change** occurs when the output does not change as the input increases. When you trace the input, x, as it increases from left to right, you will observe that the value of the output, y, does not change. That is, the output's value remains constant. The result is that the graph is a horizontal line. Here are graphical examples.

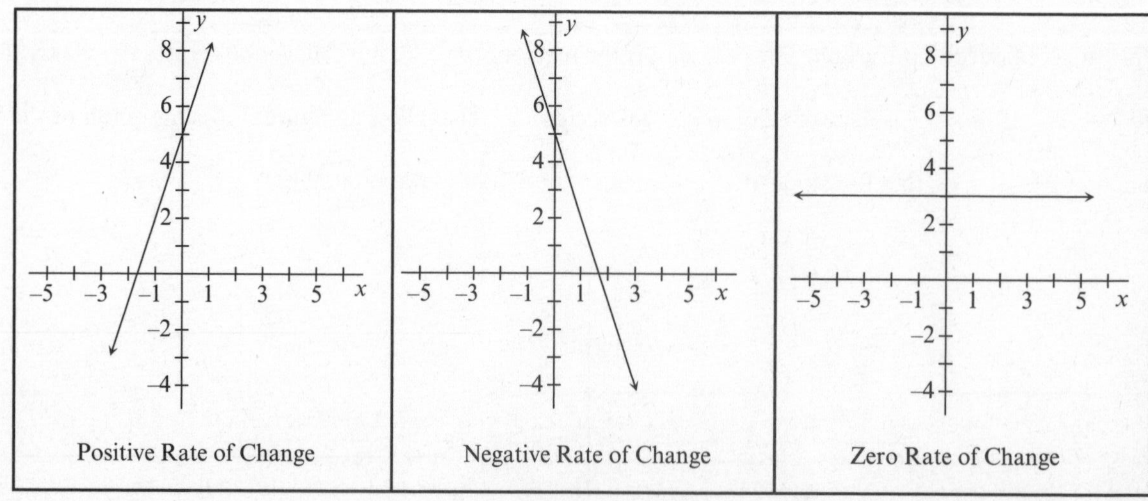

Therefore, linear functions are either increasing, decreasing, or remaining constant, from left to right, at a steady rate. Their graphs do not change direction.

Note: See "Average Rate of Change and Difference Quotient" later in this chapter for a general discussion about rate of change.

Quadratic Functions

Quadratic functions are defined by equations of the form $f(x) = ax^2 + bx + c$, $(a \neq 0)$. The domain is R and the range is a subset of R. The zeros are the roots of the quadratic equation $ax^2 + bx + c = 0$. The quantity $b^2 - 4ac$ is the **discriminant** of the quadratic equation. It determines three cases for the zeros: If $b^2 - 4ac > 0$, the quadratic function has two real *unequal* zeros; if $b^2 - 4ac = 0$, the quadratic function has one real zero (of multiplicity 2; see "Polynomial Functions" below for a discussion of multiplicity); and if $b^2 - 4ac < 0$, the quadratic function has no real zeros.

The graph of $f(x) = ax^2 + bx + c$ is a parabola. The vertex is $\left(-\frac{b}{2a}, f\left(-\frac{b}{2a}\right)\right)$. When $a > 0$, the parabola opens upward and the y-coordinate of the vertex is an **absolute minimum** of f. When $a < 0$, the parabola opens downward and the y-coordinate of the vertex is an **absolute maximum** of f. The parabola is symmetric about its **axis of symmetry,** a vertical line through its vertex that is parallel to the y-axis.

Depending on the solution set of $ax^2 + bx + c = 0$, the parabola might or might not intersect the x-axis. Three cases occur:

- If $ax^2 + bx + c = 0$ has *two* real *unequal* roots, the parabola will intersect the x-axis at those *two* points.
- If $ax^2 + bx + c = 0$ has exactly *one* real root, the parabola will be tangent to the x-axis at only that *one* point.
- If $ax^2 + bx + c = 0$ has *no* real roots, the parabola will *not* intersect the x-axis.

See the following figure.

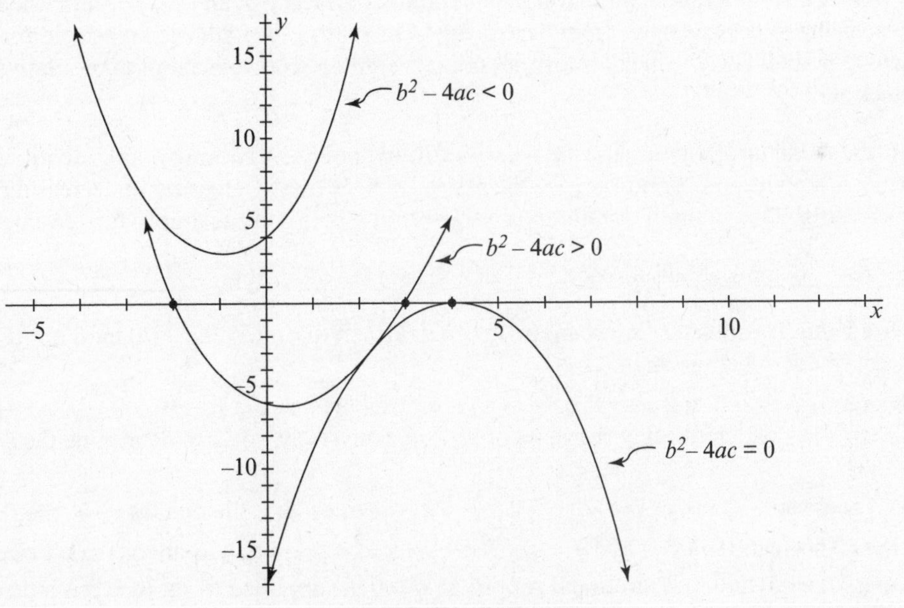

Graphs of Quadratic Functions

The **standard form** for the equation of a parabola that opens upward or downward is $f(x) = y = a(x - h)^2 + k$, $(a \neq 0)$ with vertex (h, k). Any quadratic function can be put in standard form by using the process of completing the square. (See "Solving Quadratic Equations by Completing the Square" in Chapter 3 for a discussion of completing the square.) When $a < 0$, the range of f is $(-\infty, k]$. The function is increasing on $(-\infty, h)$ and decreasing on (h, ∞). When $a > 0$, the range of f is $[k, \infty)$. The function is decreasing on $(-\infty, h)$ and increasing on (h, ∞).

Polynomial Functions

Polynomial functions are defined by equations of the form $P(x) = a_n x^n + a_{n-1}x^{n-1} + \cdots + a_2x^2 + a_1x + a_0$, with **leading coefficient** $a_n \neq 0$. The **degree** of the polynomial function is n, a nonnegative integer. Linear and quadratic functions are polynomial functions of degree one and two, respectively. A constant polynomial function, defined by $P(x) = c$ (a nonzero constant), has degree zero. The degree of the zero polynomial function, defined as $P(x) = 0$, is undefined. The domain of any polynomial function is R. When n is odd, the range is R. When n is even, the range is a subset of R. The zeros are the roots of the equation $P(x) = 0$.

A number r is a zero of a polynomial function P that is defined by $y = P(x)$ if and only if $P(r) = 0$. If $r \in R$, the graph of $y = P(x)$ crosses the x-axis at the point $(r, 0)$ and has an x-intercept at r. The graph of a polynomial function P is a continuous smooth curve (or line) with no breaks of any kind; moreover, it has no **cusps** (meaning sharp corners). The y-intercept of the graph is $P(0)$. The x-intercepts correspond to the real zeros (if any) of P. As the degree of polynomial functions increases, their graphs become more complex. The graph below shows a polynomial function that has zeros (and x-intercepts) –1, 0, 2, and 3, and y-intercept 0.

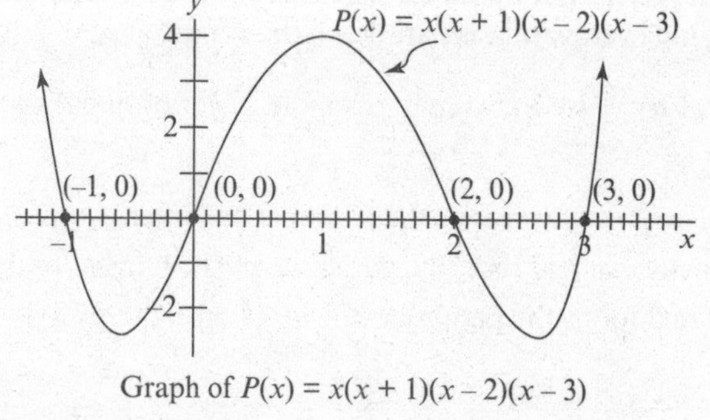

Graph of $P(x) = x(x + 1)(x - 2)(x - 3)$

The graph of a polynomial function might have turning points. A **turning point** (x, y) occurs whenever the graph changes from increasing to decreasing or from decreasing to increasing. An nth degree polynomial function has at most $(n - 1)$ turning points. The y value of a turning point is either a relative maximum or relative minimum value for the function.

Tip: Do not confuse maximum or minimum values with turning points. A turning point, identified by an ordered pair (x, y), is a point on the graph where the graph changes from increasing to decreasing (or from decreasing to increasing). A maximum or minimum value is not a point on the graph. It is a value of the function.

Some useful theorems to know about polynomial functions are the following:

- **Intermediate Value Theorem for Polynomials:** If $a, b \in R$ such that $P(a)$ and $P(b)$ have opposite signs, then P has at least one zero between a and b.
- **Factor Theorem:** $P(r) = 0$ if and only if $x - r$ is a factor of $P(x) = a_n x^n + a_{n-1}x^{n-1} + \cdots + a_2x^2 + a_1x + a_0$. Thus, you can factor $P(x)$ by determining the zeros of P; and, conversely, you can determine the zeros of P by factoring $P(x)$.
- **Remainder Theorem:** If $P(x) = a_n x^n + a_{n-1}x^{n-1} + \cdots + a_2x^2 + a_1x + a_0$ is divided by $x - r$, the remainder is $P(r)$.
- **Rational Root Theorem:** If $P(x) = a_n x^n + a_{n-1}x^{n-1} + \cdots + a_2x^2 + a_1x + a_0$ with integer coefficients a_i (and both a_n and a_0 are not zero) and $\frac{p}{q}$ is a rational root of $P(x) = 0$ in simplified form, then p is a factor of a_0 and q is a factor of a_n.
- **Descartes' Rule of Signs:** If $P(x)$ has real coefficients and is written in descending (or ascending) powers of x, then the number of positive real roots of $P(x) = 0$ is either the number of sign changes, from left to right, occurring in the coefficients of $P(x)$, or it is less than this number by an even number. Similarly, the number of negative real roots of $P(x) = 0$ is either the number of sign changes, from left to right, occurring in the coefficients of $P(-x)$, or it is less than this number by an even number. ***Note:*** When using this rule, ignore missing powers of x.

- **Fundamental Theorem of Algebra:** Over the complex numbers, every polynomial function P of degree $n \geq 1$ has at least one zero. It follows that if you allow complex zeros and count a zero again each time it occurs more than once, a polynomial function of degree n has exactly n zeros. This theorem guarantees that for every polynomial function P of degree $n \geq 1$ there exist complex zeros $r_1, r_2, \ldots,$ and r_n, so that you can factor $P(x)$ completely as $P(x) = a_n(x - r_1)(x - r_2) \ldots (x - r_n)$, where a_n is the leading coefficient of $P(x)$. In general, a zero r of a polynomial function P has **multiplicity *k*,** meaning it occurs as a zero exactly k times, if $(x - r)^k$ is a factor of $P(x)$ and $(x - r)^{k+1}$ is not a factor of $P(x)$. Hence, the n zeros of a polynomial function P are not necessarily all different from each other. For example, 3 is a zero of multiplicity 2 for the second degree polynomial function P defined by $P(x) = x^2 - 6x + 9 = (x - 3)(x - 3)$.
- **Complex Conjugate Rule:** If $P(x)$ has real coefficients and $a + bi$, $(b \neq 0)$, is a complex root of $P(x) = 0$, then its complex conjugate $a - bi$ is also a root of $P(x) = 0$.

Tip: Go to http://www.infinitysw.com/exams/tutorials to view a tutorial on the ETS graphing calculator's Solver tool. Be careful when using this tool. It returns only one value for the solution. It determines the answer closest to your guess or within your specified interval. It does not return complex zeros. You must use your knowledge of the concepts discussed in this section to make sure you determine the correct number of zeros of a function.

Here are examples of finding the zeros of a polynomial function.

Find the real zeros of the polynomial function P defined by $P(x) = 2x^3 - 3x^2 - 11x + 6$.

Using Descartes' rule of signs, the number of sign changes in $P(x) = 2x^3 - 3x^2 - 11x + 6$ is two. So, there are two or zero positive real roots. The number of sign changes in $P(-x) = -2x^3 - 3x^2 + 11x + 6$ is one. So, there is at most one negative real root. If $\frac{p}{q}$ is a rational root of $P(x) = 0$, then possible values for p are factors of 6 and possible values for q are factors of 2. Thus, p could be $\pm 1, \pm 2, \pm 3$, or ± 6 and q could be ± 1 or ± 2. Hence, $\frac{p}{q}$ is possibly ± 1, $\pm 2, \pm 3, \pm 6, \pm \frac{1}{2}$, or $\pm \frac{3}{2}$. Substituting into $P(x)$, $P(1) = -6$, $P(-1) = 12$, $P(2) = -12$, and $P(-2) = 0$. Thus, -2 is a zero, and $(x + 2)$ is a factor of $P(x)$ by the factor theorem. There are no other negative zeros, so eliminate $-3, -6, -\frac{1}{2}$, and $-\frac{3}{2}$ as possible zeros.

Using the remainder theorem and synthetic division, test $x = 3$ (see Appendix D for an explanation of synthetic division).

$$\begin{array}{r|rrrr} 3 & 2 & -3 & -11 & 6 \\ & & 6 & 9 & -6 \\ \hline & 2 & 3 & -2 & 0 \end{array}$$

So, 3 is a zero, and $(x - 3)$ is a factor of $P(x)$. From the coefficients displayed in the synthetic division, the other factor is the trinomial $2x^2 + 3x - 2$. Given that $(x + 2)$ is a factor of $P(x)$, you can quickly determine that $P(x) = 2x^3 - 3x^2 - 11x + 6 = (x - 3)(2x^2 + 3x - 2) = (x - 3)(x + 2)(2x - 1)$. Therefore, the real zeros of the polynomial function P are $-2, \frac{1}{2}$, and 3. There are no complex zeros. ***Tip:*** This solution is one way to determine the zeros, but other approaches also could be used to yield the same result.

Find the zeros of the polynomial function P defined by $P(x) = x^3 - 1$.

The zeros of P are the roots of $x^3 - 1 = 0$. Since $P(x)$ has degree 3, the equation $x^3 - 1 = 0$ has exactly three roots. Solve by factoring the difference of two cubes and then using the quadratic formula to determine the roots of the trinomial factor.

$$x^3 - 1 = 0$$
$$(x-1)(x^2+x+1) = 0$$
$$(x-1) = 0 \text{ or } (x^2+x+1) = 0$$
$$x = 1 \text{ or } x = \frac{-1 \pm \sqrt{1^2 - 4(1)(1)(1)}}{2(1)} = \frac{-1 \pm \sqrt{-3}}{2} = -\frac{1}{2} \pm \frac{\sqrt{3}}{2}i$$

Thus, 1, $-\frac{1}{2}+\frac{\sqrt{3}}{2}i$, and $-\frac{1}{2}-\frac{\sqrt{3}}{2}i$ are the zeros of P.

Tip: When a polynomial function *P* has only real coefficients, the complex zeros of *P* occur in conjugate pairs (as shown in this example).

In the above example, even though P has three zeros, it has only one real zero, namely, 1, so its graph will intersect the x-axis only once—at $x = 1$, as shown in the following figure.

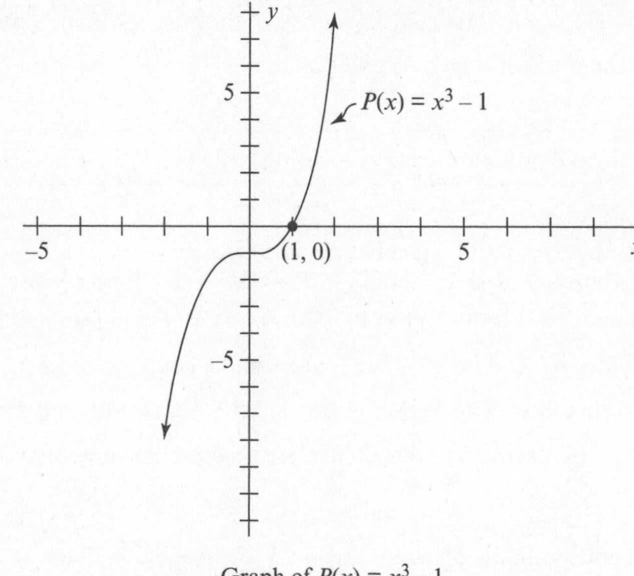

Graph of $P(x) = x^3 - 1$

To determine the behavior of a polynomial function defined by $P(x) = a_nx^n + a_{n-1}x^{n-1} + \cdots + a_2x^2 + a_1x + a_0$ as x approaches ∞ or $-\infty$, factor out a_nx^n, the term with highest degree. Then as x approaches ∞ or $-\infty$, $P(x)$ behaves as a_nx^n does.

For example, suppose $P(x) = 3x^4 - 500{,}000x^3 + 40x^2 + 100x - 80$. Factoring out $3x^4$ yields $P(x) = 3x^4 - 500{,}000x^3 + 40x^2 + 100x - 80 = 3x^4\left(1 - \frac{500{,}000}{3x} + \frac{40}{3x^2} + \frac{100}{3x^3} - \frac{80}{3x^4}\right)$. As x approaches ∞ or $-\infty$, the quantity in parentheses approaches 1, so $P(x)$ will behave as $3x^4$ does. Given that $3x^4$ is always positive, then as x approaches ∞, $P(x)$ will become increasingly positive, and as x approaches $-\infty$, again $P(x)$ will become increasingly positive.

Rational Functions

Rational functions are defined by equations of the form $f(x) = \frac{P(x)}{Q(x)} = \frac{a_nx^n + a_{n-1}x^{n-1} + \cdots + a_1x + a_0}{b_mx^m + b_{m-1}x^{m-1} + \cdots + b_1x + b_0}$, where $P(x)$ and $Q(x)$ are polynomials and $Q(x) \neq 0$. The domain is $\{x \in R \mid Q(x) \neq 0\}$. The range is a subset of R. When $f(x)$ is in simplified form (that is, when the numerator and denominator polynomials have no common factors), the zeros of f, if any, occur at x values for which $P(x) = 0$. If 0 is in the domain of f, the y-intercept is $f(0)$. When $f(x)=\frac{P(x)}{Q(x)}$ is in simplified form, the x-intercepts occur at real values for which $P(x) = 0$.

To graph $f(x)=\frac{P(x)}{Q(x)}$, first factor $P(x)$ and $Q(x)$ to identify possible "holes" in the graph of f. Intuitively, a **hole** is a missing point in the graph. If $P(x)$ and $Q(x)$ have a common factor, $(x - h)$, that will divide out completely from the denominator when $f(x)$ is simplified, then the graph will have a hole at $(h, f(h))$, where $f(h)$ is calculated after $f(x)$ is simplified.

For example, let $f(x)=\frac{x+2}{x^2-4}=\frac{x+2}{(x+2)(x-2)}$. The common factor, $(x + 2)$, will divide out completely from the denominator when $f(x)$ is simplified to $f(x)=\frac{1}{x-2}$. Therefore, the graph of f has a hole at $\left(-2,-\frac{1}{4}\right)$, given that f is undefined when $x = -2$. After identifying possible holes, next use the simplified form of $f(x)$ to determine asymptotes of the graph (see "Asymptotes" earlier in this chapter for a discussion of this topic). Because $f(x)=\frac{1}{x-2}$ is undefined when x is 2, the graph has a vertical asymptote at $x = 2$. The degree of the numerator of $f(x)=\frac{1}{x-2}$ is less than the degree of its denominator, so the x-axis is a horizontal asymptote of the graph. See the following figure.

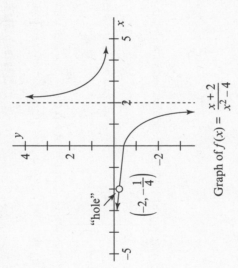

Graph of $f(x) = \frac{x+2}{x^2-4}$

To determine the behavior of the rational function f defined by $f(x)=\frac{P(x)}{Q(x)}=\frac{a_nx^n+a_{n-1}x^{n-1}+\cdots+a_1x+a_0}{b_mx^m+b_{m-1}x^{m-1}+\cdots+b_1x+b_0}$, as x approaches ∞ or $-\infty$, separately factor out a_nx^n, the term with highest degree in the numerator, and b_mx^m, the term with highest degree in the denominator. Then as x approaches ∞ or $-\infty$, $f(x)=\frac{P(x)}{Q(x)}$ behaves as $\frac{a_nx^n}{b_mx^m}$ does.

Tip: Use the ETS graphing calculator to explore rational functions. Enter the function, using parentheses around both the numerator and denominator polynomials. Use trial and error and the Zoom feature to find a good viewing window; otherwise, you might be misled by the graph displayed.

Square Root Functions

Square root functions are defined by equations of the form $f(x)=\sqrt{ax+b}$. The domain is $\{x \in R|\ ax+b \geq 0\}$. The range is $\{y \in R|\ y \geq 0\}$. The graph is nonnegative with the only zero at $x=-\frac{b}{a}$. The following figure shows the square root function $f(x)=\sqrt{x}$.

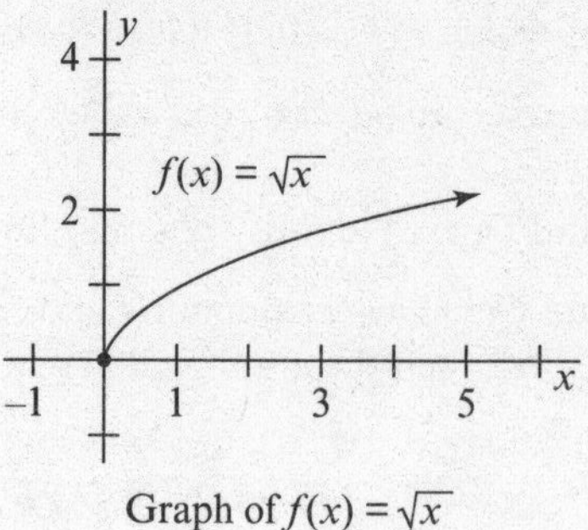

Graph of $f(x) = \sqrt{x}$

Power Functions

Power functions are defined by equations of the form $f(x) = x^a$, where a is a real number (provided that 0^0 does not occur). If a is a rational number $\frac{p}{q}$ [with p and q integers ($q \neq 0$) and $\frac{p}{q}$ simplified], then the domain is $[0, \infty)$ when q is even and is $(-\infty, \infty)$ when q is odd. If a is an irrational number, the domain is $[0, \infty)$. The range will vary depending on the value of a, and so will the zeros.

Absolute Value Functions

Absolute value functions are defined by equations of the form $f(x) = |ax + b|$. The domain is R, and the range is $\{y \in R | \, y \geq 0\}$. The only zero occurs at $x = -\frac{b}{a}$, and the y-intercept is located at $|b|$. The absolute value function $f(x) = |ax + b|$ is a piecewise function because you can write it as $f(x) = \left\{ \begin{array}{c} ax + b \text{ if } x \geq -\frac{b}{a} \\ -(ax + b) \text{ if } x < -\frac{b}{a} \end{array} \right\}$. ***Tip:*** **A piecewise function** is defined by different equations over a sequence of intervals. The following figure shows the absolute value function $f(x) = |x|$.

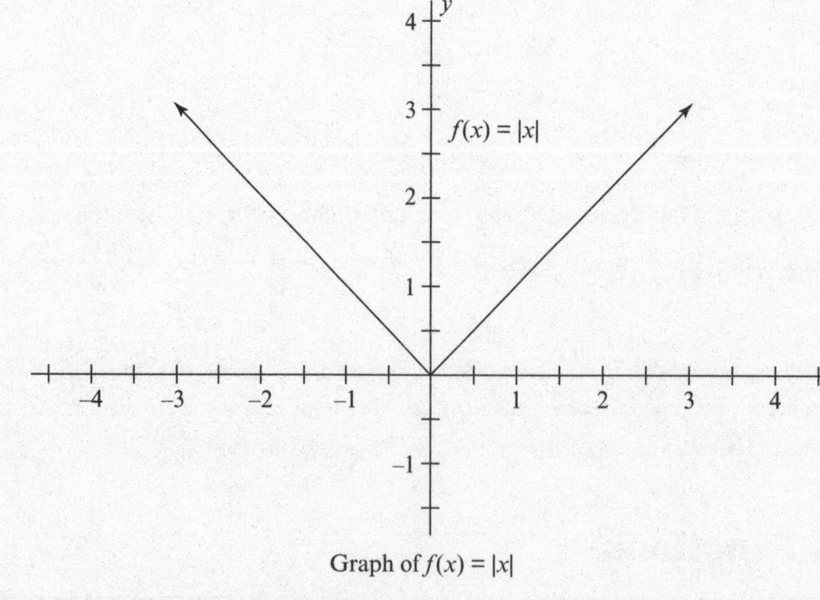

Graph of $f(x) = |x|$

The absolute value function has the following properties.

$|x| \geq 0$

$|x| = |-x|$

$|uv| = |u||v|$

$$\left|\frac{u}{v}\right| = \frac{|u|}{|v|},\ v \neq 0$$

$$|u + v| \leq |u| + |v|$$

$$\sqrt{x^2} = |x|$$

Note: Always perform computations inside absolute value bars *before* you evaluate the absolute value.

For $c > 0$,

$|x| = c$ if and only if either $x = c$ or $x = -c$

$|x| < c$ if and only if $-c < x < c$

$|x| > c$ if and only if either $x < -c$ or $x > c$

Note: Properties involving < and > hold if you replace < with ≤ and > with ≥.

Greatest Integer Functions

The **greatest integer function** (also called **step function**) is defined by $f(x) = [\![x]\!]$, where the brackets denote finding the greatest integer n such that $n \leq x$. The domain is R, and the range is the integers. The zeros lie in the interval $[0, 1)$. The y-intercept is 0. The x-intercepts lie in the interval $[0, 1)$. The graph of the function is constant between the integers, but "jumps" at each integer. The following figure shows the greatest integer function.

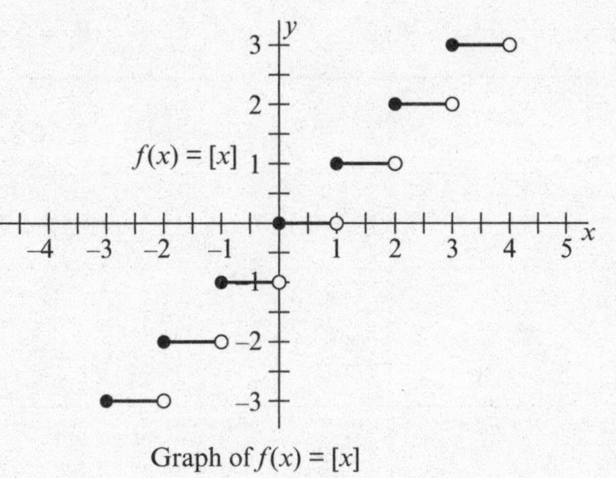

Graph of $f(x) = [x]$

Exponential Functions

Exponential functions are defined by equations of the form $f(x) = b^x$ ($b > 0$, $b \neq 1$), where b, a constant, is the base of the exponential function. The domain is R, and the range is $(0, \infty)$, which is to say that $b^x > 0$ for every real number x. Because $f(x) = b^x = 0$ has no solution, there are no zeros.

The graph of $f(x) = b^x(b > 0, b \neq 1)$ is a smooth, continuous curve. The graph passes through the points (0, 1) and (1, b) and is located in the first and second quadrants only. The y-intercept is 1. The graph of the function does not cross the x-axis, so it has no x-intercepts. The x-axis is a horizontal asymptote.

If $b > 1$, the function is increasing. As x approaches ∞, $f(x) = b^x$ approaches ∞. As x approaches $-\infty$, $f(x) = b^x$ approaches 0, but never reaches 0. If $0 < b < 1$, the function is decreasing. As x approaches ∞, $f(x) = b^x$ approaches 0, but never reaches 0. As x approaches $-\infty$, $f(x) = b^x$ approaches ∞.

The following figure shows the graph of the exponential function $f(x) = 2^x$.

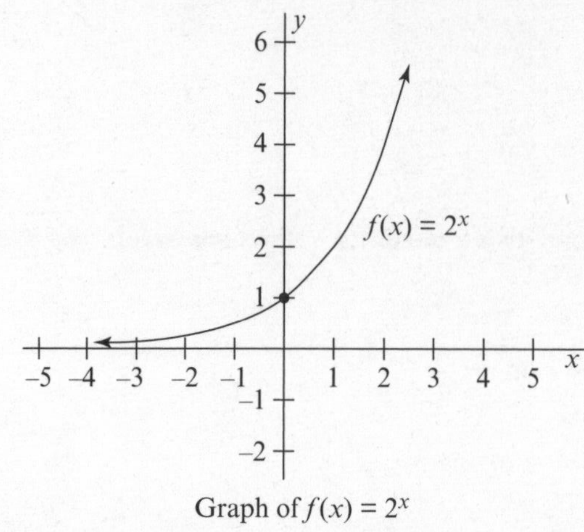

Graph of $f(x) = 2^x$

The **natural exponential function** is defined by $f(x) = e^x$, where the base e is the irrational number whose rational decimal approximation is 2.718281828 (to nine digits).

The **base-10 exponential function** is defined by $f(x) = 10^x$.

Exponential functions have the following properties for the function f defined by $f(x) = b^x (b > 0, b \neq 1)$.

Property	Examples
$f(x) = b^x > 0$, for all real numbers	$2^5 = 32 > 0$; $\left(\frac{1}{3}\right)^2 = \frac{1}{9} > 0$; $4^{-2} = \frac{1}{4^2} = \frac{1}{16} > 0$
$f(0) = b^0 = 1$	$25^0 = 1$; $\left(\frac{3}{5}\right)^0 = 1$; $(1.4)^0 = 1$; $\left(\sqrt{2}\right)^0 = 1$
$f(1) = b^1 = b$	$130^1 = 130$; $\left(\frac{4}{9}\right)^1 = \frac{4}{9}$; $(2.5)^1 = 2.5$; $\left(\sqrt{2}\right)^1 = \sqrt{2}$
$f(-x) = b^{-x} = \frac{1}{b^x}$	$2^{-5} = \frac{1}{2^5} = \frac{1}{32}$; $\left(\frac{1}{3}\right)^{-2} = \frac{1}{\left(\frac{1}{3}\right)^2} = 9$
$f(u) \cdot f(v) = b^u \cdot b^v = b^{u+v} = f(u+v)$	$2^3 \cdot 2^4 = 2^7$; $\left(\frac{3}{4}\right)^2\left(\frac{3}{4}\right) = \left(\frac{3}{4}\right)^3$; $\left(4^{-2}\right)\left(4^5\right) = 4^3$; $\left(6^{\frac{1}{2}}\right)\left(6^{\frac{1}{2}}\right) = 6$
$\frac{f(u)}{f(v)} = \frac{b^u}{b^v} = b^{u-v} = f(u-v)$	$\frac{5^8}{5^6} = 5^2$; $\frac{(1.75)^4}{(1.75)^3} = 1.75$; $\frac{10^{-5}}{10^{-7}} = 10^2$; $\frac{3^{-2}}{3^2} = 3^{-4} = \frac{1}{3^4}$; $\frac{32^{\frac{1}{5}}}{32^{-\frac{4}{5}}} = 32$
$(f(x))^p = \left(b^x\right)^p = b^{xp} = f(xp)$	$\left(2^3\right)^4 = 2^{12}$; $\left(\left(\frac{3}{4}\right)^2\right)^3 = \left(\frac{3}{4}\right)^6$; $\left(4^{-2}\right)^{-1} = 4^2$; $\left((0.5)^3\right)^{-4} = (0.5)^{-12}$
One-to-one property: $f(u) = f(v)$ if and only if $u = v$; that is, $b^u = b^v$ if and only if $u = v$.	$e^{3x} = e^{12}$ if and only if $3x = 12$ $4^{2x+1} = 4^5$ if and only if $2x + 1 = 5$

(See "Exponents" in Chapter 2 for a review of exponents.)

Tip: Do not confuse exponential functions with power functions. The exponents in exponential functions are *variables*, whereas the exponents in power functions are *constants*. For example, $f(x) = 3^x$ defines an exponential function and $g(x) = x^3$ defines a power function.

Logarithmic Functions

Logarithmic functions are defined by equations of the form $f(x) = \log_b x$, where $y = \log_b x$ if and only if $b^y = x$ ($b > 0$, $b \neq 1$). The constant b is the base of the logarithmic function. The domain is $(0, \infty)$, and the range is R. The function has one zero at $x = 1$.

Logarithms are exponents. If $y = \log_b x$, the output y is the exponent that is used on the base b to obtain the input x. Here are examples.

If $f(x) = \log_2(x)$, then $f(8) = \log_2(8) = 3$ because $2^3 = 8$.

If $g(x) = \log_{\frac{1}{3}}(x)$, then $g(9) = \log_{\frac{1}{3}}(9) = -2$ because $\left(\frac{1}{3}\right)^{-2} = 3^2 = 9$.

If $h(x) = \log_5(x)$, then $h\left(\frac{1}{125}\right) = \log_5\left(\frac{1}{125}\right) = -3$ because $5^{-3} = \frac{1}{5^3} = \frac{1}{125}$.

The graph of $f(x) = \log_b x$ ($b > 0$, $b \neq 1$) is a smooth, continuous curve. The graph passes through $(1, 0)$ and $(b, 1)$ and is located in the first and fourth quadrants only. The graph of the function does not cross the y-axis, so it does not have a y-intercept. The y-axis is a vertical asymptote.

If $b > 1$, the function is increasing. As x approaches ∞, $f(x) = \log_b x$ approaches ∞. As x approaches 0, $f(x) = \log_b x$ approaches $-\infty$. If $0 < b < 1$, the function is decreasing. As x approaches ∞, $f(x) = \log_b x$ approaches $-\infty$. As x approaches 0, $f(x) = \log_b x$ approaches ∞. The **natural logarithmic function** is defined by $f(x) = \log_e x$. This function is denoted $f(x) = \ln x$. The **common logarithmic function** is defined by $f(x) = \log_{10} x$.

For a given base, the logarithmic function is the inverse of the corresponding exponential function, and the reverse is true. The logarithm function $f(x) = \log_{10} x$ (common logarithmic function) is the inverse of the exponential function $g(x) = 10^x$. The logarithm function $g(x) = \ln x$ (natural logarithmic function) is the inverse of the exponential function $f(x) = e^x$. (See "Inverses of Functions" later in this chapter for an explanation of inverses.)

The following figure shows the graphs of the logarithmic function defined by $g(x) = \ln x$ and its mutually inverse exponential function defined by $f(x) = e^x$.

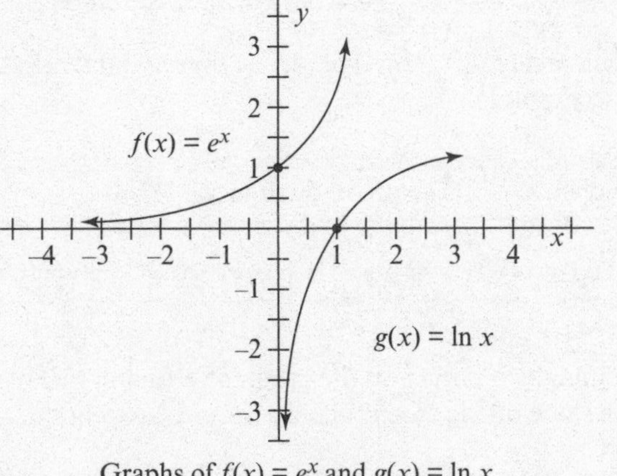

Graphs of $f(x) = e^x$ and $g(x) = \ln x$

Logarithmic functions have the following properties for the function f defined by $f(x) = \log_b x$ ($b > 0$, $b \neq 1$).

Property	Examples
$f(1) = \log_b 1 = 0$	$\log_{25}(1) = 0$; $\log_{\frac{3}{5}}(1) = 0$; $\log_{1.4}(1) = 0$; $\log_{\sqrt{2}}(1) = 0$
$f(b) = \log_b b = 1$	$\log_{130}(130) = 1$; $\log_{\frac{4}{9}}\left(\frac{4}{9}\right) = 1$; $\log_{2.5}(2.5) = 1$; $\log_{\sqrt{2}}\left(\sqrt{2}\right) = 1$

Continued

Property	Examples
$f(b^x) = \log_b b^x = x$	$\log_2 2^5 = 5$; $\log_{\frac{1}{3}}\left(\frac{1}{3}\right)^2 = 2$; $\log_4 4^{-2} = -2$; $\log_6 6^{\frac{1}{2}} = \frac{1}{2}$
$f\left(\frac{1}{x}\right) = \log_b \frac{1}{x} = -\log_b x$	$\log_2\left(\frac{1}{8}\right) = -\log_2(8) = -3$; $\log_3\left(\frac{1}{9}\right) = -\log_3(9) = -2$
$f(uv) = \log_b(uv) = \log_b u + \log_b v$	$\log_2(8 \cdot 16) = \log_2(8) + \log_2(16) = 3 + 4 = 7$
$f\left(\frac{u}{v}\right) = \log_b\left(\frac{u}{v}\right) = \log_b u - \log_b v$	$\log_3\left(\frac{243}{27}\right) = \log_3(243) - \log_3(27) = 5 - 3 = 2$
$f(x^p) = \log_b(x^p) = p\log_b x$	$\log_2(8^{12}) = 12\log_2(8) = 12 \cdot 3 = 36$
Change-of-base formula: $f(x) = \log_b x = \frac{\log_a x}{\log_a b} = \frac{\ln x}{\ln b} = \frac{\log_{10} x}{\log_{10} b}$ $(a > 0,\ a \neq 1)$	$\log_5 600 = \frac{\ln 600}{\ln 5} \approx 3.97$; $\log_2 100 = \frac{\log_{10} 100}{\log_{10} 2} \approx 6.64$
One-to-one property: $f(u) = f(v)$ if and only if $u = v$; that is, $\log_b u = \log_b v$ if and only if $u = v$	$\ln(4x) - \ln(80)$ if and only if $4x = 80$; $\log_{10}(5x + 100) = \log_{10}(1{,}000)$ if and only if $5x + 100 = 1{,}000$

(See "Logarithms" in Chapter 2 for a review of logarithms.)

Tip: Logarithms are exponents, so think about the rules for exponents when you are working with logarithms.

Note: See Chapter 5, "Trigonometry," for a discussion of the trigonometric functions.

Average Rate of Change and Difference Quotient

If (x_1, y_1) and (x_2, y_2) are two distinct points on the graph of a function f, the **average rate of change** of f as x goes from x_1 to x_2 is given by $\frac{\Delta y}{\Delta x} = \frac{y_2 - y_1}{x_2 - x_1} = \frac{f(x_2) - f(x_1)}{x_2 - x_1}$, where Δy is the change in y values and Δx is the change in x values. The average rate of change measures the "speed," *on average,* at which a function is changing over an interval of its domain. Here is an example.

Find the average rate of change of $f(x) = x^2$ on the interval [1, 4].

$$\frac{\Delta y}{\Delta x} = \frac{f(x_2) - f(x_1)}{x_2 - x_1} = \frac{f(4) - f(1)}{4 - 1} = \frac{4^2 - 1^2}{3} = \frac{15}{3} = 5$$

A **secant line** is a straight line joining two points on the graph of a function. The average rate of change of a function between two points and the slope of the secant line between the two points are the same thing. Thus, the slope of the secant line between x_1 and x_2 = the average rate of change between the two points $= \frac{f(x_2) - f(x_1)}{x_2 - x_1}$.

If $(x + h, f(x + h))$ and $(x, f(x))$ are two ordered pairs in a function f, the difference quotient is the expression $\frac{f(x+h) - f(x)}{(x+h) - (x)} = \frac{f(x+h) - f(x)}{h}$, where $h \neq 0$. The **difference quotient** is the average rate of change of f as x goes from x to $x + h$. Here is an example.

Find and simplify the difference quotient for $f(x) = x^2$.

$$\frac{f(x+h) - f(x)}{h} = \frac{(x+h)^2 - (x)^2}{h} = \frac{x^2 + 2xh + h^2 - x^2}{h} = \frac{2xh + h^2}{h} = 2x + h$$

Composition and Inverses of Functions

For this topic, you must be able to determine the composition of two functions, find the inverse of a one-to-one function in simple cases, and understand that only one-to-one functions have inverses.

Arithmetic of Functions and Composition

Suppose that both $f(x)$ and $g(x)$ exist. For all real numbers x such that $x \in D_f \cap D_g$, the following definitions for the arithmetic of functions hold:

the **sum of *f* and *g*** is the function $f + g$, defined by $(f + g)(x) = f(x) + g(x)$;

the **difference of *f* and *g*** is the function $f - g$, defined by $(f - g)(x) = f(x) - g(x)$;

the **product of *f* and *g*** is the function fg, defined by $(fg)(x) = f(x) \cdot g(x)$; and

the **quotient of *f* and *g*** is the function $\frac{f}{g}$, defined by $\left(\frac{f}{g}\right)(x) = \frac{f(x)}{g(x)}$, where $g(x) \neq 0$.

Here is an example.

> Let $f(x) = x^2 + 1$ and $g(x) = \sqrt{x} - 3$. **(a)** Find the domain of $\frac{f}{g}$, and **(b)** write a simplified expression for $\left(\frac{f}{g}\right)(x)$.

(a) The domain of $\frac{f}{g}$ must exclude negative values of x and also values of x for which $g(x) = \sqrt{x} - 3 = 0$. Solving $\sqrt{x} - 3 = 0$ yields $x = 9$, so the domain of $\frac{f}{g}$ is $\{x|\ x \geq 0, x \neq 9\}$.

(b) $\left(\frac{f}{g}\right)(x) = \frac{f(x)}{g(x)} = \frac{x^2 + 1}{\sqrt{x} - 3}$

The **composition of *f* and *g*** is the function $f \circ g$ defined by $(f \circ g) = f(g(x))$, provided that $g(x) \in D_f$. (***Note:*** Read $f(g(x))$ as "f of g of x.") The domain of $f \circ g$ is all x in the domain of g such that $g(x)$ is defined and $g(x)$ is in the domain of f. Here are examples.

> If $f = \{(-3, -5), (-2, -4), (0, -5), (1, 3), (2, 0), (4, 7)\}$ and $g = \{(-4, 8), (-3, -8), (-2, -3), (0, 1), (1, 4)\}$, find **(a)** $f \circ g$ and **(b)** $g \circ f$ and, if possible, evaluate **(c)** $(f \circ g)(1)$, **(d)** $(g \circ f)(-3)$, **(e)** $(f \circ g)(-4)$, and **(f)** $(g \circ f)(2)$.

(a) $f \circ g = \{(-2, -5), (0, 3), (1, 7)\}$

(b) $g \circ f = \{(-2, 8), (2, 1)\}$

(c) $(f \circ g)(1) = f(g(1)) = f(4) = 7$

(d) $(g \circ f)(-3) = g(f(-3)) = g(-5) =$ undefined because -5 is not in the domain of g.

(e) $(f \circ g)(-4) = f(g(-4)) = f(8) =$ undefined because 8 is not in the domain of f.

(f) $(g \circ f)(2) = g(f(2)) = g(0) = 1$

> Let $f(x) = x^2$ and $g(x) = \sqrt{x + 3}$. **(a)** Determine the domain of $f \circ g$, **(b)** write a simplified expression for $(f \circ g)(x)$, and **(c)** if possible, evaluate $(f \circ g)(6)$, $(f \circ g)(-1)$, and $(f \circ g)(-6)$.

(a) The domain of $f \circ g$ is all x in the domain of g such that $g(x)$ is defined and $g(x)$ is in the domain of f. The function g defined by $g(x) = \sqrt{x+3}$ has the domain $D_g = \{x | x \geq -3\}$. In the composition, $g(x)$ must be in the domain of f. The domain of f is all real numbers, so $g(x)$ is definitely in the domain of f. Therefore, the domain of $f \circ g$ is the same as the domain of g; that is, the domain of $f \circ g = \{x | x \geq -3\}$.

(b) $(f \circ g)(x) = f(g(x)) = f\left(\sqrt{x+3}\right) = \left(\sqrt{x+3}\right)^2 = x+3,\ x \geq -3$

(c) $(f \circ g)(6) = f(g(6)) = f\left(\sqrt{6+3}\right) = f\left(\sqrt{9}\right) = f(3) = 3^2 = 9$;

$(f \circ g)(-1) = f(g(-1)) = f\left(\sqrt{-1+3}\right) = f\left(\sqrt{2}\right) = \left(\sqrt{2}\right)^2 = 2$; $(f \circ g)(-6)$ is undefined because -6 is not in the domain of $f \circ g$.

Composition of functions is not commutative; that is, in general, $(f \circ g)(x) \neq (g \circ f)(x)$.

Also, the product function fg is fundamentally different from the composition function $f \circ g$. For example, if $f(x) = 3x$ and $g(x) = x^2$, $fg(x) = f(x) \cdot g(x) = (3x) \cdot (x^2) = 3x^3$; but $(f \circ g)(x) = f(g(x)) = f(x^2) = 3(x^2) = 3x^2$.

Inverses of Functions

If f is a one-to-one function, its **inverse,** denoted f^{-1} (read "f inverse"), is the function such that $(f^{-1} \circ f)(x) = x$ for all x in the domain of f and $(f \circ f^{-1})(x) = x$ for all x in the domain of f^{-1}, and $D_{f^{-1}} = R_f$ and $R_{f^{-1}} = D_f$. Graphically, f^{-1} is a reflection of f over the line $y = x$.

Tip: Do not interpret f^{-1} to mean $\frac{1}{f}$. The $^{-1}$ that is attached to f is not an exponent; it is a notation that denotes the inverse of a function.

If a function f defined by a set of ordered pairs is one-to-one, then you can find f^{-1} by interchanging x and y in each of the ordered pairs of f. Here is an example.

Given $f = \{(-1, 2), (3, 5), (6, -1)\}$, find f^{-1}.

$$f^{-1} = \{(2, -1), (5, 3), (-1, 6)\}$$

If a function is one-to-one, its inverse exists. When a one-to-one function f is defined by an equation, two ways you can find the equation of f^{-1} are the following:

Method 1. Set $(f \circ f^{-1})(x) = x$ and solve for $f^{-1}(x)$. Here is an example.

Given $y = f(x) = 3x$, find $f^{-1}(x)$.

$$\left(f \circ f^{-1}\right)(x) = x$$
$$f\left(f^{-1}(x)\right) = x$$
$$3f^{-1}(x) = x$$
$$f^{-1}(x) = \frac{x}{3}$$

Method 2. First, interchange x and y in $y = f(x)$, and then solve $x = f(y)$ for y. Here is an example.

Given $y = f(x) = 3x$, find $f^{-1}(x)$.

First, interchanging x and y gives $x = 3y$. Next, solving for y gives $\frac{x}{3} = y$ or $y = \frac{x}{3}$. Thus, $y = f^{-1}(x) = \frac{x}{3}$, the same as obtained through Method 1.

Only one-to-one functions have inverses that are functions. However, when a function f is not one-to-one, it might be possible to restrict its domain so that f is one-to-one in the restricted domain. Then, f will have an inverse function in the restricted domain.

Modeling with Functions

For this topic you must be able to find an appropriate family of functions to model particular phenomena (for example, population growth, cooling, or simple harmonic motion).

Some common families of functions that are used to model phenomena in the real world are the families of linear functions, quadratic functions, exponential functions, and trigonometric functions.

Linear functions model processes in which the rate of change is constant. For example, a linear function can be used to describe the distance a moving object travels at a constant rate of speed.

Quadratic functions are used to model processes that involve a maximum or a minimum value. For example, in business, a quadratic function can be used to model a company's profit or revenue, which depends on the number of units sold.

Exponential functions are used to model physical phenomena such as population growth and population decay. This family of functions is also used in business for determining the growth of money when interest is compounded.

Trigonometric functions are used to model periodic processes. For example, physical phenomena such as light waves, sound waves, and the movement of a pendulum or a weight attached to a coiled spring can be modeled using the trigonometric sine or cosine function.

Here are examples.

A water tank that holds 1,000 gallons of water is one-fourth full. Suppose water is added to the tank at a constant rate of 150 gallons per hour. Let $f(t)$ be the amount of water (in gallons) in the tank after t hours.

(a) What is the rate of change of the function f?

(b) What is the amount of water in the tank at time $t = 0$?

(c) Write a formula for $f(t)$.

(d) At what time t will the water tank be filled to capacity?

(a) The amount of water in the tank changes at a constant rate of 150 gallons per hour. Thus, the rate of change of f is 150 gallons per 1 hour of time.

(b) At time $t = 0$, the initial amount of water in the tank is $\frac{1}{4}(1{,}000 \text{ gallons}) = 250$ gallons.

(c) Omitting units, $f(t) = 150t + 250$, a linear function.

(d) Find t, when $f(t) = 1{,}000$.

$$\begin{aligned} 1{,}000 &= 150t + 250 \\ 750 &= 150t \\ 5 &= t \end{aligned}$$

The water tank is filled to capacity at time $t = 5$ hours.

A homeowner has 100 feet of fencing to enclose a rectangular region for a small garden. The homeowner will use a portion of the side of a large shed as one side of the rectangle, as shown in the following figure.

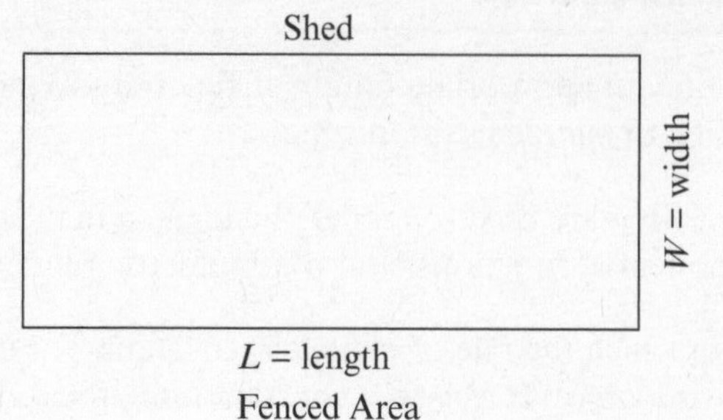

Let $f(W)$ be the area of the rectangular region expressed in terms of its width, W.

(a) Write a formula for $f(W)$.

(b) Find the dimensions of the rectangle that give the maximum area for the garden.

(a) The fence does not go along the shed, so (omitting units) $100 = 2W + L$, which implies that $L = 100 - 2W$. The area of the rectangular region equals length times width. Thus, $f(W) = (100 - 2W)W = 100W - 2W^2 = -2W^2 + 100W$, a quadratic function.

(b) The graph of $f(W)$ is a parabola opening downward. The vertex formula is $\left(-\frac{b}{2a}, f\left(-\frac{b}{2a}\right)\right)$, so the maximum value for $f(W)$ occurs when $W = -\frac{b}{2a} = -\frac{100}{2(-2)} = 25$. The corresponding value of $L = 100 - 2W = 100 - 2 \cdot 25 = 100 - 50 = 50$. The dimensions that maximize the area are 50 feet by 25 feet.

Functions of Two Variables

For this topic, you must be able to interpret representations of functions of two variables, such as three-dimensional graphs.

A **real-valued function of two variables** is a function f that associates with each pair (x, y) of real numbers of a set $D_f \subseteq R^2$ one and only one real number $z = f(x, y)$. The set D_f is the domain of f, and the set of all real numbers $z = f(x, y)$ is D_f, the range of f.

As with functions of one variable, functions of two variables can be represented numerically (using a table of values), algebraically (using a formula), and sometimes graphically (using a graph).

The graph of the function f of two variables is the set of all points $(x, y, f(x, y))$ defining a region or curved surface in three-dimensional space, where you restrict the values of (x, y) to lie in the domain of f. In other words, the graph is the set of all points (x, y, z) with $z = f(x, y)$.

Chapter 5

Trigonometry

The Six Basic Trigonometric Functions

For this topic, you must be able to define and use the six basic trigonometric functions using the degree or radian measure of angles and know their graphs and be able to identify their periods, amplitudes, phase displacements or shifts, and asymptotes.

Right Triangle Ratios

To define the six **basic trigonometric (trig) ratios,** begin with a right triangle ABC and label its six parts as follows:

Right Triangle ABC

$m\angle A$

$m\angle B = 90° - m\angle A$

$m\angle C = 90°$

a = length of side opposite $\angle A$

b = length of side adjacent to $\angle A$

c = length of side opposite the right angle C = length of the hypotenuse

Note: $m\angle X$ denotes "the measure of angle X."

The ratios relative to angle A in the right triangle ABC are as follows:

sine of $\angle A = \sin A = \frac{\text{side opposite}}{\text{hypotenuse}} = \frac{a}{c}$

cosine of $\angle A = \cos A = \frac{\text{side adjacent}}{\text{hypotenuse}} = \frac{b}{c}$

tangent of $\angle A = \tan A = \frac{\text{side opposite}}{\text{side adjacent}} = \frac{a}{b}$

cosecant of $\angle A = \csc A = \frac{\text{hypotenuse}}{\text{side opposite}} = \frac{c}{a}$

secant of $\angle A = \sec A = \frac{\text{hypotenuse}}{\text{side adjacent}} = \frac{c}{b}$

cotangent of $\angle A = \cot A = \frac{\text{side adjacent}}{\text{side opposite}} = \frac{b}{a}$

Note: When no confusion can occur, "side opposite," "side adjacent," and "hypotenuse" refer to the length of the side opposite an angle, the length of the side adjacent to an angle, and the length of the hypotenuse, respectively.

From the preceding formulas, you can see that sine and cosecant are reciprocals of each other, that cosine and secant are reciprocals of each other, and that tangent and cotangent are reciprocals of each other. Therefore, it is necessary to remember only the sine, cosine, and tangent ratios because the other ratios can be determined by using the reciprocal relationships.

Tip: The mnemonic SOH-CAH-TOA (soh-kuh-toh-uh) can help you remember that S (sine) is O (opposite) over H (hypotenuse), that C (cosine) is A (adjacent) over H (hypotenuse), and T (tangent) is O (opposite) over A (adjacent).

Typically, when working with right triangles on the Praxis Math CK test, you need to find the measure of a missing angle or of a missing side of a right triangle. If you are given two sides of the right triangle, you should use the Pythagorean theorem to find the missing side. (See Chapter 7, "Geometry," for a discussion of the Pythagorean theorem.) If you are given a side and one of the acute angles, label the sides as follows: opposite side (the side across from the given angle), the hypotenuse (across from the right angle), and the adjacent side (the leftover side). Then select the trig ratio that best fits the information you are given.

Tip: When solving a right triangle in which the angles are given in degrees, be sure to set the Trig Mode of the ETS graphing calculator to degrees mode.

Two special right triangles of trigonometry that are useful to know are the **30°-60°-90° right triangle** and the **45°-45°-90° right triangle** shown here.

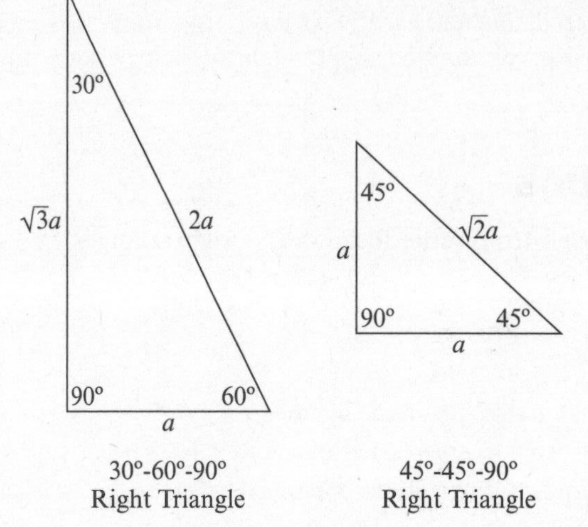

30°-60°-90° Right Triangle

45°-45°-90° Right Triangle

The trigonometric ratios associated with these triangles are given in the following table.

Special Trigonometric Ratios

Angle	30°	45°	60°
Sine	$\frac{1}{2}$	$\frac{1}{\sqrt{2}}=\frac{\sqrt{2}}{2}$	$\frac{\sqrt{3}}{2}$
Cosine	$\frac{\sqrt{3}}{2}$	$\frac{\sqrt{2}}{2}$	$\frac{1}{2}$
Tangent	$\frac{1}{\sqrt{3}}=\frac{\sqrt{3}}{3}$	1	$\sqrt{3}$

Rather than trying to memorize this table, it is better to remember the triangles and how the ratios are defined. All triangles similar to these two have the same ratio values. Here is an example of using the special trig ratios.

Given $m\angle C = 90°$, $m\angle A = 60°$, and $b = 5$, find a and c for the triangle shown.

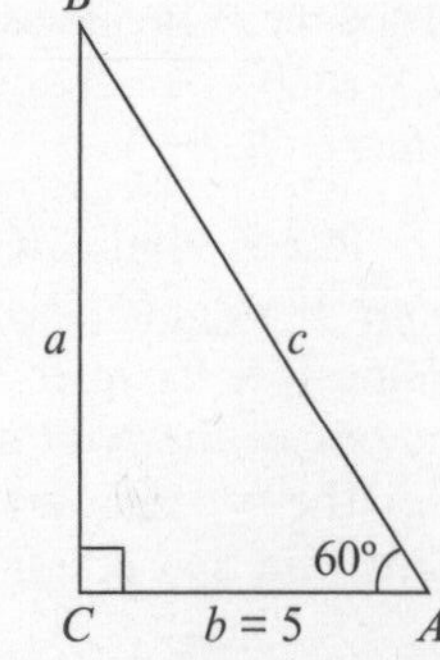

Given $m\angle A = 60°$, then $m\angle B = 90° - 60° = 30°$. The triangle is a 30°-60°-90° right triangle; thus, $\cos\angle A = \frac{b}{c} = \frac{5}{c} = \frac{1}{2}$. Hence, $c = 10$. Also, $\sin\angle A = \frac{a}{c} = \frac{a}{10} = \frac{\sqrt{3}}{2}$. Hence, $a = 5\sqrt{3}$.

The Unit Circle and Trigonometric Functions

The unit circle is a circle centered at (0, 0) with radius equal to 1. If the unit circle is plotted in the Cartesian coordinate plane, then the sine and cosine trig functions are associated with the circle in the manner shown.

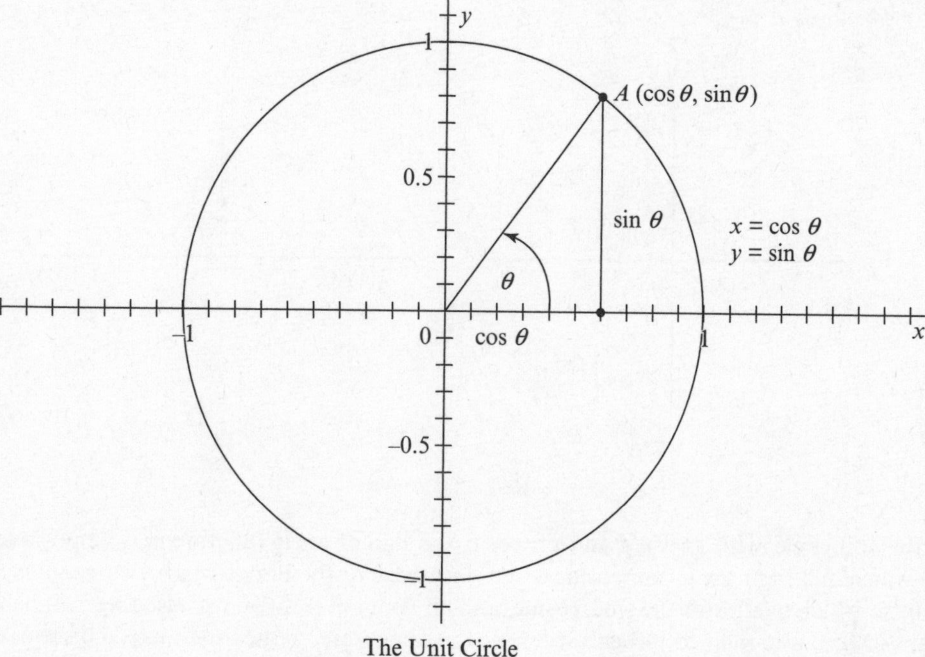

The Unit Circle

Because the radius is 1, cos θ is the x-coordinate and sin θ is the y-coordinate of the point on the circle intercepted by the ray determined by the central angle θ.

If the point on the circle is rotated counterclockwise to the y-axis, then $\sin\theta = 1$ and $\cos\theta = 0$. Thus, $\sin(90°) = 1$ and $\cos(90°) = 0$. By the same token, $\sin(0°) = 0$ and $\cos(0°) = 1$.

If an angle θ is placed in the Cartesian coordinate plane such that the vertex is at the origin and one side is along the x-axis, then θ is said to be in **standard position.** The side along the x-axis is the **initial side,** and the other side is the terminal side. An angle can be thought of as being formed by a rotation of the **terminal side.** If the rotation is counterclockwise, the angle is positive; if the rotation is clockwise, the angle is negative.

As the terminal side of θ moves around the unit circle passing through the four quadrants of the coordinate plane, the values of the trig functions $y = \sin\theta$, $y = \cos\theta$, $y = \tan\theta$, $y = \csc\theta$, $y = \sec\theta$, and $y = \cot\theta$ can be determined by using the appropriate reference angle. The **reference angle** for an angle in standard position is the positive acute angle formed by the x-axis and the terminal side of the angle (disregarding direction of rotation). For example, the reference angle for 120° is 60°. The following figure illustrates angle $\angle A$ and its associated reference angle $\angle A_r$ in the four quadrants.

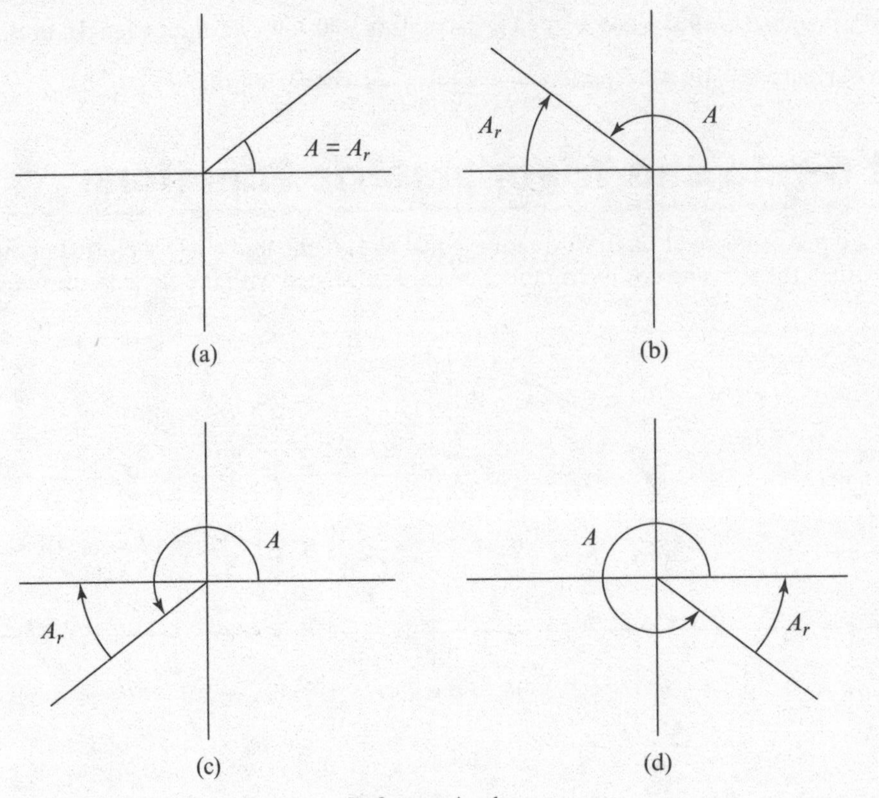

Reference Angles

Referring to the unit circle, with $y = \sin \theta$ and $x = \cos \theta$, the sign of a trig function may be positive or negative, depending in which quadrant the terminal side of θ is located. For the Praxis Math CK test, it is necessary to remember only in which quadrants the sine, cosine, and tangent are positive because they will be negative in the other quadrants. Moreover, their reciprocals will have the same signs as the functions themselves do. The sine function is positive in Quadrant I and Quadrant II; the cosine function is positive in Quadrant I and Quadrant IV; and the tangent function is positive in Quadrant I and Quadrant III.

Tip: Use the mnemonic "All Students Take Calculus" to help you remember the correct sign of a function as you move in a counterclockwise direction from Quadrant I to Quadrant IV. The initial letters A-S-T-C in the mnemonic remind you that All the functions are positive in Quadrant I; the Sine function is positive in Quadrant II; the Tangent function is positive in Quadrant III; and the Cosine function is positive in Quadrant IV.

Here is an example of determining the values of trig functions using reference angles.

Determine $\sin \theta$, $\cos \theta$, and $\tan \theta$ for $\theta = 315°$.

The angle $\theta = 315°$ is in Quadrant IV. The reference angle is $360° - 315° = 45°$. Thus, $\sin 315° = -\sin 45° = -\frac{\sqrt{2}}{2}$, $\cos 315° = \cos 45° = \frac{\sqrt{2}}{2}$, and $\tan 315° = -\tan 45° = -1$.

The trig functions, of course, can be associated with any circle of radius r. The ratios then take on the following forms: $\sin\theta = \frac{y}{r}$, $\cos\theta = \frac{x}{r}$, $\tan\theta = \frac{y}{x}$. Note that $y = r \sin \theta$ and $x = r \cos \theta$. These connections will be used later in this chapter in the discussion on polar coordinates.

The angle θ can be expressed in **degrees** or **radians**. In the radian system of angular measurement, $360° = 2\pi$ radians. Thus, $1° = \frac{\pi}{180}$ radians and 1 radian $= \frac{180°}{\pi}$. If $\theta = x$ radians, where x is a real number, the six basic trignometric functions of x are $y = \sin x$, $y = \cos x$, $y = \tan x$, $y = \csc x$, $y = \sec x$, and $y = \cot x$.

Trigonometric Function	Domain	Range	Vertical Asymptote
	Let k be any integer		**Let k be any integer**
$y = \sin x$	all reals	$[-1, 1]$	none
$y = \cos x$	all reals	$[-1, 1]$	none
$y = \tan x$	$\left\{x \in \text{reals}, x \neq \frac{\pi}{2} + k\pi\right\}$	all reals	$x = \frac{\pi}{2} + k\pi$
$y = \csc x$	$\{x \in \text{reals}, x \neq k\pi\}$	$(-\infty, -1] \cup [1, \infty)$	$x = k\pi$
$y = \sec x$	$\left\{x \in \text{reals}, x \neq \frac{\pi}{2} + k\pi\right\}$	$(-\infty, -1] \cup [1, \infty)$	$x = \frac{\pi}{2} + k\pi$
$y = \cot x$	$\{x \in \text{reals}, x \neq k\pi\}$	all reals	$x = k\pi$

Tip: Switch to radians mode when the argument of the trigonometric function is a real number.

The following table summarizes the values of the trigonometric functions for some **special angles**.

Angle (°)	Angle (radians)	Sine	Cosine	Tangent	Cotangent	Secant	Cosecant
0°	0	0	1	0	undefined	1	undefined
30°	$\frac{\pi}{6}$	$\frac{1}{2}$	$\frac{\sqrt{3}}{2}$	$\frac{1}{\sqrt{3}}$	$\sqrt{3}$	$\frac{2}{\sqrt{3}}$	2
45°	$\frac{\pi}{4}$	$\frac{1}{\sqrt{2}}$	$\frac{1}{\sqrt{2}}$	1	1	$\sqrt{2}$	$\sqrt{2}$
60°	$\frac{\pi}{3}$	$\frac{\sqrt{3}}{2}$	$\frac{1}{2}$	$\sqrt{3}$	$\frac{1}{\sqrt{3}}$	2	$\frac{2}{\sqrt{3}}$
90°	$\frac{\pi}{2}$	1	0	undefined	0	undefined	1

Graphs of the Trigonometric Functions

A function f is **periodic** if there is a positive number P such that $f(x + P) = f(x)$ for all x in the domain. The least number P for which this is true is the **period** of f. The sine, cosine, secant, and cosecant functions are periodic with period 2π. The tangent and cotangent functions are periodic with period π.

Note: In graphing the trig functions, commonly the radian measure for angles is used.

The graphs of $y = \sin x$, $y = \cos x$, and $y = \tan x$—the three main trigonometric functions—are shown in the following figures.

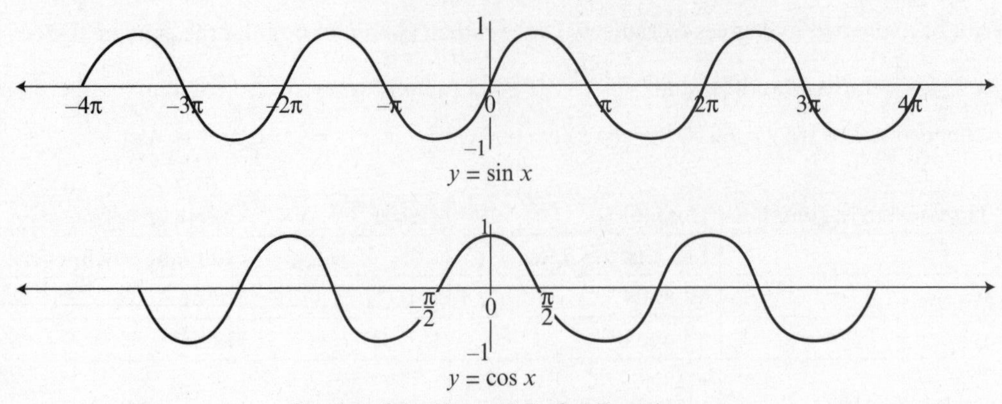

Graphs of the Sine and Cosine Functions

Notice that the graphs of the sine and cosine functions have a wave pattern. The **amplitude** of the function is the height of the wave. It equals one-half the absolute difference between the function's maximum value (max) and minimum value (min); that is, amplitude $= \frac{1}{2}|\text{max} - \text{min}|$.

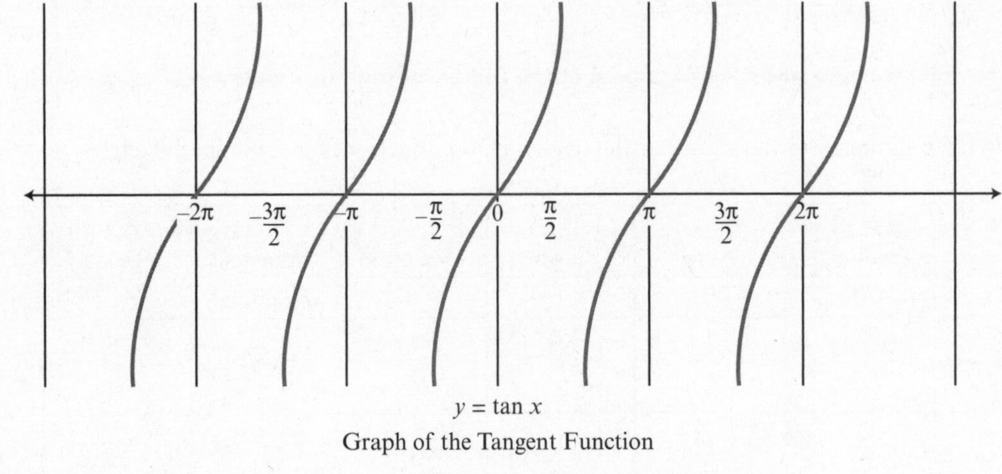

Graph of the Tangent Function

The graphs of the other three trig functions are shown in the following figures.

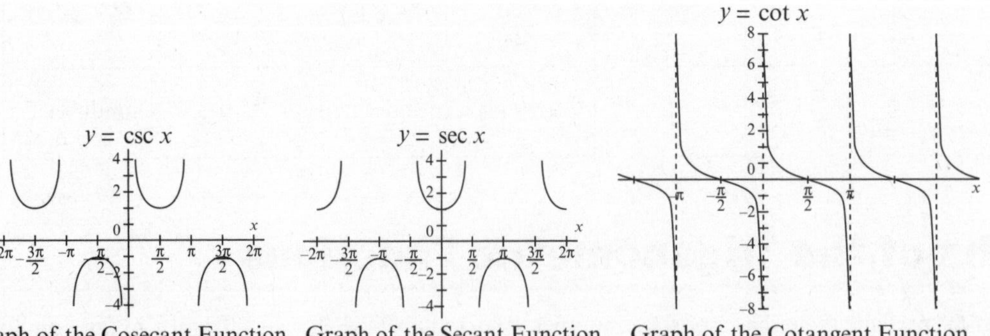

Graph of the Cosecant Function Graph of the Secant Function Graph of the Cotangent Function

Knowing the shapes of the graphs of the basic trig functions will help you graph functions that are similar but are variations of the basic graphs.

Transformations of the Trigonometric Functions

If $b > 0$, the general forms for the sine and cosine functions, $y = a\sin(bx + c) + k$ and $y = a\cos(bx + c) + k$, have graphs with amplitude $= |a|$, period $= \frac{2\pi}{b}$, a horizontal or phase shift of $\frac{|c|}{b}$ units (to the left of the origin if $\frac{c}{b}$ is positive; to the right of the origin if $\frac{c}{b}$ is negative), and a vertical shift of $|k|$ units (up from the origin if k is positive; down from the origin if k is negative). Graphically, the coefficient a causes the function to be "stretched" *away* from the x-axis or "compressed" *toward* the x-axis in the vertical direction by the multiple $|a|$. For the sine and cosine functions, the maximum height of the graph is $|a| + k$ and the minimum height is $-|a| + k$. If $a < 0$, the graph is reflected over $y = k$, and over the x-axis when $k = 0$.

If $b > 0$, the general form for the tangent function, $y = a\tan(bx + c) + k$, has a graph with period $= \frac{\pi}{b}$, a horizontal or phase shift of $\frac{|c|}{b}$ units (to the left of the origin if $\frac{c}{b}$ is positive; to the right of the origin if $\frac{c}{b}$ is negative), and a vertical shift of $|k|$ units (up from the origin if k is positive; down from the origin if k is negative). Graphically, the coefficient a causes the function to be "stretched" *away* from the x-axis or "compressed" *toward* the x-axis in the vertical direction by the multiple $|a|$; however, unlike the sine and cosine functions, the tangent function has neither a maximum nor a minimum value. If $a < 0$, the graph is reflected over $y = k$, and over the x-axis when $k = 0$.

Here are examples.

The graph of $y = 2\cos(3x)$ has an amplitude $= |2| = 2$, period $= \frac{2\pi}{3}$, and no phase or vertical shift.

The graph of $y = -2\cos(3x - \pi)$ has an amplitude $= |-2| = 2$, period $= \frac{2\pi}{3}$, a phase shift to the right of $\frac{|-\pi|}{3} = \frac{\pi}{3}$, no vertical shift, and is a reflection over the x-axis.

The graph of $y = \frac{1}{2}\sin\left(4x - \frac{\pi}{3}\right)$ has an amplitude $= \left|\frac{1}{2}\right| = \frac{1}{2}$, period $= \frac{2\pi}{4} = \frac{\pi}{2}$, a phrase shift to the right of $\frac{\left|-\frac{\pi}{3}\right|}{4} = \frac{\pi}{12}$, and no vertical shift.

The graph of $y = -\cos(2x + \pi) + 3$ has an amplitude $= |-1| = 1$, period $= \frac{2\pi}{2} = \pi$, a phase shift to the left of $\frac{|\pi|}{2} = \frac{\pi}{2}$, a vertical shift of $|3| = 3$ units up, and is reflected over $y = 3$.

If $b < 0$, rewrite the argument of the function as -1 times a factor, then use the even-odd identities in the section "Special Angle Formulas and Identities" later in this chapter to write the function as an equivalent function with $b > 0$. For example, the graph of $y = -2\cos(\pi - 3x) = -2\cos[(-1)(3x - \pi)] = -2\cos(3x - \pi)$ because cosine is an even function.

The Law of Sines and the Law of Cosines

The formulas for the law of sines and the law of cosines are on the Notations, Definitions, and Formulas reference sheet that you can access by clicking the Help button when you are taking the Praxis Math CK test.

The **law of sines** and the **law of cosines** are given below for the triangle ABC labeled as shown here.

Law of Sines: $\frac{\sin A}{a} = \frac{\sin B}{b} = \frac{\sin C}{c}$

Law of Cosines: $c^2 = a^2 + b^2 - 2ab \cos C$

$a^2 = b^2 + c^2 - 2bc \cos A$

$b^2 = a^2 + c^2 - 2ac \cos B$

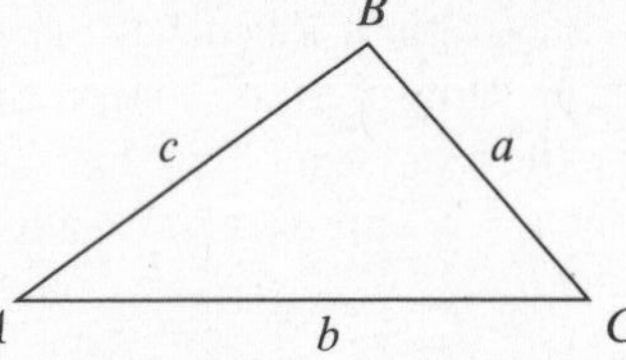

Every triangle has six parts: three sides and three angles. To **solve a triangle** means to determine all missing measures of the six parts. The law of sines and the law of cosines are used to find missing measures of parts of **oblique triangles** (triangles that are not right triangles). Three possibilities can result: one solution, two solutions (called the ambiguous case), or no solution. The following table summarizes when to use the two laws.

Situation in the Problem	Use	Number of Solutions
You are given the measures of three sides (SSS), and the sum of the lengths of the two smaller sides is greater than the length of the larger side.	law of cosines	one
You are given the measures of three sides (SSS), and the sum of the lengths of the two smaller sides is less than or equal to the length of the larger side.	neither	no solution
You are given the measures of two sides and the included angle (SAS).	law of cosines	one solution
You are given the measures of two angles and the included side (ASA), and the sum of the given angles is less than 180°.	law of sines	one solution
You are given the measures of two angles and a nonincluded side (AAS), and the sum of the given angles is less than 180°.	law of sines	one solution
You are given the measures of two angles and either the included side (ASA) or a nonincluded side (AAS), and the sum of the given angles is greater than or equal to 180°.	neither	no solution
You are given the measures of two sides and a nonincluded obtuse angle (SSA), and the length of the side opposite the given angle is greater than the length of the side adjacent to the given angle.	law of sines	one solution
You are given the measures of two sides and a nonincluded obtuse angle, and the length of the side opposite the given angle is less than or equal to the length of the side adjacent to the given angle.	neither	no solution
You are given the measures of two sides and a nonincluded acute angle (SSA), and the length of the side opposite the given angle is greater than or equal to the length of the side adjacent to the given angle.	law of sines	one solution
You are given the measures of two sides and a nonincluded acute angle (SSA), and the length of one side falls between the length of the altitude from the vertex where the two given sides meet and the length of the other side.	law of sines	two solutions
You are given the measures of two sides and a nonincluded acute angle (SSA), and the length of the altitude from the vertex where the two given sides meet falls between the lengths of the two given sides.	neither	no solution
You are given the measures of three angles (AAA).	neither	no unique solution

Here is an example of using the law of sines.

> Solve triangle ABC, given $m\angle A = 40°$, $a = 50$, and $b = 30$.

Sketch a figure.

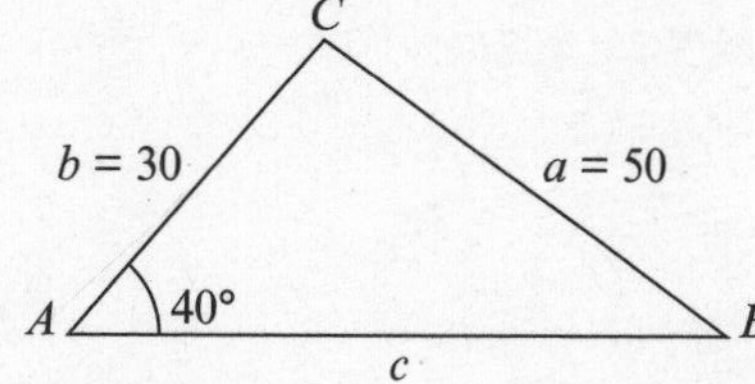

You are given the measures of two sides and a nonincluded acute angle (SSA), and the length of the side opposite the given angle is greater than the length of the side adjacent to the given angle, so there is one solution.

Using the law of sines, $\frac{\sin B}{30} = \frac{\sin 40°}{50}$. Thus, $\sin B = \frac{30 \sin 40°}{50} \approx 0.3857$. Using the asin function key (which is the inverse sine function key) on the ETS graphing calculator yields $m\angle B_r \approx 22.7°$. Thus, either $m\angle B \approx 22.7°$ or $m\angle B \approx 180° - 22.7° = 157.3°$. The latter value will not work because $40° + 157.3° > 180°$. It follows that $m\angle C \approx 180° - 40° - 22.7° = 117.3°$. Using this result and again applying the law of sines, $\frac{\sin 40°}{50} = \frac{\sin 117.3°}{c}$; so $c = \frac{50 \sin 117.3°}{\sin 40°} \approx 69.1$. Therefore, the triangle is solved.

Here is an example of using the law of cosines.

> Solve triangle ABC, given $a = 15$, $b = 25$, and $c = 28$.

Sketch a figure.

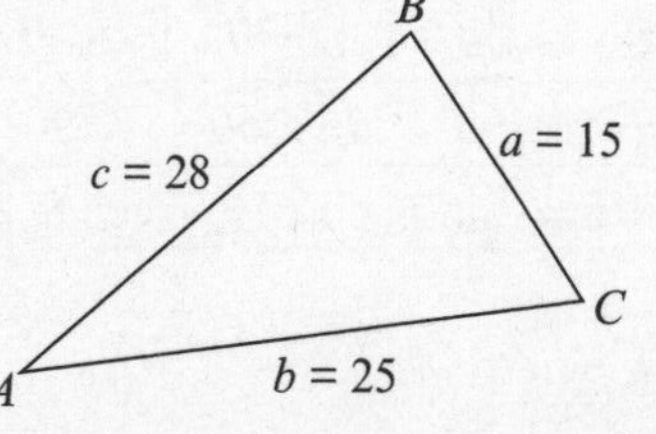

You are given the measures of three sides (SSS), and the sum of the lengths of the two smaller sides is greater than the length of the larger side, so there is one solution. Applying the law of cosines, solve for $m\angle A$.

$$15^2 = 25^2 + 28^2 - 2(25)(28)\cos A$$
$$225 = 625 + 784 - 1400\cos A$$
$$225 = 1409 - 1400\cos A$$
$$-1184 = -1400\cos A$$
$$\cos A \approx 0.8457$$

Using the acos function key (which is the inverse cosine function key) on the ETS graphing calculator yields

$$m\angle A \approx 32.25°$$

Applying the law of cosines a second time, solve for $m\angle B$.

$$\begin{aligned} 25^2 &= 15^2 + 28^2 - 2(15)(28)\cos B \\ 625 &= 225 + 784 - 840\cos B \\ 625 &= 1009 - 840\cos B \\ -384 &= -840\cos B \\ \cos B &\approx 0.4571 \\ m\angle B &\approx 62.80° \end{aligned}$$

Then $m\angle C \approx 180° - 32.25° - 62.8° \approx 84.95°$.

Therefore, the triangle is solved.

Tip: When solving an oblique triangle, be sure to set the mode of the ETS graphing calculator to degrees mode if the angle measurements are in degrees and to radians mode if the angle measurements are given in radians.

Special Angle Formulas and Identities

For the Praxis Math CK test, you need to know certain fundamental identities and formulas that can be used to simplify or change trigonometric expressions. The following is a list of important identities to commit to memory before the test.

Reciprocal Identities	$\sec\theta = \frac{1}{\cos\theta}$, $\csc\theta = \frac{1}{\sin\theta}$, and $\cot\theta = \frac{1}{\tan\theta}$
Ratio Identities	$\tan\theta = \frac{\sin\theta}{\cos\theta}$ and $\cot\theta = \frac{\cos\theta}{\sin\theta}$
Pythagorean Identities	$\sin^2\theta + \cos^2\theta = 1$, $\tan^2\theta + 1 = \sec^2\theta$, and $1 + \cot^2\theta = \csc^2\theta$
Cofunction Identities	$\cos\theta = \sin(90° - \theta)$, $\csc\theta = \sec(90° - \theta)$, and $\cot\theta = \tan(90° - \theta)$
Even-Odd Identities	$\sin(-\theta) = -\sin\theta$, $\cos(-\theta) = \cos\theta$, and $\tan(-\theta) = -\tan\theta$

Tip: The notation $\sin^2\theta = (\sin\theta)^2$. Similarly, $\cos^2\theta = (\cos\theta)^2$, $\tan^2\theta = (\tan\theta)^2$, and so forth.

The following formulas are given on the Notations, Definitions, and Formulas reference sheet that is provided.

Sum/Difference Formulas	$\sin(x \pm y) = \sin x\cos y \pm \cos x\sin y$, $\cos(x \pm y) = \cos x\cos y \mp \sin x\sin y$, and $\tan(x \pm y) = \frac{\tan x \pm \tan y}{1 \mp \tan x\tan y}$
Half-Angle Formulas (sign depends on the quadrant of $\frac{\theta}{2}$)	$\sin\frac{\theta}{2} = \pm\sqrt{\frac{1-\cos\theta}{2}}$, $\cos\frac{\theta}{2} = \pm\sqrt{\frac{1+\cos\theta}{2}}$, from which you can obtain $\tan\frac{\theta}{2} = \pm\sqrt{\frac{1-\cos\theta}{1+\cos\theta}}$ or $\tan\frac{\theta}{2} = \frac{\sin\theta}{1+\cos\theta} = \frac{1-\cos\theta}{\sin\theta}$

Even though you can derive the following formulas from the sum formulas, it is a good idea to be familiar with them.

Double Angle Formulas	$\sin(2\theta) = 2\sin\theta\cos\theta$, $\cos(2\theta) = \cos^2\theta - \sin^2\theta = 2\cos^2\theta - 1 = 1 - 2\sin^2\theta$, and $\tan 2\theta = \dfrac{2\tan\theta}{1-\tan^2\theta}$

For the Praxis Math CK test, you might have to select which trigonometric expression is an identity for a given trigonometric expression. Here are some helpful strategies.

- Change all the trigonometric functions in the given expression to sines and cosines and simplify.
- Combine fractions and simplify.
- If the numerator or denominator of a fraction has the form $f(x) + 1$, multiply the numerator and denominator by $f(x) - 1$ to obtain the difference of two squares, and then look for a Pythagorean identity; for $f(x) - 1$ multiply by $f(x) + 1$.
- Evaluate the given trigonometric expression for a convenient value of the angle, and then evaluate each of the answer choices for the same value of the angle to find one that evaluates to be the same value you obtained for the given trigonometric expression.

Trigonometric Equations and Inequalities

Trigonometric equations and inequalities are solved in a manner similar to the way that algebraic equations and inequalities are solved. (See Chapter 3, "Algebra," for a discussion on solving algebraic equations and inequalities.) The main difference is that because of the periodic nature of the trigonometric functions, there might be multiple solutions to the equation, depending on the specifications in the problem. For example, to solve $\cos\theta = \frac{1}{2}$, you must find all values of θ that make the equation true. For simplicity, suppose you want to express the answer in radians. Because $\frac{1}{2}$ is the cosine of a special angle (see "The Six Basic Trigonometric Functions" at the beginning of this chapter for a summary of special angles), you know that $\frac{\pi}{3}$ is a value for θ that makes the equation true. However, the cosine function is also positive in Quadrant IV. The angle in Quadrant IV with reference angle $\frac{\pi}{3}$ is $\frac{5\pi}{3}$, which is also a value for θ that makes the equation true. Because the cosine function is periodic with period 2π, you have many more values for θ that satisfy $\cos\theta = \frac{1}{2}$. To list all of them, add multiples of 2π to each of the values $\frac{\pi}{3}$ and $\frac{5\pi}{3}$. Thus, the solutions are $\theta = \frac{\pi}{3} + k \cdot 2\pi$ and $\frac{5\pi}{3} + k \cdot 2\pi$, where k is any integer. If the problem specifies that you are to find only values in a particular interval, then you omit any values outside the given interval.

Solving equations frequently involves using the concept and properties of inverse functions. (See Chapter 4, "Functions," for a discussion of inverses of functions.) For trigonometric equations, some restrictions must be made to allow you to use inverses. The restrictions in this case are on the domains, so that the inverse will be a function. The **restricted domains** of the three basic functions are shown in the following table.

Restricted Domains of Trig Functions

$\sin\theta$	$-\frac{\pi}{2} \le \theta \le \frac{\pi}{2}$
$\cos\theta$	$0 \le \theta \le \pi$
$\tan\theta$	$-\frac{\pi}{2} < \theta < \frac{\pi}{2}$

On the restricted domains, the functions are one-to-one and have inverses. The graphs of each function and its inverse are shown in the following figure. In the figure, $\sin^{-1}x$ denotes the inverse sine function, $\cos^{-1}x$ denotes the inverse cosine function, and $\tan^{-1}x$ denotes the inverse tangent function. ***Note:*** Other notations can be used to denote the inverse trigonometric functions. For example, three common notations for the inverse sine function are $\sin^{-1}x$, arcsin x, and ArcSin x.

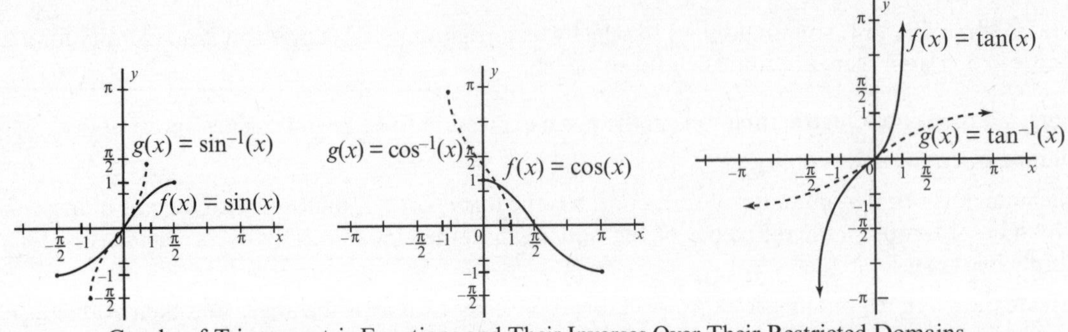

Graphs of Trigonometric Functions and Their Inverses Over Their Restricted Domains

Observe that the domain of both $\sin^{-1}x$ and $\cos^{-1}x$ is the interval $[-1,1]$, and the domain of $\tan^{-1}x$ is $(-\infty,\infty)$.

You can use the ETS graphing calculator to solve trigonometric equations by using the keys for the inverse trigonometric functions, $y=\sin^{-1}x$ (use the asin key), $y=\cos^{-1}x$ (use the acos key), and $y=\tan^{-1}x$ (use the atan key). The range for an inverse trigonometric function is restricted. When you use the keys for the inverse functions, the values returned will be in the restricted ranges. You will have to use your knowledge of reference angles and the periodicity of the functions to determine other values in the solution set, if needed.

Note: The restricted ranges for $\sin^{-1}x$, $\cos^{-1}x$, and $\tan^{-1}x$ are on the Notations, Definitions, and Formulas reference sheet.

Tip: If the answer choices are given as radians expressed in terms of π, set the ETS graphing calculator to degrees mode when obtaining the angle's value, and then convert the angle into radians using the relationship that $1° = \frac{\pi}{180}$ radians. If you set the calculator to radians mode, the solution's value will be displayed as a real number. You will have to convert the answer choices to real numbers to decide which answer is the same as your solution.

Here is an example of solving a trig equation.

Solve $2\sin\theta-\sqrt{2}=0$ for all solutions in $[0,3\pi]$.

$$2\sin\theta-\sqrt{2}=0$$
$$\sin\theta=\frac{\sqrt{2}}{2}$$
$$\sin^{-1}(\sin\theta)=\sin^{-1}\left(\frac{\sqrt{2}}{2}\right)$$
$$\theta=\frac{\pi}{4}$$

All solutions are $\frac{\pi}{4}, \frac{3\pi}{4}, \frac{9\pi}{4}$, and $\frac{11\pi}{4}$.

Tip: You will find that visualizing the unit circle and the algebraic sign of the given function in the various quadrants is helpful when you are determining all solutions for trig equations.

Rectangular and Polar Coordinate Systems

For this topic, you must be able to convert between rectangular and polar coordinate systems.

Polar Coordinates

Polar coordinates are based on a directed distance and an angle relative to a fixed point. As illustrated in the following figure, a fixed ray, called the **polar axis,** emanating from a fixed point O, the **origin,** is the basis for the coordinate system. A point in the plane is located by **polar coordinates** (r, θ).

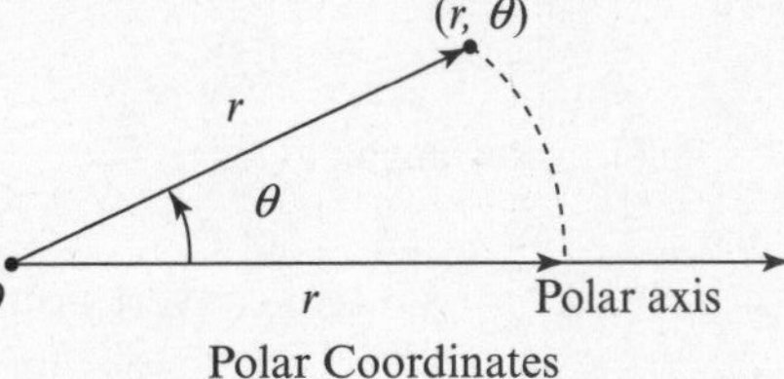

Polar Coordinates

The quadrant in which a point lies is determined by the sign of r and the magnitude of θ. If r is positive, the point is in the same quadrant as θ; if r is negative, the point is in the opposite quadrant.

Here is an example of plotting polar coordinates.

> Plot the points $\left(3, \frac{\pi}{4}\right)$, (2, 30°), (4, 75°), $(-3, \pi)$, and (3, −60°) in the polar plane.

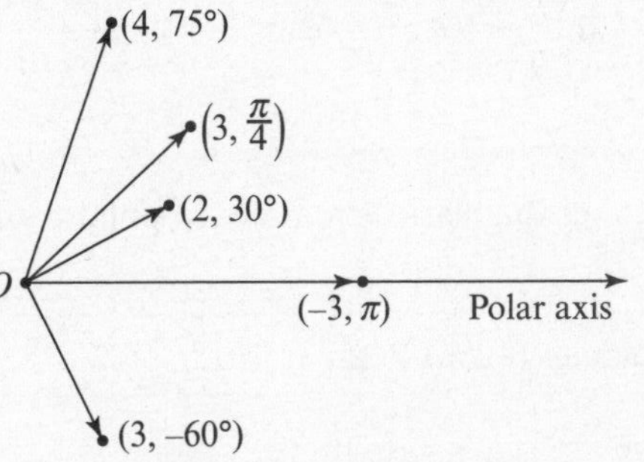

One feature of this coordinate system is that, unlike rectangular coordinates in which the coordinates are unique, a point has an unlimited number of representations in polar coordinates. For example, $(r, \theta) = (r, \theta + 2n\pi)$, for n an integer. Also, $(r, \theta) = (-r, \pi + \theta) = (-r, -\pi + \theta)$. See the following figure.

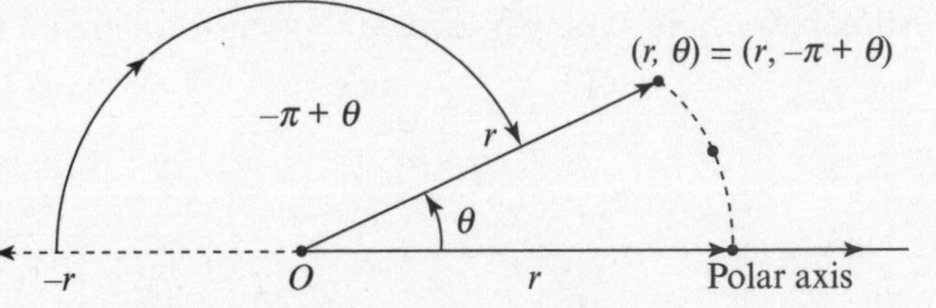

Nonunique Representation of Polar Coordinates

Converting Between Coordinate Systems

The right triangle trigonometric relationships are central to converting between coordinate systems, as shown in the following figure.

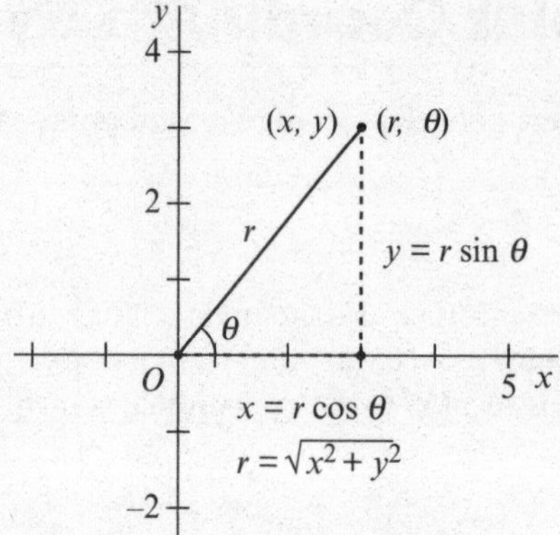

Polar-to-Rectangular Conversion

You use the conversion equations $x = r\cos\theta$ and $y = r\sin\theta$ to convert from polar coordinates to rectangular coordinates.

You use the conversion equations $r = \sqrt{x^2 + y^2}$ and $\theta = \tan^{-1}\frac{y}{x}$ $(x \neq 0)$ to convert from rectangular coordinates to polar coordinates.

Here is an example of converting from polar coordinates to rectangular form.

> Convert the polar coordinates (6, 240°) to rectangular form.

$x = r\cos\theta = 6\cos(240°) = 6\left(-\frac{1}{2}\right) = -3$ and $y = r\sin\theta = 6\sin(240°) = 6\left(-\frac{\sqrt{3}}{2}\right) = -3\sqrt{3}$.

Thus, $(6, 240°) = (-3, -3\sqrt{3})$.

Here is an example of converting from rectangular coordinates to polar form.

> Convert the rectangular coordinates (–2, 6) to polar form.

The point (–2, 6) is in Quadrant II. $r = \sqrt{(-2)^2 + 6^2} = \sqrt{40} \approx 6.3$. $\theta_r = \tan^{-1}\left(\frac{6}{-2}\right) = \tan^{-1}(-3) \approx -71.6°$.

$\theta \approx 180° - 71.6° = 108.4°$; thus, $(-2, 6) \approx (6.3, 108.4°)$.

Note: The formulas for converting between rectangular form and polar form are on the Notations, Definitions, and Formulas reference sheet.

Trigonometric Form of a Complex Number

The trigonometric form of a complex number $z = x + yi$ is $r\cos\theta + ir\sin\theta = r(\cos\theta + i\sin\theta)$, where $r = \sqrt{x^2 + y^2}$ and $\tan\theta = \frac{y}{x}$, provided $x \neq 0$. Because z also can be represented by the ordered pair (x, y), the similarity to formulas for polar coordinates is not surprising.

De Moivre's theorem says that $(\cos\theta + i\sin\theta)^k = \cos(k\theta) + i\sin(k\theta)$. This theorem is useful for finding powers and roots of complex numbers. Here is an example.

$$\left(-3 - i3\sqrt{3}\right)^3 = (6\cos 240° + i6\sin 240°)^3 = 6^3(\cos 240° + i\sin 240°)^3 = 216(\cos 720° + i\sin 720°) = 216(1+0) = 216$$

Note: De Moivre's theorem is on the Notations, Definitions, and Formulas reference sheet.

Chapter 6

Calculus

Limits

The study of calculus begins with the study of limits. For the Praxis Math CK test, the following definitions and properties of limit are essential to know.

Definition of Limit

Let f be a function defined on an open interval containing a, except possibly at a, then the $\lim\limits_{x \to a} f(x) = L$ (read "the limit of $f(x)$ as x approaches a equals L") if for every number $\varepsilon > 0$, there exists a number $\delta > 0$ such that if $0 < |x - a| < \delta$, then $|f(x) - L| < \varepsilon$ for every x in the domain of f. That is, a function f has a limit L as x approaches a, written, $\lim\limits_{x \to a} f(x) = L$, provided the error between $f(x)$ and L, written $|f(x) - L|$, can be made less than any preassigned positive number ε by making x sufficiently close to, but not equal to, a. ***Note:*** ε and δ are the lowercase Greek letters *epsilon* and *delta,* respectively.

Intuitively, the $\lim\limits_{x \to a^-} f(x) = M$ is the **left-hand limit** of $f(x)$ provided $f(x)$ approaches M as x approaches a from the left, and $\lim\limits_{x \to a^+} f(x) = N$ is the **right-hand limit** of $f(x)$ provided $f(x)$ approaches N as x approaches a from the right.

The limit $\lim\limits_{x \to a} f(x) = L$ *exists* only if the following conditions are satisfied:

1. the limit L is a single finite real number; and
2. the left-hand and right-hand limits of $f(x)$ as x approaches a both exist; and
3. $\lim\limits_{x \to a^-} f(x) = \lim\limits_{x \to a^+} f(x) = L.$

If no such L exists, then the $\lim\limits_{x \to a} f(x)$ *does not exist.* Common situations that occur when the limit of a function f as x approaches a does *not* exist are the following:

- $\lim\limits_{x \to a^+} f(x) \neq \lim\limits_{x \to a^-} f(x),$
- $f(x)$ increases or decreases without bound as x approaches a, or
- $f(x)$ oscillates between two fixed values as x approaches a.

Here is an example.

> Determine $\lim\limits_{x \to 5} \dfrac{10}{x - 5}$.

From the limit definition, $\lim\limits_{x \to 5} \dfrac{10}{x - 5}$ exists only if $\dfrac{10}{x - 5}$ approaches a single finite value as x approaches 5 from both the left and right. As x approaches 5 from the left, the number $\dfrac{10}{x - 5}$ is decreasing without bound; symbolically, you indicate this behavior as $\lim\limits_{x \to 5^-} \dfrac{10}{x - 5} = -\infty$. As x approaches 5 from the right, the number $\dfrac{10}{x - 5}$ is increasing without bound, indicated as $\lim\limits_{x \to 5^+} \dfrac{10}{x - 5} = \infty$. Since $\dfrac{10}{x - 5}$ does not approach a single finite value as x approaches 5 from both the left and right of 5, $\lim\limits_{x \to 5} \dfrac{10}{x - 5}$ does not exist.

Intuitively, the "ε-δ" definition of limit means that if the values of $f(x)$ get arbitrarily close to a single value L as x approaches a from both sides, then $\lim_{x \to a} f(x) = L$. When $\lim_{x \to a} f(x)$ exists, the limit is unique. Furthermore, its value is independent of the value of f at a.

Here is an example.

> Determine $\lim_{x \to 5}\left(x^2 + 3\right)$ using an intuitive approach.

If x gets very close to but unequal to 5 in value, either from the left or right, $(x^2 + 3)$ is very close to 28 in value (for example, when $x = 4.99$, $x^2 + 3 = 27.9001$; and when $x = 5.01$, $x^2 + 3 = 28.1001$). Thus, $(x^2 + 3)$ approaches a single finite value, namely 28, as x approaches 5 from either the left or right. Therefore, $\lim_{x \to 5}\left(x^2 + 3\right) = 28$.

When $\lim_{x \to a} f(x)$ exists, three situations that might occur at a are the following:

- $f(a) = \lim_{x \to a} f(x)$;
- $f(a)$ is undefined; or
- $f(a)$ is defined, but $f(a) \neq \lim_{x \to a} f(x)$.

Limits of Continuous Functions

Notice that in the limit concept, you do not consider what happens at $x = a$, only what happens when x is close to the value of a. Therefore, you must be cautious about assuming that $\lim_{x \to a} f(x) = f(a)$; that is, that you determine the limit by substituting $x = a$ into the expression that defines $f(x)$ and then evaluating. However, when a function is continuous at a point a, you have the situation whereby the limit *can* be calculated by actually evaluating the function at the point a. Thus, when a function f is *continuous* at $x = a$, then $\lim_{x \to a} f(x) = f(a)$, so you can find the limit by direct substitution (see "Continuity" later in this chapter for a discussion of the term *continuous*). Here are some common limits that can be evaluated using direct substitution.

$$\lim_{x \to a} b = b$$

$$\lim_{x \to a} x = a$$

$$\lim_{x \to a} \frac{1}{x} = \frac{1}{a},\ a \neq 0$$

$$\lim_{x \to a} x^2 = a^2$$

$\lim_{x \to a} x^n = a^n$, for n a positive integer

$$\lim_{x \to a} \sqrt{x} = \sqrt{a},\ a \geq 0$$

$\lim_{x \to a} \sqrt[n]{x} = \sqrt[n]{a}$, for n a positive integer with the restriction that if n is even, $a \geq 0$

$$\lim_{x \to a} |x| = |a|$$

$\lim_{x \to a} e^x = e^a$ and $\lim_{x \to a} b^x = b^a$, $b > 0$, $b \neq 1$

$\lim_{x \to a} \ln x = \ln a$, $a > 0$ and $\lim_{x \to a} \log_b x = \log_b a$, $a > 0$, $b > 0$, $b \neq 1$

If f is a polynomial function given by $f(x) = c_n x^n + c_{n-1} x^{n-1} + c_{n-2} x^{n-2} + \cdots + c_2 x^2 + c_1 x + c_0$, then $\lim_{x \to a} f(x) = c_n a^n + c_{n-1} a^{n-1} + c_{n-2} a^{n-2} + \cdots + c_2 a^2 + c_1 a + c_0$.

If f is a rational function given by $f(x)=\frac{p(x)}{q(x)}$, then $\lim_{x\to a} f(x)=\frac{p(a)}{q(a)}$, provided $q(a) \neq 0$.

For a in the domain of the function,

$$\lim_{x\to a} \sin x = \sin a \qquad \lim_{x\to a} \csc x = \csc a$$
$$\lim_{x\to a} \cos x = \cos a \qquad \lim_{x\to a} \sec x = \sec a$$
$$\lim_{x\to a} \tan x = \tan a \qquad \lim_{x\to a} \cot x = \cot a$$

Here are illustrations.

$$\lim_{x\to 5} \frac{1}{x} = \frac{1}{5}$$
$$\lim_{x\to 3} x^4 = 3^4 = 81$$
$$\lim_{x\to 36} \sqrt{x} = \sqrt{36} = 6$$
$$\lim_{x\to 32} \log_2 x = \log_2 32 = 5$$
$$\lim_{x\to 3} 4^x = 4^3 = 64$$
$$\lim_{x\to \frac{\pi}{6}} \sin x = \sin\left(\frac{\pi}{6}\right) = \frac{1}{2}$$

Limit of a composite function: If f and g are functions such that g is continuous at a and f is continuous at $g(a)$, then $\lim_{x\to a} f \quad g(x) = \lim_{x\to a} f(g(x)) = f\left(\lim_{x\to a} g(x)\right) = f(g(x))$.

Here is an illustration with $f(x) = |x|$ and $g(x) = \tan x$.

$$\lim_{x\to \frac{7\pi}{4}} |\tan x| = \left| \lim_{x\to \frac{7\pi}{4}} \tan x \right| = |-1| = 1$$

L'Hôpital's Rule

If $\lim_{x\to a} p(x) = 0$ and $\lim_{x\to a} q(x) = 0$, then direct substitution into $\lim_{x\to a} \frac{p(x)}{q(x)}$ yields $\frac{0}{0}$, which is an indeterminate form. When this problem occurs, try factoring $(x - a)$ from $p(x)$ and $q(x)$, reducing the algebraic fraction $\frac{p(x)}{q(x)}$, and then finding the limit of the resulting expression, if it exists. Here is an example.

Find $\lim_{x\to 4} \frac{x^2-16}{x-4}$.

Direct substitution into $\lim_{x\to 4} \frac{x^2-16}{x-4}$ yields $\frac{0}{0}$. Reducing $\frac{x^2-16}{x-4}$ first and then finding the limit results in the following: $\lim_{x\to 4} \frac{x^2-16}{x-4} = \lim_{x\to 4} \frac{(x+4)\cancel{(x-4)}}{\cancel{(x-4)}} = \lim_{x\to 4} (x+4) = 8$.

Another way to approach problems that result in an indeterminate form is to apply **L'Hôpital's rule** using derivatives (see "Derivatives" later in this chapter for an explanation of derivatives and related terminology). A function is **differentiable** if its derivative exists. By L'Hôpital's rule, if p and q are differentiable at every number x in an open interval I, except possibly at a, and $\lim\limits_{x\to a} p(x)=0$ and $\lim\limits_{x\to a} q(x)=0$, then $\lim\limits_{x\to a}\frac{p(x)}{q(x)}=\lim\limits_{x\to a}\frac{p'(x)}{q'(x)}$, provided $q'(x)\neq 0$ for all $x\neq a$ in I and $\lim\limits_{x\to a}\frac{p'(x)}{q'(x)}$ exists. (***Note:*** $p'(x)$ and $q'(x)$ are the derivatives of p and q, respectively.)

L'Hôpital's rule also applies when $\lim\limits_{x\to a} p(x)=\pm\infty$ and $\lim\limits_{x\to a} q(x)=\pm\infty$.

Here are illustrations (refer to "Differentiation Formulas" later in this chapter).

$$\lim_{x\to 4}\frac{x^2-16}{x-4}=\lim_{x\to 4}\frac{D_x\left(x^2-16\right)}{D_x(x-4)}=\lim_{x\to 4}\frac{2x}{1}=8$$

$$\lim_{x\to 0}\frac{\sin x}{6x}=\lim_{x\to 0}\frac{D_x(\sin x)}{D_x(6x)}=\lim_{x\to 0}\frac{\cos x}{6}=\frac{1}{6}$$

Note: $D_x f(x)=f'(x)$

Properties of Limits

Assuming that the functions f and g have limits that exist as x approaches a, the following fundamental properties of limits hold.

Sum or Difference	$\lim\limits_{x\to a}[f(x)\pm g(x)]=\lim\limits_{x\to a} f(x)\pm\lim\limits_{x\to a} g(x)$
Product	$\lim\limits_{x\to a}[f(x)\cdot g(x)]=\lim\limits_{x\to a} f(x)\cdot\lim\limits_{x\to a} g(x)$
Quotient	$\lim\limits_{x\to a}\frac{f(x)}{g(x)}=\frac{\lim\limits_{x\to a} f(x)}{\lim\limits_{x\to a} g(x)}$, provided $g(x)\neq 0$ and $\lim\limits_{x\to a} g(x)\neq 0$
Power	$\lim\limits_{x\to a}[f(x)]^n=[\lim\limits_{x\to a} f(x)]^n$
Root	$\lim\limits_{x\to a}\sqrt[n]{f(x)}=\sqrt[n]{\lim\limits_{x\to a} f(x)}$ for n a positive integer, provided both $f(x)\geq 0$ and $\lim\limits_{x\to a} f(x)\geq 0$ when n is even
Scalar Multiplication	$\lim\limits_{x\to a} k\,f(x)=k\lim\limits_{x\to a} f(x)$, for any real number k

Here are illustrations.

$$\lim_{x\to 2}\frac{3x-5}{5x+2}=\frac{\lim\limits_{x\to 2}(3x-5)}{\lim\limits_{x\to 2}(5x+2)}=\frac{\lim\limits_{x\to 2}3x-\lim\limits_{x\to 2}5}{\lim\limits_{x\to 2}5x+\lim\limits_{x\to 2}2}=\frac{3\lim\limits_{x\to 2}x-\lim\limits_{x\to 2}5}{5\lim\limits_{x\to 2}x+\lim\limits_{x\to 2}2}=\frac{3(2)-5}{5(2)+2}=\frac{1}{12}$$

$$\lim_{x\to 4}\left(3x+\sqrt{16x}\right)=\lim_{x\to 4}3x+\lim_{x\to 4}\sqrt{16x}=3\lim_{x\to 4}x+\sqrt{\lim_{x\to 4}16x}=3\lim_{x\to 4}x+\sqrt{16\lim_{x\to 4}x}=3(4)+\sqrt{16(4)}=12+\sqrt{64}$$
$$=12+8=20$$

Derivatives

For this topic, you must demonstrate an understanding of the derivative of a function as a limit, as the slope of a curve, and as a rate of change.

Definition of Derivative

The derivative f' (read "f prime") of the function f at the number x is defined as $f'(x) = \lim\limits_{h \to 0} \frac{f(x+h) - f(x)}{h}$, provided this limit exists. If this limit does not exist, then f does not have a derivative at x. Here is an example.

> Given the function f defined by $f(x) = -2x + 3$, use the definition of the derivative to find $f'(x)$.

$$f'(x) = \lim_{h \to 0} \frac{f(x+h) - f(x)}{h} = \lim_{h \to 0} \frac{(-2(x+h)+3) - (-2x+3)}{h} =$$

$$\lim_{h \to 0} \frac{(-2x-2h+3)+2x-3}{h} = \lim_{h \to 0} \frac{-2x-2h+3+2x-3}{h} = \lim_{h \to 0} \frac{-2h}{h} = \lim_{h \to 0}(-2) = -2$$

A *differentiable* function is a function that has a derivative. If $f'(c)$ exists, then f is differentiable at c; otherwise, f does not have a derivative at c. Various symbols are used to represent the derivative of a function f. For the notation $y = f(x)$, you can symbolize the derivative of f by $f'(x)$, $\frac{dy}{dx}$, $D_x f(x)$, y', $D_x y$, or $\frac{d}{dx} f(x)$.

The derivative $f'(x)$ is the **first derivative** of f. The derivative of $f'(x)$ is the **second derivative** of f and is denoted $f''(x)$. Similarly, the derivative of $f''(x)$ is the **third derivative** of f and is denoted $f'''(x)$. In general, the ***n*th derivative** of f is denoted $f^{(n)}(x)$.

Slope of Tangent Line

If $f'(a)$ exists, then the tangent line to the graph of the function f at the point $P(a, f(a))$ is the line through P that has slope $m = f'(a)$. Here is an example (refer to "Differentiation Formulas" later in this chapter).

> Find the slope of the tangent line to the parabola $y = f(x) = x^2 + 1$ at the point (2, 5).

Given that $f(x) = x^2 + 1$, then $f'(x) = 2x$.

Therefore, the slope at point $(2, 5) = m = f'(2) = 4$. See the following figure.

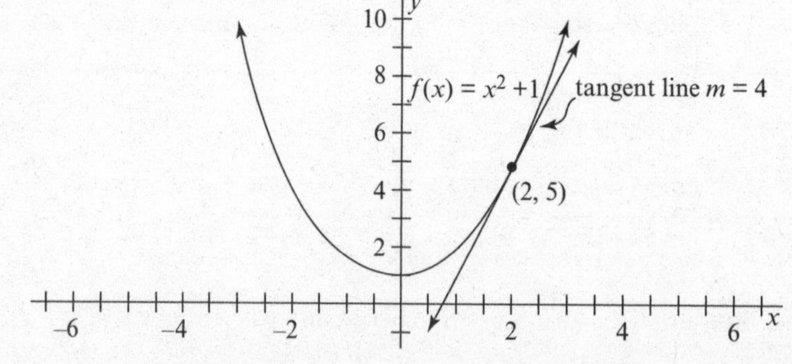

Slope of Tangent Line to $f(x) = x^2 + 1$ at (2, 5)

Instantaneous Rate of Change

If $f'(t)$ exists, then the **instantaneous rate of change** of f at t is $f'(t)$. For example, if $s(t)$ is the **position function** of a moving object, then the **velocity** (the instantaneous rate of change) of the object at time t is $s'(t)$. Additionally, the **acceleration** of the object at time t is $s''(t)$. Here is an example (refer to "Differentiation Formulas" later in this chapter).

> Suppose $s(t) = 100t^2 + 100t$ describes the position (in feet) of a moving object as a function of time t (in seconds). Find the velocity (in feet per second) and acceleration (in feet per second^2) of the object at time $t = 2$ seconds.

Velocity $= s'(t) = 200t + 100$, so at time $t = 2$ seconds, velocity $= s'(2) = 200(2) + 100 = 500$ feet per second.

Acceleration $= s''(t) = 200$, so at time $t = 2$ seconds, acceleration $= 200$ feet per second^2.

Continuity

For this topic, you must be able to show that a particular function is continuous and demonstrate an understanding of the relationship between continuity and differentiability.

Definition of Continuous Function

The function f is **continuous at the point $x = a$** in the domain of f if *all three* of the following conditions are met:

1. $f(a)$ is defined;
2. $\lim\limits_{x\to a} f(x)$ exists; and
3. $\lim\limits_{x\to a} f(x) = f(a)$.

A function that does not satisfy the above conditions is **discontinuous at a.**

Here are examples.

> Given $f(x) = \sqrt{2x+17}$, is f continuous at $x = 4$?

$\lim\limits_{x\to 4} \sqrt{2x+17} = \sqrt{\lim\limits_{x\to 4}(2x+17)} = \sqrt{25} = 5$ exists and is equal to $f(4) = \sqrt{2(4)+17} = \sqrt{25} = 5$; therefore, f is continuous at 4.

> Given $g(x) = \dfrac{15}{x-2}$, is g continuous at $x = 2$?

$\lim\limits_{x\to 2} \dfrac{15}{x-2}$ does not exist; therefore, g is discontinuous at 2.

A function f is **continuous** if for every value a in its domain, $f(a)$ exists and $\lim\limits_{x\to a} f(x) = f(a)$. Otherwise, f is **discontinuous.**

A function f is **continuous in an open interval** if it is continuous at each point in the interval. If a function is continuous on the entire real line, the function is **continuous everywhere;** that is to say, its graph is a single, unbroken curve that has no holes, jumps, or gaps in it.

Common Continuous Functions

A function is a continuous function if it is continuous on its domain. The following types of functions are continuous at every point in their domains.

Constant Functions	$f(x) = k$, where k is a constant
Identity Functions	$f(x) = x$
Reciprocal Functions	$f(x) = \frac{1}{x},\ x \neq 0$
Power Functions	$f(x) = x^n$, where n is a real number
Quadratic Functions	$f(x) = x^2$
Square Root Functions	$f(x) = \sqrt{x},\ x \geq 0$
Radical Functions	$f(x) = \sqrt[n]{x}$, for n a positive integer, provided that if n is even, $x \geq 0$
Absolute Value Functions	$f(x) = \lvert x \rvert$
Polynomial Functions	$f(x) = c_n x^n + c_{n-1}x^{n-1} + c_{n-2}x^{n-2} + \cdots + c_2 x^2 + c_1 x + c_0$
Rational Functions	$f(x) = \frac{p(x)}{q(x)},\ q(x) \neq 0$
Exponential Functions	$f(x) = b^x,\ b > 0,\ b \neq 1$
Logarithmic Functions	$f(x) = \log_b x,\ b > 0,\ b \neq 1,\ x > 0$
Trigonometric Functions	$f(x) = \sin x, f(x) = \cos x, f(x) = \tan x, f(x) = \csc x, f(x) = \cot x$, and $f(x) = \sec x$

Properties of Continuity

If f and g are continuous at $x = a$, then the following functions are also continuous at $x = a$.

Sum and Difference	$f \pm g$
Product	fg
Scalar Multiple	kf, for k a real number
Quotient	$\frac{f}{g},\ g(a) \neq 0$
Composition	If g is continuous at a and f is continuous at $g(a)$, then $f \circ g$ is continuous at a, where $(f \circ g)(x) = f(g(x))$.

If a function f is differentiable at $x = a$, then f is continuous at $x = a$; in other words, *differentiability implies continuity*. Therefore, if f is *not* continuous at $x = a$, then f is also *not* differentiable at $x = a$. ***Caution:*** Continuity does *not* imply differentiability. A function can be continuous at a point $x = a$ even though $f'(x)$ does not exist at $x = a$. This circumstance occurs when there is a cusp (a sharp corner) or a vertical tangent line at a. For example, the absolute value function (shown below) is continuous at $x = 0$; however, $f'(x)$ does not exist at $x = 0$.

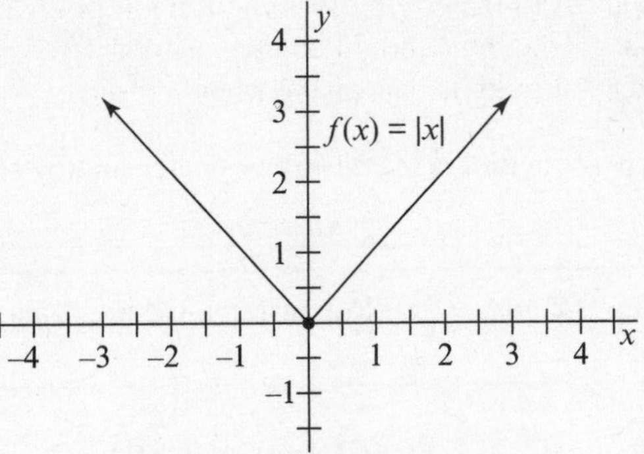

Absolute Value Function

Analyzing the Behavior of a Function

For this topic, you must be able to analyze the behavior of a function (for example: find relative extrema, concavity), solve problems involving related rates, and solve applied extrema problems.

Increasing and Decreasing Behavior

If f is continuous on a closed interval $[a, b]$ and differentiable on the open interval (a, b), then

- f is **increasing** on $[a, b]$ if $f'(x) > 0$ on (a, b);
- f is **decreasing** on $[a, b]$ if $f'(x) < 0$ on (a, b); and
- f is **constant** on $[a, b]$ if $f'(x) = 0$ on (a, b).

Tip: The sign of $f'(x)$ determines the increasing or decreasing behavior of ***f***. Here is an example.

Describe the behavior of the function f defined by $f(x) = x^2 + 1$ in the interval $[-3, 3]$.

The function f defined by $f(x) = x^2 + 1$ is a quadratic function, so it is continuous everywhere. Given $f(x) = x^2 + 1$, then $f'(x) = 2x$. For any $x \in (-3, 0)$, $f'(x) = 2x < 0$; and for any $x \in (0, 3)$, $f'(x) = 2x > 0$. Therefore, f is decreasing on $(-3, 0)$ and increasing on $(0, 3)$.

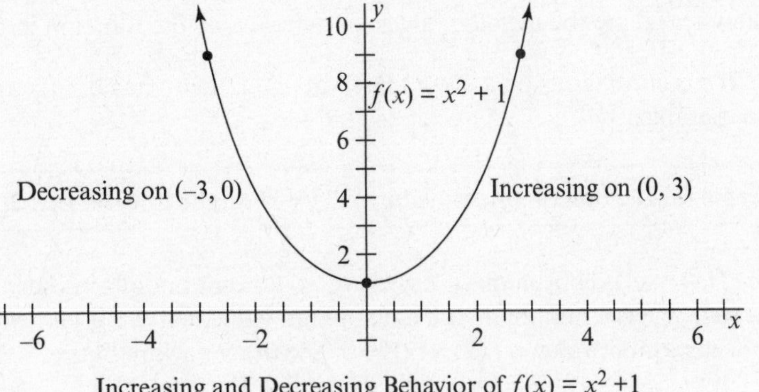

Increasing and Decreasing Behavior of $f(x) = x^2 +1$

Tip: Recall that the slope of the tangent to the graph of a function f at point $P(a, f(a))$ equals $f'(a)$. If the tangent line's slope, $f'(a)$, is positive at $x = a$, then f should be increasing when $x = a$. Similarly, if the tangent line's slope, $f'(a)$, is negative at $x = a$, then f should be decreasing when $x = a$.

You can find the intervals on which a function is increasing or decreasing by solving the inequalities $f'(x) > 0$ and $f'(x) < 0$. Here is an example.

> For the function f defined by $f(x) = x^2 + 2x + 1$, determine the intervals on which f is increasing or decreasing.

$f'(x) = 2x + 2$, so solving the inequalities $2x + 2 > 0$ and $2x + 2 < 0$ yields $x > -1$ and $x < -1$, respectively. Therefore, $f'(x)$ is positive when $x \in (-1, \infty)$ and negative when $x \in (-\infty, -1)$. Thus, f is increasing on $(-1, \infty)$ and decreasing on $(-\infty, -1)$. Here are side-by-side graphs of $f(x)$ and $f'(x)$. Notice that the graph of $f(x) = x^2 + 2x + 1$ is decreasing to the left of -1 and increasing to the right of -1. The graph of $f'(x) = 2x + 2$ is negative to the left of -1 and positive to the right of -1.

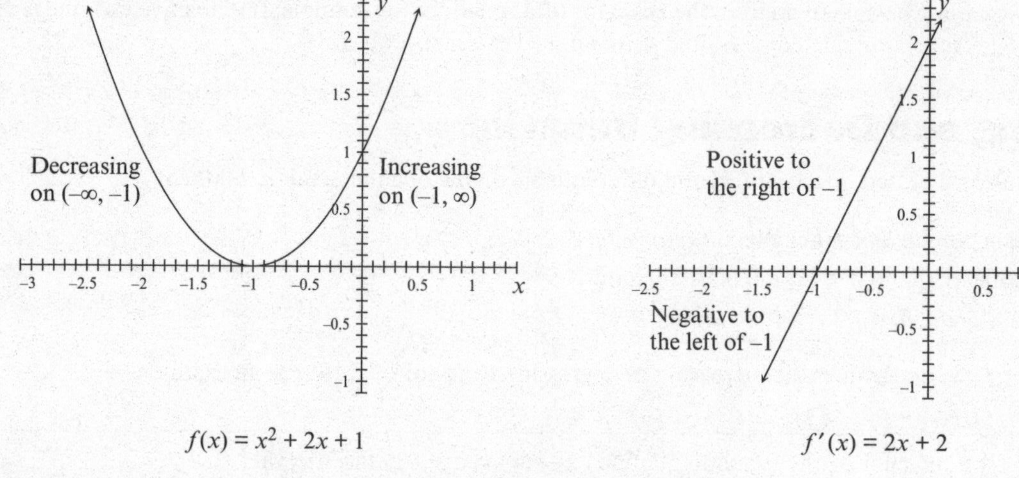

$f(x) = x^2 + 2x + 1$ $\qquad$ $f'(x) = 2x + 2$

Extrema and the Extreme Value Theorem

Let f be defined on an interval containing c. The value $f(c)$ is a **minimum** (also called the absolute minimum) of f in the interval if $f(c) \le f(x)$ for every number x in the interval; similarly, $f(c)$ is a **maximum** (also called the absolute maximum) of f in the interval if $f(c) \ge f(x)$ for every number x in the interval. The minimum and maximum values of a function in an interval are the **extreme values,** or **extrema,** of the function in the interval.

Extreme Value Theorem: If f is continuous on a closed interval $[a, b]$, then f has both a minimum and a maximum value in $[a, b]$. Here is an example.

> Describe the extrema for the function f defined by $f(x) = x^3$ on the interval $[-2, 2]$.

The function f defined by $f(x) = x^3$ is continuous everywhere, so it is continuous in the interval $[-2, 2]$. By the extreme value theorem, f has a minimum and a maximum value in $[-2, 2]$. The minimum value is $f(-2) = (-2)^3 = -8$, and the maximum value is $f(2) = (2)^3 = 8$. See the following figure.

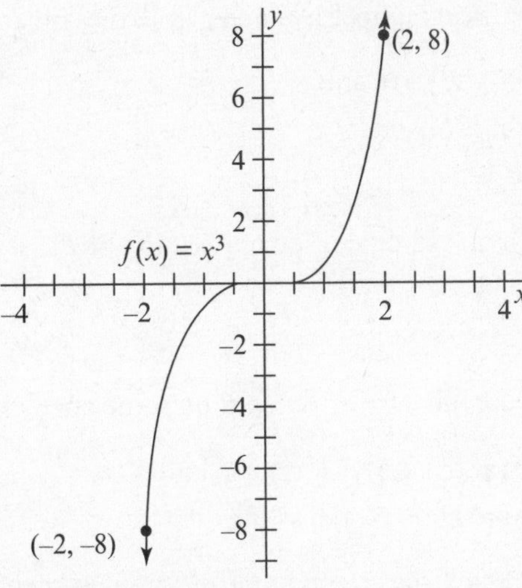

Minimum and Maximum Behavior of $f(x) = x^3$ on the Interval [–2, 2]

Tip: The extreme value theorem tells you when the minimum and maximum of a function exist, but not how to find these values. You can use the ETS graphing calculator's minimum and maximum analysis modes to find the extreme values of a function.

The number $f(c)$ is a **relative minimum** of a function f if there exists an open interval containing c in which $f(c)$ is a minimum; similarly, the number $f(c)$ is a **relative maximum** of a function f if there exists an open interval containing c in which $f(c)$ is a maximum. If $f(c)$ is a relative minimum or maximum of f, it is called a **relative extremum** of f. If f has a relative extremum at c, then either $f'(c) = 0$ or $f'(c)$ does not exist.

First and Second Derivative Tests

Given c is in the domain of f, then c is a **critical number** of f if either $f'(c) = 0$ or $f'(c)$ does not exist. The critical numbers determine points at which $f'(x)$ can change signs; that is, these are the only numbers for which the graph of f can have turning points, cusps, or discontinuities. If c is a critical number for f, then $f(c)$ is a **critical value** of f and the point $(c, f(c))$ is a **critical point** of the graph.

A **sign diagram** for $f'(x)$ is a diagram along the real line showing the signs for $f'(x)$ between critical numbers for f. You can use a sign diagram to predict the shape of the graph of f. (See the next section, "Concavity," for an example of a sign diagram.)

First Derivative Test: Given c is a critical number of a function f that is continuous on an open interval I containing c, then

- if $f'(x)$ changes sign at c from negative (for x values in I less than c) to positive (for x values in I greater than c), then $f(c)$ is a relative minimum of f; and
- if $f'(x)$ changes sign at c from positive (for x values in I less than c) to negative (for x values in I greater than c), then $f(c)$ is a relative maximum of f.

(See the next section for an example of an application of the first derivative test.)

Second Derivative Test: Given c is a critical number of f and $f''(c)$ exists on an open interval containing c, then

- $f(c)$ is a relative minimum of f if $f''(c) > 0$; and
- $f(c)$ is a relative maximum of f if $f''(c) < 0$.
- If $f''(c) = 0$, the test is inconclusive.

(See the next section, "Concavity," for an example of an application of the second derivative test.)

Concavity

Given f is a function whose first and second derivatives exist on some open interval containing the number c, then

- the graph of f is **concave upward** at $(c, f(c))$ if $f''(c) > 0$; and
- the graph of f is **concave downward** at $(c, f(c))$ if $f''(c) < 0$.

The point $(c, f(c))$ is a point of **inflection** if the concavity of the graph of f changes at $(c, f(c))$. If a graph has an inflection point at $x = c$, then either $f''(c)$ is 0 or does not exist.

Tip: When a curve is concave up, it looks like it could hold water; when a curve is concave down, it looks like it would spill water.

A methodical way to analyze the behavior of a function is to proceed as follows:

1. First, find the critical number(s) of f by using $f'(c)$.
2. Next, use the first derivative test, a sign diagram, and, if applicable, the second derivative test to find relative extrema.
3. And then use $f''(c)$, if it exists, to investigate concavity and identify points of inflection.

Here is an example.

Given $f(x) = 2x^3 - 9x^2 + 2$, discuss critical points, the sign diagram, turning points, extrema, concavity, and points of inflection with regard to f.

If $f(x) = 2x^3 - 9x^2 + 2$, then $f'(x) = 6x^2 - 18x$. Set $f'(x)$ equal to zero. If $f'(x) = 6x^2 - 18x = 6x(x - 3) = 0$, then $x = 0$ and $x = 3$ are critical numbers. The sign diagram for $f'(x)$ is shown here.

	$x < 0$	$x = 0$	$0 < x < 3$	$x = 3$	$x > 3$
$f'(x)$	+	0	–	0	+
$f(x)$	increasing	2	decreasing	–25	increasing

Next, evaluate the second derivative $f''(x) = 12x - 18$ at the critical numbers, 0 and 3, to obtain $f''(0) = 12(0) - 18 = -18$ and $f''(3) = 12(3) - 18 = 18$. Thus, by the second derivative test, $f(0) = 2(0)^3 - 9(0)^2 + 2 = 2$ is a relative maximum because $f''(0) = -18 < 0$, and $f(3) = 2(3)^3 - 9(3)^2 + 2 = -25$ is a relative minimum because $f''(3) = 18 > 0$. For $x < 0, f''(x) = 12x - 18 < 0$, so the graph of f is concave downward in that interval. For $x > 3, f''(x) = 12x - 18 > 0$, so the graph of f is concave upward in that interval. Solving $f''(x) = 12x - 18 = 0$ yields $x = 1.5$ as a possible point of inflection. For $0 < x < 1.5, f''(x) = 12x - 18 < 0$, so the graph of f is concave downward from 0 to 1.5. From $1.5 < x < 3, f''(x) = 12x - 18 > 0$, so the graph of f is concave upward from 1.5 to 3. The concavity of the graph of f changes at (1.5, –11.5), so (1.5, –11.5) is a point of inflection. See the graph below.

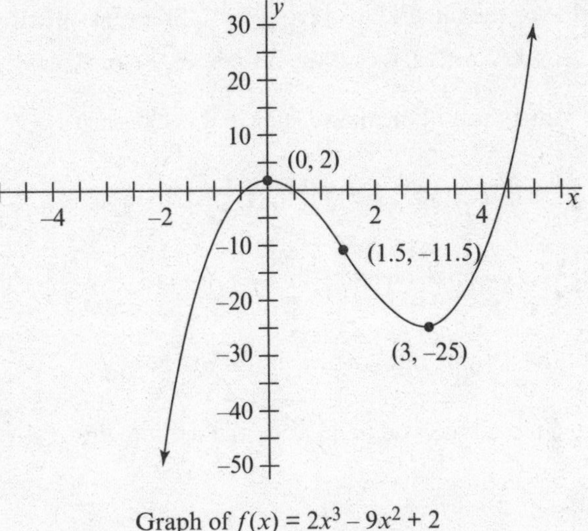

Graph of $f(x) = 2x^3 - 9x^2 + 2$

The Mean Value Theorem for Derivatives

Mean Value Theorem for Derivatives: If the function f is continuous on a closed interval $[a, b]$ and $f'(x)$ exists on the open interval (a, b), then there exists a number c in (a, b) such that $f'(c) = \frac{f(b) - f(a)}{b - a}$.

This theorem tells you that if f is continuous on $[a, b]$ and differentiable on (a, b), there exist some value c in (a, b) where the slope of the tangent line at $(c, f(c))$ is equal to the slope of the secant line between $(a, f(a))$ and $(b, f(b))$.

Here is an example.

> Find the value of c, if any, in the interval $(1, 3)$ that satisfies the mean value theorem for derivatives for the function f defined by $f(x) = x^2$.

The function f is quadratic and, therefore, is continuous on $[1, 3]$ and differentiable on $(1, 3)$. Find c such that $f'(c) = \frac{f(3) - f(1)}{3 - 1} = \frac{9 - 1}{3 - 1} = 4$. Because $f'(x) = 2x$, you have $2c = 4$, which yields $c = 2$.

The Fundamental Theorems of Calculus and the Mean Value Theorem for Integrals

Fundamental Theorems of Calculus

The function F is called an **antiderivative** (or **indefinite integral**) of the function f if $F'(x) = f(x)$.

First Fundamental Theorem of Calculus: If f is continuous on the closed interval $[a, b]$ and F is an antiderivative of f on $[a, b]$, then the evaluation of the definite integral $\int_a^b f(x)\,dx$ is given by $\int_a^b f(x)\,dx = F(b) - F(a)$. (See "Integration as a Limiting Sum" later in this chapter for a discussion of definite integrals.)

The following notations are used when applying the first fundamental theorem of calculus:

$$\int_a^b f(x)\,dx = F(b) - F(a) = F(x)\Big|_a^b = F(x)\Big]_a^b = \Big[F(x)\Big]_a^b = \Big[F(x)\Big]_{x=a}^{x=b}$$

Thus, to find the numerical value of the integral $\int_a^b f(x)\,dx$, you first find an antiderivative, say $F(x)$, for $f(x)$, evaluate that antiderivative at a and b, and then find the difference, $F(b) - F(a)$.

Here are illustrations (refer to "Integration Formulas" later in this chapter).

$$\int_1^4 15x^2\,dx = 5x^3\Big|_1^4 = 5(4)^3 - 5(1)^3 = 320 - 5 = 315$$

$$\int_3^6 \frac{1}{x}\,dx = \ln|x|\Big|_3^6 = \ln|6| - \ln|3| = \ln 6 - \ln 3 = \ln\left(\frac{6}{3}\right) = \ln 2$$

The following statements about the definite integral are useful to know:

If a function f is continuous on a closed interval $[a, b]$, then the definite integral $\int_a^b f(x)\,dx$ is a value that always exists.

If the function f is continuous on the closed interval $[a, b]$, then the average value of f on $[a, b]$ is $\frac{1}{b-a}\int_a^b f(x)\,dx$.

Second Fundamental Theorem of Calculus: If f is continuous on an open interval containing c, then for every x in the interval, $D_x\left[\int_c^x f(t)\,dt\right] = f(x)$. Here are illustrations.

$$D_x\int_3^x \left(3t^2 - 7\right)dt = 3x^2 - 7$$

$$D_x\int_0^x \sin t\;dt = \sin x$$

Try this problem.

Suppose f is a continuous function in the closed interval $[0, 3]$ and $F(x) = \int_0^x f(t)\,dt$, where $0 \le x \le 3$; then $F'(x) = D_x\int_0^x f(t)\,dt = f(x)$. If f has the graph shown, at which of the labeled points is F increasing?

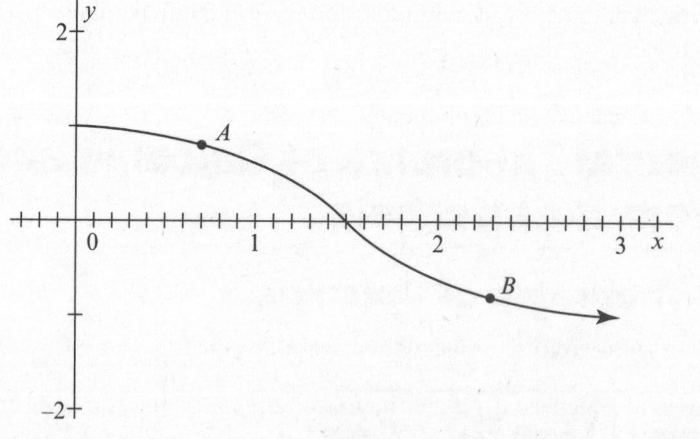

Given f is the first derivative of F, its graph tracks the slope of the tangent line to F at any point $x \in [0, 3]$. Thus, F is increasing when the graph of f is positive and decreasing when the graph of f is negative. Therefore, F is increasing at the point A.

Note: The expression $\int_c^x f(t)\,dt$ is an integral with a variable upper limit. The t appearing in this expression is called a "dummy variable" and can be replaced with any other letter not already being used.

The Mean Value Theorem for Integrals

Mean Value Theorem for Integrals: If the function f is continuous on a closed interval $[a, b]$, then there exists a number c in (a, b) such that $\int_a^b f(x)\,dx = f(c)(b-a)$.

This theorem tells you that if f is continuous on a closed interval $[a, b]$, there exists a number c in (a, b) such that the area of the region bounded by the graph of f, the x-axis, and the vertical lines $x = a$ and $x = b$ is the same as the area of a rectangle of height $f(c)$ and width $(b - a)$.

Here is an example.

> Find the value of c, if any, in the interval (1, 3) that satisfies the mean value theorem for integrals for the function f defined by $f(x) = x^2$.

The function f is quadratic and, therefore, is continuous on [1, 3]. Find c such that $\int_1^3 x^2\,dx = f(c)(3-1)$. Solving for $f(c)$ yields $f(c) = \frac{1}{2}\int_1^3 x^2\,dx = \frac{1}{2}\left(\frac{x^3}{3}\right)\Big|_1^3 = \frac{1}{2}\left(\frac{3^3}{3}\right) - \frac{1}{2}\left(\frac{1^3}{3}\right) = \frac{27}{6} - \frac{1}{6} = \frac{26}{6} = \frac{13}{3}$. Because $f(x) = x^2$, you have $c^2 = \frac{13}{3}$, which implies $c = \pm\sqrt{\frac{13}{3}}$. However, because c must lie in (1, 3) and is therefore positive, $c = \sqrt{\frac{13}{3}}$.

Properties of the Definite Integral

- If f is defined at $x = a$, then $\int_a^a f(x)\,dx = 0$.
- If f is integrable on $[a, b]$, then $\int_a^b f(x)\,dx = -\int_b^a f(x)\,dx$.
- If f is integrable on $[a, b]$ and k is a constant, then the function kf is integrable on $[a, b]$ and $\int_a^b kf(x)\,dx = k\int_a^b f(x)\,dx$.
- If f and g are integrable on $[a, b]$, then the functions $f \pm g$ are integrable on $[a, b]$ and $\int_a^b (f(x) \pm g(x))\,dx = \int_a^b f(x)\,dx \pm \int_a^b g(x)\,dx$.
- If f is integrable on $[a, b]$, $[a, c]$, and $[c, b]$, then $\int_a^b f(x)\,dx = \int_a^c f(x)\,dx + \int_c^b f(x)\,dx$.
- If f is integrable and nonnegative on $[a, b]$, then $\int_a^b f(x)\,dx \geq 0$.
- If f and g are integrable on $[a, b]$, and $f(x) \leq g(x)$ for $a \leq x \leq b$, then $\int_a^b f(x)\,dx \leq \int_a^b g(x)\,dx$.
- If f is integrable on $[-a, a]$ and f is even, then $\int_{-a}^a f(x)\,dx = 2\int_0^a f(x)\,dx$.
- If f is integrable on $[-a, a]$ and f is odd, then $\int_{-a}^a f(x)\,dx = 0$.
- If k is a constant, then $\int_a^b k\;dx = k(b-a)$.

Integration as a Limiting Sum

If a function f is a continuous function defined on the closed interval $[a, b]$, then the definite integral of f from $x = a$ to $x = b$ is defined as a **limiting sum** as follows: $\int_a^b f(x)\,dx = \lim\limits_{\max \Delta x_i \to 0} \sum_{i=1}^{n} f(c_i)\Delta x_i$, where $[a, b]$ is divided into n subintervals (not necessarily equal), c_i is a point in the ith subinterval $[x_{i-1}, x_i]$, and $\Delta x_i = x_i - x_{i-1}$, provided this limit exists.

The limiting sum, $\lim_{\max \Delta x_i \to 0} \sum_{i=1}^{n} f(c_i)\Delta x_i$, in the definition of definite integral is a **Riemann sum.** The Riemann sum might be positive, negative, or zero, depending upon the behavior of the function f in the interval $[a, b]$.

If f is a nonnegative, continuous function on the closed interval $[a, b]$, then the **area of the region** bounded by the graph of f, the x-axis, and the vertical lines $x = a$ and $x = b$ is $\int_a^b f(x)dx$.

If f and g are continuous functions on the closed interval $[a, b]$ and $f(x) \geq g(x)$ on $[a, b]$, then the area of the region bounded by $y = f(x)$, $y = g(x)$, and the vertical lines $x = a$ and $x = b$ is $\int_a^b (f(x) - g(x))dx$.

Here is an example (refer to "Integration Formulas" later in this chapter).

> Find the area in the first quadrant enclosed by the curves $y = x^2$ and $y = x^3$.

The graphs of $y = x^2$ and $y = x^3$ intersect when $x^3 = x^2$. See the following figure.

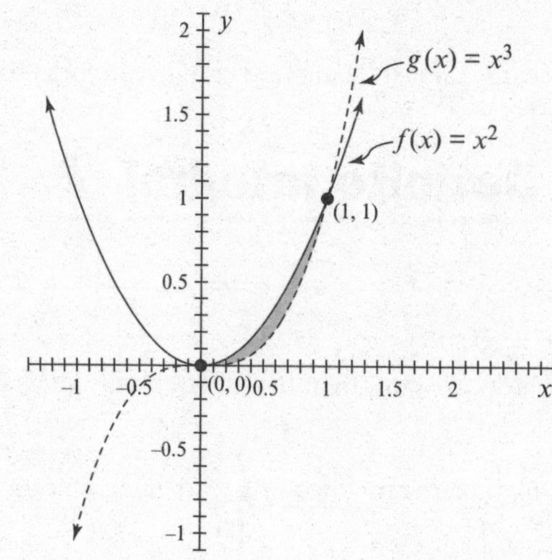

Solving this equation yields

$$\begin{aligned} x^3 &= x^2 \\ x^3 - x^2 &= 0 \\ x^2(x-1) &= 0 \\ x &= 0 \text{ or } x = 1 \end{aligned}$$

Since $x^2 \geq x^3$ on the interval from $x = 0$ to $x = 1$, the shaded area enclosed by the two curves is $\int_0^1 (x^2 - x^3)dx = \left(\frac{x^3}{3} - \frac{x^4}{4}\right)\Big|_0^1 = \frac{1}{3} - \frac{1}{4} = \frac{1}{12}$.

Tip: For the Praxis Math CK test, if asked to find the area enclosed by two curves, first, you might need to find the points of intersection of the two curves to determine *a* and *b*. You can use the intersection analysis mode of the ETS graphing calculator to find where the curves intersect, or you might elect to find the points of intersection algebraically. After determining *a* and *b*, you can numerically evaluate the integral.

The definite integral can be used to compute the area under a curve or between two curves, as shown in this section. It can also be used to compute the volume of three-dimensional figures, accumulated distance, accumulated production, the total of a continuous income stream, and the results of other limiting sum processes.

Differentiation and Integration Techniques

For this topic, you must be able to use standard differentiation and integration techniques.

Differentiation Formulas

The process of finding the derivative of a function is called **differentiation.** You should know the following differentiation formulas for the Praxis Math CK test.

$D_x k = 0$, for k a real number

$D_x x = 1$

$D_x (mx) = m$

$D_x x^n = nx^{n-1}$, for n a rational number

$D_x \ln x = \frac{1}{x},\ x > 0$

$D_x e^x = e^x$

$D_x \sin x = \cos x$

$D_x \cos x = -\sin x$

$D_x \tan x = \sec^2 x$

$D_x \sec x = \sec x \tan x$

$D_x \csc x = -\csc x \cot x$

$D_x \cot x = -\csc^2 x$

If f and g are differentiable at x, then the following derivative formulas are true.

Scalar Multiplication	$D_x(kf(x)) = k \cdot f'(x)$ for k a real number
Sum and Difference	$D_x(f(x) \pm g(x)) = f'(x) \pm g'(x)$
Product	$D_x(f(x)g(x)) = f(x) \cdot g'(x) + g(x) \cdot f'(x)$
Quotient	$D_x\left(\frac{f(x)}{g(x)}\right) = \frac{g(x) \cdot f'(x) - f(x) \cdot g'(x)}{(g(x))^2},\ g(x) \neq 0$
Chain Rule	$D_x [f(g(x))] = f'(g(x)) \cdot g'(x)$

Here are illustrations. ***Note:*** Recall that $D_x f(x)$ can be written as $\frac{d}{dx} f(x)$.

$$D_x(-2x + 3) = -2 + 0 = -2$$
$$\frac{d}{dx}\left(x^2 + 1\right) = 2x + 0 = 2x$$
$$D_t(100t^2 + 100t) = 200t + 100$$
$$\frac{d}{dt}(200t + 100) = 200 + 0 = 200$$
$$D_x(2x^3 - 9x^2 + 2) = 6x^2 - 18x + 0 = 6x^2 - 18x$$
$$\frac{d}{dx}\left(6x^2 - 18x\right) = 12x - 18$$
$$D_x \ln x = \frac{1}{x},\ x > 0$$

$$\frac{d}{dx}\left(x^2\sin x\right) = x^2 \cdot \cos x + \sin x \cdot 2x = x^2\cos x + 2x\sin x$$

$$D_x\left(\frac{1}{\sqrt{x}}\right) = \frac{\sqrt{x}\,(D_x(1)) - 1\left(D_x x^{\frac{1}{2}}\right)}{\left(\sqrt{x}\right)^2} = \frac{\sqrt{x}\,(0) - 1\left(\frac{1}{2}x^{-\frac{1}{2}}\right)}{x} = \frac{-1\left(\frac{1}{2}x^{-\frac{1}{2}}\right)}{x} = -\frac{1}{2x^{\frac{3}{2}}}$$

$$\frac{d}{dx}\left(x^{-\frac{1}{2}}\right) = -\frac{1}{2}x^{-\frac{3}{2}} = -\frac{1}{2x^{\frac{3}{2}}}$$

$$D_x(x^2 - 1)^3 = 3(x^2 - 1)^2 \cdot 2x = 6x(x^2 - 1)^2$$

Note: The formulas for $D_x(f(x)g(x))$, $D_x\left(\frac{f(x)}{g(x)}\right)$, and $D_x f(g(x))$ are given on the Notations, Definitions, and Formulas reference sheet.

Integration Formulas

The process of integrating a function is called **integration.** You should know the following integration formulas for the Praxis Math CK test. The constant C in the formulas is the **constant of integration.**

$\int dx = x + C$	$\int k\,dx = kx + C$	$\int x^n\,dx = \frac{x^{n+1}}{n+1} + C,\ n \neq -1$
$\int \frac{1}{x}dx = \ln x + C,\ x > 0$	$\int e^x\,dx = e^x + C$	
$\int \cos x dx = \sin x + C$	$\int \sin x\,dx = -\cos x + C$	$\int \sec^2 x\,dx = \tan x + C$
$\int \sec x \tan x\,dx = \sec x + C$	$\int \csc x \cot x\,dx = -\csc x + C$	$\int \csc^2 x\,dx = -\cot x + C$

Change of Variable: $\int_a^b f(g(x))g'(x)\,dx = \int_{g(a)}^{g(b)} f(u)\,du$, where $u = g(x)$ and $du = g'(x)dx$

Integration by Parts: $\int u\ dv = u \cdot v - \int v\ du$

Here are illustrations.

$$\int\left(x^e + e^x\right)dx = \int x^e dx + \int e^x dx = \frac{x^{e+1}}{e+1} + e^x + C$$

$$\int\left(x^2+1\right)\sqrt{x}\ dx = \int\left(x^2+1\right)x^{\frac{1}{2}}\ dx = \int\left(x^{\frac{5}{2}} + x^{\frac{1}{2}}\right)dx = \int x^{\frac{5}{2}}dx + \int x^{\frac{1}{2}}\ dx = \frac{x^{\frac{7}{2}}}{\frac{7}{2}} + \frac{x^{\frac{3}{2}}}{\frac{3}{2}} + C = \frac{2}{7}x^{\frac{7}{2}} + \frac{2}{3}x^{\frac{3}{2}} + C$$

Try this problem.

> Find $\int x\sin(3x)\,dx$.

Let $u = x$ and $dv = \sin 3x dx$.

Then $du = dx$ and $v = \int \sin(3x)\,dx = -\frac{1}{3}\cos(3x)$.

Note: The constant of integration is added at the end of the process.

Now, using the integration by parts formula, you have

$$\int u\ dv = u\cdot v - \int v\ du = \int x\sin(3x)\,dx = (x)\left(-\frac{1}{3}\cos(3x)\right) - \int\left(-\frac{1}{3}\cos(3x)\right)\cdot dx = -\frac{1}{3}x\cos(3x) + \frac{1}{3}\int \cos(3x)dx$$

$$= -\frac{1}{3}x\cos(3x) + \frac{1}{3}\cdot\frac{1}{3}\sin(3x) = -\frac{1}{3}x\cos(3x) + \frac{1}{9}\sin(3x) + C$$

Note: The formula for integration by parts is given on the Notations, Definitions, and Formulas reference sheet.

Numerical Approximation of Derivatives and Integrals

For this topic, you must be able to numerically approximate derivatives and integrals.

Numerical Approximation of Derivatives

If $f'(x)$ exists, then the numerical value of f' at c is $f'(c)$. Analytically, this means that to find the numerical value of the derivative of a function at a point c, you must first find the derivative of the function, and then evaluate the function at the point c. Given a table of values, you can use the slope of the secant line to approximate $f'(c)$.

Here is an example.

A function is continuous on [1, 5] and differentiable on (1, 5). Approximate $f'(3)$ given the following table of values:

x	1	2	3	4	5
$f(x)$	4	7	12	19	28

The derivative of f at 3 is the slope of the tangent line at the point (3, 12). To calculate the slope of a line, you need two points on the line. You have only one point on the tangent line, so to approximate its slope, find the slope of the secant line connecting two points on the graph. Excluding (3, 12), systematically select pairs of points and calculate the slope of the secant line between them until you exhaust the possibilities. Then average the results to obtain the approximation.

Using (1, 4) and (5, 28), $f'(3) \approx \frac{28-4}{5-1} = \frac{24}{4} = 6$; using (1, 4) and (4, 19), $f'(3) \approx \frac{19-4}{4-1} = \frac{15}{3} = 5$; using (1, 4) and (2, 7), $f'(3) \approx \frac{7-4}{2-1} = \frac{3}{1} = 3$; using (2, 7) and (5, 28), $f'(3) \approx \frac{28-7}{5-2} = \frac{21}{3} = 7$; using (2, 7) and (4, 19), $f'(3) \approx \frac{19-7}{4-2} = \frac{12}{2} = 6$; using (4, 19) and (5, 28), $f'(3) \approx \frac{28-19}{5-4} = \frac{9}{1} = 9$. Averaging the results yields $f'(3) \approx \frac{6+5+3+7+6+9}{6} = \frac{36}{6} = 6$.

Numerical Approximation of Integrals

In addition to the Riemann sum formula, the following two techniques are numerical methods that can be used to approximate a definite integral for a function f that is continuous on a closed interval $[a, b]$, where $[a, b]$ is divided into n subintervals $[x_{k-1}, x_k]$ with $x_0 = a$ and $x_n = b$; $\Delta x = \frac{b-a}{n}$; and $x_k = a + k\Delta x$.

Trapezoid Rule: $\int_a^b f(x)dx \approx \frac{b-a}{2n}\left[f(x_0) + 2f(x_1) + 2f(x_2) + \quad + 2f(x_{n-1}) + f(x_n)\right]$

Midpoint Rule: $\int_a^b f(x)dx \approx \frac{b-a}{n}\left[f\left(\frac{x_0+x_1}{2}\right) + f\left(\frac{x_1+x_2}{2}\right) + f\left(\frac{x_2+x_3}{2}\right) + \quad + f\left(\frac{x_{n-1}+x_n}{2}\right)\right]$

Here is an example of using the midpoint rule to approximate $\int_1^3 x^2\,dx$, where $\Delta x = \frac{3-1}{4} = \frac{1}{2} = 0.5$ and [1, 3] is divided into 4 subintervals [1, 1.5], [1.5, 2], [2, 2.5], and [2.5, 3].

$$\begin{aligned}\int_1^3 x^2\,dx &\approx 0.5\left[f\left(\frac{1+1.5}{2}\right)+f\left(\frac{1.5+2}{2}\right)+f\left(\frac{2+2.5}{2}\right)+f\left(\frac{2.5+3}{2}\right)\right]\\ &= 0.5[f(1.25)+f(1.75)+f(2.25)+f(2.75)]\\ &= 0.5[1.5625+3.0625+5.0625+7.5625]\\ &= 0.5[17.25]\\ &= 8.625\end{aligned}$$

Thus, using the midpoint rule, $\int_1^3 x^2\,dx \approx 8.625$.

Limits of Sequences

An **infinite sequence** is a function whose domain is the set of positive integers. (Hereafter, when no confusion can occur, an infinite sequence will be called simply *sequence*.) The notation a_n denotes the image of the integer n, and a_n is the ***n*th term** (or element) **of the sequence.** You use $\{a_n\}$ to denote the sequence $a_1, a_2, \ldots, a_n, \ldots$

The sequence $a_1, a_2, \ldots, a_n, \ldots$ has limit L, written $\lim_{n\to\infty} a_n = L$ if for every number $\varepsilon > 0$, there exists a number M such that $|a_n - L| < \varepsilon$ whenever $n > M$. A sequence that has a limit is said to **converge** to that limit. Sequences that do not converge are said to **diverge.**

Three important limits of sequences you need to know for the Praxis Math CK test are the following:

$\lim_{n\to\infty} k = k$, for k a real number

$\lim_{n\to\infty} \frac{1}{n} = 0$

$\lim_{n\to\infty} \frac{k}{n^p} = 0$, for k a real number and p any positive rational number

Assuming that the sequences $\{a_n\}$ and $\{b_n\}$ have limits that exist, the following fundamental properties hold.

Sum or Difference	$\lim_{n\to\infty}[a_n \pm b_n] = \lim_{n\to\infty} a_n \pm \lim_{n\to\infty} b_n$
Product	$\lim_{n\to\infty}[a_n \cdot b_n] = \lim_{n\to\infty} a_n \cdot \lim_{n\to\infty} b_n$
Quotient	$\lim_{n\to\infty} \frac{a_n}{b_n} = \frac{\lim_{n\to\infty} a_n}{\lim_{n\to\infty} b_n}$, provided $b_n \neq 0$ and $\lim_{n\to\infty} b_n \neq 0$
Scalar Multiplication	$\lim_{n\to\infty} ka_n = k \lim_{n\to\infty} a_n$, for any real number k

Some useful theorems about limits of sequences are the following:

Squeeze Theorem: If $a_n \le c_n \le b_n$ for each integer n and if $\lim_{n\to\infty} a_n = \lim_{n\to\infty} b_n = L$, then $\lim_{n\to\infty} c_n = L$.

If $\lim_{n\to\infty} a_n = L$, then $\lim_{n\to\infty} |a_n| = |L|$.

If $\lim_{n\to\infty} |a_n| = 0$, then $\lim_{n\to\infty} a_n = 0$.

A sequence $\{a_n\}$ is **monotonic** if either

- its terms are nondecreasing ($a_1 \le a_2 \le a_3 \ldots \le a_n \le \ldots$); or
- its terms are nonincreasing ($a_1 \ge a_2 \ge a_3 \ldots \ge a_n \ge \ldots$).

A sequence $\{a_n\}$ is **bounded above** if there is a real number b_{upper} such that $a_n \le b_{upper}$ for all *n*. A sequence $\{a_n\}$ is **bounded below** if there is a real number b_{lower} such that $b_{lower} \le a_n$ for all *n*. A sequence is **bounded** if it is bounded above and bounded below.

If a sequence is monotonic and bounded, then it converges.

Limits of Series

If $\{a_n\}$ is an infinite sequence, then $\sum_{n=1}^{\infty} a_n = a_1 + a_2 + a_3 + \cdots + a_n + \cdots$ is an **infinite series** (also called series). The notation a_n denotes the ***n*th term of the series**. You also can represent the series $\sum_{n=1}^{\infty} a_n$ as $\sum a_n$.

Associated with each infinite series is its sequence **of partial sums:** $S_1 = a_1$, $S_2 = a_1 + a_2$, $S_3 = a_1 + a_2 + a_3$, $S_n = a_1 + a_2 + a_3 + \cdots + a_n$,.... An infinite series with partial sums $S_1, S_2, S_3, \ldots, S_n, \ldots$ converges if and only if $\lim_{n\to\infty} S_n$ exists. If the limit does not exist, then the infinite series diverges. For a convergent series, if $\lim_{n\to\infty} S_n = S$, the number *S* is called the **sum of the series.**

If $\sum_{n=1}^{\infty} a_n$ and $\sum_{n=1}^{\infty} b_n$ converge, then the following properties hold.

Sum or Difference	$\sum_{n=1}^{\infty} (a_n \pm b_n) = \sum_{n=1}^{\infty} a_n \pm \sum_{n=1}^{\infty} b_n$
Scalar Multiplication	$\sum_{n=1}^{\infty} ka_n = k\sum_{n=1}^{\infty} a_n$, for any real number k

An infinite series of the form $\sum_{n=1}^{\infty} ar^{n-1} = a_1 + a_2 r + a_3 r^2 + \cdots + a_n r^{n-1} + \cdots$ is an **infinite geometric series** with ratio *r*. This series diverges if $|r| \ge 1$ and converges if $|r| < 1$. The sum of a geometric series that converges is given by $\sum_{n=1}^{\infty} ar^{n-1} = \frac{a}{1-r}$, where $|r| < 1$.

Here are illustrations.

The series $\sum_{n=1}^{\infty} 3\left(\frac{1}{2}\right)^{n-1}$ converges because $|r| = \left|\frac{1}{2}\right| < 1$. Its sum is $\frac{3}{1-\frac{1}{2}} = 6$.

The series $\sum_{n=1}^{\infty} 5(-0.99)^{n-1}$ converges because $|r| = |-0.99| = 0.99 < 1$. Its sum is $\frac{5}{1-(-0.99)} = \frac{5}{1.99} = \frac{500}{199}$.

The series $\sum_{n=1}^{\infty} 100\left(\frac{5}{4}\right)^{n-1}$ diverges because $|r| = \left|\frac{5}{4}\right| > 1$. It has no sum.

If the series $\sum a_n$ converges, then the sequence $\{a_n\}$ converges to 0. Thus, if the sequence $\{a_n\}$ does *not* converge to 0, then $\sum a_n$ diverges. This latter statement is sometimes called "the nth term test for divergence." That is, if the limit of the nth term of the series does *not* converge to 0, then the series diverges. ***Caution:*** Do not interpret this result to mean that if the nth term of the series does converge to 0, that the series converges. When the limit of the nth term of a series converges to 0, you can draw no conclusions about convergence or divergence of the series based solely on that information. See "Sequences" and "Arithmetic and Geometric Series" in Chapter 11 for an additional discussion of sequences and series.

Tip: Sometimes it is convenient to begin an infinite sequence or series at *n* = 0 instead of *n* = 1, so be sure to check for the starting value of *n* when you work problems involving sequences or series on the Praxis Math CK test.

Chapter 7

Geometry

Congruence, Similarity, and Symmetry

Congruent (symbolized by ≅) geometric figures have exactly the same size and same shape. They are superimposable, meaning they will fit exactly on top of each other. Corresponding parts of congruent figures are congruent, and thereby, have the same measure. That is, corresponding lengths are equal and corresponding angles have the same measure.

You can use hash marks (as in the pair of congruent triangles shown below) to draw attention to corresponding congruent parts. ***Tip:*** Corresponding parts are marked with the same number of strokes.

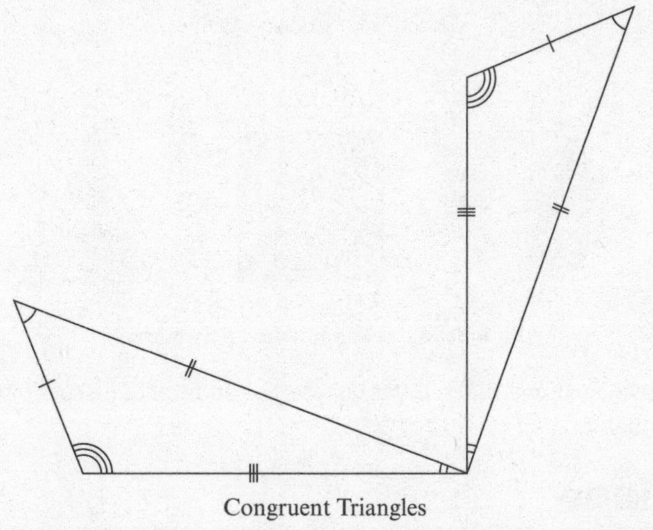

Congruent Triangles

Similar (symbolized by ~) geometric figures have the same shape but not necessarily the same size. Corresponding angles of similar shapes are congruent, and corresponding lengths of similar shapes are proportional.

Here are examples of similar figures. Notice that congruent figures are also similar figures.

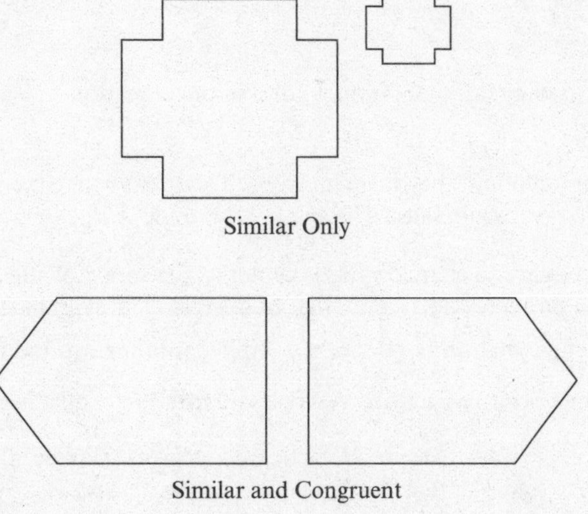

Similar Only

Similar and Congruent

Symmetry describes a characteristic of the shape of a figure or object. A figure has **reflective** (or **bilateral**) **symmetry** if it can be folded exactly in half and the resulting two parts are congruent. The line along the fold is the **line of symmetry.** A figure has **rotational symmetry** if it can be rotated onto an exact copy of itself before it comes back to its original position. The center of rotation is the **center of symmetry.** Here are examples.

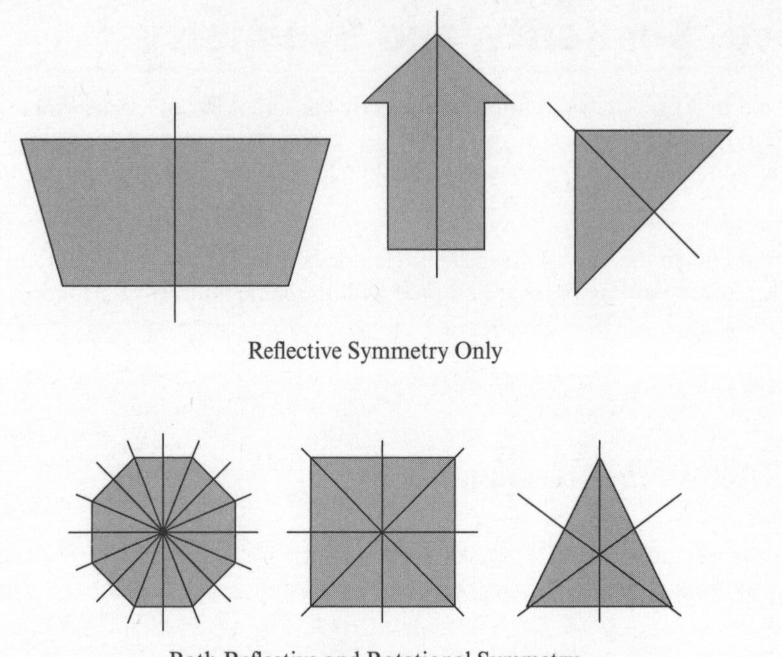

Reflective Symmetry Only
Both Reflective and Rotational Symmetry

Note: See "Geometric Transformations" later in this chapter for additional discussions on congruence, similarity, and rotation of geometric figures.

Angles and Lines

In geometry, the terms *point, line,* and *plane* are undefined. Think of a **point** as a location in space. Think of a **line** as a set of points that extends infinitely in both directions. Think of a **plane** as a set of points that forms a flat infinite surface. ***Note:*** For discussions in this chapter, unless specifically stated otherwise, all plane figures and objects are considered to lie in the same plane.

Angles

A **ray** is a portion of a line extending infinitely from a point in one direction. $\overrightarrow{AB}$ is the ray that starts at A, goes through B, and continues on.

When two rays meet at a common point, they form an **angle.** The point where the rays meet is the angle's **vertex** (the plural is vertices), and the rays are its **sides.** The symbol for angle is $\angle$.

You measure an angle with reference to a circle with its center as the vertex of the angle. The amount of rotation required to form the angle can be expressed as a number of **degrees.** The symbol for degrees is °. A full rotation around the circle is 360°. An angle that turns $\frac{1}{360}$ of a complete rotation around the circle measures 1°. A counterclockwise rotation results in a positive measure. A clockwise rotation results in a negative measure.

The number of degrees in an angle is its measure. If there are k degrees in angle A, then you write $m\angle A = k°$. An **acute angle** measures between 0° and 90°; that is, if angle A is acute, $0° < m\angle A < 90°$. An **obtuse angle** measures between 90° and 180°; that is, if angle B is obtuse, $90° < m\angle B < 180°$. A **right angle** measures exactly 90°; that is, if angle C is a right angle, $m\angle C = 90°$. A **straight angle** measures exactly 180°; that is, if angle D is a straight angle, $m\angle D = 180°$. Here are examples.

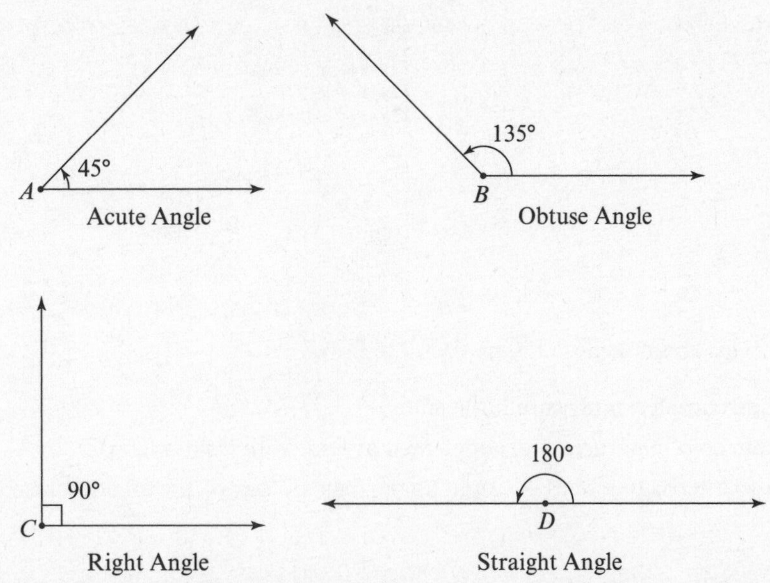

Acute Angle

Obtuse Angle

Right Angle

Straight Angle

Tip: The box in the corner of $\angle C$ denotes a right angle.

Two angles whose measures sum to 90° are **complementary angles.** Each angle is the other angle's **complement.** Two angles whose measures sum to 180° are **supplementary angles.** Each angle is the other angle's **supplement.** Here are examples.

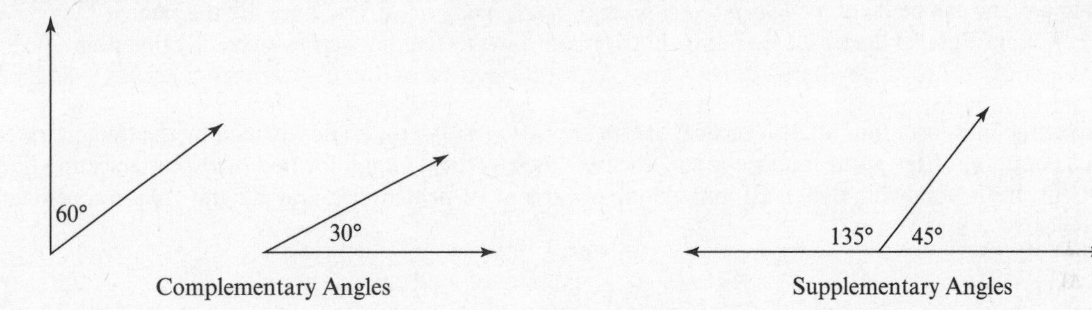

Complementary Angles

Supplementary Angles

Adjacent angles are angles that have a common vertex and a common side with no overlap. Here is an example.

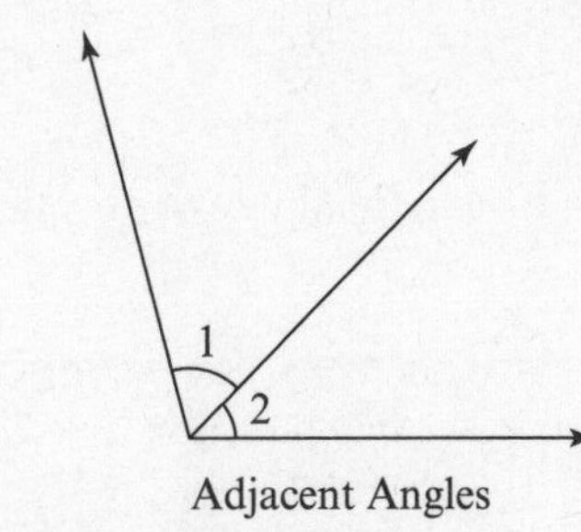

Adjacent Angles

A **bisector of an angle** is a line or ray that passes through the vertex of the angle and divides it into two congruent angles. Here is an example.

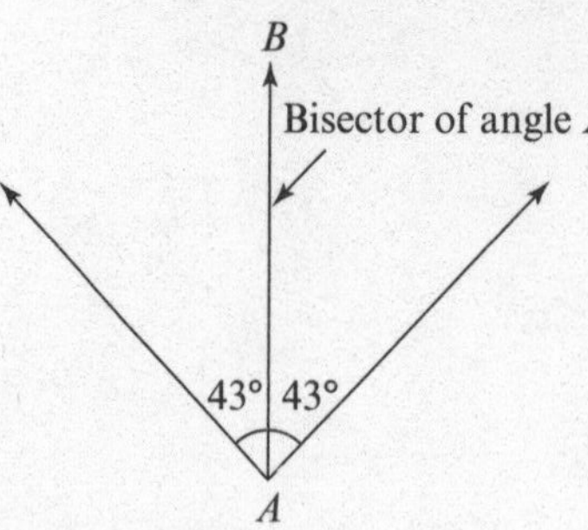

The following are theorems about angles that are useful to know.

- Two angles that are complementary are both acute.
- Two angles that are both congruent and supplementary are both right angles.
- If one angle of two intersecting lines is a right angle, then all four of the angles formed by the two lines are right angles.

Lines

The notation $\overleftrightarrow{PQ}$ denotes the line containing the points P and Q and extending infinitely in both directions.

A **line segment** $\overline{PQ}$ is a part of a line that connects the points P and Q and includes P and Q. The points P and Q are the segment's **endpoints.** Its length is denoted PQ. Congruent segments have equal lengths.

Two lines in a plane can be the *same line, parallel lines,* or *intersecting lines*. Two lines are the **same** if they have all points in common. **Parallel** lines have no points in common. **Intersecting** lines cross at exactly one point in the plane.

Two intersecting lines form four angles. **Vertical angles** are two *nonadjacent* angles formed by the two intersecting lines with a common vertex at the intersection of the two lines. Vertical angles formed by two intersecting lines are congruent. In the following figure, $\angle 1$ and $\angle 3$ are congruent vertical angles, and $\angle 2$ and $\angle 4$ are congruent vertical angles.

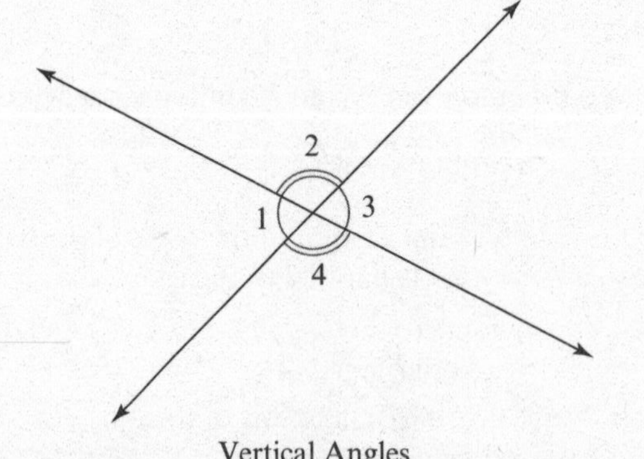

Vertical Angles

Parallel lines (in a plane) never meet. The distance between them is always the same. To indicate that line l is parallel to line m, write $l \parallel m$. A **transversal** is a straight line that intersects two or more given lines. When two parallel lines are cut by a transversal, eight angles are formed. In the following figure, parallel lines l and m are cut by a transversal n.

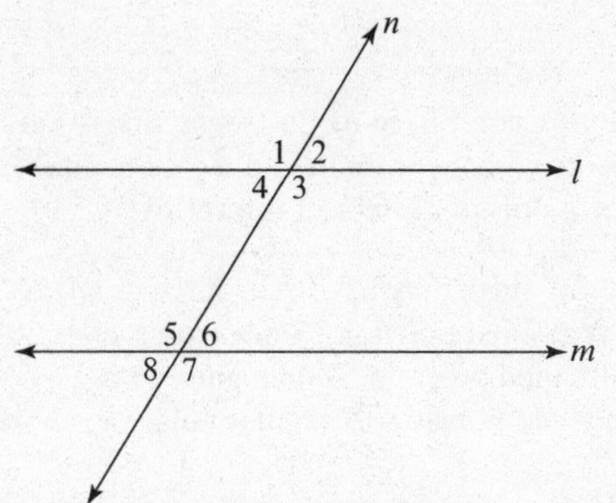

The interior angles are $\angle 3$, $\angle 4$, $\angle 5$, and $\angle 6$. The exterior angles are $\angle 1$, $\angle 2$, $\angle 7$, and $\angle 8$. The corresponding angles are the pair of angles $\angle 1$ and $\angle 5$, the pair of angles $\angle 2$ and $\angle 6$, the pair of angles $\angle 4$ and $\angle 8$, and the pair of angles $\angle 3$ and $\angle 7$. The alternate exterior angles are the pair of angles $\angle 1$ and $\angle 7$ and the pair of angles $\angle 2$ and $\angle 8$. The alternate interior angles are the pair of angles $\angle 4$ and $\angle 6$ and the pair of angles $\angle 3$ and $\angle 5$.

Perpendicular lines intersect at right angles. To indicate that line l is perpendicular to line m, write $l \perp m$. The **perpendicular bisector** of a line segment is the set of all points in the plane of the line segment that are equidistant from the endpoints of the line segment. In the following figure, line m is the perpendicular bisector of line segment $\overline{AB}$.

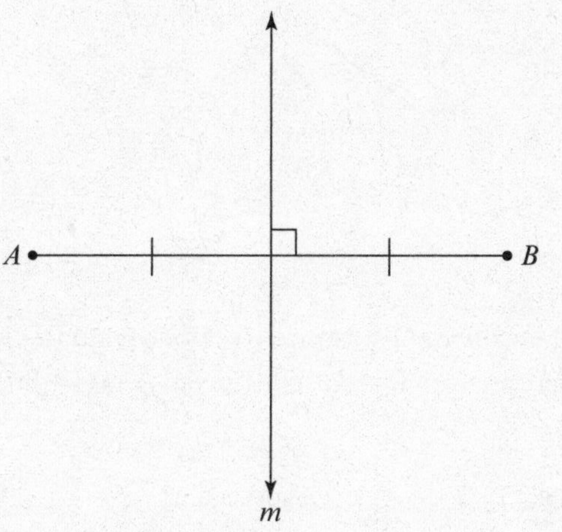

The following theorems about lines are useful to know.

- **Euclid's Parallel Postulate:** Given a line and a point in the same plane but not on the line, there is one and only one line through the given point that is parallel to the given line.
- If two parallel lines are cut by a transversal, then any pair of corresponding angles, alternate exterior angles, or alternate interior angles are congruent.
- Two lines that are cut by a transversal are parallel if any pair of corresponding angles, alternate exterior angles, or alternate interior angles are congruent.
- Two lines that are cut by a transversal are parallel if a pair of interior angles on the same side of the transversal are supplementary.
- The shortest distance from a point to a line is the length of the perpendicular line segment from the point to the line.
- Two distinct lines (in a plane) that are perpendicular to the same line are parallel.
- A line in a plane that is perpendicular to one of two parallel lines is perpendicular to the other parallel line.
- A line in a plane that intersects one of two parallel lines in exactly one point intersects the other parallel line.

Polygons

A **polygon** is a simple, closed-plane figure composed of line segments, fitted end to end. The segments meet only at their endpoints, and no two segments with a common endpoint are collinear. The segments are the polygon's **sides.** The point at which two sides of a polygon intersect is a **vertex.**

Polygons are classified by the number of sides they have. A **triangle** is a three-sided polygon. A **quadrilateral** is a four-sided polygon. A **pentagon** is a five-sided polygon. A **hexagon** is a six-sided polygon. A **heptagon** is a seven-sided polygon. An **octagon** is an eight-sided polygon. A **nonagon** is a nine-sided polygon. A **decagon** is a ten-sided polygon. In general, an ***n*-gon** is an n-sided polygon. A **regular polygon** is a polygon for which all sides and angles are congruent.

An n-sided polygon has n interior angles and n exterior angles. An **interior angle** of a polygon is formed at a vertex by two adjacent sides and lies within the polygon. The sum of the measures of an n-sided polygon's interior angles equals $(n-2)180°$. An **exterior angle** of a polygon is formed at a vertex by one side of the polygon and the extension of the adjacent side. The sum of the measures of a polygon's exterior angles equals 360°, no matter how many sides the polygon has. ***Note:*** It is possible to draw two congruent exterior angles at each vertex of a polygon, but only one is considered when speaking of the exterior angle at a particular vertex. The following figure shows an interior and exterior angle of a pentagon.

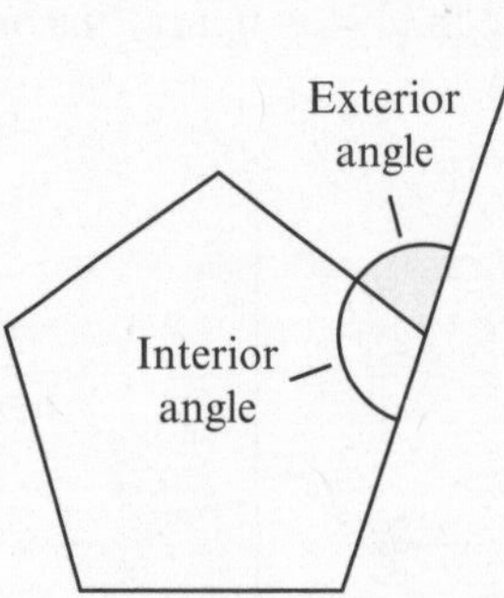

A line segment that connects two nonconsecutive vertices of a polygon is a **diagonal.** The number of diagonals of an n-sided polygon is $\frac{n(n-3)}{2}$. Here are examples of regular polygons with the number of diagonals indicated below the figure.

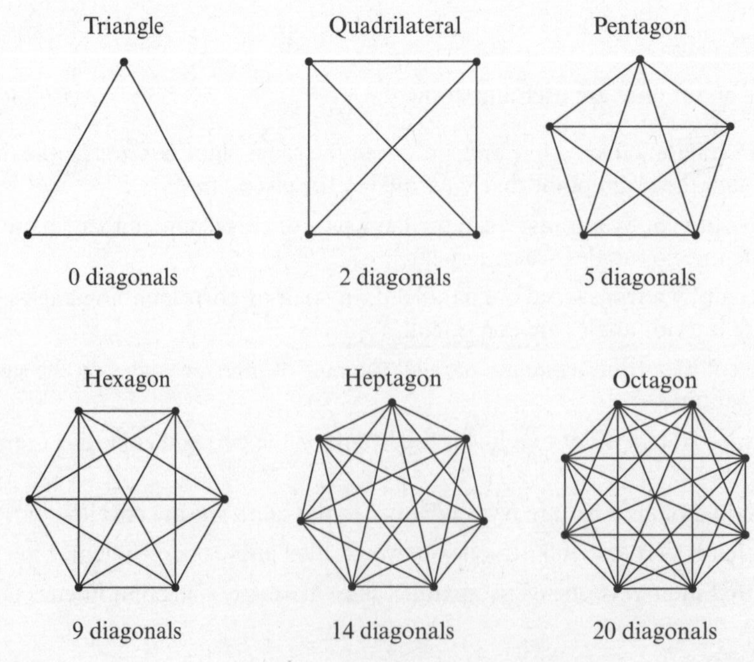

If all the diagonals of a polygon lie within the polygon's interior, the polygon is **convex;** otherwise, the polygon is **concave.** Here are examples.

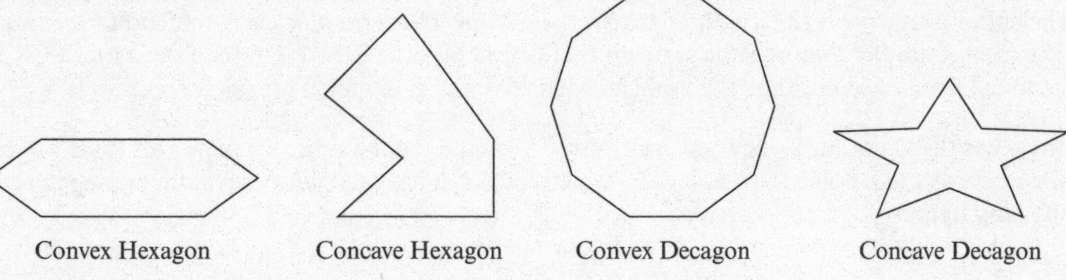

Triangles

For this topic, you must demonstrate an understanding of properties of triangles.

Triangle Classification

A **triangle** is a three-sided polygon. **Triangle inequality:** The sum of the measures of any two sides of a triangle must be greater than the measure of the third side. Essentially, for a triangle to exist, the length of the longest side must be shorter than the sum of the lengths of the other two sides.

You can classify triangles according to their sides. A **scalene triangle** has no two sides congruent. An **isosceles triangle** has at least two congruent sides (and the angles opposite the congruent sides are congruent **base angles**). An **equilateral triangle** has three congruent sides (and three congruent angles).

You can classify triangles according to the measures of their interior angles. The sum of the measures of a triangle's interior angles is 180°. An **acute triangle** has three acute interior angles. A **right triangle** has exactly one right interior angle. An **obtuse triangle** has exactly one obtuse interior angle.

Here are examples.

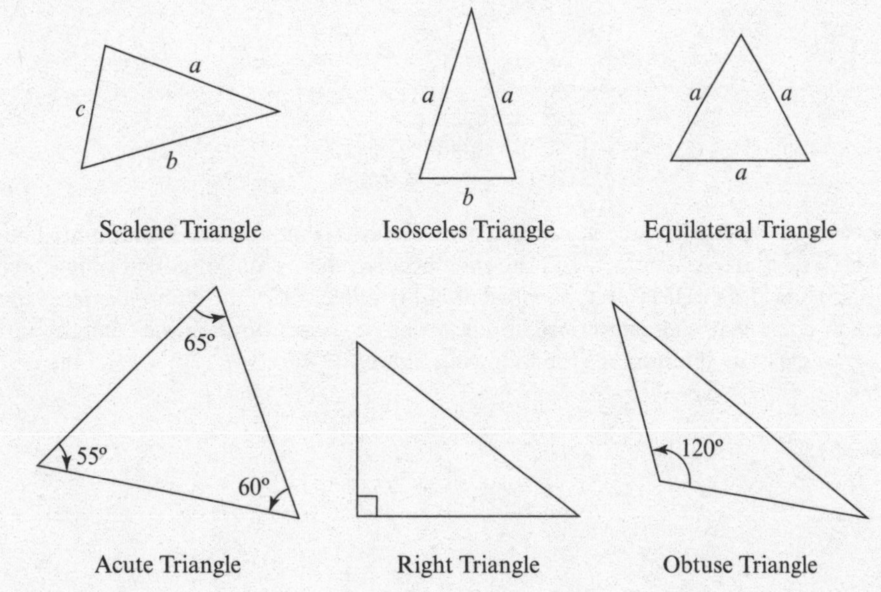

Points of Concurrency Associated with Triangles

A triangle's **altitude** is a perpendicular line segment from a vertex to a line containing the opposite side, called the **base.** The **height** of a triangle is the length of the altitude. ***Note:*** The term *altitude* is sometimes used to mean the *height* of the triangle, rather than the line segment that determines the height. On the Praxis Math CK test, you will be able to tell from the context of the problem what meaning is intended for the term altitude.

Every triangle has three altitudes, one from each vertex. The lines containing a triangle's altitudes are **concurrent,** meaning they intersect in a point. This point of concurrency of a triangle's altitudes is the triangle's **orthocenter.** See the following figure.

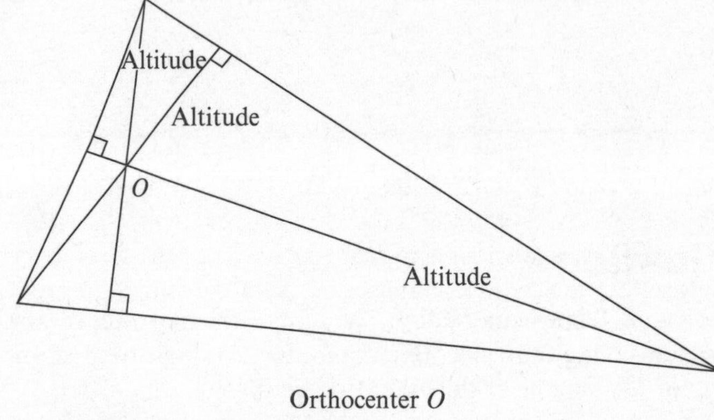

Orthocenter O

A **median** in a triangle is a line segment connecting a vertex of the triangle to the midpoint of the side opposite that vertex. The lines containing the triangle's medians are concurrent and the **centroid,** their point of concurrency, is two-thirds of the way along each median, from the vertex to the opposite side. See the following figure.

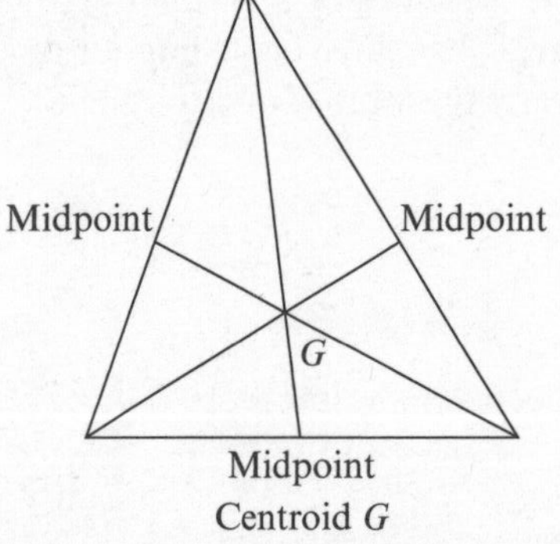

Centroid G

A **perpendicular bisector** of a triangle's side is a line perpendicular to that side at its midpoint. The perpendicular bisectors of a triangle's sides are concurrent, and the **circumcenter,** their point of concurrency, is equidistant from the triangle's vertices. Thus, if a circle is circumscribed about triangle XYZ, the circumcenter is the center of the circumscribed circle. A circle that is **circumscribed** about a triangle passes through the triangles three vertices and contains the entire triangle in its interior. See the following figure.

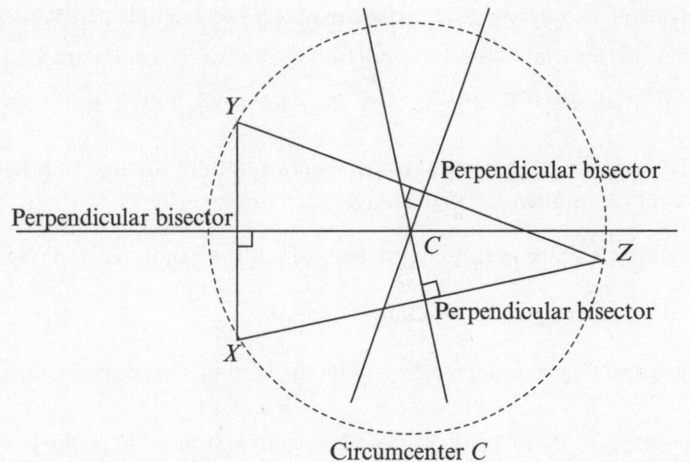

Circumcenter C

The **angle bisectors** of a triangle's interior angles are concurrent and the **incenter,** their point of concurrency, is equidistant from the three sides. Therefore, if a circle is inscribed in a triangle, the incenter is the center of the inscribed circle. A circle that is **inscribed** in a triangle touches each side of the triangle in only one point and is the largest circle contained entirely within the triangle's interior. See the following figure.

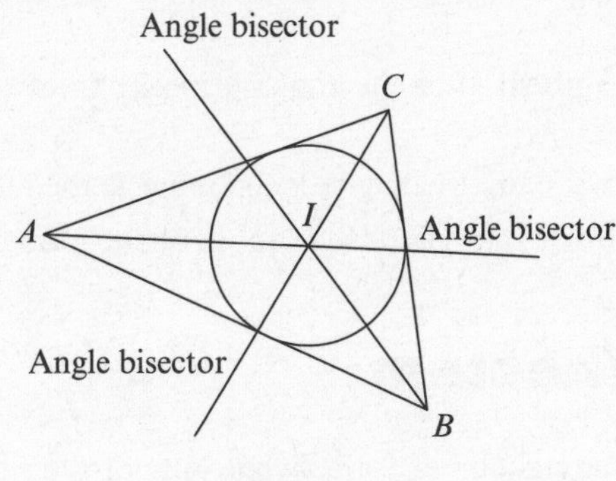

Incenter I

Congruent and Similar Triangles

Congruent triangles are triangles for which corresponding sides and corresponding angles are congruent. You can use the following theorems to prove two triangles are congruent.

- If three sides of one triangle are congruent, correspondingly, to three sides of another triangle, then the two triangles are congruent (SSS). ***Remember:*** To make sure a triangle exists, the sum of the lengths of any two sides must be greater than the length of the third side.
- If two sides and the included angle of one triangle are congruent, correspondingly, to two sides and the included angle of another triangle, then the two triangles are congruent (SAS).
- If two angles and the included side of one triangle are congruent, correspondingly, to two angles and the included side of another triangle, then the two triangles are congruent (ASA).
- If two angles and the nonincluded side of one triangle are congruent, correspondingly, to two angles and the nonincluded side of another triangle, then the two triangles are congruent (AAS).

Tip: Two methods that do NOT work for proving congruence are AAA (three corresponding angles congruent) and SSA (two corresponding sides and the nonincluded angle congruent).

Similar triangles are triangles for which corresponding sides are proportional and corresponding angles are congruent. You can use the following theorems to prove two triangles are similar.

- If corresponding angles of two triangles are congruent, the two triangles are similar.
- If corresponding sides of two triangles are proportional, the two triangles are similar.
- If two angles of one triangle are congruent to two corresponding angles of another triangle, then the two triangles are similar.
- If two sides of one triangle are proportional to two corresponding sides of another triangle, and the included angles are congruent, then the two triangles are similar.

(See "Geometric Transformations" later in this chapter for an additional discussion of *congruence* and *similarity*.)

Here are other theorems about triangles that are useful to know.

- The measure of an exterior angle of a triangle equals the sum of the measures of the nonadjacent (remote) interior angles.
- The segment between the midpoints of two sides of a triangle is parallel to the third side and half as long.
- A line that is parallel to one side of a triangle and cuts the other two sides in distinct points cuts off segments that are proportional to these two sides.
- A line that intersects two sides of a triangle and cuts off segments proportional to these two sides is parallel to the third side.
- The bisector of an interior angle of a triangle divides the opposite side in the ratio of the sides that form the angle bisected.
- If two sides of a triangle are congruent, then the angles opposite those sides are congruent, and the reverse is true.
- The ratio of the perimeters of two similar triangles is the same as the ratio of any two corresponding sides.
- The ratio of the areas of two similar triangles is the square of the ratio of any two corresponding sides.

The Pythagorean Theorem

In a right triangle, the side opposite the right angle is the **hypotenuse** of the right triangle. The hypotenuse is *always* the longest side of the right triangle. The other two sides are the right triangle's **legs.** See the following figure.

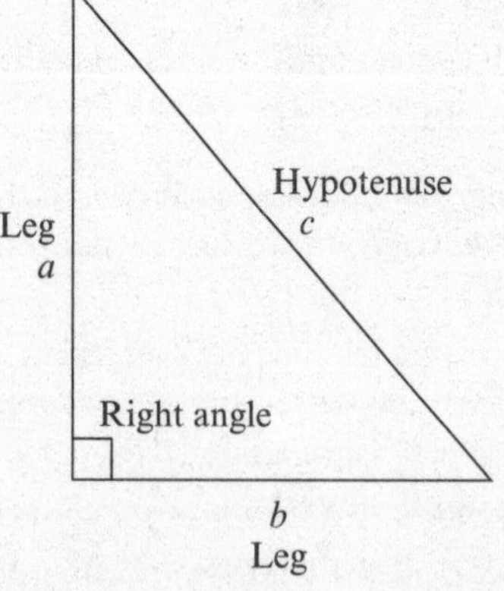

The **Pythagorean theorem** states that, in a right triangle, $c^2 = a^2 + b^2$, where c is the length of the hypotenuse and a and b are the lengths of the legs of the right triangle. This relationship applies only to right triangles. If you know any two sides of a right triangle, you can find the third side by using the formula $c^2 = a^2 + b^2$. Here is an example.

Find the hypotenuse of a right triangle that has legs 9 centimeters and 12 centimeters.

Substitute into the formula and omit units for convenience. Solve for c.

$$c^2 = a^2 + b^2$$
$$c^2 = 9^2 + 12^2$$
$$c^2 = 81 + 144$$
$$c^2 = 225$$
$$c = \sqrt{225} = 15$$

Thus, $c = 15$ centimeters.

Tip: The number 225 has two square roots, 15 and –15. The negative value is discarded because the length of the hypotenuse (or any side of a triangle) cannot be negative.

The converse of the Pythagorean theorem also is true. To be precise: If the square of the length of the longest side of a triangle equals the sum of the squares of the lengths of the other two sides, the triangle is a right triangle.

For example, a triangle with sides of lengths 3, 4, and 5 is a right triangle because $3^2 + 4^2 = 9 + 16 = 25 = 5^2$. The numbers (3, 4, 5) are a **Pythagorean triple,** so called because they are natural numbers that satisfy the relation $a^2 + b^2 = c^2$. Other well-known Pythagorean triples are (5, 12, 13) and (8, 15, 17).

After you identify a Pythagorean triple, any multiple of the three numbers is also a Pythagorean triple. That is, if each number of a Pythagorean triple is multiplied by a positive number k, the resulting triple also satisfies $a^2 + b^2 = c^2$. Thus, $(3k, 4k, 5k)$, $(5k, 12k, 13k)$, and $(8k, 15k, 17k)$ are Pythagorean triples. For example, let $k = 2$, then $(3k, 4k, 5k)$ equals (6, 8, 10). A triangle with sides of lengths 6, 8, and 10 is a right triangle because $6^2 + 8^2 = 36 + 64 = 100 = 10^2$.

Here are additional theorems about right triangles that are useful to know.

- The length of the median to the hypotenuse of a right triangle is one-half the length of the hypotenuse.
- The altitude to a right triangle's hypotenuse divides the triangle into two right triangles that are similar to each other and to the original right triangle. Furthermore, the altitude's length is the geometric mean of the lengths of the two segments into which it separates the hypotenuse. In the figure shown below, $\Delta ACB \sim \Delta AHC \sim \Delta CHB$; and $\frac{AH}{h} = \frac{h}{HB}$.

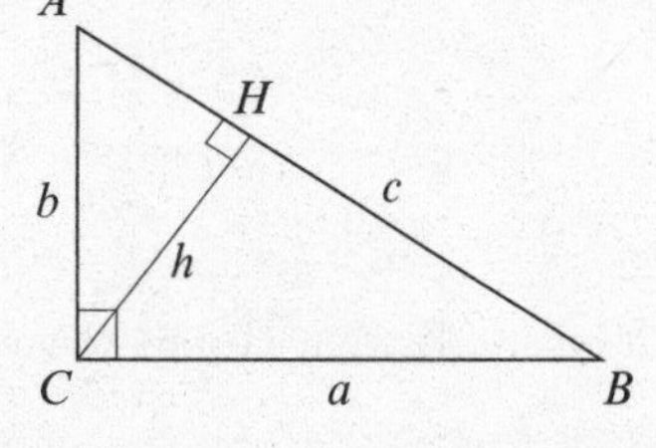

- The lengths of the sides of a 45°–45°–90° right triangle are in the ratio $\frac{1}{\sqrt{2}} : \frac{1}{\sqrt{2}} : 1$ or, equivalently, $1 : 1 : \sqrt{2}$.
- The lengths of the sides of a 30°–60°–90° right triangle are in the ratio $\frac{1}{2} : \frac{\sqrt{3}}{2} : 1$, or equivalently, $1 : \sqrt{3} : 2$, where the shortest side is opposite the 30° angle.
- Given two right triangles, if the hypotenuse and one leg of one triangle are congruent to the hypotenuse and the corresponding leg of the other triangle, then the two right triangles are congruent.

Quadrilaterals

A **quadrilateral** is a four-sided polygon. Quadrilaterals are subclassified as trapezoids or parallelograms.

A **trapezoid** has two definitions, both of which are widely accepted. One definition is that a trapezoid is a quadrilateral that has *exactly* one pair of opposite sides that are parallel. This definition would exclude parallelograms as a special case. The other definition is that a trapezoid is a quadrilateral that has *at least* one pair of parallel sides. This definition would allow any parallelogram to be considered a special kind of trapezoid. This situation is one of the few times that mathematicians do not agree on the definition of a term. For purposes of this CliffsNotes book, we will have to assume that answers to problems involving trapezoid(s) on the Praxis Math CK test will not hinge on the definition for trapezoid you choose to use during the test.

A **parallelogram** is a quadrilateral that has two pairs of opposite parallel sides. Some useful properties of parallelograms are the following:

- Opposite sides are congruent.
- The sum of the four interior angles is 360°.
- Opposite interior angles are congruent.
- Consecutive interior angles are supplementary.
- The diagonals bisect each other.
- Each diagonal divides the parallelogram into two congruent triangles.

Some parallelograms have special names because of their special properties. A **rhombus** is a parallelogram that has four congruent sides. A **rectangle** is a parallelogram that has four right angles. A **square** is a parallelogram that has four right angles and four congruent sides. These three figures have all the general properties of parallelograms. In addition, in rectangles and squares, the diagonals are congruent. In rhombuses and squares, the diagonals intersect at right angles.

Here are examples of quadrilaterals.

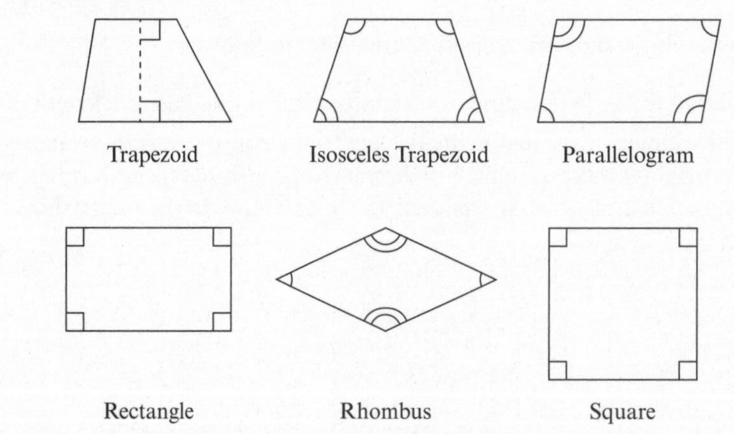

The following are theorems about quadrilaterals that are useful to know.

- The sum of the interior angles of a quadrilateral is 360°.
- If the diagonals of a quadrilateral bisect each other, the quadrilateral is a parallelogram.
- If both pairs of opposite sides of a quadrilateral are congruent, the quadrilateral is a parallelogram.
- If two sides of a quadrilateral are parallel and congruent, the quadrilateral is a parallelogram.
- If the diagonals of a quadrilateral are perpendicular bisectors of each other, the quadrilateral is a rhombus.
- If a parallelogram has one right angle, it has four right angles and is a rectangle.
- If a rhombus has one right angle, it has four right angles and is a square.

Circles

A **circle** is a closed-plane figure for which all points are the same distance from a point within, called the center. A circle's **radius** is a line segment joining the circle's center to any point on the circle (the plural of radius is **radii**). A **chord** of a circle is a line segment with both endpoints on the circle. A **diameter** is a chord that passes through the circle's center. A circle's diameter is twice the radius. Conversely, a circle's radius is half the diameter. See the following illustration.

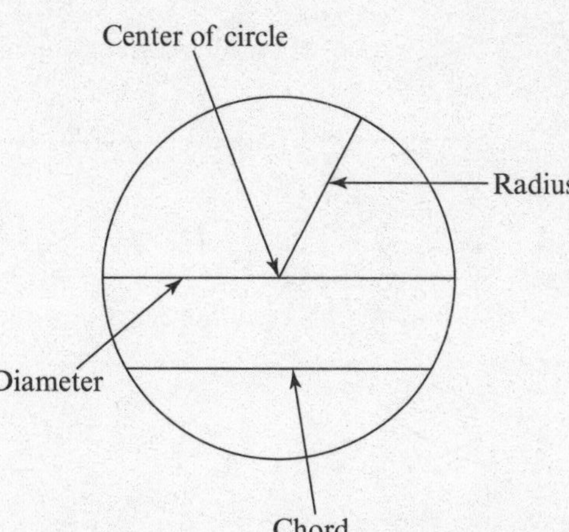

In a circle, a radius perpendicular to a chord bisects the chord. Consequently, a chord's perpendicular bisector passes through the circle's center as shown below.

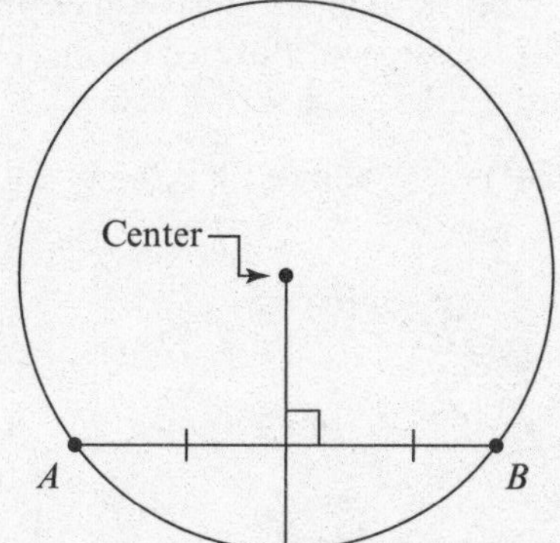

An **arc** is part of a circle; it is the set of points between and including two points on the circle. The two points determine two arcs on the circle. Arcs are measured in degrees. If the two arcs are of unequal measure, the arc with the smaller measure is the **minor arc,** and the arc with the greater measure is the **major arc.** A **semicircle** is an arc whose endpoints are the endpoints of the circle's diameter. The degree measure of a semicircle is 180°.

A **central angle** of a circle is an angle that has its vertex at the circle's center. A central angle and its **intercepted arc** have the same degree measure. In the circle shown below, the intercepted arc of the central angle is minor arc AB; its measure is 80°.

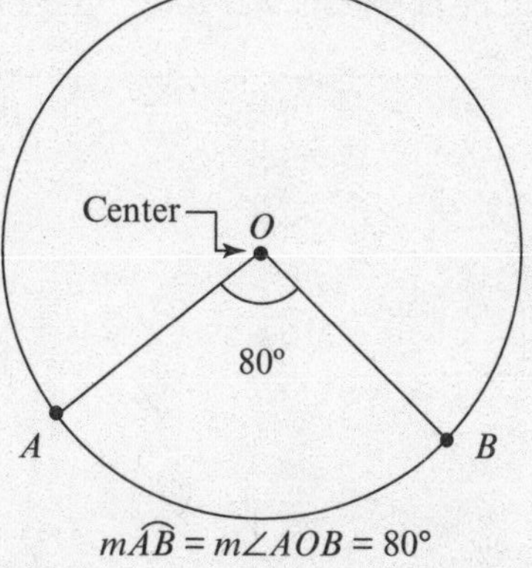

$m\widehat{AB} = m\angle AOB = 80°$

An **inscribed angle** is an angle whose vertex is on a circle and whose sides are chords of the circle. The arc of the circle that is in the inscribed angle's interior and whose endpoints are on the angle's sides is its intercepted arc.

The measure of an inscribed angle is half the measure of its intercepted arc. An angle inscribed in a semicircle is a right angle. Look at the following figures.

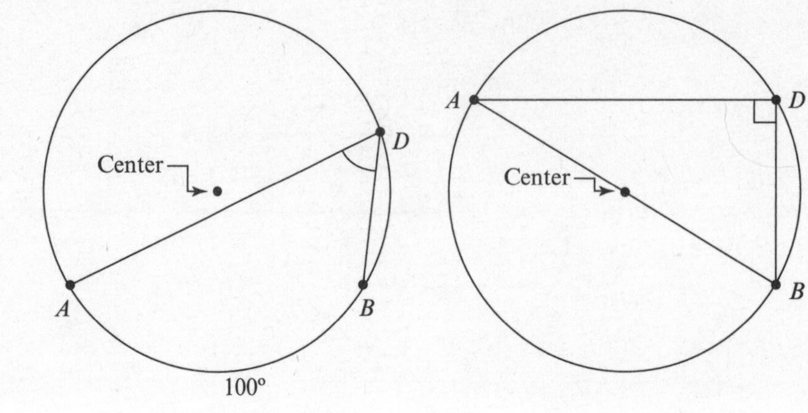

$m\angle ADB = \frac{1}{2}(100°) = 50°$ $m\angle ADB = \frac{1}{2}(180°) = 90°$

If two chords intersect within a circle, each of the angles formed equals one-half the sum of its intercepted arcs. Furthermore, the product of the lengths of the segments formed for one chord equals the product of the lengths of the segments formed for the other chord. In the circle shown below,
$m\angle RVU = m\angle SVT = \frac{1}{2}(50° + 70°) = \frac{1}{2}(120°) = 60°$; and $(RV)(VS) = (UV)(VT)$.

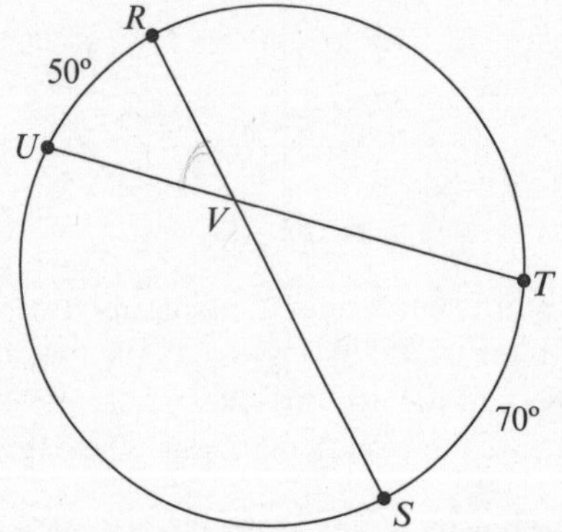

A **secant** to a circle is a line that contains a chord. A **tangent** to a circle is a line in the circle's plane that intersects the circle in only one point. The point of contact is the **point of tangency.** If a line is tangent to a circle, then the radius drawn to the point of tangency will be perpendicular to the tangent. See the following figure.

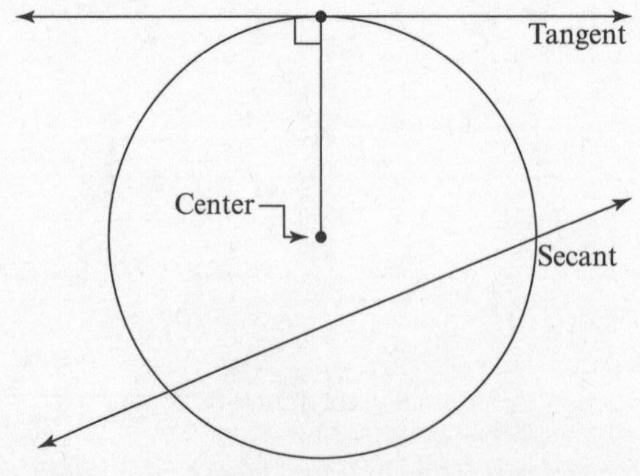

The **length,** L, of an arc that has measure $a°$ is $L = \frac{a°}{360°} \cdot 2\pi r = \frac{a}{180} \cdot \pi r$. For example, in a circle that has radius 18 cm, the length of an arc of 60° is $\frac{60}{180} \cdot \pi(18 \text{ cm}) = 6\pi$ cm.

A **sector** of a circle is a region bounded by two radii and an arc of the circle. The **area,** A, of a sector with radius r and arc measure of $a°$ is $A = \frac{a}{360} \cdot \pi r^2$. For example, in a circle that has radius 18 cm, the area of a sector whose arc has measure of 60° is $\frac{60}{360} \cdot \pi(18 \text{ cm})^2 = \frac{1}{6} \cdot \pi\left(324 \text{ cm}^2\right) = 54\pi \text{ cm}^2$.

The following are additional properties of circles that are useful to know.

- The measure of an angle formed outside a circle by the intersection of two secants, two tangents, or a tangent and a secant equals one-half the difference of the measures of the intercepted arcs.
- The measure of an angle with its vertex on a circle formed by a secant and a tangent equals one-half the measure of the intercepted arc.
- The ratio of the length of the arc intercepted by a central angle to the circumference of the circle equals the ratio of the degree measure of the central angle to 360°.
- Two tangent segments to a circle from an exterior point are congruent. ***Note:*** If a line through a point E that is exterior to a circle is tangent to the circle at point T, then $\overline{ET}$ is a **tangent segment** from E to the circle.
- If two arcs have congruent radii, then the lengths of the arcs are proportional to their measures.
- Concentric circles are circles that have the same center.
- A polygon is inscribed in a circle if each of its vertices lies on the circle.
- A polygon is circumscribed about a circle if each of its sides is tangent to the circle.
- Opposite pairs of interior angles of a quadrilateral inscribed in a circle are supplementary.

Perimeter, Area, and Volume

For this topic, you must be able to compute and reason about perimeter, area, surface area, and volume of two- or three-dimensional figures or of regions or solids that are combinations of these figures.

Geometric Formulas

The following are important formulas for perimeter (P), area (A), surface area ($S.A.$), and volume (V).

Triangle: height h, base b $A = \frac{1}{2}bh$ **Triangle:** sides a, b, and c $P = a + b + c$	**Square:** side s $A = s^2$ $P = 4s$	**Rectangle:** length l, width w $A = lw$ $P = 2l + 2w$	**Parallelogram:** height h, base b $A = bh$ $P = 2b + 2a$

Continued

Circle: radius r, diameter d
$A = \pi r^2$
P = circumference (C) = $2\pi r = \pi d$
diameter $d = 2r$

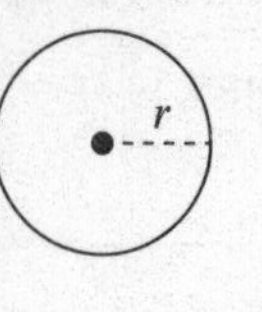

Trapezoid: height h, bases a, b
$A = \frac{1}{2}h(a+b)$
$P = a+b+c+d$

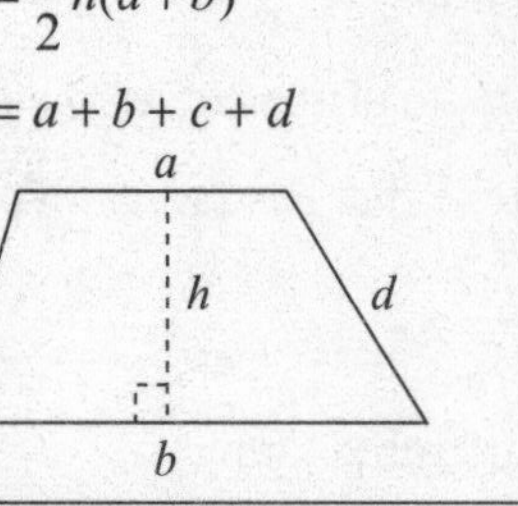

Sphere: radius r
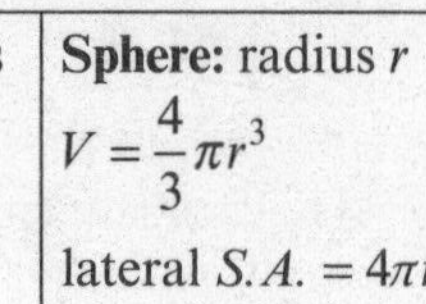
$V = \frac{4}{3}\pi r^3$
lateral $S.A. = 4\pi r^2$

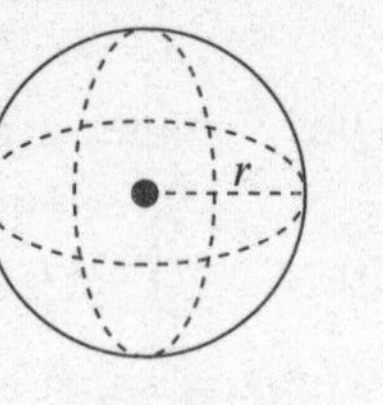

Right prism: height h, area of base B
$V = Bh$
total $S.A. = 2B$ + sum of areas of rectangular lateral faces

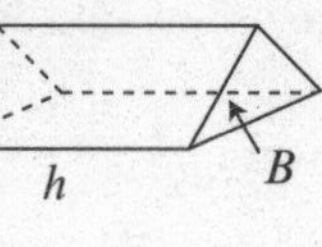

Rectangular prism: length l, width w, height h
$V = lwh$
total $S.A. = 2hl + 2hw + 2lw$

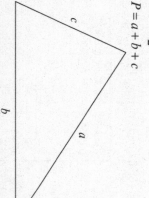

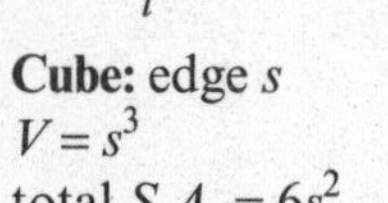

Cube: edge s
$V = s^3$
total $S.A. = 6s^2$

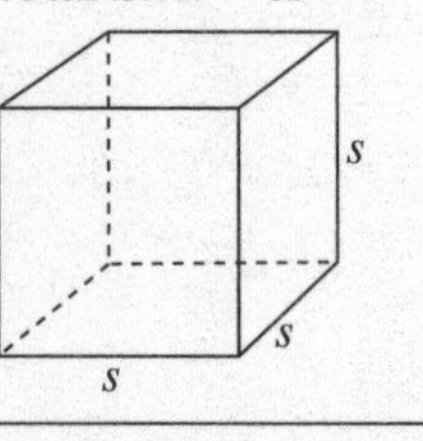

Right circular cylinder: height h, radius of base r
$V = \pi r^2 h$
lateral $S.A. = (2\pi r)h$
total $S.A. = (2\pi r)h + 2(\pi r^2)$

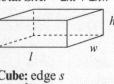

Right pyramid: height h, area of base B
$V = \frac{1}{3}Bh$
total $S.A. = B$ + sum of areas of triangular lateral faces

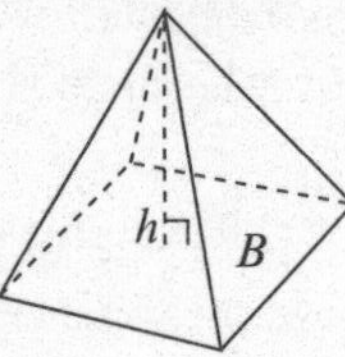

Right circular cone: height h, radius of base r
$V = \frac{1}{3}\pi r^2 h$
lateral $S.A. = \pi r\sqrt{r^2+h^2} = \pi rs$, where s is the slant height = $\sqrt{r^2+h^2}$
total $S.A. = \pi r\sqrt{r^2+h^2} + \pi r^2 = \pi rs + \pi r^2$

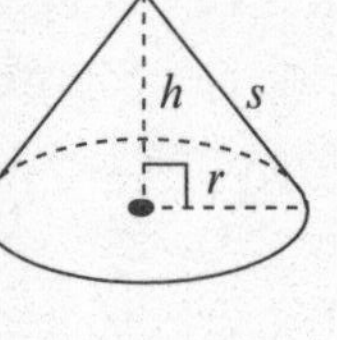

The following are additional helpful formulas.

Scalene triangle: sides a, b, and c
$A = \sqrt{s(s-a)(s-b)(s-c)}$
where
$s = \frac{a+b+c}{2}$
$P = a+b+c$

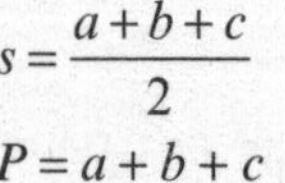
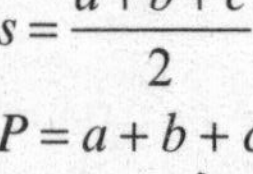
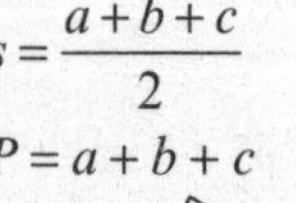
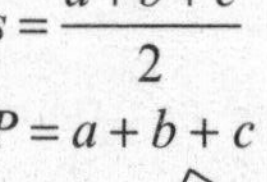
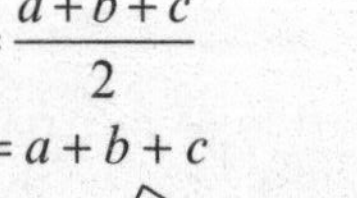
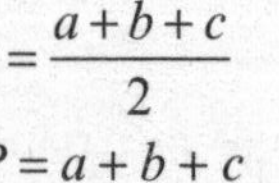
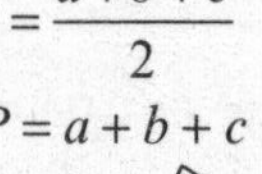
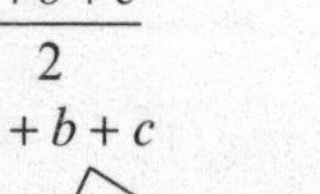
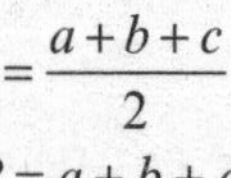
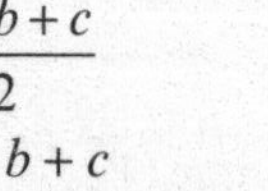
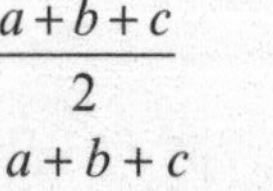
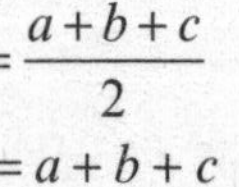

Equilateral triangle: side a
$A = \frac{\sqrt{3}}{4}a^2$
$P = 3a$

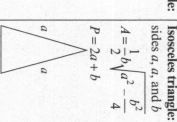

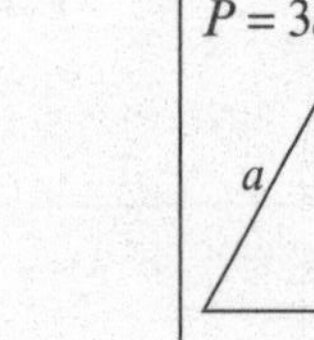

Isosceles triangle: sides a, a, and b
$A = \frac{1}{2}b\sqrt{a^2 - \frac{b^2}{4}}$
$P = 2a + b$

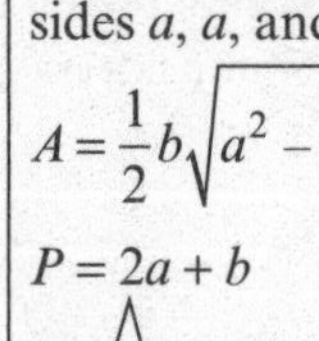

Sector of circle: radius r, θ measure of subtended central angle in radians
$A = \frac{\theta r^2}{2}$
arc length $= s = r\theta$

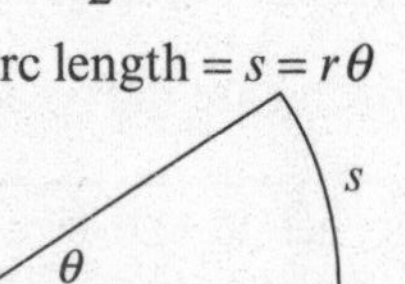

Tip: Rather than memorizing the formulas for the areas of equilateral and isosceles triangles, you may find it easier to construct a suitable altitude, use the Pythagorean theorem to determine its length, and then compute the area of the triangle using the formula area = $\frac{1}{2}bh$.

Tip: In the radian system of angular measurement, 360° = 2π radians. Thus, you have $1° = \frac{\pi}{180}$ radians and 1 radian = $\frac{180°}{\pi}$. See Chapter 5, "Trigonometry," for an additional discussion of radian measurement.

Perimeter and Circumference

A figure's **perimeter** is the distance around it. A circle's perimeter is called its **circumference.** You measure perimeter in units of length, such as inches, feet, yards, miles, kilometers, meters, centimeters, and millimeters. Here is an example of finding the perimeter of a figure that is a combination of figures.

> The figure shown consists of a semicircle of radius r and an attached rectangle whose longer side is $2r$ and whose shorter side is r. What is the perimeter of the figure in terms of r?
>
> 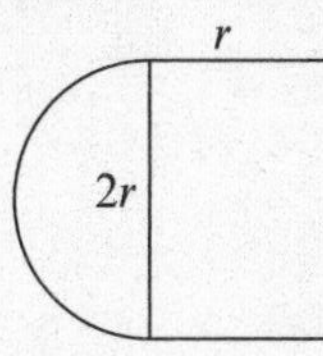
>

The perimeter equals the circumference of the semicircle plus 2 times the shorter side and 1 times the longer side of the attached rectangle.

$$\text{Perimeter} = \frac{1}{2}(2\pi r) + 2 \cdot r + 2r = \pi r + 4r$$

Area

The **area** (A) of a plane figure is the amount of surface enclosed by the figure's boundary. You measure area in square units, such as square inches (in^2), square feet (ft^2), square miles (mi^2), square kilometers (km^2), square meters (m^2), square centimeters (cm^2), and square millimeters (mm^2). The area is always described in terms of square units, regardless of the figure's shape.

A figure's boundary measurements are measured in two dimensions (for example: length and width, base and height). The units for the boundary measurements are linear units (for example: inches, feet, miles, meters, and so on). You obtain the square units needed to describe area when you multiply the unit by itself. For example, $(1 \text{ in})(1 \text{ in}) = 1 \text{ in}^2 = 1$ square inch. Here is an example of finding the area of a triangle.

> Find the area of the triangle with a base of 8 feet and the height to that base of 7 feet.

From the list of formulas, you know that to find the area of a triangle you must know the measure of the triangle's base and height. The base can be any of the triangle's three sides; you can pick any convenient side of the triangle to serve as the base. The height for the base is the length of the perpendicular line segment from the opposite vertex. The formula is $A = \frac{1}{2}bh$, where b is the length of a base of the triangle and h is the height for that base.

Sketch a figure.

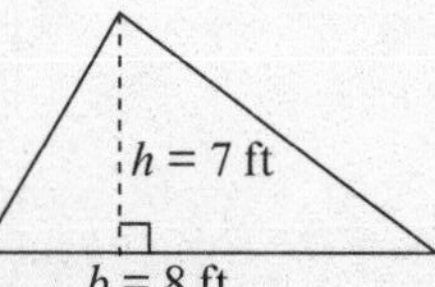

Tip: When you work problems involving geometric figures, sketch a diagram if no diagram is given.

Apply the formula to your figure and compute the area.

$$A = \frac{1}{2}(8\text{ ft})(7\text{ ft}) = 28\text{ ft}^2$$

Here is an example of finding the area of a triangle in the coordinate plane.

The vertices of the triangle shown are $A(-3, 3)$, $B(1, 5)$, and $C(4, 2)$. Determine the area of triangle ABC.

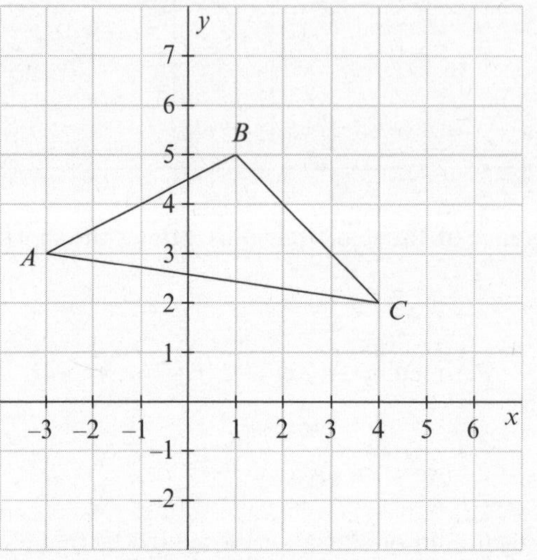

The figure has no horizontal or vertical sides, so you cannot easily find the lengths of the sides or altitudes. To determine the area, enclose the triangle in a rectangle as shown below. Make the rectangle's top side parallel to the x-axis, passing through vertex B of the triangle. Make the rectangle's bottom side parallel to the x-axis, passing through vertex C of the triangle. Make the left side of the rectangle perpendicular to its top and bottom sides, passing through vertex A. Make the right side of the rectangle perpendicular to its top and bottom sides, passing through vertex C. To help keep track of your work, label the coordinates of the vertices in the figure.

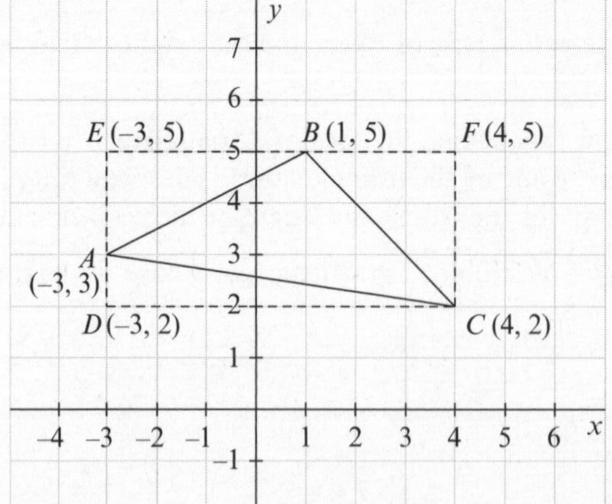

The area of triangle ABC is the area of rectangle $EDCF$ minus the sum of the areas of right triangles ADC, CFB, and BEA. In the figure, you can find the lengths of the sides of the figures by counting the units.

Rectangle $EDCF$ has dimensions 7 by 3 units. Triangle ADC has base 7 units and height 1 unit. Triangle CFB has base 3 units and height 3 units. And triangle BEA has base 4 units and height 2 units.

$$
\begin{aligned}
A &= (7 \text{ units})(3 \text{ units}) - \frac{1}{2}(7 \text{ units})(1 \text{ units}) - \frac{1}{2}(3 \text{ units})(3 \text{ units}) - \frac{1}{2}(4 \text{ units})(2 \text{ units}) \\
&= 21 \text{ units}^2 - 3.5 \text{ units}^2 - 4.5 \text{ units}^2 - 4 \text{ units}^2 \\
&= 9 \text{ units}^2
\end{aligned}
$$

Triangle ABC has area of 9 units^2.

Surface Area

When you have a solid figure such as a rectangular prism (a box), a cylinder, or a pyramid, you can find the area of every face (surface) and add the areas together. The sum is the solid figure's **surface area** (*S.A.*).

Here is an example of finding the surface area of a rectangular box.

What is the surface area of the box shown?

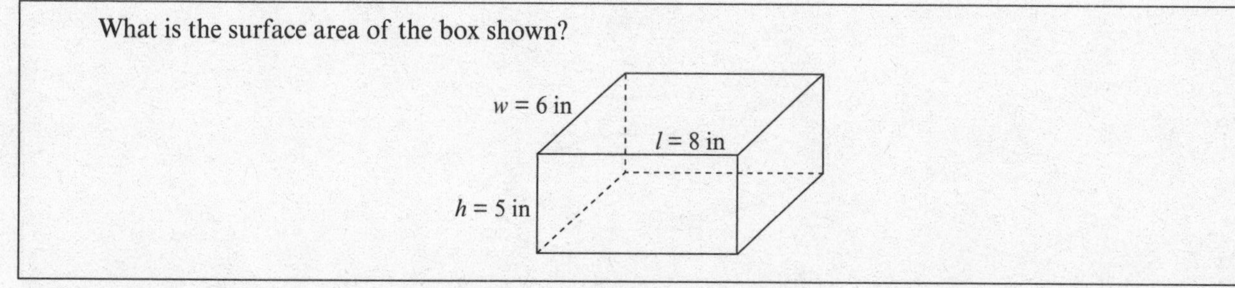

The box is composed of six faces, all of which are rectangles. Use the length and height to find the areas of the front and back faces. Use the length and width to find the areas of the top and bottom faces. Use the width and height to find the areas of the two side faces.

$$S.A. = 2(8 \text{ in})(5 \text{ in}) + 2(8 \text{ in})(6 \text{ in}) + 2(6 \text{ in})(5 \text{ in}) = 80 \text{ in}^2 + 96 \text{ in}^2 + 60 \text{ in}^2 = 236 \text{ in}^2$$

Nets are helpful when you want to find the surface area of a solid figure. A **net** is a two-dimensional shape that can be folded to make a three-dimensional solid figure in which each face is a flat surface. Here are six three-dimensional solids and a corresponding net for each. ***Note:*** Nets are not unique. A solid can have more than one net configuration.

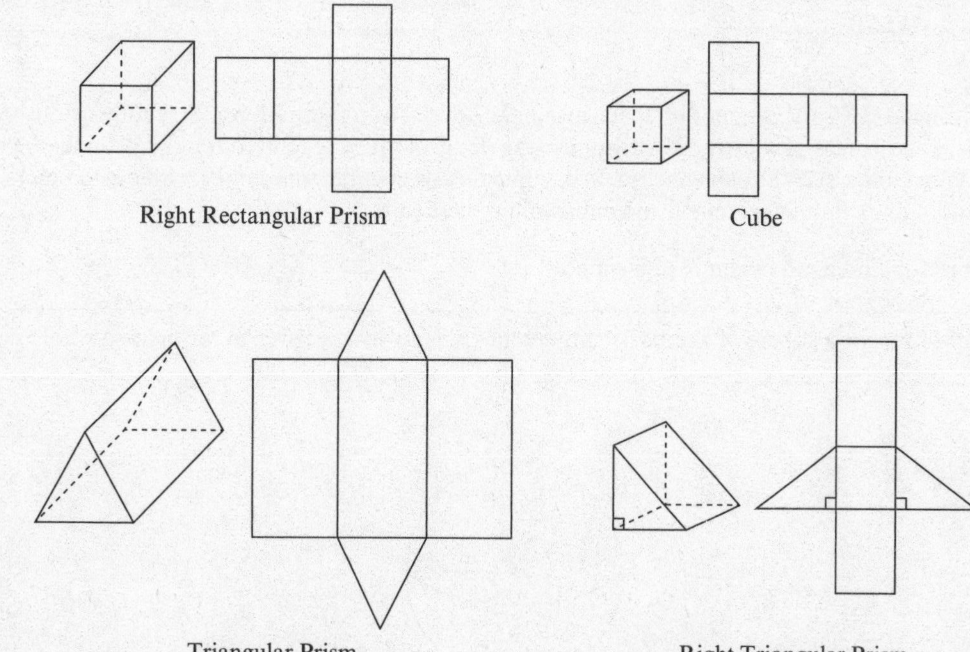

Right Rectangular Prism

Cube

Triangular Prism

Right Triangular Prism

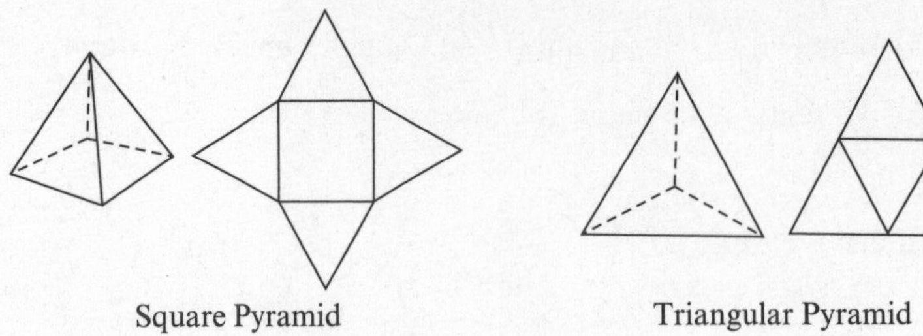

Here is an example of using a net to find surface area.

The grid shows the net for a square pyramid. Find the surface area of the pyramid. Assume each grid box represents a 1-inch by 1-inch square.

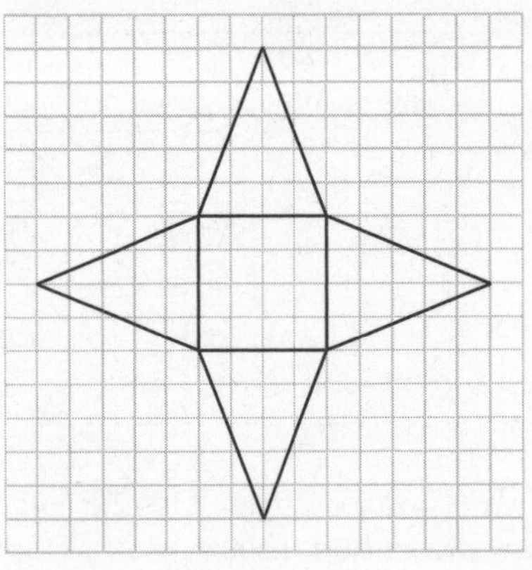

The surface area of the pyramid is the sum of the area of its square base and the areas of its four triangular faces. The square measures 4 inches by 4 inches. Each triangle has base 4 inches and height 5 inches.

$$S.A. = (4\text{ in})(4\text{ in}) + 4\left(\frac{1}{2}\right)(4\text{ in})(5\text{ in}) = 16\text{ in}^2 + 40\text{ in}^2 = 56\text{ in}^2$$

Volume

A solid figure's **volume** (V) is the amount of space inside the solid. Solid figures have three dimensions (for example: length, width, and height of a box). When you use the dimensions of a solid to find its volume, the units for the volume are cubic units, such as cubic inches (in^3), cubic feet (ft^3), cubic miles (mi^3), cubic kilometers (km^3), cubic meters (m^3), cubic centimeters (cm^3), and cubic millimeters (mm^3).

Here is an example of finding the volume of a sphere.

Find the volume of a sphere of radius 6 centimeters. (Round your answer to the nearest whole number.)

Sketch a figure.

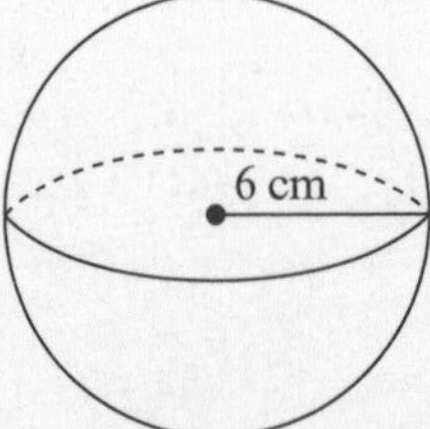

From the list of formulas, you know that the formula for a sphere's volume is $V = \frac{4}{3}\pi r^3$.

Apply the formula to the problem and compute the volume.

$$V = \frac{4}{3}(\pi)(6\text{ cm})^3 \approx 905\text{ cm}^3$$

Note: In the context of rounding, the symbol "≈" is read "is approximately equal to."

Geometric Transformations

A **geometric transformation** is a one-to-one mapping between the points of the plane and themselves. A transformation maps a **preimage** point, P, onto a unique **image** point, P'. Each point is associated with itself or with some other point in the plane. In symbols, this mapping is represented as $P \to P'$ and is read as "the image of P is P prime." In this section, you will learn about four common transformations in the plane: reflections, translations, rotations, and dilations.

Reflections

A **reflection over a line** is a geometric transformation in which every point P is mapped to a new point P' that is the same distance from a fixed line, but on the opposite side of the line. The fixed line is the **line of reflection.** This line is the perpendicular bisector of the segment joining any point to its image. ***Note:*** Any line in the plane can serve as a line of reflection.

A **reflection over the *x*-axis** is a transformation in which $P(x, y) \to P'(x, -y)$. Corresponding points are equidistant from the x-axis as shown below.

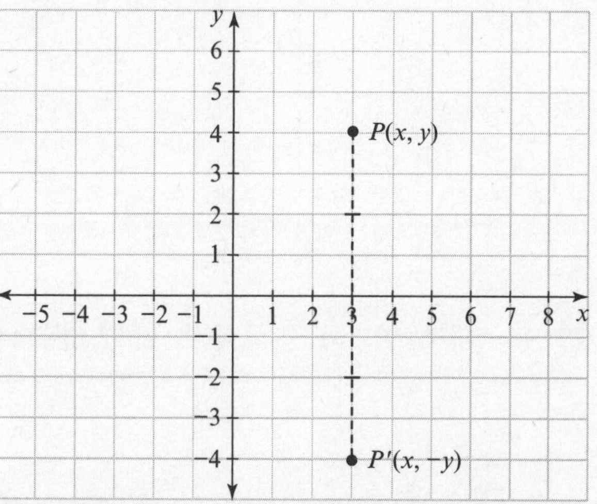

Tip: Under a reflection over the *x*-axis, every *x*-coordinate stays the same and every *y*-coordinate is changed to its opposite.

Here is an illustration.

In the diagram below, triangle $A'B'C'$ is the image of triangle ABC under a reflection over the x-axis. Observe that $A(-4, 3) \to A'(-4, -3)$, $B(-4, 1) \to B'(-4, -1)$, and $C(2, 1) \to C'(2, -1)$.

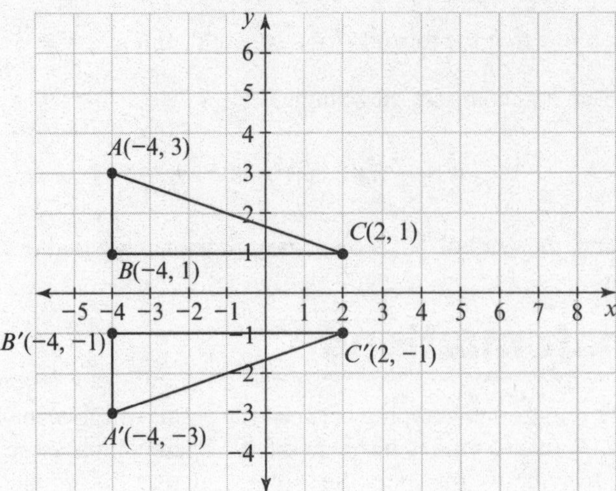

A **reflection over the *y*-axis** is a transformation in which $P(x, y) \to P'(-x, y)$. Corresponding points are equidistant from the *y*-axis as shown below.

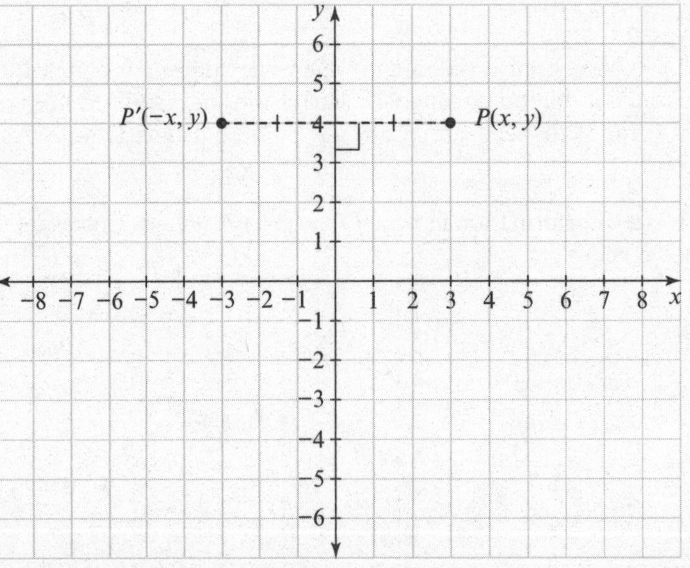

Tip: Under a reflection over the *y*-axis, every *y*-coordinate stays the same and every *x*-coordinate is changed to its opposite.

Here is an illustration.

In the diagram below, segment $\overline{A'B'}$ is the image of segment $\overline{AB}$ under a reflection over the *y*-axis. Observe that $A(2, 4) \to A'(-2, 4)$ and $B(5, 1) \to B'(-5, 1)$.

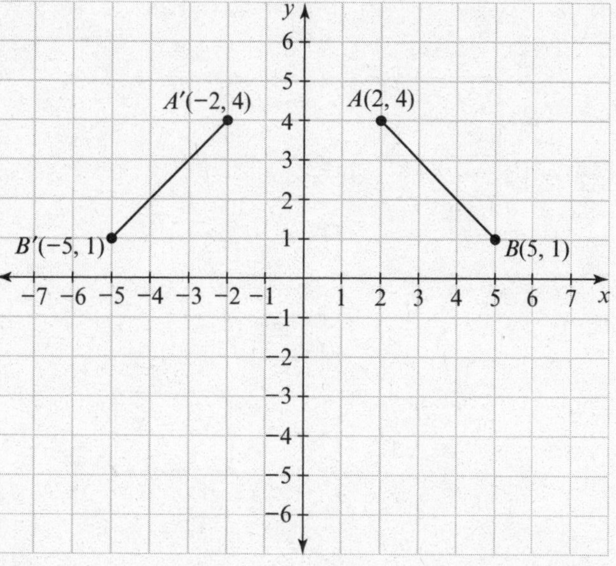

A **reflection in a point** is a geometric transformation about a fixed **point of reflection** for which every point P is mapped to a new point P' directly opposite it on the other side of the point of reflection, so that the point of reflection is the midpoint of the segment joining the original point with its image. ***Note:*** Any point in the plane can serve as a point of reflection.

A **reflection in the origin** is a transformation in which $P(x, y) \rightarrow P'(-x, -y)$. The origin is the midpoint of segment $\overline{PP'}$ joining corresponding points as shown below.

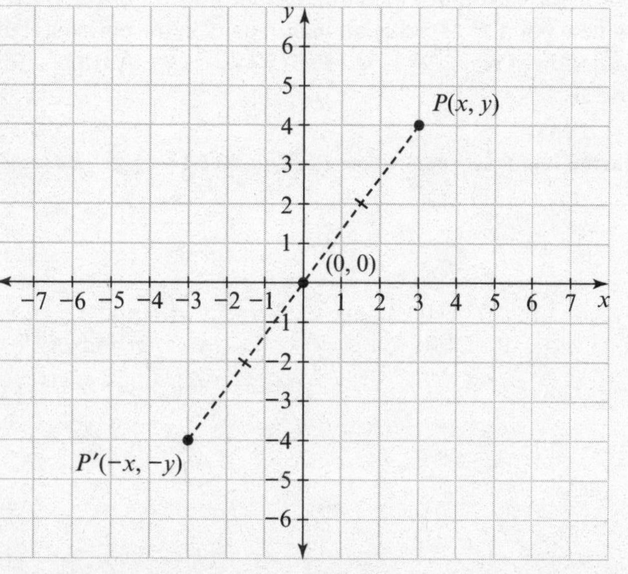

Tip: Under a reflection in the origin, every *x*-coordinate and every *y*-coordinate is changed to its opposite.

Here is an illustration.

In the diagram below, rectangle $A'B'C'D'$ is the image of rectangle $ABCD$ under a reflection in the origin. Observe that $A(2, -3) \rightarrow A'(-2, 3)$, $B(2, -5) \rightarrow B'(-2, 5)$, $C(5, -5) \rightarrow C'(-5, 5)$, and $D(5, -3) \rightarrow D'(-5, 3)$.

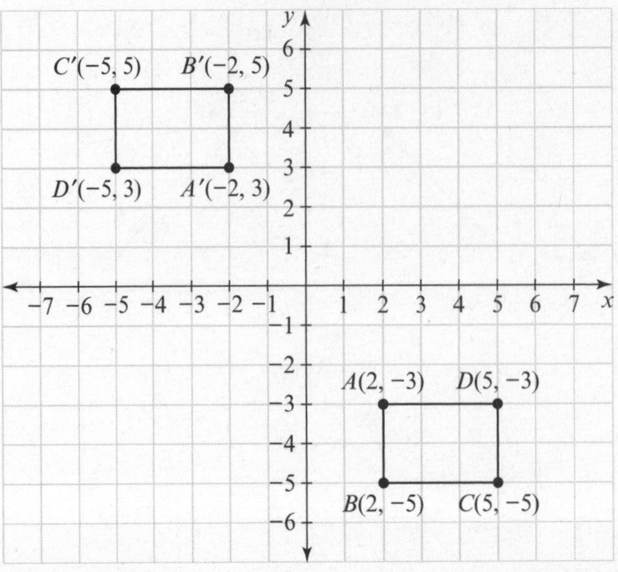

Tip: As the illustrations in this discussion of reflections show, you can think of reflections as "flips." The image is the result of flipping the preimage over the line of reflection so that the new figure is a mirror image of the original.

Translations

A **translation** is a geometric transformation in which every point P is mapped a fixed distance in the same direction along a straight line to a new point P'. A **translation of h units in the horizontal direction and k units in the vertical direction** is a transformation in which $P(x, y) \to P'(x + h, y + k)$. A translation moves every point h units horizontally and k units vertically.

Tip: In a translation, you merely add h to each x-coordinate and k to each y-coordinate.

Here is an illustration.

In the diagram below, segment $\overline{A'B'}$ is the image of segment $\overline{AB}$ under a translation of 3 units horizontally and –2 units vertically. Observe that $A(2, 4) \to A'(5, 2)$ and $B(3, 1) \to B'(6, -1)$.

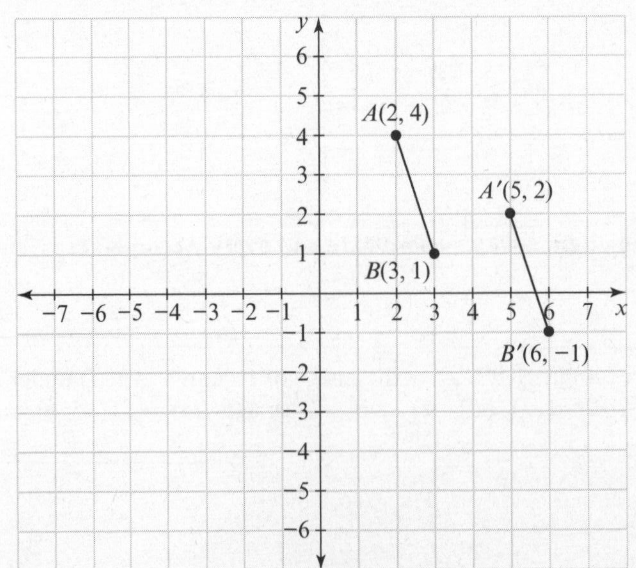

Tip: You can think of translations as "slides," which is shown in the previous illustration. You slide the preimage right or left or up or down, or a combination of these moves. The result is the image.

Rotations

A **rotation** is a geometric transformation in which every point P is "rotated" through an angle around a fixed point, called the **center of rotation.** A figure has **rotational symmetry** if there is a rotation of less than 360° in which the image and its preimage coincide under the rotation.

The following discussion presents coordinate rules for three types of rotations about the origin O: a counterclockwise rotation of 90° about O, a counterclockwise rotation of 180° about O, and a counterclockwise rotation of 270° about O.

Tip: Think of rotations as "turns" around a point.

A **counterclockwise rotation of 90° about the origin O** is a transformation in which $P(x, y) \to P'(-y, x)$. The angle POP' is a right angle as shown below.

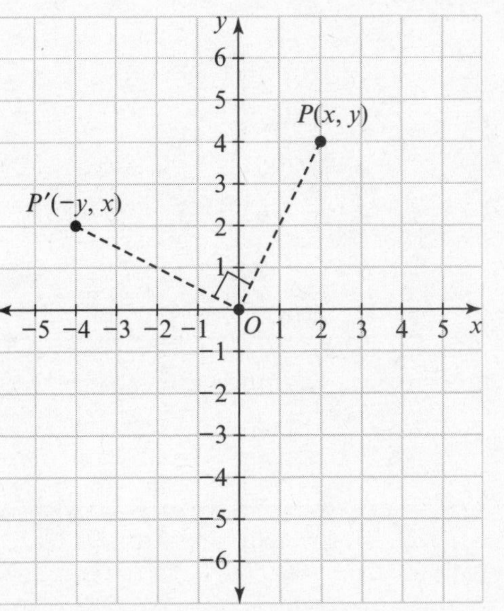

Here is an illustration.

In the diagram below, rectangle $A'B'C'D'$ is the image of rectangle $ABCD$ under a rotation of 90° about the origin. Observe that $A(2, -3) \to A'(3, 2)$, $B(2, -5) \to B'(5, 2)$, $C(5, -5) \to C'(5, 5)$, and $D(5, -3) \to D'(3, 5)$.

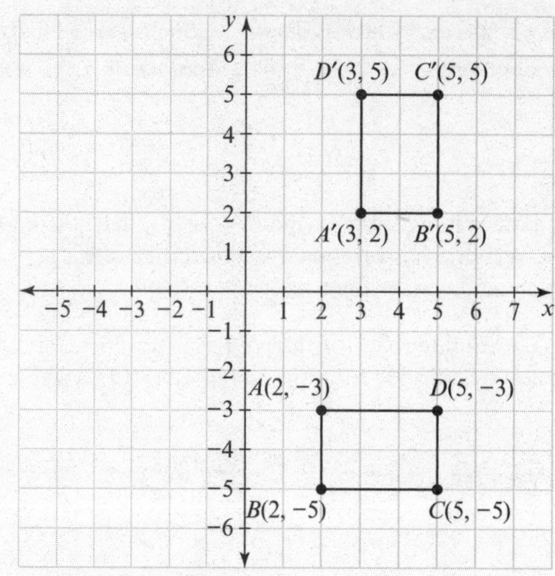

A **counterclockwise rotation of 180° about the origin** O is a transformation in which $P(x, y) \rightarrow P'(-x, -y)$. The measure of angle POP' is 180° as shown below.

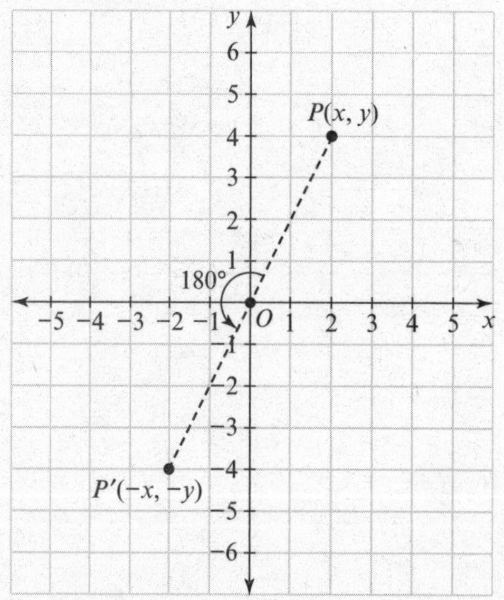

Tip: A counterclockwise rotation of 180° about the origin O is equivalent to a reflection in the origin.

Here is an illustration.

In the diagram below, segment $\overline{A'B'}$ is the image of segment $\overline{AB}$ under a rotation of 180° about the origin. Observe that $A(2, 4) \rightarrow A'(-2, -4)$ and $B(5, 1) \rightarrow B'(-5, -1)$.

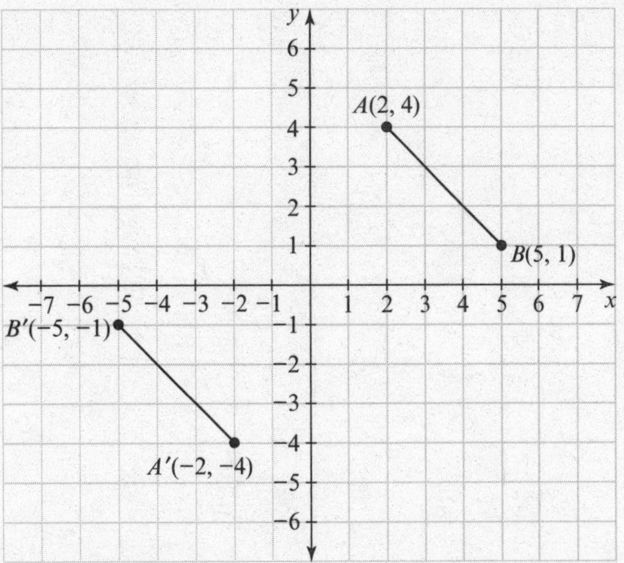

A **counterclockwise rotation of 270° about the origin *O*** is a transformation in which $P(x, y) \rightarrow P'(y, -x)$. The measure of angle POP' is 270° as shown below. The angle is measured *counterclockwise* from $\overline{OP}$ to $\overline{OP'}$.

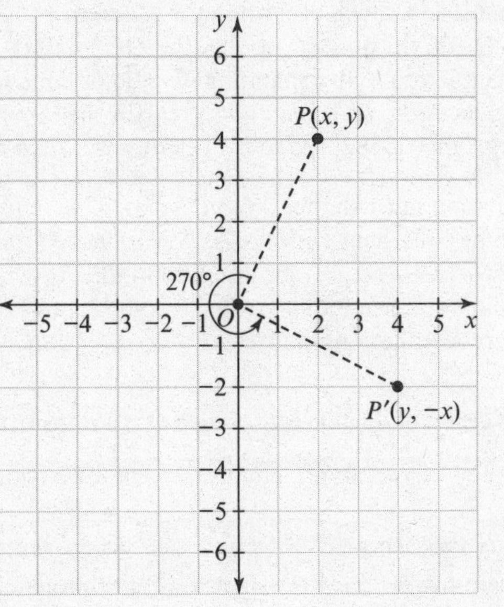

Here is an illustration.

In the diagram below, triangle $A'B'C'$ is the image of triangle ABC under a rotation of 270° about the origin. Observe that $A(3, -2) \rightarrow A'(-2, -3)$, $B(2, -5) \rightarrow B'(-5, -2)$, and $C(5, -5) \rightarrow C'(-5, -5)$.

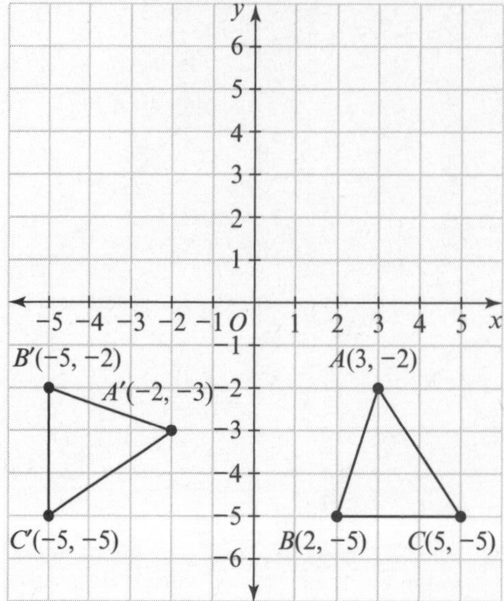

Dilations

A **dilation** is a geometric transformation in which every point P is mapped to a new point P', where the point P' lies on a ray through a fixed point O and the point P, so that the $\overline{OP'} = |k|\overline{OP}$, where k is a nonzero real number, called the **scale factor.** Informally, a dilation is an expanding ($|k| > 1$) or contracting ($|k| < 1$) of a geometric shape using a scale factor, while its shape, location, and orientation remain the same. In the case that $|k| = 1$, the dilated image is congruent to the original geometric shape, and the dilation is a rigid motion.

Note: Some sources insist that a dilation must change a figure's size. This requirement would exclude the scale factor k, where $|k| = 1$. However, to be consistent with the *2008 National Mathematics Advisory Panel Report of the Task Group on Learning Processes* (www.ed.gov/about/bdscomm/list/mathpanel/index.html), which suggests the use of dilation in defining similarity, the case that results in congruency between the image and preimage must be included (given that similar figures can be congruent).

A **dilation of scale factor r where the center of dilation is the origin O** is a transformation in which $P(x, y) \to P'(rx, ry)$, where $r > 0$. Under a dilation, the ratio of OP' to OP equals the dilation's scale factor r. That is, $\frac{OP'}{OP} = r$.

Note: Any point can be chosen as the center of dilation. Also, scale factors can be negative. In this book, dilations are limited to those where the origin is the center of dilation and scale factors are positive.

Under a dilation, if the scale factor r is greater than 1, the image is an **enlargement** of the preimage and has the same shape. If the scale factor is between 0 and 1, the image is a **reduction** of the preimage and has the same shape. If the scale factor equals 1, the preimage and image are the same size and shape.

Here are illustrations.

In the diagram below, segment $\overline{A'B'}$ is the image of segment $\overline{AB}$ under a dilation of 2. Observe that $A(2, 1) \to A'(4, 2)$ and $B(3, -2) \to B'(6, -4)$.

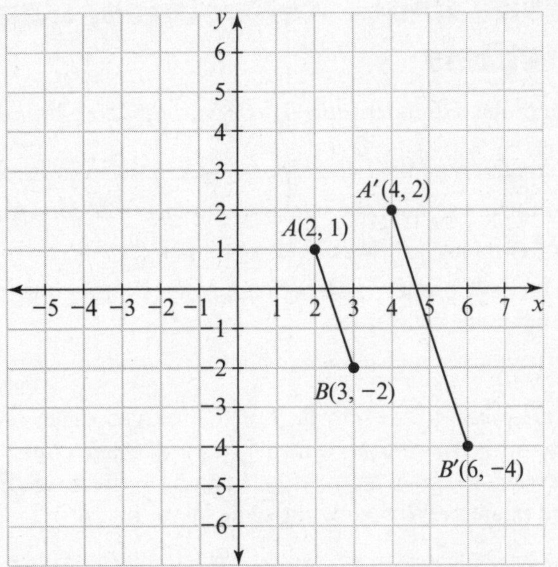

In the diagram below, rectangle $A'B'C'D'$ is the image of rectangle $ABCD$ under a dilation of $\frac{1}{2}$. Observe that $A(-4, 5) \rightarrow A'(-2, 2.5)$, $B(-4, -5) \rightarrow B'(-2, -2.5)$, $C(4, -5) \rightarrow C'(2, -2.5)$, and $D(4, 5) \rightarrow D'(2, 2.5)$.

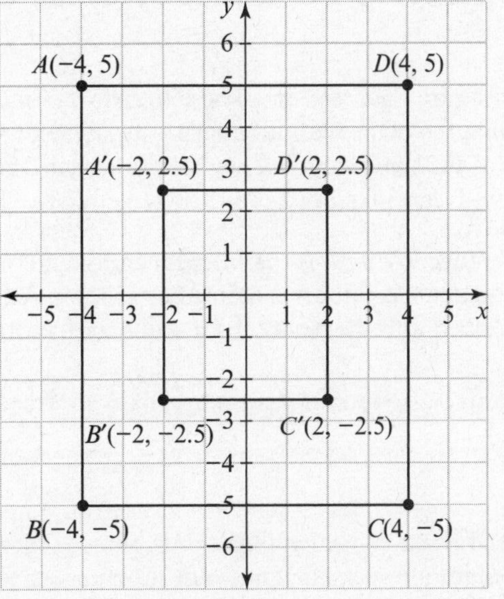

Summary of Coordinate Rules for Geometric Transformations

The following is a summary of the coordinate rules for the common transformation types presented in this chapter.

Transformation	Coordinate Rule
Reflection over the x-axis	$P(x, y) \rightarrow P'(x, -y)$
Reflection over the y-axis	$P(x, y) \rightarrow P'(-x, y)$
Reflection in the origin	$P(x, y) \rightarrow P'(-x, -y)$
Counterclockwise rotation of 90° about the origin	$P(x, y) \rightarrow P'(-y, x)$
Counterclockwise rotation of 180° about the origin	$P(x, y) \rightarrow P'(-x, -y)$
Counterclockwise rotation of 270° about the origin	$P(x, y) \rightarrow P'(y, -x)$
Translation of h units in the horizontal direction and k units in the vertical direction	$P(x, y) \rightarrow P'(x+h, y+k)$
Dilation of scale factor r where center of dilation is the origin	$P(x, y) \rightarrow P'(rx, ry)$, $r > 0$

Properties Preserved Under Reflections, Translations, Rotations, and Dilations

The following five properties are preserved under *reflections, translations,* and *rotations*:

- Distance—Lengths in the image equal their corresponding lengths in the preimage.
- Angle measure—Angles in the image have the same measure as their corresponding angles in the preimage.
- Parallelism—The images of two parallel lines are also parallel lines.
- Collinearity—The images of three or more points that lie on a straight line (that is, the points are collinear) will also lie on a straight line in the same order.
- Midpoint—The image of the midpoint of a line segment is the midpoint of the line segment's image.

The properties preserved under *dilations* include only four of the five properties preserved under reflections, translations, and rotations. These properties are angle measure, parallelism, collinearity, and midpoint. Dilations do not preserve distance (except when the scale factor is 1). Lengths in the image figure are equal to their corresponding lengths in the preimage figure multiplied by the scale factor r.

Tip: A dilation maps a line not containing the center of dilation to a parallel line.

Congruence and Similarity in the Context of Geometric Transformations

Reflections, translations, and rotations are **rigid motions.** These transformations are rigid motions because they move a figure to a different location in the plane without altering its shape or size. They take lines to lines. They take line segments to line segments of the same length. They take angles to angles of the same measure. They take parallel lines to parallel lines. And they take points to their same relative locations.

Under reflections, translations, and rotations, figures (preimages) and their corresponding images are congruent. Therefore, **congruence** of two plane geometric figures is defined as follows: A two-dimensional figure is congruent to another if the first can be transformed into the second by a sequence of rotations, reflections, and translations.

Tip: The sequence of transformations that results in two congruent figures is not necessarily unique.

Here is an illustration.

> In the diagram, trapezoids I and II are congruent. One possible sequence of transformations whereby Trapezoid I can be transformed into Trapezoid II is a reflection across the y-axis, followed by a translation of 1 unit right and 8 units down. Specifically, $(-5, 5) \to (5, 5) \to (6, -3)$; $(-5, 3) \to (5, 3) \to (6, -5)$; $(-2, 3) \to (2, 3) \to (3, -5)$; $(-3, 5) \to (3, 5) \to (4, -3)$.

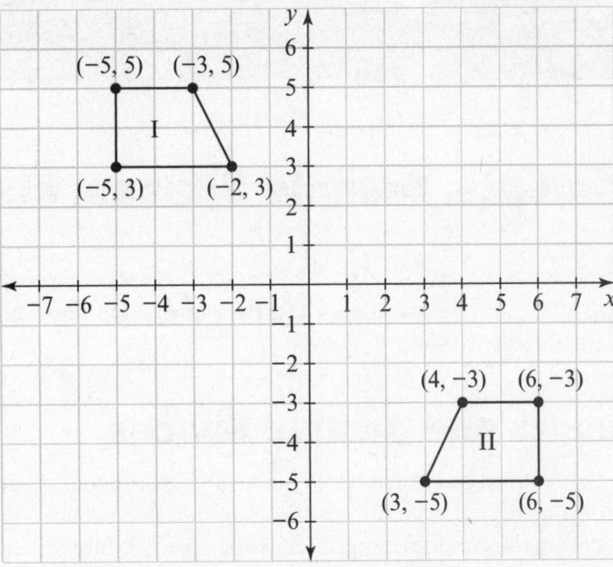

Dilations are *not* rigid motions. However, dilations *do* take angles to angles of the same measure. They take parallel lines to parallel lines. And they take points to their same relative locations. Under dilations, figures (preimages) and their images are similar. Therefore, **similarity** of two plane geometric figures is defined as follows: A two-dimensional figure is similar to another if the first can be transformed into the second by a sequence of rotations, reflections, translations, and dilations.

Tip: The sequence of transformations that results in two similar figures is not necessarily unique.

Here is an illustration.

In the diagram, triangles I and II are similar. A possible sequence of transformations that transforms Triangle I into Triangle II is a counterclockwise rotation of 90°, followed by a dilation of 1.5. Specifically, $(2, 5) \rightarrow (-5, 2) \rightarrow (-7.5, 3)$; $(3, 2) \rightarrow (-2, 3) \rightarrow (-3, 4.5)$; $(6, 4) \rightarrow (-4, 6) \rightarrow (-6, 9)$.

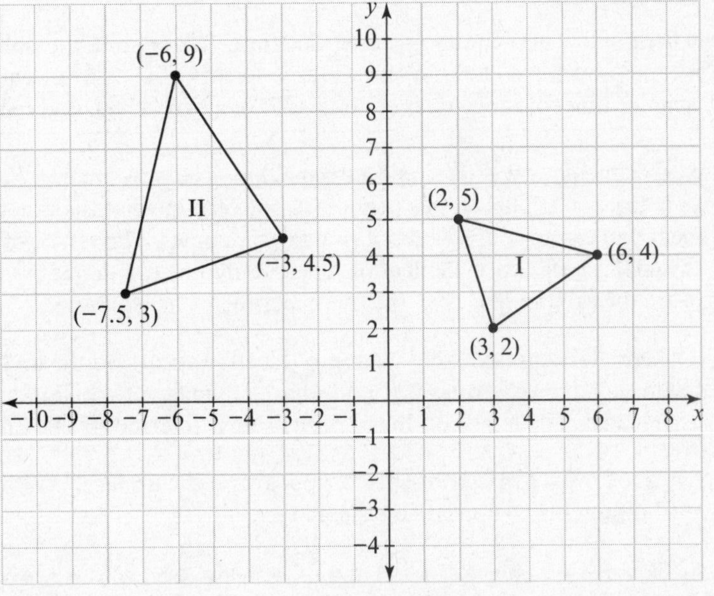

Note: See "Congruence, Similarity, and Symmetry" and "Congruent and Similar Triangles" earlier in this chapter for additional discussions of congruence and similarity. Also, see "Representation of Geometric Transformations" in Chapter 10, "Matrices," for an additional discussion of geometric transformations.

Chapter 8

Probability

Random Experiments, Sample Spaces, and Probability Measures

This topic presents the concepts of random experiments and their corresponding sample spaces and introduces you to probability measures associated with sample spaces.

Random Experiments and Sample Spaces

A **chance process** gives results that cannot be determined beforehand. A **random experiment** is a chance process such that, on any single repetition of the experiment, exactly one outcome occurs. It is assumed that all the possible outcomes are known before the random experiment is performed, but which of the possibilities will in fact occur is uncertain. Here are examples. (***Note:*** To facilitate the discussion that follows, the experiments are numbered; when no confusion might occur, experiment means "random experiment.")

Experiment 1: Flip a U.S. coin one time and observe the coin's up face.

Experiment 2: Perform one toss of a number cube, whose six faces are numbered 1 through 6, and observe the up face.

Experiment 3: Draw one card (without looking) from a well-shuffled standard deck of 52 playing cards and observe which card was drawn. (***Note:*** When you draw without looking you are making a random selection.)

Experiment 4: Draw one tile (without looking) from a box containing five wooden, 1-inch square tiles numbered 1 through 5, and observe the up face.

Experiment 5: Spin the pointer of a circular spinner one time. In one spin, the pointer will turn a random number of times and stop. The spinner has three sectors. The color of each sector and the percentage of the spinner that color occupies are blue (25%), green (25%), and red (50%).

For each of these random experiments you get a single **outcome** that occurs by chance. You cannot determine with certainty the outcome beforehand. That is, you cannot say for certain what the exact outcome will be. However, for each experiment you can produce its set of *possible* outcomes. The set, S, of possible outcomes of a random experiment is its **sample space.** Each element of S is an outcome (or **simple event, sample point,** or **elementary outcome**). Here are the sample spaces of the five experiments listed above.

Experiment 1: $S = \{H, T\}$, where "H" represents the outcome "Heads appears on the up face" and "T" represents the outcome "Tails appears on the up face." ***Note:*** U.S. coins have an image of a historical figure (person) on one side, which is referred to as "Heads." The image on the opposite side is referred to as "Tails."

Experiment 2: $S = \{1, 2, 3, 4, 5, 6\}$, where "1" represents "1 appears on the up face," "2" represents "2 appears on the up face," and so on to "6" represents "6 appears on the up face."

Experiment 3: S = {♣A, ♣2, ♣3, ♣4, ♣5, ♣6, ♣7, ♣8, ♣9, ♣10, ♣J, ♣Q, ♣K, ♠A, ♠2, ♠3, ♠4, ♠5, ♠6, ♠7, ♠8, ♠9, ♠10, ♠J, ♠Q, ♠K, ♥A, ♥2, ♥3, ♥4, ♥5, ♥6, ♥7, ♥8, ♥9, ♥10, ♥J, ♥Q, ♥K, ♦A, ♦2, ♦3, ♦4, ♦5, ♦6, ♦7, ♦8, ♦9, ♦10, ♦J, ♦Q, ♦K}, where ♣A represents the ace of clubs, ♣2 represents the 2 of clubs, ... ♣J represents the jack of clubs, ♣Q represents the queen of clubs, ♣K represents the king of clubs, and so on to ♦A represents the ace of diamonds, ♦2 represents the 2 of diamonds, ... ♦J represents the jack of diamonds, ♦Q represents the queen of diamonds, and ♦K represents the king of diamonds. ***Note:*** A standard deck of 52 playing cards consists of four suits: clubs (♣), spades (♠), hearts (♥), and diamonds (♦). Clubs and spades are black-colored suits; hearts and diamonds are red-colored suits. Each suit has 13 cards consisting of three face cards (king, queen, and jack) and number cards from 1 (ace) to 10 as shown in the following black and white illustration.

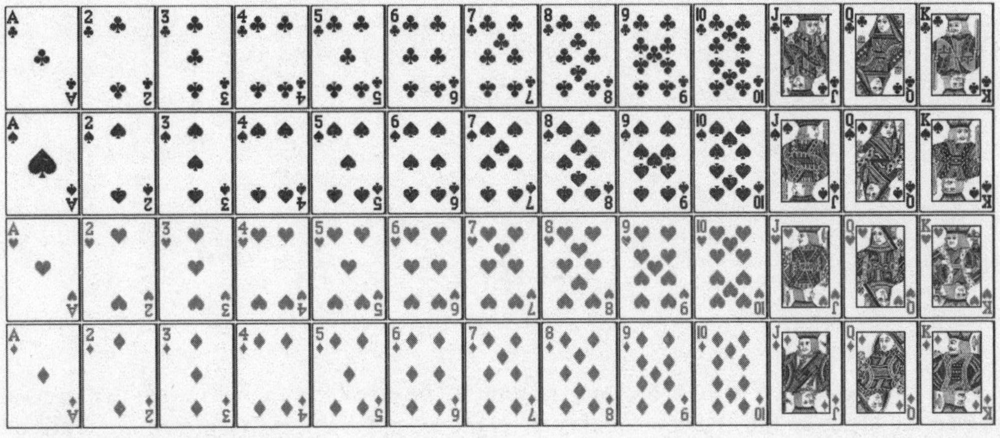

Source: *www.jfitz.com/cards/*

Experiment 4: $S = \{1, 2, 3, 4, 5\}$, where "1" represents the outcome "the tile drawn shows a 1," "2" represents the outcome "the tile drawn shows a 2," and so on to "5" represents the outcome "the tile drawn shows a 5."

Experiment 5: $S = \{B, G, R\}$, where "B" represents the outcome "the pointer stops on blue," "G" represents the outcome "the pointer stops on green," and "R" represents the outcome "the pointer stops on red."

Note: A sample space can be finite or infinite. In this book, only finite sample spaces are considered.

Sometimes random experiments have several stages. For example, consider the experiment of flipping two coins and observing the up faces. Think of the experiment as having two stages. First, flip the first coin and observe the up face. Next, flip the second coin and observe the up face. Three common methods for generating the possible outcomes for such an experiment are organized lists, tables, and tree diagrams.

Here is an example of using an **organized list** to generate the possible outcomes.

Proceed systematically. First, list H twice on the first coin with each of the possibilities (H, T) for the second coin. Next, list T twice on the first coin with each of the possibilities (H, T) for the second coin.

First Coin	Second Coin
H	H
H	T
T	H
T	T

Tip: When you use an organized list to count possibilities, be careful to proceed in a systematic manner, as shown in the example above. Otherwise, you might overlook a possibility or count one more than once.

Here is an example of using a **table** to generate the possible outcomes.

	First Coin	
Second Coin	H	T
H	HH	HT
T	TH	TT

Here is an example of using a **tree diagram** to generate the possible outcomes.

First, draw a branch for each possibility for the first stage (in this case, the first coin). Next, attach branches for each possibility for the second stage (in this case, the second coin) to each of the possibilities for the first stage. Then, list the possible outcomes by tracing along the branches.

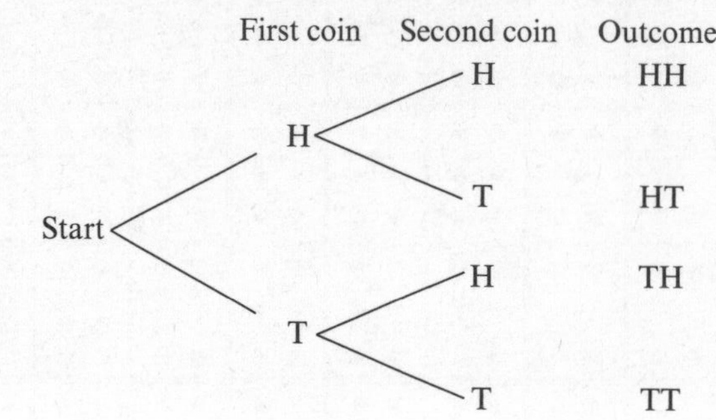

Each of the three methods results in the same four outcomes. The possible outcomes when two coins are flipped are HH (representing heads on the first coin and heads on the second coin), HT (representing heads on the first coin and tails on the second coin), TH (representing tails on the first coin and heads on the second coin), and TT (representing tails on the first coin and tails on the second coin). Therefore, S = {HH, HT, TH, TT} is the sample space for flipping two coins.

Notice that HT and TH are *not* the same outcome. HT is the outcome of heads on the first coin and tails on the second coin, but TH is the outcome of tails on the first coin and heads on the second coin.

You can extend organized lists and tree diagrams to three or more stages. Here is a tree diagram for flipping three coins.

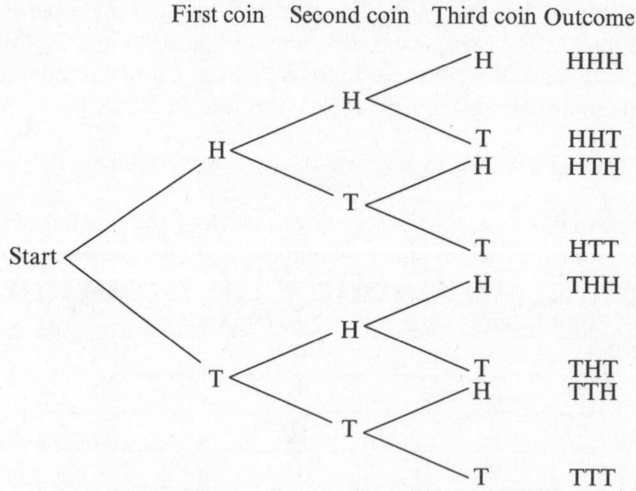

S = {HHH, HHT, HTH, HTT, THH, THT, TTH, TTT} is the sample space for flipping three coins. The number of possible outcomes is 8.

Determining the outcomes in a sample space is a critical step in solving a probability problem. For simple experiments, organized lists, tables, and tree diagrams are useful ways to generate a list of the outcomes. More sophisticated counting techniques, which include the fundamental counting principle, permutations, and combinations, are needed for problems that are less straightforward. See "Counting Techniques" in Chapter 11 for a discussion of these methods.

Probability Measures

A **probability measure** on a sample space, S, is a function that assigns to each outcome in S a real number between 0 and 1, inclusive, so that the values assigned to the outcomes in S sum to 1. (For a general discussion of functions, see Chapter 4.). The value assigned to an outcome in S is the **probability value** of that outcome.

Consider the sample space $S = \{1, 2, 3, 4, 5\}$ from Experiment 4 of drawing one tile (without looking) from a box containing five wooden, 1-inch square tiles numbered 1 through 5. Given that the tiles are physically identical and the drawing is performed without looking (that is, randomly), each tile has a 1 in 5 chance of being drawn. Thus, a logical probability value for each of the five outcomes in S is $\frac{1}{5}$. The sum of the probability values of the five outcomes in S is $\frac{1}{5}+\frac{1}{5}+\frac{1}{5}+\frac{1}{5}+\frac{1}{5}=\frac{5}{5}=1$.

Consider the sample space $S = \{B, G, R\}$ from Experiment 5 of spinning the pointer of a circular spinner one time, where the spinner has three sectors that are colored blue (25%), green (25%), and red (50%). A logical probability value for the outcome B is $\frac{1}{4}$, for the outcome G is $\frac{1}{4}$, and for the outcome R is $\frac{1}{2}$. The sum of the probability values of the three outcomes in S is $\frac{1}{4}+\frac{1}{4}+\frac{1}{2}=\frac{4}{4}=1$.

Consider the sample space $S = \{HHH, HHT, HTH, HTT, THH, THT, TTH, TTT\}$ from the experiment of flipping three coins. A logical probability value for each of the eight outcomes in S is $\frac{1}{8}$. The sum of the probability values of the eight outcomes in S is $\frac{1}{8}+\frac{1}{8}+\frac{1}{8}+\frac{1}{8}+\frac{1}{8}+\frac{1}{8}+\frac{1}{8}+\frac{1}{8}=\frac{8}{8}=1$.

Tip: For a sample space resulting from a real-world chance experiment, usually there is only one probability measure that is considered appropriate. In particular, objects such as coins and number cubes are considered to be fair; that is, such objects do not favor one outcome over another.

According to the frequency theory of probability, the probability values assigned to the outcomes of a sample space are the limiting values of the proportions of times over many repetitions that the experiment will result in the different possible outcomes. (See "Frequency Theory of Probability" later in this chapter for a discussion of this topic.)

Random Variables, Probability Distributions, and Expected Value

This topic presents the concept of random variables and their related probability distributions. You will calculate the expected value of a random variable and interpret the result as the mean of the probability distribution.

Random Variables and Probability Distributions

A **random variable** is a function X that assigns a real number x, determined by chance, to each and every outcome in a sample space S. The number x is the **value** of the random variable. It is determined by the outcome of a random experiment.

Note: Random variables are usually denoted by uppercase letters, often X, Y, or Z.

Like probability measures, a random variable is a function over a sample space; however (unlike probability measures), there are no restrictions on the values assigned to the outcomes of S, nor to their sum.

Note: Random variables can be discrete or continuous. This chapter deals only with discrete random variables. A discrete random variable is one in which its values can be counted or listed.

The **probability distribution** of a discrete random variable gives the probability for each of the random variable's values in a graph, chart, or table, or by means of a formula.

Consider the sample space $S = \{1, 2, 3, 4, 5\}$ from Experiment 4 (given previously) of drawing one tile (without looking) from a box containing five wooden, 1-inch square tiles numbered 1 through 5. Define the random variable X as the function that assigns the value 1 to the outcomes that show an even number on the drawn tile and the value 6 to the outcomes that show an odd number on the drawn tile. The possible values for the random variable X are 1 and 6. Specifically, $X(1) = 6$, $X(2) = 1$, $X(3) = 6$, $X(4) = 1$, and $X(5) = 6$. Notice that a random variable can assign the same value to more than one outcome in the sample space. The following table represents the probability distribution for X.

x	$P(X = x)$
1	$\frac{2}{5}$
6	$\frac{3}{5}$

The entries in the $P(X = x)$ column sum to 1 (that is, $\frac{2}{5} + \frac{3}{5} = \frac{5}{5} = 1$) because X assigns every outcome in S one and only one of the values 1 or 6.

Consider the sample space $S = \{$HHH, HHT, HTH, HTT, THH, THT, TTH, TTT$\}$ from the experiment (given previously) of flipping three coins. Define the random variable Y as the number of heads observed in an outcome. The possible values for the random variable Y are 0, 1, 2, and 3. Specifically, Y(HHH) = 3, Y(HHT) = 2, Y(HTH) = 2, Y(HTT) = 1, Y(THH) = 2, Y(THT) = 1, Y(TTH) = 1, and Y(TTT) = 0. The following graph represents the probability distribution for Y.

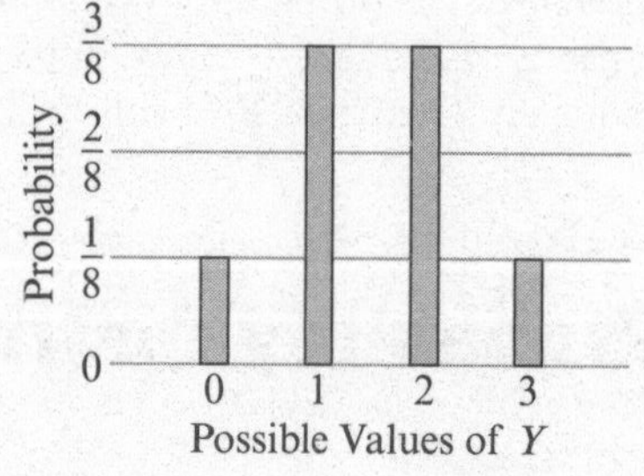

The probabilities for the possible values of Y sum to 1 (that is, $\frac{1}{8} + \frac{3}{8} + \frac{3}{8} + \frac{1}{8} = \frac{8}{8} = 1$) because Y assigns every outcome in S one and only one of the values 0, 1, 2, or 3.

Expected Value

If X is a discrete random variable that takes on values $x_1, x_2, \ldots, x_n$, with respective probabilities $P(x_1), P(x_2), \ldots, P(x_n)$, the **expected value**, denoted $E(X)$, is the **theoretical mean** μ of X and is given by

$$\mu = E(X) = x_1P(x_1) + x_2P(x_2) + \ldots + x_nP(x_n)$$

Suppose X is the random variable that has the probability distribution shown.

x	$P(X = x)$
1	$\frac{2}{5}$
6	$\frac{3}{5}$

The expected value of X is given by

$$\mu = E(x) = x_1P(x_1) + x_2P(x_2) = 1\left(\frac{2}{5}\right) + 6\left(\frac{3}{5}\right) = \frac{20}{5} = 4$$

You can use your understanding of probability distributions and expected value to decide whether a game is fair. For example, suppose you pay 5 chips to play a game with the numbered tiles. You receive 6 chips if the tile drawn shows an odd number and 1 chip if the tile drawn shows an even number. Your expected value for the game is 4 chips. Because you are paying a 5-chip fee to play the game, on average, you lose 1 chip per play. The game is not fair, since you, the player, can expect to lose.

Events

For this topic, you will learn basic concepts related to events and use the classical method for computing probabilities of simple events.

Basic Concepts Related to Events

An **event,** E, is a collection of outcomes from a sample space S; that is, an event E is a subset of S. (See "Basic Set Theory" in Chapter 11 for a discussion of sets and subsets.) E can consist of no outcomes (the null set) or from a single outcome up to all the outcomes in S. ***Note:*** By convention, capital letters are used to designate events, with the word *event* being omitted in cases where the meaning is clear.

An event E is said to **occur** if a member of E occurs when the experiment is performed. The **probability of E,** denoted $P(E)$, is the sum of the probability values assigned to the outcomes in E. It is a numerical value between 0 and 1, inclusive, that quantifies the chance or likelihood that E will occur.

An **impossible event** is one that cannot occur. The probability of an impossible event is 0. A **certain event** is one that is guaranteed to occur. The probability of a certain event is 1. A probability near zero indicates an unlikely event; a probability around $\frac{1}{2}$ is neither likely nor unlikely; and a probability near 1 indicates a likely event. Thus, the lowest probability you can have is 0, and the highest probability you can have is 1. All other probabilities fall between 0 and 1. Symbolically, $0 \le P(E) \le 1$, for any event E.

Tip: If you determine a probability and your answer is greater than 1 or your answer is negative, you've made a mistake! Go back and check your work.

Here are examples of events and their corresponding probabilities for the sample space $S = \{1, 2, 3, 4, 5\}$, the set of outcomes from Experiment 4, the tile-drawing experiment.

If $E_1 = \{1\}$, then $P(E_1) = P(\{1\}) = \frac{1}{5}$. ***Note:*** Hereafter, probability of single outcomes, such as $P(\{1\})$ will be written as $P(1)$.

If $E_2 = \{1, 3, 5\}$, the event that the tile drawn shows an odd number, then $P(E_2) = P(1) + P(3) + P(5) = \frac{1}{5} + \frac{1}{5} + \frac{1}{5} = \frac{3}{5}$.

If $E_3 = \{4, 5\}$, the event that the tile drawn shows a number greater than 3, then $P(E_3) = P(4) + P(5) = \frac{1}{5} + \frac{1}{5} = \frac{2}{5}$.

If E_4 is the event that the tile drawn shows a number greater than 5, then E_4 is an impossible event; thus, $P(E_4) = 0$.

If E_5 is the event that the tile drawn shows a whole number, then E_5 is a certain event; thus, $P(E_5) = 1$.

Classical Method for Computing Probabilities

When each of the possible outcomes in a sample space has an equal chance of occurring, the sample space has **equally likely outcomes.** The probability distribution for a sample space with equally likely outcomes is a **uniform probability distribution.** The probability of each outcome is $\frac{1}{n}$, where n is the number of possible outcomes.

If all outcomes in the sample space are equally likely, the **classical method** for computing the **probability of an event E** is given by $P(E) = \frac{\text{Number of outcomes in } E}{\text{Total number of outcomes in the sample space}}$.

For example, if the sample space is $S = \{1, 2, 3, 4, 5\}$, the set of outcomes from the tile-drawing experiment, and E is the event the tile drawn shows an odd number, then $P(E) = \frac{\text{Number of outcomes in } E}{\text{Total number of outcomes in the sample space}} = \frac{3}{5}$.

Tip: In a probability problem involving equally likely outcomes, the number of total outcomes possible will always be greater than or equal to the number of outcomes in the event, so check to make sure that the denominator is *larger than or equal* to the numerator when you plug into the formula.

Probabilities can be expressed as fractions, decimals, or percents. In the example given, the probability of drawing an odd-numbered tile can be expressed as $\frac{3}{5}$, 0.6, or 60 percent.

Keep in mind that the rule for the classical method of computing probability will *not* apply to sample spaces in which the events are not equally likely. For example, the sample space for spinning the pointer of the spinner shown is $S = \{\text{green, red, yellow}\}$.

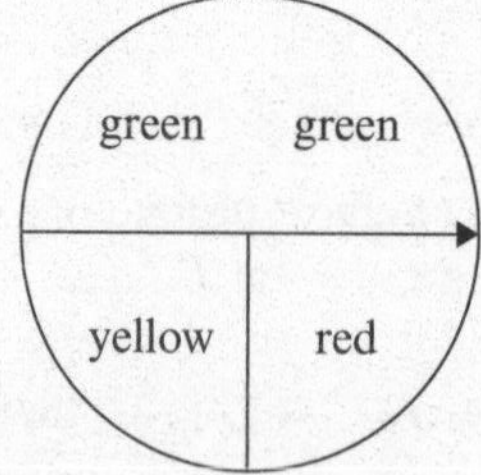

The probabilities for the different outcomes are the following: $P(\text{red}) = \frac{1}{4}$, $P(\text{yellow}) = \frac{1}{4}$, and $P(\text{green}) = \frac{1}{2}$. The three outcomes are not equally likely because the green section is larger than the other two sections.

Tip: Always remember to check whether the outcomes are equally likely before using the rule for the classical method of computing probability.

Combinations of Events

For this topic, you must demonstrate an understanding of complements, unions, and intersections of events.

Complement of an Event

The **complement of an event E,** denoted E^c, is the event that E does not occur. The probability of the complement of an event E is $P(E^c) = 1 - P(E)$. For example, if $P(E) = 0.06$, then $P(E^c) = 1 - P(E) = 1 - 0.06 = 0.94$.

Conversely, $P(E) = 1 - P(E^c)$. For example, if the probability of not guessing correctly on a multiple-choice test question is $\frac{3}{4}$, then the probability of guessing correctly on that question is $1 - \frac{3}{4} = \frac{1}{4}$.

Compound Events

Suppose A and B are two events in a sample space S.

The event $A \cup B$ (read "**A union B**") is the event consisting of all outcomes in S that are in at least one of the events A or B. That is, the event $A \cup B$ includes all the outcomes that are in only one or the other of the two events as well as those that are common to both events.

Then, $P(A \cup B)$ is the probability that event A occurs or event B occurs or that both events occur simultaneously.

Tip: You will find it helpful to know that $P(A \cup B)$ is the probability that at least one of the events A or B occurs.

The event $A \cap B$ (read "**A intersection B**") is the event consisting of all outcomes in S that are in both events A and B. That is, the event $A \cap B$ includes all the outcomes that are common to both events.

Then, $P(A \cap B)$ is the probability that events A and B both occur simultaneously.

The Addition Rule and Mutually Exclusive Events

For this topic, you will demonstrate an understanding of the addition rule and mutually exclusive events.

Addition Rule

Addition Rule: Given events A and B, $P(A \cup B) = P(A) + P(B) - P(A \cap B)$. For the addition rule, the events under consideration are associated with one task (getting a job offer, drawing one card, selecting one number, and so on). Here is an example.

> Jaiden, a recent college graduate, applies for jobs at two different companies, Company X and Company Y. Let $P(X)$ be the probability that Jaiden gets a job offer from Company X, $P(Y)$ be the probability Jaiden gets a job offer from Company Y, and $P(X \cap Y)$ be the probability Jaiden gets job offers from both companies. Suppose $P(X) = 0.8$, $P(Y) = 0.6$, and $P(X \cap Y) = 0.5$. What is the probability that Jaiden will get a job offer from at least one of the companies?

The probability that Jaiden will get a job offer from at least one of the companies is $P(X \cup Y) = P(X) + P(Y) - P(X \cap Y) = 0.8 + 0.6 - 0.5 = 0.9$.

In many situations, you must calculate the probabilities used in the addition rule. Here is an example.

> Suppose a card is drawn at random from a well-shuffled standard deck of 52 playing cards. What is the probability that the card drawn is a face card or a diamond? (See page 165 for an illustration of a standard deck of 52 playing cards.)

There are 12 face cards, so $P(\text{face card}) = \frac{12}{52}$. There are 13 diamonds, so $P(\text{diamond}) = \frac{13}{52}$. There are 3 diamond face cards, so $P(\text{face card} \cap \text{diamond}) = \frac{3}{52}$; thus, $P(\text{face card or diamond}) = P(\text{face card} \cup \text{diamond}) = P(\text{face card}) + P(\text{diamond}) - P(\text{face card} \cap \text{diamond}) = \frac{12}{52} + \frac{13}{52} - \frac{3}{52} = \frac{22}{52} = \frac{11}{26}$.

In applying the addition rule, you can reduce fractions as you go along or wait until your final computation to reduce fractions. Waiting until the final computation to reduce fractions (as shown in this example) can save time. Given that the number of elements in S is the same for $P(A)$, $P(B)$, and $P(A \cap B)$, the denominators for these probabilities in the computation will be the same number if you do not reduce fractions beforehand.

When you can determine the possible outcomes for the sample space, an efficient and straightforward way to find $P(A \cup B)$ is to sum the number of ways that event A can occur and the number of ways that event B can occur, *being sure to add in such a way that no outcome is counted twice,* and then to divide by the total number of outcomes in the sample space.

Employing this strategy for the example given above, you have the following: There are 12 face cards. There are 10 diamonds that are *not* face cards. Thus, there are $12 + 10 = 22$ distinct cards in the event "face card or diamond." Therefore, $P(\text{face card} \cup \text{diamond}) = \frac{12+10}{52} = \frac{22}{52} = \frac{11}{26}$.

Mutually Exclusive Events and the Addition Rule

Two events A and B are **mutually exclusive** if they cannot occur at the same time; that is, they have no outcomes in common. Therefore, events A and B are mutually exclusive if and only if $P(A \cap B) = 0$. For example, suppose you draw one card from a standard deck of 52 playing cards; the event of drawing a king and the event of drawing an ace are mutually exclusive. Thus, $P(\text{king} \cap \text{ace}) = 0$.

When two events A and B are mutually exclusive, the addition rule is $P(A \cup B) = P(A) + P(B)$. Here is an example.

> One card is randomly drawn from a well-shuffled standard deck of 52 playing cards. Find the probability that the card drawn is a king or an ace. (See page 165 for an illustration of a standard deck of 52 playing cards.)

There are 4 kings in the deck, so $P(\text{king}) = \frac{4}{52}$. There are 4 aces in the deck, so $P(\text{ace}) = \frac{4}{52}$. The event of drawing a king and the event of drawing an ace are mutually exclusive (because you cannot draw both at the same time on one draw from the deck). Hence, $P(\text{king or ace}) = P(\text{king} \cup \text{ace}) = P(\text{king}) + P(\text{ace}) = \frac{4}{52} + \frac{4}{52} = \frac{1}{13} + \frac{1}{13} = \frac{2}{13}$.

Conditional Probability

The probability of an event E, given that an event A has occurred, is a **conditional probability,** denoted $P(E|A)$ (read as "the probability of E given A").

One way to obtain the conditional probability, $P(E|A)$, is to compute the probability of event E in a "reduced" sample space that you determine after taking into account that the event A has already occurred. Here is an example.

Suppose you draw one card at random from a well-shuffled standard deck of 52 playing cards. Find the probability that the card drawn is a 6, given that the card drawn is greater than 2 and less than 8. (See page 165 for an illustration of a standard deck of 52 playing cards.)

Let E be the event "the card drawn is a 6" and A be the event "the card drawn is greater than 2 and less than 8." There are 20 cards between 2 and 8 (four 3s, four 4s, four 5s, four 6s, and four 7s). Of these 20 cards, four are 6s. Hence, $P(E|A) = \frac{4}{20} = \frac{1}{5}$.

Here is an example using a summary table.

The table below shows the gender and type of residence of 2,000 senior students at a university.

Gender and Type of Residence of Senior Students ($n = 2{,}000$)

	Female	Male	Row Total
Apartment	229	180	409
Dorm	203	118	321
House	258	272	530
With Parent(s)	200	201	401
Sorority/Fraternity House	241	98	339
Column Total	1,131	869	2,000

(a) What is the probability that a senior selected at random lives in a dorm given that the senior is female? Express your answer as a decimal to the nearest hundredth.

(b) What is the probability that a senior selected at random is a female given that the senior lives in a dorm? Express your answer as a decimal to the nearest hundredth.

(a) Let D be the event "the senior selected lives in the dorm" and F be the event "the senior selected is female." The total number of female seniors is 1,131. Of that total, 203 live in a dorm; thus, $P(D|F) = \frac{203}{1{,}131} \approx 0.18$.

(b) Let F be the event "the senior selected is female" and D be the event "the senior selected lives in the dorm." The total number of seniors living in a dorm is 321. Of that total, 203 are female; thus, $P(F|D) = \frac{203}{321} \approx 0.63$.

Note: Notice that in the above examples, the total number of outcomes under consideration is "reduced" to a lower number than the original problem began with.

Another way to obtain the conditional probability, $P(E|A)$, is to use the following formula:

$$P(E|A) = \frac{P(E \cap A)}{P(A)}, \text{ provided } P(A) > 0$$

Here is the formula applied to the previously shown examples.

> Suppose you draw one card at random from a well-shuffled standard deck of 52 playing cards. Find the probability that the card drawn is a 6, given that the card drawn is greater than 2 and less than 8. (See page 165 for an illustration of a standard deck of 52 playing cards.)

Let E be the event "the card drawn is a 6" and A be the event "the card drawn is greater than 2 and less than 8."

$$P(E \cap A) = \frac{4}{52} \text{ and } P(A) = \frac{20}{52}. \text{ Hence, } P(E|A) = \frac{P(E \cap A)}{P(A)} = \frac{\frac{4}{52}}{\frac{20}{52}} = \frac{4}{20} = \frac{1}{5}.$$

> The table shows the gender and type of residence of 2,000 senior students at a university.
>
> **Gender and Type of Residence of Senior Students ($n = 2{,}000$)**
>
> | | Female | Male | Row Total |
> |---|---|---|---|
> | Apartment | 229 | 180 | 409 |
> | Dorm | 203 | 118 | 321 |
> | House | 258 | 272 | 530 |
> | With Parent(s) | 200 | 201 | 401 |
> | Sorority/Fraternity House | 241 | 98 | 339 |
> | **Column Total** | 1,131 | 869 | 2,000 |
>
> **(a)** What is the probability that a senior selected at random lives in a dorm given that the senior is female? Express your answer as a decimal to the nearest hundredth.
>
> **(b)** What is the probability that a senior selected at random is a female given that the senior lives in a dorm? Express your answer as a decimal to the nearest hundredth.

(a) Let D be the event "the senior selected lives in the dorm" and F be the event "the senior selected is female."

$$P(D \cap F) = \frac{203}{2{,}000} \text{ and } P(F) = \frac{1{,}131}{2{,}000}; \text{ thus } P(D|F) = \frac{P(D \cap F)}{P(F)} = \frac{\frac{203}{2{,}000}}{\frac{1{,}131}{2{,}000}} = \frac{203}{1{,}131} \approx 0.18.$$

(b) Let F be the event "the senior selected is female" and D be the event "the senior selected lives in the dorm."

$$P(F \cap D) = \frac{203}{2{,}000} \text{ and } P(D) = \frac{321}{2{,}000}; \text{ thus, } P(F|D) = \frac{P(F \cap D)}{P(D)} = \frac{\frac{203}{2{,}000}}{\frac{321}{2{,}000}} = \frac{203}{321} \approx 0.63.$$

As you can see, for both examples, you get the same answers as previously obtained.

The Multiplication Rule and Independent and Dependent Events

For this topic, you must demonstrate an understanding of the multiplication rule and independent and dependent events.

Multiplication Rule

Multiplication Rule: Given events A and B, $P(A \cap B) = P(A)P(B|A)$. For the multiplication rule, the events under consideration are associated with two or more tasks (drawing two cards, flipping a coin followed by tossing a number cube, and so on). Here are examples.

Suppose you draw two cards at random, one after the other, from a standard deck of 52 playing cards. Let J be the event "a jack is drawn on the first draw" and K be the event "a king is drawn on the second draw." (See page 165 for an illustration of a standard deck of 52 playing cards.)

(a) What is the probability of drawing a jack on the first draw, without replacement, and a king on the second draw? ***Note:*** **"Without replacement"** means the first item selected is *not* put back before the second selection takes place.

(b) What is the probability of drawing a jack on the first draw, with replacement, and a king on the second draw? ***Note:*** **"With replacement"** means the first card is put back before the second drawing takes place.

(a) $P(J) = \frac{4}{52} = \frac{1}{13}$ (this is true because there are 4 jacks in the deck of 52 cards) and $P(K|J) = \frac{4}{51}$ (this is true because after the jack is drawn and not put back in the deck, there are 4 kings in the remaining deck of 51 cards). Therefore, $P(J \cap K) = \frac{1}{13} \cdot \frac{4}{51} = \frac{4}{663}$.

(b) $P(J) = \frac{4}{52} = \frac{1}{13}$ (this is true because there are 4 jacks in the deck of 52 cards) and $P(K|J) = \frac{4}{52} = \frac{1}{13}$ (this is true because after the jack is drawn and put back in the deck, there are 4 kings in the remaining deck of 52 cards). Therefore, $P(J \cap K) = \frac{1}{13} \cdot \frac{1}{13} = \frac{1}{169}$.

Tip: For the Praxis Math CK test, remember that to obtain the probability that event *A* occurs followed by event *B*, you multiply the probability of event *A* times the *conditional* probability of event *B*. This means you must take into account that event *A* has already occurred when determining the second factor.

Independent and Dependent Events and the Multiplication Rule

Two events A and B are **independent** if $P(A|B) = P(A)$ and $P(B|A) = P(B)$. This definition means events A and B are independent if the occurrence of one does not affect the probability of the occurrence of the other. It follows that if events A and B are independent, then the multiplication rule is $P(A \cap B) = P(A)P(B)$. Here are examples.

Suppose you flip a coin, and then toss a number cube, whose faces are numbered 10, 20, 30, 40, 50, and 60. Find the probability that a head appears on the up face of the coin and the number 50 appears on the up face of the number cube.

Let H be the event "a heads appears on the up face of the coin" and F be the event "the number 50 appears on the up face of the number cube." $P(H|F) = P(H) = \frac{1}{2}$ (this is true because what happens with the coin is not affected by what happens with the number cube) and $P(F|H) = P(F) = \frac{1}{6}$ (this is true because what happens with the number cube is not affected by what happens with the coin). Therefore, $P(H \cap F) = P(H)P(F) = \frac{1}{2} \cdot \frac{1}{6} = \frac{1}{12}$.

You can extend the multiplication rule for two independent events to any number of independent events. For example, suppose you flip a coin three times; the probability of obtaining three heads is $P(H) \cdot P(H) \cdot P(H) = \frac{1}{2} \cdot \frac{1}{2} \cdot \frac{1}{2} = \frac{1}{8}$.

> Suppose you draw 2 marbles, one after the other, from a box containing 6 red marbles and 4 blue marbles. Find the probability of drawing a red marble, with replacement, on the first draw and then drawing a blue marble on the second draw.

Let R be the event "the first marble drawn is red" and B be the event "the second marble drawn is blue." $P(R) = \frac{6}{10} = \frac{3}{5}$ (this is true because on the first draw, there are 6 red marbles in the box of 10 marbles) and $P(B|R) = P(B) = \frac{4}{10} = \frac{2}{5}$ (this is true because after the red marble is drawn and replaced, the probability of drawing a blue marble has not changed given there are still 4 blue marbles and 6 red marbles in the box). Therefore, $P(R \cap B) = P(R)P(B) = \frac{3}{5} \cdot \frac{2}{5} = \frac{6}{25}$.

If events A and B are not independent, they are said to be **dependent.** Here is an example.

> Suppose you draw 2 marbles, one after the other, from a box containing 6 red marbles and 4 blue marbles. Find the probability of drawing a red marble, without replacement, on the first draw and then drawing a blue marble on the second draw.

Let R be the event "the first marble drawn is red" and B be the event "the second marble drawn is blue." $P(R) = \frac{6}{10} = \frac{3}{5}$ (this is true because on the first draw, there are 6 red marbles in the box of 10 marbles) and $P(B|R) = \frac{4}{9}$ (this is true because after the red marble is drawn without replacement, there are 4 blue marbles and 5 red marbles remaining in the box). Therefore, $P(R \cap B) = P(R)P(B|R) = \frac{3}{5} \cdot \frac{4}{9} = \frac{4}{15}$.

Notice that selecting "with replacement" results in independent events, while selecting "without replacement" results in dependent events.

The Complement Rule

For some problems, you might find it convenient to determine the probability that at least one of something of interest occurs by using the following **complement rule:** P(at least one) = 1 – P(none). Here is an example.

> A coin is flipped three times. Find the probability that at least one tails occurs.

The sample space is {HHH, HHT, HTH, HTT, THH, THT, TTH, TTT}. Thus, P(at least one tails) = 1 – P(no tails) = 1 – P(HHH) $= 1 - \frac{1}{8} = \frac{7}{8}$. By looking at the sample space, you can see that this answer is correct because there are seven outcomes in which tails occurs. In fact, you could have worked the problem directly as follows: P(at least one tails) $= \frac{7}{8}$. With larger sample spaces, rather than working out the probability directly, it is often more convenient to determine the probability of "at least one" by using 1 – P(none).

Odds

The **odds in favor of an event *E*** are given by $\frac{P(E)}{1-P(E)}$, usually expressed in the form p: q (or p to q), where p and q are integers with no common factors and $\frac{P(E)}{1-P(E)} = \frac{p}{q}$. The **odds against an event *E*** are given by $\frac{1-P(E)}{P(E)}$, usually expressed in the form q: p (or q to p), where p and q are integers with no common factors and $\frac{1-P(E)}{P(E)} = \frac{q}{p}$. Here is an example.

> Suppose you perform one toss of a number cube, whose six faces are numbered 1 through 6, and observe the up face. What are the odds of observing a 2 on the up face?

The probability of observing a 2 on the up face is $\frac{1}{6}$ (this is true because 2 has a 1 in 6 chance of showing on the up face). Therefore, the odds in favor of observing a 2 on the up face are $\frac{\frac{1}{6}}{1-\frac{1}{6}} = \frac{\frac{1}{6}}{\frac{5}{6}} = \frac{1}{5}$, which is 1 to 5. The odds against observing a 2 on the up face are 5 to 1.

Frequency Theory of Probability

An empirical way to assign probability to a random experiment is to view probability as long-run relative frequency. The **frequency theory of probability** assumes that as the numbers of trials increases, the proportion of times that E occurs approaches E's true probability. For example, as a coin is flipped repeatedly, the proportion of heads obtained gets closer and closer to $\frac{1}{2}$ as the number of repetitions increases. The value of $\frac{1}{2}$ is the limiting value of this process and, as a result, is called the probability of heads.

In general, the **probability of an event *E*** is interpreted to mean the limiting value of the relative frequency of the occurrence of E if the experiment were conducted an indefinitely large number of times. It is the proportion of times the event would occur in a large number of repetitions (called trials) of the experiment.

In some situations, the only feasible way to assign a probability to an event is to make a relative frequency interpretation of probability. This way of assigning probability is the **relative frequency method.** The probability of an event E is estimated by conducting the experiment a large number of times and counting the number of times that event E actually occurred. Based on these results, the probability of E is estimated as $P(E) \approx \frac{\text{Number of times } E \text{ occurred}}{\text{Total number of trials}}$. Here is an example.

Out of 100 light bulbs tested at Company *X*, two are defective. What is the estimated probability that a Company *X* light bulb is defective?

$$P(\text{Company } X \text{ light bulb is defective}) \approx \frac{2}{100} = 0.02 = 2\%$$

Geometric Probability

Geometric probability involves determining probabilities associated with geometric objects. Here is an example.

The figure shown is a circle inscribed in a 10-inch square. A point is randomly selected within the square. What is the probability that the point will be inside the circle as well? Round your answer to three decimal places.

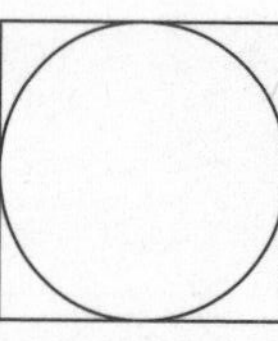

To calculate the probability that the point will be inside the circle, calculate the ratio of the area of the circle to the area of the square. (See "Perimeter, Area, and Volume" in Chapter 7 for formulas for the area of geometric shapes.)

$$P(\text{point is inside circle}) = \frac{\text{area of circle}}{\text{area of square}} = \frac{\pi r^2}{s^2} = \frac{\pi(5\text{ in})^2}{(10\text{ in})^2} = \frac{25\pi}{100} \approx 0.785$$

Chapter 9

Statistics

Statistical Questions and Types of Data

When you have a statistical question, you need information, called **data,** to answer it. A **statistical question** is one that anticipates the data collected to answer it will vary. The question does not have a specific predetermined answer. For example, "What is the average salary of teachers in your state?" is a statistical question. You expect the salaries of teachers to vary from teacher to teacher. However, "What is the salary of the high school band director at a particular school in your state?" is *not* a statistical question. The band director has a specific salary. There is no variability in the answer at the time of the question. Accounting for the **variability** in data is the main purpose of statistical analysis.

The salary of a randomly selected teacher in your state is a **variable.** In statistics, a **variable** is a characteristic (or attribute) that describes an object, person, or thing. The variable's value varies from entity to entity. When you collect data related to a variable, the data are qualitative data or quantitative data.

Qualitative data (also called **categorical data**) are non-numerical data such as names, labels, codes, colors, race, educational level, and other qualities that result from sorting objects, things, or people into categories.

Quantitative data are numerical data that represent a measurement (such as lengths, heights, weights, temperature, test scores, and other amounts) or a count (such as family size, number of pets, and so forth). Quantitative data that results from taking a measurement is **measurement data.**

The **distribution** of a variable is a representation of a variable's data that shows what values the variable assumes and the frequency of those values.

Graphical Representations of Data

Graphical representations of data show the distributions of variables. For the Praxis Math CK test, you should be able to read and interpret information about variables from tables, pictographs, circle graphs, bar graphs, line graphs, dot plots, stem-and-leaf plots, and histograms.

Tables

A **table** organizes information as entries in rows and columns. Row and column labels explain the data recorded in the table. A **frequency table** is a tabular representation of data that shows the frequency of each value in the data set. A **relative frequency table** shows the frequency of each value as a proportion or percentage of the whole data set. The total of all relative frequencies should be 1.00 or 100 percent (but instead might be very close to 1.00 or 100 percent due to round-off error). Here is an example.

Grade Distribution of 25 Students for Test 1

Grade	Frequency	Relative Frequency
A	5	0.20
B	8	0.32
C	9	0.36
D	2	0.08
F	1	0.04
Total	**25**	**1.00**

According to the information in the table, $0.20 + 0.32 + 0.36 = 0.88$ or 88% of the students received a C or better on Test 1.

Pictographs

A **pictograph** (or **picture graph**) uses symbols or pictures to represent data. Each symbol stands for a definite number of a specific item. This information should be stated on the graph. To read a pictograph, you count the number of symbols shown and then multiply by the number it represents. Fractional portions of symbols are approximated and used accordingly. Here is an example.

According to the graph, $4 \times 5 = 20$ of the 75 dog owners surveyed responded "yes" to the survey question.

Circle Graphs

A **circle graph** (or **pie chart**) is a graph in the shape of a circle. A circle graph visually displays the relative contribution of each category of data within a set of data belonging to a whole, which is represented by the circle. A circle graph can only compare parts of a whole. Circle graphs are also called "pie" charts because each looks like a pie cut into wedges. The wedges are labeled to show the categories for the graph. Usually the portion of the graph that corresponds to each category is shown as a percent. The total amount of percentage on the graph is 100 percent. The graph is made by dividing the 360 degrees of the circle into portions that are proportional to the percentages for each category. You read a circle graph by reading the percents displayed on the graph for the different categories. Here is an example.

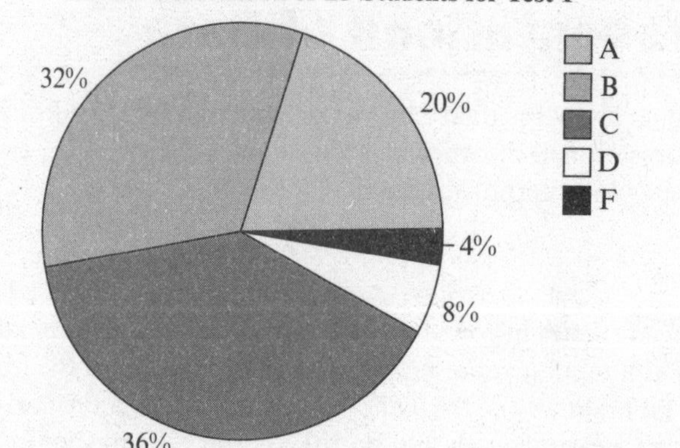

According to the graph, over half of the students ($32\% + 20\% = 52\%$) received a B or better on Test 1.

Bar Graphs

A **bar graph** is a useful way to organize and represent categorical data. Bar graphs can display categories that are not parts of a whole as well as categories that are parts of a whole. A bar graph uses rectangular bars of the same width to show the frequency (or relative frequency) of the different categories in which the data are classified. Labels at the base of the bars specify the categories. The bars are equally spaced from each other and may be oriented vertically or horizontally. (***Note:*** For ease of discussion, the following explanation is limited to bar graphs that are oriented vertically; the explanation for bar graphs that are oriented horizontally is similar.) The categories for the data are labeled on the horizontal axis. The horizontal axis is not a scale as such, meaning the ordering of the categories and their horizontal positions are not dictated by the data. A bar's length or height indicates the frequency (or relative frequency) for the category represented by that particular bar. A vertical scale, marked in whole numbers for determining the frequency counts (or marked as proportions/percentages for determining relative frequencies) corresponding to the bars' categories is shown on the graph. To read a bar graph, examine the vertical scale to determine the count (or relative frequency) represented by each tick mark. Then determine where the bars' heights fall relative to the scale. Here is an example.

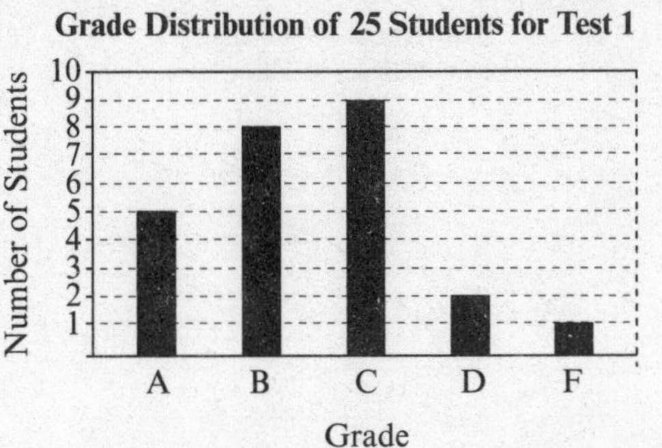

The graph shows that 9 + 8 + 5 = 22 students received a grade of C or better on Test 1.

Two or more sets of data can be displayed on the same graph to facilitate comparison of the data sets to each other. Here is an example.

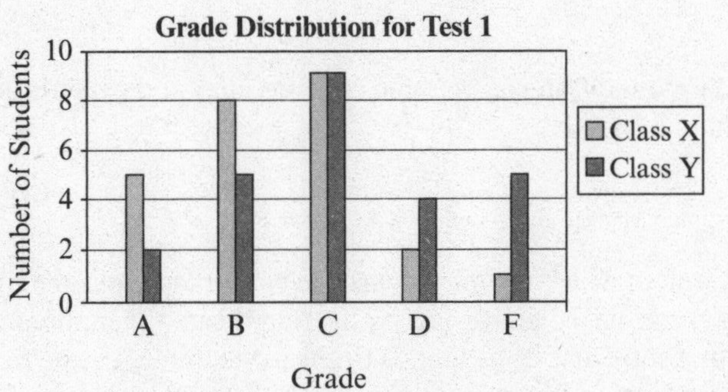

The graph shows that Class X had more As and Bs and fewer Ds and Fs than did Class Y; so, in general, Class X performed better on Test 1 than did Class Y.

Line Graphs

A **line graph** displays measurement data that have been collected over equal consecutive time intervals. The data values are plotted as ordered pairs on a grid that has a horizontal time scale. The vertical scale corresponds to the measurement scale that was used to obtain the data. Consecutive points are connected by line segments to aid the eye in identifying changes over time. The slants of the line segments between points indicate which direction the data might be trending. Upward slants from left to right indicate increasing data values, downward slants from left to right indicate decreasing data values, and line segments with no slant (horizontal line) indicate that the data values are remaining constant. **Trends** are patterns of (relatively) long-term upward or downward changes. Here is an example.

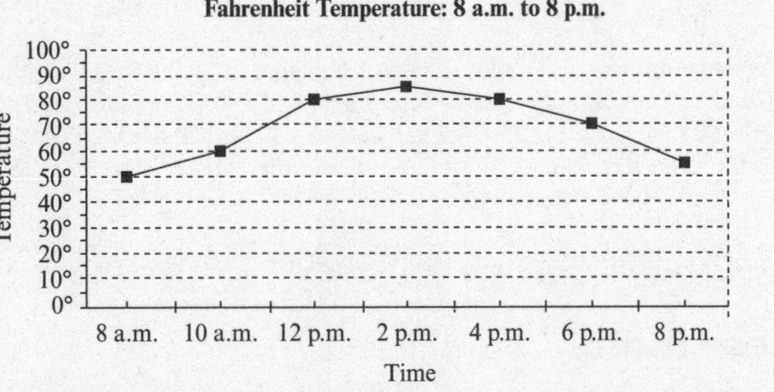

The graph shows that the temperature steadily increased between 8 a.m. and 2 p.m. (upward trend), and then steadily decreased between 2 p.m. and 8 p.m. (downward trend).

You can plot two or more sets of data on the same graph, a display that facilitates comparisons between the data sets. Here is an example.

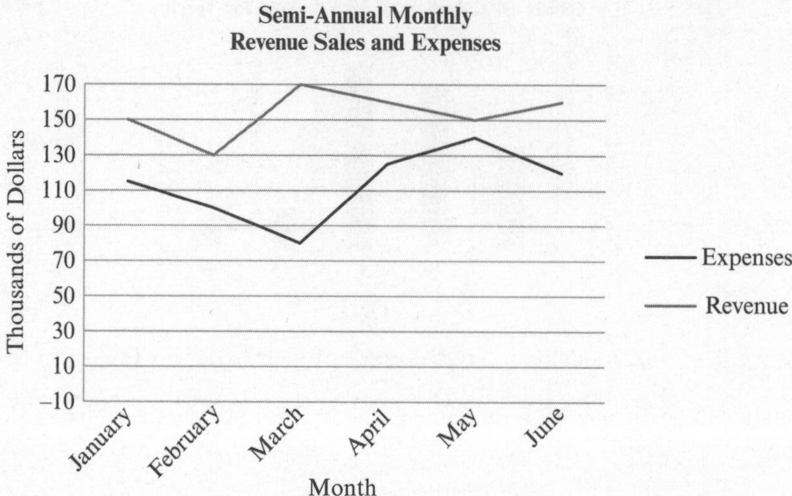

The graph shows that the maximum difference between revenue sales and expenses occurred in March, and the minimum difference occurred in May.

Dot Plots

A **dot plot** (or **line plot**) is a graph in which the data's possible values are indicated along the horizontal axis, and dots (or other similar symbols) are placed above each value to indicate the number of times that particular value occurs in the data set. The horizontal axis corresponds to the measurement scale that was used to obtain the data. An important advantage of dot plots is that they show a symbol for every data value. You can easily determine the minimum (least) and the maximum (greatest) data values, and the frequency of occurrence of values. Features of the data's distribution including clusters, gaps, and outliers are visually apparent. A **cluster** is a group of data that are close together. A **gap** is an interval where no data are plotted. An **outlier** is a data value that is extremely high or extremely low in comparison to most of the other data values. Here is an example.

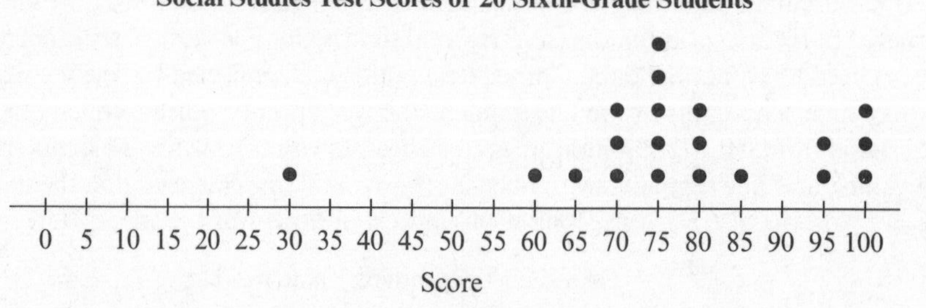

The dot plot provides visual information about the shape and spread of the data distribution. It shows a cluster of scores between 60 and 85 and a smaller cluster between 95 and 100. There is a large gap between 30 and 60 and a smaller one between 85 and 95. Because the gap between 30 and 60 is very large (indicating 30 is extremely low in comparison to the other data values), 30 is an outlier in the data set. The score that occurs most frequently is 75. The least score is 30 and the greatest score is 100.

Tip: Dot plots are used mostly with small data sets (those with fewer than 50 data values).

Stem-and-Leaf Plots

A **stem-and-leaf plot** is a graphical display of data in which each data value is separated into two parts: a stem and a leaf. For a given data value, the leaf is the last digit, and the stem, the remaining digits. For example, for the data value 198, 19 is the stem and 8 is the leaf. A stem-and-leaf plot includes a legend that explains what the stem and leaf represent so the reader can interpret the information in the plot; for example, 19|8 = 198. Usually, the stems are listed vertically, from smallest to largest, in a column labeled "Stem." The leaves are listed horizontally, from smallest to largest, in the row of their corresponding stem under a column labeled "Leaves." Each leaf is listed to the right of its corresponding stem as many times as it occurs in the original data set. A feature of a stem-and-leaf plot is that the original data are retained and displayed in the plot. Reading information from a stem-and-leaf plot is a matter of interpreting the plot's stems and leaves. Here is an example.

Ages of 40 Attendees at a Retirement Party

Stem	Leaves
4	0 3 3 5 6 9
5	3 4 4 5 6 6 7 7 7 7 7 8 8 8 9
6	0 0 0 1 1 1 2 3 3 3 7
7	1 4 7 8
8	1 3
9	0 1
Legend: 4|6 = 46	

According to the plot, 40 people attended the retirement party. Of the 40 attendees, 6 were in their 40s, 15 were in their 50s, 11 were in their 60s, 4 were in their 70s, 2 were in their 80s, and 2 were in their 90s.

Histograms

A **histogram** summarizes measurement data that have been grouped by nonoverlapping **class intervals.** Histograms have two scales: a measurement scale, corresponding to the measurement scale used to obtain the data, and a frequency (or relative frequency) scale. The histogram displays the data's frequencies (or relative frequencies) within the successive class intervals that lie along the measurement scale. Class intervals are of equal width and cover from the lowest to the highest data value. The left and right endpoints for the class intervals are selected so that each data value clearly falls within one and only one class interval. The frequency or relative frequency of the data's occurrence within a class interval is represented by a rectangular bar, whose width is the same as the width of the class interval. The height of the bar is proportional to the data's frequency (or relative frequency) within that interval. ***Tip:*** There are no horizontal spaces between the bars of a histogram unless a bar's height is zero, meaning no data values fall in its class interval.

In a **frequency histogram,** the scale for measuring the bars' heights is marked with actual frequencies (or counts). In a **relative frequency histogram,** the scale is marked with relative frequencies instead of actual frequencies. The total of the relative frequencies corresponding to the class intervals should be 1.00 or 100 percent (but might instead be very close to 1.00 or 100 percent due to round-off error). Here is an example.

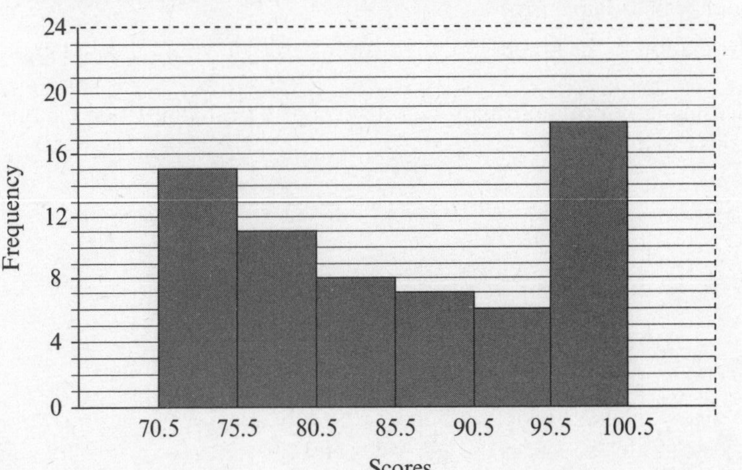

The histogram shows that the data are clustered between 70.5 and 100.5 with no student scoring below 70. There are no gaps in the data and no outliers.

Misleading Graphs

Drawing valid conclusions from graphical representations of data requires that you have read the graph accurately and analyzed the graphical information correctly. Sometimes a graphical representation will distort the data in some way, leading you to draw an invalid conclusion. Here is an example.

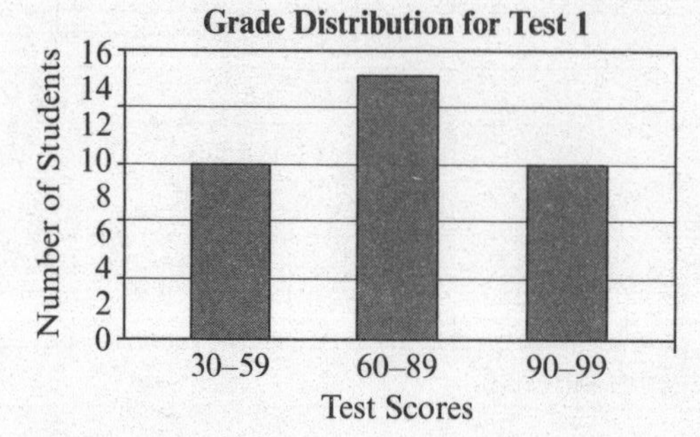

At first glance, the data for this graph look evenly distributed. However, upon closer examination, you can see that each of the first two intervals covers a 29-point spread, but the last interval covers only a 9-point spread, making it difficult to draw conclusions from the graph.

Guidelines for Interpreting Graphs

When you interpret graphical information on the Praxis Math CK test, follow these suggestions:

- Make sure you understand the graph's title.
- Read the labels on the graph's parts to understand what is being represented.
- Make sure you know what each symbol in a pictograph represents; check that the symbols are a uniform size.
- Examine carefully the horizontal and vertical scales; make sure the numbers are equally spaced.
- Look for trends such as rising values (upward slanting line segments), falling values (downward slanting line segments), and periods of inactivity (horizontal line segments) in line graphs.
- Look for clusters, gaps, and outliers and note the general shape of dot plots, stem-and-leaf plots, and histograms.
- Be ready to do simple arithmetic computations.
- Make sure the numbers add up correctly.
- Use only the information in the graph. Do not answer based on your personal knowledge or opinion.

Here is an example of using graphical information to determine a probability (see Chapter 8, "Probability," for a further discussion of this topic).

Given the frequency histogram for the scores of 65 tenth graders (shown below), find the probability that a student randomly selected from the 65 tenth graders scored 90.5 or higher.

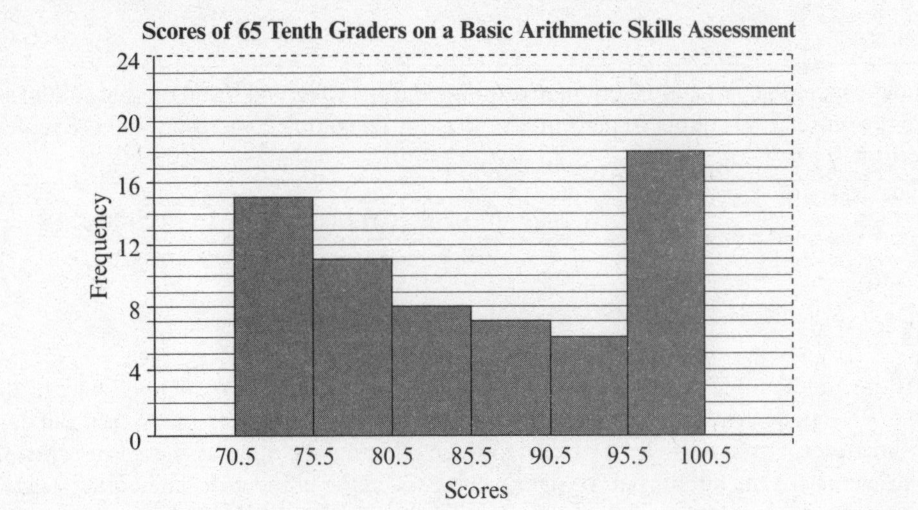

According to the graph, $6 + 18 = 24$ of the 65 students scored 90.5 or higher. Thus, since the student is randomly selected $P(\text{score is 90.5 or higher}) = \dfrac{\text{number of outcomes in the event}}{\text{total number of outcomes}} = \dfrac{24}{65}$.

Measures of Central Tendency

A measure of **central tendency** is a numerical value that describes a data set by attempting to provide a "central" or "typical" value of the data set. It is a single number that summarizes all the values in the data set. Three common measures of central tendency are the mean, median, and mode. Each of these measures represents a way to describe a set of data's central value.

Tip: Measures of central tendency should have the same units as those of the data values from which they are determined. If no units are specified for the data values, no units are specified for the measures of central tendency.

Mean

A data set's **mean** is the data values' arithmetic average; thus, $\text{mean} = \dfrac{\text{sum of the data values}}{\text{number of data values}}$. Here is an example.

Find the mean of the following data set: 21, 35, 34, 30, 32, 36, 24, 35, 28, 35.

$$\text{mean} = \frac{\text{sum of the data values}}{\text{number of data values}} = \frac{21+24+28+30+32+34+35+35+35+36}{10} = \frac{310}{10} = 31$$

Tip: When solving a central tendency problem, it's a good practice to list the values of a data set in order from least to greatest (or greatest to least). While reordering the values of a data set isn't necessary to find the mean, doing so is helpful in identifying the mode and *imperative* to finding the median.

A **weighted mean** is a mean computed by assigning weights to the data values. To find a weighted mean, first, multiply each data value by its assigned weight, and then sum the results. Next, divide the sum obtained by the sum of the weights. Thus, for data values $x_1, x_2, \ldots, x_n$ with respective assigned weights $w_1, w_2, \ldots, w_n$, the weighted mean $= \frac{\sum w_i x_i}{\sum w_i}$. Here is an example.

> A student scores 80, 60, and 50 on three exams. Find the weighted mean of the student's three scores, where the score of 80 counts 20 percent, the score of 60 counts 20 percent, and the score of 50 counts 60 percent.

$$\text{weighted mean} = \frac{\sum w_i x_i}{\sum w_i} = \frac{20\%(80) + 20\%(60) + 60\%(50)}{20\% + 20\% + 60\%} = \frac{16 + 12 + 30}{100\%} = \frac{58}{1} = 58$$

Median

The **median** is the middle value or the average of the middle pair of values in an *ordered* set of data. For a small data set, you easily can determine a data set's median using a two-step process. First, put the data values in order from least to greatest (or greatest to least). Next, find the middle data value. If there is no single middle data value, find the average of the middle pair of data values. When the number of data values is *odd,* the median is the middle value. When the number of data values is *even,* the median is the average of the middle pair of values. Here is an example.

> Find the median of the data set consisting of the 10 values 21, 35, 34, 30, 32, 36, 24, 35, 28, 35.

Step 1. Put the data values in order: 21, 24, 28, 30, 32, 34, 35, 35, 35, 36.

Step 2. The number of data values is even, so find the average of the middle pair of values: $\frac{32 + 34}{2} = 33$; therefore, the median is 33.

Tip: When you are finding a median, don't make the common mistake of neglecting to put the numbers in order first.

In terms of position, the median is the $\frac{(n+1)}{2}$ data value in an ordered set of discrete values. You can find the median by counting up from the least data value to the $\frac{(n+1)}{2}$ position, which is the middle position of the ordered set of data. When n is odd, there is one number at the $\frac{(n+1)}{2}$ position. When n is even, the median is halfway between the two numbers on either side of the $\frac{(n+1)}{2}$ position. Here is an example.

> Find the median of the data in the following stem-and-leaf plot.

Ages of 40 Attendees at a Retirement Party

Stem	Leaves
4	0 3 3 5 6 9
5	3 4 4 5 6 6 7 7 7 7 7 8 8 8 9
6	0 0 0 1 1 1 2 3 3 3 7
7	1 4 7 8
8	1 3
9	0 1
Legend: 4|6 = 46	

The median for the stem-and-leaf plot shown is in the $\frac{(40+1)}{2} = 20.5$th position. Thus, the median is halfway between the 20th data value, 58, and the 21st data value, 59. The median is 58.5.

Tip: $\frac{(n+1)}{2}$ does not give a median's value; it gives the median's position in an ordered data set.

Mode

The **mode** is the data value or values that occur with the highest frequency in a data set. A data set can have one mode, more than one mode, or no mode. If exactly two data values occur with the same frequency that is more often than that of any of the other data values, then the data set is bimodal. If three or more data values occur with the same frequency that is more often than that of any of the other data values, then the data set is multimodal. A data set in which each data value occurs the same number of times has no mode. Here is an example.

Find the mode of the following data set: 21, 35, 34, 30, 32, 36, 24, 35, 28, 35.

The value 35 occurs 3 times, which is the highest frequency of occurrence for any one value in the data set. Thus, the mode is 35.

Selecting the Most Appropriate Measure of Central Tendency

The mean, median, and mode are ways to describe a data set's central value. To know which of these measures of central tendency you should use to describe a data set, consider the following information.

Mean

- The mean is preferred when the distribution of the data has a symmetric shape (or close to it). ***Tip:*** A distribution is **symmetric** if its lower half and upper half are mirror images of each other.
- The actual data values are used in the computation of the mean. If any one number is changed, the mean's value will change. For example, the mean of the data set consisting of 50, 50, 87, 78, and 95 is 72. If the 95 in this set is changed to 100, the new data set's mean is 73.
- Although the mean represents a data set's central or typical value, the mean does not necessarily have the same value as one of the numbers in the set. For example, the mean of 50, 50, 87, 78, and 95 is 72, yet none of the five numbers in this data set equals 72.
- A disadvantage of the mean is that it is influenced by outliers, especially in a small data set. It tends to be "pulled" toward an extreme value, much more so than does the median. (An **outlier** is a data value that is extremely high or extremely low in comparison to most of the other data values.)
  - If a data set contains extremely high values that are not balanced by corresponding low values, the mean is misleadingly high. The mean of the data set consisting of 15, 15, 20, 25, and 25 is 20. If the 20 in this set is changed to 100, the mean of the new data set is 36. The value 36 does not represent the data set consisting of 15, 15, 100, 25, and 25 very well, since four of the data values are less than 30.
  - If a data set contains extremely low values that are not balanced by corresponding high values, the mean is misleadingly low. The mean of the data set consisting of 100, 100, 130, and 150 is 120. If the 150 in this set is changed to 10, the mean of the new data set is 85. The value 85 does not represent the data set consisting of 100, 100, 130, and 10 very well, since three of the data values are greater than or equal to 100.

Median

- The median is the most useful alternative to the mean as a measure of central tendency. The median is preferred when the data distribution is "lopsided" with unbalanced extreme values or outliers on one side. Such distributions are **skewed. Right-skewed** distributions have unbalanced extreme values on the right side. **Left-skewed** distributions have unbalanced extreme values on the left side. (See "Skewness" later in this chapter for an additional discussion of this topic.)

- Like the mean, the median does not necessarily have the same value as one of the numbers in the set. If the data set contains an odd number of data values, the median will be the middle number; however, for an even number of data values, the median is the arithmetic average of the middle pair of numbers.
- The median is not strongly influenced by outliers. For example, the median of the data set consisting of 10, 15, 20, 25, and 30 is 20. If the 30 in this set is changed to 100, the new data set's median remains 20.
- A disadvantage of the median as an indicator of a central value is that it is based on relative size rather than on the actual numbers in the set. For example, a student who has test scores of 44, 47, and 98 shows improved performance that would not be reflected if the median of 47, rather than the mean of 63, was reported as the representative score.

Mode

- The mode is the simplest measure of central tendency to calculate.
- If a data set has a mode, the mode (or modes) is one of the data values.
- The mode is the only appropriate measure of central tendency for data that are strictly nonnumeric, like data on ice cream flavor preferences (vanilla, chocolate, strawberry, and so on). Although it makes no sense to determine a mean or median ice cream flavor for the data, the ice cream flavor that was named most frequently would be the modal flavor.
- For numeric data, the mode is not a preferred measure of central tendency.
- A disadvantage of the mode as an indicator of a central value is that it is based on relative frequency, rather than on all the values in the set. For example, a student who has test scores of 45, 45, and 99 shows improved performance that would not be reflected if the mode of 45, rather than the mean of 63, was reported as the representative score.

When you are summarizing data, you might want to report more than one measure of central tendency, if appropriate. For numeric data, if you select only one measure, the mean is preferred for data sets in which outliers are not present. The median is the preferred measure when outliers are present. The mode is the preferred measure for nonnumeric categorical data.

Percentiles and Quartiles

Percentiles and quartiles are additional measures that are used to describe numerical data. The ***P*th percentile** is a value at or below which *P* percent of the data fall. For example, the median is the 50th percentile because 50 percent of the data fall at or below the median. **Quartiles** are values that divide an ordered data set into four portions, each of which contains approximately one-fourth of the data. About 25 percent of the data values are at or below the first quartile (also called the 25th percentile). About 50 percent of the data values are at or below the second quartile (also called the 50th percentile), which is the same as the median. About 75 percent of the data values are at or below the third quartile (also called the 75th percentile).

The **first quartile,** denoted Q_1, is the median of the lower half of an ordered data set, and the **third quartile,** denoted Q_3, is the median of the upper half. When the number of data values is odd, exclude the median to create the two halves of the data set. Here are examples.

Given the data set 21, 24, 28, 30, 32, 34, 35, 35, 35, 36, Q_1 is 28, the median is 33, and Q_3 is 35.

Given the data set 10, 12, 12, 13, 14, 15, 16, 17, 20, Q_1 is 12, the median is 14, and Q_3 is 16.5.

Note: Determining Q_1 and Q_3 by excluding the median to create the two halves when the number of data values is odd is not the only approach currently in use. You might encounter other methods for dividing the data set into two halves for the purposes of calculating Q_1 and Q_3 when the number of data values is odd.

Tip: Percentiles and quartiles are numbers along the horizontal axis. They are not percentages.

Measures of Variability

A measure of **variability** is a single value that describes the spread of a data set about its central value. Measures of center are important for describing data sets. However, their interpretation is enhanced when the variability about the central value is known. For example, one set of scores may be extremely consistent, with scores like 60, 62, 65, 68, 70, 70, 72, 75, 78, and 80; while another set of scores may be very erratic, with scores like 40, 40, 50, 55, 60, 80, 85, 90, 100, and 100. The scores in the first set cluster more closely together than do the scores in the second set; the scores in the second set are more spread out.

For the Praxis Math CK test, measures of variability you should know are the range, standard deviation, variance, and interquartile range (IQR).

Range

The **range** of a data set is the difference between the maximum value (the greatest value) and the minimum value (least value) in the data set; that is, range = maximum value – minimum value. ***Tip:*** The range should have the same units as those of the data values from which it is computed. If no units are specified, then the range will not specify units. Here is an example.

> Find the range of the following data set: 21, 35, 34, 30, 32, 36, 24, 35, 28, 35.

Range = maximum value – minimum value = 36 – 21 = 15.

The range gives an indication of the spread of the values in a data set, but its value is determined by only two of the data values. The extent of spread of the other data values is not considered.

Standard Deviation and Variance

The **standard deviation** is a measure of the variability of a set of data values about the mean of the data set. If there is no variability in a data set, each data value equals the mean, giving a standard deviation of 0. The more the data values vary from the mean, the greater the standard deviation, meaning the data set has more spread. ***Tip:*** The standard deviation should have the same units as those of the data values from which it is computed. If no units are specified, then the standard deviation will not specify units. The **variance** is the square of the standard deviation.

Tip: The standard deviation and variance are used for data in which the mean is the appropriate measure of center.

The formula for the standard deviation σ of a population of size N with mean μ is $\sigma = \sqrt{\frac{\sum (x-\mu)^2}{N}}$, where the x in the formula represents the population's N data values. The formula for the standard deviation, s, of a sample of size n with mean $\bar{x}$ (read as "x-bar") is $s = \sqrt{\frac{\sum (x-\bar{x})^2}{n-1}}$, where x in the formula represents the sample's n data values. The variance of a population, σ^2, is the square of the standard deviation of the population. The variance of a sample, s^2, is the square of the standard deviation of the sample. (See "Statistical Inference" later in this chapter for definitions of the terms *population* and *sample.*)

> **Tip: For the Praxis Math CK test, if a problem requires that you calculate a standard deviation or variance, check whether the data are from a population or a sample to make sure you use the correct formula.**

When you are given two data sets, the standard deviation of the one whose data values are clustered closer to the mean of the data is less than the standard deviation of the other data set. Here is an example.

The following two data sets both have a mean of 50. Which data set has the lesser standard deviation?

Set 1: 30, 40, 50, 60, 70

Set 2: 10, 10, 50, 90, 90

It is not necessary to calculate the actual standard deviations for the two data sets because, by inspection, the data values in Set 1 cluster more closely around the mean of 50 than do the data values in Set 2. Therefore, the standard deviation of Set 1 is less than the standard deviation of Set 2. ***Note:*** Even though the two data sets have the same mean, the data in Set 2 have more spread than the data in Set 1.

Visually, in a manner of speaking, data sets whose distributions are "tall and thin" have standard deviations that are less than the standard deviations of data sets whose distributions are "short and wide." Here is an example.

The dot plots show the scores of 30 seventh graders on the mathematics beginning-of-year (BOY) assessment and on the mathematics end-of-year (EOY) assessment. Which set of scores has the lesser standard deviation?

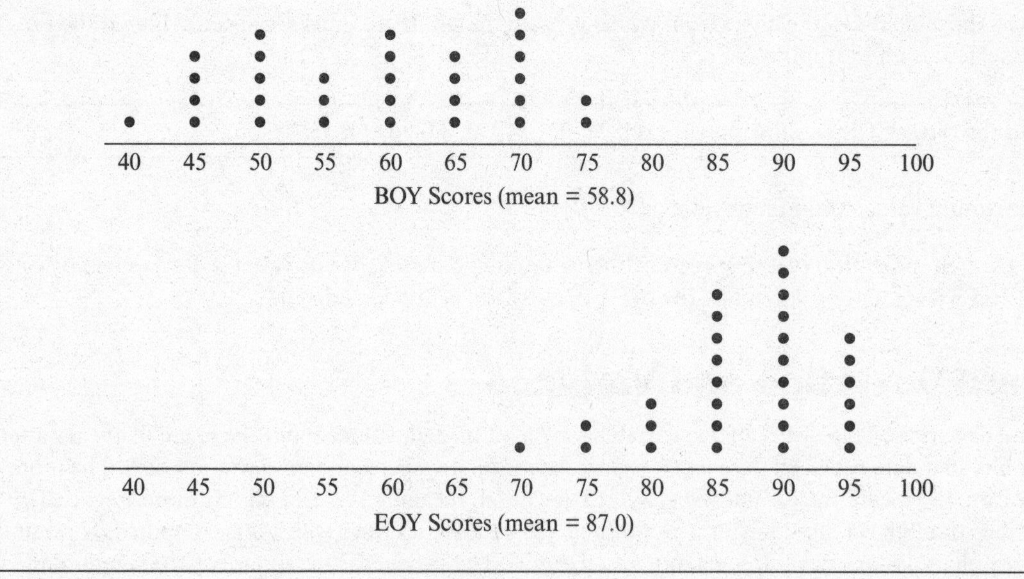

The BOY scores show more variability than do the EOY scores. The BOY distribution looks shorter and wider than the EOY distribution. The EOY scores are clustered more closely around the EOY mean of 87.0 than are the BOY scores around the BOY mean of 58.8. Therefore, by visual inspection, the standard deviation of the EOY scores is less than the standard deviation of the BOY scores.

Interquartile Range

The **interquartile range (IQR)** is the difference between the upper and lower quartiles of a data set. That is, $\text{IQR} = Q_3 - Q_1$.

The IQR is the range of the middle 50 percent of the data. A small IQR indicates the middle half of the data cluster around the median. A large IQR indicates the middle half of the data are spread out away from the median.

Tip: The IQR is used for data in which the median is the appropriate measure of center.

To determine the IQR, you will need to do three steps. First, determine the data set's median. Next, determine the upper and lower quartiles. Then, compute the difference between the upper and lower quartiles. Here are examples using the data sets given in "Percentiles and Quartiles" earlier in this chapter.

Given the data set 21, 24, 28, 30, 32, 34, 35, 35, 35, 36, Q_1 is 28, the median is 33, and Q_3 is 35. Thus, the IQR = 35 − 28 = 7.

Given the data set 10, 12, 12, 13, 14, 15, 16, 17, 20, Q_1 is 12, the median is 14, and Q_3 is 16.5. Thus, the IQR = 16.5 − 12 = 4.5.

z-Scores

The ***z*-score** for a data value is its distance in standard deviations from the mean of the data values. To compute a *z*-score, use the following formula:

$$z\text{-score} = \frac{\text{data value} - \text{mean}}{\text{standard deviation}}$$

If a *z*-score is positive, the data value is greater than the mean; if a *z*-score is negative, the data value is less than the mean. The mean has a *z*-score of 0. Here is an example.

Suppose a student scored 80 on a chemistry test and 90 on a biology test. The mean and standard deviations of the scores from the entire class on the two tests are shown in the table below.

On which test did the student perform better relative to the mean performance of the class on the test?

Course	Mean	Standard Deviation
Chemistry	70	5
Biology	84	6

The student's *z*-score for the chemistry test is $\frac{\text{score} - \text{mean}}{\text{standard deviation}} = \frac{80 - 70}{5} = 2$, indicating the student scored two standard deviations above the class mean on the chemistry test. The student's *z*-score for the biology test is $\frac{\text{score} - \text{mean}}{\text{standard deviation}} = \frac{90 - 84}{6} = 1$, indicating the student scored one standard deviation above the class mean on the biology test. Therefore, relative to the mean performance of the class, the student performed better on the chemistry test.

Five-Number Summary and Box Plots

For a set of data, the **five-number summary** consists of five measures: the minimum data value (Min), the first quartile (Q_1), the median, the third quartile (Q_3), and the maximum value (Max), written in order from smallest to largest. A **box plot** (shown below) is a graphical representation of the five-number summary for a data set. Box plots are also called **box-and-whisker plots.** Here is an example. (***Note:*** The dashed vertical lines are used for clarity but would not be included as part of the box plot.)

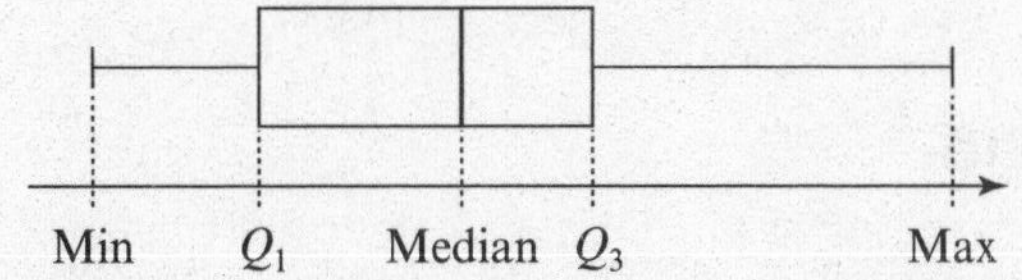

This box plot shows a rectangular box between Q_1 and Q_3, above the horizontal axis. The median is indicated with a vertical line in the interior of the box. The minimum value is at the end of the horizontal line extending from the left end of the box, and the maximum value is at the end of the horizontal line extending from the right end of the box. ***Note:*** Box plots also may be oriented vertically.

The box plot is a visual summary of the data. The five numbers of the five-number summary determine four groups from left to right, starting at the minimum value position in the box plot. Each group contains approximately 25% of the data values.

Skewness

Skewness describes the "lopsidedness" of a distribution. A distribution that is **symmetric,** meaning the lower half is a mirror image of the upper half, has no skew. A distribution is **skewed to the right** (or **positively skewed**) if it has a longer tail to the right, toward larger values. A distribution is **skewed to the left** (or **negatively skewed**) if it has a longer tail to the left. In a right-skewed distribution, the mean lies to the right of the median. In a left-skewed distribution, the mean lies to the left of the median. The mean and median coincide for a symmetric distribution (no skew).

Here are examples.

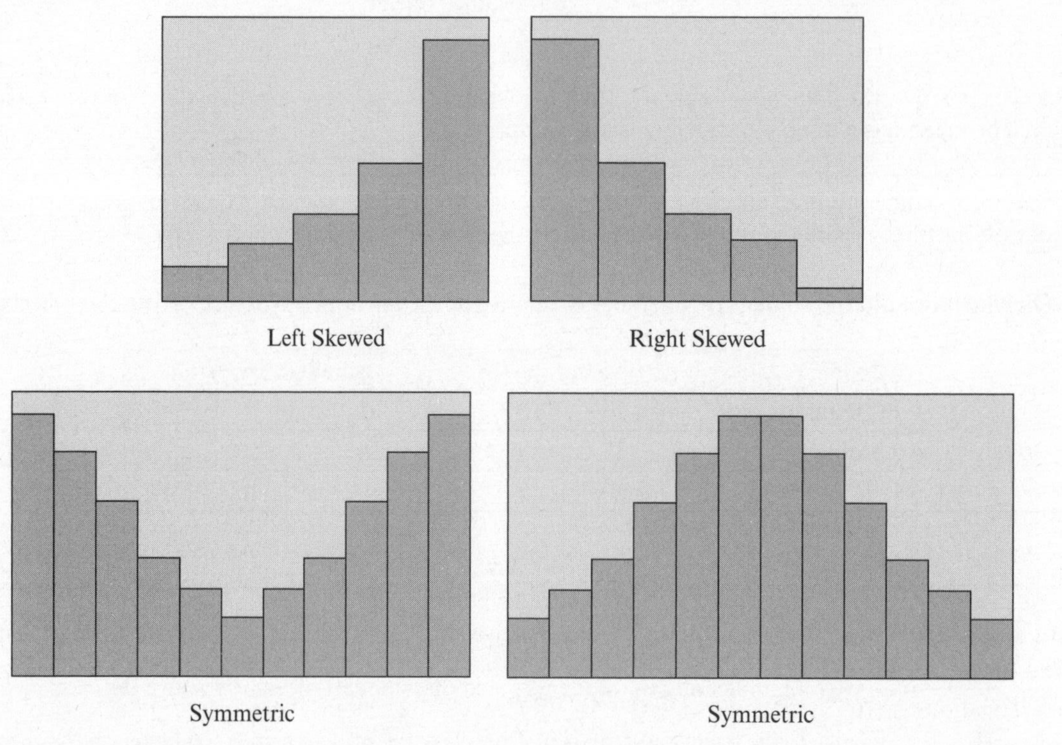

In box plots, skewness is detected by the position of the median. If the median is farther from the first quartile than it is from the third quartile, the distribution is skewed to the left. If the median is farther from the third quartile than it is from the first quartile, the distribution is skewed to the right. If the median is equidistant from the first and third quartiles, the distribution is symmetric. Here are examples.

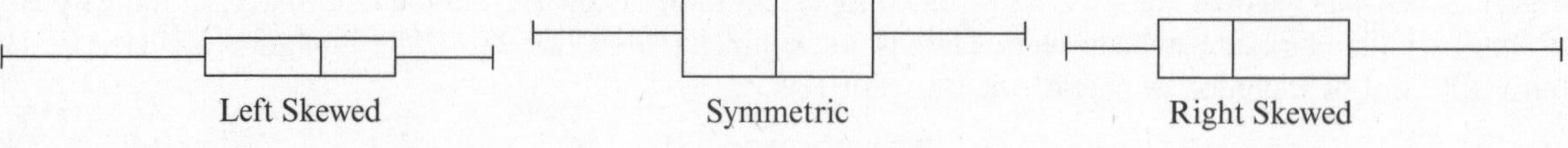

Normal Distributions

A **normal distribution** is a bell-shaped curve that is symmetric about its mean, μ. The standard deviation, σ, is the distance from μ to where the curvature of the bell-shaped graph changes on either side. The distribution is continuous, extending from $-\infty$ to ∞, and its mean, median, and mode coincide.

The mean, μ, of a normal distribution is a *location* parameter because it determines where the center of the distribution is located along the horizontal axis. The standard deviation is a measure of the variability (or spread) of the distribution about its mean. Essentially, σ is a *shape* parameter because it determines whether the distribution is tall and thin (corresponding to small values of σ) or short and wide (corresponding to large values of σ). The distribution is completely defined by its mean, μ, and standard deviation, σ.

The bell-shape of the curve means that most of the data will fall in the middle of the distribution with the amount of data tapering off evenly in both directions as you move away from the center of the distribution. This characteristic of normal distributions can be expressed in a more accurate way, by the **68-95-99.7 rule.** According to this rule, approximately 68 percent of the values of a normal distribution fall within one standard deviation of the mean, about 95 percent fall within two standard deviations of the mean, and about 99.7 percent fall within three standard deviations of the mean. In other words, about 68 percent of the values of a normal distribution fall between $\mu - 1\sigma$ and $\mu + 1\sigma$, 95 percent between $\mu - 2\sigma$ and $\mu + 2\sigma$, and 99.7 percent between $\mu - 3\sigma$ and $\mu + 3\sigma$.

A result of the 68-95-99.7 rule is that a normal distribution with mean μ and standard deviation σ can be subdivided as shown in the following figure.

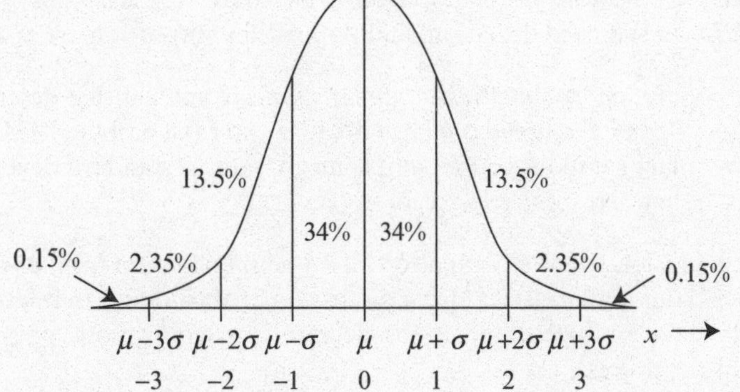

The numbers written horizontally along the bottom of the figure are measures of standard deviations from the mean, called *z*-scores.

Here is an example of using the 68-95-99.7 rule.

> The Wechsler Adult Intelligence Scale (WAIS) is a test designed to measure intelligence in adults. A subject's overall score on the test is called the subject's intelligence quotient (IQ). The WAIS IQ scores have a normal distribution with mean, $\mu = 100$, and standard deviation, $\sigma = 15$.
>
> Based on the WAIS IQ test, approximately what percent of adults have IQs between 85 and 115, between 70 and 130, and between 55 and 145?

According to the 68-95-99.7 rule, about 68 percent of WAIS IQ scores will fall between 100 – 1(15) and 100 + 1(15), 95 percent between 100 – 2(15) and 100 + 2(15), and 99.7 percent between 100 – 3(15) and 100 + 3(15). Thus, based on the WAIS IQ test, about 68 percent of adults have IQs between 85 and 115, about 95 percent have IQs between 70 and 130, and about 99.7 percent have IQs between 55 and 145.

In working problems involving normal distributions, you often will find it necessary to convert data values into *z*-scores using the formula $z\text{-score} = \frac{\text{data value} - \text{mean}}{\text{standard deviation}} = \frac{\text{data value} - \mu}{\sigma}$. The *z*-score expresses the position of the data value *relative to the mean.* (See "*z*-Scores" earlier in this chapter for an additional discussion of this topic.) Furthermore, *z*-scores are in terms of standard deviations. For example, a data value that has a *z*-score of –1 is one standard deviation below the mean, and a data value that has a *z*-score of 1 is one standard deviation above the mean.

Here is an example.

> If scores on a national exam are normally distributed with mean, $\mu = 500$, and standard deviation, $\sigma = 100$, find the *z*-score for a score of 800. Interpret the *z*-score in terms of standard deviations relative to the mean.

The *z*-score for $800 = \frac{\text{data value} - \mu}{\sigma} = \frac{800 - 500}{100} = 3$. Thus, 800 is three standard deviations above the mean.

Statistical Inference

This section presents basic terminology and concepts of statistical inference. In statistical inference, data are collected, summarized, and analyzed to answer questions or to inform decision making. The data provide information about the world around you.

Populations and Samples

A **population** is the entire group of objects, persons, or things (subjects, experimental units) that you are interested in and want to know something about. A **parameter** is a numerical measurement that describes a population. It is a fixed number. However, in investigations of the population, its value often is *unknown*. Customary symbols for the population mean, population standard deviation, and population proportion are μ, σ, and p, respectively.

A **sample** is a subset of the population. A **statistic** is a numerical measurement that describes a sample. Once you have data from a sample, the value of a **statistic** is *known* because you can compute it. However, its value varies from sample to sample. Customary symbols for the sample mean, sample standard deviation, and sample proportion are $\bar{x}$, s, and $\hat{p}$ (read as "p-hat"), respectively.

A **statistical inference** is a conclusion about a population based on information from a statistical study. (See "Types of Statistical Studies" later in this chapter for a discussion of this topic.) In inferential statistics, information from samples is used to make estimates, predictions, decisions, generalizations, or comparisons about populations. Here is a diagram of the process.

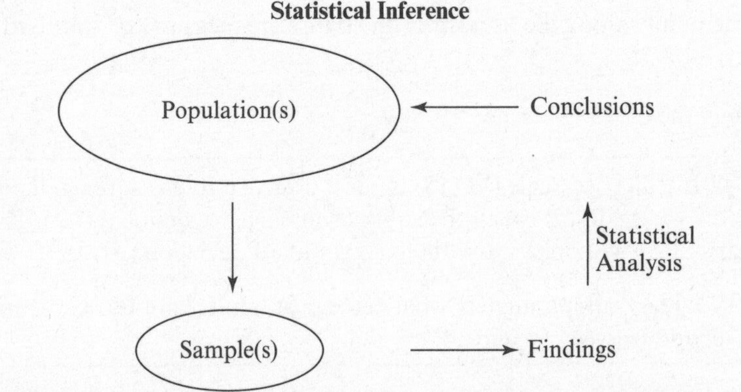

Tip: Conclusions of statistical inference are *always* about populations, *not* about samples.

Random Samples

When you select a sample from a population, you use a **random sample** of adequate size so that it will be representative of the population from which it was selected. A **representative sample** has characteristics that mirror those of the population from which it was selected. Suppose your population is all teachers in your state. Your sample, for example, should have a similar age, race, and gender makeup as this population. It also should be of adequate size. The **sample size** is the number of entities in the sample. Statistical formulas or guidelines are available for determining adequate sample size for various types of studies. In general, increasing the sample size leads to more accurate results (because it reduces variability in the data). A sample is most likely to be a representative sample when it has been chosen randomly from the population, and it is of adequate size.

Note: Conclusions about populations should not be based on samples that are far too small (for example, an opinion survey that uses fewer than 10 subjects).

In a **simple random sample** (or just **random sample**), every member of the population has an equal chance of being selected. Drawing without looking from a bowl containing names written on slips of paper is a way to obtain a random sample. For many situations, however, this method is impractical. Computer-generated random digits or a table of random digits can be used to choose a random sample (see Appendix E for a description of the process).

An important advantage of random samples is that they guard against bias. **Bias** in a statistical study is a type of systematic error that favors particular results.

The powerful techniques of inferential statistics allow you to take sample data and draw inferences about the entire population. Of course, you can't be positive your conclusions are correct because your data are not from the entire population. Fortunately, though, random sampling tends to produce representative samples. Representative samples provide meaningful results that will support valid inferences you make about populations. Making inferences about populations from information in samples is known as **generalizing.**

Sampling Distributions

A **sampling distribution** is the probability distribution of the different values of a sample statistic obtained (theoretically) from all possible random samples of the same size. (See "Random Variables, Probability Distributions, and Expected Value" in Chapter 8 for an explanation of probability distributions.) The variation in the value of the sample statistic from sample to sample is **sampling variability.** Sampling distributions underlie all of statistical inference. You use probabilistic reasoning based on sampling distributions to make decisions about population parameters. Two important sampling distributions are the sampling distribution of the sample mean and the sampling distribution of the sample proportion.

When you repeatedly calculate the sample mean $\bar{x}$ from random samples of size n from a population with mean μ, the value of the sample mean will vary from sample to sample. Therefore, the sample mean is a random variable and has a probability distribution. (See "Random Variables, Probability Distributions, and Expected Value" in Chapter 8 for an explanation of random variables.) The sample mean's probability distribution is known as the **sampling distribution of the sample mean** and has the following properties:

- Its mean is the same as the mean of the sampled population μ.
- Its standard deviation is $\frac{\sigma}{\sqrt{n}}$, the standard deviation σ of the sampled population divided by the square root of the sample size n.
- Its shape approaches a normal distribution as the sample size n increases (**Central Limit Theorem**). ***Tip:*** If the sample size is at least 30, then the sampling distribution of the sample mean is approximately normally distributed. (See "Normal Distributions" earlier in this chapter for a discussion of this topic.)

When you repeatedly calculate the sample proportion $\hat{p}$ from random samples of size n from a population with population proportion p, the value of the sample proportion will vary from sample to sample. Therefore, the sample proportion is a random variable and has a probability distribution. Its probability distribution is known as the **sampling distribution of the sample proportion** $\hat{p}$ and has the following properties:

- Its mean is the same as the population proportion p.
- Its standard deviation is $\sqrt{\frac{p(1-p)}{n}}$, where n is the sample size.
- It has approximately a normal distribution when the sample size is large. ***Tip:*** The sample size n is considered "large" if both np and $n(1-p)$ are both at least 5.

In practice, when you want to estimate an unknown population parameter, you select just *one* sample from the population. You calculate the sample statistic and use it as your best estimate of the population parameter. If you use a random sample of adequate size, your estimate should be close to the true value of the population parameter. Statistical techniques allow to you to calculate a **margin of error,** a measure of sampling error based on the sampling distribution of the sample statistic. The margin of error lets you determine how far the estimate is likely to be from the true value. The sample statistic plus or minus the margin of error produces an interval that may or may not contain the true value. However, information from the sampling distribution allows you to make a statement of confidence that the true value is within the margin of error. For example, you might state that you are "95% confident" that the true value of the population parameter lies in the interval. Technically, "95% confident" means that the true value will lie within 95 percent of all possible intervals constructed in this manner.

Types of Statistical Studies

For this topic, you must demonstrate an understanding of the purposes and differences among survey, experimental, and observational studies.

Survey Studies

In **survey studies,** the purpose is to gather information from a representative sample in order to estimate or make decisions about parameters of populations. Specifying a well-defined, fixed population, using an appropriate method for randomly selecting a sample of adequate size, and ensuring accurate "measurement" of the variable of interest (for example, making sure questions are fair and unbiased) are essential components of a survey study.

Tip: In designing survey studies, you use random sampling to avoid bias, and you manage variability by selecting samples of adequate size.

Examples of this type of study include opinion surveys, fact-finding surveys, questionnaires, and interview studies. Results are summarized and reported. Generalization of the survey results to the population is appropriate only when the sample has been randomly chosen from the population. (See "Random Samples" earlier in this chapter for a discussion of this topic.)

Experimental Studies

In **experimental studies,** the purpose is to investigate possible cause-and-effect relationships by exposing an experimental group to a **treatment** condition and comparing the results to a control group not receiving the treatment. The study is set up in such a way that one group of **experimental units** (for example, people, animals, plants) gets the treatment (the **experimental group**) and another group (the **control group**) does not, and then comparisons are made to see whether the treatment had an influence on the variable of interest. For such comparisons to be valid, other sources of variation (such as extraneous variables) must be controlled. An **extraneous variable** influences the outcome of an experiment, but is not accounted for in the study design. Hallmarks of rigorous experimental studies are well-defined treatments, suitable experimental units, a sound plan for random assignment of the treatment, and accurate measurement of the experiment's results.

Examples of such studies include investigating the effectiveness of a new method of teaching reading on reading ability, the effect of a new drug on cancer patients, and the effect of a new type of fertilizer on plant growth. In a well-designed experimental study, experimental units are randomly assigned to either the treatment or control group to ensure that groups are similar in all respects *except* for the treatment. Therefore, any difference in the two groups can be attributed to the treatment. Only through well-designed experimental studies are cause-and-effect conclusions valid and generalizable.

Note: Experimental studies can involve comparisons of multiple treatments.

Observational Studies

Observational studies involve collecting and analyzing data without changing existing conditions. Observational studies are conducted when it is not possible (or, perhaps, not ethical) to randomly assign experimental units to some treatment condition (for example, being a smoker). Such studies are conducted in a setting that does not permit the investigator to manipulate or control all relevant variables. The main shortcoming of observational studies is that the experimenter cannot randomize a treatment condition to experimental units. The nonrandomness in sampling and the constraint imposed by observing a predetermined condition limit drawing cause-and-effect conclusions. There is a possibility that results are due to one or more variables other than the variables being studied.

Examples of observational studies include exploring the relationship between gum disease and smoking, between SAT scores and college grade point average, or between geographic location and family size. In observational studies, estimating population parameters or making statements about differences among treatments is not recommended. Nevertheless, the results of observational studies can point to patterns in data and relationships between variables.

Well-Designed Studies

Well-designed studies follow the process of **scientific inquiry.** Scientists use scientific inquiry to obtain reliable and valid information about variables of interest. In statistical studies, scientific inquiry has five main steps:

1. **Define the problem:** Pose a statistical question about a topic or variable of interest that can be answered with data.
2. **Formulate a hypothesis:** Make an educated guess about an aspect of the topic or variable.
3. **Gather evidence:** Design and perform a study to test the hypothesis; collect data about the hypothesis.
4. **Analyze the data:** Using appropriate statistical techniques, analyze the data collected.
5. **Draw conclusions:** Interpret the results and decide whether the hypothesis is supported or not supported by the results.

To provide results worthy of consideration, carefully plan well-designed studies, investigate issues that are clear and unambiguous, clearly identify populations of study, use randomization and select samples of adequate size, use well-defined variables of interest, avoid bias, and control for outside factors, such as extraneous variables, that could jeopardize the validity of conclusions. Only when investigators use well-designed studies can reliable and valid conclusions be drawn.

Two-Way Frequency Tables of Categorical Data

When you collect data on two categorical variables from a sample of subjects, randomly selected from a population of interest to you, display the frequencies for the data in a two-way table. Then calculate row and column totals. Use relative frequencies (or proportions) to describe possible associations between the two variables. Here is an example.

A random selection of 400 university students (200 freshmen students and 200 senior students) from a university of about 40,000 students was surveyed and asked whether they have a personal online social media account. One hundred fifty of the freshmen students and 112 of the senior students responded "yes" to the survey question.

The following two-way table summarizes the information given. Do the data suggest that there is an association between classification as a freshman or senior and having a personal online social media account?

Responses of 400 Students to the Survey Question:
Do you have a personal online social media account?

Classification	Yes	No	Total
Freshmen	150	50	200
Seniors	112	88	200
Total	262	138	**400**

The proportion of freshmen who have a personal online social media account is $\frac{150}{200} = 0.75$ or 75%. The proportion of seniors who have a social media online account is $\frac{112}{200} = 0.56$ or 56%. Using an informal inferential approach, note that the two proportions are based on an equal number of students and observe that 0.75 and 0.56 differ by 0.19 or 19%. This difference seems noteworthy. These findings suggest that, for students in that university, classification as a freshman or senior is associated with having a personal online social media account. It appears that freshmen are more likely than seniors to have a social media account.

Note: Statistical formulas are available to quantify and statistically evaluate information in two-way categorical tables. However, based on the content category descriptions for the Praxis Math CK test, you are not expected to know these formulas. (See the *Mathematics: Content Knowledge (5161) Study Companion* at https://www.ets.org/s/praxis/pdf/5161.pdf for detailed descriptions of each content category topic.)

Investigating Bivariate Data

For the Praxis Math CK test, you should have a basic understanding of how to detect relationships between two quantitative variables based on data that have been collected on both variables. These data are bivariate data. **Bivariate data** are paired values of data from two quantitative variables. The data are paired in a way that matches each value from one variable with a corresponding value from the other variable. Scatter plots, lines of best fit, simple linear regression, and correlation coefficients are used to investigate this type of data.

Scatter Plots

A **scatter plot** is a graph of the ordered pairs of a set of bivariate data plotted on a coordinate grid. The scale for one of the variables is along the horizontal axis and the scale for the other variable is along the vertical axis. Each plotted ordered pair represents a **data point** in the scatter plot. (*Note:* Do not connect the data points in a scatter plot.) Always plot the **predictor variable** (also called the **explanatory variable** or **independent variable**), if there is one, on the horizontal axis and the **response variable** (also called the **dependent variable**) on the vertical axis. The scatter plot's pattern provides visual cues as to whether there is a relationship between the two variables; and, if there is, the nature of that relationship.

For the Praxis Math CK test, you should be able to examine scatter plots and distinguish between those that suggest linear relationships and those that suggest nonlinear relationships between two variables. The data points are often described as forming a "cloud." When the data points in a scatter plot appear to cluster around an imagined line passing through the points, the scatter plot suggests a **linear** relationship between the two variables. Here is an example.

Which scatter plot clearly shows a nonlinear relationship between variables X and Y?

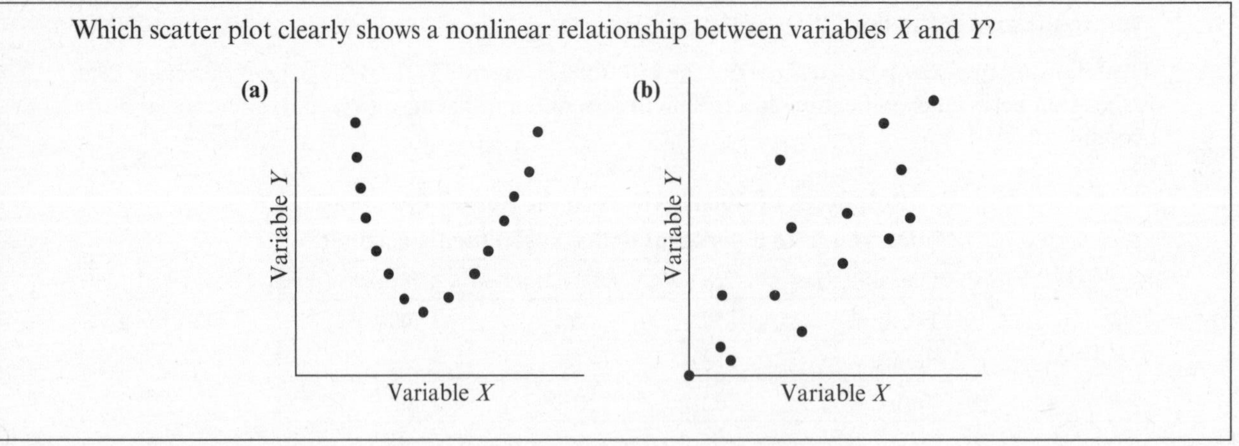

The scatter plot in (a) shows a recognizable curved pattern. This pattern suggests a curved relationship between the variables X and Y. It is clearly nonlinear. The scatter plot in (b) shows a recognizable linear pattern. This pattern suggests a linear relationship between the variables X and Y.

A scatter plot that has no recognizable pattern points to no relationship between the two variables. Here is an example.

Which scatter plot suggests that there is no relationship between the two variables?

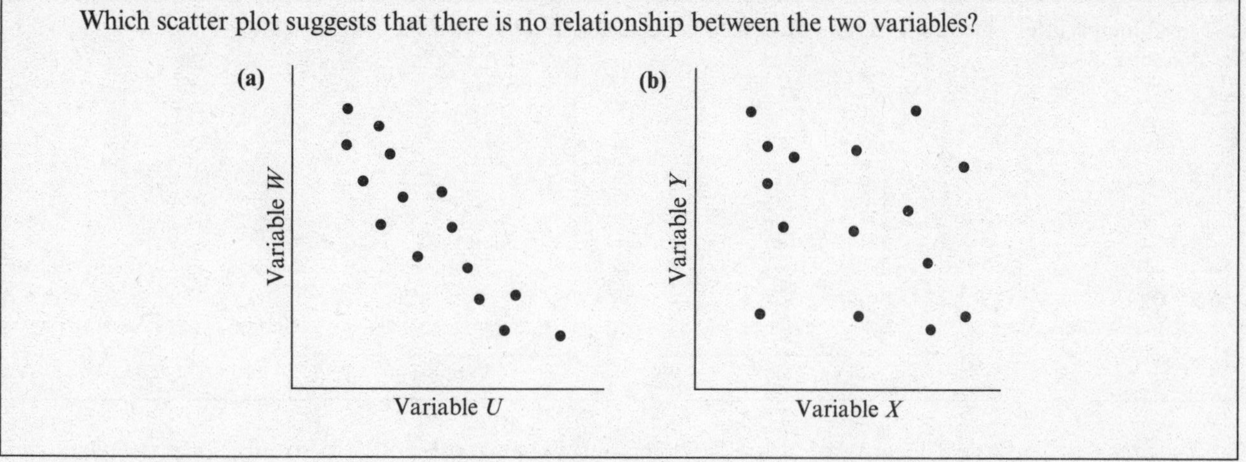

The scatter plot in (a) shows a recognizable linear pattern that suggests a linear relationship between variables *U* and *W*. The scatter plot in (b) does not show a recognizable pattern to suggest a relationship between variables *X* and *Y*.

If the relationship between two variables is linear, it can be positive or negative. For linear relationships, scatter plots that slant upward from left to right indicate positive linear relationships. In **positive linear relationships,** above-average values of one variable tend to be associated with above-average values of the other, and below-average values of the two variables also tend to be associated. Scatter plots that slant downward from left to right indicate negative linear relationships. In **negative linear relationships,** above-average values of one variable tend to be associated with below-average values of the other, and the reverse is true. Here is an example.

Describe the scatter plots as having positive or negative linear relationships.

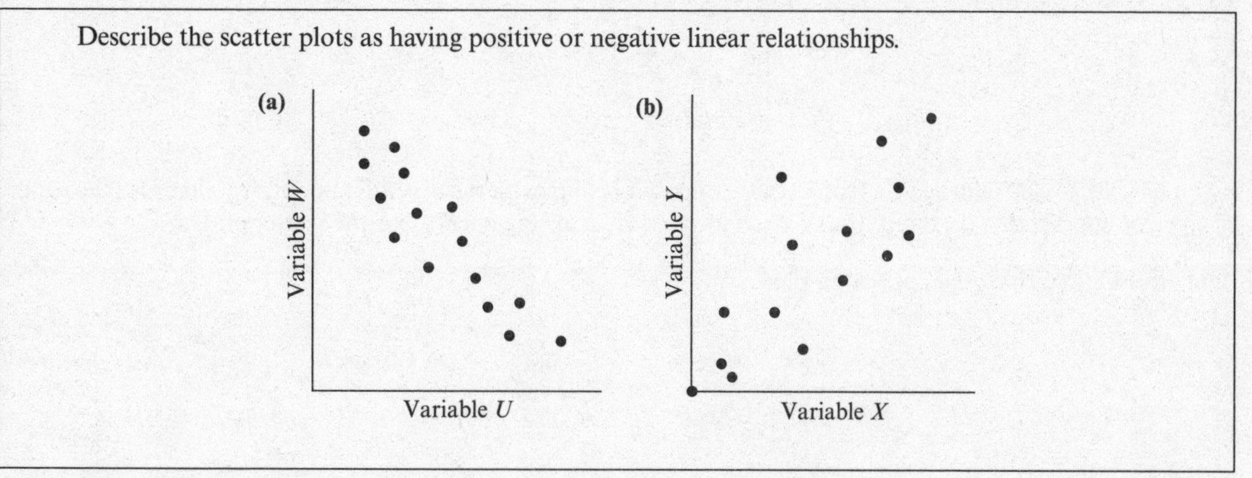

The scatter plot in (a) suggests a negative linear relationship between *U* and *W*. The scatter plot in (b) suggests a positive linear relationship between *X* and *Y*.

The closer the data points in a scatter plot cluster around an imagined line passing through the points, the stronger the linear relationship is between the two variables. Here is an example.

Which scatter plot suggests the stronger linear relationship between the two variables?

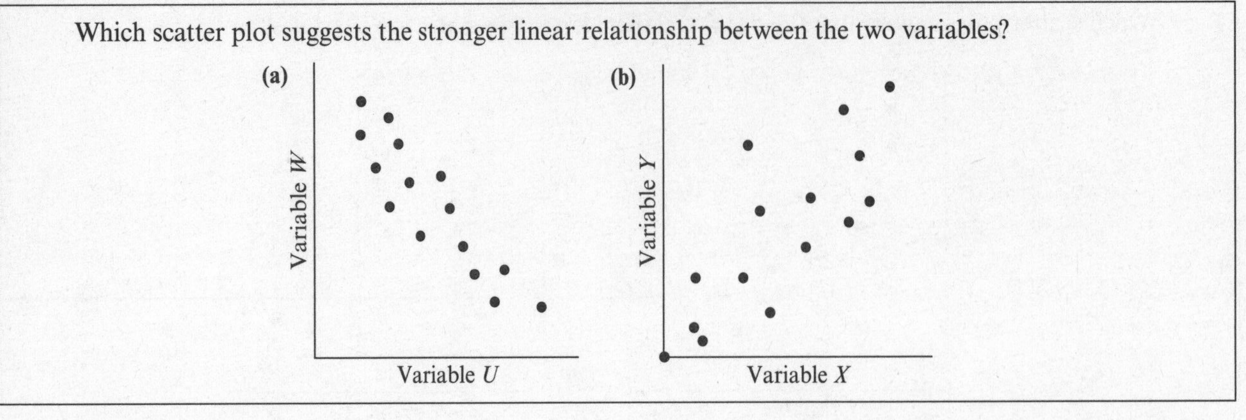

Both scatter plots indicate a linear relationship. The relationship between U and W is stronger than the relationship between X and Y because the data points in the scatter plot in (a) are clustered closer around an imagined line passing through the points than are the data points in the scatter plot in (b).

In a scatter plot, an **outlier** is a data point that is relatively far away from the rest of the points in the scatter plot. For example, in the scatter plot shown below, the data point marked with an asterisk is a noticeable outlier.

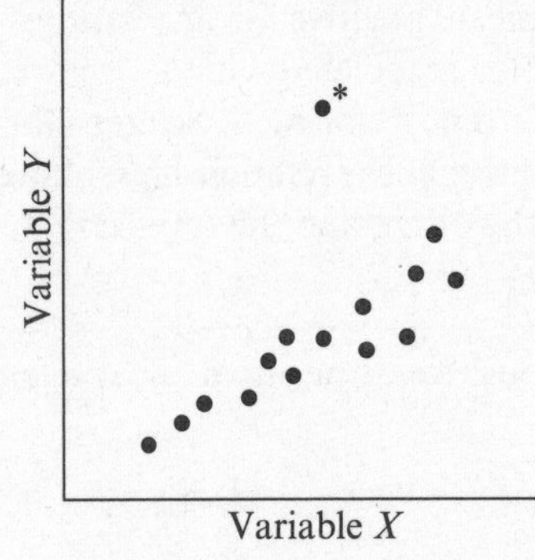

If you have *believable* information that an outlier doesn't belong with the other data points (perhaps it's the result of an error in collecting the data), you can exclude it when assessing linearity of the scatter plot.

Here are additional examples of scatter plots.

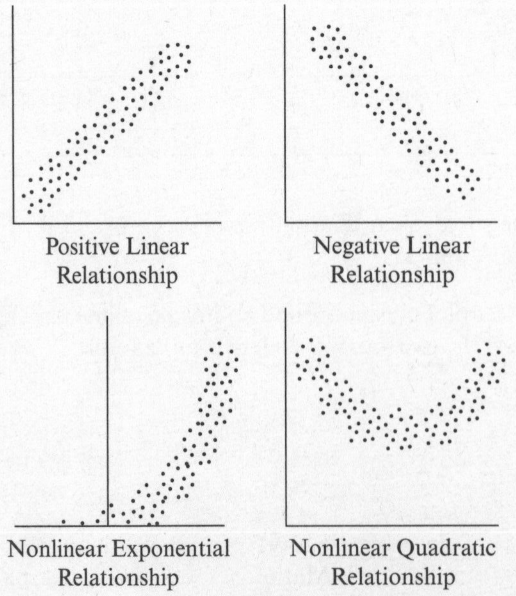

Line of Best Fit and Simple Linear Regression

If the scatter plot seems approximately linear, the **line of best fit** (or **regression line**) is a straight line that best represents the data. It might pass through some of the points, none of the points, or even all of the points. It will always pass through the point whose coordinates are the means of the two variables.

If X and Y are the two variables under consideration, the equation of the line of best fit is given by the **simple linear regression equation** $\hat{Y} = a + bX$, where $\hat{Y}$ (read as "Y-hat") is the predicted value of the response variable, Y, a is a constant (corresponding to $X = 0$), and b is the regression coefficient. For statistical reasons, to be safe, you should predict only within the range of the predictor variable. When you predict within the range of the plotted data, you are **interpolating.**

The coefficient b is the **slope** of the regression line. The interpretation of the slope, b, is that if the X variable increases by 1 unit, it is predicted that the Y variable will change by b units. The interpretation of the **intercept,** a, is that when the X variable is zero, the Y variable is a units. However, if values for the X variable near zero would not make sense, then typically the interpretation of the intercept will seem unrealistic in the real world. Nevertheless, the coefficient a is a necessary part of the equation of the line of best fit.

The **residuals** are the differences between the actual y values in the scatter plot and the $\hat{Y}$ values predicted by the regression equation. Visually, they are the vertical distances of the data points from the regression line. The line of best fit minimizes the sum of the squares of the residuals and is the **least-squares regression line.** The closer the plotted data points are to the regression line, the smaller the residual sum of squares. Here is a detailed example to clarify your understanding of simple linear regression.

The following table contains 10 bivariate data points for the variables X and Y.

X	10	8	13	9	11	14	6	4	12	5
Y	8.1	6.9	7.5	8.8	8.3	9.9	7.2	4.3	10.8	5.7

The scatter plot and line of best fit are shown below.

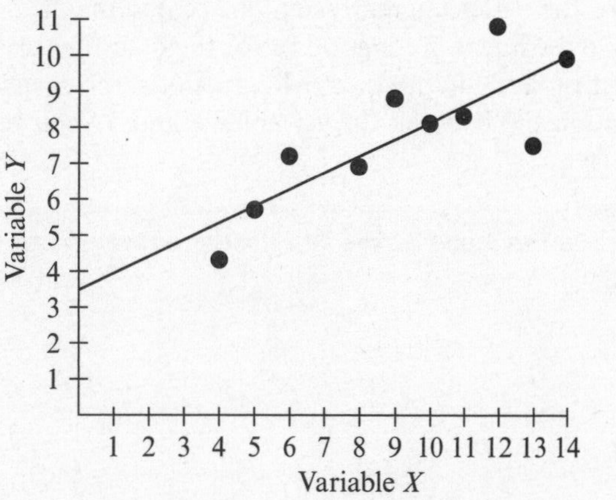

The linear regression equation of the line of best fit is $\hat{Y} = 3.5 + 0.46X$. The interpretation of the slope of 0.46 is that if the X variable increases by 1 unit, it is predicted that the Y variable will increase by 0.46 units. The interpretation of the intercept, 3.5, is that when the X variable is zero, the Y variable is 3.5 units.

The predicted Y value for $X = 12$ is $\hat{Y} = 3.5 + 0.46(12) = 9.0$. The residual for the data point (12, 10.8) is $10.8 - 9.0 = 1.8$.

The predicted Y value for $X = 7$ is $\hat{Y} = 3.5 + 0.46(7) = 6.7$. The value 7 is within the range of the available data, so it is permissible to predict its Y value.

Note: The linear regression equation in this example is provided to you because it was obtained using technology that is unavailable to you when you take the Praxis Math CK test. The ETS graphing calculator does not have a menu for performing statistical analysis. Based on this fact, (currently) it is assumed you will not be expected to produce a regression equation when you take the test. However, it is important that you understand the function of a regression equation and that you can interpret its slope and intercept.

Tip: Regression is strongly affected by outliers. Be cautious in your interpretation of regression results if the scatter plot shows clear-cut outliers.

Correlation Coefficient

Scatter plots visually show the direction, shape, and strength of the relationship between two quantitative variables. If the relationship is linear, the **correlation coefficient** ***r*** is a numerical measure that describes the direction and strength of the linear relationship between the two variables.

Correlation coefficients range from -1 to $+1$, with -1 indicating a "perfect" negative linear relationship and $+1$ indicating a "perfect" positive linear relationship. Correlation values very close to either -1 or $+1$ indicate very strong relationships, meaning the data points in the scatter plot lie close to a straight line. Correlations of precisely -1 or $+1$ occur only when the data points lie exactly along a straight line. If the two variables have no *relationship* to each other, then the correlation coefficient will be 0. The farther the correlation coefficient is from 0, the stronger the relationship. (Remember, however, that you cannot have correlation coefficients below -1 or above $+1$.)

The existence of a recognizable correlation between two variables does *not* imply that changes in one variable cause changes in the other variable. The correlation might be a reflection of outside variables that affect both variables under study. ***Tip:*** For the Praxis Math CK test, you are expected to be able to distinguish between correlation and causation.

In simple linear regression, the correlation coefficient is a measure of the strength of the linear relationship between the predictor variable and the response variable of the linear regression equation. Therefore, it can be used to assess the regression line's "goodness of fit." The closer $|r|$ is to 1, the more perfect the linear relationship is between X and Y, and therefore, the better the regression line represents the data points. If r is close to 0, there is little or no linear relationship, so the line is not a good fit for the data. For example, for the bivariate data shown previously in "Line of Best Fit and Simple Linear Regression," the correlation coefficient is 0.82, indicating a somewhat strong linear relationship between the variables X and Y. This result suggests that the regression line is a good fit for the data.

Tip: The correlation coefficient and the slope of the regression equation are not the same measure; however, their signs are always the same.

Chapter 10

Matrices

Basic Matrix Concepts

A **matrix** is a rectangular array of **elements** (usually) enclosed in brackets. For the Praxis Math CK test, the elements of a matrix are real or complex numbers or expressions representing real or complex numbers. A matrix with m rows and n columns is an $m \times n$ matrix. Matrices are commonly denoted by uppercase letters and their elements by the corresponding lowercase letters, which are subscripted to indicate the location of the elements in the matrix. For a matrix A, the notation a_{ij} denotes the element in the ith row and jth column of the matrix. It is also customary to denote an $m \times n$ matrix A by $\left[a_{ij}\right]_{(m,\,n)}$ or simply by $\left[a_{ij}\right]$, if the order is clear.

The **order** of a matrix is the number of rows and columns it contains; thus, an $m \times n$ matrix has order $m \times n$. A $1 \times n$ matrix is a **row vector** of order n. An $m \times 1$ matrix is a **column vector** of order m. Here are examples.

$$\begin{bmatrix} 5 & 0 & 4 \\ 6 & -2 & 9 \end{bmatrix}_{2\times 3} \text{ is a } 2 \times 3 \text{ matrix.}$$

$$\begin{bmatrix} -1 & 2 \\ 0 & 0 \\ 5 & 4 \end{bmatrix}_{3\times 2} \text{ is a } 3 \times 2 \text{ matrix.}$$

$$\begin{bmatrix} 2 & -3 & 1 \end{bmatrix}_{1\times 3} \text{ is a row vector of order 3.}$$

$$\begin{bmatrix} 5 \\ 1 \\ -1 \end{bmatrix}_{3\times 1} \text{ is a column vector of order 3.}$$

If $m = n$, the matrix is a **square matrix** of order n. Here is an example of a 3×3 square matrix.

$$\begin{bmatrix} 1 & 2 & 0 \\ 2 & 0 & -3 \\ 0 & -3 & 5 \end{bmatrix}_{3\times 3}$$

The **main diagonal** of a square matrix of order n is the diagonal of elements $a_{11}, a_{22}, \ldots, a_{nn}$ from the top-left corner to the bottom-right corner of the matrix. The elements on the main diagonal of the square matrix shown directly above are 1, 0, and 5.

A **diagonal matrix** is a square matrix whose only nonzero elements are on the main diagonal. A diagonal matrix that has only ones on the main diagonal is an **identity matrix.** The identity matrix of order n is denoted I_n. Here is an example of an identity matrix of order 2.

$$I_2 = \begin{bmatrix} 1 & 0 \\ 0 & 1 \end{bmatrix}$$

A square matrix containing only 0 elements is the zero matrix, denoted 0 (or $0_{n\times n}$).

The **negative of a matrix** $A = \left[a_{ij}\right]$ is the matrix $-A = \left[-a_{ij}\right]$, whose elements are the negatives of their corresponding elements in A.

Two matrices A and B are **equal** if and only if they have the same order and their corresponding elements are equal. Therefore, if two matrices $A=\left[a_{ij}\right]$ and $B=\left[b_{ij}\right]$ are equal, then $a_{ij}=b_{ij}$, for $1 \le i \le m$ and $1 \le j \le n$. For example:

$$\begin{bmatrix} 2 & 8 \\ -7 & 1 \end{bmatrix} = \begin{bmatrix} \sqrt{4} & 2^3 \\ \frac{-21}{3} & 1 \end{bmatrix}, \begin{bmatrix} 1 & 0 & 0 \\ 0 & 1 & 0 \\ 0 & 0 & 1 \end{bmatrix} \neq \begin{bmatrix} 1 & 0 \\ 0 & 1 \end{bmatrix}, \begin{bmatrix} 2 & 4 & 6 \end{bmatrix} \neq \begin{bmatrix} 2 \\ 4 \\ 6 \end{bmatrix}$$

The **transpose** of an $m \times n$ matrix A is an $n \times m$ matrix, denoted A^T (read as "A transpose"), obtained by interchanging the rows and columns of A. The transpose of a matrix A is also denoted A'. Here is an example.

$$\text{Given } A = \begin{bmatrix} 5 & 0 & 4 \\ 6 & -2 & 9 \end{bmatrix}_{2\times 3}, \text{ then } A^T = \begin{bmatrix} 5 & 6 \\ 0 & -2 \\ 4 & 9 \end{bmatrix}_{3\times 2}.$$

A square matrix A is said to be **symmetric** if $A = A^T$. Here is an example.

$$A = \begin{bmatrix} 1 & 2 & 0 \\ 2 & 0 & -3 \\ 0 & -3 & 5 \end{bmatrix}_{3\times 3} = A^T$$

Operations with Matrices

For this topic, you must be able to perform scalar multiplication and add, subtract, and multiply vectors and matrices and find inverses of matrices.

Scalar Multiplication

A **scalar** is a number or numerical quantity.

The **scalar product**, kA, of an $m \times n$ matrix $A=\left[a_{ij}\right]$ and a scalar k is the $m \times n$ matrix $R = kA$, where $\left[r_{ij}\right]=\left[ka_{ij}\right]$.

Note: Any size matrix can be multiplied by a scalar. Here is an example.

$$3\begin{bmatrix} 5 & 2 \\ 0 & -1 \end{bmatrix} = \begin{bmatrix} 15 & 6 \\ 0 & -3 \end{bmatrix}$$

Matrix Addition and Subtraction

Two matrices are **conformable for matrix addition or subtraction** if they have the same order. *Addition or subtraction of matrices with unlike orders is not defined.*

The **sum**, $A + B$, of two $m \times n$ matrices $A=\left[a_{ij}\right]$ and $B=\left[b_{ij}\right]$ is the $m \times n$ matrix $S = A + B$, where $\left[s_{ij}\right]=\left[a_{ij}+b_{ij}\right]$. Here is an example.

Given $A = \begin{bmatrix} 4 & 1 \\ -3 & 6 \end{bmatrix}$ and $B = \begin{bmatrix} 2 & -5 \\ 0 & 3 \end{bmatrix}$, find $A + B$.

$$A + B = \begin{bmatrix} 4 & 1 \\ -3 & 6 \end{bmatrix} + \begin{bmatrix} 2 & -5 \\ 0 & 3 \end{bmatrix} = \begin{bmatrix} 6 & -4 \\ -3 & 9 \end{bmatrix}$$

With respect to matrix addition, the 0 matrix is the **additive identity** element and $-A$ is the **additive inverse** for the matrix A. That is, if A and 0 have the same order, then $A + 0 = 0 + A = A$ and $A + -A = -A + A = 0$.

The **difference**, $A - B$, of two matrices is defined to be $A + (-B)$. In practice, to subtract two matrices, subtract corresponding elements of the two matrices.

$$A - B = \begin{bmatrix} 4 & 1 \\ -3 & 7 \end{bmatrix} - \begin{bmatrix} 2 & -5 \\ 0 & 3 \end{bmatrix} = \begin{bmatrix} 2 & 6 \\ -3 & 4 \end{bmatrix}$$

The Inner Product

The **inner product** (also called the **dot product**), $A \cdot B$, *in that order* of a $1 \times m$ row vector $A = [a_{11}, a_{12}, \dots a_{1m}]$ and an $m \times 1$ column vector $B = \begin{bmatrix} b_{11} \\ b_{21} \\ \vdots \\ b_{m1} \end{bmatrix}$, is the scalar $a_{11}b_{11} + a_{12}b_{21} + \dots + a_{1m}b_{m1}$. Notice that you multiply *row by column*: Multiply each element of the row times the corresponding element of the column and then sum the products. Here is an example.

Find the inner product of $A = \begin{bmatrix} 1 & 0 & 5 & -2 \end{bmatrix}$ and $B = \begin{bmatrix} 3 \\ -1 \\ 0 \\ 4 \end{bmatrix}$.

$$A \cdot B = \begin{bmatrix} 1 & 0 & 5 & -2 \end{bmatrix} \cdot \begin{bmatrix} 3 \\ -1 \\ 0 \\ 4 \end{bmatrix} = 1 \cdot 3 + 0 \cdot (-1) + 5 \cdot 0 + -2 \cdot 4 = -5$$

Matrix Multiplication

Two matrices, A and B, are **conformable for matrix multiplication** in the order AB, only if the number of columns of matrix A is equal to the number of rows of matrix B. In the product, AB, we say B is **premultiplied** by A and A is **postmultipled** by B. *Multiplication of matrices that are not conformable is not defined.*

The **product**, AB, *in that order* of an $m \times k$ matrix $A = \left[a_{ij} \right]$ and a $k \times n$ matrix $B = \left[b_{ij} \right]$ is the $m \times n$ matrix $C = \left[c_{ij} \right] = \left[a_{i1}b_{1j} + a_{i2}b_{2j} + \cdots + a_{ik}b_{kj} \right]$, for $1 \le i \le m$ and $1 \le j \le n$. Notice that the element c_{ij} is the inner product of the ith row of A and the jth column of B. Here is an example.

Given $A = \begin{bmatrix} 1 & 5 \\ 3 & -5 \end{bmatrix}$ and $B = \begin{bmatrix} 0 & 4 & 2 \\ -5 & 3 & 1 \end{bmatrix}$, compute AB.

$$AB = \begin{bmatrix} 1 & 5 \\ 3 & -5 \end{bmatrix} \begin{bmatrix} 0 & 4 & 2 \\ -5 & 3 & 1 \end{bmatrix} = \begin{bmatrix} 1 \cdot 0 + 5 \cdot (-5) & 1 \cdot 4 + 5 \cdot 3 & 1 \cdot 2 + 5 \cdot 1 \\ 3 \cdot 0 + (-5) \cdot (-5) & 3 \cdot 4 + (-5) \cdot 3 & 3 \cdot 2 + (-5) \cdot 1 \end{bmatrix} = \begin{bmatrix} -25 & 19 & 7 \\ 25 & -3 & 1 \end{bmatrix}$$

Tip: Because of the distinctive way that matrix multiplication is defined, in general, matrix multiplication is not commutative, not even for square matrices of the same order. Because of this noncommutative feature of matrix arithmetic, you must pay careful attention to the order of the factors in any product of matrices when you are taking the Praxis Math CK test.

With respect to matrix multiplication, the matrix I is the **multiplicative identity** element; that is, if A is an $m \times n$ matrix, then $AI_n = A$ and $I_m A = A$.

Matrix Inverses

If A is a square matrix of order n and there exists a square matrix B of order n such that $AB = BA = I$, then B is called the **inverse** of A. A matrix A that has an inverse is said to be **invertible** (or **nonsingular**). If no such matrix B exists, then A is **singular.**

Not all square matrices have inverses, but when the inverse for a square matrix exists, the inverse is unique and is designated A^{-1}. Thus, $AA^{-1} = A^{-1}A = I$.

The inverse of a 2×2 nonsingular matrix $A = \begin{bmatrix} a_{11} & a_{12} \\ a_{21} & a_{22} \end{bmatrix}$ is given by $A^{-1} = \frac{1}{\det(A)}\begin{bmatrix} a_{22} & -a_{12} \\ -a_{21} & a_{11} \end{bmatrix}$, where $\det(A) = a_{11}a_{22} - a_{12}a_{21} \neq 0$. The scalar $\det(A) = a_{11}a_{22} - a_{12}a_{21}$ is the determinant of A. (See the section "Determinants" later in this chapter for an additional discussion on determinants.) The procedure, which works *only* for nonsingular 2×2 matrices, can be stated in four steps:

1. Compute $\det(A) = a_{11}a_{22} - a_{12}a_{21}$.
2. Switch a_{11} and a_{22}.
3. Change the signs of a_{12} and a_{21} (but don't switch them!).
4. Multiple each element by $\frac{1}{\det(A)}$.

The reason you must understand the process is that a question might ask about the process rather than for you to find the inverse. Here is an example.

Let $A = \begin{bmatrix} 1 & 1 \\ 4 & 2 \end{bmatrix}$, find A^{-1}.

$$A^{-1} = \frac{1}{\det(A)}\begin{bmatrix} 2 & -1 \\ -4 & 1 \end{bmatrix} = \frac{1}{-2}\cdot\begin{bmatrix} 2 & -1 \\ -4 & 1 \end{bmatrix} = \begin{bmatrix} -1 & \frac{1}{2} \\ 2 & -\frac{1}{2} \end{bmatrix}$$

The matrix $A = \begin{bmatrix} a_{11} & a_{12} \\ a_{21} & a_{22} \end{bmatrix}$ has an inverse if and only if $\det(A) = a_{11}a_{22} - a_{12}a_{21} \neq 0$.

Another process for finding the inverse of a nonsingular 2×2 matrix $A = \begin{bmatrix} a_{11} & a_{12} \\ a_{21} & a_{22} \end{bmatrix}$ is

1. Create the 2×4 **partitioned matrix** $\left[\begin{array}{cc:cc} a_{11} & a_{12} & 1 & 0 \\ a_{21} & a_{22} & 0 & 1 \end{array}\right]$, which contains A as a **submatrix** on the left and I as a submatrix on the right.
2. Through a series of elementary row operations, convert the submatrix A into an identity matrix. (See the next section for a discussion of elementary row operations.)

This process will yield the matrix $\left[\begin{array}{cc:cc} 1 & 0 & \frac{a_{22}}{a_{11}a_{22} - a_{12}a_{21}} & \frac{-a_{12}}{a_{11}a_{22} - a_{12}a_{21}} \\ 0 & 1 & \frac{-a_{21}}{a_{11}a_{22} - a_{12}a_{21}} & \frac{a_{11}}{a_{11}a_{22} - a_{12}a_{21}} \end{array}\right]$, which shows I on the left and A^{-1} on the right. This latter process will also work for higher-order matrices.

With respect to arithmetic operations, matrices *that contain elements that are complex numbers or real numbers* have some properties in common with the properties of their elements. With respect to the operation of matrix addition, the set of $m \times n$ matrices is closed, commutative, and associative, and has an additive identity and an additive inverse for each $m \times n$ matrix. For the operation of matrix multiplication, certain restrictions on the order of the matrices involved in the multiplication must be met before the operation is defined. For situations in which matrix multiplication is defined, matrix multiplication is closed, associative, has a multiplicative identity, and distributes over addition. In general, matrix multiplication is *not* commutative, nor does there always exist multiplicative inverses.

Tip: The ETS graphing calculator does not have matrix features. Use the techniques in this section to perform any matrix computations that you might be required to perform on the Praxis Math CK test.

Matrix Solutions of Systems of Linear Equations

For this topic, you use matrix techniques to solve systems of linear equations.

A **system** of three linear equations with three variables x, y, and z is given by $\begin{array}{l} a_{11}x + a_{12}y + a_{13}z = c_1 \\ a_{21}x + a_{22}y + a_{23}z = c_2 \\ a_{31}x + a_{32}y + a_{33}z = c_3 \end{array}$, where the coefficients a_{ij} and c_i are constants.

This system can be solved using the algebraic methods of substitution and elimination (which are presented in the section "Systems of Equations and Inequalities" in Chapter 3) or the system can be solved using a technique called **transformation of the augmented matrix**, which will be presented in this section. The system is said to be **consistent** if it has a solution; otherwise, the system is **inconsistent.**

The augmented matrix for the system is the matrix $\begin{bmatrix} a_{11} & a_{12} & a_{13} & c_1 \\ a_{21} & a_{22} & a_{23} & c_2 \\ a_{31} & a_{32} & a_{33} & c_3 \end{bmatrix}$.

To solve the system, use **elementary row operations** (interchanging two rows, multiplying a row by a nonzero scalar, adding two rows, multiplying a row by a scalar, and adding the result to a row) to transform the submatrix of coefficients a_{ij} as close as possible into the identity matrix. When the system is consistent, the results will be one of the following reduced row-echelon forms:

$\begin{bmatrix} 1 & 0 & 0 & x_0 \\ 0 & 1 & 0 & y_0 \\ 0 & 0 & 1 & z_0 \end{bmatrix}$, which yields the unique solution $x = x_0$, $y = y_0$, $z = z_0$;

$\begin{bmatrix} 1 & 0 & k_1 & x_0 \\ 0 & 1 & k_2 & y_0 \\ 0 & 0 & 0 & 0 \end{bmatrix}$, which yields the nonunique solution $x = x_0 - k_1t$, $y = y_0 - k_2t$, $z = t$, where t is an arbitrarily chosen value for the "free" variable z; or

$\begin{bmatrix} 1 & j_1 & k_1 & x_0 \\ 0 & 0 & 0 & 0 \\ 0 & 0 & 0 & 0 \end{bmatrix}$, which yields the nonunique solution $x = x_0 - j_1s - k_1t$, $y = s$, $z = t$, where s and t are arbitrarily chosen values for the free variables y and z.

Here is an example.

Solve the system: $\begin{array}{r} x - 2y + 3z = 1 \\ x + 3y - z = 4 \\ 2x + y - 2z = 13 \end{array}$.

The augmented matrix for the system is the matrix $\begin{bmatrix} 1 & -2 & 3 & 1 \\ 1 & 3 & -1 & 4 \\ 2 & 1 & -2 & 13 \end{bmatrix}$. Proceed with elementary row operations.

$$\begin{bmatrix} 1 & -2 & 3 & 1 \\ 1 & 3 & -1 & 4 \\ 2 & 1 & -2 & 13 \end{bmatrix} \xrightarrow{\text{Multiply row 1 by } -1 \text{ and add to row 2}} \begin{bmatrix} 1 & -2 & 3 & 1 \\ 0 & 5 & -4 & 3 \\ 2 & 1 & -2 & 13 \end{bmatrix}$$

$$\xrightarrow{\text{Multiply row 1 by } -2 \text{ and add to row 3}} \begin{bmatrix} 1 & -2 & 3 & 1 \\ 0 & 5 & -4 & 3 \\ 0 & 5 & -8 & 11 \end{bmatrix}$$

$$\xrightarrow{\text{Multiply row 2 by } \frac{1}{5}} \begin{bmatrix} 1 & -2 & 3 & 1 \\ 0 & 1 & -0.8 & 0.6 \\ 0 & 5 & -8 & 11 \end{bmatrix}$$

$$\xrightarrow{\text{Multiply row 2 by 2 and add to row 1}} \begin{bmatrix} 1 & 0 & 1.4 & 2.2 \\ 0 & 1 & -0.8 & 0.6 \\ 0 & 5 & -8 & 11 \end{bmatrix}$$

$$\xrightarrow{\text{Multiply row 2 by } -5 \text{ and add to row 3}} \begin{bmatrix} 1 & 0 & 1.4 & 2.2 \\ 0 & 1 & -0.8 & 0.6 \\ 0 & 0 & -4 & 8 \end{bmatrix}$$

$$\xrightarrow{\text{Multiply row 3 by } -\frac{1}{4}} \begin{bmatrix} 1 & 0 & 1.4 & 2.2 \\ 0 & 1 & -0.8 & 0.6 \\ 0 & 0 & 1 & -2 \end{bmatrix}$$

$$\xrightarrow{\text{Multiply row 3 by } -1.4 \text{ and add to row 1}} \begin{bmatrix} 1 & 0 & 0 & 5 \\ 0 & 1 & -0.8 & 0.6 \\ 0 & 0 & 1 & -2 \end{bmatrix}$$

$$\xrightarrow{\text{Multiply row 3 by 0.8 and add to row 2}} \begin{bmatrix} 1 & 0 & 0 & 5 \\ 0 & 1 & 0 & -1 \\ 0 & 0 & 1 & -2 \end{bmatrix}$$

The solution is $x = 5$, $y = -1$, $z = -2$.

The technique of solving a system of linear equations by transformation of the augmented matrix can be applied to a system of n equations with n variables such as

$$\begin{array}{l} a_{11}x_1 + a_{12}x_2 + \cdots + a_{1n}x_n = c_1 \\ a_{21}x_1 + a_{22}x_2 + \cdots + a_{2n}x_n = c_2 \\ \cdots \quad \cdots \quad \cdots \quad \cdots \quad \cdots \\ a_{n1}x_1 + a_{n2}x_2 + \cdots + a_{nn}x_n = c_n \end{array}.$$

You would proceed in the same manner as shown for systems with three equations and three variables.

Determinants

For every square matrix A there is a unique corresponding scalar called the **determinant** of A, denoted det(A) (or $|a_{ij}|$), which is a well-defined combination of products of the elements of A. ***Tip:*** Only square matrices have determinants.

The determinant of a 2×2 matrix $A = \begin{bmatrix} a_{11} & a_{12} \\ a_{21} & a_{22} \end{bmatrix}$ is $\det(A) = \begin{vmatrix} a_{11} & a_{12} \\ a_{21} & a_{22} \end{vmatrix} = a_{11}a_{22} - a_{12}a_{21}$.

For example, the determinant of $A = \begin{bmatrix} 4 & 2 \\ -2 & 1 \end{bmatrix}$ is $\begin{vmatrix} 4 & 2 \\ -2 & 1 \end{vmatrix} = (4)(1) - 2(-2) = 4 + 4 = 8$.

One way to obtain the determinant of a 3 × 3 matrix $A = \begin{bmatrix} a_{11} & a_{12} & a_{13} \\ a_{21} & a_{22} & a_{23} \\ a_{31} & a_{32} & a_{33} \end{bmatrix}$ is given by $\det(A) = \begin{vmatrix} a_{11} & a_{12} & a_{13} \\ a_{21} & a_{22} & a_{23} \\ a_{31} & a_{32} & a_{33} \end{vmatrix} =$

$$a_{11}\begin{vmatrix} a_{22} & a_{23} \\ a_{32} & a_{33} \end{vmatrix} - a_{12}\begin{vmatrix} a_{21} & a_{23} \\ a_{31} & a_{33} \end{vmatrix} + a_{13}\begin{vmatrix} a_{21} & a_{22} \\ a_{31} & a_{32} \end{vmatrix} = a_{11}(a_{22}a_{33} - a_{23}a_{32}) - a_{12}(a_{21}a_{33} - a_{23}a_{31}) + a_{13}(a_{21}a_{32} - a_{22}a_{31}).$$

Tip: A common error in applying this definition is to forget the negative sign on the second term.

This method is by **expansion along the first row** (actually, with some adjustments you can use any row or column). A simple way to identify the elements in the 2 × 2 determinant that is multiplied by a_{1j} is to do the following: In the 3 × 3 matrix, cross out the row and column containing a_{1j}. The remaining array of elements are the elements of the determinant. Here is an example of finding the determinant of a 3 × 3 matrix.

Find the determinants of $B = \begin{bmatrix} 3 & 0 & 4 \\ -1 & 6 & 2 \\ 5 & -3 & 6 \end{bmatrix}$.

$$\det(B) = \begin{vmatrix} 3 & 0 & 4 \\ -1 & 6 & 2 \\ 5 & -3 & 6 \end{vmatrix} = 3\begin{vmatrix} 6 & 2 \\ -3 & 6 \end{vmatrix} - 0\begin{vmatrix} -1 & 2 \\ 5 & 6 \end{vmatrix} + 4\begin{vmatrix} -1 & 6 \\ 5 & -3 \end{vmatrix} = 3(36+6) - 0(-6-10) + 4(3-30) = 126 - 108 = 18$$

Here are some properties of determinants for a given square matrix A.

- If A has a row or column consisting of only 0s, then $\det(A) = 0$.
- If $A = [a_{ij}]$, then $|ka_{ij}| = k|a_{ij}|$.
- $\det(A) = \det(A^T)$
- The matrix A has an inverse if and only if $\det(A) \neq 0$.
- If the **coefficient matrix** $A = [a_{ij}]$ of the system of n linear equations with n unknowns given by

$$\begin{aligned} a_{11}x_1 + a_{12}x_2 + \cdots + a_{1n}x_n &= c_1 \\ a_{21}x_1 + a_{22}x_2 + \cdots + a_{2n}x_n &= c_2 \\ \cdots \quad \cdots \quad \cdots \quad \cdots \quad &\cdots \\ a_{n1}x_1 + a_{n2}x_2 + \cdots + a_{nn}x_n &= c_n \end{aligned}$$

  has a nonzero determinant (that is, if $\det(A) \neq 0$), then the system has exactly one solution. If $\det(A) = 0$, then the system might have no solution or infinitely many solutions.

Representation of Geometric Transformations

Four geometric transformations are translations, reflections, rotations, and dilations. You can think of geometric transformations as ways to change geometric figures without changing their basic properties. (See "Geometric Transformations" in Chapter 7 for an additional discussion of geometric transformations.)

A convenient way to represent geometric transformations is by using matrices. A geometric figure in the plane can be represented by a 2 × n **vertex matrix** whose columns' elements are the n vertices of the figure. For example, the triangle T with vertices (x_1, y_1), (x_2, y_2), and (x_3, y_3) shown in the following figure can be represented as

$$T = \begin{bmatrix} x_1 & x_2 & x_3 \\ y_1 & y_2 & y_3 \end{bmatrix}.$$

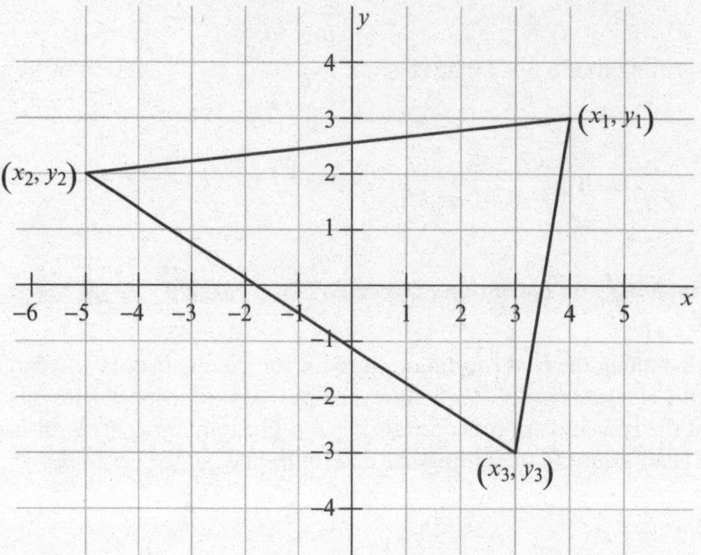

A translation h units horizontally and k units vertically is accomplished by adding the 2×3 translation matrix $\begin{bmatrix} h & h & h \\ k & k & k \end{bmatrix}$ to T as shown below.

$$\begin{bmatrix} x_1 & x_2 & x_3 \\ y_1 & y_2 & y_3 \end{bmatrix} + \begin{bmatrix} h & h & h \\ k & k & k \end{bmatrix} + = \begin{bmatrix} x_1+h & x_2+h & x_3+h \\ y_1+k & y_2+k & y_3+k \end{bmatrix}$$

A reflection over the x-axis is accomplished by premultiplying T by the 2×2 matrix $\begin{bmatrix} 1 & 0 \\ 0 & -1 \end{bmatrix}$ as shown below.

$$\begin{bmatrix} 1 & 0 \\ 0 & -1 \end{bmatrix}\begin{bmatrix} x_1 & x_2 & x_3 \\ y_1 & y_2 & y_3 \end{bmatrix} = \begin{bmatrix} x_1 & x_2 & x_3 \\ -y_1 & -y_2 & -y_3 \end{bmatrix}$$

A reflection over the y-axis is accomplished by premultiplying T by the 2×2 matrix $\begin{bmatrix} -1 & 0 \\ 0 & 1 \end{bmatrix}$ as shown below.

$$\begin{bmatrix} -1 & 0 \\ 0 & 1 \end{bmatrix}\begin{bmatrix} x_1 & x_2 & x_3 \\ y_1 & y_2 & y_3 \end{bmatrix} = \begin{bmatrix} -x_1 & -x_2 & -x_3 \\ y_1 & y_2 & y_3 \end{bmatrix}$$

A reflection in the origin is accomplished by premultiplying T by the 2×2 matrix $\begin{bmatrix} -1 & 0 \\ 0 & -1 \end{bmatrix}$ as shown below.

$$\begin{bmatrix} -1 & 0 \\ 0 & -1 \end{bmatrix}\begin{bmatrix} x_1 & x_2 & x_3 \\ y_1 & y_2 & y_3 \end{bmatrix} = \begin{bmatrix} -x_1 & -x_2 & -x_3 \\ -y_1 & -y_2 & -y_3 \end{bmatrix}$$

A reflection over the line $y = x$ is accomplished by premultiplying T by the 2×2 matrix $\begin{bmatrix} 0 & 1 \\ 1 & 0 \end{bmatrix}$ as shown below.

$$\begin{bmatrix} 0 & 1 \\ 1 & 0 \end{bmatrix}\begin{bmatrix} x_1 & x_2 & x_3 \\ y_1 & y_2 & y_3 \end{bmatrix} = \begin{bmatrix} y_1 & y_2 & y_3 \\ x_1 & x_2 & x_3 \end{bmatrix}$$

A counterclockwise rotation of θ degrees about the origin is accomplished by premultiplying T by the 2×2 matrix $\begin{bmatrix} \cos\theta & -\sin\theta \\ \sin\theta & \cos\theta \end{bmatrix}$.

For a counterclockwise rotation of 90° about the origin, premultiply T by the 2×2 matrix $\begin{bmatrix} \cos 90° & -\sin 90° \\ \sin 90° & \cos 90° \end{bmatrix} = \begin{bmatrix} 0 & -1 \\ 1 & 0 \end{bmatrix}$ as shown below.

$$\begin{bmatrix} 0 & -1 \\ 1 & 0 \end{bmatrix}\begin{bmatrix} x_1 & x_2 & x_3 \\ y_1 & y_2 & y_3 \end{bmatrix} = \begin{bmatrix} -y_1 & -y_2 & -y_3 \\ x_1 & x_2 & x_3 \end{bmatrix}$$

For a counterclockwise rotation of 180° about the origin, premultiply T by the 2×2 matrix $\begin{bmatrix} \cos 180° & -\sin 180° \\ \sin 180° & \cos 180° \end{bmatrix} = \begin{bmatrix} -1 & 0 \\ 0 & -1 \end{bmatrix}$ as shown below.

$$\begin{bmatrix} -1 & 0 \\ 0 & -1 \end{bmatrix}\begin{bmatrix} x_1 & x_2 & x_3 \\ y_1 & y_2 & y_3 \end{bmatrix} = \begin{bmatrix} -x_1 & -x_2 & -x_3 \\ -y_1 & -y_2 & -y_3 \end{bmatrix}$$

For a counterclockwise rotation of 270° about the origin, premultiply T by the 2×2 matrix $\begin{bmatrix} \cos 270° & -\sin 270° \\ \sin 270° & \cos 270° \end{bmatrix} = \begin{bmatrix} 0 & 1 \\ -1 & 0 \end{bmatrix}$ as shown below.

$$\begin{bmatrix} 0 & 1 \\ -1 & 0 \end{bmatrix}\begin{bmatrix} x_1 & x_2 & x_3 \\ y_1 & y_2 & y_3 \end{bmatrix} = \begin{bmatrix} y_1 & y_2 & y_3 \\ -x_1 & -x_2 & -x_3 \end{bmatrix}$$

A dilation by a nonzero scale factor k is accomplished by premultiplying T by the 2×2 matrix $\begin{bmatrix} k & 0 \\ 0 & k \end{bmatrix}$ as shown below.

$$\begin{bmatrix} k & 0 \\ 0 & k \end{bmatrix}\begin{bmatrix} x_1 & x_2 & x_3 \\ y_1 & y_2 & y_3 \end{bmatrix} = \begin{bmatrix} kx_1 & kx_2 & kx_3 \\ ky_1 & ky_2 & ky_3 \end{bmatrix}$$

Here is an example of using matrix multiplication to determine the coordinates of the image, $\overline{A'B'}$, of the segment $\overline{AB}$, with endpoints $A(2, 4)$ and $B(5, 1)$, after it is rotated 90° counterclockwise about the origin.

The vertex matrix for $\overline{AB}$ is $\begin{bmatrix} 2 & 5 \\ 4 & 1 \end{bmatrix}$. Premultiplying by $\begin{bmatrix} 0 & -1 \\ 1 & 0 \end{bmatrix}$ yields $\begin{bmatrix} 0 & -1 \\ 1 & 0 \end{bmatrix}\begin{bmatrix} 2 & 5 \\ 4 & 1 \end{bmatrix} = \begin{bmatrix} -4 & -1 \\ 2 & 5 \end{bmatrix}$.

Therefore, $\overline{A'B'}$ has coordinates $A'(-4, 2)$ and $B'(-1, 5)$. See the following figure.

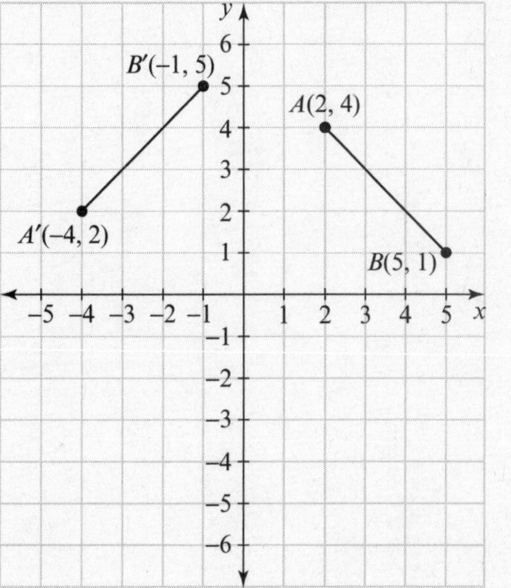

To accomplish translations in combination with rotations, reflections, or dilations using one transformation matrix, write the vertex matrix as a $3 \times n$ matrix with ones as the elements in the third row. Then, for example, to reflect over the line $y = x$, and then translate h units horizontally and k units vertically, premultiply by the 3×3 matrix $\begin{bmatrix} 0 & 1 & h \\ 1 & 0 & k \\ 0 & 0 & 1 \end{bmatrix}$ as shown below.

$$\begin{bmatrix} 0 & 1 & h \\ 1 & 0 & k \\ 0 & 0 & 1 \end{bmatrix}\begin{bmatrix} x_1 & x_2 & x_3 \\ y_1 & y_2 & y_3 \\ 1 & 1 & 1 \end{bmatrix} = \begin{bmatrix} y_1 + h & y_2 + h & y_3 + h \\ x_1 + k & x_2 + k & x_3 + k \\ 1 & 1 & 1 \end{bmatrix}$$

The technique of premultiplying the vertex matrix by either a 2×2 or a 3×3 **transformation matrix** can be applied when the number of vertices is extended to $n > 3$. You would proceed in the same manner as shown for a figure with three vertices.

Tip: When you are working problems involving geometric transformations on the Praxis Math CK test, sketch a figure to help you visualize the situation.

Chapter 11

Discrete Mathematics

Discrete and Continuous Representations

For this topic, you must demonstrate an understanding of discrete and continuous representations and fields in which they are used to model various phenomena.

Discrete Processes

Discrete mathematics (also called **finite mathematics**) is the study of processes that involve discrete or unconnected objects. Discrete mathematics does not require the notion of continuity. (See "Continuity" in Chapter 6 for a discussion of the term *continuity.*) Generally, processes studied in discrete mathematics have a finite (or countable) number of objects. Discrete mathematics has widespread uses in a variety of areas such as number theory, computer security, networking, robotics, social choice theory, and linear programming, to name a few.

The techniques of algebra and the powerful tools of calculus are needed for dealing with continuous processes. For example, functions with graphs that have no gaps, jumps, or holes are continuous functions. Applications of continuous functions are found in many fields such as in the sciences and in business and industry.

Difference Equations

A **difference equation** is an equation that describes sequential, step-by-step change. A difference equation has the form $f(n+1) - f(n) = g(n)$, where n is a positive integer.

Note: Difference equations are the discrete mathematics analog to derivatives in calculus. (See "Derivatives" in Chapter 6 for a discussion of this topic.)

A difference equation for the **first difference,** call it Δa_n, of a sequence $\{a_n\}$ is given by $a_{n+1} - a_n = \Delta a_n$. The first difference describes the rate of growth or decline of the sequence. When Δa_n is positive, the terms of the sequence are increasing; when Δa_n is negative, the terms of the sequence are decreasing. When Δa_n is constant, the sequence is growing or declining at a constant rate and the relationship between terms is linear. The **second difference** of a sequence is given by $\Delta a_{n+1} - \Delta a_n$. When the second difference is constant, the relationship between terms of the sequence is quadratic.

Vertex-Edge Graphs

A **vertex-edge graph** is a discrete structure consisting of a nonempty, finite set of **vertices** (also called **nodes**) and a set of **edges** (also called **lines**) connecting these vertices. Vertex-edge graphs are commonly used to model and solve problems involving optimal situations for networks, paths, schedules, and relationships among finitely many objects. The following figure is a vertex-edge graph with six vertices and seven edges.

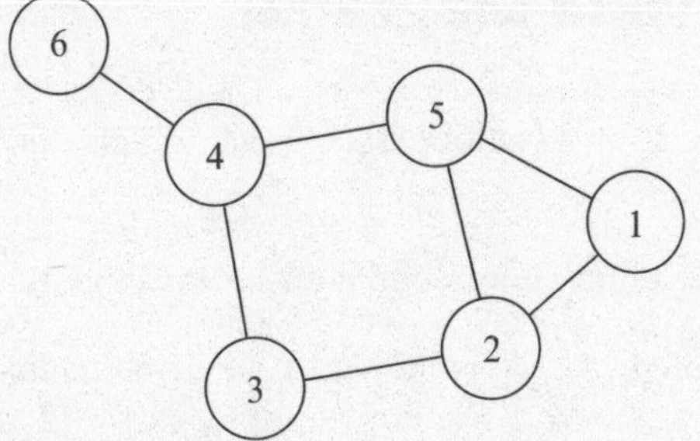

Basic Set Theory

This topic presents basic concepts of set theory (for example, terminology, unions, intersections, and Venn diagrams).

Set Terminology

A **set** is a collection of objects or things. Commonly, uppercase letters, such as A and B, are used to name sets. The objects in a set A are its **elements** (or **members**). To show that x is an element of A, write $x \in A$ (read "x is an element of set A"). If y is *not* an element of A, write $y \notin A$. (Note that a diagonal slash through a symbol negates the original meaning of the symbol.) A set is defined by means of braces in which you describe the members of the set by roster (that is, a list of the elements separated by commas), a verbal description, or mathematical symbolism. For example, the set D of digits used in the base-ten place value system can be defined in the following ways: $D = \{0, 1, 2, 3, 4, 5, 6, 7, 8, 9\}$, $D = \{\text{digits used in the base-ten place value system}\}$, or $D = \{x \in \text{Integers} \mid 0 \le x < 10\}$. You can read the third way as "The set of all x that are elements of the integers such that x is greater than or equal to zero and less than ten." The vertical line, |, is read "such that." This latter way of describing a set is **set builder notation.** The set that contains no objects is the **empty set** and is designated by the symbol $\varnothing$ or $\{\ \}$.

Tip: The symbol for the empty set is $\varnothing$, not $\{\varnothing\}$. The set $\{\varnothing\}$ is not an empty set; it has one element, namely $\varnothing$.

Sets should be **well-defined.** This term means that if you are given a set, you can tell which objects belong in the set and which objects do not belong in the set. For example, the set $I = \{\text{important people}\}$ is *not* well-defined because you are not given enough information to know who qualifies as an "important person." On the other hand, the set P = (Presidents of the United States who were elected before 2016} is well-defined because you can decide whether a given individual does or does not belong in set P.

Two sets A and B are **equal,** written $A = B$, if and only if they contain *exactly* the same elements, without regard to the order in which the elements are listed in the two sets or whether elements are repeated. For example, $\{1, 4, 8\} = \{1, 8, 4\} = \{4, 1, 8\} = \{4, 8, 1\} = \{8, 1, 4\} = \{8, 4, 1\}$ and $\{1, 4, 8\} = \{1, 1, 4, 4, 8, 8\}$. A set A is a **subset** of set B, denoted $A \subseteq B$, if every element of A is an element of B. For example, $\{1, 4\} \subseteq \{1, 4, 8\}$. Additionally, if B contains at least one element that is not in A, then A is a **proper subset** of B, denoted $A \subset B$. Thus, $\{1, 4\} \subset \{1, 4, 8\}$. You can show two sets A and B are equal by showing that $A \subseteq B$ and $B \subseteq A$. In a discussion, all the sets under consideration are subsets of a **universal set** (commonly denoted U), and the empty set is a subset of every set.

Tip: Do not confuse the relationship "is an element of" with the relationship "is a subset of." For example, $4 \in \{1, 4, 8\}$, but $\{4\} \notin \{1, 4, 8\}$; on the other hand, $\{4\} \subseteq \{1, 4, 8\}$, but $4 \not\subset \{1, 4, 8\}$.

The number of elements in a set A is the **cardinality** (or cardinal number) of A, denoted $|A|$ (read as "the cardinality of set A."). ***Note:*** Other notations for the cardinality of a set are $n(A)$ and $\#A$. The cardinality of a set can be **finite,** meaning the set has a definite number of elements that can be counted, or **infinite,** meaning the set has an unlimited number of elements. Throughout this book, the cardinality of a finite set A will be denoted $|A|$. For example, if $A = \{1, 4, 8\}$, $|A| = 3$.

Set Operations and Venn Diagrams

If in a discussion all the sets under consideration are subsets of a given set U, then U is the universal set of discourse, or simply, the universal set. In this section, assume that all sets under consideration are subsets of a given universal set U.

The three basic operations for sets are union, intersection, and complement.

The **union** of two sets A and B, denoted, $A \cup B$, is the set of all elements that are in A or in B or in both. In set-builder notation, $A \cup B = \{x \mid x \in A \text{ or } x \in B\}$. For example, if $A = \{2, 4, 6, 8\}$ and $B = \{1, 2, 4, 5, 6\}$, then

$A \cup B = \{1, 2, 4, 5, 6, 8\}$. When you form the union of two sets, do not list an element more than once because it is unnecessary to do so. Note that the word *or* is used in the *inclusive* sense; that is, *or* means "one or the other, or possibly both at the same time."

The **intersection** of two sets A and B, denoted, $A \cap B$, is the set of all elements that are in both A and B. That is, the intersection of two sets is the set of elements that are common to both sets. In set-builder notation, $A \cap B = \{x \mid x \in A \text{ and } x \in B\}$. For example, if $A = \{2, 4, 6, 8\}$ and $B = \{1, 2, 4, 5, 6\}$, then $A \cap B = \{2, 4, 6\}$. When two sets have no elements in common, their intersection is the empty set, and the sets are said to be **disjoint.** For example, for $A = \{2, 4, 6, 8\}$ and $C = \{1, 3, 5\}$, $A \cap C = \varnothing$, and A and C are disjoint.

The **complement** of a set A, denoted A^C, is the set of all elements in the universal set U that are *not* in A. In set-builder notation, $A^C = \{x \mid x \in U, x \notin A\}$. For example, if $U = \{x \in \text{Integers} \mid 0 < x \leq 10\}$ and $A = \{2, 4, 6, 8\}$, then $A^C = \{1, 3, 5, 7, 9, 10\}$.

A **Venn diagram** is a visual depiction of a set operation or relationship. In a Venn diagram, the universal set is usually represented by a rectangular region, which encloses everything else in the diagram. The sets in U are represented by circles. Shading depicts relationships or the results of a set operation. Here are examples of Venn diagrams.

Verbal Description	Symbolism	Venn Diagram
x is an element of A	$x \in A$	U A x
C is a proper subset of A	$C \subset A$	U A x C
A and B are disjoint	$A \cap B = \varnothing$	U A B
The union of A and B	$A \cup B$	U A B

continued

Verbal Description	Symbolism	Venn Diagram
The intersection of A and B	$A \cap B$	U A B
The complement of A	A^C	U A

Note: An x in a diagram means the region in which it is located is not empty.

Logic

For this topic, you are expected to understand basic terminology and symbols of logic, evaluate the truth of statements, and use logic to evaluate the equivalence of statements.

Basic Concepts of Logic

A **statement** (or **proposition**) is a declarative sentence that can be meaningfully assigned a **truth value** of either true or false. For example, "The sum of 1 and 2 is 3" is a statement whose truth value is true, but "The sum of 1 and 2 is 5" is a statement whose truth value is false. Other examples of statements are "It is raining," "The moon is made of green cheese," and "The number $\frac{1}{2}$ is a fraction." The following examples are *not* statements because their truth values cannot be determined without further specification: "She is married," "The number x is irrational," and "The set A is a subset of the set B." Sentences that are questions ("What is your name?") or commands ("Come here.") are *not* statements because they cannot be classified as either true or false. Commonly, single letters (either lower- or uppercase) are used to designate statements.

Simple statements are statements that are simple declarative sentences. Five basic **logical connectives** can be used to construct **compound statements** from simple statements. The resulting compound statements have special names. Given the simple statements P and Q, the following table summarizes compound statements constructed from P and Q.

Compound Statements

Logical Connective	Compound Statement	Name	*This compound statement is true …*	*This compound statement is false …*
not	not P	**negation**	if and only if P is false.	if and only if P is true.
or	P or Q	**disjunction**	if either P is true, or Q is true, or both are true.	only if both P and Q are false.
and	P and Q	**conjunction**	only if both P and Q are true.	if either P is false, or Q is false, or both are false.

continued

Logical Connective	Compound Statement	Name	*This compound statement is true …*	*This compound statement is false …*
If …, then …	If P, then Q	**conditional**	if either both P and Q are true, or if P is false (regardless of the truth value of Q).	only when P is true and Q is false.
if and only if	P if and only if Q	**biconditional**	only when P and Q are either both true or both false.	only when P and Q have opposite truth values.

Here are examples.

Given P = "1 + 2 = 3," Q = "4 is an even number," R = "1 + 2 = 5," and S = "4 is an odd number," classify each of the following compound statements as true or false.

(1) P and Q.
(2) Not R.
(3) P or S.
(4) If R, then Q.
(5) R or S.
(6) If P, then S.
(7) P and S.
(8) (Not P) or Q.

True	False	Statement
✓		(1) P and Q. Answer: P is true, and Q is true, so "P and Q" is true.
✓		(2) Not R. Answer: R is false so "Not R" is true.
✓		(3) P or S. Answer: P is true, and S is false, so "P or S" is true.
✓		(4) If R, then Q. Answer: R is false, so "If R, then Q" is true.
	✓	(5) R or S. Answer: R is false, and S is false, so "R or S" is false.
	✓	(6) If P, then S. Answer: P is true, and S is false, so "If P, then S" is false.
	✓	(7) P and S. Answer: P is true, and S is false, so "P and S" is false.
✓		(8) (Not P) or Q. Answer: "Not P" is false, and Q is true, so "(Not P) or Q" is true.

A **tautology** is a compound statement that is always true regardless of the truth-value combinations of the simple statements from which it is constructed. A **contradiction** is a compound statement that is always false regardless of the truth-value combinations of the simple statements from which it is constructed. For example, the statement, "P or not P" is a tautology; but the statement, "P and not P" is a contradiction.

Tautologies that are biconditional statements are **logical equivalences.** That is to say, when a biconditional statement is a tautology, the statement on the left of "if and only if" is logically equivalent to the statement on the right of "if and only if." From a logical standpoint, the two statements have exactly the same meaning.

Statements Associated with a Conditional Statement

Associated with any conditional statement, "If P, then Q," are three other conditional statements: the converse, the inverse, and the contrapositive. The **converse** is the statement, "If Q, then P." The **inverse** is the statement, "If not P, then not Q." The **contrapositive** is the statement, "If not Q, then not P." A conditional statement is *not* logically equivalent to either its converse or to its inverse. However, a conditional statement and its contrapositive *are* logically equivalent. That is, a contrapositive and the conditional from which it is derived have exactly the same meaning.

Here is an example of a conditional statement and its converse, inverse, and contrapositive, along with an explanation of the truth value of each.

Conditional: If a geometric shape is a square, then it is a polygon. True, because all squares are polygons.

Converse: If a geometric shape is a polygon, then it is a square. False, because the shape could be a polygon that is not a square such as a trapezoid, hexagon, and so on.

Inverse: If a geometric shape is not a square, then it is not a polygon. False, because there are geometric shapes (for example, triangles) that are not squares but are polygons.

Contrapositive: If a geometric shape is not a polygon, then it is not a square. True, because there are no squares that are not polygons.

Conditional statements are used extensively in mathematics. Some ways you can express that the statement, "If P, then Q" is true are the following:

If P is true, then Q is also true.

Q is true, if P is true.

P is true implies Q is true.

Q is true whenever P is true.

P is true only if Q is also true.

For Q to be true, it is sufficient that P is true.

For P to be true, it is necessary that Q is true.

Quantifiers and Negation

Quantifiers are phrases that include words such as *all, every, no, some, at least one, there exists,* and *there is at least one.* Quantifiers are used in statements to clarify the generality or existence of the objects in the statements relative to the universe of discourse. For example, if the universe of discourse is the set of polygons, P, then the quantifier, *All,* in the statement, "All squares are rectangles," signifies that, for the statement to be true, it must be true for each and every square $\in P$, no exceptions. In contrast, the quantifier, *Some,* in the statement, "Some rectangles are squares," signifies that, for the statement to be true, there must be at least one rectangle $\in P$ that is a square.

When a quantifier signals that for a statement to be true, *all* objects in the universe of discourse must make the statement true, the quantifier is a **universal quantifier,** symbolized by $\forall$. When a quantifier signals that for a statement to be true, there must *exist at least one* object in the universe of discourse that makes the statement true, the quantifier is an **existential quantifier,** symbolized by $\exists$.

Tip: To help you remember the symbols for the quantifiers, notice that the symbol $\forall$ looks like an inverted uppercase A (for *all*), and the symbol $\exists$ looks like a backward uppercase E (for *exists*).

The following table classifies common phrases as universal or existential quantifiers.

Quantifiers

Universal Quantifiers, Symbolized by $\forall$	Existential Quantifiers, Symbolized by $\exists$
all, for all, every, for every, each, for each, everything, no, nothing, not any, not all, none of these	some, for some, at least one, there exists at least one, there is at least one, there is, there are, something

For example:

All flowers are plants. (universal)

Some flowers are roses. (existential)

It is common for statements to omit quantifiers when the meaning is clear and the universal set is obvious. For example, the statement, "Triangles are polygons" means "All triangles are polygons." Also, a quantifier might be disguised as another phrase. For example, the phrases, "If x" and "whenever x" are denoted symbolically as $\forall x$. Be on the alert for such hidden quantifiers.

Negating statements involving quantifiers can be a challenge. Use the following conventions:

- To negate a statement that involves a universal quantifier, use an existential quantifier in a statement that contradicts the original statement.
- To negate a statement that involves an existential quantifier, use a universal quantifier in a statement that contradicts the original statement.

Four important forms involving quantifiers that you should be able to negate, with an example of each, are shown below.

Important Statement Forms

Statement Form	Negation of Statement Form	Example Statement	Negation of Example Statement
All *A*s are *B*s.	Some *A*s are not *B*s.	All polygons are squares.	Some polygons are not squares.
Some *A*s are *B*s.	No *A*s are *B*s.	Some triangles are right triangles.	No triangles are right triangles.
No *A*s are *B*s.	Some *A*s are *B*s	No real numbers are rational.	Some real numbers are rational.
Some *A*s are not *B*s.	All *A*s are *B*s.	Some primes are not odd.	All primes are odd.

The four statement forms are illustrated in the following Venn diagrams.

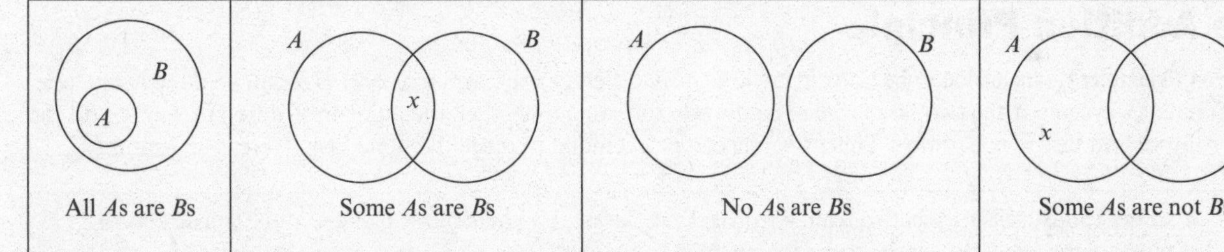

Note: An x in a diagram means the region in which it is located is not empty.

Counting Techniques

For this topic, you must be able to solve basic problems that involve counting techniques, including the fundamental counting principle, permutations, and combinations (for example, the number of arrangements of a set of objects or the number of ways to choose a committee from a club's membership).

The Fundamental Counting Principle

Fundamental Counting Principle: If one of two tasks can be done in any one of m different ways, and, for each of these ways, a subsequent second task can be done in any one of n different ways, then the first task *and* the second task can both be done, in the order given, in $m \cdot n$ ways.

You can extend the fundamental counting principle to any number of tasks. Thus, in general, for a sequence of k tasks, if a first task can be done in any one of n_1 different ways, and, for each of these ways, a subsequent second task can be done in any one of n_2 different ways, and, for each of these ways, a subsequent third task can be done in any one of n_3 different ways, and so on to the kth task, which can be done in any one of n_k different ways, then the total number of different ways the sequence of k tasks can be done, in the order given, is $n_1 \cdot n_2 \cdot n_3 \cdot \ldots \cdot n_k$. ***Note:*** This counting technique produces results in which *order determines different outcomes.* Here are examples.

> How many different 10-digit telephone numbers can begin with area code 510 and prefix 569?

Four additional digits are needed to complete telephone numbers that begin with (510) 569-. Therefore, in this problem, there are four tasks to do; namely, determine each of the four digits. Think of each of the positions of the four digits as a slot to fill. In this example, you make your selection for each slot from the same set, the digits 0 to 9. Since digits in a telephone number can repeat, you say that "repetitions are allowed." There are 10 ways to fill the first slot, and for each of these ways, 10 ways to fill the second slot, and for each of these, 10 ways to fill the third slot, and, for each of these, 10 ways to fill the fourth slot. Thus, the total number of different telephone numbers that begin with (510) 569- is $10 \cdot 10 \cdot 10 \cdot 10 = 10{,}000$.

> In how many possible ways can a president, vice president, secretary, and membership chairperson be selected from 25 members of a club if all members are eligible for each position and no member can hold more than one office?

In this problem, there are four tasks; namely, selecting each of the four officers. Think of each of the officer positions as a slot to fill. Since the officers must all be different, repetitions are not allowed in the selection process. There are 25 ways to fill the president's slot; after that, there are 24 ways remaining to fill the vice president's slot; after that, there are 23 ways remaining to fill the secretary's slot; and, finally, there are 22 ways remaining to fill the membership chairperson's slot. Thus, there are $25 \cdot 24 \cdot 23 \cdot 22 = 303{,}600$ possible ways to select a president, vice president, secretary, and membership chairperson from the 25 members of the club.

The Addition Principle

Addition Principle: If one task can be done in any one of m different ways and a second task can be done in any one of n different ways and if the two tasks *cannot* be done at the same time, then the number of different ways to do the first *or* the second task is $m + n$ ways. This principle can be extended to more than one task. Here is an example.

> A student must select 1 elective from a list of 3 art classes, 10 kinesiology classes, and 2 music classes. How many possible classes are there from which to choose?

The student can choose an elective from the art classes in 3 ways, from the kinesiology classes in 10 ways, and from the music classes in 2 ways. Therefore, there are $3 + 10 + 2 = 15$ classes from which to choose.

You can modify the addition principle for situations in which two tasks overlap; that is, when the two tasks can be done at the same time. If one task can be done in any one of m different ways and a second task can be done in any one of n different ways and if the two tasks *can* be done at the same time in k different ways, then the number of different ways to do the first or the second task is $m + n - k$. Here is an example.

> A person selects one card at random from a well-shuffled standard deck of 52 playing cards. In how many different ways can a king or a diamond be selected?

In a random drawing of a card from a well-shuffled deck of standard playing cards, there are 52 possible outcomes: ace, 2, 3, 4, 5, 6, 7, 8, 9, 10, jack, queen, and king of clubs (♣); ace, 2, 3, 4, 5, 6, 7, 8, 9, 10, jack, queen, and king of spades (♠); ace, 2, 3, 4, 5, 6, 7, 8, 9, 10, jack, queen, and king of hearts (♥); and ace, 2, 3, 4, 5, 6, 7, 8, 9, 10, jack, queen, and king of diamonds (♦). Clubs and spades have black coloration, and hearts and diamonds have red coloration. Jacks, queens, and kings are face cards. Here is a black and white illustration of a standard deck of playing cards.

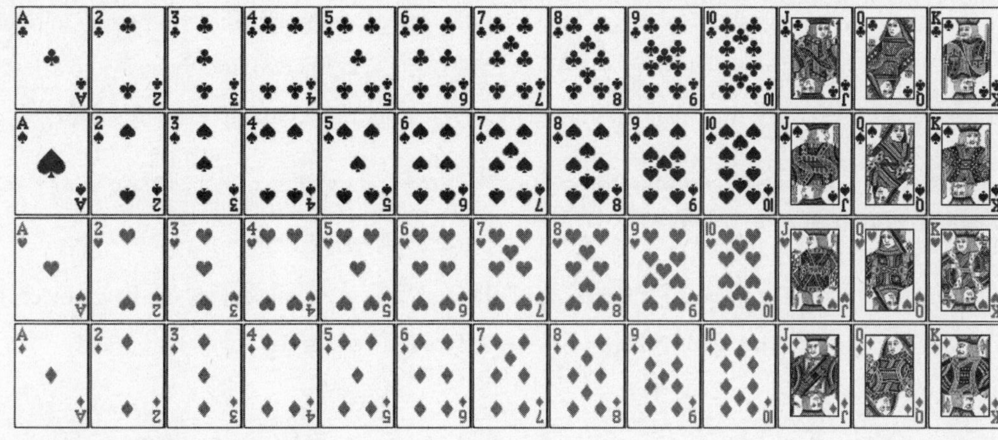

Source: *www.jfitz.com/cards/*

There are 4 ways to select a king, 13 ways to select a diamond, and 1 way to select a king and a diamond at the same time (the king of diamonds). Therefore, there are 4 + 13 – 1 = 16 ways to select a king or a diamond.

Permutations

A **permutation** is an ordered arrangement of a set of distinctly different objects. For permutations, different orderings of the same objects are counted as different permutations. For example, two different permutations of the numbers 1 through 4 are 1234 and 4213. Thus, when the order of the objects in an arrangement is a differentiating factor in a problem, you are working with permutations.

Through a direct application of the fundamental counting principle, the number of permutations of n distinct objects is $n! = n(n-1)(n-2)\ldots(2)(1)$.

Note: The notation $n!$ is read "n factorial." A factorial is the product of all positive integers less than or equal to a given positive integer. By definition $0! = 1$.

Here is an example of a permutation problem.

> In how many different ways can five people be seated in a row of five seats?

You can work this problem using the fundamental counting principle, or you can recognize that the seating arrangement is the permutation of five distinct objects (people). Thus, there are $5! = 5 \cdot 4 \cdot 3 \cdot 2 \cdot 1 = 120$ different ways for the five people to be seated in the five chairs.

Tip: On the ETS graphing calculator, fact(value) returns the factorial of a value (for example, fact(5) returns 120).

The number of permutations of r objects selected from n distinct objects is ${}_nP_r = \frac{n!}{(n-r)!}$. When you apply the formula, it is important that you make sure the following conditions are met: The n objects must be n *distinct* objects, the r objects must be selected *without repetition* from the same set, and you must count different orderings of the same objects as *different* outcomes. Here is an example.

> In how many possible ways can a president, vice president, secretary, and membership chairperson be selected from 25 members of a club if all members are eligible for each position and no member can hold more than one office?

This problem was previously worked using the fundamental counting principle, but now you can recognize that this problem satisfies the conditions for a permutation; that is, the 25 members of the club are distinct, the 4 officers are selected without repetition from the same set of 25 members, and different orderings of the same people are counted as a different slate of officers. Thus, the number of permutations of 4 people selected from 25 people is ${}_{25}P_4 = \frac{25!}{(25-4)!} = \frac{25!}{(21)!} = \frac{25 \cdot 24 \cdot 23 \cdot 22 \cdot 21!}{21!} = 25 \cdot 24 \cdot 23 \cdot 22 = 303{,}600$ possible ways to select a president, vice president, secretary, and membership chairperson from the 25 members of the club.

Tip: On the ETS graphing calculator, the function nPr(n;r) returns the number of permutations of n taken r at a time (for example, nPr(25;4) returns 303600).

The number of permutations of n objects for which n_1 of the n objects are identical, n_2 of the n objects are identical, … , n_k of the n objects are identical is $\frac{n!}{n_1!n_2!\cdots n_k!}$. Here is an example.

How many different "words" can you make using the 11 letters in the word *MISSISSIPPI* if you use all 11 letters each time?

Because the order in which different letters appear results in different words, this is a permutation problem. The word *MISSISSIPPI* consists of 11 letters: 1 *M*, 4 *I*'s, 4 *S*'s, and 2 *P*'s. Since the 11 objects (that is, the letters) to be arranged are not all mutually different objects, the number of different words is $\frac{n!}{n_1!n_2!\cdots n_k!} = \frac{11!}{4!4!2!} = 34{,}650$.

Combinations

A combination is an arrangement of a set of distinct objects in which different orderings of the same objects are considered to be the same arrangement. For example, the set of three coins quarter, dime, and nickel is the same as the set nickel, dime, and quarter. That is, in a combination problem, different orderings of the same objects are *not* counted as separate results. Thus, when the order in which the objects are arranged does *not* determine different outcomes, you are working with combinations. The number of combinations of r objects selected from n distinct objects is ${}_nC_r = \frac{n!}{r!(n-r)!}$.

Note: The notation ${}_nC_r$ is also written $\binom{n}{r}$.

When you apply the formula ${}_nC_r$, it is important that you make sure the following conditions are met: The n objects must be *n different* objects, the r objects must be selected *without repetition* from the same set, and you must consider different orderings of the same objects to be *indistinguishable*. Here is an example.

How many ways can a 4-member committee be formed from the 25 members of a club?

Since the order in which committee members are arranged does not change the makeup of the committee, you would *not* try to work this problem using the fundamental counting principle because it produces results in which order determines different outcomes. This example satisfies the conditions for a combination problem; that is, the 25 members of the club are distinct, the 4 committee members are selected without repetition from the same set of 25 members, and different orderings of the same people are counted as the same committee. Thus, the number of combinations of 4 people selected from 25 people is ${}_{25}C_4 = \frac{25!}{4!(25-4)!} = \frac{25!}{4!(21)!} = \frac{25 \cdot 24 \cdot 23 \cdot 22 \cdot 21!}{4!21!} = \frac{25 \cdot 24 \cdot 23 \cdot 22}{4 \cdot 3 \cdot 2 \cdot 1} = 12{,}650$ possible ways to form a 4-member committee from the 25 members of the club.

Tip: On the ETS graphing calculator, the function nCr(n;r) returns the number of combinations of n taken r at a time (for example, nCr(25;4) returns 12650).

You can use the combination formula in conjunction with the fundamental counting principle to determine the number of possible outcomes in certain situations. Here is an example.

> A party planner chooses 3 toy trucks, 7 toy cars, and 10 action figures from a collection of 8 different toy trucks, 10 different toy cars, and 12 different action figures. How many different ways can the party planner make the combined selections?

Thinking in terms of the fundamental counting principle, the party planner has three tasks to do: Select 3 of the 8 toy trucks, select 7 of the 10 toy cars, and select 10 of the 12 action figures. Since the arrangement of the toy items is not a differentiating factor in the problem, you can determine the number of ways to select each of the toy items using the combination formula. Then, following those calculations, you can use the fundamental counting principle to determine the total number of different ways the party planner can make the combined selections. Thus, the number of different ways the party planner can make the combined selections is (number of ways to select 3 of 8 toy trucks) × (number of ways to select 7 of 10 toy cars) × (number of ways to select 10 of 12 action figures) =

$$_8C_3 \cdot {}_{10}C_7 \cdot {}_{12}C_{10} = \frac{8!}{3!(8-3)!} \cdot \frac{10!}{7!(10-7)!} \cdot \frac{12!}{10!(12-10)!} = \frac{8!}{3!5!} \cdot \frac{10!}{7!3!} \cdot \frac{12!}{10!2!} = 56 \cdot 120 \cdot 66 = 443{,}520$$

As you can see, the one important way that combinations differ from permutations is that different orderings of the same objects are counted as separate results for permutation problems, but not for combination problems.

The following table categorizes some situations as (most likely) indicating either a permutation or combination problem.

Permutations	Combinations
creating passwords, license plates, words, or codes assigning roles filling positions making ordered arrangements of things (people, books, colors, and so on) selecting first, second, third place, and such distributing objects among several people or things	forming a committee making a collection of things (coins, books, and so on) counting subsets of a set dealing hands from a deck of cards listing the combinations from a set of objects selecting pizza toppings selecting questions from a test selecting students for groups

For the Praxis Math CK test, you should be able to work most, if not all, of the permutation problems you might encounter by using the fundamental counting principle rather than the formula $_nP_r$. For the situations similar to those given for combinations in the table, you should use $_nC_r$ (unless you can easily list the possibilities).

Tip: The ETS graphing calculator is designed to numerically evaluate both $_nP_r$ and $_nC_r$. Make a point to practice using this timesaving feature of the calculator before you take the Praxis Math CK test.

The Binomial Theorem

The binomial theorem is used to expand a binomial to a power using the following formula:

$$(x+y)^n = \sum_{k=0}^{n} \binom{n}{k} x^{n-k} y^k$$

The values $\binom{n}{k}$ are the **binomial coefficients.**

Tip: In each term, the sum of the exponents on *x* and *y* is *n* and the exponent on *x* decreases from *n* to 0, while the exponent on *y* increases from 0 to *n*.

Here is an example.

Expand $(x+y)^3$.

$$(x+y)^3 = \sum_{k=0}^{3} \binom{3}{k} x^{3-k} y^k = \binom{3}{0} x^3 y^0 + \binom{3}{1} x^2 y^1 + \binom{3}{2} x^1 y^2 + \binom{3}{3} x^0 y^3 = x^3 + 3x^2 y + 3xy^2 + y^3$$

Tip: Notice that $\binom{3}{0} = \binom{3}{3}$ and $\binom{3}{1} = \binom{3}{2}$. In general, $\binom{n}{r} = \binom{n}{n-r}$.

You can use the binomial theorem to show that, counting the empty set, the number of subsets of a set consisting of n elements is 2^n. For example, when $n = 3$, the number of subsets of size 0 is $\binom{3}{0}$, of size 1 is $\binom{3}{1}$, of size 2 is $\binom{3}{2}$, and of size 3 is $\binom{3}{3}$ for a total of $= \binom{3}{0} + \binom{3}{1} + \binom{3}{2} + \binom{3}{3} = \sum_{k=0}^{3} \binom{3}{k} 1^{3-k} 1^k = (1+1)^3 = 2^3$ (which is 8).

Binomial Experiments

In a **binomial experiment,** there are n independent **trials** where at each trial there are exactly two mutually exclusive outcomes, often referred to as **success** and **failure.** The probability, p, of a success is constant from trial to trial as is the probability of failure, $1 - p$.

The probability of getting exactly r successes in n independent trials is $\binom{n}{r} p^r (1-p)^{n-r}$.

Here are examples.

What is the probability of getting exactly three heads in five tosses of a coin?

$n = 5$; $r = 3$; $n - r = 2$; $p = \frac{1}{2} = 0.5$; and $(1 - p) = 1 - 0.5 = 0.5$

The probability of exactly three heads in five tosses is $\binom{5}{3} (0.5)^3 (0.5)^2 = (10)(0.5)^5 = 0.3125$.

A quiz consists of five multiple choice questions with four answer choices for each question. Suppose an unprepared student guesses on each and every question without even reading the question. What is the probability the student will get exactly three questions correct? (Round your answer to 2 decimal places.)

$n = 5$; $r = 3$; $n - r = 2$; $p = \frac{1}{4} = 0.25$ (this is true because the student has a 1 in 4 chance of guessing correctly on each question); and $(1 - p) = 1 - 0.25 = 0.75$

The probability of exactly three correct answers is $\binom{5}{3}(0.25)^3(0.75)^2 = (10)(0.25)^3(0.75)^2 \approx 0.09$.

Note: The word *success* as used in a binomial experiment is not meant to convey the message that the targeted success outcome is something you would ordinarily consider successful, good, or even desirable. It is simply used to designate whichever outcome is being counted in the n trials. Either outcome can be designated the "success" outcome. However, once the success outcome is identified, then its probability is designated as p.

Equivalence Relations

The **Cartesian product** of two sets A and B, denoted $A \times B$, is the set of all ordered pairs (x, y) such that $x \in A$ and $y \in B$.

A **binary relation** (also called simply relation) from a set A to a set B is a subset of $A \times B$. If $A = B$, then we say the relation is on A. That is, a relation on the set A is a subset of $A \times A$.

For a relation $\mathfrak{R}$, the notation $x \,\mathfrak{R}\, y$ (read "x is related to y") is used to denote that the ordered pair $(x, y) \in \mathfrak{R}$.

A relation $\mathfrak{R}$ on a set S is

reflexive if $x \,\mathfrak{R}\, x$ for all $x \in S$;
symmetric if $x \,\mathfrak{R}\, y$ implies $y \,\mathfrak{R}\, x$ for all $x, y \in S$;
transitive if ($x \,\mathfrak{R}\, y$ and $y \,\mathfrak{R}\, z$) implies $x \,\mathfrak{R}\, z$ for all $x, y, z \in S$; or
antisymmetric if ($x \,\mathfrak{R}\, y$ and $y \,\mathfrak{R}\, x$) implies $x = y$ for all $x, y \in S$.

An **equivalence relation** is a reflexive, symmetric, and transitive relation. For example, the relation "has the same birthday as" is an equivalence relation. That is, if x, y, and z are any three people, then the relation is

- reflexive because "x has the same birthday as x" for all x;
- symmetric because "x has the same birthday as y" implies "y has the same birthday as x" for all x, y;
- transitive because ("x has the same birthday as y") and ("y has the same birthday as z") implies "x has the same birthday as z" for all x, y, z.

The relation "is the son of" is not an equivalence relation because it is not reflexive or symmetric. For example, if x and y are any two people, then the statement "x is the son of x" is not true, and the statement "x is the son of y" implies "y is the son of x" also is not true.

Note: The definitions for *reflexive, symmetric, transitive, antisymmetric,* and *equivalence relation* are given on the Notations, Definitions, and Formulas reference sheet that is provided during the test.

Sequences

A **sequence** is a function whose domain is a subset of the integers, usually the natural numbers $N = \{1, 2, 3, \ldots\}$ or the whole numbers $W = \{0, 1, 2, \ldots\}$. (For this section, sequences are restricted, without loss of generality, to domains equal to N.) The notation a_n denotes the image of the integer n; that is, a_n is the nth term (or element) of the sequence. The initial term of the sequence is denoted a_1. When a_n can be expressed as a formula that can be used to generate any term of the sequence, it is conventional to call a_n the **general term of the sequence.** Even though a sequence is a function (a set of ordered pairs), it is customary to describe a sequence by listing the terms in the order in which they correspond to the natural numbers. For example, the list of terms of the sequence with initial term a_1 is $a_1, a_2, a_3, a_4, \ldots, a_n, \ldots$.

Note: The three dots (…) indicate that the sequence continues in the same manner.

In an **arithmetic sequence,** the same number, called the **common difference,** is added (algebraically) to each term to obtain the subsequent term in the sequence. An arithmetic sequence (also called arithmetic progression) has the form $a_1, a_1 + d, a_1 + 2d, \ldots, a_1 + (n-1)d, \ldots$, where a_1 is the initial term, d is the common difference between terms, and $a_n = a_1 + (n-1)d$ is the general term. Here are examples.

> What is the next term in the sequence 4, 9, 14, 19, 24, …?

The number 5 is added to a term to obtain the term that follows it, so the next term in the sequence is $24 + 5 = 29$.

> What is the next term in the sequence 10, 6, 2, –2, –6, …?

The number –4 is added to a term to obtain the term that follows it, so the next term in the sequence is $-6 + -4 = -10$.

> What is the 50th term in the sequence –2, 2, 6, 10, 14, …?

The first term a_1 is –2. The common difference is 4. The general term is $a_n = a_1 + (n-1)d = -2 + (n-1)(4)$. Thus, the 50th term is $a_{50} = -2 + (50-1)(4) = -2 + (49)(4) = -2 + 196 = 194$.

In a **geometric sequence,** each term is multiplied by the same number, called the **common ratio,** to obtain the subsequent term in the sequence. A geometric sequence (also called geometric progression) has the form $a_1, a_1r, a_1r^2, \ldots, a_1r^{n-1}, \ldots$, where a_1 is the initial term, r is the common ratio between terms, and $a_n = a_1r^{n-1}$ is the general term. Here are examples.

> What is the next term in the sequence 4, 8, 16, 32, 64, …?

Each term is multiplied by 2 to obtain the term that follows it, so the next term in the sequence is $64 \cdot 2 = 128$.

> What is the next term in the sequence $25, 5, 1, \frac{1}{5}, \frac{1}{25}, \ldots$?

Each term is multiplied by $\frac{1}{5}$ to obtain the term that follows it, so the next term in the sequence is $\frac{1}{25} \cdot \frac{1}{5} = \frac{1}{125}$.

> What is the 9th term in the sequence –1, –2, –4, –8, –16, …?

The first term a_1 is –1. The common ratio is 2. The general term is $a_n = a_1r^{n-1} = (-1)2^{n-1}$. Thus, the 9th term is $a_9 = (-1)2^{9-1} = (-1)2^8 = (-1)(256) = -256$.

Of course, you could have worked this problem by continuing to multiply by 2 until you reached the 9th term as shown below.

–1,	–2,	–4,	–8,	–16,	–32,	–64,	–128,	–256
1st	2nd	3rd	4th	5th	6th	7th	8th	9th

Tip: If you use this approach, count the terms to be sure you have the correct term.

Some sequences consist of **figurate numbers,** so-called because they can be displayed as geometric shapes. Here is an example of a sequence of triangular numbers with their corresponding geometric shapes. The nth term is $\frac{n(n+1)}{2}$.

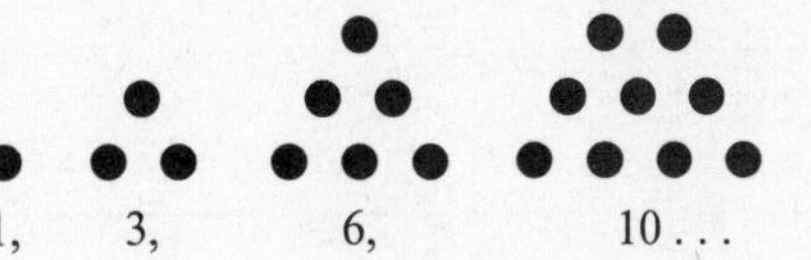

Here is an example of a sequence of square numbers with their corresponding geometric shapes. The nth term is n^2.

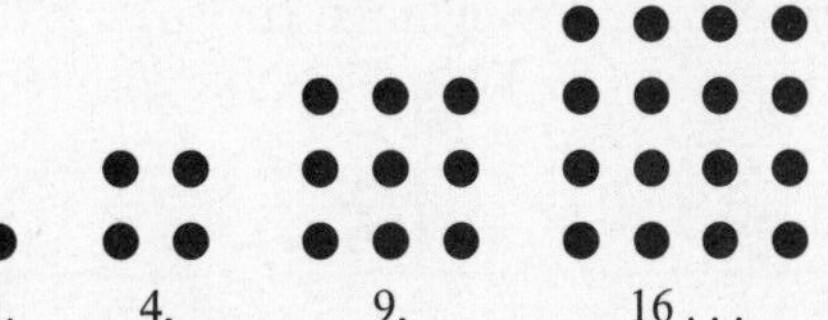

A **recursive definition for a sequence** is a definition that includes the value of one or more initial terms of the sequence and a formula that tells you how to find each term from previous terms. Here is an example.

> List the first four terms of the sequence defined as follows: $f(1) = 1, f(n) = 3f(n - 1) + 1$ for $n \geq 2$.

For the recursive formula given in the problem, you will need to find the previous term before you can find the next term. You proceed as shown below.

$f(1) = 1$
$f(2) = 3f(1) + 1 = 3(1) + 1 = 3 + 1 = 4$
$f(3) = 3f(2) + 1 = 3(4) + 1 = 12 + 1 = 13$
$f(4) = 3f(3) + 1 = 3(13) + 1 = 39 + 1 = 40$

Thus, the first four terms are 1, 4, 13, and 40.

A **Fibonacci sequence** is defined by the recursive definition: $a_1 = 1$, $a_2 = 1$, and $a_n = a_{n-1} + a_{n-2}$, $n \geq 3$. A list showing its first seven terms is 1, 1, 2, 3, 5, 8, 13, … .

A recursive form of the arithmetic sequence 4, 9, 14, 19, 24, … is $a_1 = 4$ and $a_n = a_{n-1} + 5$, $n \geq 2$.

A recursive form of the geometric sequence 4, 8, 16, 32, 64, … is $a_1 = 4$ and $a_n = 2a_{n-1}$, $n \geq 2$.

For the Praxis Math CK test, you might be asked to determine the general term or the next term of a sequence when a few terms of the sequence are given. Even though, in reality, the initial terms do not necessarily determine a unique sequence, you will have to assume there is a pattern that continues in the same manner, and then you can make an educated guess about the general term or the next term. Look for an identifiable pattern such as the following:

- Arithmetic: $a_1 + (n - 1)d$ (Is there a common difference?)
- Geometric: a_1r^{n-1} (Is there a common ratio?)
- Figurate: $\frac{n(n+1)}{2}$ or n^2 (Are the terms perfect squares or triangular numbers?)
- Quadratic: $n^2 \pm c$ or $kn^2 \pm c$ (Are the terms perfect squares or a multiple of perfect squares plus or minus a constant?)

- Cubic: $n^3 \pm c$ or $kn^3 \pm c$ (Are the terms perfect cubes or a multiple of perfect cubes plus or minus a constant?)
- Exponential: $2^n \pm c$, $3^n \pm c$, $k2^n \pm c$, or $k3^n \pm c$ (Are the terms powers of 2 or 3 or a multiple of powers of 2 or 3 plus or minus a constant?)
- Factorial: $n!$ (Are the terms obtained by multiplying the previous terms in some way?)
- Recursive: $a_n = a_{n-1} \pm a_{n-2}$ (Are the terms obtained by adding or subtracting the previous terms in some way?)

Here are examples.

Find the 20th term in the sequence 2, 5, 8, 11, 14, … .

The terms shown have a common difference of 3 with initial term $a_1 = 2$. If this pattern continues in the same manner, the general term is $a_1 + (n-1)d = 2 + (n-1)(3)$. Thus, the 20th term is $2 + (20-1)(3) = 2 + (19)(3) = 59$.

Find the 10th term in the sequence 2, 6, 18, 54, 162, … .

The terms shown have a common ratio of 3 with initial term $a_1 = 2$. If this pattern continues in the same manner, the general term is $a_1 r^{n-1} = 2 \cdot 3^{n-1}$. Thus, the 10th term is $2 \cdot 3^{10-1} = 2 \cdot 3^9 = 39{,}366$.

Find the 8th term in the sequence 2, 5, 10, 17, 26, … .

The terms shown can be rewritten as $1^2 + 1, 2^2 + 1, 3^2 + 1, 4^2 + 1, 5^2 + 1, \ldots$. If this pattern continues in the same manner, the general term is $n^2 + 1$. Thus, the 8th term is $8^2 + 1 = 64 + 1 = 65$.

Tip: Sometimes it is convenient to begin an arithmetic or geometric sequence at $n = 0$ instead of $n = 1$, so be sure to check for the starting value of n when you work problems involving sequences on the Praxis Math CK test.

Arithmetic and Geometric Series

Given a finite number of terms of a sequence, $a_1, a_2, a_3, a_4, \ldots, a_n$, the sum of the terms $s_n = a_1 + a_2 + a_3 + a_4 + \ldots + a_n$ is a **finite series.** You can write this sum using the **sigma (summation) notation** as $s_n = \sum_{k=1}^{n} a_k$, where k is the **summing index.** Some useful properties of sigma notation are the following:

$$\sum_{k=1}^{n} c = nc \qquad \sum_{k=1}^{n}(a_k \pm b_k) = \sum_{k=1}^{n} a_k \pm \sum_{k=1}^{n} b_k$$

$$\sum_{k=1}^{n} ca_k = c\sum_{k=1}^{n} a_k \qquad \sum_{k=1}^{n} a_k = \sum_{k=1}^{m} a_k + \sum_{k=m+1}^{n} a_k, \text{ where } 1 \le m \le n$$

$$\sum_{k=1}^{n} a_k = a_1 + a_2 + \sum_{k=3}^{n-1} a_k + a_n$$

Here is an example of using the sigma notation.

> Expand and then sum: $\sum_{k=1}^{4}(5k-3)$.

$$\sum_{k=1}^{4}(5k-3)=(5\cdot 1-3)+(5\cdot 2-3)+(5\cdot 3-3)+(5\cdot 4-3)=2+7+12+17=38$$

The sum of a finite arithmetic series is given by $s_n = a_1 + a_2 + \ldots + a_n = \sum_{k=1}^{n} a_k = \frac{n(a_1+a_n)}{2}$.

The sum of a finite geometric series is given by $s_n = a_1 + a_1 r + \ldots + a_1 r^{n-1} = \sum_{k=1}^{n} a_1 r^{k-1} = \frac{a_1 - a_1 r^n}{1-r} = \frac{a_1(1-r^n)}{1-r}$, provided $r \neq 1$. If $r = 1$, then $s_n = na_1$.

Here is an example of summing a finite series.

> Find the sum of the first 60 positive odd numbers.

The odd numbers are an arithmetic sequence with general term $a_n = 2n - 1$. Therefore,

$$s_{60} = 1+3+5+\ldots+119 = \frac{n(a_1+a_n)}{2} = \frac{60(a_1+a_{60})}{2} = \frac{60(1+119)}{2} = 3{,}600.$$

If $|r| < 1$, then the sum of the infinite geometric series $a_1 + a_1 r + \ldots + a_1 r^{n-1} + \ldots$ is given by $S = \frac{a_1}{1-r}$.

Here is an example.

> Find the sum of the infinite geometric series $4+2+1+\frac{1}{2}+\cdots$, if possible.

The first term $a_1 = 4$ and the common ratio $r = \frac{1}{2}$. Because $|r| < 1$, $4+2+1+\frac{1}{2}+\cdots = S = \frac{a_1}{1-r} = \frac{4}{1-\frac{1}{2}} = \frac{4}{\frac{1}{2}} = 8$.

If $|r| \geq 1$, then the infinite geometric series $a_1 + a_1 r \ldots + a_1 r^{n-1} + \ldots$ does not have a sum.

Note: See "Limits of Sequences" and "Limits of Series" in Chapter 6 for an additional discussion of sequences and series.

Praxis Mathematics: Content Knowledge (5161) Practice Test Materials

Notations, Definitions, and Formulas

Notations

(a, b)	$\{x: a < x < b\}$
$[a, b)$	$\{x: a \leq x < b\}$
$(a, b]$	$\{x: a < x \leq b\}$
$[a, b]$	$\{x: a \leq x \leq b\}$
$\text{gcf}(m, n)$	greatest common factor of two integers m and n
$\text{lcm}(m, n)$	least common multiple of two integers m and n
$[x]$	greatest integer n such that $n \leq x$
$m \equiv n \pmod{k}$	m and n are congruent modulo k (m and n have the same remainder when divided by k, or equivalently, $m - n$ is a multiple of k)
f^{-1}	inverse of a one-to-one function f; (*not* equal to $\frac{1}{f}$)
$\lim_{x \to a^+} f(x)$	right-hand limit of $f(x)$; limit of $f(x)$ as x approaches a from the right (if it exists)
$\lim_{x \to a^-} f(x)$	left-hand limit of $f(x)$; limit of $f(x)$ as x approaches a from the left (if it exists)
$\varnothing$ or $\{\ \}$	the empty set
$x \in A$	x is an element of set A
$A \subset B$	set A is a proper subset of set B
$A \subseteq B$	either set A is a proper subset of set B or $A = B$
$A \cup B$	union of sets A and B
$A \cap B$	intersection of sets A and B

Definitions

Discrete Mathematics

A relation $\Re$ on a set A is

reflexive if $x \Re x$ for all $x \in A$
symmetric if $x \Re y \Rightarrow y \Re x$ for all $x, y \in A$
transitive if $(x \Re y$ and $y \Re z) \Rightarrow x \Re z$ for all $x, y, z \in A$
antisymmetric if $(x \Re y$ and $y \Re x) \Rightarrow x = y$ for all $x, y \in A$

An *equivalence* relation is a reflexive, symmetric, and transitive relation.

Formulas

Angle Sum and Difference Identities	$\sin(x \pm y) = \sin x \cos y \pm \cos x \sin y$ $\cos(x \pm y) = \cos x \cos y \mp \sin x \sin y$ $\tan(x \pm y) = \dfrac{\tan x \pm \tan y}{1 \mp \tan x \tan y}$
Half-Angle Identities (sign depends on the quadrant of $\frac{\theta}{2}$)	$\sin\frac{\theta}{2} = \pm\sqrt{\frac{1-\cos\theta}{2}}$; $\cos\frac{\theta}{2} = \pm\sqrt{\frac{1+\cos\theta}{2}}$
Range of Inverse Trigonometric Functions	$\sin^{-1} x: \left[-\frac{\pi}{2}, \frac{\pi}{2}\right]$; $\cos^{-1} x: [0, \pi]$; $\tan^{-1} x: \left(-\frac{\pi}{2}, \frac{\pi}{2}\right)$
Law of Sines	$\dfrac{\sin A}{a} = \dfrac{\sin B}{b} = \dfrac{\sin C}{c}$ 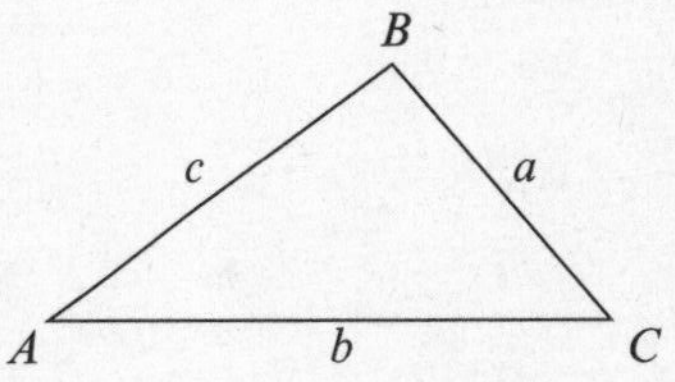
Law of Cosines	$c^2 = a^2 + b^2 - 2ab(\cos C)$
De Moivre's Theorem	$(\cos\theta + i\sin\theta)^k = \cos(k\theta) + i\sin(k\theta)$
Coordinate Transformation	
Rectangular (x, y) to polar (r, θ):	$r^2 = x^2 + y^2$; $\tan\theta = \frac{y}{x}$, provided $x \neq 0$
Polar (r, θ) to rectangular (x, y):	$x = r\cos\theta$; $y = r\sin\theta$
Distance from point (x_1, y_1) to line $Ax + By + C = 0$	$d = \dfrac{\lvert Ax_1 + By_1 + C\rvert}{\sqrt{A^2 + B^2}}$

Continued

Volume	
Sphere: radius r	$V = \frac{4}{3}\pi r^3$
Right circular cone: height h, base of radius r	$V = \frac{1}{3}\pi r^2 h$
Right circular cylinder: height h, base of radius r	$V = \pi r^2 h$
Pyramid: height h, base of area B	$V = \frac{1}{3}Bh$
Right prism: height h, base of area B	$V = Bh$
Surface Area	
Sphere: radius r	$A = 4\pi r^2$
Right circular cone: radius r, slant height s	$A = \pi rs + \pi r^2$
Differentiation	
$(f(x)g(x))' = f(x)g'(x) + g(x)f'(x)$; $\left(\frac{f(x)}{g(x)}\right)' = \frac{g(x)f'(x) - f(x)g'(x)}{(g(x))^2}$ provided $g(x) \neq 0$; $(f(g(x)))' = f'(g(x))g'(x)$	
Integration by Parts	$\int u\,dv = uv - \int v\,du$

Scoring Your Practice Tests

Step 1. Determine your raw score. Count how many questions you answered correctly. (Remember, for selected-response questions with one or more correct answers, no credit is given unless all correct answers and no others are selected.)

Step 2. Determine your percent correct: $\frac{\text{raw score}}{60}$

Note: For the official exam, your percent correct is $\frac{\text{raw score}}{50}$ because 10 of the test questions do not contribute toward your score.

Step 3. Use the table below to determine your approximate scaled score.*

Percent Correct	Scaled Score
0%–18%	100
20%	103
22%	106
24%	108
26%	111
28%	113
30%	116
32%	119
34%	121
36%	124
38%	126
40%	129
42%	131
44%	134
46%	137
48%	139
50%	142
52%	145
54%	147
56%	150
58%	152

Percent Correct	Scaled Score
60%	155
62%	157
64%	160
66%	162
68%	165
70%	168
72%	170
74%	173
76%	175
78%	178
80%	180
82%	183
84%	186
86%	188
88%	191
90%	193
92%	196
94%	199
96%	200
98%	200
100%	200

*The testing company does not reveal exactly how scaled scores are determined. The values in this table are approximate scaled scores only (current in 2015). Scaled scores for the official test may vary from form to form of the test.

Caution: Do not let your scaled score give you a false sense of security. The practice tests include questions similar to what might appear on the official test. However, you should not use your practice tests results to predict your score on the official test. You should try to achieve your personal best on the official test.

Chapter 12

Practice Test 1

Time: 150 Minutes

60 Questions

Directions: Read the directions for each question carefully. This test has several different question types. For each question, select a single answer choice unless written instructions preceding the question state otherwise. For each selected-response question, select the best answer or answers from the choices given. For each numeric-entry question, enter an answer in the answer box. Enter the exact answer unless you are told to round your answer. If a question asks specifically for the answer as a fraction, there will be two boxes—a numerator box and a denominator box. Do not use decimal points in fractions.

1. Rose took a cab from the airport to her home. She gave the cab driver $38.50, which included the fare and a tip of $5. The cab company charges $3.50 for the first mile and $1.50 for each additional half-mile after that. How many miles is Rose's home from the airport?

Ⓐ 10 miles
Ⓑ 11 miles
Ⓒ 20 miles
Ⓓ 21 miles

For the following question, select <u>all</u> that apply.

2. The whole number *y* is exactly three times the whole number *x*. The whole number *z* is the sum of *x* and *y*. Which of the following could be the value of *z*?

[A] 314
[B] 416
[C] 524
[D] 1,032

For the following question, enter your numeric answer in the box below the question.

Determination of Course Grade	Percent
Average (mean) of 3 major exams	50%
Average (mean) of weekly quizzes	10%
Final exam score	40%

3. A student is trying to achieve an average of at least 80 to earn a grade of B in a college course. In determining the course grade, the instructor calculates a weighted average as shown in the table above. The student has scores of 72, 81, and 75 on the 3 major exams and an average of 92 on weekly quizzes. To the nearest tenth, what is the *lowest* score the student can make on the final exam and still receive a B in the course?

[ ]

4. Which of the following true statements can be proven using the principle of mathematical induction?

Ⓐ $\sin^2\theta + \cos^2\theta = 1$, where θ is a real number
Ⓑ $\lim_{x \to 0} \frac{\sin x}{x} = 1$, where x is a real number
Ⓒ $\sum_{k=1}^{n} k = \frac{n(n+1)}{2}$, where n is a natural number
Ⓓ $\int_a^b f(x)\,dx = F(b) - F(a)$, where $F'(x) = f(x)$ and a, b are real numbers

GO ON TO THE NEXT PAGE

5. Working alone at its constant rate, Machine 1 produces $40x$ electrical components in 10 hours. Working alone at its constant rate, Machine 2 produces $40x$ electrical components in 15 hours. How many hours does it take machines 1 and 2, working simultaneously at their respective constant rates, to produce $40x$ electrical components?

Ⓐ 5 hours
Ⓑ 6 hours
Ⓒ $8\frac{1}{4}$ hours
Ⓓ $12\frac{1}{2}$ hours

6. Each edge of a solid cube of silver measures 4 centimeters. A metallurgist melts the cube and uses all the molten silver to make two smaller identical solid cubes. What is the length of an edge of one of the smaller cubes?

Ⓐ 2 centimeters
Ⓑ $2\sqrt{2}$ centimeters
Ⓒ $2\sqrt[3]{2}$ centimeters
Ⓓ $2\sqrt[3]{4}$ centimeters

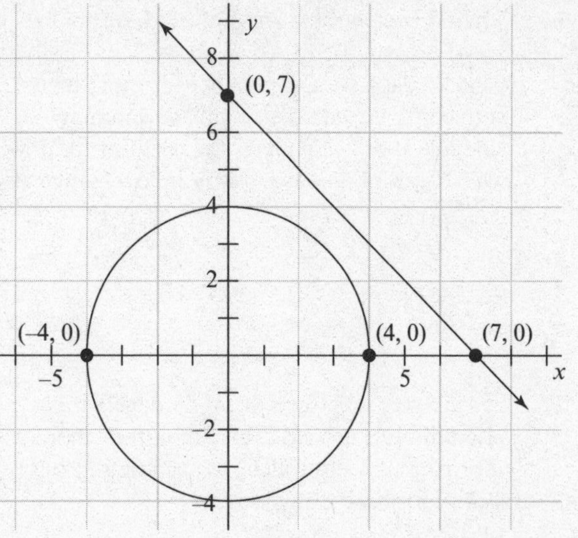

7. Which of the following statements is true about the solution set of the system of equations represented by the graphs of the circle and line shown above?

Ⓐ The system of equations has no solution because the two graphs do not intersect.
Ⓑ The solution set is $\{-4, 4, 7\}$.
Ⓒ An x-value that satisfies the system is $\frac{7}{2}+i\frac{\sqrt{41}}{2}$.
Ⓓ An x-value that satisfies the system is $\frac{7}{2}-i\frac{\sqrt{17}}{2}$.

8. A line l passes through the point (0, 5) and is perpendicular to the line that has equation $x - 3y = 10$. Which of the following equations represents the line l?

Ⓐ $x + 3y = 5$
Ⓑ $x - 3y = 5$
Ⓒ $3x + y = 5$
Ⓓ $-3x + y = 5$

9. In the xy plane, what is the center of the circle that has equation $x^2 + 6x + y^2 - 8y = 24$?

Ⓐ $(-3, 4)$
Ⓑ $(3, -4)$
Ⓒ $(-6, 8)$
Ⓓ $(3, -4)$

GO ON TO THE NEXT PAGE

10. Ari and Izzie both swam in the indoor pool at Stay-Fit Gym today. Ari swims at Stay-Fit Gym every 12 days. Izzie swims there every 15 days. If both continue with their regular swimming schedule at Stay-Fit Gym, the next time both will swim there on the same day is in how many days?

Ⓐ 12
Ⓑ 15
Ⓒ 30
Ⓓ 60

11. For disaster relief in a flood-damaged area, \$1.6 billion is needed. This amount of money is approximately equivalent to spending \$1 per second for how many years?

Ⓐ 10
Ⓑ 50
Ⓒ 100
Ⓓ 500

12. A carpenter needs to drill a hole in a triangular piece of wood so that the center of the hole is equidistant from each side of the triangle. Which of the following constructions should the carpenter do to determine the hole's location?

Ⓐ Find the intersection of the bisectors of the three angles.
Ⓑ Find the intersection of the three altitudes of the triangle.
Ⓒ Find the intersection of the perpendicular bisectors of the three sides.
Ⓓ Find the intersection of the three medians of the triangle.

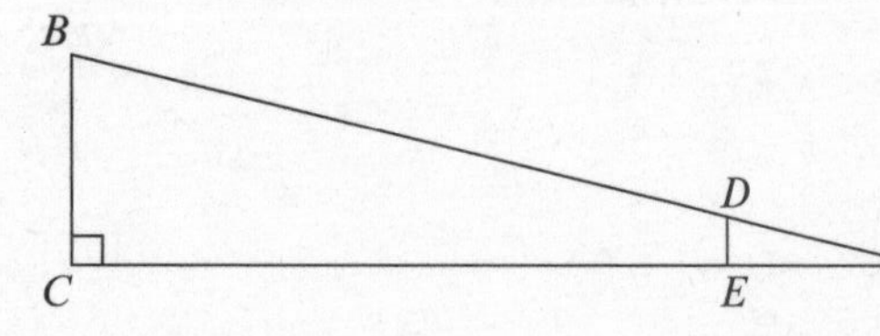

13. In triangle ABC shown above, $\overline{CE}$ has length 50 units, $\overline{EA}$ has length 25 units, and $\overline{DE}$ is perpendicular to $\overline{AC}$ and has length 10 units. What is the area of triangle ABC?

Ⓐ 750 square units
Ⓑ 1,125 square units
Ⓒ 1,500 square units
Ⓓ 2,250 square units

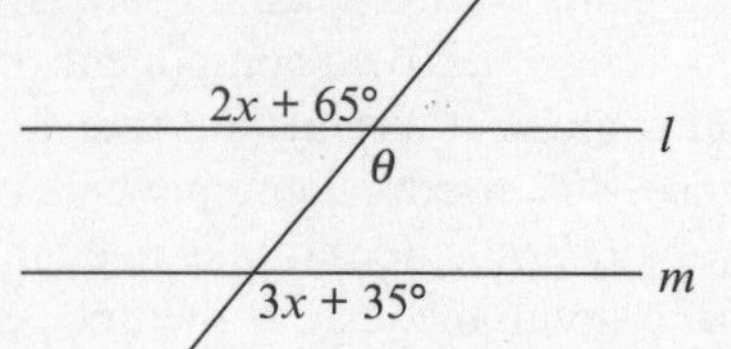

14. In the preceding figure, lines l and m are parallel. What is the measure of angle θ?

Ⓐ 125°
Ⓑ 97°
Ⓒ 30°
Ⓓ 16°

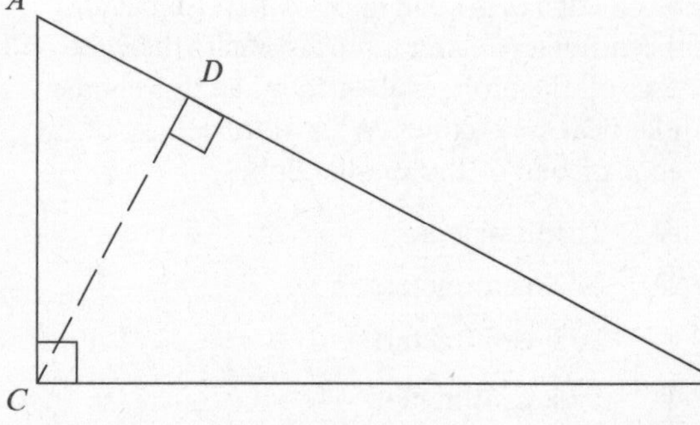

15. In the figure above, $\overline{CD}$ is an altitude of right triangle ABC, $AD = 2$, and $DB = 8$. Find the perimeter of triangle ABC.

Ⓐ $16\sqrt{5}$
Ⓑ $10+6\sqrt{5}$
Ⓒ $10+2\sqrt{5}$
Ⓓ It cannot be determined from the information given.

16. In the xy plane, Point K lies on l and has coordinates $(-3, 5)$. If l is rotated counterclockwise 90° about the origin and then translated 4 units right and 7 units down, what will be the coordinates of K', the image of K, under this series of transformations?

Ⓐ $(-1, -12)$
Ⓑ $(-1, -10)$
Ⓒ $(-1, -7)$
Ⓓ $(-1, -4)$

GO ON TO THE NEXT PAGE

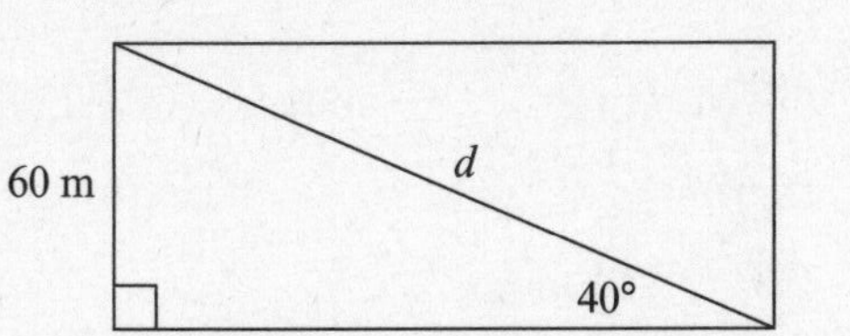

17. In the rectangle shown above, what is the length of the diagonal d, to the nearest tenth of a meter?

Ⓐ 71.5 m
Ⓑ 78.3 m
Ⓒ 80.5 m
Ⓓ 93.3 m

18. Which of the following is an identity for the trigonometric expression $10\sin(4\theta)\cos(-4\theta)$?

Ⓐ $5\sin(4\theta)$
Ⓑ $5\sin(8\theta)$
Ⓒ $10\sin(8\theta)$
Ⓓ $-5\sin(4\theta)$

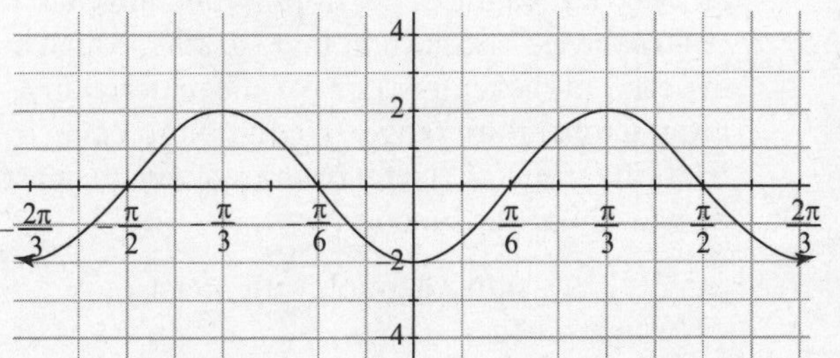

19. The graph above shows a representation of a sound wave on an oscilloscope. Describe the function that best models the curve.

Ⓐ Sine function with amplitude = 2, period = 2π, and phrase shift = $\frac{\pi}{3}$ to the right of the origin.
Ⓑ Cosine function with amplitude = 2, period = 2π, and phrase shift = $\frac{\pi}{3}$ to the right of the origin.
Ⓒ Sine function with amplitude = 2, period = $\frac{2\pi}{3}$, and phrase shift = $\frac{\pi}{6}$ to the right of the origin.
Ⓓ Cosine function with amplitude = 2, period = $\frac{2\pi}{3}$, and phrase shift = $\frac{\pi}{6}$ to the right of the origin.

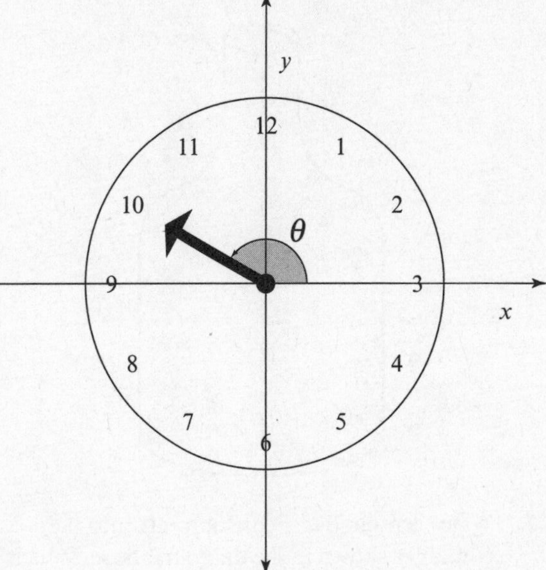

20. The diagram above shows a clock on an xy plane with the center of the clock at the origin. If the hour hand has a length of 5 centimeters, what are the coordinates of the tip of the hour hand at 10:00?

Ⓐ $\left(5\cos\frac{\pi}{6}, 5\sin\frac{\pi}{6}\right)$
Ⓑ $\left(5\cos\frac{5\pi}{6}, 5\sin\frac{5\pi}{6}\right)$
Ⓒ $\left(5\sin\frac{\pi}{6}, 5\cos\frac{\pi}{6}\right)$
Ⓓ $\left(5\sin\frac{5\pi}{6}, 5\cos\frac{5\pi}{6}\right)$

GO ON TO THE NEXT PAGE

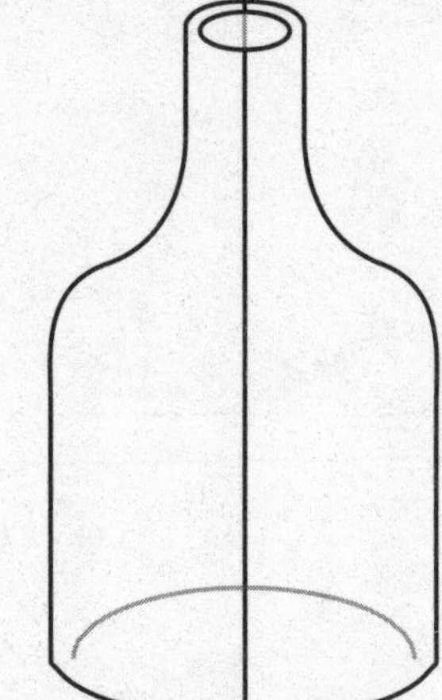

21. Water is poured at a constant rate into the container shown in the diagram above. Which of the following graphs best represents the height of the water in the container as a function of time?

Ⓐ Height / Time

Ⓑ

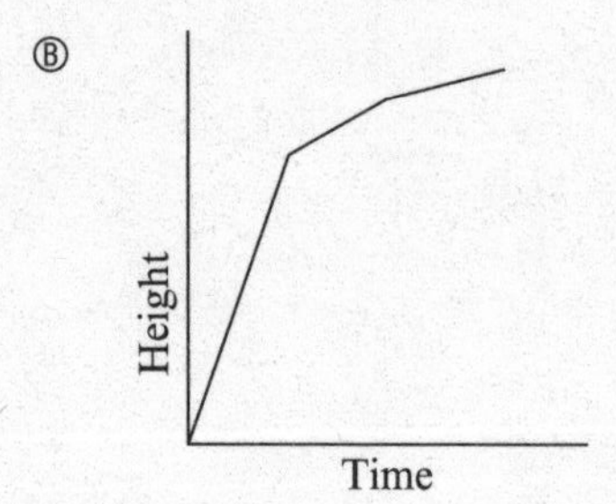

Ⓒ Ⓓ

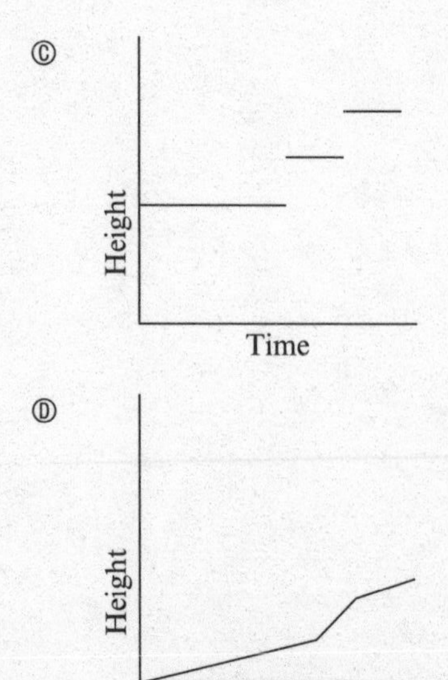

22. Given $f(x) = \frac{3x+4}{x+3}$ and $g(x) = x + 2$, find $f(g(a))$.

Ⓐ $\frac{3a+6}{a+2}$

Ⓑ $\frac{3a+4}{a+3}$

Ⓒ $\frac{3a+6}{a+3}$

Ⓓ $\frac{3a+10}{a+5}$

23. Which of the following statements is a negation of "Some books are entertaining"?

Ⓐ Some books are not entertaining.
Ⓑ All books are entertaining.
Ⓒ No books are entertaining.
Ⓓ No books are not entertaining.

24. Using data collected through experimentation, an electrical engineer develops a function that relates the electric current that passes through a material to the temperature of the material in a given temperature range. In addition to being a relation, which of the following statements must be true about the function?

Ⓐ It has a smooth graph with no cusps or jagged edges.
Ⓑ It is continuous and takes on values at all points in the temperature range.
Ⓒ It is differentiable at all points in the temperature range.
Ⓓ It gives a single value for the current at each point in the temperature range.

GO ON TO THE NEXT PAGE

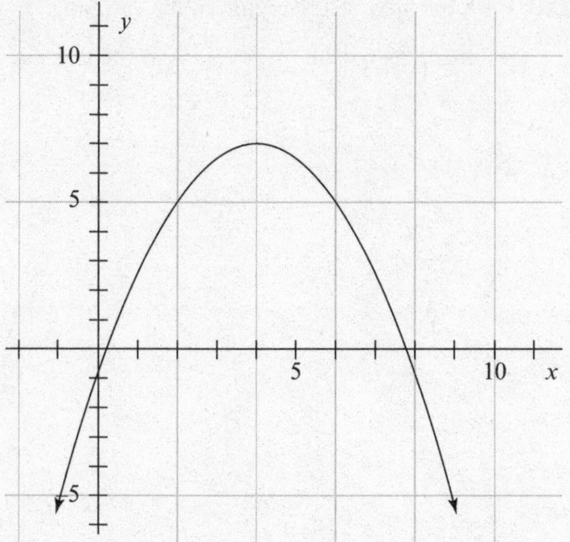

25. A quadratic function $f(x) = ax^2 + bx + c$ has the graph shown above. Which of the statements about the discriminant of $f(x) = 0$ is true?

Ⓐ $b^2 - 4ac < 0$
Ⓑ $b^2 - 4ac = 0$
Ⓒ $b^2 - 4ac > 0$
Ⓓ $b^2 - 4ac$ is undefined

26. Given the cubic function $f(x) = x^3$, which of the following best describes the function $g(x) = (x - 3)^3 + 8$?

Ⓐ the same as the graph of $f(x) = x^3$ shifted right by 3 units and up by 8 units
Ⓑ the same as the graph of $f(x) = x^3$ shifted left by 3 units and up by 8 units
Ⓒ the same as the graph of $f(x) = x^3$ shifted right by 3 units and down by 8 units
Ⓓ the same as the graph of $f(x) = x^3$ shifted left by 3 units and down by 8 units

27. In the xy plane, the graphs defined by $f(x) = \dfrac{x^2 + x - 6}{(x+3)}$ and $g(x) = 2.5x + 2.5$ intersect in how many distinct points?

Ⓐ 0
Ⓑ 1
Ⓒ 2
Ⓓ 4

x	$f(x)$	$g(x)$
1	3	3
2	1	4
3	4	2
4	2	1

28. Selected values of the functions f and g are given in the table shown above. What is the value of $g(f(3))$?

Ⓐ 1
Ⓑ 2
Ⓒ 3
Ⓓ 4

29. A quality control engineer has determined that a machine can produce $Q(d)$ units per day after d days in operation, where $Q(d) = \dfrac{5(6d+14)}{d+7}$. Assuming the machine continues to work efficiently, approximately how many components is the machine able to produce per day after being in operation for an extended period of time?

Ⓐ 6 components
Ⓑ 10 components
Ⓒ 14 components
Ⓓ 30 components

GO ON TO THE NEXT PAGE

30. The value of the first derivative for the graph of an acceleration curve $a(t)$ at numbers t_1, t_2, t_3, and t_4 is as follows:

$a'(t_1) = -0.8$
$a'(t_2) = -0.35$
$a'(t_3) = 0.5$
$a'(t_4) = 0.72$

At which number is the acceleration changing most rapidly?

Ⓐ t_1
Ⓑ t_2
Ⓒ t_3
Ⓓ t_4

31. Find the area of the region in the xy plane bounded by the curve $y = \frac{x^2}{2}$ and the line $y = 2$.

Ⓐ $\frac{8}{3}$
Ⓑ $\frac{16}{3}$
Ⓒ $\frac{24}{3}$
Ⓓ $\frac{40}{3}$

GO ON TO THE NEXT PAGE

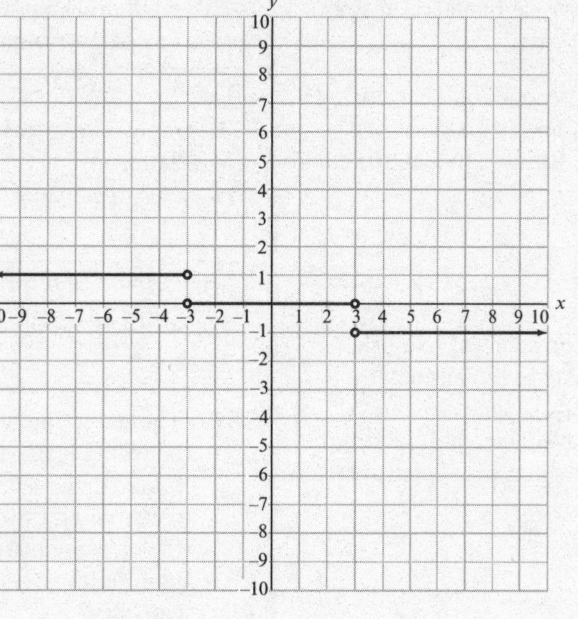

32. The figure above is a graph of $y = f'(x)$. Which of the following graphs is a possible representation of f?

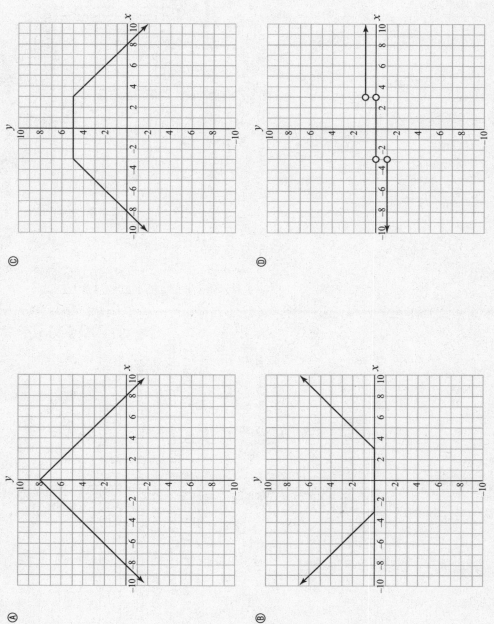

Ⓐ

Ⓑ

Ⓒ

Ⓓ

GO ON TO THE NEXT PAGE

For the following question, enter your numeric answer in the box below the question.

33. The velocity, in feet per second, of a car during the first 10 seconds of a test run is given by $v(t) = 0.9t^2$. What is the distance, in feet, the car has traveled after 10 seconds?

[ ] feet

34. A rectangular pen is to be adjacent to a brick wall and is to have fencing on three sides, the side on the brick wall requiring no fencing. If 550 yards of fencing is available, find the length parallel to the wall of the pen with largest area.

Ⓐ 110 yards
Ⓑ 137.5 yards
Ⓒ 183.3 yards
Ⓓ 275 yards

Scaled Scores of 35 Students on a Mathematics Test

Stem	Leaves
12	3 8 8
13	1 3 4 4 5 6 8
14	0 0 2 4 5 5 7 7 7 8 9
15	0 1 3 3 5 6 7 8 9 9
16	1 2 2 9
Legend: 12|3 = 123	

35. The stem-and-leaf plot above displays the scaled scores of 35 students on a standardized mathematics test. What is the median scaled score of the 35 students?

Ⓐ 137
Ⓑ 140
Ⓒ 147
Ⓓ 149

For the following question, enter your numeric answer in the box below the question.

Genre	Number of Students
Biography/Historical Nonfiction	22
Historical Fiction	29
Mystery	32
Science/Nature Informational	25
Science Fiction/Fantasy	52
Total	160

36. The preceding table shows the results of a poll of young readers who were asked what genre of books they read most often. If a circle graph is constructed using the data in the table, what is the measure of the central angle that should be used to represent the Science Fiction/Fantasy category?

[ ] °

Group	Mean	Standard Deviation
A	30 cm	5 cm
B	30 cm	8 cm
C	25 cm	10 cm
D	25 cm	9 cm

37. The data in the preceding table are based on five repetitions of the same experiment performed by four different groups of students: Group A, Group B, Group C, and Group D. The data of which group are most reliable?

Ⓐ Group A
Ⓑ Group B
Ⓒ Group C
Ⓓ Group D

38. The lifetime of a certain type of disposable razor is normally distributed with a mean of 16.8 shavings and a standard deviation of 2.4 shavings. What percentage of disposable razors of this type will last more than 19.2 shavings?

Ⓐ 2.5%
Ⓑ 16%
Ⓒ 34%
Ⓓ 68%

GO ON TO THE NEXT PAGE

39. A researcher analyzes data from a study using a simple linear regression model. Using statistical software, the researcher enters the data and runs a least-squares linear regression. In addition to providing the regression coefficients, the software output shows a correlation coefficient of 0.03. What can the researcher infer from this coefficient?

Ⓐ The linear model is not a good fit for the data.

Ⓑ The predictor and response variables have a strong positive correlation.

Ⓒ The linear model has a 3% probability of fitting the data.

Ⓓ The slope of the regression equation is 0.03.

Grade Level	Cell Phone	No Cell Phone
Ninth	55	45
Tenth	70	30
Eleventh	78	22
Twelfth	95	5

40. The data in the preceding table show cell phone status by grade level of 400 high school students. If 1 of the 400 students is randomly selected, what is the probability that the student has a cell phone given that the student is a ninth grader?

Ⓐ $\frac{149}{800}$

Ⓑ $\frac{11}{100}$

Ⓒ $\frac{11}{80}$

Ⓓ $\frac{11}{20}$

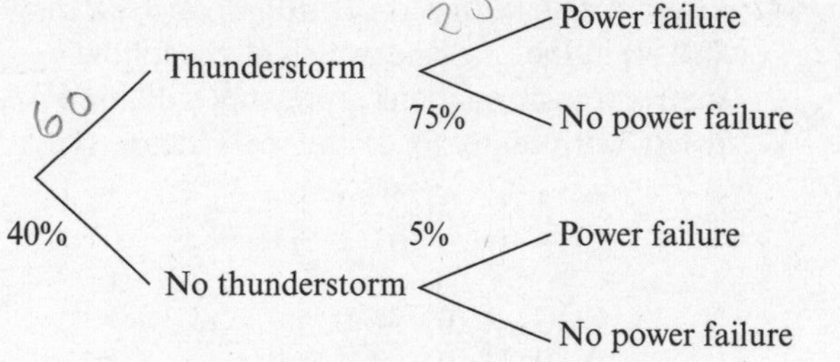

41. The partially completed probability diagram shown above represents the incidence of power failure during weather in which a thunderstorm might or might not develop. What is the probability that a thunderstorm develops and a power failure occurs?

Ⓐ 2%

Ⓑ 15%

Ⓒ 65%

Ⓓ 85%

42. Only 1 of 10 remote controls in a box is defective. The remote controls are tested one at a time. If the first three remote controls tested are not defective, what is the probability that the fourth remote control tested is defective?

Ⓐ $\frac{1}{10}$

Ⓑ $\frac{1}{7}$

Ⓒ $\frac{7}{10}$

Ⓓ $\frac{9}{10}$

43. The mean of six different positive integers is 73. Four of the integers are 48, 53, 61, and 82. What is the maximum possible value of the largest of the six integers?

Ⓐ 82

Ⓑ 83

Ⓒ 193

Ⓓ 194

GO ON TO THE NEXT PAGE

44. Given ΔABC with vertices $A(0, 0)$, $B(3, 0)$, and $C(0, 4)$ in the xy plane, which of the following matrix transformations represents a dilation of ΔABC with center (0, 0) and scale factor 3?

Ⓐ $\begin{bmatrix} 0 & 3 \\ 0 & 3 \end{bmatrix}\begin{bmatrix} 0 & 3 & 0 \\ 0 & 0 & 4 \end{bmatrix}$

Ⓑ $\begin{bmatrix} 3 & 3 \\ 0 & 0 \end{bmatrix}\begin{bmatrix} 0 & 3 & 0 \\ 0 & 0 & 4 \end{bmatrix}$

Ⓒ $\begin{bmatrix} 3 & 3 \\ 3 & 3 \end{bmatrix}\begin{bmatrix} 0 & 3 & 0 \\ 0 & 0 & 4 \end{bmatrix}$

Ⓓ $\begin{bmatrix} 3 & 0 \\ 0 & 3 \end{bmatrix}\begin{bmatrix} 0 & 3 & 0 \\ 0 & 0 & 4 \end{bmatrix}$

For the following question, select <u>all</u> that apply.

45. Under which of the following transformations will the lengths of the sides of a triangle be unchanged?

- [A] A rotation of $\theta°$ about the origin
- [B] A translation of h units to the right and k units up
- [C] A dilation with center at the origin by a scale factor of m
- [D] A reflection over the y-axis

$$\begin{bmatrix} 5 & 1.5 \\ 2 & d \end{bmatrix}$$

46. For what value of d is the 2×2 matrix shown above NOT invertible?

Ⓐ −0.6
Ⓑ 0
Ⓒ 0.6
Ⓓ 3

47. Given the recursive function defined by

$$f(0) = 3,$$
$$f(n) = 2f(n-1) + 3 \text{ for } n \geq 1,$$

what is the value of $f(3)$?

Ⓐ 9
Ⓑ 21
Ⓒ 45
Ⓓ 93

For the following question, enter your fractional answer in the boxes below the question.

48. The enrollment at a small community college for the fall semester is 10% higher than the enrollment in the fall semester a year ago. The number of female students increased by 5%, and the number of male students increased by 20%. Female students make up what fraction of the current enrollment at the community college?

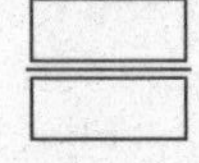

49. How many different ways can four people be seated in four of seven empty identical chairs that are placed in a row?

Ⓐ 24
Ⓑ 35
Ⓒ 840
Ⓓ 5,040

For the following question, select <u>all</u> that apply.

50. The relation "is a subset of" satisfies which of the following properties?

- [A] reflexive
- [B] symmetric
- [C] transitive
- [D] antisymmetric

For the following question, enter your numeric answer in the box below the question.

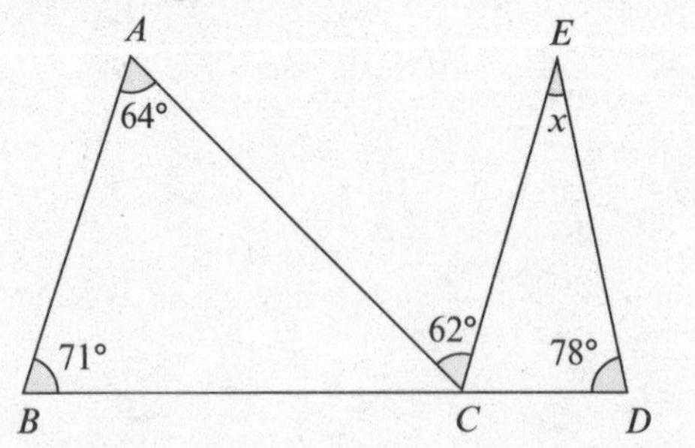

51. In the diagram with the measures of the angles as shown above, what is the measure of angle E?

[ ]°

GO ON TO THE NEXT PAGE

For the following question, enter your numeric answer in the box below the question.

52. If $x = \left(1 + \left(1 + 2^{-1}\right)^{-1}\right)^{-1}$, then $50x =$

[ ]

53. Which of the following expressions is equivalent to $3^x + 12^x$?

Ⓐ $3^x(1 + 4^x)$
Ⓑ $3(5^x)$
Ⓒ 15^x
Ⓓ 15^{2x}

For the following question, enter your numeric answer in the box below the question.

54. What is the least integer k such that $\frac{1}{4^k} < 0.001$?

[ ]

55. The number 144 has how many positive factors?

Ⓐ 6
Ⓑ 8
Ⓒ 15
Ⓓ 30

For the following question, select <u>all</u> that apply.

56. The number 200 lies between $\frac{1}{4}x$ and $\frac{1}{3}x$. Which of the following numbers could be values of x?

[A] 550
[B] 650
[C] 750
[D] 850

57. If $\frac{1}{3^x} = \frac{1}{3^n} + \frac{1}{3^n} + \frac{1}{3^n}$, then x expressed in terms of n is

Ⓐ $n - 1$
Ⓑ $n + 1$
Ⓒ $3n$
Ⓓ n^3

58. Given the equation $y = \frac{k}{x}$, where $x > 0$, $y > 0$, and k is a constant, if y increases by $\frac{1}{2}$ of its value, then the value of x decreases by what fraction of its value?

Ⓐ $\frac{1}{4}$
Ⓑ $\frac{1}{3}$
Ⓒ $\frac{1}{2}$
Ⓓ $\frac{2}{3}$

For the following question, enter your numeric answer in the box below the question.

59. If $\log_{(2x+3)}(125) = 3$, $x > 0$, what is the value of x?

[ ]

60. When $-4 - i$ is multiplied by its conjugate, the result is

Ⓐ −17
Ⓑ −15
Ⓒ 15
Ⓓ 17

STOP

Answer Key for Practice Test 1

Question Number	Correct Answer	Reference Chapter	Question Number	Correct Answer	Reference Chapter
1.	B	Algebra	31.	B	Calculus
2.	B, C, D	Number and Quantity	32.	C	Calculus
3.	82	Statistics	33.	300	Calculus
4.	C	Number and Quantity	34.	D	Calculus
5.	B	Algebra	35.	C	Statistics
6.	D	Geometry	36.	117	Statistics
7.	D	Algebra	37.	A	Statistics
8.	C	Algebra	38.	B	Statistics
9.	A	Algebra	39.	A	Statistics
10.	D	Number and Quantity	40.	D	Probability
11.	B	Number and Quantity	41.	B	Probability
12.	A	Geometry	42.	B	Probability
13.	B	Geometry	43.	C	Statistics
14.	A	Geometry	44.	D	Matrices
15.	B	Geometry	45.	A, B, D	Geometry
16.	B	Geometry	46.	C	Matrices
17.	D	Trigonometry	47.	C	Discrete Mathematics
18.	B	Trigonometry	48.	$\frac{7}{11}$	Algebra
19.	C	Trigonometry	49.	C	Discrete Mathematics
20.	B	Trigonometry	50.	A, C, D	Discrete Mathematics
21.	A	Functions	51.	29	Geometry
22.	D	Functions	52.	30	Algebra
23.	C	Discrete Mathematics	53.	A	Algebra
24.	D	Functions	54.	5	Algebra
25.	C	Functions	55.	C	Number and Quantity
26.	A	Functions	56.	B, C	Number and Quantity
27.	A	Functions	57.	A	Algebra
28.	A	Functions	58.	B	Algebra
29.	D	Calculus	59.	1	Algebra
30.	A	Calculus	60.	D	Number and Quantity

Answer Explanations for Practice Test 1

1. B. The fare is \$3.50 for the first mile plus \$1.50 for each additional half-mile.

Method 1. To solve the problem, break the distance into a 1-mile portion plus a portion composed of half-mile segments. Then write and solve an equation that models the situation.

Let n = the number of half-mile segments.

Distance from the bus station to Rose's home = 1 mile + n half-miles

$\text{Fare} = \$3.50 \text{ (for the first mile)} + n \cdot \dfrac{\$1.50}{\text{half-mile}}$

Write an equation that represents the facts given.

Fare + Tip = \$38.50

$$\left(\$3.50 + n \cdot \frac{\$1.50}{\text{half-mile}}\right) + \$5 \text{ (tip)} = \$38.50$$

Solve the equation, omitting the units for convenience.

$$\begin{aligned}(3.50 + n \cdot 1.50) + 5 &= 38.50\\ 3.50 + 1.5n + 5 &= 38.50\\ 1.5n &= 30\\ n &= \frac{30}{1.5}\\ n &= 20 \text{ half-mile segments}\end{aligned}$$

Distance from the bus station to Rose's home = 1 mile + 20 half-miles = 1 mile + 10 miles = 11 miles, choice B.

Method 2. Check the answer choices (a smart test-taking strategy for multiple-choice questions).

Check A: If the distance to Rose's home is 10 miles, then the trip is broken into a 1-mile portion plus 9 miles = 1 mile + 18 half-miles. The fare for the trip = \$3.50 (for the first mile) + (18 half-miles)$\left(\dfrac{\$1.50}{\text{half-mile}}\right)$ = \$3.50 + \$27.00 = \$30.50. When you add the \$5 tip, the total is \$35.50, which is not equal to \$38.50, so eliminate choice A.

Check B: If the distance to Rose's home is 11 miles, then the trip is broken into a 1-mile portion plus 10 miles = 1 mile + 20 half-miles. The fare for the trip = \$3.50 (for the first mile) + (20 half-miles)$\left(\dfrac{\$1.50}{\text{half-mile}}\right)$ = \$3.50 + \$30.00 = \$33.50. When you add the \$5 tip, the total is \$38.50, which is correct. Choice B is the correct response.

In a test situation, go on to the next question because you have found the correct answer. You would not check choices C and D; but for your information, choice C gives \$65.50 and choice D gives \$68.50, both of which are too high.

2. B, C, D. Given that x and y are whole numbers and $z = x + y = x + 3x = 4x$, then z is a multiple of 4. Therefore, z represents a whole number that is divisible by 4. A number is divisible by 4 only if the last 2 digits form a number that is divisible by 4. Of the answer choices, only choice A fails the test for divisibility by 4—because the last 2 digits of 314 are 14, which is not divisible by 4. Choices B, C, and D are divisible by 4, so each could be the value of z.

3. 82 The question asks: What is the *lowest* score the student can make on the final exam and still receive a B in the course? Examine the table below to review the instructor's grading guidelines.

Determination of Course Grade	Percent
Average (mean) of 3 major exams	50%
Average (mean) of weekly quizzes	10%
Final exam score	40%

From the table, you can see that you first must calculate the mean of the student's 3 major exam scores:

$\text{mean} = \frac{72+81+75}{3} = \frac{228}{3} = 76.$

Let x = the lowest score the student can make on the final and still have at least an 80 average.

Solve the following equation for x.

$$\begin{aligned} 50\%(76)+10\%(92)+40\%(x) &= 80 \\ 0.5(76)+0.1(92)+0.4(x) &= 80 \\ 38+9.2+0.4x &= 80 \\ 0.4x &= 32.8 \\ x &= 82 \end{aligned}$$

The lowest score that will yield an average of at least 80 is 82.

4. **C.** The principle of mathematical induction states that any set of counting numbers that contains the number 1 and also contains $(k + 1)$ whenever it contains the counting number k, contains all the counting numbers. Eliminate A, B, and D, which are statements about the real numbers. Choice C is a statement about the sum of the first n natural numbers. The natural numbers is another name for the counting numbers, so the statement in choice C can be proven using the principle of mathematical induction. Choice A can be proven using trigonometric concepts and the Pythagorean theorem. Choices B and D can be proven using techniques from calculus.

5. **B.** Let t = the time it takes the two machines when they work together. Omitting the units and using the quick solution method, $t = \frac{(10)(15)}{10+15} = \frac{150}{25} = 6$. The time it takes machines 1 and 2, working simultaneously at their respective constant rates, to produce $40x$ electrical components is 6 hours.

Tip: You should eliminate choice D at the outset because the time for the two machines working together should be less than either of their times working alone.

6. **D.** The volume V of a cube with edge s is given by $V = s^3$. The volume of the original cube will equal the sum of the volumes of the two smaller cubes.

The volume V_o of the original cube is $V_o = (4\text{ cm})^3 = 64\text{ cm}^3$.

The volume V_s of one of the smaller cubes $= \frac{1}{2}V_o = \frac{1}{2}\cdot 64\text{ cm}^3 = 32\text{ cm}^3$.

Let e = the length of an edge of one of the smaller cubes. Then $e^3 = 32\text{ cm}^3$, so

$e = \sqrt[3]{32\text{ cm}^3} = \sqrt[3]{8\text{ cm}^3 \cdot 4} = 2\sqrt[3]{4}$ centimeters, choice D.

7. **D.** The figure shows a circle centered at 0 with radius 4 units and a line that passes through the points (0, 7) and (7, 0).

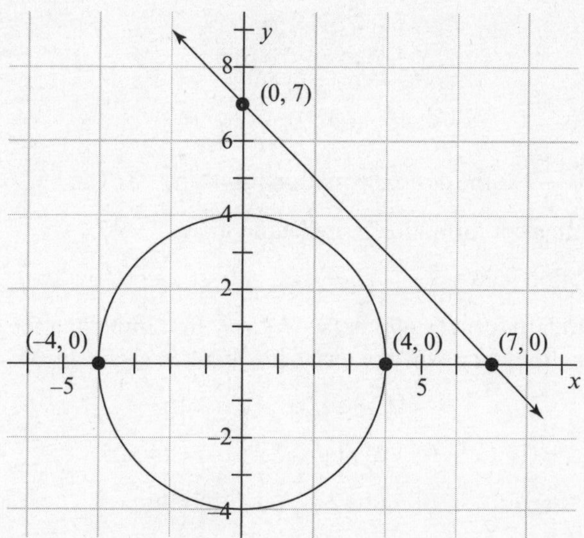

Write equations that represent each of the graphs shown, and then find the simultaneous solution of the two equations.

The equation of a circle centered at 0 with radius 4 is $x^2 + y^2 = 16$.

The slope of the line that passes through the points (0, 7) and (7, 0) is $m = \frac{0-7}{7-0} = \frac{-7}{7} = -1$. The y-intercept b is 7. The equation of the line is $y = -x + 7$.

The system of two equations is

$x^2 + y^2 = 16$

$y = -x + 7$

Caution: When an equation or a system of equations has real solutions, you can use features of the ETS graphing calculator to find a solution. This method will not work when the graphs do not intersect, as in this problem.

Substitute $y = -x + 7$ into the equation $x^2 + y^2 = 16$ to obtain

$$x^2 + (-x+7)^2 = 16$$
$$x^2 + x^2 - 14x + 49 = 16$$
$$2x^2 - 14x + 33 = 0$$

Using the quadratic formula,

$$a = 2,\ b = -14,\ c = 33$$

$$x = \frac{-(-14) \pm \sqrt{(-14)^2 - 4(2)(33)}}{2(2)} = \frac{14 \pm \sqrt{196-264}}{4} = \frac{14 \pm \sqrt{-68}}{4} = \frac{14 \pm 2i\sqrt{17}}{4} = \frac{7}{2} \pm i\frac{\sqrt{17}}{2}$$

Thus, $\frac{7}{2} - i\frac{\sqrt{17}}{2}$ is an x-value that satisfies the system, choice D.

8. C. When two lines are perpendicular, their slopes are negative reciprocals of each other.

Solve $x - 3y = 10$ for y to find its slope.

$$\begin{aligned} x-3y&=10 \\ -3y&=-x+10 \\ y&=\frac{1}{3}x-\frac{10}{3} \end{aligned}$$

The slope of $x-3y=10$ is $\frac{1}{3}$, so the desired equation has slope −3. The line passes through (0, 5), so 5 is the y-intercept. In slope-intercept form, the desired equation is $y=-3x+5$.

In standard form the equation is $3x+y=5$, choice C.

9. **A.** Put the equation in standard form $(x-h)^2+(y-k)^2=r^2$ by completing the square for the terms involving x and completing the square for the terms involving y.

$$\begin{aligned} x^2+6x+y^2-8y&=24 \\ (x^2+6x+9)+(y^2-8y+16)&=24+25 \\ (x+3)^2+(y-4)^2&=49 \end{aligned}$$

Therefore, the circle's center is (−3, 4), choice A.

10. **D.** The number of days until the next time is the least common multiple of 12 and 15, which is 60. It will be 60 days before Ari and Izzie both will swim at Stay-Fit Gym on the same day.

11. **B.** Perform the following calculation to determine how many years it would take to spend \$1.6 billion at the rate of \$1 per second.

$$\frac{\$1{,}600{,}000{,}000}{1}\cdot\frac{1\ \cancel{\text{sec}}}{\$1}\cdot\frac{1\ \cancel{\text{min}}}{60\ \cancel{\text{sec}}}\cdot\frac{1\ \cancel{\text{hr}}}{60\ \cancel{\text{min}}}\cdot\frac{1\ \cancel{\text{day}}}{24\ \cancel{\text{hr}}}\cdot\frac{1\text{ yr}}{365\ \cancel{\text{days}}}=50.73566\ldots$$ or approximately 50 years,

choice B.

12. **A.** The angle bisectors of a triangle are concurrent in a point that is equidistant from the three sides, which means choice A is the correct response. Choice B is incorrect because the altitudes of a triangle are concurrent in a point; but, in general, the point of concurrency is not equidistant from the three sides. Choice C is incorrect because the perpendicular bisectors of a triangle are concurrent in a point that is equidistant from the vertices of the triangle; but, in general, the point of concurrency is not equidistant from the three sides. Choice D is incorrect because the medians of a triangle are concurrent in a point; but, in general, the point of concurrency is not equidistant from the three sides.

13. **B.** Triangles ABC and ADE are similar right triangles because they share the common angle A.

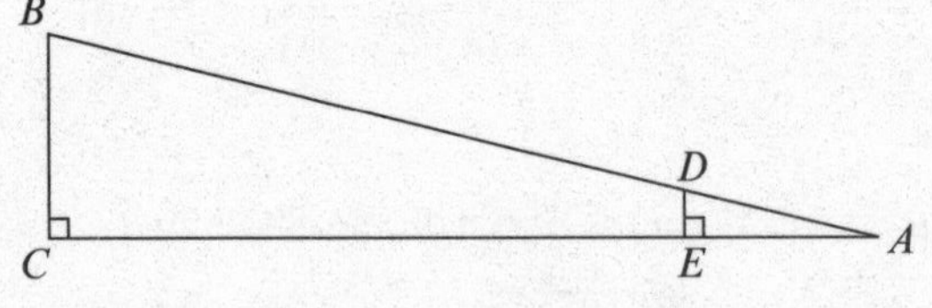

The area of triangle $ABC=\frac{1}{2}(\text{length of }\overline{CA})(\text{length of }\overline{BC})=\frac{1}{2}(CA)(BC)$. To find the area, determine CA and BC.

$$CA=CE+EA=50\text{ units}+25\text{ units}=75\text{ units}$$

Let $x=BC$. Set up a proportion based on corresponding sides of similar triangles. Solve for x, omitting the units for convenience.

$$\begin{aligned} \frac{x}{75}&=\frac{10}{25} \\ x&=\frac{(75)(10)}{25} \\ x&=30\text{ units} \end{aligned}$$

Thus, the area of triangle $ABC=\frac{1}{2}(75\text{ units})(30\text{ units})=1{,}125$ square units, choice B.

14. **A.** The measure of angle θ equals $2x + 65°$ because vertical angles have the same measure. The measure of angle θ equals $3x + 35°$ because corresponding angles of parallel lines have the same measure.

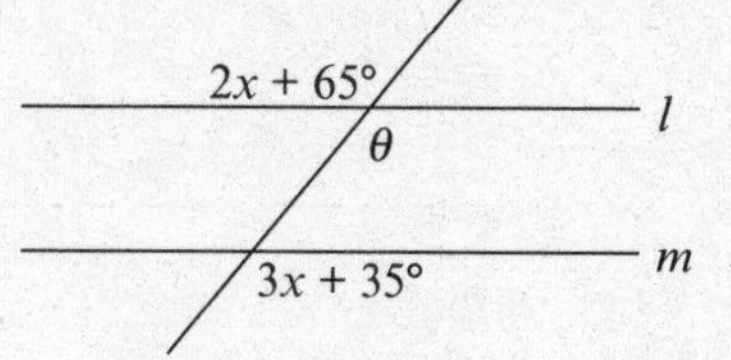

Thus, $2x + 65°$ and $3x + 35°$ are equal. Solve the following equation for x.

$$3x + 35° = 2x + 65°$$
$$x = 30°$$

Substituting this value for x into $2x + 65°$ yields the measure of angle $\theta = 2x + 65° = 2(30°) + 65° = 125°$, choice A.

15. **B.** Let x = length of $\overline{CD} = CD$. Sketch the figure and mark the information given.

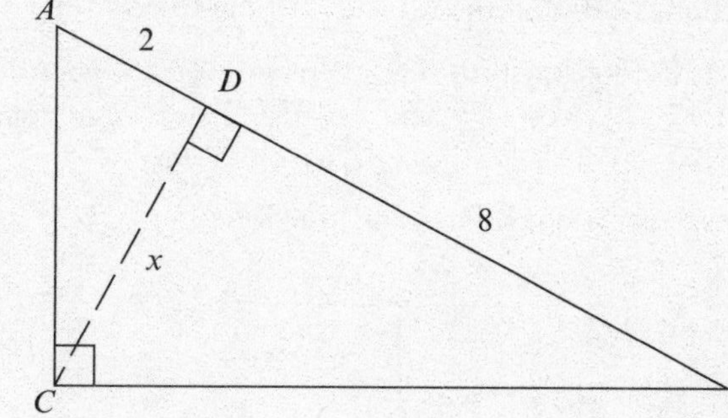

The perimeter of $\Delta ABC = \left(\text{length of } \overline{AB}\right) + \left(\text{length of } \overline{BC}\right) + \left(\text{length of } \overline{AC}\right) = AB + BC + AC$. From the information given, $AB = AD + DB = 2 + 8 = 10$. Now, determine BC and AC to find the perimeter.

The altitude to the hypotenuse of a right triangle is the geometric mean of the lengths of the two segments into which it separates the hypotenuse. Therefore, $\frac{AD}{x} = \frac{x}{DB}$. Substitute $AD = 2$ and $DB = 8$ and solve for x.

$$\frac{2}{x} = \frac{x}{8}$$
$$x^2 = 16$$
$$x = 4$$

Tip: The number −4 is also a solution, but is rejected because length is nonnegative.

Using the Pythagorean theorem, solve for BC and AC.

$BC = \sqrt{4^2 + 8^2} = \sqrt{80} = 4\sqrt{5}$ and

$AC = \sqrt{4^2 + 2^2} = \sqrt{20} = 2\sqrt{5}$

Thus, the perimeter of $\Delta ABC = 10 + 4\sqrt{5} + 2\sqrt{5} = 10 + 6\sqrt{5}$, choice B.

16. **B.** The image of (−3, 5) under a counterclockwise rotation of 90° about the origin is (−5, −3). The image of (−5, −3) under a translation of 4 units right and 7 units down is is (−1, −10). Therefore, the image K' of K under the series of transformations is (−1, −10), choice B.

17. **D.** The diagonal divides the rectangle into two right triangles.

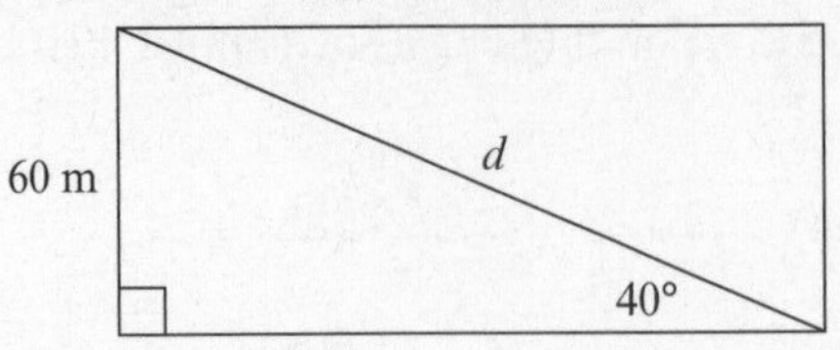

In the lower right triangle, the side 60 m is opposite the angle 40°.

To find d, use the definition of the sine function, and then solve.

$$\sin 40° = \frac{\text{length of side opposite } 40° \text{ angle}}{\text{length of hypotenuse}} = \frac{60 \text{ m}}{d}$$

$$d = \frac{60 \text{ m}}{\sin 40°} \approx 93.3 \text{ m}$$ (rounded to the nearest tenth of a meter), choice D.

Tip: Be sure to check that your ETS graphing calculator is in degrees mode when the angle given is in degrees.

18. **B.** The cosine is an even function, so $10\sin(4\theta)\cos(-4\theta) = 10\sin(4\theta)\cos(4\theta)$.

Rewrite $10\sin(4\theta)\cos(4\theta)$ as $5 \cdot 2\sin(4\theta)\cos(4\theta)$. The expression $2\sin(4\theta)\cos(4\theta)$ has the form of the double-angle formula $\sin(2x) = 2\sin(x)\cos(x)$, where $x = 4\theta$ and $2x = 8\theta$; therefore, $5 \cdot 2\sin(4\theta)\cos(4\theta) = 5 \cdot \sin(8\theta) = 5\sin(8\theta)$, choice B.

19. **C.** The graph's shape indicates either a sine or a cosine function.

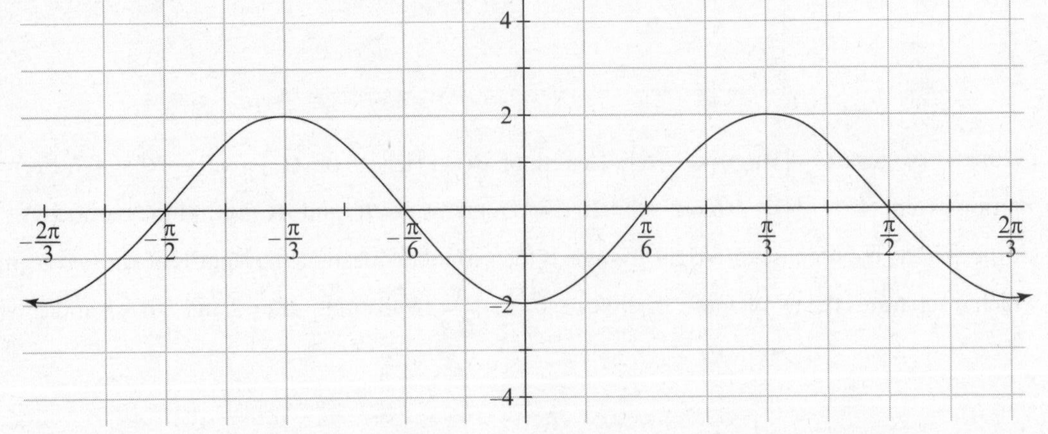

If $b > 0$, the general forms for the sine and cosine functions, $y = a\sin(bx + c) + k$ and $y = a\cos(bx + c) + k$, have graphs with amplitude $= |a|$, period $= \frac{2\pi}{b}$, a horizontal (or phase) shift of $\frac{|c|}{b}$ units (to the left of the origin if $\frac{c}{b}$ is positive; to the right of the origin if $\frac{c}{b}$ is negative), and a vertical shift of $|k|$ units (up from the origin if k is positive; down from the origin if k is negative).

Regardless whether you view the graph as a sine or a cosine function, the graph has amplitude 2, period $= \frac{2\pi}{3}$, and no vertical shift (that is, $k = 0$). Eliminate choices A and B because the period in these choices is 2π. If you view the graph as a sine function, the graph has a phase shift of $\frac{\pi}{6}$ units to the right of the origin, making choice C the correct response. Choice D is incorrect because if you view the graph as a cosine function, the phase shift is $\frac{\pi}{3}$ units, not $\frac{\pi}{6}$ units, to the right of the origin.

20. **B.** The hour hand is at 10:00. The angle θ from the positive x-axis to the hour hand is $120° = \frac{5\pi}{6}$.

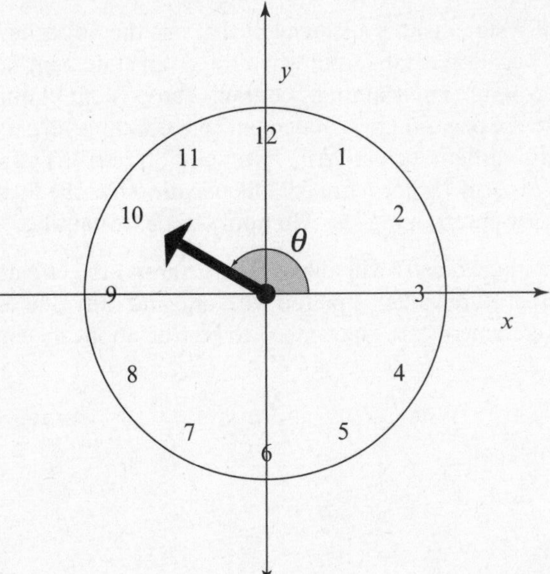

The length of the hour hand is 5 centimeters. In polar coordinates, the tip of the hour hand is located at $\left(5, \frac{5\pi}{6}\right)$. To change from polar (r, θ) to rectangular (x, y), use $x = r\cos\theta$ and $y = r\sin\theta$. (These formulas are included in the provided Notations, Definitions, and Formulas reference sheet.) Substituting into the formulas, the coordinates of the tip of the hour hand are $\left(5\cos\frac{5\pi}{6}, 5\sin\frac{5\pi}{6}\right)$, choice B.

21. **A.** Analyze the figure.

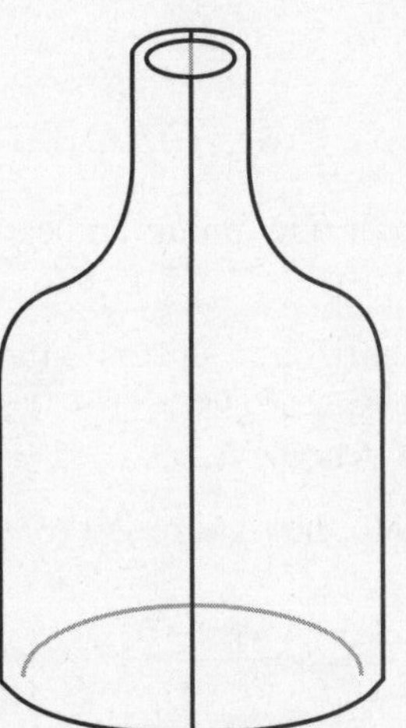

As water is poured into the container at a constant rate, the height of the water rises at a constant rate until it reaches the point near the top where the bottle narrows. At that point, the water rises at a faster (but still constant) rate until it reaches the bottle's neck, where it rises at an even faster rate. The graph that corresponds to this analysis is given in choice A. Choice B is incorrect because it indicates that the rate at which the water rises slows down as the water reaches the top of the bottle. Choice C is incorrect because it indicates that the height of the water in the bottle is constant at first, then suddenly leaps to a higher level and remains constant at that level for a while and, finally, leaps to an even higher level, where it remains constant. Choice D is incorrect because it indicates that the rate at which the water rises initially is the same as the rate at which it rises when it reaches the bottle's neck.

22. D. $f(g(a)) = f(a+2) = \frac{3(a+2)+4}{(a+2)+3} = \frac{3a+6+4}{a+2+3} = \frac{3a+10}{a+5}$, choice D.

23. C. In logic, the negation of a statement is a statement that has the opposite truth value. That is, when the given statement is true, its negation is false, and when the given statement is false, its negation is true. The given statement, "Some books are entertaining," contains the existential quantifier "Some." You can eliminate choice A because the negation of a statement that contains an existential quantifier is a statement that contains a universal quantifier (such as "All, "No," and "None"). The statement, "Some books are entertaining" has the logical form "Some *b* are *e*." The negation has the form "No *b* are *e*." Therefore, the negation of "Some books are entertaining" is "No books are entertaining," choice C.

24. D. Only the statement given in choice D will always be true about the engineer's function. By definition, each first component (temperature value) is paired with one and only one second component (current value). None of the other statements are guaranteed to be true about the engineer's function.

25. C. Examine the graph.

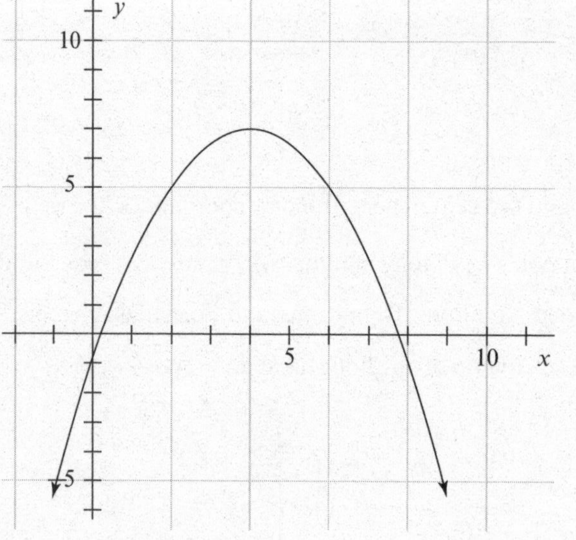

The graph intersects the real axis at two distinct points, indicating the function has two distinct real zeros. Therefore, $b^2 - 4ac > 0$, choice C.

26. A. Subtracting 3 from *x* will result in a horizontal shift of 3 units to the right. Adding 8 to $f(x)$ will result in a vertical shift of 8 units up. Thus, the graph of $g(x) = (x-3)^3 + 8$ is the same as the graph of $f(x) = x^3$ shifted right by 3 units and up by 8 units, choice A.

Tip: If you are unsure whether a shift is to the right or left (or up or down), graph the functions using the ETS graphing calculator to check.

27. A. The rational function *f* defined by $f(x) = \frac{x^2+x-6}{(x+3)} = \frac{(x+3)(x-2)}{(x+3)}$ is undefined when $x = -3$.

Simplified $f(x) = \frac{(x+3)(x-2)}{(x+3)} = x-2$, so the graph of *f* is the line whose equation is $y = x - 2$, but with a "hole" at the point $(-3, -5)$. The graph of the linear function *g* defined by $g(x) = 2.5x + 2.5$ is the line $y = 2.5x + 2.5$ that intersects the line $y = x - 2$ at $(-3, -5)$. That is, $(-3, -5)$ satisfies both $y = x - 2$ and $y = 2.5x + 2.5$. However, since -3 is not in the domain of *f*, the graphs of *f* and *g* do not intersect, choice A.

Caution: Using the ETS graphing calculator for problems involving holes in graphs can lead to incorrect answers.

28. A. Examine the table.

x	$f(x)$	$g(x)$
1	3	3
2	1	4
3	4	2
4	2	1

According to the table, $f(3) = 4$ and $g(4) = 1$. Therefore, $g(f(3)) = g(4) = 1$, choice A.

29. **D.** The phrase "an extended period of time" is a clue that this is a calculus problem involving the limit of a function as the variable approaches infinity. To answer the question, find the limit of the function

$Q(d) = \frac{5(6d+14)}{d+7}$ as d approaches infinity: $\lim_{d\to\infty} \frac{5(6d+14)}{d+7} = \lim_{d\to\infty} \frac{30d+70}{d+7} = \lim_{d\to\infty} \frac{30+\frac{70}{d}}{1+\frac{7}{d}} = \frac{30+0}{1+0} = \frac{30}{1} = 30$.

Thus, after being in operation for an extended period of time, the machine is able to produce 30 components per day, choice D.

30. **A.** The value of the first derivative at each number t_1, t_2, t_3, and t_4 is the instantaneous rate of change of the acceleration curve at that number. The acceleration is changing most rapidly at the number t_1 because the magnitude of the change is greatest at this number, choice A.

Tip: To avoid making a careless mistake, add 0s to make the number of decimal places in each value the same before making a comparison: $a'(t_1) = -0.80$, $a'(t_2) = -0.35$, $a'(t_3) = 0.50$, $a'(t_4) = 0.72$.

31. **B.** Make a quick sketch and shade the area bounded by $y = \frac{x^2}{2}$ and $y = 2$.

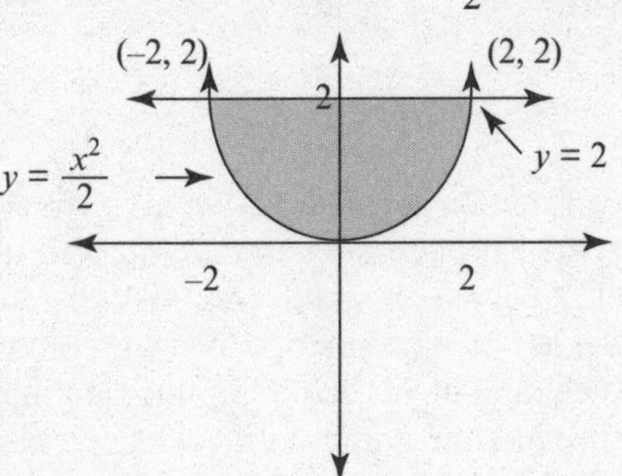

The curve and the line intersect at the points $(-2, 2)$ and $(2, 2)$, and $y = 2$ lies above $y = \frac{x^2}{2}$ between $x = -2$ and $x = 2$. To find the area of the shaded region, evaluate the integral $\int_{-2}^{2}\left(2-\frac{x^2}{2}\right)dx$.

$$\int_{-2}^{2}\left(2-\frac{x^2}{2}\right)dx = \left(2x-\frac{x^3}{6}\right)\Bigg|_{-2}^{2} = \left(2(2)-\frac{(2)^3}{6}\right)-\left(2(-2)-\frac{(-2)^3}{6}\right) = \left(4-\frac{8}{6}\right)-\left(-4-\frac{-8}{6}\right)$$

$$= 4-\frac{4}{3}+4-\frac{4}{3} = 8-\frac{8}{3} = \frac{24}{3}-\frac{8}{3} = \frac{16}{3}, \text{ choice B}$$

32. C. Analyze the graph of f'.

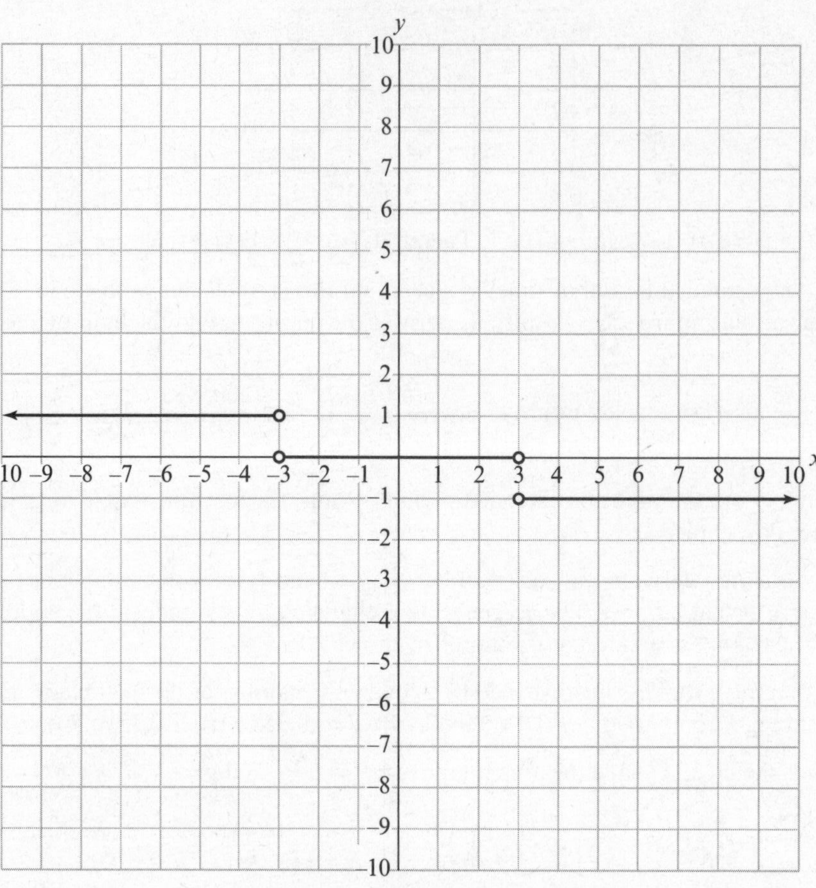

Recall that the first derivative of a function at a point is equal to the slope of the graph of the function at that point. If $f'(x) > 0$ on an interval, f is increasing on that interval. If $f'(x) < 0$ on an interval, f is decreasing on that interval. And if $f'(x) = 0$ on an interval, f is constant on that interval. By inspecting the graph of f', you can see that to the left of -3, the slope of the graph of f is a constant value of positive 1, indicating that to the left of -3 the graph of f is a straight line slanting upward from left to right with slope of 1. Eliminate choices B and D because the graphs in these answer choices do not meet this condition. Between -3 and 3, according to the graph of f', the slope of the graph of f is a constant value of 0, indicating that between -3 and 3 the graph of f is a horizontal line. Eliminate choice A because the graph in this answer choice does not have a horizontal component. Therefore, choice C is the correct response. The graph in choice C is the only graph shown in the answer choices that is consistent with the behavior of f'.

33. **300** Recall that the first derivative of a position function is the velocity function. To find the distance traveled after 10 seconds, find the numerical integral of the velocity function between 0 and 10 seconds.

That is, evaluate the integral $\int_0^{10} 0.9t^2\,dt$.

$\int_0^{10} 0.9t^2\,dt = \frac{0.9t^3}{3}\Big|_0^{10} = 0.3t^3\Big|_0^{10} = 0.3(10)^3 - 0.3(0)^3 = 0.3(1{,}000) - 0.3(0) = 300 - 0 = 300$. Therefore, the distance the car has traveled after 10 seconds is 300 feet.

34. **D.** Let the two sides of the pen that are perpendicular to the brick wall each have length of x yards. The side parallel to the wall has length 550 yards $-2x$ because the sum of the three sides is 550 yards. Sketch a diagram to illustrate the problem.

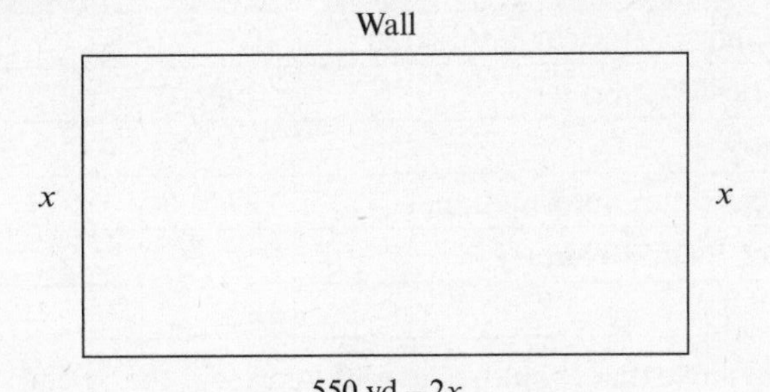

The area of the pen is width times length and is given by the function f, where $f(x) = x(550 - 2x) = 550x - 2x^2$.

The pen will have maximum area when $f(x)$ is the maximum value of f. To find the length of the pen with largest area, first solve $f'(x) = 0$ to find the critical number(s) for f.

$f(x) = 550x - 2x^2$

$f'(x) = 550 - 4x = 0$

$x = 137.5$ is a critical number of f.

Then check $f''(137.5)$ to determine whether $f(137.5)$ is a maximum.

$f''(x) = -4$

Therefore, $f''(137.5) = -4 < 0$

By the second derivative test, $f(137.5)$ is the maximum area of the pen. The length of the pen that encloses the maximum area is 550 yards – 2(137.5 yards) = 275 yards, choice D.

35. **C.** In an ordered set of data values, the median is the value in the $\left(\frac{n+1}{2}\right)$ position.

Scaled Scores of 35 Students on a Mathematics Test

Stem	Leaves
12	3 8 8
13	1 3 4 4 5 6 8
14	0 0 2 4 5 5 7 7 7 8 9
15	0 1 3 3 5 6 7 8 9 9
16	1 2 2 9
Legend: 12|3 = 123	

There are 35 data values, so the median is the $\frac{35+1}{2} = \frac{36}{2} = 18\text{th}$ data value. Counting from the least score, the 18th score in the stem-and-leaf plot is 147, choice C.

36. **117** A circle graph is made by dividing the 360 degrees of the circle that makes the graph into portions that correspond to the proportion for each category.

Genre	Number of Students
Biography/Historical Nonfiction	22
Historical Fiction	29
Mystery	32
Science/Nature Informational	25
Science Fiction/Fantasy	52
Total	160

The measure of the central angle that should be used to represent the Science Fiction/Fantasy category $= \frac{52}{160}(360°) = 117°$.

37. **A.** Analyze the information in the table.

Group	Mean	Standard Deviation
A	30 cm	5 cm
B	30 cm	8 cm
C	25 cm	10 cm
D	25 cm	9 cm

The standard deviation for the data obtained by Group A is less than the standard deviations of the data from the other groups. This result means the data from Group A have less variability and are, therefore, more reliable. Thus, choice A is the correct response.

38. **B.** According to the 68-95-99.7 rule, approximately 68% of the values of a normal distribution fall within 1 standard deviation of the mean, about 95% fall within 2 standard deviations of the mean, and about 99.7% fall within 3 standard deviations of the mean. The mean number of shavings for the razors is 16.8 with a standard deviation of 2.4 shavings.

The z-score for $19.2 = \frac{\text{data value} - \text{mean}}{\text{standard deviation}} = \frac{19.2 - 16.8}{2.4} = 1$. Therefore, 19.2 is 1 standard deviation above the mean.

Find the percentage of the normal distribution that is 1 standard deviation above the mean.

By the 68-95-99.7 rule, 68% of the distribution is within 1 standard deviation of the mean. Since the normal curve is symmetric, about $\frac{1}{2}$ of $68\% = 34\%$ of the distribution is between the mean and 1 standard deviation. Make a sketch to illustrate the problem.

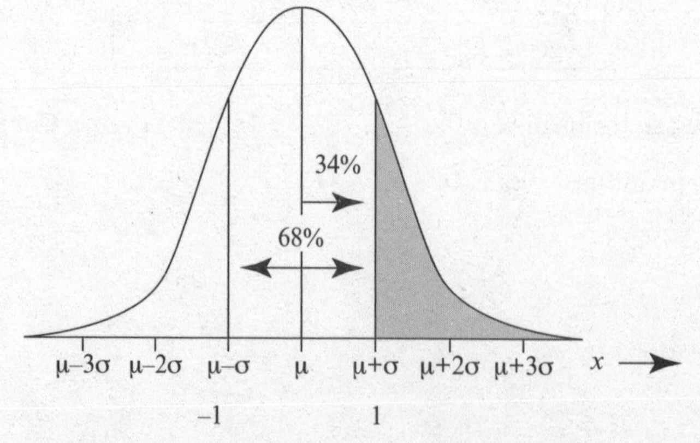

Again, due to symmetry, 50% of the distribution is above the mean. Thus, approximately 50% – 34% = 16% of the distribution is above 1 standard deviation above the mean. Thus, about 16% of the razors will last more than 19.2 shavings, choice B.

39. **A.** Because the correlation coefficient measures the linear relationship between the predictor and response variables of the simple-linear regression model, it can be used as an estimate of the "goodness of fit" of the regression model. Given the value 0.03 of the correlation coefficient is near 0, it fails to support a linear relationship between the variables of the linear regression, indicating that the linear model is not a good fit for the data, choice A.

40. **D.** Fill in the row and column totals for the table.

Grade Level	Cell Phone	No Cell Phone	Row Total
Ninth	55	45	100
Tenth	70	30	100
Eleventh	78	22	100
Twelfth	95	5	100
Total	298	102	400

This question asks you to find a conditional probability; that is, you are to find the probability when you already know that the student is a ninth grader. Thus, when computing the probability, the number of possible students under consideration is no longer 400, but is reduced to the total number of ninth graders, which is 100. According to the table, 55 of the 100 ninth graders have a cell phone.

Therefore, P(the student has a cell phone given that the student is a ninth grader) $= \frac{55}{100} = \frac{11}{20}$, choice D.

41. **B.** Fill in the missing probabilities.

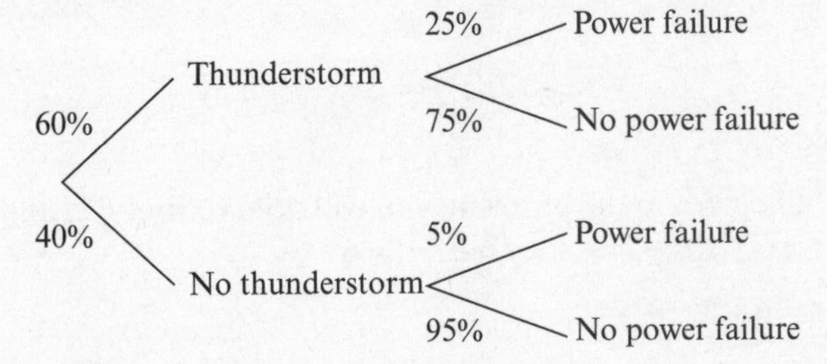

This problem requires an application of the multiplication rule, which states that $P(A \text{ and } B) = P(A)P(B|A)$. P(thunderstorm and power failure) = P(thunderstorm) · P(power failure given a thunderstorm has developed) = 60% · 25% = 15%, choice B.

42. **B.** Because there are only seven remote controls left in the box, one of which is defective, the probability that the next remote control is defective $= \frac{1}{7}$, choice B.

43. **C.** Let x and y be the two positive integers whose values you are not given and, for convenience, let $x < y$. Given that 73 is the mean of the six numbers, $\frac{48+53+61+82+x+y}{6} = 73$. Solve this equation for $x + y$.

$$\frac{48+53+61+82+x+y}{6} = 73$$
$$48+53+61+82+x+y = (6)(73)$$
$$244+x+y = 438$$
$$x+y = 194$$

Because x and y are positive integers, the least that x can be is 1. Therefore, the greatest that y can be is 193, choice C.

44. **D.** You can represent the triangle ABC with vertices $A(0, 0)$, $B(3, 0)$, and $C(0, 4)$ using a 2×3 matrix, with each column $\begin{bmatrix} x \\ y \end{bmatrix}$ representing a vertex: $\begin{bmatrix} 0 & 3 & 0 \\ 0 & 0 & 4 \end{bmatrix}$. The dilation of ABC, using a scale factor of 3, is represented by the matrix $\begin{bmatrix} 0 & 9 & 0 \\ 0 & 0 & 12 \end{bmatrix}$. Look at the answer choices and select the 2×2 matrix that will multiply times $\begin{bmatrix} 0 & 3 & 0 \\ 0 & 0 & 4 \end{bmatrix}$ to give $\begin{bmatrix} 0 & 9 & 0 \\ 0 & 0 & 12 \end{bmatrix}$. A quick way to work this problem is to check the answer choices.

Check A: $\begin{bmatrix} 0 & 3 \\ 0 & 3 \end{bmatrix}\begin{bmatrix} 0 & 3 & 0 \\ 0 & 0 & 4 \end{bmatrix} = \begin{bmatrix} 0 & 0 & \\ & & \end{bmatrix}$, eliminate choice A because the element in the first row second column is not 9. There is no need to complete the multiplication.

Check B: $\begin{bmatrix} 3 & 3 \\ 0 & 0 \end{bmatrix}\begin{bmatrix} 0 & 3 & 0 \\ 0 & 0 & 4 \end{bmatrix} = \begin{bmatrix} 0 & 9 & 12 \\ & & \end{bmatrix}$, eliminate choice B because the element in the first row third column is not 0. There is no need to complete the multiplication.

Check C: $\begin{bmatrix} 3 & 3 \\ 3 & 3 \end{bmatrix}\begin{bmatrix} 0 & 3 & 0 \\ 0 & 0 & 4 \end{bmatrix} = \begin{bmatrix} 0 & 9 & 12 \\ & & \end{bmatrix}$, eliminate choice C because the element in the first row third column is not 0. There is no need to complete the multiplication.

Thus, choice D is the correct response since you've eliminated choices A, B, and C.

45. **A, B, D.** Length is preserved only under rotations (choice A), translations (choice B), and reflections (choice D). Length is not preserved under dilations (choice C).

46. **C.** The matrix $\begin{bmatrix} 5 & 1.5 \\ 2 & d \end{bmatrix}$ is not invertible if its determinant is equal to 0. Set the determinant of the matrix equal to 0 and solve for d.

$$5d - (2)(1.5) = 5d - 3 = 0$$

Thus, $d = \frac{3}{5} = 0.6$, choice C.

47. **C.** For the recursive formula given in the problem, you will need to find $f(2)$ and $f(1)$ before you can find $f(3)$. Given $f(0) = 3$ and $f(n) = 2f(n-1) + 3$ for $n \geq 1$, then

$f(1) = 2f(0) + 3 = 2(3) + 3 = 6 + 3 = 9$

$f(2) = 2f(1) + 3 = 2(9) + 3 = 18 + 3 = 21$

$f(3) = 2f(2) + 3 = 2(21) + 3 = 42 + 3 = 45$, choice C.

48. $\mathbf{\frac{7}{11}}$ Let f = the number of female students enrolled in the fall semester a year ago.

Then, $f + 0.05f = 1.05f$ = the number of female students currently enrolled.

Let m = the number of male students enrolled in the fall semester a year ago.

Then, $m + 0.20m = 1.20m$ = the number of male students currently enrolled.

$f + m$ = the total enrollment in the fall semester a year ago.

And $(f + m) + 0.10(f + m) = 1.10(f + m)$ = the current enrollment at the community college.

The current enrollment also equals $1.05f + 1.20m$.

Therefore, $1.05f + 1.20m = 1.10(f + m)$, which implies that $0.10m = 0.05f$, or equivalently, $2m = f$. This result tells you that in the fall semester a year ago, there were twice as many female students as male students. Pick convenient values for m and f that satisfy this relationship. For example, let $m = 100$ and $f = 200$. With these values, the total enrollment a year ago was 300. You can check that $1.20(100) + 1.05(200) = 120 + 210 = 330$, which is the same as $1.10(300)$.

Thus, the fraction of the current enrollment at the community college that is female students is

$$\frac{1.05(200)}{1.10(300)} = \frac{210}{330} = \frac{7}{11}.$$

Tip: When you work with ratios (fractions), proportions, and percents, you often can pick convenient numbers to work with. Just make sure the numbers you pick satisfy all the conditions of the problem.

49. **C.** There are two tasks to be accomplished. The first task is to select 4 of the 7 chairs. Noting that different ordering of the chairs does not produce different arrangements, the number of ways to select 4 of 7 identical chairs is ${}_7C_4$. The second task is to arrange the 4 people in the 4 chairs. Since different orderings of the people results in different arrangements, the number of ways to seat 4 people in 4 chairs is $(4)(3)(2)(1) = 4!$ because there are 4 ways to seat someone in the first chair, 3 ways to seat someone in the second chair, and so on. Therefore, by the fundamental counting principle, the total number of ways to seat 4 people in 4 of 7 empty identical chairs is

$${}_7C_4 \cdot 4! = \frac{7!}{4!3!} \cdot 4! = 35 \cdot 24 = 840, \text{ choice C.}$$

50. **A, C, D.** A relation $\Re$ on a set S is reflexive if $x \Re x$ for all $x \in S$; symmetric if $x \Re y$ implies $y \Re x$ for all $x, y \in S$; transitive if ($x \Re y$ and $y \Re z$) implies $x \Re z$ for all $x, y, z \in S$; or antisymmetric if ($x \Re y$ and $y \Re x$) implies $x = y$ for all $x, y \in S$.

Recall that set A is a subset of set B, written $A \subseteq B$, if and only if $x \in A$ implies that $x \in B$, for every $x \in A$.

The relation "is a subset of" is reflexive (choice A) because every set is a subset of itself; that is, $A \subseteq A$. The relation "is a subset of" is not symmetric (choice B) because, for example, $\{1, 3\} \subseteq$ Integers, but Integers $\not\subseteq \{1, 3\}$. The relation "is a subset of" is transitive (choice C) because if $A \subseteq B$ and $B \subseteq C$, then $A \subseteq C$. The relation "is a subset of" is antisymmetric (choice D) because if $A \subseteq B$ and $B \subseteq A$, then $A = B$.

51. **29** Start with the angles for which you can find the measure by using the given information. As you determine the measure of each angle, you will gain enough information to find the solution.

$m\angle ACB = 180° - 64° - 71° = 45°$ (because the sum of the measures of the interior angles of a triangle is 180°)

$m\angle BCE = 45° + 62° = 107°$

The measure of an exterior angle of a triangle equals the sum of the measures of the nonadjacent interior angles. Thus, $m\angle BCE = 107° = 78° + x$; hence, $x = 107° - 78° = 29° = m\angle E$.

52. **30** Substitute the given value of x, and use your knowledge of exponents to solve for $50x$.

$$50x = 50\left(1+\left(1+2^{-1}\right)^{-1}\right)^{-1}$$

$$= 50\left(1+\left(1+\frac{1}{2}\right)^{-1}\right)^{-1} = 50\left(1+\left(\frac{3}{2}\right)^{-1}\right)^{-1} = 50\left(1+\frac{2}{3}\right)^{-1} = 50\left(\frac{5}{3}\right)^{-1} = \cancel{50}^{10}\left(\frac{3}{\cancel{5}}\right) = 30$$

53. **A.** Follow the rules for exponents.

$$3^x + 12^x = 3^x + (3 \cdot 4)^x = 3^x + 3^x4^x = 3^x(1 + 4^x), \text{ choice A}$$

54. **5** The inequality $\frac{1}{4^k} < 0.001$ implies that $4^k > 1{,}000$. Solve $4^k > 1{,}000$ for k.

$$4^k > 1{,}000$$

Take the log (base 10) of both sides of the equation, simplify, and solve for k.

$$\begin{aligned} &4^k > 1{,}000 \\ &\log\left(4^k\right) > \log(1{,}000) \\ &k\log(4) > 3 \\ &k > \frac{3}{\log(4)} \approx 4.98 \end{aligned}$$

Therefore, $k = 5$ is the least integer that satisfies the inequality.

55. **C.** The prime factorization of 144 is $2^4 \cdot 3^2$. Therefore, the number 144 has $(4 + 1)(2 + 1) = (5)(3) = 15$ positive factors, choice C.

56. **B, C.** $\frac{1}{4}x < 200 < \frac{1}{3}x$ implies that $12\left(\frac{1}{4}x\right) < 12(200) < 12\left(\frac{1}{3}x\right)$, which is equivalent to $3x < 2400 < 4x$. Check the answer choice for numbers that satisfy this double inequality.

Check A: $3(550) = 1{,}650$ and $4(550) = 2{,}200$, so reject choice A because 550 is too low.

Check B: $3(650) = 1{,}950$ and $4(650) = 2{,}600$, so select choice B because $x = 650$ satisfies the double inequality.

Check C: $3(750) = 2{,}250$ and $4(750) = 3{,}000$, so select choice C because $x = 750$ satisfies the double inequality.

Check D: $3(850) = 2{,}550$, so reject choice D because $x = 850$ is too high.

Tip: Eliminating fractions at the outset simplified the calculations for this problem.

57. **A.** Simplify the equation.

$$\begin{aligned} &\frac{1}{3^x} = \frac{1}{3^n} + \frac{1}{3^n} + \frac{1}{3^n} \\ &\frac{1}{3^x} = \frac{3}{3^n} \\ &\frac{1}{3^x} = \frac{1}{3^{n-1}}, \text{ which implies} \\ &x = n - 1, \text{ choice A} \end{aligned}$$

58. **B.** Given that $y = \frac{k}{x}$, then $xy = k$, where k is a constant. If y is increased by $\frac{1}{2}$ of its value to $\frac{3}{2}y$, then x must be decreased to $\frac{2}{3}x$ so that the product $\left(\frac{2}{3}x\right)\left(\frac{3}{2}y\right) = xy = k$ remains constant. Thus, if y is increased by $\frac{1}{2}$ of its value, then x is decreased by $\frac{1}{3}$ of its value. For example, suppose $x = 3$, $y = 6$, and $k = 18$, then $(3)(6) = 18$. Suppose 6 increases by $\frac{1}{2}$ of 6; that is, suppose 6 increases to 9. Then 3 must decrease to 2, to keep the product xy equal to 18. So, 3 must decrease by 1, which is $\frac{1}{3}$ of its value, choice B.

59. **1** The equation $\log_{(2x+3)}(125) = 3$ is equivalent to $(2x + 3)^3 = 125$. Solve this equation by taking the cube root of both sides to obtain $2x + 3 = 5$, which yields $x = 1$.

60. **D.** The conjugate of $-4 - i$ is $-4 + i$. The product is $(-4 - i)(-4 + i) = (-4)^2 - (i)^2 = 16 - (-1) = 16 + 1 = 17$, choice D.

Chapter 13

Practice Test 2

Time: 150 Minutes

60 Questions

Directions: Read the directions for each question carefully. This test has several different question types. For each question, select a single answer choice unless written instructions preceding the question state otherwise. For each selected-response question, select the best answer or answers from the choices given. For each numeric-entry question, enter an answer in the answer box. Enter the exact answer unless you are told to round your answer. If a question asks specifically for the answer as a fraction, there will be two boxes—a numerator box and a denominator box. Do not use decimal points in fractions.

1. In the *xy* plane, which of the following points lies inside the circular region of radius 4 centered at (–2, 3)?

Ⓐ (–6, 3)
Ⓑ (–2, –1)
Ⓒ (1, 5)
Ⓓ (2, 3)

For the following question, select all that apply.

2. Which of the following sets are closed with respect to the given operation?

[A] The set of perfect squares with respect to multiplication
[B] The set of whole numbers with respect to subtraction
[C] The set of odd numbers with respect to addition
[D] The set of integers with respect to division

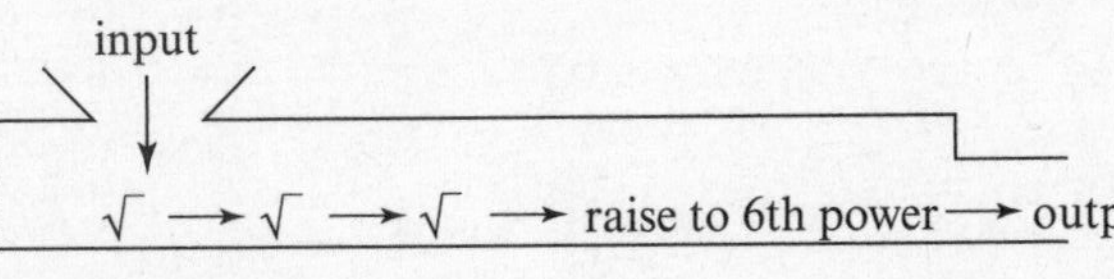

3. If a positive number x is used as the input for the function machine shown above, which of the following is equivalent to the output?

Ⓐ $x^{\frac{1}{24}}$
Ⓑ $x^{\frac{3}{4}}$
Ⓒ x
Ⓓ $x^{\frac{3}{2}}$

4. For what value of k will the graph of the function defined by $y = \dfrac{k}{16x^2 + kx + 9}$ have exactly one vertical asymptote?

Ⓐ 0
Ⓑ 12
Ⓒ 24
Ⓓ 48

5. Definition: The *normal line* to the curve $y = f(x)$ at the point T is the line perpendicular to the tangent line to the curve at T. If an equation of the normal line to the graph of the function defined by $y = f(x)$ at the point (3, 1) is $y = \frac{5}{6}x - \frac{3}{2}$, find the equation of the tangent line at (3, 1).

Ⓐ $5x - 6y = 9$
Ⓑ $-6x + 5y = -13$
Ⓒ $6x + 5y = 23$
Ⓓ $6x + 5y = 21$

For the following question, enter your numeric answer in the box below the question.

6. Given $f(x) = -x^2 + 12\sqrt{x}$, find the slope of the tangent line to the graph of f at $x = 4$.

[ ]

GO ON TO THE NEXT PAGE

7. The operation $\oplus$ is defined on the set R of real numbers by $x \oplus y = 3x + xy$, where x and y are real numbers and the operations on the right side of the equal sign denote the standard operations for the real number system. Which of the following questions tests whether the operation $\oplus$ is commutative?

- Ⓐ Does $x + y = y + x$ for all real numbers x and y?
- Ⓑ Does $3x + xy = 3x + yx$ for all real numbers x and y?
- Ⓒ Does $3x + x^2 = 3y + y^2$ for all real numbers x and y?
- Ⓓ Does $3x + xy = 3y + yx$ for all real numbers x and y?

8. The exterior of a spherical tank with radius 12 feet is to be painted with one coat of paint. The paint sells for $22.40 per gallon and can be purchased in 1-gallon cans only. If a can of paint will cover approximately 400 square feet, what is the cost of the paint needed to paint the exterior of the tank?

- Ⓐ $22.40
- Ⓑ $44.80
- Ⓒ $101.36
- Ⓓ $112.00

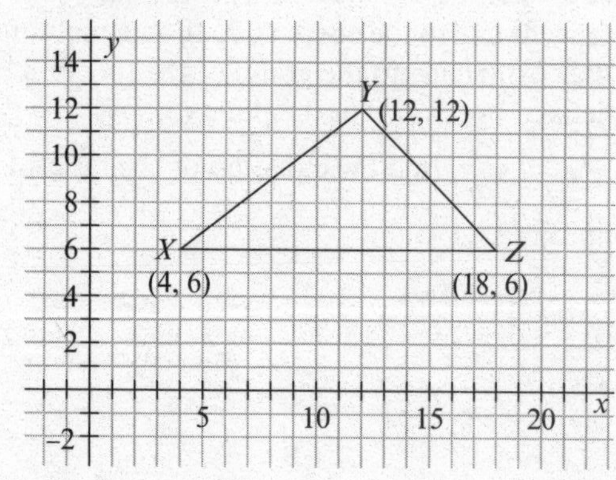

9. Which of the following properties associated with triangle XYZ shown above is an irrational quantity?

- Ⓐ perimeter of triangle XYZ
- Ⓑ area of triangle XYZ
- Ⓒ length of side $\overline{XY}$
- Ⓓ midpoint of side $\overline{XZ}$

10. To estimate the population of fish in a lake, a parks and recreation team captures and tags 500 fish and then releases the tagged fish back into the lake. One month later, the team returns and captures 100 fish from the lake, 20 of which have tags that identify them as being among the previously captured fish. If all the tagged fish are still active in the lake when the second group of fish is captured, what is the best estimate of the fish population in the lake based on the information obtained through this capture-recapture strategy?

- Ⓐ 100 fish
- Ⓑ 1,500 fish
- Ⓒ 2,500 fish
- Ⓓ 3,000 fish

11. Which of the following statements follows logically from the statement "If it is Monday, then I will go to work"?

- Ⓐ It is not Monday, so I am not going to work.
- Ⓑ It is Monday, so I am going to work.
- Ⓒ I am going to work, so it must be Monday.
- Ⓓ I am not going to work, so it is not Monday.

12. Given $\frac{a}{b} = 10$ and $\frac{b}{c} = 5$, with $b \cdot c \neq 0$, what is the value of $\frac{a}{b+c}$?

- Ⓐ $\frac{25}{6}$
- Ⓑ $\frac{25}{3}$
- Ⓒ $\frac{5}{3}$
- Ⓓ 12

13. $(2 \cos 10° + 2i \sin 10°)^3$ equals

- Ⓐ $4\sqrt{3} + 4i$
- Ⓑ $4 + 4\sqrt{3}i$
- Ⓒ $8 \cos 1{,}000° + 8i \sin 1{,}000°$
- Ⓓ $8 \sin 1{,}000° + 8i \cos 1{,}000°$

GO ON TO THE NEXT PAGE

14. A family on vacation in an RV leaves home at 9 a.m., travels at an average speed of 50 miles per hour, and arrives at the vacation destination at 2 p.m., with no stops along the way. At approximately what time would the family have arrived if the average speed of the trip had been 65 miles per hour?

Ⓐ 12:24 p.m.
Ⓑ 12:51 p.m.
Ⓒ 1:24 p.m.
Ⓓ 1:51 p.m.

15. Triangle ABC has vertices (2, 1), (–3, 4), and (5, –3). Which of the following matrix multiplications would result in a reflection of ΔABC over the x-axis?

Ⓐ $\begin{bmatrix} -1 & 0 \\ 0 & 1 \end{bmatrix}\begin{bmatrix} 2 & -3 & 5 \\ 1 & 4 & -3 \end{bmatrix}$

Ⓑ $\begin{bmatrix} 0 & 1 \\ -1 & 0 \end{bmatrix}\begin{bmatrix} 2 & -3 & 5 \\ 1 & 4 & -3 \end{bmatrix}$

Ⓒ $\begin{bmatrix} 1 & 0 \\ 0 & -1 \end{bmatrix}\begin{bmatrix} 2 & -3 & 5 \\ 1 & 4 & -3 \end{bmatrix}$

Ⓓ $\begin{bmatrix} 0 & 1 \\ 1 & 0 \end{bmatrix}\begin{bmatrix} 2 & -3 & 5 \\ 1 & 4 & -3 \end{bmatrix}$

For the following question, select <u>all</u> that apply.

16. Which of the following relations is an equivalence relation?

[A] "is similar to" over the set of all parallelograms
[B] "is equal to" over the set of all $m \times n$ matrices
[C] "is perpendicular to" over the set of all lines in the xy plane
[D] "is congruent to" over the set of all triangles

17. For which of the following data sets is the median clearly a preferred alternative to the mean as a measure of central tendency?

Ⓐ The data set contains some extremely high, without corresponding extremely low, data values.
Ⓑ The data set has a somewhat symmetrical distribution.
Ⓒ The data set is very large in number and has no mode.
Ⓓ The data set is very small in number and has no mode.

18. A box contains 50, 1-inch square wooden tiles numbered 1 through 50. If one tile is drawn at random from the box, what is the probability that the number on the tile is a prime number?

Ⓐ $\frac{1}{50}$
Ⓑ $\frac{1}{15}$
Ⓒ $\frac{3}{10}$
Ⓓ $\frac{8}{25}$

19. To find the distance across the lake between two houses separated by the lake, a surveyor measures the angle between the houses from a distant point, X, on dry land. The surveyor then measures the straight line distance on dry land from X to each of the two houses. The distance from X to the first house is 60 feet and from X to the second house is 75 feet. If the angle measured at point X between the two houses is 60°, approximately how far apart are the two houses?

Ⓐ 39 feet
Ⓑ 69 feet
Ⓒ 96 feet
Ⓓ 4,725 feet

20. The density of lead is 11.3 grams per cubic centimeter. What is the mass (to the nearest tenth of a gram) of a lead cube that measures 1.5 centimeters on an edge?

Ⓐ 3.3 grams
Ⓑ 17.0 grams
Ⓒ 25.4 grams
Ⓓ 38.1 grams

For the following question, enter your numeric answer in the box below the question.

21. The original price of a suit was 30 percent less than the suit's suggested retail price of $500. The price at which the suit was sold was 30 percent more than the original price. What is the price at which the suit was sold?

$ 

GO ON TO THE NEXT PAGE

22. Given the functions $f = \{(-2, -8), (-1, 3), (0, 1), (1, 4), (2, 8)\}$ and $g = \{(-2, -7), (-1, 4), (0, -2), (1, 2), (2, 0), (3, 8)\}$, find $g \circ f$, where $(g \circ f)(x) = g(f(x))$.

Ⓐ $\{(0, -8), (1, 8), (2, 1)\}$
Ⓑ $\{(-1, 8), (0, 2)\}$
Ⓒ $\{(-2, 56), (-1, -12), (0, -2), (1, 8), (2, 0)\}$
Ⓓ $\{(-2, -15), (-1, -1), (0, -1), (1, 6), (2, 8)\}$

23. A team of biologists introduces a herd of 250 deer onto an uninhabited island. If the deer population doubles every 8 years, which of the following functions models the growth of the deer population on the island if t is the time in years?

Ⓐ $(250)^{0.125t}$
Ⓑ $(250)2^{0.125t}$
Ⓒ $(250)^{8t}$
Ⓓ $(250)2^{8t}$

For the following question, select <u>all</u> that apply.

24. For what values of x in the interval $0 \le x \le 2\pi$ does $\sin^2 x - 5 \sin x + 4 = 0$?

[A] 1, 4
[B] π
[C] $\frac{\pi}{2}$
[D] $\frac{3\pi}{2}$

25. If $f(x) = -x^{-2}$, then $f'(2)$ is

Ⓐ -1
Ⓑ $-\frac{1}{4}$
Ⓒ $\frac{1}{4}$
Ⓓ 1

Correlation Table for Variables *A*, *B*, *C*, and *D*

	A	*B*	*C*	*D*
A	1			
B	–0.88	1		
C	0.65	0.15	1	
D	–0.59	0.50	0.78	1

26. The preceding correlation table shows the correlations between pairs of variables from among the four variables *A*, *B*, *C*, and *D*. The correlation coefficient between which of the following pairs of variables shows the strongest relationship?

Ⓐ *A* and *B*
Ⓑ *A* and *C*
Ⓒ *A* and *D*
Ⓓ *C* and *D*

For the following question, select <u>all</u> that apply.

27. In general, with respect to matrix multiplication on the set of $n \times n$ matrices whose elements are real numbers only, which of the following properties hold?

[A] closure
[B] commutativity
[C] associativity
[D] distributive property

$$b2_{\text{seven}} = 134_{\text{five}}$$

28. In the preceding equation, the subscript of each number identifies the base in which the number is expressed. What base-seven number does $b2_{\text{seven}}$ represent?

Ⓐ 82_{seven}
Ⓑ 26_{seven}
Ⓒ 52_{seven}
Ⓓ 62_{seven}

GO ON TO THE NEXT PAGE

29. What are the units of the quantity $Y = \frac{Adv}{t}$, where A is measured in square centimeters (cm^2), d is expressed in grams per cm^3 $\left(\frac{g}{cm^3}\right)$, v is expressed in centimeters per second $\left(\frac{cm}{s}\right)$, and t is given in seconds (s)?

Ⓐ g
Ⓑ $\frac{g}{s^2}$
Ⓒ $\frac{g-cm}{s}$
Ⓓ $\frac{g-cm}{s^2}$

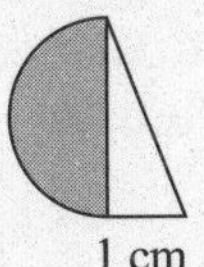

30. The figure above consists of a semicircle of radius 1 cm and an attached right triangle with one leg equal to the radius of the semicircle as shown. What is the figure's perimeter to the nearest tenth of a centimeter?

Ⓐ 5.4 cm
Ⓑ 5.9 cm
Ⓒ 6.4 cm
Ⓓ 9.5 cm

For the following question, select <u>all</u> that apply.

31. If x and y are real numbers, which of the following statements must be true?

[A] $-|-x| = x$
[B] $|xy| = |x||y|$
[C] $\left|\frac{x}{y}\right| = \frac{|x|}{|y|}$, provided $y \neq 0$
[D] $|x + y| \leq |x| + |y|$

32. What is the value of $\lim_{x \to 3} \frac{2x-6}{x^2-9}$?

Ⓐ The limit does not exist.
Ⓑ $\frac{1}{6}$
Ⓒ $\frac{1}{3}$
Ⓓ 1

33. The velocity function for a particle moving in a straight line is given by $v(t) = 1.8t^2$. How far does the particle move between time $t = 0$ and $t = 5$?

Ⓐ 15
Ⓑ 45
Ⓒ 75
Ⓓ 225

34. Find a, b, c, and d if

$$\begin{bmatrix} a & 5 \\ 4b & d \end{bmatrix} - \begin{bmatrix} 3a & 2c \\ -6 & -2d \end{bmatrix} = \begin{bmatrix} -8 & 7 \\ b & 9 \end{bmatrix}.$$

Ⓐ $a = -4, b = 2, c = -1, d = 3$
Ⓑ $a = 4, b = -2, c = -1, d = 3$
Ⓒ $a = 4, b = -2, c = 1, d = -3$
Ⓓ $a = -4, b = 2, c = 1, d = 3$

35. At an appliance store's grand-opening sale, 152 customers bought a washer or a dryer. Looking at the inventory, the store manager found that 94 washers and 80 dryers were sold. Of the 152 customers, how many bought only a washer?

Ⓐ 22
Ⓑ 58
Ⓒ 72
Ⓓ 130

36. The equation of the line tangent to the graph of $y = 2x^3 - x + 3$ at the point where $x = 1$ is given by

Ⓐ $6x - y = 2$
Ⓑ $5x - y = 1$
Ⓒ $5x - y = 5$
Ⓓ $5x - y = -1$

37. What is the area of the region bounded by the graph of $f(x) = 3x^2 + 1$ and the x-axis over the closed interval [1, 3]?

Ⓐ 26
Ⓑ 28
Ⓒ 30
Ⓓ 32

GO ON TO THE NEXT PAGE

38. The heights of a certain type of indoor plant are normally distributed with a mean of 24 inches and a standard deviation of 3.5 inches. What is the approximate probability a plant of this type chosen at random will be between 20.5 inches and 27.5 inches tall?

Ⓐ 16%
Ⓑ 34%
Ⓒ 68%
Ⓓ 84%

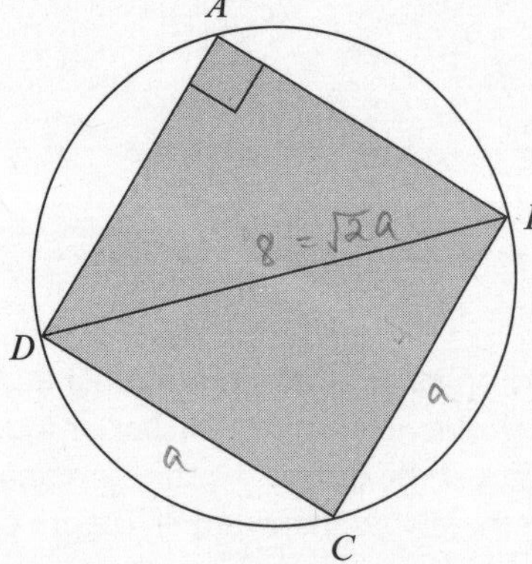

39. In the figure above, the circle circumscribed about the square $ABCD$ has a circumference of 8π cm. Find the area of the square $ABCD$.

Ⓐ 32 cm^2
Ⓑ $4\sqrt{2} \text{ cm}^2$
Ⓒ $32\pi \text{ cm}^2$
Ⓓ It cannot be determined from the information given.

	Exam 1	Exam 2	Exam 3	Exam 4
Student's Grade	65	87	92	70
Class Mean	55	88	86	60
Class Standard Deviation	5	2	4	10

40. The data in the preceding table show a student's grades on 4 exams in a college statistics class along with the means and standard deviations of the grades for all the students in the class of 50 students. On which of the exams did the student perform best relative to the performance of the student's classmates?

Ⓐ Exam 1
Ⓑ Exam 2
Ⓒ Exam 3
Ⓓ Exam 4

41. Which of the following graphs illustrates the solution to $\frac{2-x}{5} < 1$?

Ⓐ −8 −7 −6 −5 −4 −3 −2 −1 0 1 2 3 4 5 6 7 8
Ⓑ −8 −7 −6 −5 −4 −3 −2 −1 0 1 2 3 4 5 6 7 8
Ⓒ −8 −7 −6 −5 −4 −3 −2 −1 0 1 2 3 4 5 6 7 8
Ⓓ −8 −7 −6 −5 −4 −3 −2 −1 0 1 2 3 4 5 6 7 8

Time (Minutes)	Population
0	1,000
10	5,000

42. The preceding table gives the population of a beneficial bacterium at two different times. The bacteria's growth is modeled by the function defined by $Q(t) = Q_0e^{xt}$, where t is in minutes. Based on this information, what is the value of x?

Ⓐ $\frac{\ln 5}{10}$
Ⓑ $\ln 5$
Ⓒ $\ln 10 - \ln 5$
Ⓓ $\ln\frac{1}{5}$

43. Which of the following functions is the factored form of the polynomial of lowest degree with real coefficients and leading coefficient 1 that has zeros at 0, $2 - i$, 4, and -3?

Ⓐ $P(x) = x(x - 2 + i)(x - 4)(x + 3)$
Ⓑ $P(x) = x(x + 2 - i)(x + 4)(x - 3)$
Ⓒ $P(x) = x(x - 2 - i)(x - 2 + i)(x + 4)(x - 3)$
Ⓓ $P(x) = x(x - 2 + i)(x - 2 - i)(x - 4)(x + 3)$

GO ON TO THE NEXT PAGE

For the following question, enter your numeric answer in the box below the question.

44. What is the value of k such that $x - i$ is a factor of the polynomial $P(x) = k^2x^4 - 8kx^2 + 16$?

For the following question, select all that apply.

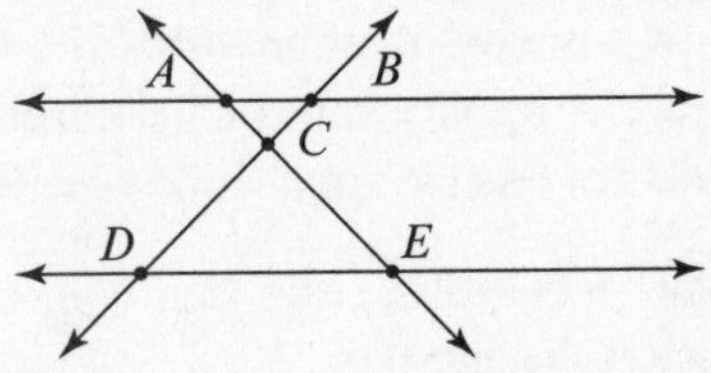

45. In the preceding figure $\overleftrightarrow{AB} \parallel \overleftrightarrow{DE}$, which of the following geometric theorems would most likely be used in proving that $\Delta ABC \sim \Delta EDC$?

[A] Vertical angles of intersecting lines are congruent.

[B] If two parallel lines are cut by a transversal, then any pair of alternate interior angles is congruent.

[C] If two angles of one triangle are congruent to two corresponding angles of another triangle, then the triangles are similar.

[D] The measure of an exterior angle of a triangle equals the sum of the measures of the remote interior angles.

46. In the xy plane, triangle ABC has vertices (0, 0), (8, 0), and (0, 15). A dilation of triangle ABC with center (0, 0) and scale factor 5 is achieved by premultiplying the vertex matrix $\begin{bmatrix} x_i \\ y_i \end{bmatrix}$ by which of the following transformation matrices?

Ⓐ $\begin{bmatrix} 5 & 5 \\ 5 & 5 \end{bmatrix}$

Ⓑ $\begin{bmatrix} 5 & 0 \\ 5 & 0 \end{bmatrix}$

Ⓒ $\begin{bmatrix} 5 & 0 \\ 0 & 5 \end{bmatrix}$

Ⓓ $\begin{bmatrix} 0 & 5 \\ 0 & 5 \end{bmatrix}$

47. What is the approximate volume of a right hexagonal prism that is 30 centimeters in height and whose bases are regular hexagons that are 6 centimeters on a side?

Ⓐ 468 cm^3

Ⓑ 1,080 cm^3

Ⓒ 2,806 cm^3

Ⓓ 3,240 cm^3

For the following question, enter your numeric answer in the box below the question.

48. Squaring both sides of the equation $2x = \sqrt{3x+1}$ and then solving for x gives rise to what extraneous solution?

49. Find the area enclosed by the curve $y = 2x - x^2$ and the line $y = 2x - 4$.

Ⓐ $\frac{16}{3}$

Ⓑ $\frac{32}{3}$

Ⓒ 16

Ⓓ $\frac{64}{3}$

Resident Status of Second–Year Students ($n = 500$)

Gender	On-Campus	Off-Campus
Female	114	135
Male	156	95

50. The preceding table shows the resident status, by sex, of 500 second-year students at a community college. If 1 of the 500 students is randomly selected, which of the following calculations yields the probability that the student resides off-campus, given that the student selected is a male student?

Ⓐ $1 - \frac{156}{500}$

Ⓑ $\frac{95}{500}$

Ⓒ $\frac{251}{500} \cdot \frac{95}{500}$

Ⓓ $\frac{95}{251}$

GO ON TO THE NEXT PAGE

51. If a prime number p is a factor of both $(14k + 13)$ and $(7k + 1)$, what is the value of p?

Ⓐ 7
Ⓑ 11
Ⓒ 13
Ⓓ It cannot be determined from the information given.

52. What is the third term in the binomial expansion of $(x + 2y)^5$?

Ⓐ $10x^2y^3$
Ⓑ $10x^3y^2$
Ⓒ $40x^3y^2$
Ⓓ $80x^2y^3$

53. If the function f is defined by $f(x) = \frac{x+1}{x-2}$, $x \neq 2$, then f^{-1}, the inverse of f, is defined by which of the following equations?

Ⓐ $f^{-1}(x) = -\frac{x-1}{x+2}$, $x \neq -2$
Ⓑ $f^{-1}(x) = \frac{x-2}{x+1}$, $x \neq -1$
Ⓒ $f^{-1}(x) = -\frac{2x+1}{x-1}$, $x \neq 1$
Ⓓ $f^{-1}(x) = \frac{2x+1}{x-1}$, $x \neq 1$

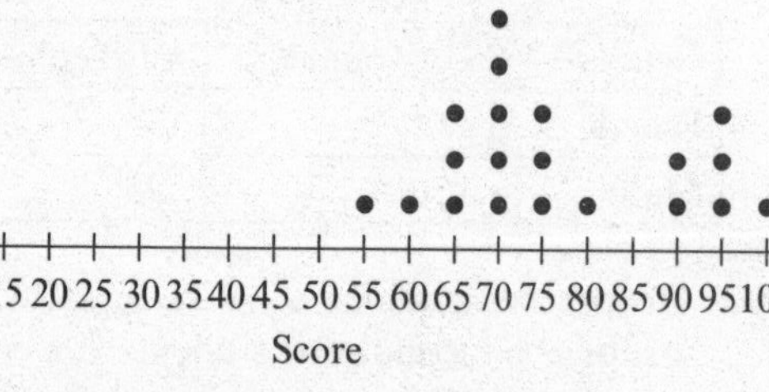

54. The preceding dot plot displays the scores of 20 students on a biology exam. The standard deviation of these data is approximately 12.8. Determine the number of students whose scores are within 1 standard deviation of the mean.

Ⓐ 11
Ⓑ 12
Ⓒ 13
Ⓓ 14

55. To investigate the effect of Fertilizer X on plant growth, a researcher decides to conduct an experimental study with 80 identical plant seedlings (a plant seedling is a young plant) and two plots of identical soil. The seedlings are randomly assigned to either the treatment plot or the control plot (40 plants in each plot). The plant seedlings in the treatment plot will be those that

Ⓐ have plant growth.
Ⓑ do not have plant growth.
Ⓒ receive applications of Fertilizer X.
Ⓓ do not receive applications of Fertilizer X.

For the following question, enter your numeric answer in the box below the question.

56. Given $x^2 + kx + c = (x + h)^2$, where c, k, and h are real numbers, if $k = 6$, what is the value of c?

57. Treasure coins in a video game are distributed among five locations in the ratio 1:2:3:4:5. To win the game, a player must acquire at least 50% of the coins in each of three or more of the five locations. To win, a player must acquire what minimum percent of the total coins?

Ⓐ 10%
Ⓑ 15%
Ⓒ 20%
Ⓓ 25%

For the following question, select <u>all</u> that apply.

58. If f is a real–valued function, which of the following values are NOT in the domain of f, where $f(x) = \frac{\sqrt{x+2}}{2x^3 + x^2 - 2x - 1}$?

[A] -3
[B] -1
[C] $-\frac{1}{2}$
[D] 1

59. Find $\lim_{h \to 0} \frac{\left(\frac{1}{2}+h\right)^8 - \left(\frac{1}{2}\right)^8}{h}$.

Ⓐ 0
Ⓑ $\frac{1}{2}$
Ⓒ $\frac{1}{16}$
Ⓓ The limit does not exist.

GO ON TO THE NEXT PAGE

60. If f is a function such that, for all x, $f'(x) > 0$ and $f''(x) < 0$, which of the following could be a portion of the graph of f?

Ⓐ

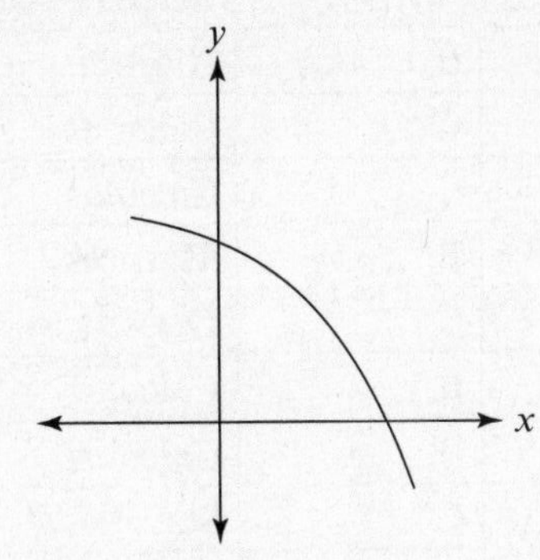

Ⓑ

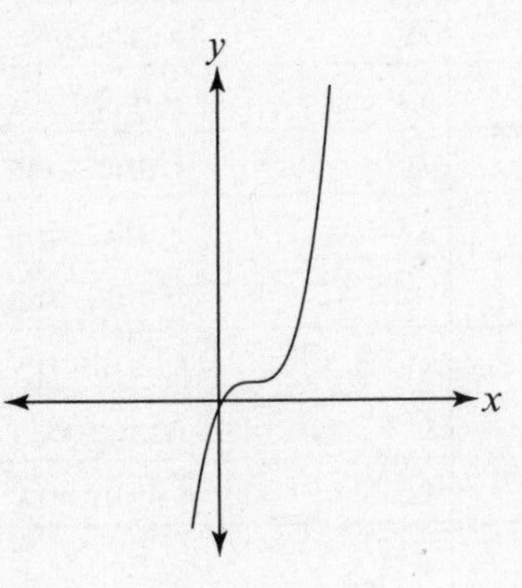

Ⓒ

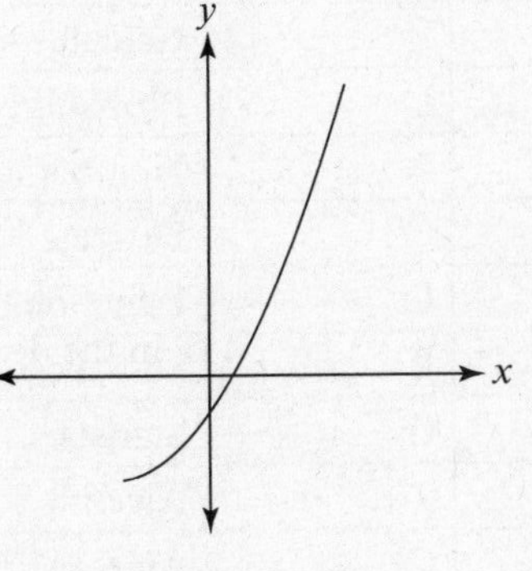

Ⓓ

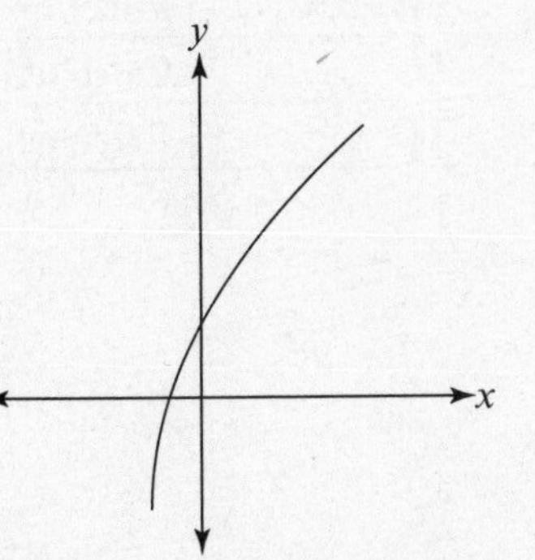

Answer Key for Practice Test 2

Question Number	Correct Answer	Reference Chapter	Question Number	Correct Answer	Reference Chapter
1.	C	Geometry	31.	B, C, D	Algebra
2.	A	Number and Quantity	32.	C	Calculus
3.	B	Algebra	33.	C	Calculus
4.	C	Functions	34.	B	Matrices
5.	C	Algebra	35.	C	Discrete Mathematics
6.	–5	Calculus	36.	B	Calculus
7.	D	Algebra	37.	B	Calculus
8.	D	Geometry	38.	C	Statistics
9.	A	Geometry	39.	A	Geometry
10.	C	Statistics	40.	A	Statistics
11.	D	Discrete Mathematics	41.	D	Algebra
12.	B	Functions	42.	A	Functions
13.	A	Trigonometry	43.	D	Functions
14.	B	Algebra	44.	–4	Functions
15.	C	Matrices	45.	A, B, C	Geometry
16.	A, B, D	Discrete Mathematics	46.	C	Matrices
17.	A	Statistics	47.	C	Geometry
18.	C	Probability	48.	$-\frac{1}{4}$	Algebra
19.	B	Trigonometry	49.	B	Calculus
20.	D	Geometry	50.	D	Probability
21.	455	Algebra	51.	B	Number and Quantity
22.	B	Functions	52.	C	Discrete Mathematics
23.	B	Functions	53.	D	Functions
24.	C	Trigonometry	54.	B	Statistics
25.	C	Calculus	55.	C	Statistics
26.	A	Statistics	56.	9	Algebra
27.	A, C, D	Matrices	57.	C	Algebra
28.	D	Number and Quantity	58.	A, B, C, D	Functions
29.	B	Number and Quantity	59.	C	Calculus
30.	C	Geometry	60.	D	Calculus

Answer Explanations for Practice Test 2

1. **C.** Make a sketch of the circle and plot the points given in the answer choices.

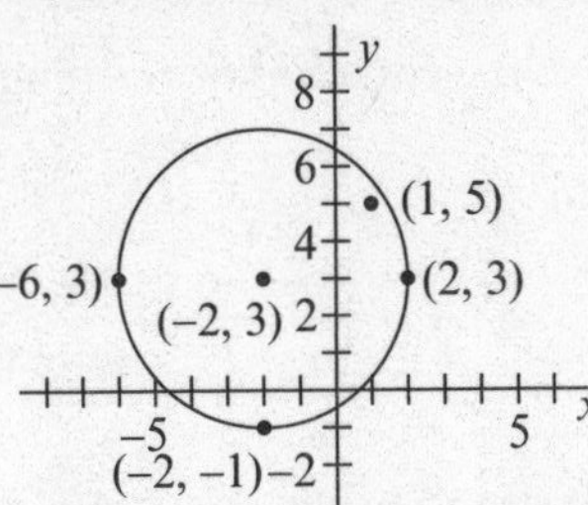

The center of the circle is at (–2, 3) with radius 4, so its equation is $(x + 2)^2 + (y - 3)^2 = 16$. The points (–6, 3), (–2, –1), (2, 3) lie on the circle. When you substitute the coordinates of these points into the equation of the circle, they satisfy the equation as shown below:

$((-6) + 2)^2 + ((3) - 3)^2 = (-4)^2 + (0)^2 = 16 + 0 = 16$

$((-2) + 2)^2 + ((-1) - 3)^2 = (0)^2 + (-4)^2 = 0 + 16 = 16$

$((2) + 2)^2 + ((3) - 3)^2 = (4)^2 + (0)^2 = 16 + 0 = 16$

Because $((1) + 2)^2 + ((5) - 3)^2 = (3)^2 + (2)^2 = 9 + 4 = 13 < 16$, only (1, 5) clearly lies within the interior of the circle. Thus, choice C is the correct response.

2. **A.** A set is closed with respect to an operation if the result of performing the operation with any pair of elements in the set yields an element contained in the set. Choice A is the correct response. To show that the set of perfect squares is closed with respect to multiplication, let a^2 and b^2 be any two perfect squares. Then $(a^2)(b^2) = (ab)^2$, which is also a perfect square. You should move on to the next problem. But for your information, to show a set is *not* closed, you need to find just *one* pair of elements that does not yield an element in the set when the operation is performed with that pair of elements. Eliminate the other answer choices and show they are *not* closed by selecting arbitrary pairs of values and testing them with the given operation.

Eliminate choice B because 5 and 9 are whole numbers, but $5 - 9 = -4$, which is not a whole number. Eliminate choice C because 3 and 5 are odd numbers, but $3 + 5 = 8$, which is not an odd number. Eliminate choice D because 1 and 2 are integers, but $\frac{1}{2}$ is not.

3. **B.** The answer choices are given as exponential expressions, so a logical way to work this problem is to perform on x the sequence of operations indicated by the function machine, using the exponential form for the operation.

$$\left(\left(\left((x)^{\frac{1}{2}}\right)^{\frac{1}{2}}\right)^{\frac{1}{2}}\right)^{6} = x^{\frac{1}{2}\cdot\frac{1}{2}\cdot\frac{1}{2}\cdot 6} = x^{\frac{6}{8}} = x^{\frac{3}{4}}, \text{ choice B}$$

4. **C.** The graph of the function defined by $y = \frac{k}{16x^2 + kx + 9}$ will have vertical asymptotes at values of x for which the denominator, $16x^2 + kx + 9$, equals 0. The trinomial, $16x^2 + kx + 9$, will have exactly one 0 when it is a perfect square. The expression $16x^2 + kx + 9$ is a perfect square when the coefficient, k, of x is $2\sqrt{16}\sqrt{9} = 2(4)(3) = 24$, choice C.

Tip: You can check your answer by substituting into the equation the values for k given in the answer choices and graphing the resulting functions using the ETS graphing calculator. However, it is best that you work out the problem analytically rather than using only the calculator to determine a solution because on a graphing calculator, the graphs of functions that have asymptotes are sometimes misleading.

5. **C.** Because the normal line is perpendicular to the tangent line at (3, 1), the slope of the tangent line through the point (3, 1) is the negative reciprocal of the slope of the normal line. The slope of the normal line $y=\frac{5}{6}x-\frac{3}{2}$ is $\frac{5}{6}$. Therefore, the tangent line at (3, 1) has slope $-\frac{6}{5}$.
Use the point–slope form to determine the equation of the tangent line at (3, 1).

$$y-1=-\frac{6}{5}(x-3)$$
$$5y-5=-6x+18$$
$$6x+5y=23,\text{ choice C}$$

6. **–5** The slope of the tangent line to the graph of f at 4 is $f'(4)$. $f(x)=-x^2+12\sqrt{x}=-x^2+12x^{\frac{1}{2}}$. Then $f'(x)=-2x+\left(\frac{1}{2}\right)(12)x^{-\frac{1}{2}}=-2x+6x^{-\frac{1}{2}}$ and $f'(4)=-2(4)+6(4)^{-\frac{1}{2}}=-8+\frac{6}{\sqrt{4}}=-8+3=-5$.

7. **D.** The operation $\oplus$ is commutative on the set R of real numbers if $x\oplus y=y\oplus x$ for all real numbers x and y. By the definition of the operation, you have $x\oplus y=3x+xy$ and $y\oplus x=3y+yx$, so the question that tests commutativity is "Does $3x+xy=3y+yx$ for all real numbers x and y?," choice D.

8. **D.** To determine the cost of the paint, first find the surface area of the sphere. Next, find the number of gallons of paint needed and then find the cost of the paint.

Find the surface area ($S.A.$) of the sphere with $r = 12$ ft.

$S.A. = 4\pi r^2 = 4\pi(12\text{ ft})^2 = 576\pi\text{ ft}^2$ (Don't approximate this answer.)

Note: The formula for the surface area of a sphere is given in the Notations, Definitions, and Formulas reference sheet provided.

Find the number of gallons needed.

$576\pi\text{ ft}^2 \div \frac{400\text{ ft}^2}{1\text{ gal}} = 576\pi\text{ ft}^2 \cdot \frac{1\text{ gal}}{400\text{ ft}^2} \approx 4.52$ gallons, so 5 gallons will need to be purchased (because the paint is sold in gallon containers only).

Find the cost of 5 gallons of paint.

$5\text{ gal}\cdot\frac{\$22.40}{1\text{ gal}}=\$112.00$, choice D.

9. **A.** Make a sketch. Draw the altitude from vertex Y to side $\overline{XZ}$ and label the point of intersection P as shown below.

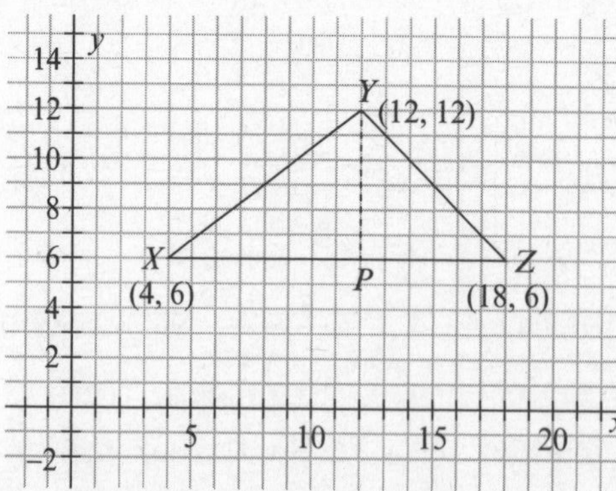

From the figure, you can determine that the length of side $\overline{XZ}$ is 14 units and that the altitude of triangle XYZ, from the vertex Y to side $\overline{XZ}$, is 6 units. The line segment $\overline{YP}$ creates two right triangles: triangles XPY and ZPY. Use the information given and the properties of right triangles to check the answer choices.

For this question, an optimum strategy is to start by eliminating answer choices that are obviously rational quantities.

Eliminate choice B because the area of triangle XYZ is $\frac{1}{2}(XZ)(YP) = \frac{1}{2}(14 \text{ units})(6 \text{ units})$, which is a rational quantity. Eliminate choice C because $\overline{XY}$ is the hypotenuse of a right triangle whose legs are 8 units and 6 units; thus, the length of $\overline{XY}$ is 10 units, a rational quantity. Eliminate choice D because the length of $\overline{XZ}$ is 14 units, a rational quantity, so its midpoint is a rational quantity as well. Therefore, choice A is the correct response. You should move on to the next problem, but just so you know, the perimeter of triangle XYZ is irrational because it has a portion, namely $\overline{YZ}$, that is the hypotenuse of a right triangle whose legs are each 6 units; thus, the length of $\overline{YZ} = \sqrt{6^2+6^2} = \sqrt{72}$ units, an irrational quantity.

10. C. If all the tagged fish are still active in the lake when the second group of fish is captured, the proportion of tagged fish in the second group should equal to the proportion of tagged fish in the whole population, P, of fish in the lake. Set up a proportion and solve for P.

$$\frac{20}{100} = \frac{500}{P}$$
$$\frac{1}{5} = \frac{500}{P}$$
$$P = (5)(500)$$
$$P = 2{,}500$$

The answer is 2,500 fish, choice C.

11. **D.** The statement "If it is Monday, then I will go to work" is a conditional statement. It has the logical form "If p, then q," where p is the statement "it is Monday" and q is the statement "I will go to work." In logic, the equivalent of "If p, then q" is its contrapositive, which is stated like so: "If not q, then not p." The contrapositive for the statement given is "If I will not go to work, then it is not Monday." Only choice D is compatible with this statement.

12. **B. Method 1.** Express $\frac{a}{b+c}$ in terms of $\frac{a}{b}$ and $\frac{b}{c}$ by dividing each term in the numerator and denominator by b. Then substitute $\frac{a}{b} = 10$ and $\frac{b}{c} = 5$ and evaluate.

$$\frac{a}{b+c} = \frac{\frac{a}{b}}{\frac{b}{b}+\frac{c}{b}} = \frac{\frac{a}{b}}{1+\frac{1}{\frac{b}{c}}} = \frac{10}{1+\frac{1}{5}} = \frac{10}{\frac{6}{5}} = \frac{50}{6} = \frac{25}{3}, \text{ choice B}$$

Method 2. Substitute values for a, b, and c that satisfy the conditions given, and then work with your substituted numbers as shown below.

Let $a = 100$, $b = 10$, and $c = 2$. Then $\frac{a}{b} = \frac{100}{10} = 10$, $\frac{10}{2} = 5$, and $\frac{a}{b+c} = \frac{100}{10+2} = \frac{100}{12} = \frac{25}{3}$, choice B.

13. **A.** $(2\cos 10° + i\,2\sin 10°)^3 = 2^3(\cos 10° + i\sin 10°)^3 = 8(\cos 10° + i\sin 10°)^3$

Evaluate the second factor of this product by using De Moivre's theorem (given in the Notations, Definitions, and Formulas reference sheet provided), to obtain

$$8(\cos(3\cdot 10°)+i\sin(3\cdot 10°)) = 8(\cos 30° + i\sin 30°) = 8\left(\frac{\sqrt{3}}{2}+i\frac{1}{2}\right) = 4\sqrt{3} + 4i, \text{ choice A}$$

14. **B.** At 50 miles per hour, it took the family 5 hours (9 a.m. to 2 p.m.) to reach their destination. The distance traveled $= (5 \cancel{\text{hr}})\left(50\ \dfrac{\text{mi}}{\cancel{\text{hr}}}\right) = 250$ miles. At an average speed of 65 miles per hour, the trip would have taken $\dfrac{250\ \cancel{\text{mi}}}{65\ \dfrac{\cancel{\text{mi}}}{\text{hr}}} \approx 3.85$ hours $= 3$ hours 51 minutes. Therefore, if the family left at 9 a.m. and traveled at an average speed of 65 miles per hour, they would have arrived at 9 a.m. plus 3 hours 51 minutes = 12:51 p.m. (approximately), choice B.

15. **C.** Triangle ABC with vertices (2, 1), (–3, 4), and (5, –3) can be represented by the 2×3 (vertex) matrix $\begin{bmatrix} 2 & -3 & 5 \\ 1 & 4 & -3 \end{bmatrix}$, where the x-coordinates are in the first row and their corresponding y-coordinates are in the second row. In a reflection over the x-axis, the x-coordinates of the image will be the same as the x-coordinates of the preimage, and the y-coordinates of the image will be the negatives of the y-coordinates of the preimage. Thus, you are looking for a matrix multiplication that will yield the product matrix $\begin{bmatrix} 2 & -3 & 5 \\ -1 & -4 & 3 \end{bmatrix}$.

A quick way to work this problem is to check the answer choices.

Mentally multiply the matrices.

Check A: $\begin{bmatrix} -1 & 0 \\ 0 & 1 \end{bmatrix}\begin{bmatrix} 2 & -3 & 5 \\ 1 & 4 & -3 \end{bmatrix} = \begin{bmatrix} -2 & & \\ & & \end{bmatrix}$. Eliminate choice A because the element in the first row first column is not 2. There is no need to complete the multiplication.

Check B: $\begin{bmatrix} 0 & 1 \\ -1 & 0 \end{bmatrix}\begin{bmatrix} 2 & -3 & 5 \\ 1 & 4 & -3 \end{bmatrix} = \begin{bmatrix} 1 & & \\ & & \end{bmatrix}$. Eliminate choice B because the element in the first row first column is not 2. There is no need to complete the multiplication.

Check C: $\begin{bmatrix} 1 & 0 \\ 0 & -1 \end{bmatrix}\begin{bmatrix} 2 & -3 & 5 \\ 1 & 4 & -3 \end{bmatrix} = \begin{bmatrix} 2 & -3 & 5 \\ -1 & -4 & 3 \end{bmatrix}$. Thus, choice C is the correct response. There is no need to check choice D. Go on to the next question.

16. **A, B, D.** An equivalence relation is a reflexive, symmetric, and transitive relation. ***Note:*** The definitions for reflexive, symmetric, transitive, and equivalence relations are given in the Notations, Definitions, and Formulas reference sheet provided. The relation in choice C, "'is perpendicular to' over the set of all lines in the xy plane," is not an equivalence relation because this relation is neither reflexive nor transitive. The relations in answer choices A, B, and D are equivalence relations.

17. **A.** When a data set contains some extremely high values that are not balanced by corresponding extremely low values, the mean for the data set will be misleadingly high as an indication of a "typical" or "central" value for the data set. The median, which is not strongly influenced by extreme values, is the preferred alternative to the mean when the situation of unbalanced extremely high values occurs in a data set, choice A. Since the data set in choice B is somewhat symmetrical, there would be no particular reason to prefer the median over the mean as a measure of central tendency. For the data sets given in choices C and D, there is not enough information to "clearly" prefer the median over the mean.

18. **C.** The box contains 50 tiles numbered 1 through 50. The primes between 1 and 50 are 2, 3, 5, 7, 11, 13, 17, 19, 23, 29, 31, 37, 41, 43, 47, which is a total of 15 primes. (Remember, the number 1 is neither prime nor composite.)

Therefore, the probability that the number on a randomly drawn tile is a prime number is $\dfrac{15}{50} = \dfrac{3}{10}$, choice C.

19. **B.** Sketch a diagram, letting d = the distance between the two houses.

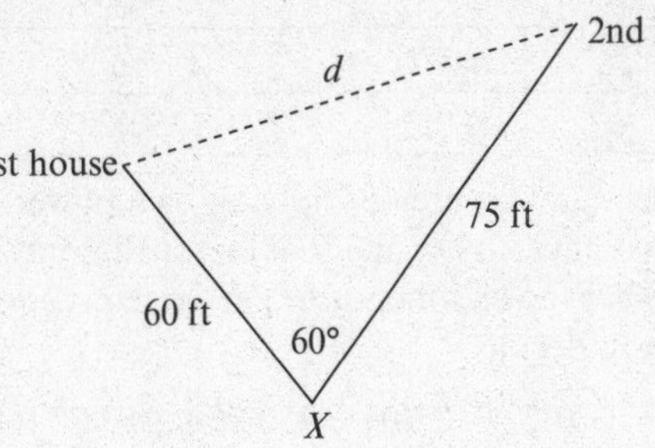

Looking at the sketch, you can see that you are given the measures of two sides and the included angle of an oblique triangle. To find the distance between the two houses, substitute the given information into the law of cosines and solve for d. ***Note:*** The law of cosines is given in the Notations, Definitions, and Formulas reference sheet.

$c^2 = a^2 + b^2 - 2ab \cos C$

The side d corresponds to c, $a = 60$ ft, and $b = 75$ ft. Substitute into the formula and solve for d, omitting the units for convenience.

$$d^2 = (60)^2 + (75)^2 - 2(60)(75)(\cos\ 60°)$$
$$d^2 = 3{,}600 + 5{,}625 - 9{,}000\left(\frac{1}{2}\right)$$
$$d^2 = 4{,}725$$
$$d = \sqrt{4{,}725} \approx 69$$

The distance between the two houses is approximately 69 feet, choice B.

Tip: Be sure to check that your calculator is in degrees mode when the angle given is in degrees.

20. **D.** You are to find the mass, in grams, of the cube. The units for density are grams per cubic centimeter $\left(\frac{\text{g}}{\text{cm}^3}\right)$, so dimensional analysis tells you that if you want to have grams as the units of your answer, then you will need to cancel cm^3 from the denominator of the density quantity. Cubic centimeters are units of volume. Therefore, find the volume of the cube, and then multiply by the density of lead.

Volume of cube = $(1.5 \text{ cm})^3 = 3.375 \text{ cm}^3$

Multiply the volume of the cube by the density of lead.

$$\left(3.375\ \cancel{\text{cm}^3}\right)\left(\frac{11.3 \text{ g}}{\cancel{\text{cm}^3}}\right) \approx 38.1 \text{ g}$$

The mass of the lead cube is approximately 38.1 grams, choice D.

21. **455** The suit's original price was 70% of \$500, which is 0.7(\$500) = \$350. The suit's selling price was 130% of \$350, which is 1.3(\$350) = \$455.

22. **B.** The domain of $g \circ f$ is the set of elements x in the domain of f for which $f(x)$, the image of x, is in the domain of g. Only the elements –1 and 0 have images that are in the domain of g. The images of –1 and 0 under $g \circ f$ are

$(g \circ f)(-1) = g(f(-1)) = g(3) = 8$ and $(g \circ f)(0) = g(f(0)) = g(1) = 2$.

Thus, $g \circ f = \{(-1, 8), (0, 2)\}$, choice B.

23. **B.** Make a table showing the growth of the deer population as a function of time, t.

Time in Years	$t = 0$	$t = 8$	$t = 16$	$t = 24$	...
Deer Population	250	$(250)2$	$(250)2^2$	$(250)2^3$	...

The table shows that at 8-year intervals, you are multiplying by a power of 2. Therefore, the function that models the population growth must have an exponential factor that has base 2 in it, so you can eliminate A and C. Now you must decide whether the exponent for 2 in the expression should be $0.125t$ (choice B) or $8t$ (choice D). Use the table to help you decide.

Checking when $t = 0$: $(250)2^{0.125t} = (250)2^0 = (250)1 = 250$ and $(250)2^{8t} = (250)2^0 = (250)1 = 250$, which matches the table.

Checking when $t = 8$: $(250)2^{0.125t} = (250)2^{0.125(8)} = (250)2$, which matches the table; but $(250)2^{8t} = (250)2^{8(8)} = (250)2^{64}$ does not match the table. Therefore, choice B is the correct response.

24. **C.** Solve the trigonometric equation $\sin^2 x - 5 \sin x + 4 = 0$.

$$\sin^2 x - 5\sin x + 4 = 0$$
$$(\sin x - 1)(\sin x - 4) = 0$$
$$\sin x = 1 \text{ or } \sin x = 4 \text{ (no solution)}$$
$$x = \sin^{-1}(1)$$
$$x = \frac{\pi}{2}$$

This is the only solution in the interval $0 \le x \le 2\pi$, choice C.

25. **C.** Find the numerical derivative using methods of calculus.

Given $f(x) = -x^{-2}$

then $f'(x) = 2x^{-3}$ and $f'(2)=2(2)^{-3} = 2\left(\frac{1}{8}\right) = \frac{1}{4}$, choice C.

26. **A.** Examine the table.

Correlation Table for Variables *A*, *B*, *C*, and *D*

	A	*B*	*C*	*D*
A	1			
B	−0.88	1		
C	0.65	0.15	1	
D	−0.59	0.50	0.78	1

Correlation values very close to either −1 or +1 indicate very *strong* correlations. The closer $|r|$ is to 1, the stronger the relationship. Thus, the correlation coefficient between A and B (choice A) indicates the strongest relationship because $|-0.88|$ is greater than the absolute values of the correlation coefficients for the pairs of variables in the other answer choices.

27. **A, C, D.** On the set of $n \times n$ matrices whose elements are real numbers, matrix multiplication is closed (choice A), associative (choice C), and the distributive property holds (choice D); but, in general, matrix multiplication is not commutative (choice B).

28. **D.** The number on the left of the equal sign is expressed in the base-seven system, while the number on the right is expressed in the base-five system. To find the value of b (and thus, $b2_{\text{seven}}$), first expand the numbers in their respective bases to convert them to the base-ten system. Next, set the resulting base-ten expressions equal to each other, solve for b, and then put its value in the expression $b2_{\text{seven}}$.

$b2_{\text{seven}} = b \cdot 7 + 2 = (7b + 2)_{\text{ten}} = 7b + 2$

$134_{\text{five}} = 1 \cdot 25 + 3 \cdot 5 + 4 = 44_{\text{ten}} = 44$

Solve for *b*.

$$\begin{aligned} 7b + 2 &= 44 \\ 7b &= 42 \\ b &= 6 \end{aligned}$$

Therefore, $b2_{\text{seven}} = 62_{\text{seven}}$, choice D.

29. **B.** Plug the units into the formula and simplify as you would for variable quantities.

$$Y = \frac{Adv}{t} = \frac{\left(\cancel{\text{cm}^2}\right)\left(\frac{\text{g}}{\cancel{\text{cm}^3}}\right)\left(\frac{\cancel{\text{cm}}}{\text{s}}\right)}{\text{s}} = \frac{\frac{\text{g}}{\text{s}}}{\text{s}} = \frac{\text{g}}{\text{s}^2}, \text{ choice B.}$$

30. **C.** Examine the figure.

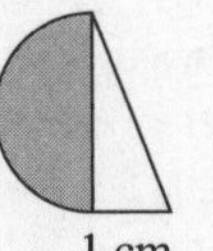

The perimeter around the figure can be broken into three portions: (one-half the circumference of a circle with radius 1 cm) plus (the hypotenuse of a right triangle with legs of 1 cm and 2 cm) plus (a horizontal segment of length 1 cm).

Find one-half the circumference of a circle with radius 1 cm.

$\frac{1}{2}(2\pi r) = \frac{1}{\cancel{2}}\left(\cancel{2}\pi(1 \text{ cm})\right) = \pi \text{ cm}$ (Don't evaluate yet.)

Find the length of the hypotenuse of a right triangle with legs of 1 cm and 2 cm.

$$\begin{aligned} c^2 &= 1^2 + 2^2 \\ c^2 &= 5 \\ c &= \sqrt{5} \end{aligned}$$

The hypotenuse of the right triangle has length of $\sqrt{5}$ cm. (Don't evaluate yet.)

Find the perimeter.

Perimeter $= 1 \text{ cm} + \pi \text{cm} + \sqrt{5} \text{ cm} \approx 6.4$ cm, choice C.

31. **B, C, D.** You must select which statements about absolute value must *always* be true. Choices B, C, and D are properties of absolute value that are always true. Only the statement in choice A is not always true. For example, when x is 8, you have $-|-x| = -|-(8)| = -|-8| = -8 \neq x = 8$.

32. **C.** Substituting 3 into the numerator and denominator yields the indeterminate form $\frac{0}{0}$.

Method 1. $\lim\limits_{x \to 3} \frac{2x - 6}{x^2 - 9} = \lim\limits_{x \to 3} \frac{2\cancel{(x-3)}}{(x+3)\cancel{(x-3)}} = \lim\limits_{x \to 3} \frac{2}{(x+3)} = \frac{2}{6} = \frac{1}{3}$, choice C.

Method 2. Because $\lim\limits_{x \to 3}(2x - 6) = 0$ and $\lim\limits_{x \to 3}(x^2 - 9) = 0$, you can use L'Hôpital's rule to evaluate the limit by taking the derivatives of the numerator and denominator before evaluating the limit.

Thus, you have $\lim\limits_{x \to 3} \frac{2x - 6}{x^2 - 9} = \lim\limits_{x \to 3} \frac{2}{2x} = \frac{2}{6} = \frac{1}{3}$, choice C.

33. **C.** The particle does not change direction because the velocity function $v(t) = 1.8\ v^2$ is always positive. Recall that the first derivative of a position function is the velocity function. To find the distance traveled between $t = 0$ and $t = 5$, evaluate the following definite integral: $\int_0^5 1.8t^2\,dt$.

Integrate the function using methods of calculus.

$\int_0^5 1.8t^2\,dt = \left.\frac{1.8t^3}{3}\right|_0^5 = \left.0.6t^3\right|_0^5 = 0.6(5)^3 - 0.6(0)^3 = 0.6(125) - 0.6(0) = 75 - 0 = 75$. Therefore, the distance traveled is 75, choice C.

34. **B.** Using the rules for matrix subtraction, you can write four equations.

$a - 3a = -8$, $4b + 6 = b$, $5 - 2c = 7$, and $d + 2d = 9$

Solving $a - 3a = -8$ yields $a = 4$, so eliminate choices A and D because these answer choices have $a = -4$. Since both of the remaining answer choices have $b = -2$, go on to the next equation. You have $5 - 2c = 7$, so $c = -1$; eliminate choice C. Thus, choice B is the correct response.

35. **C.** Let W = the set of customers who bought washers and D = the set of customers who bought dryers. Using the notation $|X|$ to represent the number of elements in a set, you have $|W| = 94$ and $|D| = 80$. Because $|W| + |D| = 94 + 80 = 174$, which is greater than 152, the total number of customers, you can conclude that some customers bought both a washer and a dryer. Draw a Venn diagram showing two overlapping circles representing W and D. Label the intersection $W \cap D$.

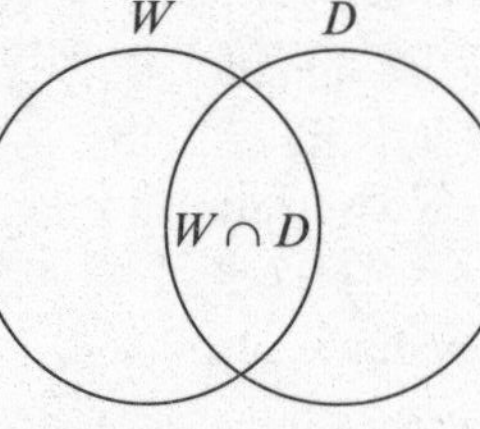

The intersection $W \cap D$ represents the set of customers who bought both a washer and a dryer. From the diagram and the information given in the problem, you have the following equation:

$152 = |W| + |D| - |W \cap D|$

Thus, $152 = 94 + 80 - |W \cap D|$

Solving for $|W \cap D|$ yields

$|W \cap D| = 94 + 80 - 152 = 22$

Therefore, the number of customers who bought only a washer equals

$|W| - |W \cap D| = 94 - 22 = 72$, choice C.

Note: The notation $|X|$ is read "the cardinality of set X." The *cardinality* of a set is the number of elements in the set.

36. **B.** Given: $y = f(x) = 2x^3 - x + 3$. The y value at the point where $x = 1$ is $f(1) = 2(1)^3 - (1) + 3 = 4$. The slope, m, of the tangent line at the point $(1, f(1))$ is given by $f'(1)$.

$f(x) = 2x^3 - x + 3$ implies $f'(x) = 6x^2 - 1$. Thus, $m = f'(1) = 6(1)^2 - 1 = 5$ when $x = 1$.

Use the point-slope form to find the equation of the tangent line at the point (1, 4).

$$y - 4 = 5(x - 1)$$
$$y - 4 = 5x - 5$$
$$1 = 5x - y \text{ or } 5x - y = 1, \text{ choice B}$$

37. **B.** Make a sketch and shade the area of interest.

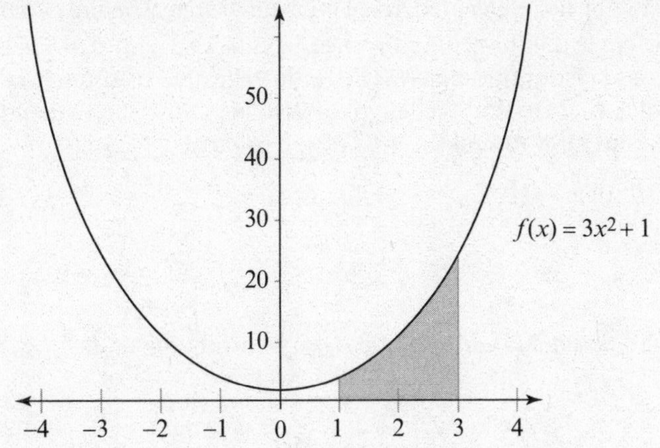

The area of the region bounded by the graph of $f(x) = 3x^2 + 1$, the x-axis, and the vertical lines $x = 1$ and $x = 3$ is given by Area $= \int_1^3 (3x^2 + 1)\,dx$.

Evaluate the definite integral using methods of calculus.

$$\int_1^3 (3x^2 + 1)\,dx = (x^3 + x)\Big|_1^3 = (3^3 + 3) - (1^3 + 1) = 30 - 2 = 28,\text{ choice B}$$

38. **C.** According to the 68-95-99.7 rule, approximately 68% of the data in a normal distribution fall within 1 standard deviation of the mean, about 95% fall within 2 standard deviations of the mean, and about 99.7% fall within 3 standard deviations of the mean. You want to find the approximate probability that a randomly chosen plant from a distribution with μ of 24 inches and standard deviation, σ, of 3.5 inches will be between 20.5 inches and 27.5 inches tall.

To find the approximate probability, first determine the z-scores for 20.5 inches and 27.5 inches, and then find the percentage of the normal distribution that is between those two z-scores.

Find the z-scores for 20.5 inches and 27.5 inches.

$z\text{-score} = \dfrac{\text{data value} - \text{mean}}{\text{standard deviation}} = \dfrac{20.5 - 24}{3.5} = -1$. Therefore, 20.5 is 1 standard deviation below the mean.

$z\text{-score} = \dfrac{\text{data value} - \text{mean}}{\text{standard deviation}} = \dfrac{27.5 - 24}{3.5} = 1$. Therefore, 27.5 is 1 standard deviation above the mean.

Now find the percentage of the normal distribution that is between the z-scores –1 and 1.

According to the 68-95-99.7 rule, about 68%, choice C, of the distribution is within 1 standard deviation of the mean.

39. **A.** Let x = length of a side of the square.

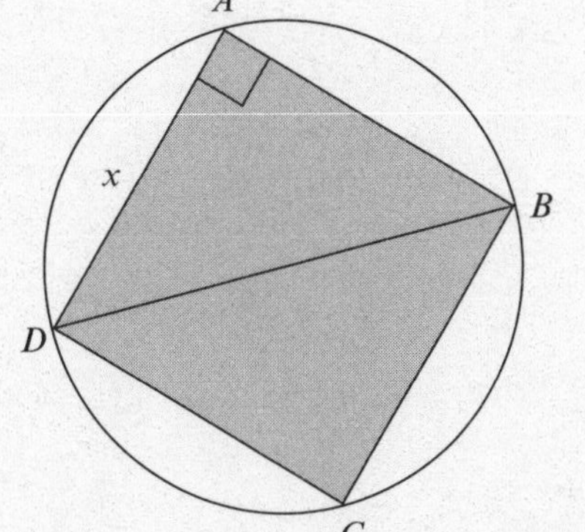

The area of square $ABCD$ is x^2. Right angle DAB is an inscribed angle. The measure of an inscribed angle is half the degree measure of its intercepted arc. Thus, the degree measure of $\overset{\frown}{DB}$ is 180°. Therefore, chord $\overline{DB}$ is a diameter of the circle that has circumference 8π cm. Also, chord $\overline{DB}$ is the diagonal of the square $ABCD$ and the hypotenuse of right triangle DAB. To find the area of square $ABCD$, first use the formula for the circumference of a circle to find the length of $\overline{DB}$. Next, use the Pythagorean theorem to find x. Finally, use the value found for x to find the area of the square.

Let d = the length of $\overline{DB}$, then

$C = \pi d = 8\pi$ cm

$d = 8$ cm

Apply the Pythagorean theorem in right triangle DAB, omitting the units for convenience.

$$\begin{aligned} x^2 + x^2 &= (8)^2 \\ 2x^2 &= 64 \\ x^2 &= 32 \\ x &= \sqrt{32} \end{aligned}$$

The area of square $ABCD = \left(\sqrt{32}\text{ cm}\right)\left(\sqrt{32}\text{ cm}\right) = 32\text{ cm}^2$, choice A.

Notice that you determine x^2, the area of the square, just before you obtain x. You should skip the final step in this problem by stopping when you find x^2.

Tip: In an isosceles right triangle, the square of the length of the hypotenuse is always twice the square of the length of a leg of the triangle.

40. **A.** To compare the student's performance on the four exams relative to the performance of the student's classmates, compute the student's z-score for each of the four exams.

Exam 1: $z\text{-score} = \dfrac{\text{data value} - \text{mean}}{\text{standard deviation}} = \dfrac{65-55}{5} = 2$. Therefore, the student scored 2 standard deviations above the mean on Exam 1.

Exam 2: $z\text{-score} = \dfrac{\text{data value} - \text{mean}}{\text{standard deviation}} = \dfrac{87-88}{2} = -0.5$. Therefore, the student scored 0.5 standard deviation below the mean on Exam 2.

Exam 3: $z\text{-score} = \dfrac{\text{data value} - \text{mean}}{\text{standard deviation}} = \dfrac{92-86}{4} = 1.5$. Therefore, the student scored 1.5 standard deviations above the mean on Exam 3.

Exam 4: $z\text{-score} = \dfrac{\text{data value} - \text{mean}}{\text{standard deviation}} = \dfrac{70-60}{10} = 1$. Therefore, the student scored 1 standard deviation above the mean on Exam 4.

Because the student's z-score for Exam 1 is greater than any of the z-scores for the other exams, the student's best performance was on Exam 1 (choice A) relative to that of the student's classmates.

41. **D.** Solve the inequality.

$$\begin{aligned} \frac{2-x}{5} &< 1 \\ 2-x &< 5 \\ -x &< 3 \\ x &> -3 \end{aligned}$$

The graph for this inequality is a ray extending to the right from the point –3 with an open dot at the point –3, choice D.

Tip: Remember to reverse the direction of the inequality when you multiply both sides by a negative quantity.

42. **A.** You are given two points (0, 1,000) and (10, 5,000) that satisfy the function $Q(t) = Q_0e^{xt}$. To find the value of x, first substitute the values for the two points into $Q(t) = Q_0e^{xt}$, and then solve the resulting system of equations for x.

$1{,}000 = Q_0e^{x(0)} = Q_0e^0 = Q_0 \cdot 1 = Q_0$

$5{,}000 = Q_0e^{x(10)} = Q_0e^{10x} = 1{,}000e^{10x}$ (Using the results from the first equation)

Solve for x.

$$\begin{aligned} 5{,}000 &= 1{,}000e^{10x} \\ 5 &= e^{10x} \\ \ln 5 &= \ln\left(e^{10x}\right) \\ \ln 5 &= 10x \ln e \\ \ln 5 &= 10x \\ \frac{\ln 5}{10} &= x \end{aligned}$$

$x = \frac{\ln 5}{10}$, choice A.

43. **D.** You are given that $P(x)$ has zeros 0, $2 - i$, 4, and –3. Because $P(x)$ has real coefficients, the complex conjugate, $2 + i$, of $2 - i$ is also a zero. Hence, $P(x)$ has five zeros (eliminate choices A and B). By the factor theorem, if r is a zero of a polynomial, $P(x)$, then $x - r$ is a factor of $P(x)$; so $P(x) = (x - 0)[x - (2 - i)][x - (2 + i)](x - 4)[x - (-3)] = x(x - 2 + i)(x - 2 - i)(x - 4)(x + 3)$, choice D.

44. **–4** By the factor theorem, $x - i$ is a factor of $P(x)$ if $P(i) = 0$. First, determine $P(i)$. Next, solve $P(i) = 0$ for k.

Determine $P(i)$.

$$\begin{aligned} P(x) &= k^2x^4 - 8kx^2 + 16 \\ P(i) &= k^2(i)^4 - 8k(i)^2 + 16 \\ P(i) &= k^2(1) - 8k(-1) + 16 \\ P(i) &= k^2 + 8k + 16 \end{aligned}$$

Solve $P(i) = 0$ for k.

$$\begin{aligned} k^2 + 8k + 16 &= 0 \\ (k+4)^2 &= 0 \\ k &= -4 \end{aligned}$$

45. **A, B, C.** The question asks which theorems most likely would be used to prove ΔABC is similar to ΔEDC. Examine the figure.

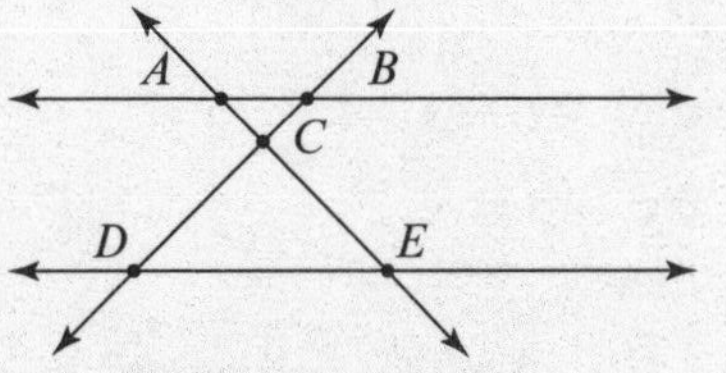

Considering the theorems given in the answer options, only choice D would be eliminated from the proof. A simple way to show two triangles are similar is to show that two angles of one triangle are congruent to two corresponding angles of the other triangle (choice C). You could proceed by showing that $\angle ACB$ is congruent to $\angle ECD$ because these angles are vertical angles of intersecting lines (choice A), and then showing $\angle ABC$ is congruent to $\angle EDC$ because these angles form a pair of alternate-interior angles of two parallel lines cut by a transversal (choice B).

46. **C.** From the 2×2 matrices in the answer choices, you want the one that premultiplies the vertex matrix $\begin{bmatrix} x_i \\ y_i \end{bmatrix}$ to yield $\begin{bmatrix} 5x_i \\ 5y_i \end{bmatrix}$, where $i = 1, 2, 3$. Check the answer choices.

Check A: $\begin{bmatrix} 5 & 5 \\ 5 & 5 \end{bmatrix}\begin{bmatrix} x_i \\ y_i \end{bmatrix} = \begin{bmatrix} 5x_i + 5y_i \\ \end{bmatrix}$, eliminate choice A.

Check B: $\begin{bmatrix} 5 & 0 \\ 5 & 0 \end{bmatrix}\begin{bmatrix} x_i \\ y_i \end{bmatrix} = \begin{bmatrix} 5x_i \\ 5x_i \end{bmatrix}$, eliminate choice B.

Check C: $\begin{bmatrix} 5 & 0 \\ 0 & 5 \end{bmatrix}\begin{bmatrix} x_i \\ y_i \end{bmatrix} = \begin{bmatrix} 5x_i \\ 5y_i \end{bmatrix}$; thus, choice C is the correct response. Go on to the next question.

47. **C.** The volume of a right prism is $V = Bh$. (***Note:*** This formula is given in the Notations, Definitions, and Formulas reference sheet provided.) To find the volume of the right hexagonal prism, first find the area, B, of one of the regular hexagonal bases, and then find the volume by multiplying B by the height of the prism, h.

Find the area of one of the regular hexagonal bases.

Sketch a diagram.

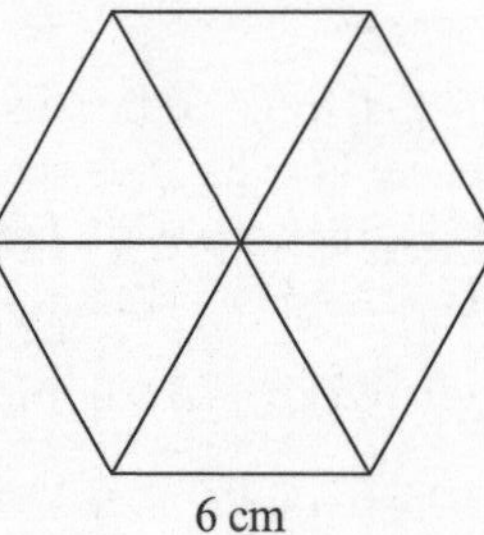

A regular hexagon with side 6 cm can be divided into 6 equilateral triangles with each side equal to 6 cm. The area of an equilateral triangle with side $s = 6$ cm is $\frac{\sqrt{3}}{4}s^2 = \frac{\sqrt{3}}{4}(6 \text{ cm})^2 = 9\sqrt{3} \text{ cm}^2$.

Tip: If you forget the formula for the area of an equilateral triangle, you can derive it by using the Pythagorean theorem or trigonometric functions to determine the height (altitude) of the triangle, and then using the formula area $= \frac{1}{2}bh$.

Thus, the area of the regular hexagonal base of the prism is $B = 6\left(9\sqrt{3} \text{ cm}^2\right) = 54\sqrt{3} \text{ cm}^2$.

Volume $= Bh = \left(54\sqrt{3} \text{ cm}^2\right)(30 \text{ cm}) \approx 2{,}806 \text{ cm}^3$, choice C.

48. $-\frac{1}{4}$ Square both sides of the equation $2x = \sqrt{3x+1}$ and solve for x.

$$(2x)^2 = \left(\sqrt{3x+1}\right)^2$$
$$4x^2 = 3x + 1$$
$$4x^2 - 3x - 1 = 0$$
$$(4x+1)(x-1) = 0$$
$$x = -\frac{1}{4} \text{(extraneous) or } x = 1$$

$-\frac{1}{4}$ is an extraneous solution because it makes the left side of the original equation negative, so it cannot equal $\sqrt{3x+1}$, which is always nonnegative.

Checking $x = 1$ shows 1 satisfies the equation.

$$2(1) \stackrel{?}{=} \sqrt{3(1)+1}$$
$$2 \stackrel{?}{=} \sqrt{4}$$
$$2 \stackrel{\checkmark}{=} 2$$

Tip: Remember to answer the question posed. The question asks for the extraneous solution.

49. **B.** Make a sketch and shade the area of interest.

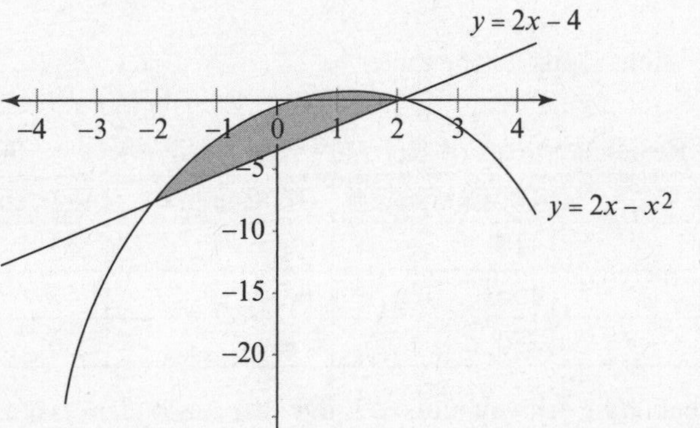

Use the ETS graphing calculator to determine that the two graphs intersect at two points and the graph of $y = 2x - x^2$ lies above $y = 2x - 4$ between the points of intersection. To find the area of the region bounded by the two graphs, first find the x values for the points of intersection of the two graphs. Next, find the difference between the two functions, being sure to subtract the equation of the lower graph from the equation of the upper graph, and then evaluate the definite integral of the difference of the two graphs between the two x values of their points of intersection.

Find the x values for the points of intersection of the two graphs.

Using substitution,

$$2x - x^2 = 2x - 4$$
$$-x^2 = -4$$
$$x^2 = 4$$
$$x = \pm 2$$

Tip: You also can use features of the ETS graphing calculator to determine the x values of the points of intersection.

Find the difference between the two functions.

Difference $= (2x - x^2) - (2x - 4) = 2x - x^2 - 2x + 4 = -x^2 + 4$

Evaluate the definite integral $\int_{-2}^{2} \left(-x^2 + 4\right) dx$.

Integrate the integral using methods of calculus.

$$\int_{-2}^{2}\left(-x^2+4\right)dx=\left(-\frac{x^3}{3}+4x\right)\Bigg|_{-2}^{2}$$
$$=\left(-\frac{(2)^3}{3}+4(2)\right)-\left(-\frac{(-2)^3}{3}+4(-2)\right)$$
$$=\left(-\frac{8}{3}+8\right)-\left(\frac{8}{3}-8\right)$$
$$=-\frac{8}{3}+8-\frac{8}{3}+8$$
$$=16-\frac{16}{3}$$
$$=\frac{32}{3}\text{, choice B}$$

50. **D.** Fill in the row and column totals for the table.

Resident Status of Second–Year Students ($n = 500$)

Gender	On-Campus	Off-Campus	Row Total
Female	114	135	249
Male	156	95	251
Total	270	230	500

You want to find a probability when you already know that the student is a male student. Thus, when computing the probability, the number of possible students under consideration is no longer 500 but is reduced to the total number of male students. In other words, once you know that the selected person is a male student, you are dealing only with the students in the second row of the table. To find the probability, first find the total number of male students. Next, among those, determine the number who reside off-campus, and then compute the conditional probability.

Among the 251 male students, 95 reside off-campus. Thus,

P(resides off-campus given student is male) $= \frac{95}{251}$, choice D.

51. **B.** If an integer is a factor of both of the integers m and n, then it is a factor of $am + bn$, for any integers a and b. Let $m = (14k + 13)$ and $n = (7k + 1)$. Because p is a factor of both $m = (14k + 13)$ and $n = (7k + 1)$, then p is a factor of $1m - 2n = (1)(14k + 13) - 2(7k + 1) = 14k + 13 - 14k - 2 = 11$. The only factors of 11 are 1 and 11. Given that p is prime, it follows that p equals 11, choice B.

52. **C.** Use the binomial theorem, $(x+y)^n = \sum_{k=0}^{n}\binom{n}{k}x^{n-k}y^k$. For this problem, $(x+2y)^5 = \sum_{k=0}^{5}\binom{5}{k}x^{5-k}(2y)^k$.

The third term is $\binom{5}{2}x^{5-2}(2y)^2 = 10x^3(2y)^2 = 10x^3\left(4y^2\right) = 40x^3y^2$, choice C.

Tip: You can use the ETS graphing calculator to compute $\binom{5}{2} = {}_5C_2$. Keying in nCr(5,2) returns 10.

53. **D.** Let $y = f(x) = \frac{x+1}{x-2}$. Interchange x and y in $y = f(x)$, and then solve for y.

$$x=\frac{y+1}{y-2}$$
$$xy-2x=y+1$$
$$xy-y=2x+1$$
$$y(x-1)=2x+1$$
$$y=\frac{2x+1}{x-1}$$
$$f^{-1}(x)=\frac{2x+1}{x-1}\text{, choice D}$$

54. B. Examine the dot plot.

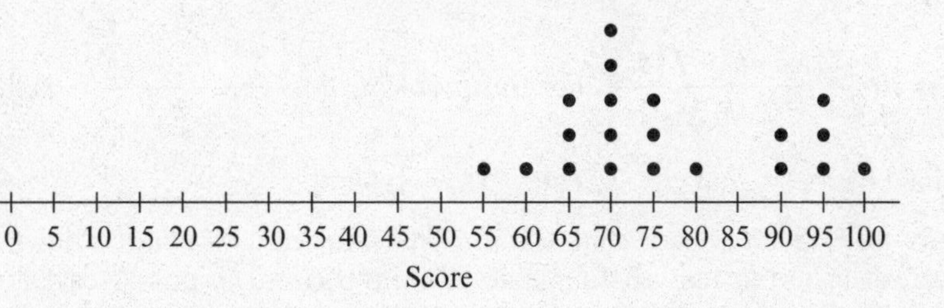

The mean of the scores is $\dfrac{55+60+3(65)+5(70)+3(75)+80+2(90)+3(95)+100}{20}=\dfrac{1{,}530}{20}=76.5$. One standard deviation below the mean is $76.5-12.8=63.7$, and 1 standard deviation above the mean is $76.5+12.8=89.3$. Exactly 12 scores fall between these two values, meaning 12 scores are within 1 standard deviation of the mean, choice B.

55. C. In this study, Fertilizer X is the treatment and plant growth is the variable of interest. In an experimental study, the treatment group receives the treatment, so the plant seedlings in the treatment plot will receive applications of Fertilizer X, choice C. Choices A and B are incorrect because these choices are related to the variable of interest, which is not manipulated by the researcher. The seedlings in the treatment plot might or might not have plant growth. The outcome depends on the effectiveness of Fertilizer X, which is what the researcher is investigating. Choice D is incorrect because the plant seedlings in the control plot, not the treatment plot, will not receive applications of Fertilizer X.

56. 9 Given $x^2+6x+c=(x+h)^2$ or equivalently $x^2+6x+c=x^2+2xh+h^2$, then $6=2h$ and $c=h^2$ (because corresponding coefficients are equal). Therefore, $h=3$ and $c=3^2=9$.

57. C. For convenience, designate the locations L1, L2, L3, L4, and L5, with treasure coins in the ratio 1:2:3:4:5, respectively. Let $n=$ the number of coins in L1, then L1, L2, L3, L4, and L5 have n, $2n$, $3n$, $4n$, and $5n$ coins, respectively. The minimum number of coins needed to win is 50% of the combined number of coins in L1, L2, and L3 (because these locations have the fewest number of coins). This minimum number is $50\%(n+2n+3n)=0.5(6n)=3n$. The total number of coins is $n+2n+3n+4n+5n=15n$. The minimum percent to win is $\dfrac{3n}{15n}=\dfrac{1}{5}=20\%$, choice C.

58. A, B, C, D. Any value of x, for which $f(x)=\dfrac{\sqrt{x+2}}{2x^3+x^2-2x-1}$ is undefined over the real numbers, is not in the domain of f. Exclude from the domain any value for which $(x+2)<0$ (or equivalently $x<-2$), so -3 (choice A) is excluded because $\sqrt{-3+2}=\sqrt{-1}$, which is not a real number. Exclude values for which the denominator evaluates to zero. Factor the denominator to identify such excluded values.
$f(x)=\dfrac{\sqrt{x+2}}{2x^3+x^2-2x-1}=\dfrac{\sqrt{x+2}}{x^2(2x+1)-(2x+1)}=\dfrac{\sqrt{x+2}}{(2x+1)\left(x^2-1\right)}=\dfrac{\sqrt{x+2}}{(2x+1)(x+1)(x-1)}$. The denominator is zero when x is -1 (choice B), $-\dfrac{1}{2}$ (choice C), or 1 (choice D), so these values are excluded.

Therefore, all of the answer choices are not in the domain of f.

Tip: You also could work this problem by substituting the values in the answer choices into $f(x)$ to check which values yield an undefined expression.

59. **C.** Recall that the derivative of f is defined as $f'(x)=\lim\limits_{h\to 0}\frac{f(x+h)-f(x)}{h}$ and the derivative of f at $x=x_0$ equals $f'(x_0)=\lim\limits_{h\to 0}\frac{f(x_0+h)-f(x_0)}{h}$. For this problem, $\lim\limits_{h\to 0}\frac{\left(\frac{1}{2}+h\right)^8-\left(\frac{1}{2}\right)^8}{h}$ is the derivative of the function f defined by $f(x)=x^8$ at $x=\frac{1}{2}$. Thus, $f'(x)=8x^7$ and $f'\left(\frac{1}{2}\right)=8\left(\frac{1}{2}\right)^7=2^3\left(\frac{1}{2^7}\right)=\frac{1}{2^4}=\frac{1}{16}$, choice C.

60. **D.** If $f'(x)>0$ for all x, then f is increasing, and if $f''(x)<0$ for all f, f is concave downward. Eliminate choice A because f is decreasing, not increasing. Eliminate choice B because f is not concave down for all x. Eliminate choice C because f is concave up, not concave down. Only choice D meets both conditions given.

Tip: The tangent lines lie below the curve when a function is concave up and lie above the curve when the function is concave down.

Chapter 14

Practice Test 3

Time: 150 Minutes

60 Questions

Directions: Read the directions for each question carefully. This test has several different question types. For each question, select a single answer choice unless written instructions preceding the question state otherwise. For each selected-response question, select the best answer or answers from the choices given. For each numeric-entry question, enter an answer in the answer box. Enter the exact answer unless you are told to round your answer. If a question asks specifically for the answer as a fraction, there will be two boxes—a numerator box and a denominator box. Do not use decimal points in fractions.

1. The greatest common factor of m and 108 is 12, and the least common multiple of m and 108 is 756. What is m?

Ⓐ 72
Ⓑ 84
Ⓒ 168
Ⓓ 216

For the following question, select <u>all</u> that apply.

$\otimes$	a	b
a	a	b
b	b	b

2. The preceding table defines an operation $\otimes$ on the set $S = \{a, b\}$. Which of the following statements about S with respect to $\otimes$ are true?

[A] S is closed.
[B] S is commutative.
[C] S contains an identity element.
[D] S contains inverses for all elements in S.

3. Sophia buys an amethyst pendant in 2007 for $500. By 2010, it has lost 10% of its value. In 2012, it is worth 10% more than in 2010. By 2015, it has lost 20% of its value from 3 years previously. What is the pendant worth in 2015?

Ⓐ $390
Ⓑ $396
Ⓒ $400
Ⓓ $404

4. If two identical machines can do a job in 10 days, how many days will take five such machines to do the same job?

Ⓐ 4 days
Ⓑ 5 days
Ⓒ 8 days
Ⓓ 25 days

5. If $y = e^{x+1}$, then $x =$

Ⓐ $\ln(y - 1)$
Ⓑ $\ln(y) - 1$
Ⓒ $\frac{y-1}{e}$
Ⓓ $\frac{y}{e} - 1$

6. Two vehicles leave the same location at 10:45 a.m., one traveling due north at 70 miles per hour and the other due south at 60 miles per hour. If the vehicles maintain their respective speeds, at what time will they be 325 miles apart?

Ⓐ 12:15 p.m.
Ⓑ 1:15 p.m.
Ⓒ 2:15 p.m.
Ⓓ 3 p.m.

GO ON TO THE NEXT PAGE

7. First prize for a television show's promotional drawing is a $24 \times 16 \times 8$-inch rectangular box filled to capacity with U.S. \$20 bills, with virtually no empty space in the box. On average, U.S. \$20 bills measure 6.14 inches long and 2.61 inches wide, and a stack of 100 \$20 bills is about 0.43-inch thick. What is the approximate total value of money in the first-prize box of \$20 bills?

Ⓐ \$45,000
Ⓑ \$890,000
Ⓒ \$1,160,000
Ⓓ \$8,920,000

8. If the surface area of a sphere is 144π cm^2, find the sphere's volume.

Ⓐ 36 cm^3
Ⓑ 288 cm^3
Ⓒ 216π cm^3
Ⓓ 288π cm^3

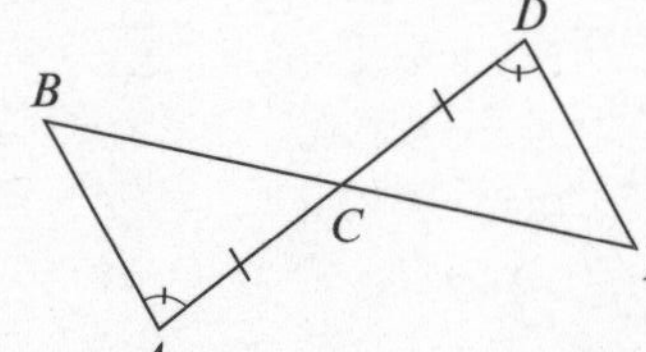

9. In the preceding figure, $\angle A \cong \angle D$ and $\overline{BE}$ bisects $\overline{AD}$. Which of the following methods should be used to show triangle ABC is congruent to triangle DEC?

Ⓐ SSS
Ⓑ SAS
Ⓒ AAA
Ⓓ ASA

10. Riqui scored at the 75th percentile on a multiple-choice history exam. The best interpretation of this information is that

Ⓐ Riqui answered 75% of the questions on the test correctly.
Ⓑ Only 25% of the other students made a lower score on the test than Riqui.
Ⓒ Riqui answered 75 questions correctly.
Ⓓ Riqui did as well or better than 75% of the students who took the exam.

11. If $\sin\theta = -\frac{5}{13}$ and $\pi < \theta < \frac{3\pi}{2}$, then $\tan\theta$ is

Ⓐ $-\frac{12}{5}$
Ⓑ $-\frac{5}{12}$
Ⓒ $\frac{12}{5}$
Ⓓ $\frac{5}{12}$

For the following question, enter your numeric answer in the box below the question.

12. If $x^2 - 13 = 12x$, what is the value of $|x - 6|$?

[ ]

13. If $y = \left|\sin x - \frac{1}{4}\right|$, what is the maximum value of y?

Ⓐ $\frac{1}{4}$
Ⓑ $\frac{3}{4}$
Ⓒ 1
Ⓓ $\frac{5}{4}$

14. Which of the following expressions is an identity for $\frac{\tan\theta + \cot\theta}{\sec\theta\csc\theta}$?

Ⓐ $\sin^2\theta + \cos^2\theta$
Ⓑ $2\cos^2\theta$
Ⓒ $2\sin\theta\cos\theta$
Ⓓ $1 - 2\sin^2\theta$

15. If $p(x) = (2x - 3)(x + k)$, and -3 is the remainder when $p(x)$ is divided by $(x - 1)$, what is the value of k?

Ⓐ -6
Ⓑ -3
Ⓒ 2
Ⓓ 6

GO ON TO THE NEXT PAGE

16. Determine k so that the function f defined by $f(x) = x + \frac{k}{x}$ has a relative minimum at $x = 2$ and a relative maximum at $x = -2$.

Ⓐ -4
Ⓑ -2
Ⓒ 2
Ⓓ 4

Mean Score	65
Median Score	73
Modal Score	77
Range	52
Standard Deviation	15
Number of Students	50

17. The data in the preceding table summarize the scores of 50 students on a chemistry exam. Which of the following statements best describes the distribution of the scores?

Ⓐ The distribution is positively skewed.
Ⓑ The distribution is negatively skewed.
Ⓒ The distribution is symmetric.
Ⓓ The distribution is bimodal.

18. A real estate agent selling houses located in an upscale housing development has determined the following probabilities for two neighboring houses, one of which is a model home: The probability that the model home will be sold is 0.50, the probability that the house next door will be sold is 0.40, and the probability that at least one of the two houses will be sold is 0.80. Find the probability that the house next door will be sold given that the model home has already been sold.

Ⓐ 10%
Ⓑ 20%
Ⓒ 30%
Ⓓ 40%

19. $i^{218} =$

Ⓐ -1
Ⓑ $-i$
Ⓒ 1
Ⓓ i

20. What is the inverse of the function defined by $y = x^5 - 3$?

Ⓐ $y = \frac{1}{\sqrt[5]{x-3}}$
Ⓑ $y = \frac{1}{x^5 - 3}$
Ⓒ $y = \sqrt[5]{x} + 3$
Ⓓ $y = \sqrt[5]{x+3}$

21. Which of the following expressions is equivalent to the expression $\log_{10}\left(\frac{x^3}{20}\right)$?

Ⓐ $(\log_{10} x)^3 - 2$
Ⓑ $3\log_{10} x - 2$
Ⓒ $(\log_{10} x)^3 - \log_{10} 20$
Ⓓ $3\log_{10} x - \log_{10} 2 - 1$

For the following question, select all that apply.

22. Which of the following matrices are nonsingular?

[A] $\begin{bmatrix} -3 & 5 \\ -6 & 10 \end{bmatrix}$

[B] $\begin{bmatrix} 4 & 0 \\ 0 & 4 \end{bmatrix}$

[C] $\begin{bmatrix} 2 & -5 & 3 \\ 6 & 1 & -4 \\ 0 & 0 & 0 \end{bmatrix}$

[D] $\begin{bmatrix} 1 & 0 & 0 \\ 0 & 1 & 0 \\ 0 & 0 & 1 \end{bmatrix}$

23. A water tank can be filled in 6 hours when the input valve is open and the outlet valve is closed. When the input valve is closed and the outlet valve is open, the same tank can be emptied in 10 hours. If a tank is filled with both valves open, how long will it take to fill the tank?

Ⓐ 4 hours
Ⓑ 8 hours
Ⓒ 15 hours
Ⓓ 16 hours

GO ON TO THE NEXT PAGE

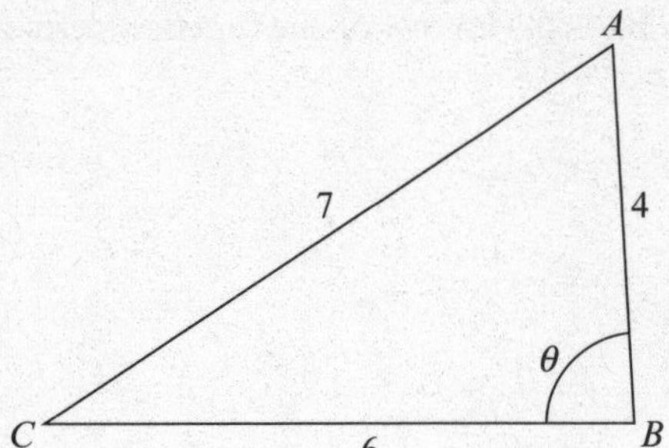

24. In triangle ABC shown above, $\cos\theta =$

Ⓐ $\frac{1}{16}$
Ⓑ $\frac{29}{56}$
Ⓒ $\frac{2}{3}$
Ⓓ $\frac{6}{7}$

25. If $f(x) = -16x^{-4}$, then $f'(2)$ is

Ⓐ -2
Ⓑ $-\frac{1}{2}$
Ⓒ $\frac{1}{2}$
Ⓓ 2

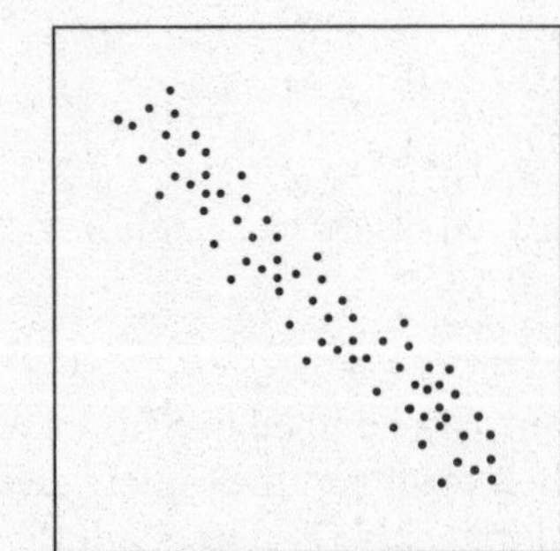

26. The preceding graph is a scatter plot for a set of bivariate data, paired values of data from two variables. What does the shape of the scatter plot most strongly suggest about the relationship between the two variables?

Ⓐ There is little relationship between the two variables.
Ⓑ There is a linear, negative relationship between the two variables.
Ⓒ There is a linear, positive relationship between the two variables.
Ⓓ There is an exponential relationship between the two variables.

27. Given $A = \begin{bmatrix} 0 & 2 \\ 1 & 3 \end{bmatrix}$ and $B = \begin{bmatrix} -2 & 3 \\ 2 & 0 \end{bmatrix}$, then $(BA)^{-1}$ is

Ⓐ $\begin{bmatrix} 3 & 5 \\ 0 & 4 \end{bmatrix}$
Ⓑ $\begin{bmatrix} \frac{1}{3} & -\frac{5}{12} \\ 0 & \frac{1}{4} \end{bmatrix}$
Ⓒ $\begin{bmatrix} 4 & 0 \\ 4 & 3 \end{bmatrix}$
Ⓓ $\begin{bmatrix} \frac{1}{4} & 0 \\ -\frac{1}{3} & \frac{1}{3} \end{bmatrix}$

28. If $f(x) = x^2 - 4$ and $g(x) = 3x + 2$, then $(f \circ g)(x) = f(g(x)) =$

Ⓐ $(x^2 - 4)(3x + 2)$
Ⓑ $9x^2$
Ⓒ $3x(3x + 4)$
Ⓓ $3x^2 - 10$

29. On a number line, if line segment x has endpoints $6\frac{1}{4}$ and $6\frac{1}{2}$ and line segment y has endpoints $\frac{5}{\sqrt{8}}$ and $\frac{3}{\sqrt{2}}$, what is the ratio of the length of y to the length of x?

Ⓐ $\frac{1}{\sqrt{2}}$
Ⓑ $\sqrt{2}$
Ⓒ $\frac{4}{\sqrt{2}}$
Ⓓ $4\sqrt{2}$

30. Suppose that the parents of a newborn child establish a savings account for the child with an investment of $10,000. Assuming no withdrawals and no additional deposits are made, approximately what interest rate compounded annually is needed to double the investment in 20 years?

Ⓐ 3.5%
Ⓑ 5.5%
Ⓒ 10.0%
Ⓓ 103.5%

GO ON TO THE NEXT PAGE

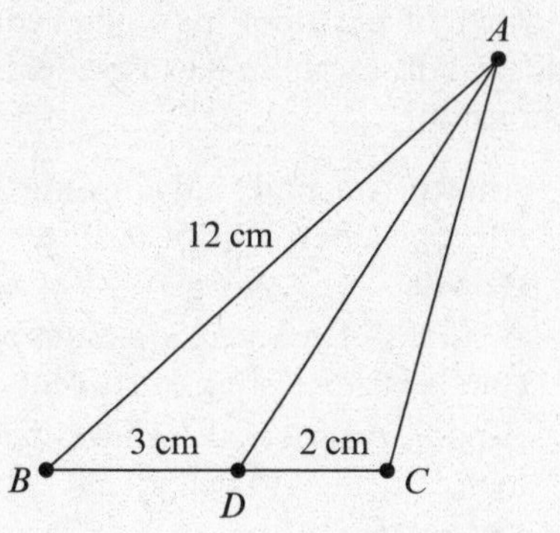

31. In triangle ABC above, $\angle DAB \cong \angle DAC$. What is the length of $\overline{AC}$?

Ⓐ 6 cm
Ⓑ 7 cm
Ⓒ 8 cm
Ⓓ It cannot be determined from the information given.

32. A manufacturing company purchases a robotic machine that can produce $Q(h)$ components per hour, where $Q(h) = \frac{10(4h+25)}{2h+5}$. Assuming the machine continues to work efficiently, approximately how many components is the machine able to produce per hour after being in operation for an extended period of time?

Ⓐ 5 components
Ⓑ 20 components
Ⓒ 40 components
Ⓓ 50 components

33. Water is running into a right cylindrical tank, which has a radius of 5 feet, at a constant rate of 30 cubic feet per minute $\left(\frac{\text{ft}^3}{\text{min}}\right)$. What is the instantaneous rate of change of the water's height after the water starts running?

Ⓐ $0.38\ \frac{\text{ft}}{\text{min}}$
Ⓑ $0.95\ \frac{\text{ft}}{\text{min}}$
Ⓒ $1.05\ \frac{\text{ft}}{\text{min}}$
Ⓓ $2.60\ \frac{\text{ft}}{\text{min}}$

For the following question, enter your numeric answer in the box below the question.

34. A student organization has 60 members, 36 boys and 24 girls. For a community activity, the organization's faculty sponsor uniformly divides the boys and girls into x groups so that each group has the same number of boys and the same number of girls as the other groups and no one is left out. What is the greatest number that x could be?

[ ]

35. In a certain small town, all the telephone numbers have the same area code, and all the 7-digit telephone numbers begin with either 560, 564, or 569 (called prefixes). Which of the following computations will yield the number of different telephone numbers that are possible if all three prefixes are used?

Ⓐ $(3)({}_{10}C_4)$
Ⓑ $(3)(10^4)$
Ⓒ 10^4
Ⓓ 10^7

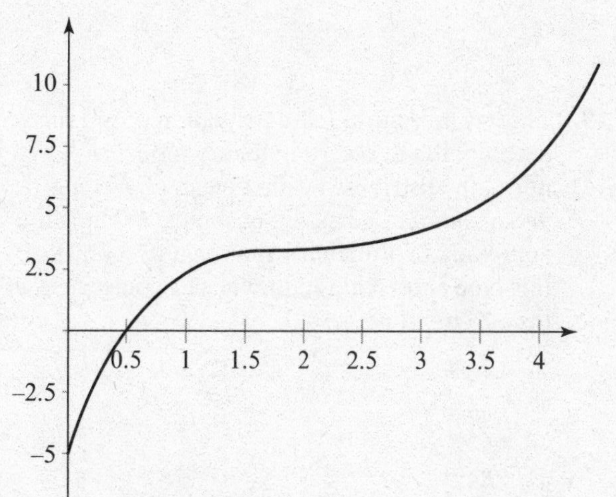

36. The graph of $y = x^3 - 6x^2 + 12x - 5$ is shown above. Which of the following statements is true about the rate of change of y with respect to x?

Ⓐ The rate of change is constant between 0 and 0.5.
Ⓑ The rate of change is increasing between 0.5 and 1.5.
Ⓒ The rate of change is decreasing between 2 and 3.
Ⓓ The rate of change is increasing between 3 and 3.5.

GO ON TO THE NEXT PAGE

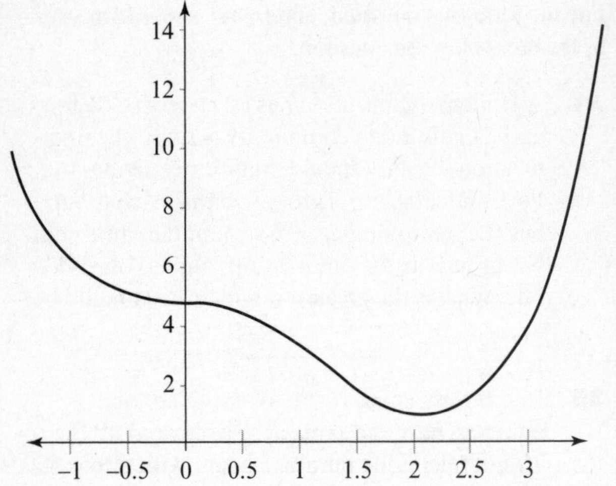

37. The function f defined by $f(x) = x^4 - 3x^3 + x^2 + 5$ has the graph shown above. What is the area of the region bounded by the graph of f and the x-axis over the closed interval [0, 2]?

Ⓐ 1
Ⓑ 5
Ⓒ $\frac{32}{5}$
Ⓓ $\frac{106}{15}$

38. The gas mileage in miles per gallon (mpg) for automobiles of a certain luxury model is normally distributed with a mean of 29 mpg and a standard deviation of 4 mpg. What is the approximate probability that an automobile of this type chosen at random has gas mileage less than 25 mpg?

Ⓐ 16%
Ⓑ 34%
Ⓒ 68%
Ⓓ 84%

39. For the point (–2, –8) on the graph of f defined by $f(x) = x^3$, give the coordinates of the corresponding point on the graph of g defined by $g(x) = f(2x)$.

Ⓐ (–1, –8)
Ⓑ (–4, –8)
Ⓒ (–2, –16)
Ⓓ (–2, –4,096)

40. For which of the following studies could the results validly establish a cause-effect relationship?

Ⓐ An experimental study investigating the effect of a new type of fertilizer on plant growth
Ⓑ A survey of teachers' opinions about standardized testing of students
Ⓒ An observational study investigating factors related to delinquent behavior in teenagers
Ⓓ An observational study investigating the relationship between college GPA and birth order

41. Which of the following sets is the solution to $2x^2 - x < 1$?

Ⓐ $\left\{x \in \text{reals}, x < -1 \text{ or } x > \frac{1}{2}\right\}$
Ⓑ $\left\{x \in \text{reals}, x < \frac{1}{2} \text{ or } x > 1\right\}$
Ⓒ $\left\{x \in \text{reals}, -\frac{1}{2} < x < 1\right\}$
Ⓓ $\left\{x \in \text{reals}, -1 < x < \frac{1}{2}\right\}$

Time (in years)	Population
0	500
5	1,500

42. The preceding table gives the population of a deer herd at two different times in years. The population's growth is modeled by the function $P(t) = P_0e^{xt}$, where t is in years. Based on this information, what is the value of x?

Ⓐ $\frac{\ln 3}{5}$
Ⓑ $\ln 3$
Ⓒ $\ln 3 - \ln 5$
Ⓓ $\ln\left(\frac{3}{5}\right)$

GO ON TO THE NEXT PAGE

43. A ball is dropped from a height of 120 feet. If each rebound is $\frac{3}{4}$ the height of the previous bounce, which of the following functions would best model the ball's height as a function of rebound number n?

Ⓐ quadratic
Ⓑ polynomial
Ⓒ linear
Ⓓ exponential

44. The graph of $y=\dfrac{x^4-81}{x^2+x-12}$ has how many asymptotes?

Ⓐ 0
Ⓑ 1
Ⓒ 2
Ⓓ 3

For the following question, enter your fractional answer in the boxes below the question.

45. Given $f(x) = 3x$ and $g(x)=\dfrac{4}{x-1}$, what is the fractional solution of $f(g(x))=g(f(x))$?

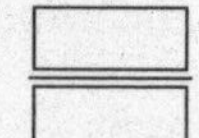

46. A sequence is defined recursively by

$a_1 = 1$

$a_n = a_{n-1} + 2n + 3$ for $n \geq 2$

The closed-form representation of the sequence is best modeled as

Ⓐ arithmetic
Ⓑ geometric
Ⓒ quadratic
Ⓓ exponential

47. What is the approximate volume of a right triangular prism that is 25 inches in height and whose bases are equilateral triangles that are 4 inches on a side?

Ⓐ 7 in^3
Ⓑ 100 in^3
Ⓒ 173 in^3
Ⓓ 200 in^3

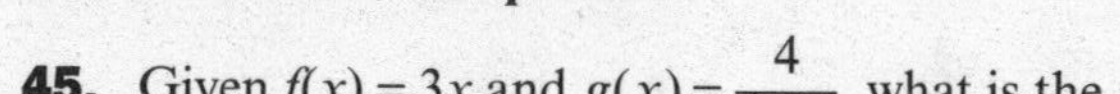

48. An experiment consists of flipping a coin and noting the up face six times. Which of the following computations will yield the number of different outcomes in the sample space for this experiment?

Ⓐ 6^2
Ⓑ 2^6
Ⓒ $6!$
Ⓓ 6^6

49. Find the area enclosed by the curves $y=\frac{1}{4}x^2$ and $y = x^2 + 3x - 9$.

Ⓐ 64
Ⓑ 118
Ⓒ 172
Ⓓ It cannot be determined from the information given.

50. A bag contains 10 blue marbles, 7 red marbles, 5 green marbles, and 3 yellow marbles. If two marbles are randomly drawn from the bag, one after the other, without replacement after the first draw, what is the probability that both marbles will be yellow?

Ⓐ $\frac{9}{625}$
Ⓑ $\frac{1}{100}$
Ⓒ $\frac{3}{25}$
Ⓓ $\frac{2}{24}$

GO ON TO THE NEXT PAGE

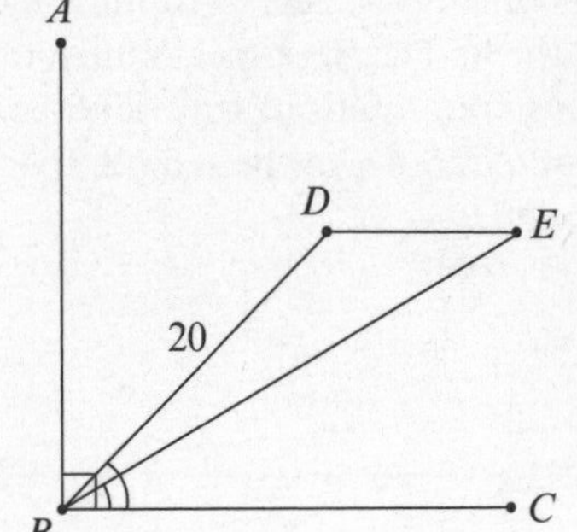

51. In the figure shown above, $\overline{AB} \perp \overline{BC}$, $\overline{DE} \parallel \overline{BC}$, $m\angle DBC = 45°$, $m\angle EBC = 30°$, and $BD = 20$. What is the perimeter of triangle DBE?

Ⓐ $10\left(2+\sqrt{2}+3\right)$

Ⓑ $10\left(2+\sqrt{2}+\sqrt{6}\right)$

Ⓒ $20\left(2+\sqrt{2}+\sqrt{3}\right)$

Ⓓ $20\left(2+2\sqrt{2}\right)$

For the following question, enter your numeric answer in the box below the question.

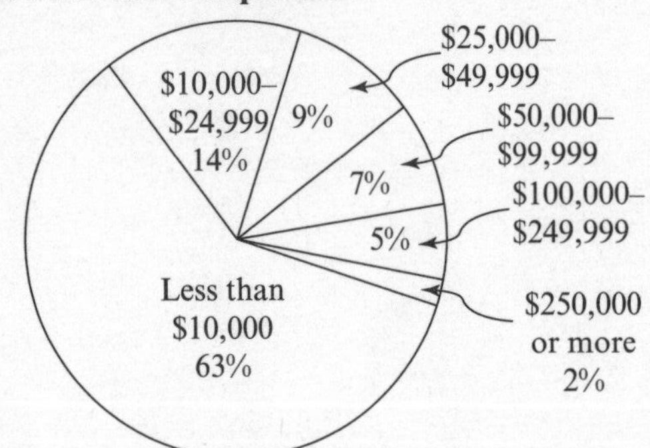

52. The circle graph above shows the distribution of 3,000 workers, ages 30 to 50, according to their total savings and investments. According to the graph, the number of workers who have less than \$10,000 in savings and investments is what percent of the number of workers who have \$100,000 or more in savings and investments?

[ ] %

53. A particle moves horizontally in a straight line with velocity $v(t) = 6t^2$. How far does the particle move between times $t = 1$ and $t = 2$?

Ⓐ 2

Ⓑ 14

Ⓒ 18

Ⓓ 42

For the following question, select <u>all</u> that apply.

54. Suppose $a = \frac{x}{4} + \frac{y}{4^2} + \frac{z}{4^3}$, where x, y, and z are each either 0 or 1. Which of the following fractions are possible values of a?

[A] $\frac{5}{64}$

[B] $\frac{13}{64}$

[C] $\frac{3}{16}$

[D] $\frac{5}{16}$

55. Given $3x + 2y + 6z = 50$ and $7x + 8y + 4z = 70$, what is the arithmetic average of x, y, and z?

Ⓐ 4

Ⓑ 10

Ⓒ 12

Ⓓ It cannot be determined from the information given.

For the following question, select <u>all</u> that apply.

56. The square root of the product of p and q is 14, where p and q are two positive integers. Which of the following integers could be a sum for $(p + q)$?

[A] 35

[B] 54

[C] 100

[D] 197

GO ON TO THE NEXT PAGE

57. Suppose f and g are differentiable functions such that

$$f(0)=1 \qquad g(0)=1$$
$$f'(0)=3 \qquad g'(0)=-3$$
$$f'(1)=-4 \qquad g'(1)=-5$$

If $h(x)=f(g(x))$, what is the value of $h'(0)$?

Ⓐ −15
Ⓑ 0
Ⓒ 12
Ⓓ 15

For the following question, enter your numeric answer in the box below the question.

58. One of the interior angles of a regular polygon measures 140°. What is the sum of the measures of the polygon's interior angles?

[ ]°

59. Two boxes each contain four tiles, numbered 1, 2, 3, and 4. The tiles are identical in shape and size. A student randomly draws one tile from each box and calculates the product of the two numbers on the tiles. Which of the following products is most likely to occur?

Ⓐ 2
Ⓑ 4
Ⓒ 6
Ⓓ 8

60. The graph of the function f defined by $f(x) = 3^x$ is reflected over the x-axis and translated 5 units to the right to become the function g. Which of the following equations defines g?

Ⓐ $g(x) = -3^{x-5}$
Ⓑ $g(x) = -3^x - 5$
Ⓒ $g(x) = 3^{-(x+5)}$
Ⓓ $g(x) = 3^{-x} - 5$

STOP

Answer Key for Practice Test 3

Question Number	Correct Answer	Reference Chapter	Question Number	Correct Answer	Reference Chapter
1.	B	Number and Quantity	**31.**	C	Geometry
2.	A, B, C	Algebra	**32.**	B	Calculus
3.	B	Algebra	**33.**	A	Calculus
4.	A	Algebra	**34.**	12	Number and Quantity
5.	B	Algebra	**35.**	B	Discrete Mathematics
6.	B	Algebra	**36.**	D	Calculus
7.	B	Number and Quantity	**37.**	D	Calculus
8.	D	Geometry	**38.**	A	Statistics
9.	D	Geometry	**39.**	A	Functions
10.	D	Statistics	**40.**	A	Statistics
11.	D	Trigonometry	**41.**	C	Algebra
12.	7	Algebra	**42.**	A	Algebra
13.	D	Trigonometry	**43.**	D	Functions
14.	A	Trigonometry	**44.**	B	Functions
15.	C	Functions	**45.**	$\frac{1}{4}$	Functions
16.	D	Calculus	**46.**	C	Discrete Mathematics
17.	B	Statistics	**47.**	C	Geometry
18.	B	Probability	**48.**	B	Probability
19.	A	Number and Quantity	**49.**	A	Calculus
20.	D	Functions	**50.**	B	Probability
21.	D	Algebra	**51.**	B	Geometry
22.	B, D	Matrices	**52.**	900	Statistics
23.	C	Algebra	**53.**	B	Calculus
24.	A	Trigonometry	**54.**	A, D	Number and Quantity
25.	D	Calculus	**55.**	A	Statistics
26.	B	Statistics	**56.**	A, C, D	Number and Quantity
27.	B	Matrices	**57.**	C	Calculus
28.	C	Functions	**58.**	1,260	Geometry
29.	B	Number and Quantity	**59.**	B	Probability
30.	A	Algebra	**60.**	A	Functions

Answer Explanations for Practice Test 3

1. **B.** The least common multiple (lcm) of two positive integers is their product divided by their greatest common factor (gcf). Use this fact about the relationship between least common multiple and greatest common factor to write an equation and solve for *m*.

$$\begin{aligned}\frac{(108)(m)}{\text{gcf}(m,\ 108)} &= \text{lcm}(m,\ 108)\\ \frac{108m}{12} &= 756\\ 9m &= 756\\ m &= 84,\ \text{choice B}\end{aligned}$$

2. **A, B, C.** Determine which of the given properties hold for $S = \{a, b\}$ with respect to $\otimes$.

$\otimes$	a	b
a	a	b
b	b	b

Using the preceding table, list the possible "products" and check for the properties given in the answer choices.

$$a \otimes a = a,\ a \otimes b = b,\ b \otimes a = b,\ \text{and } b \otimes b = b$$

Check A: *S* is closed with respect to $\otimes$ because when $\otimes$ is performed using any two elements in *S*, the result is an element in *S*. Select choice A.

Check B: Because $a \otimes b = b$ and $b \otimes a = b$, *S* is commutative with respect to $\otimes$. Select choice B.

Check C: Because $a \otimes a = a$ and $a \otimes b = b$, *S* contains an identity element, namely *a*, with respect to $\otimes$. Select choice C.

Check D: *S* does not contain an inverse for every element in *S*. In particular, the element *b* does not have an inverse because there is no element in *S* such that $b \otimes$ (that element) $= a$, the identity element. Eliminate choice D.

3. **B.** In 2007, the value is \$500.

In 2010, the value is \$500 – 10%(\$500) = 90%(\$500) = 0.90(\$500) = \$450.

In 2012, the value is \$450 + 10%(\$450) = \$450 + 0.10(\$450) = \$495.

In 2015, the value is \$495 – 20%(\$495) = 0.80(\$495) = \$396, choice B.

4. **A.** Use logical reasoning to reach the solution. The machines are identical, so if two machines can do the job in 10 days, then it should take twice as long for one machine to do the same job. So one machine can do the job in 20 days. If five such machines do the job together, they should take $\frac{1}{5}$ as long as it takes for one machine. Therefore, five machines can do the same job in $\frac{1}{5}(20\text{ days}) = 4$ days, choice A.

5. **B.** Take the natural log of both sides of the equation, and then solve for *x*.

$$\begin{aligned}y &= e^{x+1}\\ \ln y &= \ln\left(e^{x+1}\right)\\ \ln y &= (x+1)\ln(e)\\ \ln y &= x+1\\ \ln y - 1 &= x,\ \text{choice B}\end{aligned}$$

6. **B.** Let $t =$ the time it will take for the two vehicles to be 325 miles apart.

The distance traveled by vehicle traveling north = (rate)(time) = $\left(70\frac{\text{mi}}{\text{hr}}\right)(t)$.

The distance traveled by vehicle traveling south = (rate)(time) = $\left(60\frac{\text{mi}}{\text{hr}}\right)(t)$.

The two vehicles are traveling in opposite directions, so the total distance traveled is

$$70\frac{\text{mi}}{\text{hr}}t + 60\frac{\text{mi}}{\text{hr}}t = 325 \text{ miles}$$

Solve for t (omitting the units for convenience).

$$\begin{aligned} 70t + 60t &= 325 \\ 130t &= 325 \\ t &= 2.5 \end{aligned}$$

The time it will take for the two vehicles to be 325 miles apart is 2.5 hours or 2 hours 30 minutes.

The clock time = 10:45 a.m. + 2 hours 30 minutes = 1:15 p.m., choice B.

7. **B.** The capacity of the box is its volume, which equals (24 in)(16 in)(8 in). The thickness of a single U.S. $20 bill is $\frac{0.43 \text{ in}}{100} = 0.0043$ in, so the dimensions of a U.S. $20 bill are $6.14 \times 2.61 \times 0.0043$ inches. Thus, the approximate total value of money in the first-prize box of $20 bills is

$$\frac{(24 \text{ in})(16 \text{ in})(8 \text{ in})}{(6.14 \text{ in})(2.61 \text{ in})(0.0043 \text{ in})} \cdot \$20 = \frac{3072 \text{ in}^3}{0.06890922 \text{ in}^3} \cdot \$20 = \$891{,}607.83 \approx \$890{,}000, \text{ choice B.}$$

8. **D.** The formula for a sphere's surface area is $S.A. = 4\pi r^2$. The formula for a sphere's volume is $V = \frac{4}{3}\pi r^3$. (***Note:*** These formulas are provided in the Notations, Definitions, and Formulas reference sheet.) To find the sphere's volume, do two steps. First, using surface area, find the sphere's radius. Next, use the radius to find the volume.

$$\begin{aligned} 4\pi r^2 &= 144\pi \text{ cm}^2 \\ r^2 &= 36 \text{ cm}^2 \\ r &= 6 \text{ cm} \end{aligned}$$

$V = \frac{4}{3}\pi r^3 = \frac{4}{3}\pi(6 \text{ cm})^3 = 288\pi \text{ cm}^3$, choice D.

9. **D.** Eliminate choice C because this approach is not a method for proving congruence. Examine the figure.

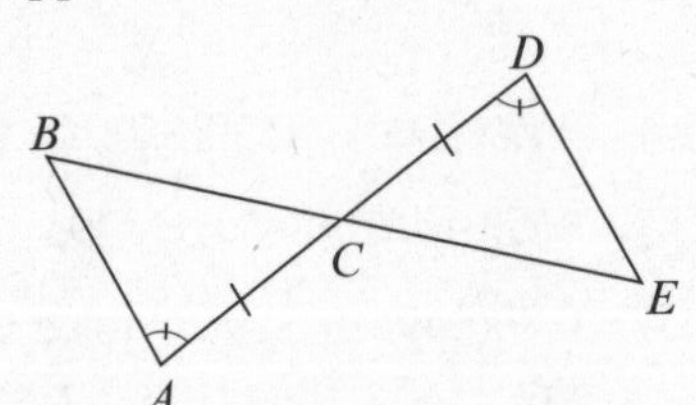

$\angle ACB \cong \angle DCE$ because they are vertical angles. $\overline{AC} \cong \overline{DC}$ because $\overline{BE}$ bisects $\overline{AD}$. You are given that $\angle A \cong \angle D$. Thus, you have two angles and the included side of triangle ABC congruent to two angles and the included side of triangle DCE. Therefore, ASA, choice D, is the correct response.

10. **D.** The 75th percentile is a value at or below which 75% of the data fall. Therefore, the best interpretation of Riqui's score is that he did as well or better than 75% of the students who took the exam, choice D.

11. **D.** Make a sketch to illustrate the problem.

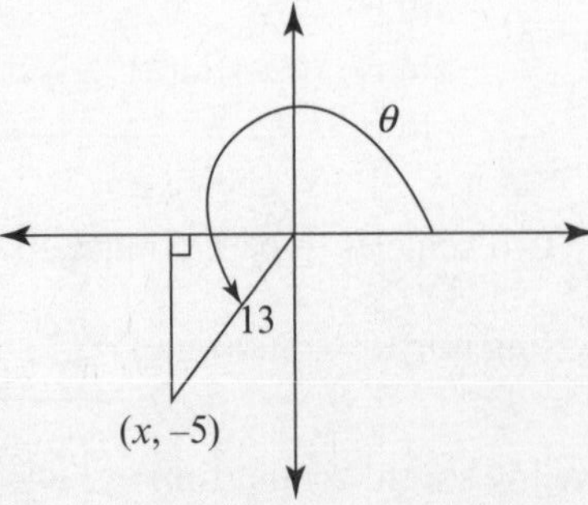

Method 1. Eliminate answer choices based on the information provided. The sketch shows that $\tan\theta = \frac{y}{x} = \frac{-5}{x}$ and that $x < 0$. Therefore, $\tan\theta > 0$ because it is the quotient of two negative numbers. Eliminate choices A and B because these answer choices contain negative values. Of the two remaining answer choices, only choice D has a 5 in the numerator for the tangent, meaning that choice D must be the correct response.

Method 2. Use the formulas $r^2 = x^2 + y^2$ and $\tan\theta = \frac{y}{x}$ (which are provided in the Notations, Definitions, and Formulas reference sheet) to determine that $x = \sqrt{13^2 - (-5)^2} = \sqrt{144} = \pm 12$. Because x is to the left of the origin, $x = -12$. Thus, $\tan\theta = \frac{y}{x} = \frac{-5}{-12} = \frac{5}{12}$, choice D.

12. 7 First, rearrange the terms so that only x terms are on the left side of the equation. Next, complete the square for the x terms. Then take the square root of both sides of the equation. ***Tip:*** Remember, $\sqrt{(x)^2} = |x|$.

$$\begin{aligned} x^2 - 13 &= 12x \\ x^2 - 12x &= 13 \\ x^2 - 12x + 36 &= 13 + 36 \\ (x-6)^2 &= 49 \\ |x-6| &= 7 \end{aligned}$$

13. **D.** You know that $|\sin x| \le 1$. Using this fact yields the following:

$$\begin{aligned} -1 \le \sin x &\le 1 \\ -1 - \frac{1}{4} \le \sin x - \frac{1}{4} &\le 1 - \frac{1}{4} \\ -\frac{5}{4} \le \sin x - \frac{1}{4} &\le \frac{3}{4} \end{aligned}$$

Thus, the maximum value of y is $\left|-\frac{5}{4}\right| = \frac{5}{4}$, choice D.

14. **A. Method 1.** Since all the answer choices are given in terms of sine and cosine, rewrite $\frac{\tan\theta + \cot\theta}{\sec\theta\csc\theta}$ as

$$\frac{\frac{\sin\theta}{\cos\theta} + \frac{\cos\theta}{\sin\theta}}{\frac{1}{\cos\theta}\cdot\frac{1}{\sin\theta}} = \frac{\frac{\sin^2\theta + \cos^2\theta}{\cos\theta\sin\theta}}{\frac{1}{\cos\theta\sin\theta}} = \sin^2\theta + \cos^2\theta, \text{ choice A.}$$

Method 2. Rewrite $\frac{\tan\theta + \cot\theta}{\sec\theta\csc\theta}$ as $\frac{\tan\theta + \frac{1}{\tan\theta}}{\frac{1}{\cos\theta}\cdot\frac{1}{\sin\theta}}$, so that you can use the trig function keys on the ETS graphing calculator to evaluate the expression for a convenient value of θ, say 30°. When you evaluate $\frac{\tan 30° + \frac{1}{\tan 30°}}{\frac{1}{\cos 30°}\cdot\frac{1}{\sin 30°}}$, you get 1 for an answer. You should recognize that $\sin^2\theta + \cos^2\theta$ (choice A) is an identity that equals 1 for all values of θ.

In a test situation, you should go on to the next question since you have found the correct answer. You would not have to check the other answer choices; but for your information, when $\theta = 30°$, choice B yields 1.5, choice C yields 0.8660…, and choice D yields 0.5.

15. **C.** By the remainder theorem, $p(1) = -3$. Substitute into $p(x)$ and solve for k.

$$\begin{aligned} p(x) &= (2x-3)(x+k) \\ p(1) &= (2(1)-3)((1)+k) \\ -3 &= (-1)(1+k) \\ -3 &= -1-k \\ k &= 2, \text{ choice C} \end{aligned}$$

16. **D.** Find $f'(x)$ and then solve $f'(2) = 0$ and $f'(-2) = 0$ for k.

$$\begin{aligned} f(x) &= x + \frac{k}{x} = x + kx^{-1} \\ f'(x) &= 1 - kx^{-2} = 1 - \frac{k}{x^2} \\ f'(2) &= 1 - \frac{k}{(2)^2} = 1 - \frac{k}{4} \\ 1 - \frac{k}{4} &= 0 \text{ implies} \\ 4 - k &= 0 \text{ implies} \\ k &= 4, \text{ choice D} \end{aligned}$$

Note: Because $f'(-2) = f'(2)$, solving $f'(-2) = 0$ for k also yields $k = 4$. When $k = 4$, $f'(x) = 1 - \frac{4}{x^2} = 1 - 4x^{-2}$, which implies $f''(x) = 8x^{-3}$. Thus, $f''(2) = 8(2)^{-3} = 1 > 0$ and $f''(-2) = 8(-2)^{-3} = -1 < 0$. This result verifies that f has a relative minimum at $x = 2$ and a relative maximum at $x = -2$.

Tip: Use the ETS graphing calculator to graph $f(x) = x + \frac{4}{x}$ to verify your results.

17. **B.** Examine the table.

Mean Score	65
Median Score	73
Modal Score	77
Range	52
Standard Deviation	15
Number of Students	50

If the data were represented using a histogram, the mean would lie to the left of both the median and the mode on the horizontal axis, indicating that the data are skewed, with a tail on the left. Thus, the distribution is negatively skewed, choice B.

18. **B.** The problem asks: Find the probability that the house next door will be sold given that the model home has already been sold. This probability is a conditional probability. If A is the event that the model home will be sold and B is the event that the house next door will be sold, then you need to find $P(B \mid A) = \frac{P(A \cap B)}{P(A)}$. You are given $P(A) = 0.50$, but you are not given $P(A \cap B)$, which is the probability that both houses are sold. The problem states "the probability that at least one of the two houses will be sold is 0.80." For this problem situation, the probability that at least one of the two houses will be sold is $P(A \cup B)$. Recall that $P(A \cup B) = P(A) + P(B) - P(A \cap B)$. Thus, since you know $P(A) = 0.50$, $P(B) = 0.40$, and $P(A \cup B) = 0.80$, you can determine $P(A \cap B)$. To find $P(B|A)$, first determine $P(A \cap B)$. Next, use the information found and information given in the problem to calculate $P(B|A)$.

$$\begin{aligned} P(A \cup B) &= P(A) + P(B) - P(A \cap B) \\ 0.80 &= 0.50 + 0.40 - P(A \cap B) \\ P(A \cap B) &= 0.90 - 0.80 \\ P(A \cap B) &= 0.10 \end{aligned}$$

Thus, $P(B \mid A) = \frac{P(A \cap B)}{P(A)} = \frac{0.10}{0.50} = 0.20 = 20\%$, choice B.

19. **A.** The powers of the complex unit i are cyclic. That is, $i = i$, $i^2 = -1$, $i^3 = -i$, $i^4 = 1$, $i^5 = i$, $i^6 = -1$, $i^7 = -i$, $i^8 = 1$, $i^9 = i$, and so on. The pattern of i, –1, $-i$, 1 repeats consecutively. In general, $i^{4k+1} = i$, $i^{4k+2} = i^2 = -1$, $i^{4k+3} = i^3 = -i$, and $i^{4k+4} = i^4 = 1$.

Therefore, to evaluate a power of i, divide its exponent by 4 and use the remainder as the exponent for i. Thus, $i^{218} = i^{4(54)+2} = i^2 = -1$, choice A.

20. **D.** Interchange x and y in $y = x^5 - 3$, and then solve for y.

$$\begin{aligned} x &= y^5 - 3 \\ x + 3 &= y^5 \\ \sqrt[5]{x+3} &= y, \text{ choice D} \end{aligned}$$

21. **D. Method 1.** Use the properties of logarithms to rewrite the expression.

$$\begin{aligned} \log_{10}\left(\frac{x^3}{20}\right) &= \log_{10} x^3 - \log_{10} 20 \\ &= 3\log_{10} x - \log_{10}(2 \cdot 10) \\ &= 3\log_{10} x - (\log_{10} 2 + \log_{10} 10) \\ &= 3\log_{10} x - \log_{10} 2 - \log_{10} 10 \\ &= 3\log_{10} x - \log_{10} 2 - 1, \text{ choice D} \end{aligned}$$

Method 2. Select a convenient value for x, say 5, and evaluate $\log_{10}\left(\frac{5^3}{20}\right)$, which is 0.79588…, and then evaluate each of the expressions given in the answer choices for x equal to 5. Choice A yields –1.65851…, choice B yields 0.09691…, choice C yields –0.95954…, and choice D yields 0.79588…. Thus, choice D is the correct response.

22. **B, D.** A matrix that has an inverse is nonsingular. A matrix has an inverse if and only if its determinant does *not* equal 0. Therefore, to determine which of the matrices are nonsingular, compute the determinant for each. If the determinant is *not* equal to 0, the matrix is nonsingular. Check the answer choices.

Check A: $\begin{vmatrix} -3 & 5 \\ -6 & 10 \end{vmatrix} = (-3)(10) - (5)(-6) = -30 - (-30) = -30 + 30 = 0$, so $\begin{bmatrix} -3 & 5 \\ -6 & 10 \end{bmatrix}$ is *not* a nonsingular matrix. Eliminate choice A.

Check B: $\begin{vmatrix} 4 & 0 \\ 0 & 4 \end{vmatrix} = (4)(4) - (0)(0) = 16 \neq 0$, so $\begin{vmatrix} 4 & 0 \\ 0 & 4 \end{vmatrix}$ is a nonsingular matrix. Select choice B.

Check C: The matrix $\begin{bmatrix} 2 & -5 & 3 \\ 6 & 1 & -4 \\ 0 & 0 & 0 \end{bmatrix}$ has a row of 0s. If a square matrix has a row or column consisting of only 0s, the determinant of the matrix equals 0. Therefore, $\begin{bmatrix} 2 & -5 & 3 \\ 6 & 1 & -4 \\ 0 & 0 & 0 \end{bmatrix}$ is *not* a nonsingular matrix. Eliminate choice C.

Check D: $\begin{bmatrix} 1 & 0 & 0 \\ 0 & 1 & 0 \\ 0 & 0 & 1 \end{bmatrix} = (1)\begin{vmatrix} 1 & 0 \\ 0 & 1 \end{vmatrix} - (0)\begin{vmatrix} 0 & 0 \\ 0 & 1 \end{vmatrix} + (0)\begin{vmatrix} 0 & 1 \\ 0 & 0 \end{vmatrix} = 1 - 0 + 0 = 1 \neq 0$, so $\begin{bmatrix} 1 & 0 & 0 \\ 0 & 1 & 0 \\ 0 & 0 & 1 \end{bmatrix}$ is a nonsingular matrix. Select choice D.

23. **C.** This problem is best analyzed as a "work problem." The key idea in a work problem is that the rate at which work is done equals the amount of work accomplished divided by the amount of time worked: $\text{rate} = \frac{\text{amount of work done}}{\text{time worked}}$. For the situation in this problem, the work to be done is to fill the tank.

However, only the input valve works to fill the tank. The output valve works counter to the input valve because it works to empty the tank. Let t = time it will take to fill the tank with both valves open. To find t, first determine the rate, r_{fill}, at which the tank can be filled when the input valve is open and the outlet valve is closed and the rate r_{empty}, at which the tank can be emptied when the input valve is closed and the outlet valve is open. Next, write an equation and solve for t.

The rate for filling the tank is $r_{fill} = \frac{1 \text{ full tank}}{6 \text{ hr}} = \frac{1}{6}$ tank/hr.

The rate for emptying the tank is $r_{empty} = \frac{1 \text{ full tank}}{10 \text{ hr}} = \frac{1}{10}$ tank/hr.

Thus, when both valves are open, $\left(\frac{1}{6} \text{ tank/hr}\right)t - \left(\frac{1}{10} \text{ tank/hr}\right)t = 1$ full tank.

Solve for t (omitting the units for convenience).

$$\begin{aligned}\frac{1}{6}t - \frac{1}{10}t &= 1\\ \frac{5}{30}t - \frac{3}{30}t &= 1\\ \frac{2}{30}t &= 1\\ \frac{1}{15}t &= 1\\ t &= 15\end{aligned}$$

It will take 15 hours to fill the tank, choice C.

24. **A.** Examine the figure.

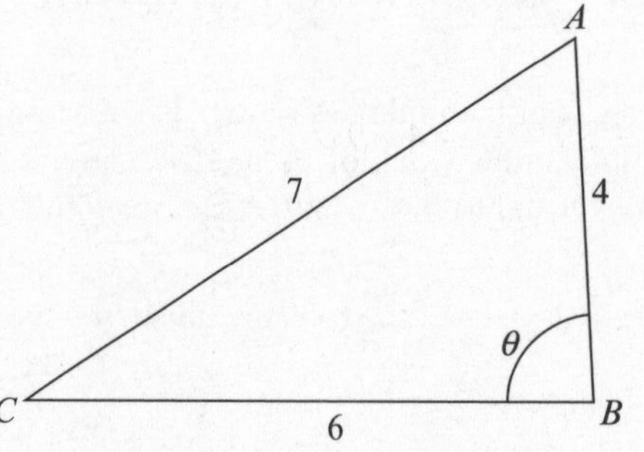

Apply the law of cosines and solve for cos θ.

$$\begin{aligned}7^2 &= 6^2 + 4^2 - 2(6)(4)\cos\theta\\ 49 &= 36 + 16 - 48\cos\theta\\ 48\cos\theta &= 3\\ \cos\theta &= \frac{3}{48} = \frac{1}{16}, \text{ choice A}\end{aligned}$$

25. **D.** First, find $f'(x)$, then determine $f'(2)$.

$f(x) = -16x^{-4}$ implies $f'(x) = 64x^{-5}$

$f'(2) = 64(2)^{-5} = 64\left(\frac{1}{32}\right) = 2$, choice D.

26. **B.** Examine the scatter plot.

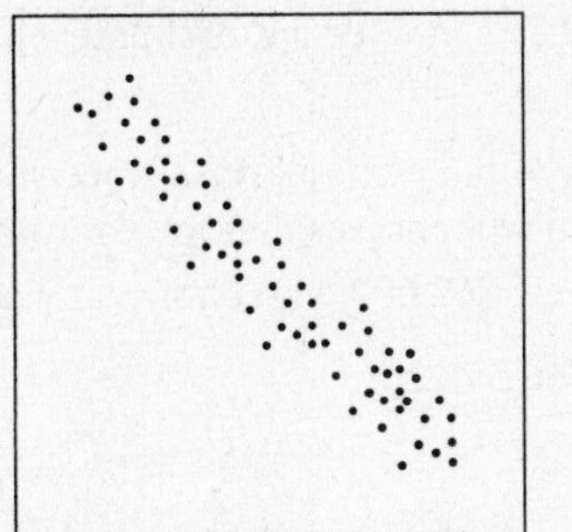

It appears that a linear relationship exists between the two variables. Since the line of best fit would slant upward to the left, the relationship is negative. Thus, choice B is the correct response. None of the statements in the other answer choices is an accurate interpretation of the scatter plot's shape.

27. **B.** Use the definition for matrix multiplication to compute the product BA, then determine $(BA)^{-1}$.

$$BA = \begin{bmatrix} -2 & 3 \\ 2 & 0 \end{bmatrix}\begin{bmatrix} 0 & 2 \\ 1 & 3 \end{bmatrix} = \begin{bmatrix} -2(0)+3(1) & -2(2)+3(3) \\ 2(0)+0(1) & 2(2)+0(3) \end{bmatrix} = \begin{bmatrix} 3 & 5 \\ 0 & 4 \end{bmatrix}$$

The determinant of $BA = (3)(4) - (5)(0) = 12$.

$$(BA)^{-1} = \begin{bmatrix} 3 & 5 \\ 0 & 4 \end{bmatrix}^{-1} = \frac{1}{\det(BA)}\begin{bmatrix} 4 & -5 \\ 0 & 3 \end{bmatrix} = \frac{1}{12}\begin{bmatrix} 4 & -5 \\ 0 & 3 \end{bmatrix} = \begin{bmatrix} \frac{1}{3} & -\frac{5}{12} \\ 0 & \frac{1}{4} \end{bmatrix}, \text{ choice B}$$

28. **C.** $(f \circ g)(x) = f(g(x)) = f(3x + 2) = (3x + 2)^2 - 4 = 9x^2 + 12x + 4 - 4 = 9x^2 + 12x = 3x(3x + 4)$, choice C.

29. **B.** Length of $x = 6\frac{1}{2} - 6\frac{1}{4} = \frac{1}{4}$.

Length of $y = \frac{3}{\sqrt{2}} - \frac{5}{\sqrt{8}} = \frac{3}{\sqrt{2}} - \frac{5}{\sqrt{4 \cdot 2}} = \frac{3}{\sqrt{2}} - \frac{5}{2\sqrt{2}} = \frac{6}{2\sqrt{2}} - \frac{5}{2\sqrt{2}} = \frac{1}{2\sqrt{2}} = \frac{1(\sqrt{2})}{2\sqrt{2}(\sqrt{2})} = \frac{\sqrt{2}}{4}$.

Ratio of the length of y to the length of x equals $\frac{\frac{\sqrt{2}}{4}}{\frac{1}{4}} = \sqrt{2}$, choice B.

30. **A.** The compound interest formula is $P = P_0(1 + r)^t$, where r is the rate, compounded annually, and P is the value after t years of an initial investment of P_0. You need to find the rate, compounded annually, that will double an investment of \$10,000 in 20 years. In other words, you need to find the rate, compounded annually, that will yield a value of \$20,000 for P in 20 years.

Method 1. Substitute into the formula (omitting the units for convenience) and solve for r.

$$\begin{aligned} P &= P_0(1+r)^t \\ 20{,}000 &= 10{,}000(1+r)^{20} \\ 2 &= (1+r)^{20} \\ \ln 2 &= \ln(1+r)^{20} \\ \ln 2 &= 20\ln(1+r) \\ \frac{\ln 2}{20} &= \ln(1+r) \\ 1+r &= e^{\frac{\ln 2}{20}} \\ r &= e^{\frac{\ln 2}{20}} - 1 \end{aligned}$$

$r = e^{\frac{\ln 2}{20}} - 1 \approx .035$ or 3.5%, choice A.

Method 2. Check the answer choices.

Check A: $\$10{,}000(1 + 0.035)^{20} = \$19{,}897.8886$ or approximately \$20,000, indicating choice A is the correct response.

In a test situation, you should go on to the next question since you have found the correct answer. You would not have to check the other answer choices; but for your information, choice B yields approximately \$30,000, choice C yields approximately \$67,000, and choice D yields approximately $\$1.5 \times 10^{10}$.

31. **C.** Given $\angle DAB \cong \angle DAC$, then $\overline{AD}$ bisects $\angle A$.

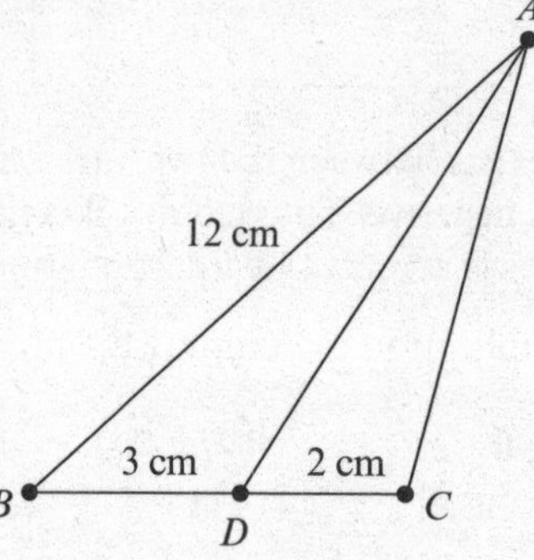

An angle bisector of an angle of a triangle divides the opposite side in the ratio of the sides that form the angle bisected. Thus, $\frac{BD}{DC} = \frac{AB}{AC}$. Substitute values from the figure into this proportion and solve for AC (omitting the units for convenience).

$$\frac{BD}{DC} = \frac{AB}{AC}$$
$$\frac{3}{2} = \frac{12}{AC}$$
$$AC = \frac{(2)(12)}{3}$$
$$AC = 8$$

The length of $\overline{AC}$ is 8 cm, choice C.

32. **B.** The phrase "an extended period of time" is a clue that this is a calculus problem in which you need to find the limit of a function as the variable approaches infinity. To answer the question, find the limit of the function $Q(h) = \frac{10(4h+25)}{2h+5}$ as h approaches infinity:

$$\lim_{h\to\infty} \frac{10(4h+25)}{2h+5} = \lim_{h\to\infty} \frac{40h+250}{2h+5} = \lim_{h\to\infty} \frac{40+\frac{250}{h}}{2+\frac{5}{h}} = \frac{40+0}{2+0} = \frac{40}{2} = 20 \text{ components, choice B.}$$

33. **A.** At any time t after the water starts running, let $h(t)$ be the height of the water in the tank. The instantaneous rate of change of the water's height is $h'(t)$. Express $h(t)$ in terms of t, then find $h'(t)$.

The volume of water at any time t is $30 \frac{\text{ft}^3}{\text{min}} t$. Substitute into the formula for the volume of a right cylinder (which is provided in the Notations, Definitions, and Formulas reference sheet) and then solve for $h(t)$, omitting the units for convenience.

$$V = \pi r^2[h(t)]$$
$$30t = \pi(5)^2[h(t)]$$
$$30t = 25\pi[h(t)]$$
$$h(t) = \frac{30t}{25\pi} \text{ implies}$$
$$h'(t) = \frac{30}{25\pi} \approx 0.38$$

The instantaneous rate of change of the height of the water at any time t is approximately $0.38\ \frac{\text{ft}}{\text{min}}$, choice A.

34. **12** The greatest number that x can be is the greatest common factor of 36 and 24, which is 12. In each of the 12 groups there are 5 students: 3 boys (36 boys ÷ 12) and 2 girls (24 girls ÷ 12). ***Tip:*** Notice that $5 \times 12 = 60$, which is the total number of students.

35. **B.** Extend the fundamental counting principle to determine the number of possible telephone numbers for each prefix as follows. After the prefix, there are 4 slots, so to speak, to fill. For each slot, 10 digits are available, which means the number of possible telephone numbers for each prefix is $10 \cdot 10 \cdot 10 \cdot 10 = 10^4$. By the addition principle, the total number of possible telephone numbers if all 3 prefixes are used is $10^4 + 10^4 + 10^4 = 3 \cdot 10^4$ or $(3)(10^4)$, choice B.

36. **D.** The rate of change of a curve at a point is described by the slope of the tangent to the curve at the point. Check each statement against the behavior of the graph of the function.

Check A: This choice is incorrect because the slope of the tangent line is decreasing between 0 and 0.5, not constant. Eliminate choice A.

Check B: This choice is incorrect because the slope of the tangent line is decreasing between 0.5 and 1.5. Eliminate choice B.

Check C: This choice is incorrect because the slope of the tangent line is increasing between 2 and 3. Eliminate choice C.

Check D: This choice is correct because the slope of the tangent line is increasing between 3 and 3.5.

37. **D.** The area of the region bounded by the graph of $f(x) = x^4 - 3x^3 + x^2 + 5$, the x-axis, and the vertical lines $x = 0$ (y-axis) and $x = 2$ is $\int_0^2 \left(x^4 - 3x^3 + x^2 + 5\right)dx$. Evaluate this definite integral using methods of calculus.

$$\int_0^2 \left(x^4 - 3x^3 + x^2 + 5\right)dx = \left(\frac{x^5}{5} - \frac{3x^4}{4} + \frac{x^3}{3} + 5x\right)\Bigg|_0^2$$
$$= \left(\frac{(2)^5}{5} - \frac{3(2)^4}{4} + \frac{(2)^3}{3} + 5(2)\right) - \left(\frac{(0)^5}{5} - \frac{3(0)^4}{4} + \frac{(0)^3}{3} + 5(0)\right)$$
$$= \frac{32}{5} - \frac{48}{4} + \frac{8}{3} + 10 = \frac{106}{15}, \text{ choice D}$$

38. **A.** According to the 68-95-99.7 rule, approximately 68% of the data in a normal distribution fall within 1 standard deviation of the mean, about 95% fall within 2 standard deviations of the mean, and about 99.7% fall within 3 standard deviations of the mean. The mean miles per gallon, μ, of the automobiles is 29 mpg with standard deviation, σ, of 4 mpg.

To find the approximate probability that a randomly chosen automobile will have gas mileage less than 25 mpg, first determine the z-score for 25 mpg, and then find the percentage of the normal distribution that is below this z-score.

z-score $= \frac{\text{data value} - \text{mean}}{\text{standard deviation}} = \frac{25 - 29}{4} = -1$. Therefore, 25 is 1 standard deviation below the mean.

Find the percentage of the normal distribution that is below a z-score of -1.

About 68% of the distribution is within standard deviation of the mean. Make a sketch to illustrate the problem.

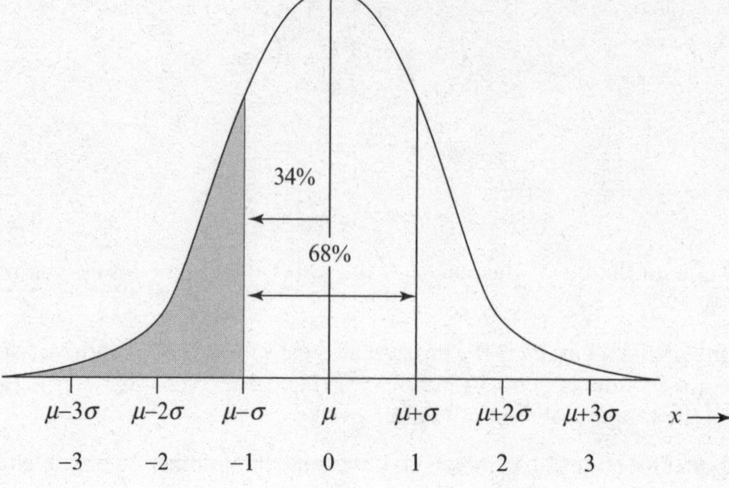

The normal curve is symmetric, so about 34% $\left(\frac{1}{2}\text{ of }68\%\right)$ of the distribution is between the mean and a z-score of –1. Again, due to symmetry, 50% of the total distribution is to the left of the mean. Thus, approximately 50% – 34% = 16% of the distribution is below a z-score of –1. The approximate probability that an automobile of this type chosen at random has gas mileage less than 25 mpg is 16%, choice A.

39. **A.** When $b > 1$, the graph defined by $g(x) = f(bx)$ is a horizontal compression toward the y-axis of the graph defined by $y = f(x)$. If (x, y) is on the graph defined by $y = f(x)$, then $\left(\frac{x}{b}, y\right)$ is on the graph defined by $g(x) = f(bx)$. Thus, if $(-2, -8)$ is on the graph of f defined by $f(x) = x^3$, then the corresponding point on the graph of g defined by $g(x) = f(2x)$ is $\left(\frac{-2}{2}, -8\right) = (-1, -8)$, choice A.

40. **A.** Only through well-designed experimental studies can investigators validly establish cause-and-effect relationships, so choice A is the correct response. Choice B is incorrect because cause-effect relationships are not established with survey studies. Choices C and D are incorrect because establishing cause-effect relationships in observational studies is problematic given that the investigators are unable to manipulate variables of interest.

41. **C.** Rewrite $2x^2 - x < 1$ as $2x^2 - x - 1 < 0$.

Factor the left side of the inequality to obtain $(2x + 1)(x - 1) < 0$. Next, determine when the product $(2x + 1)(x - 1)$ is negative. First, find the values for x at which the factors change sign; that is, find the zero for each factor.

Set each factor equal to 0 and solve for x.

$2x + 1 = 0$ implies $x = -\frac{1}{2}$ and $x - 1 = 0$ implies $x = 1$.

The two values $-\frac{1}{2}$ and 1 divide the number line into 3 intervals: $\left(-\infty, -\frac{1}{2}\right)$, $\left(-\frac{1}{2}, 1\right)$, and $(1, \infty)$.

Next, determine in which interval(s) the product of the two factors is negative.

Method 1. Make an organized table to determine the sign of $(2x + 1)(x - 1)$ for each of these intervals.

Interval	Sign of $(2x + 1)$	Sign of $(x - 1)$	Sign of $(2x + 1)(x - 1)$
$\left(-\infty, -\frac{1}{2}\right)$	negative	negative	positive
$\left(-\frac{1}{2}, 1\right)$	positive	negative	negative
$(1, \infty)$	positive	positive	positive

Thus, $(2x + 1)(x - 1)$ is negative only in the interval $\left(-\frac{1}{2}, 1\right)$, choice C.

Method 2. Use the ETS graphing calculator to graph $y = 2x^2 - x - 1$.

The graph intersects the x-axis at $x = -\frac{1}{2}$ and $x = 1$. You can see that the graph is below the x-axis (and, therefore, negative) between these two points and above the x-axis otherwise. Thus, $2x^2 - x - 1$ is negative only in the interval $\left(-\frac{1}{2}, 1\right)$, choice C.

42. **A.** You are given two points (0, 500) and (5, 1,500) that satisfy the function $P(t) = P_0e^{xt}$. First, substitute the values for the two points into $P(t) = P_0e^{xt}$ and then solve the resulting system of equations for x.

$500 = P_0e^{x(0)} = P_0e^0 = P_0(1) = P_0$

$1{,}500 = P_0e^{x(5)} = P_0e^{5x} = 500e^{5x}$ (using the results from the first equation). Solve for x.

$$\begin{aligned} 1{,}500 &= 500e^{5x} \\ 3 &= e^{5x} \\ \ln 3 &= \ln e^{5x} \\ \ln 3 &= 5x \ln e \\ \ln 3 &= 5x(1) \\ \ln 3 &= 5x \\ \frac{\ln 3}{5} &= x, \text{ choice A} \end{aligned}$$

43. **D**. Make a table showing the height of the ball as a function of rebound number.

Height of Ball (in feet)	120	$120\left(\frac{3}{4}\right)$	$120\left(\frac{3}{4}\right)\left(\frac{3}{4}\right)$	$120\left(\frac{3}{4}\right)\left(\frac{3}{4}\right)\left(\frac{3}{4}\right)$	...
Rebound Number *n*	0	1	2	3	...

Examination of the table leads to a general term for the nth bounce: $120\left(\frac{3}{4}\right)^n$, where $n = 0, 1, 2, \ldots$. Thus, an exponential function (choice D) would best model the height of the ball as a function of rebound number n. None of the functions in the other answer choices works as well as an exponential model.

44. **B.** The degree of the numerator polynomial exceeds the degree of the denominator polynomial by 2, so the graph has no horizontal or oblique asymptotes. To find vertical asymptotes, first simplify $y = \frac{x^4 - 81}{x^2 + x - 12}$, then find all values of x that make the denominator equal to zero.

$$y = \frac{x^4 - 81}{x^2 + x - 12} = \frac{(x^2+9)(x^2-9)}{(x+4)(x-3)} = \frac{(x^2+9)(x+3)\cancel{(x-3)}}{(x+4)\cancel{(x-3)}} = \frac{(x^2+9)(x+3)}{(x+4)}$$

When $x = -4$, the denominator of the simplified function is zero. So the graph has one asymptote at $x = -4$. Thus, choice B is the correct response. ***Tip:*** The graph does not have an asymptote at $x = 3$. The graph has a "hole" at $x = 3$ because the function is undefined at that point.

45. $\frac{1}{4}$ Solve $f(g(x)) = g(f(x))$ for x.

$$f(g(x)) = g(f(x))$$
$$3\left(\frac{4}{x-1}\right) = \frac{4}{(3x)-1}$$
$$\frac{12}{x-1} = \frac{4}{3x-1}$$
$$12(3x-1) = 4(x-1)$$
$$3(3x-1) = (x-1)$$
$$9x-3 = x-1$$
$$8x = 2$$
$$x = \frac{1}{4}$$

46. **C.** To determine the closed-form for a sequence requires looking for a pattern in the terms of the sequence or in the first and second differences between consecutive terms. Make a table that includes the terms of the sequence and the first and second differences between consecutive terms, and then look for a pattern.

n	a_n	1st Difference	2nd Difference
1	1	$8 - 1 = 7$	
2	8	$17 - 8 = 9$	$9 - 7 = 2$
3	17	$28 - 17 = 11$	$11 - 9 = 2$
4	28		$13 - 11 = 2$
5	41	$41 - 28 = 13$	$15 - 13 = 2$
6	56	$56 - 41 = 15$	

The preceding table shows that the second differences are constant. When the second difference is constant, the relationship between terms of the sequence is quadratic, choice C.

47. **C.** The volume of a right prism is given by $V = Bh$. (This formula is provided in the Notations, Definitions, and Formulas reference sheet.) First, find the area, B, of one of the equilateral triangular bases, and then find the volume by multiplying B by the height of the prism, h.

The area of an equilateral triangle with sides of 4 inches is given by Area $= \frac{\sqrt{3}}{4}s^2 = \frac{\sqrt{3}}{4}(4\text{ in})^2 = 4\sqrt{3}\text{ in}^2$.

Tip: If you forget the formula for the area of an equilateral triangle, you can derive it by using the Pythagorean theorem or trigonometric functions to determine the height (altitude) of the triangle, and then using the formula, area $= \frac{1}{2}bh$, to find the area of the equilateral triangle.

The volume is $Bh = \left(4\sqrt{3}\text{ in}^2\right)(25\text{ in}) \approx 173\text{ in}^3$, choice C.

48. **B.** Given the coin is to be flipped six times, work this problem by extending the fundamental counting principle to six events. There are two possibilities for each of the six coin flips, which means the total number of possible outcomes in the sample space is $2 \cdot 2 \cdot 2 \cdot 2 \cdot 2 \cdot 2 = 2^6$, choice B.

49. **A.** Make a sketch of the two curves and shade the area of interest.

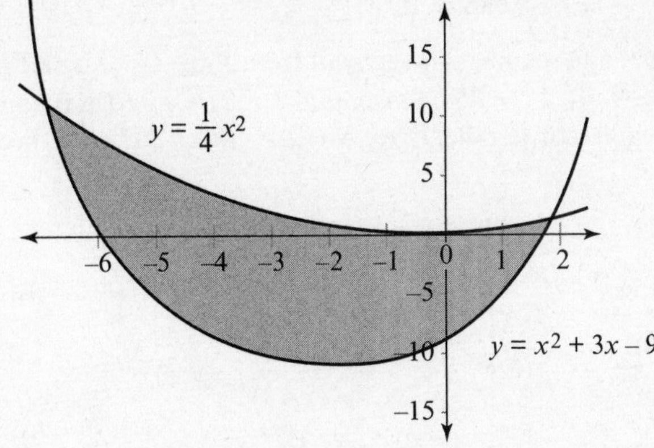

The two curves intersect at two points and $y = \frac{1}{4}x^2$ lies above $y = x^2 + 3x - 9$ between the points of intersection. First, find the x values for the points of intersection of the two curves. Next, find the difference between the two functions, being sure to subtract the equation of the lower curve from the equation of the upper curve. Then evaluate the definite integral of the difference, between the two x values of their intersection.

Step 1. Find the x values for the points of intersection of the two curves.

Use substitution and then solve for x.

$$\begin{aligned} \frac{1}{4}x^2 &= x^2 + 3x - 9 \\ 0 &= \frac{3}{4}x^2 + 3x - 9 \\ 0 &= 3x^2 + 12x - 36 \\ 0 &= x^2 + 4x - 12 \\ 0 &= (x+6)(x-2) \\ x &= -6 \text{ or } x = 2 \end{aligned}$$

Step 2. Find the difference between the two curves.

$$\text{Difference} = \left(\frac{1}{4}x^2\right) - (x^2 + 3x - 9) = \frac{1}{4}x^2 - x^2 - 3x + 9 = -\frac{3}{4}x^2 - 3x + 9$$

Step 3. Evaluate the definite integral $\int_{-6}^{2}\left(-\frac{3}{4}x^2 - 3x + 9\right)dx$ using methods of calculus.

$$\begin{aligned} \int_{-6}^{2}\left(-\frac{3}{4}x^2 - 3x + 9\right)dx &= \left(-\frac{x^3}{4} - \frac{3x^2}{2} + 9x\right)\Bigg|_{-6}^{2} \\ &= \left(-\frac{(2)^3}{4} - \frac{3(2)^2}{2} + 9(2)\right) - \left(-\frac{(-6)^3}{4} - \frac{3(-6)^2}{2} + 9(-6)\right) \\ &= (-2 - 6 + 18) - (54 - 54 - 54) \\ &= 10 + 54 = 64, \text{ choice A} \end{aligned}$$

50. **B.** The probability that a yellow marble is drawn on the first draw is

$$P(\text{yellow on first draw}) = \frac{\text{Number of yellow marbles in bag}}{\text{Total number of marbles}} = \frac{3}{25}$$

After this event occurs since the yellow marble drawn first is not put back in the bag, the probability that a yellow marble will be drawn on the second draw is

$$P(\text{yellow on second draw given first draw is yellow}) = \frac{2}{24} = \frac{1}{12}$$

Hence, the probability that both marbles will be yellow when two marbles are randomly drawn from the bag without replacement is $\frac{3}{25}\cdot\frac{1}{12}=\frac{1}{100}$, choice B.

51. **B.** Make a sketch. Construct a perpendicular segment from E to $\overline{AB}$. Angle FBD is a 45° angle because its measure is $90° - m\angle DBC = 90° - 45° = 45°$. Given that $\overline{DE} \parallel \overline{BC}$, $\angle FEB$ is congruent to $\angle EBC$ because they are alternate interior angles of parallel lines. Angle FEB is a 30° angle because it is congruent to $\angle EBC$ that has measure of 30°.

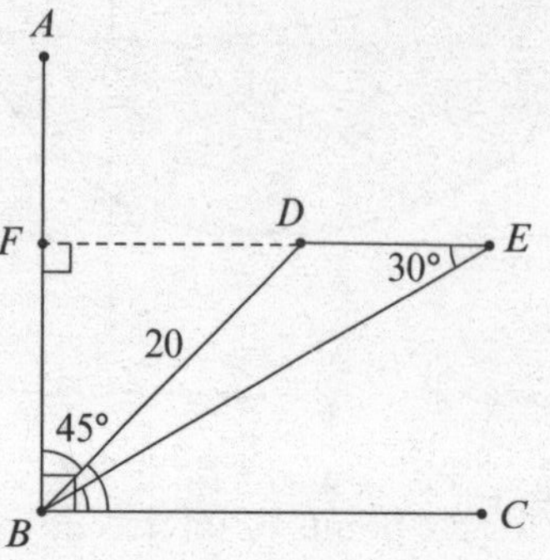

The perimeter of triangle DBE is $DB + BE + ED = 20 + BE + ED$. You need $BE + ED$. First, find BF and DF, the lengths of the legs of 45°-45°-90° right triangle DFB, which has hypotenuse of length 20. Use BF to find BE, which is the length of the hypotenuse of 30°-60°-90° right triangle EFB. Next, use BF to find EF, which is the length of the side opposite the 60° angle in 30°-60°-90° right triangle EFB. Use EF and DF to find ED, which is $EF - DF$. Then, find the perimeter.

Find BF and DF.

The length of the sides of a 45°-45°-90° right triangle are in the ratio $\frac{1}{\sqrt{2}}:\frac{1}{\sqrt{2}}:1$. Hence, $BF = DF = 20\left(\frac{1}{\sqrt{2}}\right)=\frac{20}{\sqrt{2}}=10\sqrt{2}$.

Use BF to find BE.

In 30°-60°-90° right triangle EFB, BF is the side opposite the 30° angle and BE is the hypotenuse. The lengths of the sides of a 30°-60°-90° right triangle are in the ratio $1:\sqrt{3}:2$. Therefore, $BE = (BF)(2) = (10\sqrt{2})(2) = 20\sqrt{2}$.

Use BF to find EF.

In 30°-60°-90° right triangle EFB, EF is the length of the side opposite the 60° angle and BF is the length of the other leg. The lengths of the sides of a 30°-60°-90° right triangle are in the ratio $1:\sqrt{3}:2$. So $EF = (BF)(\sqrt{3}) = (10\sqrt{2})(\sqrt{3}) = 10\sqrt{6}$.

Use EF and DF to find ED.

$$ED = EF - DF = 10\sqrt{6} - 10\sqrt{2}$$

Find the perimeter.

$\text{Perimeter} = 20 + BE + ED = 20 + 20\sqrt{2} + 10\sqrt{6} - 10\sqrt{2} = 20 + 10\sqrt{2} + 10\sqrt{6} = 10(2+\sqrt{2}+\sqrt{6})$, choice B

This explanation might seems lengthy (and, perhaps, complicated) to you. Actually, after you have created the two special right triangles, the computations are straightforward and can be done without a calculator.

Tip: When a figure has angles of 30° or 45°, consider constructions that will result in 30°-60°-90° or 45°-45°-90° right triangles.

52. **900** All of the percents in the circle graph have the same base (3,000 workers), so work with the percents, rather than the actual number of workers. The percent of workers who have less than \$10,000 in savings and investments is 63%. The percent of workers who have \$100,000 or more in savings and investments is 5% + 2% = 7%.

To answer the question, determine what percent 63% is of 7%.

$$\frac{63\%}{7\%} = 9 = 900\%$$

53. **B.** Let $s(t)$ be the position of the particle at time t. The velocity of the particle is $s'(t) = v(t) = 6t^2$. The velocity is nonnegative, so the distance the particle moves between $t = 1$ and $t = 2$ is

$$\int_1^2 v(t)\,dt = \int_1^2 6t^2\,dt = 6\int_1^2 t^2\,dt = 6\left(\frac{t^3}{3}\bigg|_1^2\right) = \left(\frac{6}{3}\right)\left(t^3\bigg|_1^2\right) = 2\left(t^3\bigg|_1^2\right) = 2\left(2^3 - 1^3\right) = 2(7) = 14, \text{ choice B}$$

Tip: The total distance traveled over the time interval a to b is $\int_a^b |v(t)|\,dt$. In this problem, the velocity is nonnegative, so the absolute value bars are not needed.

54. **A, D.** There are eight possibilities for x, y, and z. Written as ordered triples, the eight possibilities are (0, 0, 0), which yields $a = 0$; (0, 0, 1), which yields $a = \frac{1}{64}$; (0, 1, 0), which yields $a = \frac{1}{16}$; (0, 1, 1), which yields $a = \frac{5}{64}$ (select choice A); (1, 0, 0), which yields $a = \frac{1}{4}$; (1, 0, 1), which yields $a = \frac{17}{64}$; (1, 1, 0), which yields $a = \frac{5}{16}$ (select choice D); and (1, 1, 1), which yields $a = \frac{21}{64}$. The fractions in choices B and C are not possible values of a. Only the fractions in choices A and D are possible values of a.

55. **A.** The average is $\frac{x+y+z}{3}$. You have three variables and only two equations, so finding specific values for x, y, and z is problematic. Notice that if you can determine the sum $x + y + z$, you can answer the question. Observe that corresponding coefficients in the two equations add to 10. Add the two equations and solve for $(x + y + z)$.

$$\begin{aligned} 3x + 2y + 6z &= 50 \\ 7x + 8y + 4z &= 70 \\ \hline 10x + 10y + 10z &= 120 \\ 10(x + y + z) &= 120 \\ (x + y + z) &= 12 \end{aligned}$$

Thus, the average is $\frac{12}{3} = 4$, choice A.

56. **A, C, D.** $\sqrt{pq} = 14$ implies $pq = 196$. The factors of 196 are 1, 2, 4, 7, 14, 28, 49, 98, and 196. The possible two-factor combinations for p and q are 1 and 196, 2 and 98, 4 and 49, 7 and 28, and 14 and 14. The possible sums for these two-factor combinations are 197 (choice D), 100 (choice C), 53, 35 (choice A), and 28. Choice B, 54, is not a possible sum.

57. **C.** Use the chain rule, $h'(x) = f'(g(x))g'(x)$. (***Note:*** This formula is provided in the Notations, Definitions, and Formulas reference sheet under "Differentiation.")

$$h'(0) = f'(g(0))g'(0) = f'(1)g'(0) = (-4)(-3) = 12, \text{ choice C}$$

58. **1,260** The measure of an exterior angle of the regular polygon is 180° – 140° = 40°. The sum of the measures of the exterior angles of a polygon is 360°, no matter how many sides the polygon has. Because the polygon is a regular polygon, its number of sides is $\frac{360°}{40°} = 9$. The polygon has 9 sides and 9 congruent interior angles. The sum of the measures of the interior angles is (9)(140°) = 1,260°.

59. B. Show the sample space in a table.

		Box 1			
		1	**2**	**3**	**4**
Box 2	**1**	1	2	3	4
	2	2	4	6	8
	3	3	6	9	12
	4	4	8	12	16

The possible products and their frequencies are 1 (one time), 2 (two times), 3 (two times), 4 (three times), 6 (two times), 8 (two times), 9 (one time), 12 (two times), and 16 (one time). The product 4 (choice B) occurs three times, and, thus, is most likely to occur.

60. A. The function $-f(x)$ reflects $f(x)$ over the x-axis and the function $f(x-5)$ is a horizontal shift of 5 units to the right. Applying both of these transformations to f defined by $f(x) = 3^x$ results in the new function g defined by $g(x) = -3^{x-5}$, choice A.

Appendix A

Common Formulas

Temperature

F (degrees Fahrenheit) $= \frac{9}{5}C + 32$; C (degrees Celsius) $= \frac{5}{9}(F - 32)$

Percentage

$P = RB$, where P = percentage, R = rate, and B = base

Business Formulas

Simple Interest

$I = Prt$, where I = simple interest accumulated, P = principal invested or present value of a future amount S, r = annual simple interest rate, and t = time in years

$S = P(1 + rt)$ = maturity value of P

Compound Interest

$S = P\left(1 + \frac{r}{m}\right)^{mt}$, where S = maturity value, or the compound amount of P, P = original principal or the present value of S, r = stated annual percentage rate, m = number of compoundings per year, and t = time in years

$S - P$ = compound interest accumulated

Ordinary Simple Annuity

$S = R\left[\frac{(1+i)^n - 1}{i}\right]$, where S = amount of the annuity, R = periodic payment, r = stated annual percentage rate, m = number of payments (compoundings) per year, $i = \frac{r}{m}$ = interest rate per compounding period, and n = total number of payments

Rn = total of payments

$S - Rn$ = interest earned

Amortization

$A = R\left[\frac{1 - (1+i)^{-n}}{i}\right]$, where A = amount financed, R = periodic payment, r = stated annual percentage rate, m = number of payments (compoundings) per year, $i = \frac{r}{m}$ = interest rate per compounding period, and n = total number of payments

Rn = total of payments

$Rn - A$ = interest paid

Distance Formula

$d = rt$, where d = distance traveled, r = (uniform) rate of speed, and t = time

Basic Trigonometry Formulas

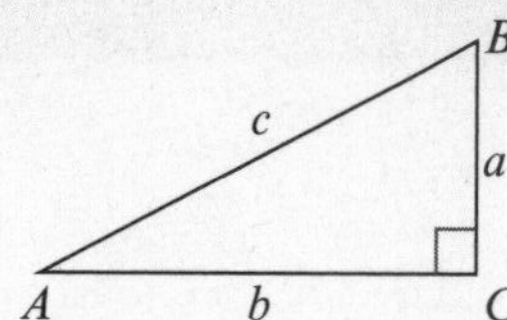

a = side opposite $\angle A$

b = side adjacent to $\angle A$

c = side opposite the right angle = hypotenuse

The basic trigonometry formulas relative to $\angle A$ in right triangle ABC are

$$\text{sine of } \angle A = \sin A = \frac{\text{side opposite}}{\text{hypotenuse}} = \frac{a}{c}$$

$$\text{cosine of } \angle A = \cos A = \frac{\text{side adjacent}}{\text{hypotenuse}} = \frac{b}{c}$$

$$\text{tangent of } \angle A = \tan A = \frac{\text{side opposite}}{\text{side adjacent}} = \frac{a}{b}$$

$$\text{cosecant of } \angle A = \csc A = \frac{\text{hypotenuse}}{\text{side opposite}} = \frac{c}{a}$$

$$\text{secant of } \angle A = \sec A = \frac{\text{hypotenuse}}{\text{side adjacent}} = \frac{c}{b}$$

$$\text{cotangent of } \angle A = \cot A = \frac{\text{side adjacent}}{\text{side opposite}} = \frac{b}{a}$$

Formulas from Science

Gas Laws

$\frac{p_1 v_1}{T_1} = \frac{p_2 v_2}{T_2}$ (General) $\frac{v_1}{T_1} = \frac{v_2}{T_2}$ (Charles's Law) $\frac{p_1}{p_2} = \frac{v_2}{v_1}$ (Boyle's Law), where v_1 = volume at pressure p_1 and temperature T_1, and v_2 = volume at pressure p_2 and temperature T_2

Specific Gravity

$$\text{Specific gravity of substance} = \frac{\text{weight of given volume of substance}}{\text{weight of equal volume of water}}$$

Lever

$\frac{W_1}{W_2} = \frac{L_2}{L_1}$, where W_1 = force at distance L_1 from fulcrum, and W_2 = force at distance L_2 from fulcrum

Pulley

$\frac{R_1}{R_2} = \frac{d_2}{d_1}$, where R_1 = revolutions per minute of pulley of diameter d_1, and R_2 = revolutions per minute of pulley of diameter d_2

Appendix B

Simplifying Radicals

A radical is simplified when

- the radicand contains no variable factor raised to a power equal to or greater than the index of the radical;
- the radicand contains no constant factor that can be expressed as a power equal to or greater than the index of the radical;
- the radicand contains no fractions;
- no fractions contain radicals in the denominator;
- and the index of the radical is reduced to its lowest value.

Here are examples.

$\sqrt[3]{24a^5b^6} = \left(\sqrt[3]{8a^3b^6}\right)\left(\sqrt[3]{3a^2}\right) = 2ab^2\left(\sqrt[3]{3a^2}\right)$ is simplified.

$\sqrt{12} = \left(\sqrt{4}\right)\left(\sqrt{3}\right) = 2\left(\sqrt{3}\right)$ is simplified.

$\frac{\sqrt{54}}{\sqrt{6}} = \sqrt{9} = 3$ is simplified.

$\frac{1}{\sqrt{2}} = \left(\frac{1}{\sqrt{2}}\right)\left(\frac{\sqrt{2}}{\sqrt{2}}\right) = \frac{\sqrt{2}}{2}$ is simplified.

$\sqrt[4]{5^2} = \sqrt{5}$ is simplified.

Because square roots occur so frequently, the remainder of the examples will use only square root radicals.

Radicals that have the same index and the same radicand are like radicals. To add or subtract like radicals, combine their coefficients and write the result as the coefficient of the common radical factor. Indicate the sum or difference of unlike radicals.

$$5\sqrt{3} + 2\sqrt{3} = 7\sqrt{3}$$

You may have to simplify the radical expressions before combining them.

$$5\sqrt{3} + \sqrt{12} = 5\sqrt{3} + \sqrt{4 \cdot 3} = 5\sqrt{3} + 2\sqrt{3} = 7\sqrt{3}$$

To multiply radicals that have the same index, multiply their coefficients to find the coefficient of the product. Multiply the radicands to find the radicand of the product. Simplify the results.

$$5\sqrt{3} \cdot 2\sqrt{3} = 10 \cdot 3 = 30$$

For a sum or difference, treat the factors as you would binomials, being sure to simplify radicals after you multiply.

$$\left(2\sqrt{3} + 5\sqrt{7}\right)\left(\sqrt{3} - 3\sqrt{6}\right) = 2\sqrt{9} - 6\sqrt{18} + 5\sqrt{21} - 15\sqrt{42} =$$
$$2(3) - 6\sqrt{9 \cdot 2} + 5\sqrt{21} - 15\sqrt{42} = 6 - 18\sqrt{2} + 5\sqrt{21} - 15\sqrt{42}$$
$$\left(1 - \sqrt{3}\right)\left(1 + \sqrt{3}\right) = 1 + \sqrt{3} - \sqrt{3} - 3 = 1 - 3 = -2$$

The technique of rationalizing is used to remove radicals from the denominator (or numerator) of a fraction. For square root radicals, if the denominator (numerator) contains a single term, multiply the numerator and denominator by the smallest radical that will produce a perfect square in the denominator (numerator). Here is an example.

$$\frac{5}{\sqrt{3}} = \frac{5}{\sqrt{3}} \cdot \frac{\sqrt{3}}{\sqrt{3}} = \frac{5\sqrt{3}}{3}$$

If the denominator (numerator) contains a sum or difference of two terms involving square roots, multiply the numerator and denominator by the conjugate, which is obtained by changing the sign between the two terms. This action causes the middle terms to sum to 0 when you multiply. Here is an example.

$$\frac{5}{1-\sqrt{3}} = \frac{5}{\left(1-\sqrt{3}\right)} \frac{\left(1+\sqrt{3}\right)}{\left(1+\sqrt{3}\right)} = \frac{5\left(1+\sqrt{3}\right)}{1-3} = -\frac{5+5\sqrt{3}}{2}$$

Appendix C

Measurement Units and Conversions

U.S. Customary Units	Conversion
Length	
Inch (in)	$1 \text{ in} = \frac{1}{12} \text{ ft}$
Foot (ft)	1 ft = 12 in $1 \text{ ft} = \frac{1}{3} \text{ yd}$
Yard (yd)	1 yd = 36 in 1 yd = 3 ft
Mile (mi)	1 mi = 5,280 ft 1 mi = 1,760 yd
Weight	
Pound (lb)	1 lb = 16 oz
Ton (T)	1 T = 2,000 lb
Capacity	
Fluid ounce (fl oz)	$1 \text{ fl oz} = \frac{1}{8} \text{ c}$
Cup (c)	1 c = 8 fl oz
Pint (pt)	1 pt = 2 c
Quart (qt)	1 qt = 32 fl oz 1 qt = 4 c 1 qt = 2 pt $1 \text{ qt} = \frac{1}{4} \text{ gal}$
Gallon (gal)	1 gal = 128 fl oz 1 gal = 16 c 1 gal = 8 pt 1 gal = 4 qt

Metric Units	Conversion
Length	
Millimeter (mm)	$1 \text{ mm} = 0.1 \text{ cm} = \frac{1}{10} \text{ cm}$ $1 \text{ mm} = 0.001 \text{ m} = \frac{1}{1000} \text{ m}$
Centimeter (cm)	1 cm = 10 mm $1 \text{ cm} = 0.01 \text{ m} = \frac{1}{100} \text{ m}$
Meter (m)	1 m = 1000 mm 1 m = 100 cm $1 \text{ m} = 0.001 \text{ km} = \frac{1}{1000} \text{ km}$
Kilometer (km)	1 km = 1000 m

Metric Units	Conversion
Mass	
Milligram (mg)	$1 \text{ mg} = 0.001 \text{ g} = \frac{1}{1000} \text{ g}$
Gram (g)	$1 \text{ g} = 1000 \text{ mg}$ $1 \text{ g} = 0.001 \text{ kg} = \frac{1}{1000} \text{ kg}$
Kilogram (kg)	$1 \text{ kg} = 1000 \text{ g}$
Capacity	
Milliliter (mL)	$1 \text{ mL} = 0.001 \text{ L} = \frac{1}{1000} \text{ L}$
Liter (L)	$1 \text{ L} = 1000 \text{ mL}$

Time	Conversion
Second (s)	$1 \text{ s} = \frac{1}{60} \text{ min}$ $1 \text{ s} = \frac{1}{3,600} \text{ hr}$
Minute (min)	$1 \text{ min} = 60 \text{ s}$ $1 \text{ min} = \frac{1}{60} \text{ hr}$
Hour (hr)	$1 \text{ hr} = 3,600 \text{ s}$ $1 \text{ hr} = 60 \text{ min}$ $1 \text{ hr} = \frac{1}{24} \text{ d}$
Day (d)	$1 \text{ d} = 24 \text{ hr}$
Week (wk)	$1 \text{ wk} = 7 \text{ d}$
Year (yr)	$1 \text{ yr} = 365 \text{ d}$ $1 \text{ yr} = 52 \text{ wk}$

Approximate Equivalents

English to Metric	Metric to English
$1 \text{ in} = 2.54 \text{ cm}$ (exactly)	$1 \text{ cm} \cong 0.3937 \text{ in}$
$1 \text{ ft} \cong 30.48 \text{ cm}$	$1 \text{ m} \cong 39.37 \text{ in}$ $\cong 1.094 \text{ yd}$
$1 \text{ yd} \cong 0.914 \text{ m}$	$1 \text{ km} \cong 0.621 \text{ mi}$
$1 \text{ mi} \cong 1.609 \text{ km}$	
$1 \text{ fl oz} \cong 28.35 \text{ g}$	$1 \text{ g} \cong 0.035 \text{ oz}$
$1 \text{ lb} \cong 0.454 \text{ kg}$	$1 \text{ kg} \cong 2.205 \text{ lb}$
$1 \text{ T} \cong 907.18 \text{ kg}$	$1000 \text{ kg} \cong 1.1 \text{ tons}$
$1 \text{ oz} \cong 29.574 \text{ mL}$ (cc)	
$1 \text{ c} \cong 237 \text{ mL}$ (cc)	
$1 \text{ qt} \cong 0.946 \text{ L}$	$1 \text{ L} \cong 1.057 \text{ qt}$

Appendix D

Long Division of Polynomials and Synthetic Division

Here is an example of long division of polynomials.

$$\frac{4x^3 + 8x - 6x^2 + 1}{2x - 1} =$$

$2x-1\overline{)4x^3 - 6x^2 + 8x + 1}$	1. Arrange the terms of both the dividend and divisor in descending powers of the variable x.
$\begin{array}{r} 2x^2 \quad\quad\quad\quad\quad \\ 2x-1\overline{)4x^3 - 6x^2 + 8x + 1} \end{array}$	2. Divide the first term of the dividend by the first term of the divisor, and write the answer as the first term of the quotient.
$\begin{array}{l} \quad\quad\;\; 2x^2 \\ 2x-1\overline{)4x^3 - 6x^2 + 8x + 1} \\ \quad\quad\;\; 4x^3 - 2x^2 \end{array}$	3. Multiply $2x^2$ by $2x - 1$ and enter the product under the dividend.
$\begin{array}{l} \quad\quad\;\; 2x^2 \\ 2x-1\overline{)4x^3 - 6x^2 + 8x + 1} \\ \quad\quad\;\; \underline{4x^3 - 2x^2} \\ \quad\quad\quad\quad -4x^2 \end{array}$	4. Subtract $4x^3 - 2x^2$ from the dividend, being sure to mentally change the signs of both terms.
$\begin{array}{l} \quad\quad\;\; 2x^2 - 2x \\ 2x-1\overline{)4x^3 - 6x^2 + 8x + 1} \\ \quad\quad\;\; \underline{4x^3 - 2x^2} \\ \quad\quad\quad\quad -4x^2 + 8x \\ \quad\quad\quad\quad \underline{-4x^2 + 2x} \\ \quad\quad\quad\quad\quad\quad\quad 6x \end{array}$	5. Bring down $8x$, the next term of the dividend, and repeat steps 2–4.
$\begin{array}{l} \quad\quad\;\; 2x^2 - 2x + 3 \\ 2x-1\overline{)4x^3 - 6x^2 + 8x + 1} \\ \quad\quad\;\; \underline{4x^3 - 2x^2} \\ \quad\quad\quad\quad -4x^2 + 8x \\ \quad\quad\quad\quad \underline{-4x^2 + 2x} \\ \quad\quad\quad\quad\quad\quad\quad 6x + 1 \\ \quad\quad\quad\quad\quad\quad\quad \underline{6x - 3} \\ \quad\quad\quad\quad\quad\quad\quad\quad\;\; 4 \end{array}$	6. Bring down 1, the last term of the dividend, and repeat steps 2–4.
$\frac{4x^3 + 8x - 6x^2 + 1}{2x - 1} = 2x^2 - 2x + 3 + \frac{4}{2x - 1}$	7. Write the answer as quotient + $\frac{\text{remainder}}{\text{divisor}}$.

Here is a completed example in which the divisor has the form $x - r$.

$$\frac{2x^3 + x^2 - 13x + 6}{x - 4} = \qquad \begin{array}{r} 2x^2 + 9x + 23 \\ x - 4\overline{)2x^3 + x^2 - 13x + 6} \\ \underline{2x^3 - 8x^2} \qquad\qquad \\ 9x^2 - 13x \quad\; \\ \underline{9x^2 - 36x} \quad\; \\ 23x + 6 \\ \underline{23x - 92} \\ 98 \end{array}$$

Thus, $\frac{2x^3 + x^2 - 13x + 6}{x - 4} = 2x^2 + 9x + 23 + \frac{98}{x - 4}$.

You can shorten the division process when the divisor has the form $x - r$ by using synthetic division.

Synthetic division is a shortcut method for dividing a polynomial by a binomial, $x - r$. You simplify the process by working only with r and the coefficients of the polynomial—being careful to use 0 as a coefficient for missing powers of x. Here is an example of the previous problem using synthetic division steps to solve.

$$\frac{2x^3 + x^2 - 13x + 6}{x - 4} =$$

$2x^3 + x^2 - 13x + 6$	1. Write the polynomial in descending powers of x, using a coefficient of 0 when a power of x is missing, if needed.
2 1 –13 6	2. Write only the coefficients as shown.
4⎸2 1 –13 6	3. Write $r = 4$ as shown.
4⎸2 1 –13 6 2	4. Bring down the first coefficient.
4⎸2 1 –13 6 8 2 9	5. Multiply the first coefficient by $r = 4$, write the product under the second coefficient, and then add.
4⎸2 1 –13 6 8 36 2 9 23	6. Multiply the sum by $r = 4$, write the product under the third coefficient, and then add.
4⎸2 1 –13 6 8 36 92 2 9 23 98	7. Repeat step 6 until you use up all the coefficients in the polynomial.
4⎸2 1 –13 6 8 36 92 2 9 23 ⎣98	8. Separate the final sum, which is the remainder, as shown.
$\frac{2x^3 + x^2 - 13x + 6}{x - 4} = 2x^2 + 9x + 23 + \frac{98}{x - 4}$	9. Write the quotient and remainder using the coefficients.

Table of Random Digits

06902	33797	30026	07243	90700	18295	81471	45296	66417	46047
92543	98296	76461	65566	15163	90376	36058	04942	34178	29469
09390	66246	60588	51890	27937	43978	34739	78542	53092	22718
06064	77426	22940	30309	39167	64104	40303	23666	08155	23600
69202	62496	77261	31794	89989	56280	76040	95364	57450	42126
01783	12202	16234	84535	36161	52932	76294	37133	02482	99160
47413	43747	88371	24814	98830	16399	91564	17606	22253	36468
86164	01581	36001	15892	57621	85239	96470	65144	53360	07616
74520	02972	56177	87580	66794	48123	48898	29724	88303	18150
01430	97022	65380	91304	32853	99729	43154	33740	11092	30661
05814	67583	01277	77815	60558	75920	94316	98015	06006	51357
80498	26935	56306	38710	77239	47139	50419	17091	78228	17665
40614	21201	75983	35695	60517	14579	70657	17096	00691	54658
70789	02628	26124	68322	01436	85994	18682	14949	15547	06416
27702	93635	69404	76323	33459	70041	63542	23946	01083	20994
09224	08984	81320	03226	60959	78246	03919	08318	19804	13837
12069	04415	78662	28295	46513	92889	25933	63964	73951	11939
46169	13070	18401	14382	48262	53177	45617	73521	12086	99420
80156	53531	36891	29620	72532	47368	32112	05166	24175	22722
18068	87733	74995	61843	88472	15736	37360	26919	95668	42417
60040	47619	57452	92819	34401	48782	60565	00452	85458	63697
92461	94060	67951	28895	79309	91897	78121	22103	57231	66277

Source: http://hcoop.net/~ntk/random/

This table shows a list of random digits. The digits appear in groups of five to make the table easier to read. You can read the digits in any order, across a row or down a column. Each digit in the table is equally likely to be any of the 10 digits, 0, 1, 2, 3, 4, 5, 6, 7, 8, 9. Similarly, each two-digit group is equally likely to be any of the 100 possible groups, 00, 01, 02, … , 99. Each three-digit group is equally likely to be any of the 1,000 possible groups, 000, 001, 002, … , 999.

To select a random sample, do the following:

Step 1. Give each member of the population a numerical label. Use the same number of digits for each one, but use the shortest possible label. Use one digit for a population up to 10 members, two digits for 11 to 99, three digits for 100 to 999, and so on. For example, labels for 100 people could be 001, 002, … , 099, 100.

Step 2. Start anywhere in the table. For convenience, count off and accept or reject groups of three successive digits at a time across a row, one group after the other. Move along the row and continue to the next row until you encounter one of the labels from Step 1. Reject all other three-digit groups. For example, if you begin in the first row, the first label you encounter is 069, then 023, 026, 072, 070, and 018 (see bolded three-digit groups below). The people labeled 069, 023, 026, 072, 070, and 018 go into the sample. Continue moving along the rows until 100 people are selected.

06902 **3**3797 30**026** **072**43 9**0700** **18**295 81471 45296 66417 46047